THE MYSTICAL CITY OF GOD

VOLUME III

"THE TRANSFIXION"

THE DIVINE HISTORY AND
LIFE OF THE VIRGIN
MOTHER OF GOD

VENERABLE MARY OF AGREDA

TRANSLATED FROM THE SPANISH BY
REVEREND GEORGE J. BLATTER

CATHOLIC WAY
PUBLISHING

IMPRIMATUR:
+H.J. Alerding
Bishop of Fort Wayne

Mystical City of God, the miracle of his omnipotence and the abyss of his grace
the divine history and life of the Virgin Mother of God our Queen and our Lady,
most holy Mary expiatrix of the fault of eve and mediatrix of grace. The history
and life of the Virgin Mother of God our Queen and our Mother and Mediatrix
of Grace, manifested to Sister Mary of Jesus, Prioress of the convent of the
Immaculate Conception in Agreda, Spain. For new enlightenment of the world,
for rejoicing of the Catholic Church, and encouragement of men. Completed in
1665.

Translation from the Original Authorized Spanish Edition by Fiscar Marison
(George J. Blatter). Begun on the Feast of the Assumption 1902, completed
1912.

The Mystical City of God consists of four volumes; The Conception, The
Incarnation, The Transfixion and The Coronation. These four Volumes and
Popular Abridgement are available from the Publisher in E-Book and Paperback.

This work is published for the greater glory of Jesus Christ through His
most holy mother Mary and for the sanctification of the Church militant.

ISBN-13: 978-1-78379-286-3

13 12 11 10 9 8 7 6 5 4

Available in E-Book.

www.catholicwaypublishing.com
London, England, UK
2013

CONTENTS

CITY OF GOD PART II
THE TRANSFIXION
BOOK VI

THE MYSTICAL CITY OF GOD

VOLUME III

THE TRANSFIXION

CITY OF GOD PART II

THE TRANSFIXION

BOOK V

Concerning the Perfection with which the most Holy Mary copied and imitated the Activity of the Soul of Christ; how the Incarnate Word Instructed Her In the Laws of grace, the Articles of Faith, the Sacraments, the Ten Commandments; and with what Alacrity and Noble Prompte She Corresponded. Also concerning the Death of Saint Joseph, the Preaching of Saint John, the Fasting and the Baptism of our Redeemer, the call of the First Disciples and the Baptism of the Virgin Mary, our Blessed Lady.

Chapter I

THE LORD STILL FARTHER TRIES THE MOST HOLY MARY BY ACTING TOWARD HER WITH A CERTAIN DISTANCE AND SEVERITY; THE REASONS FOR THIS BEHAVIOR ARE EXPLAINED.

1. Already Jesus, Mary and Joseph had settled in Nazareth and thus changed their poor and humble dwelling into a heaven. In order to describe the mysteries and sacraments which passed between the divine Child and his purest Mother before his twelfth year and later on, until his public preaching, many chapters and many books would be required; and in them all, I would be able to relate but the smallest part in view of the vastness of the subject and the insignificance of such an ignorant woman as I am. Even with the light given me by this great Lady I can speak of only a few incidents and must leave the greater part unsaid. It is not possible or befitting to us mortals to comprehend all these mysteries in this life, since they are reserved for the future life.

2. Shortly after their return from Egypt to Nazareth the Lord resolved to try his most holy Mother in the same manner as He had tried Her in her childhood and as was mentioned in the second book of the first part, chapter twenty-seventh. Although She was now vastly grown in the exercise of her love and wisdom, yet as the power of God and the

object of divine charity is infinite, and as moreover the capacity of the Queen exceeded that of all creatures, the Lord wished to raise Her to a higher level of holiness and merit. Moreover, being a true Educator of the spirit, He wished to form of Her a disciple of such exalted knowledge, that She would truly be for us a consummate Teacher and a living example of his own doctrines. For such was to be her office after the ascension of her Son and Redeemer, as I will relate in the third part. It was also befitting and necessary for the honor of Christ, our Redeemer, that the teaching of the Gospel, by which and on which He was to found the law of grace, holy, immaculate and without a wrinkle, should give full evidence of its efficacy and power in a mere creature, and that all its adequate and super eminent effects should be exhibited in some one, who could be a standard for all men. It is clear, that this creature could be none else than the most blessed Mary, who, as his Mother, stood so close to the Master and Teacher of all holiness.

3. The Most High therefore resolved that the heavenly Lady should be the first disciple of his school and the firstborn Daughter of the new Law of grace, the most perfect copy of his ideals and the most pliant material, upon which, as on liquid wax, should be set the seal of his doctrine of holiness, so that the Son and the Mother might be the two true tablets of the new law of the world (Exod. 31, 18). For this purpose of the infinite wisdom He manifested to Her all the mysteries of the evangelical law and of his doctrine; and this was the subject of his instructions from the time of their return from Egypt until his public preaching, as we shall see in the course of this history. In these hidden sacraments the incarnate Word and his holy Mother occupied themselves during the twentythree years of their stay in Nazareth. As all this concerned the heavenly Mother alone (whose life the holy Evangelists did not profess to narrate), the writers of the

Gospel made no mention of it, excepting that which was related of the Child Jesus, when, in his twelfth year, He was lost in Jerusalem. During all those years Mary alone was the disciple of Christ. In addition therefore to the ineffable gifts of grace and holiness, which He had conferred upon Her until their arrival in Nazareth, He infused into Her new light and made Her a participant in his divine knowledge, depositing and engraving into her heart the whole law and doctrine of grace, which to the end of the world was to be dispensed by his holy Church. This was moreover effected in such an exalted manner that no human thought or words can express it; and the great Lady was thereby filled with such wisdom and knowledge, that it would suffice to enlighten many worlds, if there were more than one.

4. In order to rear in the heart of the purest Virgin this edifice of holiness to a height beyond all that is not God, the Lord laid its foundations accordingly, trying the strength of her love and of all her other virtues. For this purpose the Lord withdrew Himself, causing Her to lose Him from her sight, which until then had caused Her to revel in continual joy and delight. I do not wish to say, that the Lord left Her bodily; but, still remaining with Her and in Her by an ineffable presence and grace, He hid Himself from her interior sight and suspended the tokens of his most sweet affection. The heavenly Lady in the meanwhile knew not the inward cause of this behavior, as the Lord gave Her no explanation. Moreover her divine Son, without any forewarning showed Himself very reserved and withdrew from her society. Many times He retired and spoke but few words to Her, and even these with great earnestness and majesty. But what was apt to afflict Her most, was the eclipse of the light by which She was wont to see reflected as in a crystal the human operations of his most pure soul. This light was

suddenly dimmed so much, that She could not thenceforth
distinguish them as a living copy for her own actions.

5. This unannounced and unexpected change was the
crucible in which the purest gold of the love of our Queen
was cleansed and assayed. Surprised at what was happening,
She immediately took refuge in the humble opinion She had
of Herself, deeming Herself unworthy of the vision of the
Lord, who now had hidden Himself. She attributed it all to
her want of correspondence and to her ingratitude for the
blessings She had obtained from the most generous and
exalted Father of mercies. The most prudent Queen did not
feel so much the privation of his delightful caresses, as the
dread of having displeased Him and of having fallen short in
his service. This was the arrow that pierced her heart with
grief. One filled with such true and noble love could not feel
less; for all delight of love is founded in the pleasure and
satisfaction given by the lover to the one beloved, and therefore He cannot rest, when he suspects that the beloved is not
contented or pleased. The loving sighs of his Mother were
highly pleasing to her most holy Son. He was enamored with
Her anew and the tender affection of his only and chosen
One wounded his heart (Cant. 4, 9). But whenever the sweet
Mother sought Him out in order to hold converse with Him.
He continued to show exterior reserve. Just as the flame of a
forge or a conflagration is intensified by the application of
insufficient water, so the flame of love in the heart of the
sweetest Mother was fanned to an intense blaze by this
adversity.

6. The single hearted Dove exercised Herself in heroic
acts of all the virtues. She humbled Herself below the dust;
She reverenced Her Son in deepest adoration; She blessed the
Father, thanking Him for his admirable works and blessings
and conforming Herself to his wishes and pleasure; She
sought to know his will in order to fulfill it in all things; She

unceasingly renewed her acts of faith, hope and burning love; and in all her actions and in all circumstances this most fragrant spikenard gave forth the odor of sweetness for Him, the King of kings, who rested in her heart as in his flowery and perfumed couch (Cant. 1, 11). She persevered in her tearful prayers, with continual sighing and longing from her inmost heart; She poured forth her prayers in the presence of the Lord and recounted her tribulation before the throne of the God (Ps. 141, 3). And many times She broke out in words of ineffable sweetness and loving sorrow, such as these:

7. "Creator of all the universe," She would say, "eternal and almighty God, infinite is thy wisdom and goodness, incomprehensible in essence and perfection: well do I know that my sighs are not hidden to Thee and that Thou knowest of the wound that pierces my heart. If as a useless handmaid I have fallen short in thy service and in pleasing Thee, why, 0 Life of my soul, dost Thou not afflict me and chastise me with all the pains and sufferings of this my mortal life, so that I may not be obliged to endure the turning away of thy eyes, though I have deserved this treatment through my default? All punishments would be less than this; for my heart cannot bear thy displeasure; Thou alone, 0 Lord, art my life, my happiness, my glory, and my treasure. My soul counts for nothing all that Thou hast created and their image lives not in my soul, except in order to magnify thy greatness and to acknowledge Thee as Creator and Lord of all. What shall I then do, if Thou, my blessed Lord, the light of my eyes, the goal of my desires, the north star of my pilgrimage, the life of my being and the essence of my life, fail me? Who will give fountains to my eyes to bewail my want of correspondence to all the blessings I have received and my ingratitude for my benefits? My Lord, my light, my guide and teacher on the way, who by thy most exalted and perfect operations directest my fragile and lukewarm undertakings, how can I regulate

my life, if Thou fail me as my model? Who will guide me
securely through this desert? What shall I do and whither
shall I turn, if Thou deprivest me of thy assistance ?"

8. Nor did this wounded Deer rest satisfied therewith,
but, thirsting after the purest fountains of grace, She addressed Herself also to the holy angels and held long conferences and colloquies with them, saying: "Sovereign princes
and intimate friends of the highest King, my guardians, by
your felicitous vision of his divine countenance (Matth. 18,
10) and the ineffable light (I Tim. 6, 16), I conjure you to
tell me the cause of his displeasure, if such He has conceived
against me. Intercede for me in his real presence, that
through your prayers He may pardon me, if I have offended
Him. Remind Him, my friends, that I am but dust (Job
10,9), although I am formed by his hands and have upon me
the seal of his image; beseech Him not to forget his needy
one to the end, so that she may confess and magnify his
name (Ps, 73, 19). Ask Him to give back to me the breath of
life which fails me at the dread of having lost his love. Tell
me, how and by what means I can please Him and regain the
joy of his countenance ?" The holy angels answered: "Our
Queen and Sovereign, dilated is thy heart so that Thou canst
not be vanquished by tribulation; and none is so able as
Thou to understand how near the Lord is to the afflicted,
who call upon Him (Ps. 40, 15). Without doubt He recog-
nizes thy affection and does not despise thy loving sighs (Ps.
37, 10). Even shalt Thou find Him a kind Father and his
Onlybegotten a most affectionate Son, looking upon thy
affliction." The lovelorn Mother replied: "Will it perhaps be
presumption to appear before Him and prostrate myself
before Him, asking his pardon for any fault He might find in
me? What shall I do? What relief can I find in my anxieties ?"
And the holy princes answered: "An humble heart does not
displease our King (50, 9) ; upon it He fixes his loving regard

and He is never displeased by the clamors of those who act in love."

9. These colloquies and answers of the holy angels somewhat gladdened and consolated their Queen and Mistress, since they confirmed Her in her own interior conviction, that these sweetest sighs would excite the special love and delight of the Most High. They would not speak more openly, because the Lord on his own account wished to prolong these delights (Prov. 8, 31). Although her most holy Son, on account of his natural love toward his Mother (a Mother only, not having any father), was often deeply touched with compassion at seeing Her so afflicted; yet He would not show any signs thereof, hiding his compassion under a severe countenance. Sometimes, when the most loving Mother called Him to his meals, He would delay; at other times He would partake of them without looking at Her or speaking to Her. But although the great Lady at such times shed many tears and lovingly sighed in her heart, She always put upon Herself such restraint and weighed all her actions so wisely, that, if it were possible for God to give way to wonder (which certainly He cannot), He would have yielded to such a feeling in the presence of such plenitude of holiness and perfection in this mere Creature. In as far as He was man, the Child Jesus delighted especially in seeing his divine love and grace bring forth such abundant fruits in his Virgin Mother. The holy angels sang to Him new hymns of praise for this admirable and unheard of prodigy of virtues.

10. Upon the request of the loving Mother saint Joseph had made a couch, which She covered with a single blanket and upon which the Child Jesus rested and took his sleep; for from the time in which He had left the cradle, when they were yet in Egypt, He would not accept of any other bed or of more covering. Although He did not stretch Himself out on this couch, nor even always made use of it, He sometimes

reclined in a sitting posture upon it, resting upon a poor pillow made of wool by the same Lady. When She spoke of preparing for Him a better restingplace, her most holy Son answered, that the only couch upon which He was to be stretched out, was that of his Cross, in order to teach men by his example (I Pet. 2, 21), that no one can enter eternal rest by things beloved of Babylon and that to suffer is our true relief in mortal life. Thenceforward the heavenly Lady imitated Him in this manner of taking rest with new earnestness and attention. When at night the time for repose had come the Mistress of humility had been accustomed to prostrate Herself before her Son as He reclined on his couch, asking his pardon for not having fulfilled all her duty in serving Him and for not having been sufficiently grateful for the blessings of the day. She poured out her thanks anew and with many tears acknowledged Him as true God and Redeemer of the world; and She would not rise from the ground until her Son commanded Her and gave Her his blessing. This same behavior She observed also in the morning, requesting her divine Teacher and Master to impose upon Her all that She was to do during the day in his service; which Jesus did with tokens of great love.

11. But now He changed his bearing and manner toward Her. When the most innocent Mother approached to reverence and adore Him as She was wont, although her tears and sighs issued ever more abundantly from her inmost heart, He would not answer Her a word, but listened to Her unmoved, commanding Her to betake Herself away. To see her Son, the true God and Man, so different in his behavior and so distant in his action, so sparing of words, and, in all his exterior bearing, so changed, ineffably affected the purest and dovelike heart of the loving Mother. The heavenly Lady examined her interior, searched all the conditions, circumstances and sequence of her actions and racked her memory

in her inquiry into the celestial workings of her soul and faculties. Although She could find no shadow of darkness, where all was light, holiness, purity and grace; yet, since She knew, as Job says, that neither the heavens nor the stars are pure in the eyes of God (Job 15, 15), and since He finds fault even in the angelic spirits (Job 25, 5), the great Queen feared lest She should have overlooked some defect, which was known to the Lord. In this anxiety She, though filled with supreme wisdom, suffered agonies of love. For her love, being strong as death (Cant. 8, 6), caused in Her an emulation enkindled by an unquenchable fire of suffering and tribulation. This trial of our Queen lasted many days, during which her most holy Son looked upon Her with incomparable pleasure, by which He raised Her to the position of a Teacher of all the creatures. He rewarded her loyalty and exquisite love with abundant graces in addition to those which She already possessed. Then happened what I shall relate in the following chapter.

Words of the Queen

THE VIRGIN MARY SPEAKS TO SISTER MARY OF AGREDA

12. My daughter, I see that thou art desirous of being a disciple of my most holy Son, since now thou hast understood and described my own behavior in this regard. For thy consolation take notice, that He has exercised this office of Teacher not only once and not only at the time, when He taught his holy doctrine while yet in mortal flesh, as is related in the Gospels (Matth. 28, 20) ; but that He continues to be the Teacher of souls to the end of the world. He admonishes, instructs, and inspires them, urging them to put in practice whatever is most perfect and most holy. Thus He acts toward all without exception, although according to his divine ordainment, and according to the disposition and attentive-

ness of each soul, everyone receives more or less of the benefits (Matth. 11, 5). If thou hadst always applied this truth, thou wouldst have known by abundant experience, that the Lord does not refuse to act as the Teacher of the poor, of the despised and of the sinners, if they wish to listen to his secret doctrines. As thou now desirest to know what disposition He requires of thee in order to have Him teach Thee to thy heart's content, I shall in his name inform thee of it. I assure thee, that if He shall find thee well disposed He will, as a true and wise Teacher, communicate to thee the plenitude of his wisdom and enlightenment.

13. First of all thou must keep thy conscience pure, undefiled, serene and quiet, keeping a constant watch against falling into any sin or imperfection throughout all the events of this life. At the same time thou must withdraw thyself and disentangle thyself from all that is earthly, so much so that (as I have already formerly admonished thee) thou do not retain any image or memory of human or visible things, but maintain the utmost sincerity, purity and serenity of heart. When thou thus hast cleared thy interior from the images and shadows of earthly things, then thou wilt pay attention to the voice of thy God like a beloved daughter, forgetting the voice of Babylon, the house of her father Adam and all the aftertastes of sin. I assure thee, that He will speak to thee words of eternal life (John 6, 69). It will be thy duty to listen to Him with reverence and humble gratitude; to appreciate his teachings, and to follow them in practice with all diligence and punctuality. Nothing can be hid from this great Master and Teacher (Heb. 4, 13), and He withdraws in disgust from those who are ungrateful and disobedient. No one must think that these withdrawals of the Most High always happen in the same way as they happened to me. For the Lord withdrew from me, not on account of any fault of mine, but out of exceeding love. He is accustomed to with-

draw from other creatures in order to visit them with merited punishment for their many sins, outrages, ingratitudes and negligences.

14. Therefore, my daughter, in gauging thy reverence and esteem for the teaching and enlightenment of thy divine Master and for my own exhortations, thou must take into account thy omissions and faults. Moderate thy inordinate fears and do not any more doubt that it is the Lord, who speaks to thee and teaches thee, since his doctrine of itself gives testimony of its own truth and assures thee, that God is its Author; for thou seest that it is holy, pure, perfect and without error. It inculcates whatever is best and reprehends thy least fault, and it is moreover approved by thy instructors and spiritual directors. As I am thy Teacher, I wish that thou also, in imitation of me, come every morning and night humbly and sorrowfully to confess thy faults, in order that I may intercede for thee and as thy Mother obtain for thee the pardon of the Lord. As soon as thou commitest any imperfection, acknowledge it without delay and ask the Lord pardon, promising to amend. If thou attend to these things, which I here tell thee, thou wilt be a disciple of the Most High and of me as thou desirest to be. Purity of soul and the divine grace is the most exquisite and adequate preparation for partaking of the influences of divine light and science, and the Redeemer of the world communicates it to his true disciples.

Chapter II

THE OPERATIONS OF THE SOUL OF HER MOST HOLY SON
AND ALL THAT HAD BEEN HIDDEN TO HER AGAIN BECOMES
VISIBLE TO MOST HOLY MARY SHE IS INSTRUCTED IN THE
LAW OF GRACE.

15. Human ingenuity has made long and copious inquisi-
tions into the nature and properties of love and into its cause
and effects. In order to explain the holy and divine love of
our blessed Mother, I was compelled to add much to all that
has been written and said concerning love; for, with the
exception of the love existing in the soul of Christ our Redeemer, there was none in all the human creatures, which
was equal to that possessed by that heavenly Lady, who
merited the name of beautiful love (Eccli. 24, 24). The
object and end of holy love is the same in all, namely God in
Himself and all the other creatures for his sake; but the
subject in which it exists, the source from which it flows, the
effects which it produces, are widely different. Now in our
great Queen all these elements of love attained their highest
perfection. Purity of heart, faith, hope, filial and holy fear,
knowledge and wisdom, remembrance and gratitude for the
greatest benefits, and all the other sources of a most exalted
love were hers in boundless affluence and proportion. The
flame of her love was not enkindled or enflamed by the
foolishness of the senses, which are without the guide and

control of reason. Her holy and pure love entered by way of her most exalted understanding of the infinite goodness and ineffable sweetness of God; for since God is wisdom and goodness, He wishes to be loved not only with sweetness, but also with wisdom and knowledge of the one that loves.

16. These loving affections are more alike to themselves in their effects than in their causes; for if they once take possession and subject to themselves the heart, they are hard to expel. From this fact arises the suffering of the human heart in seeing itself forsaken and unnoticed by the one beloved; for this want of proper correspondence implies the obligation of rooting out its own love. As this love has taken such entire possession of the heart, that it dreads a dispossession, although on the other hand reason urges it, such a violent strife is caused, as will resemble the agony of death. In the blind and worldly love this agony is but frenzy and madness. But in divine love this agony is highest wisdom; for, since no reason can be found for expelling love, it is the height of prudence to search after means of loving more ardently and seeking to please the Beloved more zealously. As also the will therein acts with fullest liberty, it happens, that the more freely it loves the highest Good, so much the more does it lose the power of not loving Him. In this glorious strife, the will, being the master and sovereign of the soul, becomes happily the slave of its love; it neither seeks, nor is it able to deny itself this free servitude. On account of this free violence, if the soul finds avoidance or withdrawal of the highest Good which it loves, it suffers the pains and agonies of death, in the same manner as if its life were ebbing away. The soul's whole life is in its love and in the knowledge that it is loved.

17. Hence one can understand a little of the sufferings of the most ardent and pure heart of our Queen in the absence of the Lord and in the eclipse of the light of his love: it caused in Her agonies of doubt, whether perhaps She had

not displeased Him. For as She was so to say a vast abyss of humility and love and as She knew not whence the austerity and reserve of her Beloved originated, She suffered a martyrdom so entrancing and yet so severe, as no human or angelic powers will ever be able to fathom. Mary who is the Mother of the most holy love (Eccli. 24, 24) and who reached the pinnacle of created perfection, alone knew how and was able to bear this martyrdom, and in it She exceeded all the sufferings of all the martyrs and the penances of all the confessors added together. In Her was fulfilled, what is said in the Canticles: "I f a man should give all the substance of his house for love, he shall despise it as nothing" (Cant. 8, 7). For in it She forgot all the visible and created things and her own life, accounting it all for nought, until She again found the grace and love of her most holy and divine Son, whom She feared to have lost although She continued to possess Him. No words can equal her care and solicitude, her watchfulness and diligence in trying to please her sweetest Son and the eternal Father.

18. Thirty days passed in this conflict; and they equaled many ages in the estimation of Her, who deemed it impossible to live even one moment without the love and without the Beloved of her soul. After such delay (according to our way of speaking), the heart of the Child Jesus could no longer contain itself or resist further the immense force of his love for his sweetest Mother; for also the Lord suffered a delightful and wonderful violence in thus holding Her in such a suspense and affliction. It happened that the humble and sovereign Queen one day approached her Son Jesus, and, throwing Herself at his feet, with tears and sighs coming from her inmost heart, spoke to Him as follows: "My sweetest Love and highest Good, of what account am I, the insignificant dust and ashes, before thy vast power? What is the misery of a creature in comparison with thy endless afflu-

ence? In all things Thou excellest our lowliness and thy immense sea of mercy overwhelms our imperfections and defects. If I have not been zealous in serving Thee, as I am constrained to confess, do Thou chastise my negligence and pardon it. But let me, my Son and Lord, see the gladness of thy countenance, which is my salvation and the wished for light of my life and being. Here at thy feet I lay my poverty, mingling it with the dust, and I shall not rise from it until I can again look into the mirror, which reflects my soul."

19. These and other pleadings, full of wisdom and most ardent love, the great Queen poured humbly forth before her most holy Son. And as his longings to restore Her to his delights were even greater than those of the blessed Lady, He pronounced with great sweetness these few words: "My Mother, arise." As these words were pronounced by Him, who is Himself the Word of the eternal Father, it had such an effect, that the heavenly Mother was instantly transformed and elevated into a most exalted ecstasy, in which She saw the Divinity by an abstractive vision. In it the Lord received Her with sweetest welcome and embraces of a Father and Spouse, changing her tears into rejoicing, her sufferings into delight and her bitterness into highest sweetness. The Lord manifested to Her great secrets of the scope of his new evangelical law. Wishing to write it entirely into her purest heart, the most holy Trinity appointed and destined Her as his firstborn Daughter and the first disciple of the incarnate Word and set Her up as the model and pattern for all the holy Apostles, Martyrs, Doctors, Confessors, Virgins and other just of the new Church and of the law of grace, which the incarnate Word was to establish for the Redemption of man.

20. To this mystery must be referred all that the heavenly Lady says of Herself and which the holy Church applies to Her in the twenty fourth chapter of Ecclesiasticus under the

figure of divine wisdom. I will not detain myself in explaining it, as by proceeding to describe this mysterious event, I shall make plain, what the holy Spirit says in this chapter of our great Queen. It is sufficient to quote some of the sayings therein contained, so that all may understand something of this admirable mystery. "I came out of the mouth of the Most High" says this Lady, "the firstborn before all creatures; I made that in the heavens there should arise light that never faileth, and as a cloud I covered all the earth; I dwelt in the highest places and my throne is in a pillar of cloud. I alone have compassed the circuit of heaven, and have penetrated into the bottom of the deep, and have walked in the waves of the sea, and have stood in all the earth: and in every people, and in every nation I have had the chief rule: and by my power I have trodden under my feet the hearts of all the high and low: and in all these I sought rest, and I shall abide in the inheritance of the Lord. Then the Creator of all things commanded, and said to me: and He that made me, rested in my tabernacle, and He said to me: Let thy dwelling be in Jacob, and thy inheritance in Israel, and take root in my elect. From the beginning (ab initio), and before the world, was I created, and unto the world to come I shall not cease to be, and in the holy dwellingplace I have ministered before Him. And so was I established in Sion, and in the holy city likewise I rested, and my power was in Jerusalem. And I took root in an honorable people, and in the portion of my God his inheritance, and my abode is in the full assembly of his saints" (Eccli, 24, 516).

21. A little farther on Ecclesiasticus continues to enumerate the excellences of Mary, saying: "I have stretched out my branches as the turpentine tree, and my branches are of honor and of grace. As the vine I have brought forth a pleasant odor: and my flowers are the fruit of honor and riches. I am the mother of fair love, and of fear, and of knowledge

and of holy hope. In me is all the grace on the way and the truth, in me is all hope of life and of virtue. Come over to me, all ye that desire me and be filled with my fruits. For my spirit is sweet above honey, and my inheritance above honey and the honeycomb. My memory is unto everlasting generations. They that eat me shall yet hunger, and they that drink me shall yet thirst. He that harkened to me, shall not be confounded: and they that work by me, shall not sin. They that shall explain me shall have life everlasting" (Eccli. 24, 2231). Let these words of Scripture suffice for pious souls; for in them they will immediately recognize such a pregnancy of mysteries and sacraments referring to most holy Mary, that their hearts will at once be lifted up and they will understand and feel to what an inexplicable greatness and excellence the teaching and instruction of her Son have exalted the sovereign Mother. By the decree of the most holy Trinity this Princess of heaven was made the true Ark of the covenant in the new Testament (Apoc. 11, 19); and from the abundance of her wisdom and grace, as from an immense ocean, all sorts of blessings, which were received and shall be received by the other saints until the end of the world, have overflowed.

22. The heavenly Mother came out of her trance and again adored her most holy Son, asking his forgiveness for any negligence that She might have been guilty of in his service. The Child Jesus, raising Her up from the ground where She lay prostrate, said to Her: "My Mother, I am much pleased with the affection of thy heart and I wish thee to dilate it and prepare it for new tokens of my love. I will fulfill the will of my Father, record in thy bosom the evangelical law, which I came to teach in this world. And thou, Mother, shalt put it in practice, with the perfection desired by Me." The most pure Queen responded: "My Son and Lord, may I find grace in thy eyes; and do Thou govern my faculties in the ways of thy rectitude and pleasure. Speak, my

Lord, for thy servant hears, and will follow Thee unto death"
(Kings III 3, 10). During this conference of the divine Child
and his holy Mother, the great Lady began again to see the
most holy soul of Christ and its interior operations; and from
that day on this blessing increased as well subjectively as
objectively; for She continued to receive more clear and more
exalted light and in her most holy Son She saw mirrored the
whole of the new law of the Gospel, with all its mysteries,
sacraments and doctrines, according as the divine Architect
of the Church had conceived it and as He had, in his quality
of Redeemer and Teacher, predisposed it for the benefit of
men. In addition to this clear vision of this law, which was
reserved to Mary alone, He added another kind of instruction; for also in his own living words He taught and instructed Her in the hidden things of his wisdom (Ps. SO, 8), such
as all men and angels could never comprehend. This wisdom
of which Mary partook without deceit, She also communicated without envy, both before and still more after the
ascension of Christ our Lord.

23. I well know that it belongs to this history to manifest
the most hidden mysteries, which passed between Christ our
Lord and his Mother during the years of his boyhood and
youth until his preaching; for all these years were spent in
teaching his heavenly Mother: but I must confess again, as I
have done above that I, as well as all other creatures, are
incapable of such exalted discourse. In order to do justice to
these mysteries and secrets it would be necessary to explain all
the mysteries of the holy Scriptures, the whole Christian
doctrine, all the virtues, all the traditions of the holy Church,
all the arguments against errors and sects, the decrees of all
the holy councils, all that upholds the Church and preserves
her to the end of the world, and also the great mysteries of
the glorious lives of the saints. For all this was written in the
purest heart of our great Queen and it would be necessary to

add thereto all the works of the Redeemer and Teacher in multiplying the blessings and instructions of the Church; also all that the holy Evangelists, Apostles, Prophets and ancient Fathers have recorded, and that which afterwards was practiced by the saints; the light vouchsafed to the doctors; the sufferings of the martyrs and virgins; and all the graces which they received for bearing their sufferings and accomplishing their works of holiness. All this, and much more that cannot be enumerated here, most holy Mary knew and personally comprehended and witnessed; She it was that gave proper thanks for it and corresponded with it in her actions as much as is possible for a mere creature, cooperating with the eternal Father as the Author of it all and with Her his onlybegotten Son as the head of the Church. These things I will explain farther on, in so far as it will be possible.

24. Nor, in attending to the instructions of her Son and Teacher and in fulfilling all her works with the highest perfection, did She ever fail in what concerned the outward service and the bodily wants of her Son and saint Joseph; but to all her duties She applied Herself without failing or neglect, providing for their food and their comforts, always prostrate on her knees before her most holy Son with ineffable reverence. She also sought to procure for saint Joseph the consoling intercourse of the Child Jesus as if he had been his natural father. In this the divine Child obeyed his Mother, many times bearing saint Joseph company in the hard labor, which the saint pursued with tireless diligence in order to support with the sweat of his brow the Son of the eternal Father and his Mother. When the divine Child grew larger He sometimes helped saint Joseph as far as his strength would permit; at other times, as his doings were always kept a secret in the family, He would perform miracles, disregarding the natural forces in order to ease and comfort him in his labors.

Words of the Queen

THE VIRGIN MARY SPEAKS TO SISTER MARY OF AGREDA

25. My daughter, I call thee anew to be, from this day on, my disciple and my companion in the practice of the celestial doctrine, which my divine Son teaches his Church by means of the holy Gospels and other Scriptures. I desire of thee to prepare thy heart with new diligence and attention, so that like a chosen soil, it may receive the living and holy seed of the word of the Lord producing fruits a hundredfold (Luke 8, 8). Make thy heart attentive to my words; and at the same time, let thy reading of the Holy Gospels be continual; meditate and ponder within thyself the doctrines and mysteries which thou perceivest therein. Hear the voice of thy Spouse and Master. He calls all men and invites them to the feast of his words of eternal life (John 6, 69). But so great is the dangerous deception of this mortal life, that only very few souls wish to hear and understand the way of light (Matth. 7, 14). Many follow the delights presented to them by the prince of darkness; and those that follow them know not whither they are led (John 12, 35). But thou art called by the Most High to the paths of true light; follow them by imitating me, and thou wilt have thy longings fulfilled. Deny thyself to all that is earthly and visible; ignore it and refuse to look upon it; have no desire for it and pay no attention to it; avoid being known, and let no creatures have any part in thee; guard thou thy secret (Is. 24, 16), and thy treasure (Matth. 13, 44) from the fascination of men and from the devil. In all this wilt thou have success, if, as a disciple of my most holy Son and of me, thou puttest in perfect practice the evangelical doctrine inculcated by Us. In order to compel thyself to such an exalted undertaking always be mindful of the blessing of being called by divine Providence to the imitation of my life and virtues and to the following of my

footsteps through my instruction. From this state of a novice, thou must pass on to a more exalted state and to the full profession of the Catholic faith, conforming thyself to the evangelical law and to the example of thy Redeemer, running after the odor of his ointments and by his truth in the paths of rectitude. By first being my disciple thou shouldst prepare thyself for becoming a disciple of my Son; and both these states should lead thee to the perfect union with the immutable being of God. These three stages are favors of peerless value, which place thee in a position to become more perfect than the exalted seraphim. The divine right hand has conceded them to thee in order to dispose, prepare and enable thee to receive proper light and intelligence for recording the works, virtues, mysteries and sacraments of my life. Freely and without thy merit the Lord has shown thee this great mercy, yielding to my petitions and intercessions. I have procured thee this favor, because thou didst subject thyself in fear and trembling to the will of the Lord in obedience to thy superiors, who continued to give thee express commands for the writing of this history. Thy greatest reward is that thou hast learnt of the three stages or ways, which are so mysterious, hidden and exalted above carnal prudence and so pleasing to thy divine Master (Is. 24, 16). They contain most abundant instruction as thou thyself hast learnt and experienced for the attainment of still higher ends. Do thou record them separately in a treatise for itself, according to the will of my most holy Son. Let its title be the same as what thou hast already mentioned in the introduction to this history: "Laws of the Spouse, crumbs of his chaste love, and fruits collected from the tree of life in this history."

Chapter III

MOST HOLY MARY AND JOSEPH GO TO JERUSALEM EVERY
YEAR ACCORDING TO THE REQUIREMENT OF THE LAW AND
THEY TAKE WITH THEM THE CHILD JESUS.

26. Some days after our Queen and Lady with her most holy
Son and saint Joseph had settled in Nazareth, the time of the
year in which the Jews were obliged to present themselves
before the Lord in the temple of Jerusalem, was at hand. This
commandment obliged the Jews to this duty three times each
year, as can be seen in Exodus and Deuteronomy. But it
obliged only the men, not the women (Exod. 23, 17); therefore the women could go or not, according to their devotion;
for it was neither commanded nor prohibited to them. The
heavenly Lady and her spouse conferred with each other as to
what they should do in this regard. The holy husband much
desired the company of the great Queen, his wife, and of her
most holy Son; for he wished to offer Him anew to the
eternal Father in the temple. The most pure Mother also was
drawn by her piety to worship the Lord in the temple; but as
in things of that kind She did not permit Herself to decide
without the counsel and direction of the incarnate Word, her
Teacher, She asked his advice upon this matter. They finally
arranged, that two times a year saint Joseph was to go to
Jerusalem by himself, while on the third occasion They
would go together. The Israelites visited the temple on the

feast of the Tabernacles (Deut. 16, 13), the feast of the Weeks, or Pentecost, and the feast of the unleavened Breads or the Pasch of the preparation. To this latter the sweetest Jesus, most pure Mary, and Joseph went up together. It lasted seven days and during that time happened what I shall relate in the next chapter. For the other solemnities saint Joseph went alone, leaving the Child and the Mother at home.

27. The holy spouse Joseph made these pilgrimages for himself and his Spouse in the name of the incarnate Word. Instructed by Him and furnished with his graces the saint journeyed to the temple, offering there to the eternal Father the gifts always reserved for this occasion. Being the substitute of the Son and Mother, who remained at home praying for him, he offered up the mysterious sacrifices of his prayers and as he therein represented Jesus and Mary, his offering was more acceptable to the eternal Father than the offerings of the whole Jewish people. But whenever he was accompanied by the incarnate Word and the Virgin Mother at the feast of the Pasch, the journey was a most wonderful one to him and to the heavenly courtiers, who, as I have already recorded of similar occasions, formed for them a most solemn procession. The ten thousand angels accompanied the three pilgrims, Jesus, Mary and Joseph, in human forms, refulgent in their beauty and full of profoundest reverence, serving their Creator and their Queen. The distance between Nazareth and Jerusalem was in the neighborhood of thirty leagues and the holy angels, according to the command and disposition of the incarnate Word, observed the same mode of accompaniment both in going and returning.

28. They consumed more time in these journeys than in previous ones; for after they had come back from Egypt the Child Jesus desired that they journey on foot; and therefore all three, the son and the parents made the pilgrimage afoot.

And it was necessary to proceed slowly; for already the Child Jesus began to assume hardships in the service of his eternal Father and for our advantage. He refused to make use of his immense power for lessening the difficulties of the journey, but undertook it as a man subject to suffering and allowed all the natural causes to produce their effects. One of these effects was the fatigue and exhaustion caused by travel. Although in his first journey the heavenly Mother and saint Joseph eased his fatigue by sometimes carrying Him in their arms; yet this was but a slight alleviation and later on He always made the whole journey on foot. The sweetest Mother did not interfere, since She knew his desire of suffering; but ordinarily She led Him by the hand, and sometimes this was also done by saint Joseph. Many times, when the Child was fatigued and overheated, the loving and prudent Mother was moved to tenderest and tearful compassion. She inquired about his sufferings and fatigue and wiped his divine countenance, which was more beautiful than the heavens and all its stars. She was wont to do this on her knees and with ineffable reverence. The divine Child would respond with much pleasure and speak of the delight with which He accepted these hardships for the glory of the eternal Father and for the good of men. With these conversations and conferences, varied by canticles of divine praise, they shortened much of their journey, as I have already mentioned in other places.

29. At other times, when the great Queen and Lady beheld on the one hand the interior activity of the soul of Christ and on the other hand the perfection of his deified humanity, the beauty and activity of which manifested itself in the operations of divine grace and in his growth as true man, and when She pondered upon all this in her heart (Luke 2, 19), She exercised Herself in heroic acts of all the virtues and was inflamed with divine love. She beheld also the Child as the Son of the eternal Father and as the true

God; without ever failing in the love of a true and natural Mother, She showed Him all the reverence due to Him as her God and Creator. All this flowed naturally from her spotless and pure heart. Very often the wind would flutter through the hair of the Child Jesus as He walked along. His hair grew to no greater length than was necessary and He lost none of it, except what the executioners tore out later on. Such little incidents were noticed by the sweetest Mother and they afforded Her subjects for affectionate and sweet meditation. In all her interior and exterior conduct, She was wonderful to the angels and pleasing to her most holy Son and Creator.

30. During these journeys of the holy Family Jesus and Mary performed heroic works of charity for the benefit of souls; They converted many to the knowledge of the Lord, freed them from their sins and justified them, leading them on the way of life eternal. But as it was not yet time for the Teacher of virtue to manifest Himself, all these works were done in secret (John 12, 49). As the heavenly Lady knew that such activity was enjoined upon her Son by the eternal Father, and that for the present it was to remain hidden, She concurred therein as the instrument of the Redeemer's will, though in a covered and hidden manner. In order to govern Herself according to the dictates of the highest wisdom, the most prudent Lady always consulted the divine Child concerning all her doings on the way and concerning their stopping places and their lodginghouses on their journey. The heavenly Princess well knew that her Son prearranged the occasions for his admirable works, which He foresaw and foreordered in his wisdom.

31. Hence they passed their nights sometimes in lodging places, sometimes on the open fields; but the divine Child and his purest Mother never separated. At all times the great Lady attended upon her Son and Master, watching his

actions in order to imitate and follow them closely. The same
She did in the temple, where She joined in the prayers and
petitions of the incarnate Word to his eternal Father and was
witness to the humble and profound reverence, by which his
humanity acknowledged the gifts flowing from the Divinity.
A few times the most blessed Mother heard the voice of the
Father saying: "This is my beloved Son in whom I am well
pleased" (Matth. 17, 5). At other times She perceived and
witnessed, how her most holy Son prayed for Her to the
eternal Father and how He offered Her to Him as his true
Mother: and this knowledge was inexpressibly joyful to Her.
She perceived also how He prayed for the whole human race
and how He offered up all his works and labors for all these
ends. In these petitions and offerings She accompanied,
imitated and followed Him at all times.

32. It happened also at other times that the holy angels
intoned hymns of sweetest harmony in honor of the incarnate Word, as well when they entered the temple as on their
journey. The most fortunate Mother saw them and listened
to them, understanding all the mysteries and being filled
thereby with new light and wisdom. Her purest heart was
inflamed and blazed up in divine love. The Most High
showered upon Her new gifts and blessings, such as my
inadequate tongue cannot clothe in words. But by them He
prepared Her for the adversities, which She was to suffer.
For, many times after these consolations, She beheld as in a
panorama all the affronts, ignominies, and sufferings awaiting her most holy Son in that same city of Jerusalem. In
order that She might, already at that time, see all this with so
much the more vivid sorrow, He was wont to enter upon his
prayers in the presence of his sweetest Mother; and, as She
was filled with the light of divine wisdom and with a divine
love for God and her Son, She was pierced with the sword of
sorrow mentioned by Simeon (Luke 2, 35); She shed many

tears in anticipation of the injuries to be borne by her sweetest Son and at the thought of the sufferings and the ignominious Death to which He was destined (Is. 53, 3). Her soul was filled with anguish, when She remembered, that the beauty of the Son of God, greater than that of all men, was to be disfigured worse than with leprosy (Wis. 2, 20; Ps. 44, 3); and that She herself was to see all this with her own eyes. In order to lessen her sore rows the divine Child was wont to turn toward Her, telling Her to dilate her heart with charity for the human race and together with Him offer to the eternal Father all these sufferings for the salvation of men. Thus both Son and Mother made delightful offerings to the holy Trinity, applying them for the benefit of the faithful, and especially for the predestined who would profit by their merits and by the Redemption through the incarnate Word. Principally in these occupations the sweetest Jesus and his Mother spent the days of their visits to the temple of Jerusalem.

Words of the Queen

THE VIRGIN MARY SPEAKS TO SISTER MARY OF AGREDA

33. My daughter, if thou wilt deeply and attentively weigh thy obligations, thou wilt find very easy and sweet all the labors enjoined upon thee by the commands and precepts of the holy law of the Lord. This must be the first step of thy pilgrimage, as the beginning and foundation of all Christian perfection. But I have already many times reminded thee, that the fulfillment of the precepts of the Lord must not be cold and lukewarm, but most fervent and devoted. For this favor will prevent thee from being satisfied with common virtue, and excite thee to undertake works of purest love beyond that which God imposes upon thee by command. For this is one of the artifices of His wisdom, that He seeks

to be obliged by his true servants and friends, in order that He may reward them, and this is what I desire of thee. Remember, dearest, that the journey from the mortal to the eternal life is long, painful and dangerous (Matth. 7, 14): long, because it takes up the whole life, painful, on account of the hardships, dangerous, on account of human frailty and the astuteness of the enemies. In addition to this the time is short (I Cor. 7, 29), the end uncertain (Eccli. 9, 2), being either very happy, or most unfortunate (Matth. 25, 31), while the one as well as the other termination is irrevocable (Eccli. 11, 3). Since the sin of Adam the animal and earthly life of man is burdensome for all those that subject themselves to it (Job 7, 29), the chains of the passions are strong, the war against the lower nature continual; sensible pleasures are always present and easily fascinate the faculties of man, while that which is noble, as well as its immediate consequences, is often hidden from the gaze. All this fills the pilgrimage of life with hazardous dangers and difficulties.

34. Among all these dangers and difficulties not the least are those of the flesh; for its human weakness, always present and always active, withdraws many from grace. The shortest and the most secure course to follow, both for thee and for all men, is to welcome bitterness and sorrow and put aside ease and pleasure of the senses, and inviolably to resolve not to allow them to become dissipated or enjoy greater freedom than the strict rule of reason permits. In addition to this thou must continually seek after the greater pleasure of the Lord and aspire to the great last end of all thy longings. For this purpose thou must always be solicitous to imitate me, for to this I call and invite thee, desiring that thou arrive at the summit of virtue and holiness. Consider the punctuality and fervor with which I achieved so many and so great results; not because the Lord urged me on by his commands, but because I wished to please Him more: Do thou also multiply

thy deeds of fervor, thy devotions, thy spiritual exercises and in all things increase thy prayers and sacrifices to the eternal Father for the benefit of mortals. Help them also by the example and thy exhortations wherever thou canst. Console the sorrowful, encourage the weak, help the fallen to arise; and for all of them offer, if necessary, thy own lifeblood. Above all strive to please my most holy Son, who suffers so kindly the ingratitude of men, preserving them in existence and continuing to shower his favors upon them. Consider his invincible love toward them and how I imitated Him, and even now show toward them the same love. I desire of thee, that thou follow thy sweet Spouse in his exalted charity, and also me, who am thy Teacher.

Chapter IV

AT TWELVE YEARS OF AGE THE CHILD JESUS GOES WITH HIS
PARENTS TO JERUSALEM AND HE CONCEALS HIMSELF FROM
THEM IN THE TEMPLE.

35. As I have said, Mary and Joseph repeated their visit to the
temple at the feast of the unleavened Bread every year. Also
when the divine Child was twelve years old and when it was
time to allow the splendors of his inaccessible and divine
light to shine forth, They went to the temple for this feast
(Luke 2, 42). This festival of the unleavened Bread lasted
seven days, according to the command of the divine law; and
the more solemn days were the first and the last. On this
account our heavenly Pilgrims remained in Jerusalem during
the whole week, spending their time in acts of worship and
devotion as the rest of the Jews, although on account of the
sacraments connected with each of Them their worship and
devotion was entirely different and greatly exalted above that
of the others. The blessed Mother and holy Joseph received
during these days favors and blessings beyond the conception
of the human mind.

36. Having thus spent all the seven days of the feast They
betook themselves on their way home to Nazareth. When his
parents departed from Jerusalem and were pursuing their way
homeward, the Child Jesus withdrew from them without
their knowledge. For this purpose the Lord availed Himself

of the separation of the men and women, which had become customary among the pilgrims for reasons of decency as well as for greater recollection during their return homeward. The children which accompanied their parents were taken in charge promiscuously either by the men or the women, since their company with either was a matter of indifference. Thus it happened that saint Joseph could easily suppose that the Child Jesus had remained with his most holy Mother; with whom He generally remained. The thought that She would go without Him was far from his mind, since the heavenly Queen loved and delighted in Him more than any other creature human or angelic. The great Lady did not have so many reasons for supposing that her most holy Son was in the company of saint Joseph: but the Lord himself so diverted her thoughts by holy and divine contemplations, that She did not notice his absence at first. When afterwards She became aware of her not being accompanied by her sweetest and beloved Son, She supposed that the blessed Joseph had taken Him along and that the Lord accompanied his foster father for his consolation.

37. Thus assured, holy Mary and Joseph pursued their home journey for an entire day, as saint Luke tells us. As the pilgrims proceeded onwards they gradually thinned out, each taking his own direction and joining again with his wife or family. The most holy Mary and saint Joseph found themselves at length in the place where they had agreed to meet on the first evening after leaving Jerusalem. When the great Lady saw that the Child was not with saint Joseph and when the holy Patriarch found that He was not with his Mother, the two were struck dumb with amazement and surprise for quite a while. Both, governed in their judgment by their most profound humility, felt overwhelmed with self reproach at their remissness in watching over their most holy Son and thus blamed themselves for his absence; for neither of them

had any suspicion of the mysterious manner in which He had been able to elude their vigilance. After a time they recovered somewhat from their astonishment and with deepest sorrow took counsel with each other as to what was to be done (Luke 2, 45). The loving Mother said to saint Joseph: "My spouse and my master, my heart cannot rest, unless we return with all haste to Jerusalem in order to seek my most holy Son." This they proceeded to do, beginning their search among their relations and friends, of whom, however, none could give them any information or any comfort in their sorrow; on the contrary their answers only increased their anxiety, since none of them had so much as seen their Son since their departure from Jerusalem.

38. The afflicted Mother turned to her holy angels. Those that carried the escutcheons inscribed with the most holy name of Jesus (of which I spoke at the Circumcision), had accompanied the Lord, while the other angels still remained with the purest Mother; this was the order maintained whenever the Son separated from the Mother. These, who numbered ten thousand, She asked, saying: "My friends and companions, you well know the cause of my sorrow: in this bitter affliction be my consolation and give me some information concerning my Beloved, so that I may seek and find Him (Cant. 3, 2). Give some relief to my wounded heart, which, torn from its happiness and life, bounds from its place in search of Him." The holy angels, who, though they never lost sight of the Creator and Redeemer, were aware that the Lord wished to furnish his Mother this occasion of great merit, and that it was not yet time to reveal the secret to Her, answered by speaking to her words of consolation without manifesting to Her the whereabouts and the doings of their Lord. This evasive answer raised new doubts in the most prudent Lady. Her anxiety of heart caused Her to break out in tears and sighs of inmost grief, and urged Her onward in

search, not of the lost drachm, like the woman in the Gospel, but of the whole treasure of heaven and earth (Luke 15, 8).

39. The Mother of wisdom then began to discuss within her heart the different possibilities. The first thought which presented itself to Her, was the fear lest Archelaus, imitating the cruelty of his father Herod, should have obtained notice of the presence of Jesus and have taken Him prisoner. Although She knew from the holy Scriptures and revelations, and by her conversations with her most holy Son and Teacher, that the time for his Passion and Death had not yet come and that the king would not take away his life, yet She was filled with dread at the thought, that they should have taken Him prisoner and might illtreat Him. In her profoundest humility She also had misgivings, lest perchance She had in any way displeased Him by her conduct and therefore deserved that He should leave Her and take up his abode in the desert with his precursor saint John. At other times, addressing her absent Love, She exclaimed: "Sweet Love and Delight of my soul! Thou art impelled by thy desire of suffering for men and by thy immense charity to avoid no labor or pain; but on the contrary, I fear, 0 Lord and Master, that Thou seekest it on purpose (Is. 53, 7). ·Whither shall I go and whither shall I find Thee, Light of my eyes? (Tob. 10, 4). Dost Thou wish to deprive me of life by the sword of severance from thy presence? But I do not wonder, 0 my highest Good: Thou chastisest by thy absence her who did not know how to profit by thy company. Why, 0 my Lord, hast Thou enriched me with the delights of thy infancy, if I am so soon to lose the assistance of thy loving instruction? But, woe is me! since, not being worthy to retain and enjoy Thee as my Son, I must confess, that I am obliged to thank Thee even for the favor of condescending to accept me as thy slave! If the privilege of being thy unworthy Mother can be of any avail in finding Thee, my God and my highest Good, do Thou, 0

Lord, permit it, and make me worthy of again finding Thee, so that I may go with Thee in the desert, to sufferings, labors, tribulations, or whatever Thou wilt. My Lord, my soul desires to merit at least in part to share thy sorrows and torments, to die, if I do not find Thee, or to live in thy service and presence. When thy Divinity hid Itself from my gaze, thy amiable humanity at least remained; and, although Thou wast austere and less kind to me than Thou hadst been, I could throw myself at thy feet; but now this happiness is taken away from me and I have lost sight entirely of the Sun which enlightens me, left only to groans and sighs. Ah Love of my soul! What sighs from the inmost of my heart can I send Thee as messengers? But I am not worthy of thy clemency, since my eyes find no traces of Thee."

40. Thus this sincerest Dove persevered in her tears and groans without cessation or rest, without sleeping or eating anything for three whole days. Although the ten thousand angels accompanied Her in corporeal forms and witnessed her affliction and sorrow, yet they gave Her no clue to find her lost Child. On the third day the great Queen resolved to seek Him in the desert where saint John was; for since She saw no indications that Archelaus had taken Him prisoner, She began to believe more firmly, that her most holy Son was with saint John. When She was about to execute her resolve and was on the point of departing for the desert, the holy angels detained Her, urging Her not to undertake the journey, since the divine Word was not there. She wanted also to go to Bethlehem, in the hope of finding Him in the cave of the Nativity; but this the holy angels likewise prevented, telling Her that He was not so far off. Although the blessed Mother heard these answers and well perceived that the holy angels knew the whereabouts of the Child Jesus, She was so considerate and reserved in her humility and prudence, that She gave no response, nor asked where She could find Him;

for She understood that they withheld this information by command of the Lord. With such magnanimous reverence did the Queen of the angels treat the sacraments of the Most High and of his ministers and ambassadors (II Mach. 2, 9). This was one of the occasions in which the greatness of her queenly and magnanimous heart was made manifest.

41. Not all the sorrows suffered by all the martyrs ever reached the height of the sorrows of most holy Mary in this trial; nor will the patience, resignation and tolerance of this Lady ever be equaled, nor can they; for the loss of Jesus was greater to Her than the loss of anything created, while her love and appreciation of Him exceeded all that can be conceived by any other creature. Since She did not know the cause of the loss, her anxiety was beyond all measure, as I have already said. Moreover, during these three days the Lord left Her to her natural resources of nature and of grace, deprived of special privileges and favors; for, with the exception of the company and intercourse of the angels, He suspended all the other consolations and blessings so constantly vouchsafed to her most holy soul. From all this we can surmise what sorrow filled the loving heart of the heavenly Mother. But, 0 prodigy of holiness, prudence, fortitude and perfection! in such unheard of affliction and sorrow She was not disturbed, nor lost her interior or exterior peace, nor did She entertain a thought of anger or indignation, nor allowed Herself any improper movement or expression, nor fell into any excess of grief or annoyance, as is so common in great affliction with other children of Adam, who allow all their passions and faculties to be disarranged, yea even in small difficulties! The Mistress of all virtue held all her powers in heavenly order and harmony; though her sorrow was without comparison great and had pierced her inmost heart, She failed not in reverence and in the praise of the Lord, nor

ceased in her prayers and petitions for the human race, and
for the finding of her most holy Son.

42. With this heavenly wisdom and with greatest diligence She sought Him for three successive days, roaming
through the streets of the city, asking different persons and
describing to the daughters of Jerusalem the marks of her
Beloved, searching the byways and the open squares of the
city and thereby fulfilling what was recorded in the Canticles
of Solomon (Cant. 5, 10). Some of the women asked Her
what were the distinctive marks of her lost and only Son; and
She answered all the words of the Spouse: "My Beloved is
white and ruddy, chosen out of thousands." One of the
women, hearing Her thus describing Him, said: "This Child,
with those same marks, came yesterday to my door to ask for
alms, and I gave some to Him; and his grace and beauty have
ravished my heart. And when I gave Him alms, I felt myself
overcome by compassion to see a Child so gracious in poverty and want." These were the first news the sorrowful
Mother heard of her Onlybegotten in Jerusalem. A little
respited in her sorrow, She pursued her quest and met other
persons, who spoke of Him in like manner, Guided by this
information She directed her steps to the hospital of the city,
thinking that among the afflicted She would find the Spouse
and the Originator of patient poverty among his own legitimate brethren and friends (Matth. 5, 40). Inquiring at that
place, She was informed that a Child of that description had
paid his visits to the inmates, leaving some alms and speaking
words of much consolation to the afflicted.

43. The report of these doings of her Beloved caused sentiments of sweetest and most tender affection in the heart of
the heavenly Lady, which She sent forth from her inmost
heart as messengers to her lost and absent Son. Then the
thought struck Her, that, since He was not with the poor,
He no doubt tarried in the temple, as in the house of God

and of prayer. The holy angels encouraged Her and said: "Our Queen and Lady, the hour of thy consolation is at hand: soon wilt Thou see the Light of thy eyes; hasten thy footsteps and go to the temple." The glorious patriarch saint Joseph at this moment again met his Spouse, for, in order to increase their chance of finding the divine Child, they had separated in different directions. By another angel he had now been likewise ordered to proceed to the temple. During all these three days he had suffered unspeakable sorrow and affliction, hastening from one place to another, sometimes without his heavenly Spouse, sometimes with Her. He was in serious danger of losing his life during this time, if the hand of the Lord had not strengthened him and if the most prudent Lady had not consoled him and forced him to take some food and rest. His sincere and exquisite love for the divine Child made him so anxious and solicitous to find Him, that he would have allowed himself no time or care to take nourishment for the support of nature. Following the advice of the holy princes, the most pure Mary and Joseph betook themselves to the temple, where happened what I will relate in the next chapter.

Words of the Queen

THE VIRGIN MARY SPEAKS TO SISTER MARY OF AGREDA

44. My daughter, by oft repeated experience mortals know, that they do not lose without sorrow what once they have possessed with delight. This truth, so well established, should convince men what little love they have for their God and Creator; since among the many who lose Him, there are so few who heartily grieve at this loss, and thereby show, that they have never possessed or loved Him with a love flowing from grace. Just as they fail to grieve at losing the highest Good, which they do not hold in loving possession, so they

also fail to seek after their God when they have lost Him. But there is a great difference in the manner in which men lose sight of their highest Good; for it is not the same to lose sight of God for the purpose of being tried in virtue and love and to lose sight of Him in punishment for sins committed. The first is a contrivance of divine love and a means of communicating itself more abundantly to the one that longs for it and merits it. The second is a just punishment for outrages committed against the Divinity. In the first kind of absence the Lord humiliates the soul by holy fear and filial love leaving it uncertain, whether it has not given cause for his withdrawal (Prov. 28, 13). Although its conscience does not reprehend it, the loving and ingenuous heart knows its danger, feels the loss and thus, as the wise man says, is blessed (Eccli. 9, 1); for it then lives in constant fear and dread of such a loss, knowing that man, until the end of this life, is uncertain, whether he deserves love or hate in the sight of God. During their mortal existence the just man and the sinner commonly share the same good and evil lot without much distinction.

45. This is the great evil which the wise man mentions as among the happenings under the sun; that the impious and the wicked harden their hearts in their malice and false security, seeing that the same mishaps befall both themselves and others, and that no one can tell with certainty who are the chosen or the reprobate, the friends or enemies, of God, the just or the sinners; who are worthy of love and who of hatred. But if men would dispassionately and without deceit appeal to their conscience, it would answer each one truthfully what he should know (Luke 12, 58); for when it cries out against sins committed, they would be foolish not to attribute the evils and adversities to themselves, or to fail to see themselves forsaken by grace and deprived of the highest Good. If their reason were unbiased, the greatest source of

misgiving would be, to be unmoved by the loss or by the cessation of the spiritual joys of grace. For the want of this misgiving in a soul created and destined for eternal happiness is a strong indication that the soul neither desires nor loves this happiness, and therefore it is a sign, that it does not seek it in earnest, so as to enjoy a well founded prospect of once possessing the highest Good. For thou must remember, that this well founded assurance, of not having forfeited it in this mortal life, can be attained by all faithful souls.

46. I was deprived of the bodily presence of my most holy Son; but, although I was in hope of again finding Him, yet, in my great love, the uncertainty as to the cause of his withdrawal gave me no rest until I found Him. In this I wish that thou, my dearest, imitate me, whether thou lose Him through thy own fault or by the disposition of his own will. So great should be thy dread of losing Him through thy fault, that neither tribulation, nor trouble, nor necessity, nor danger, nor persecution, nor the sword, neither height nor depth should ever withhold thee from seeking after thy God (Rom. 8, 35) ; for if thou art faithful as thou shouldst be, and if thou dost not wish to lose Him, neither the angels, nor the principalities, nor the powers, nor any other creature can ever deprive thee of Him. So strong are the bonds of his love and its chains, that no one can burst them, except thy own free will.

Chapter V

AFTER THREE DAYS MOST HOLY MARY AND SAINT JOSEPH
FIND THE CHILD JESUS IN THE TEMPLE DISPUTING WITH
THE TEACHERS.

47. In the foregoing chapter a partial answer might be found
to the question raised by some, as to how the heavenly
Queen, who was so diligent and solicitous in attending upon
and serving her most holy Son, could ever so far lose Him
out of sight as to leave Him in Jerusalem. Although it would
be a sufficient answer to say that the Lord himself brought it
about, yet I will now explain more fully how it could have
happened without any voluntary negligence or oversight of
the loving Mother. It is certain, that besides availing Himself
of the great concourse of people, our Lord was obliged to use
also supernatural means to elude the attention of his solicitous Mother; for without it She could no more have lost
sight of Him than of the sun, that lighted Her on the way.
Therefore, at the parting of the men and the women which I
mentioned, the almighty Lord visited his heavenly Mother
with an abstractive vision of the Divinity, which with divine
power centered and withdrew all her faculties toward her
interior. She thus remained so abstracted, inflamed and
deprived of her senses, that She could make use of them only
in so far as was necessary to pursue her way. As to all the rest,
She was entirely lost in the sweetness and consolation of the

divine vision. Saint Joseph was guided in his behavior by the circumstances already mentioned; although he also was wrapped in a most exalted contemplation, which made more easy and mysterious his error in regard to the whereabouts of the Child. Thus Jesus withdrew Himself from both of them, remaining in Jerusalem. When after a considerable while the Queen came to Herself and found Herself without the company of her most holy Son, She supposed Him to be with his reputed father.

48. It was very near to the gate of the city, that the divine Child turned and hastened back through the streets. Foreseeing in his divine foreknowledge all that was to happen, He offered it up to his eternal Father for the benefit of souls. He asked for alms during these three days in order to ennoble from that time on humble mendicity as the firstborn of holy poverty. He visited the hospitals of the poor, consoling them and giving them the alms which He had received; secretly He restored bodily health to some and spiritual health to many, by enlightening them interiorly and leading them back to the way of salvation. On some of the benefactors, who gave Him alms, He performed these wonders with a greater abundance of grace and light; thus fulfilling from that time on the promise, which He was afterwards to make to his Church; that he who gives to the just and to the prophet in the name of a prophet, shall receive the reward of the just (Matth. 10, 41).

49. Having thus busied Himself with these and other works of his Father, He betook Himself to the temple. On the day which the Evangelist mentions it happened that also the rabbis, who were the learned and the teachers of the temple, met in a certain part of the buildings in order to confer among themselves concerning some doubtful points of holy Scriptures. On this occasion the coming of the Messias was discussed; for on account of the report of the wonderful

events, which had spread about since the birth of the Baptist
and the visit of the Kings of the east, the rumor of the coming of the Redeemer and of his being already in the world,
though yet unknown, had gained ground among the Jews.
They were all seated in their places filled with the sense of
authority customary to those who are teachers and considered as learned. The Child Jesus came to the meeting of these
distinguished men; and He that was the King of kings, and
Lord of lords (Apoc. 19, 16), the infinite Wisdom itself (I
Cor. 1, 24), and who corrects the wise (Wis. 7, 15), presented Himself before the teachers of this world as an humble
disciple, giving them to understand that He had come to
hear the discussion and inform Himself on the question
treated of, namely: whether the Messias was already come, or,
if not, concerning the time in which He should come into
the world.

50. The opinions of the scribes were much at variance on
this question, some of them answering in the affirmative,
others in the negative. Those in the negative quoted some
testimonies of holy Scriptures and prophecies with the coarse
interpretation reprehended by the Apostle: namely, killing
the spirit by the letter (II Cor. 3, 6). They maintained that
the Messias was to come with kingly magnificence and
display in order to secure the liberty of his people by the
exercise of great power, rescuing them in a temporal manner
from the slavery of the gentiles; yet, that there were no
indications of this power and freedom in the present state of
the Hebrews and no possibility of throwing off the yoke of
the Romans. This outward circumstance was an argument of
great force among this carnal and blinded people; for they
presumed, that the coming greatness and majesty of the
promised Messias and the Redemption was intended for
themselves only; and they believed this Redemption to be
temporal and earthly, just as even now the Jews, in the

obscurity which envelops their hearts (Is. 6, 10), continue to believe. For to the present day they have not yet come to realize, that the glory, the majesty, and the power of the Redeemer, and the liberty which He is to bring to the world, is not of an earthly, temporal and perishable kind, but heavenly, spiritual and eternal; and that it is not intended alone for the Jews, although offered to them before all other nations, but indiscriminately for the whole human race descended from Adam (I Cor. 3, 15).

51. The teacher of truth, Jesus, foresaw that the discussion would end with the confirmation of this error; for although some of the learned men inclined to the contrary opinion, they were but few; and they had now been silenced by the authority and specious arguments of the others. As the Lord had come into the world in order to give testimony of the truth (John 18, 37), which was He Himself, He would not on this occasion, when it was so important to manifest the truth, allow that the deceit and error opposed to it should be confirmed and established by the authority of the learned. His measureless charity could not pass by unnoticed this ignorance of his works and high purposes in these men, who were set as teachers of the people in matters concerning eternal life and its Author, our Redeemer. Therefore the divine Child presented Himself to the disputants, manifesting the grace poured out over his lips (Ps. 44, 3). He stepped into their midst with exceeding majesty and grace, as one who would propose some doubt or solution. By his pleasing appearance He awakened in the hearts of these learned men a desire to hear Him attentively.

52. The divine Child spoke to them as follows: "The question concerning the coming of the Messias and the answer given to it, I have heard and understood completely. In order to propose my difficulty in regard to its solution, I presuppose what the Prophets say, that his coming shall be in

great power and majesty, which has also been confirmed by the testimonies brought forward. For Isaias says, that He shall be our Lawgiver and King, who shall save his people (Is. 30, 27), and David, that He shall crush all his enemies (Ps. 94, 3), Daniel, that all tribes and nations shall serve Him (Dan. 7, 14), Ecclesiasticus} that He shall come with a great multitude of the saints (Eclus. 24, 3). All the Prophets and Scriptures are full of similar promises, manifesting his characteristics clearly and decisively enough for all those that study them with enlightened attention. But the doubt arises from the comparison of these with other passages in the Prophets, since all of them must be equally true, though on account of their brevity they may appear to contradict each other. Therefore they must agree with each other in another sense, which can and must be found equally applicable in all the passages. How then shall we understand what this same Isaias says of Him, that He shall come from the land of the living, and when He asks: who shall declare his generation? (Is. 53, 8), that He shall be satiated with reproach; that He shall be led as a sheep to the slaughter, and that He shall not open his mouth ? Jeremias states that the enemies of the Messias shall join hands to persecute Him and mix poison with his bread, and they shall wipe out his name from the earth, although they shall not prevail in their attempt (Jer. 11, 19). David says that He shall be the reproach of the people and of men, and shall be trodden under foot and shall be despised as a worm (Ps. 21, 78); Zachary, that He shall come meek and humble seated upon an insignificant beast (Zach. 9, 9). All the Prophets say the same concerning the signs of the promised Messias."

53. "Hence," added the divine Child, "how will it be possible to reconcile these prophecies, if we suppose that the Messias is to come with the power and majesty of arms in order to conquer all the kings and monarchs by violence and

foreign bloodshed? We cannot fail to see that He is to come twice; once to redeem the world and a second time to judge it; the prophecies must be applied to both these comings, giving to each one its right explanation. As the purposes of these comings are different so must also the conditions be different; for He is not to exercise the same office in both, but widely divergent and opposite offices. In the first advent He is to overthrow the demon, hurling him from his sovereignty over souls obtained through the first sin. And therefore He must first render satisfaction to God for the whole human race; then also teach men by his word and example the way of eternal life, how they are to overcome their enemies, serve and adore their God and Redeemer; how they must correspond to the gifts and use well the blessings of his right hand. All these requirements the Messias must fulfill in the first coming. The second coming is for the purpose of exacting an account from all men in the general judgment, of giving to each one the return for his works, good or bad, chastising his enemies in his wrath and indignation. This is what the Prophets say of his second coming."

54. "Accordingly, when we wish to understand how his first coming shall be in power and majesty, or as David says, that He shall reign from sea to sea, that in his advent He shall be glorious, as said by the other Prophets: all this cannot be interpreted as referring to visible and terrestrial sovereignty, with all its outward show of pomp and majesty; but of a spiritual reign in a new Church, which would be extended over all the earth with sovereign power and riches of grace and virtue in opposition to the demon. By this interpretation the whole Scripture becomes dear, while in another sense its different parts cannot be made to harmonize. That the people of the Jews ate under dominion of the Romans and are in no condition to restore their sovereignty, not only cannot be held as a proof of his not having come, but on the

contrary, it is an infallible sign that He is already come into
the world. For our patriarch Jacob has pointed out this very
sign for the guidance of his posterity, commanding them to
expect the Messias as soon as they should see the tribe of
Juda deprived of the sceptre and sovereignty of Israel (Gen.
49, 10) ; and you must confess that neither Juda nor any
other tribe of Israel can hope to recover or hold it. The same
is also proved by the weeks of Daniel (Dan. 9, 25) ; which
must certainly be now complete. Those who wish can also
remember, that a few years ago a light was seen in Bethlehem
at midnight and that some poor shepherds heard the message
of the newborn Redeemer; and soon after some Kings of the
East came guided by a star, seeking the King of the Jews in
order to adore Him. All this had been prophesied. Herod,
the father of Archelaus, believing it an established fact, took
away the life of so many children, hoping thereby to destroy
the newborn King, whom he feared as his rival in the government of Israel."

55. Other arguments did the Child Jesus add, and while
seeming to ask questions He taught with a divine efficacy.
The scribes and learned men who heard Him were all dumbfounded. Convinced by his arguments they looked at each
other and in great astonishment asked: "What miracle is this?
and what prodigy of a boy! Whence has He come and who is
the Child ?" But though thus astonished, they did not recognize or suspect who it was, that thus taught and enlightened
them concerning such an important truth. During this time
and before Jesus had finished his argument, his most holy
Mother and saint Joseph her most chaste spouse arrived, just
in time to hear him advance his last arguments. When He
had finished, all the teachers of the law arose with stupendous amazement. The heavenly Lady, absorbed in joy, approached her most loving Son and in the presence of the
whole assembly, spoke to Him the words recorded by saint

Luke: "Son, why hast Thou done so to us? Behold thy father and I have sought Thee sorrowing (Luke 4, 48). This loving complaint the heavenly Mother uttered with equal reverence and affection, adoring Him as God and manifesting her maternal affliction. The Lord answered: "Why is it that you sought Me? Did you not know that I must be about my Father's business?"

56. The Evangelist says that they did not understand the mystery of these words (Luke 2, 50); for it was hidden at the time to most holy Mary and saint Joseph. And for two reasons; on the one hand, the interior joy of now reaping what they had sown in so much sorrow, and the visible presence of their precious Treasure, entirely filled the faculties of their souls; and on the other hand, the time for the full comprehension of what had just been treated of in this discussion had not yet arrived for them. Moreover, for the most solicitous Queen there was another hindrance just at that time, and it was, that the veil, concealing the interior of her most holy Son had again intervened and was not removed until some time later. The learned men departed, commenting in their amazement upon the wonderful event, by which they had been privileged to hear the teaching of eternal Wisdom, though they did not recognize it. Being thus left almost alone, the blessed Mother, embracing Him with maternal affection, said to Him : "Permit my longing heart, my son, to give expression to its sorrow and pain; so that it may not die of grief as long as it can be of use to Thee. Do not cast me off from thy sight; but accept me as thy slave. If it was my negligence, which deprived me of thy presence, pardon me and make me worthy of thy company, and do not punish me with thy absence." The divine Child received Her with signs of pleasure and offered Himself as her Teacher and Companion until the proper time should arrive. Thus was

the dovelike and affectionate heart of the great Lady appeased, and They departed for Nazareth.

57. But at some distance from Jerusalem, when They were alone upon the road, the most prudent Lady fell on her knees before her Son and adored Him, asking his benediction; for She had not thus reverenced Him openly in presence of the people in the temple, being always anxious to conduct Herself with the perfection of holiness. With loving tenderness the Child Jesus raised Her from the ground and spoke to Her words of sweetest comfort. Immediately the veil fell, revealing anew his most holy soul with greater depth and clearness than ever before. Then the heavenly Mother read and perceived in the interior of her most holy Son all the mysteries of his doings during those three days in Jerusalem. She understood also all that had passed in the dispute with the doctors, what Jesus had said and why He did not manifest Himself more clearly as the true Messias. Many other sacramental secrets He revealed to his Virgin Mother, depositing them with Her as in an archive of all the treasures of the incarnate Word, in order that thence He might receive for all of them the return of honor and praise due to Him as Author of such great wonders. And She, the Virgin Mother, fulfilled all the expectations of the Lord. Then She asked Him to rest a while in the field and partake of some nourishment, and He accepted it from the hands of the great Lady, the attentive Mother of divine Wisdom (Eccli. 24, 24).

58. During the rest of the journey the heavenly Mother discoursed with her sweetest Son on the mysteries, interiorly manifested to Her concerning the discussion with the teachers. He repeated by word of mouth, what He had shown Her interiorly. In particular He told Her, that these doctors had not recognized Him as the Messias because they were inflated and arrogant in their own knowledge. Their understanding was obscured by the darkness of their pride, so that they

could not perceive the divine light shining forth in such profusion from Him; while, if they had had the humble and loving desire of seeing the truth, his reasoning would have sufficiently convinced them. On account of these obstacles they saw it not, though it was open before their eyes. Our Redeemer converted many souls to the way of salvation on this journey and, as his most holy Mother was with Him, He used Her as an instrument of his wonderful works. By means of her most prudent words and holy admonitions He enlightened the hearts of all to whom She spoke. They restored health to many of the sick; They consoled the afflicted and sorrowful; and everywhere They scattered grace and mercy without ever losing an occasion for doing good. Since I have described more particularly some of the wonders performed during other of their journeys, I do not stop to describe any more here; for many chapters and much time would be necessary to relate them all and there are other things more to the point to be related in this history.

59. They arrived at Nazareth, where they occupied themselves in what I shall record later on. The evangelist Luke compendiously mentions all the mysteries in few words, saying the Child Jesus was subject to his parents, namely most holy Mary and saint Joseph, and that his heavenly Mother noted and preserved within her heart all these events; and that Jesus advanced in wisdom, and age, and grace with God and men (Luke 2, 52), of which, as far as my understanding goes, I will speak later on. Just now I wish only to mention, that the humility and obedience of our God and Master toward his parents were the admiration of the angels. But so was also the dignity and excellence of his most blessed Mother, who thus merited that the incarnate God should subject Himself and resign Himself to her care; so much so, that She, with the assistance of saint Joseph, governed Him and disposed of Him as her own. Although his subjection

and obedience was to a certain extent a natural result of her motherhood; yet, in order to make proper use of this maternal right and superiority, a different grace was necessary than the one by which She conceived and gave birth to Him. The graces necessary for such ministry and office were given to most holy Mary in such abundance, that they overflowed into the soul of saint Joseph, making Him worthy of being the reputed father of Jesus and the head of this family.

60. To the obedience and subjection of her most holy Son the great Lady on her part responded by heroic works. Among her other excellences She conceived as it were an incomprehensible humility and a most heartfelt gratitude for having regained the companionship of her Son. This blessing, of which the heavenly Queen deemed Herself unworthy, vastly increased in her most pure heart her love and her anxiety to serve her divine Son. And She was so constant in showing her gratitude, so punctual and solicitous to serve Him, kneeling before Him and lowering Herself to the dust, that it excited the admiration of the highest seraphim. Moreover, She sought with the closest attention to imitate Him in all his actions as they became known to Her and exerted Herself most anxiously to copy them and reproduce them in her own life. The plenitude of her perfection wounded the heart of our Christ and Lord, and, according to our way of speaking, held him bound to Her with chains of invincible love. (Osee 11, 4). His being thus bound as God and as Son to this heavenly Princess, gave rise to such an interchange and divine reciprocity of intense love, as surpasses all created understanding. For into the ocean of Mary's soul entered all the vast floods of the graces and blessings of the incarnate Word; and this ocean did not overflow (Eccles. 1, 7), because it contained the depth and expanse necessary to receive them. But these currents turned back to their source like ebbs and tides of the Divinity held between two shores, the Son of

God and his Mother. This explains the many repetitions of the humble acknowledgment of the Spouse: "My beloved to me, and I to him, who feedeth among the lilies, till the day break and shadows retire." (Cant. 2, 16). And elsewhere: "I to my beloved, and my beloved to me" (Cant. 6, 2); "I to my beloved, and his turning is to me" (Cant. 7, 10).

61. The fire of divine love, which burned In the heart of our Redeemer and which He came to spread upon the earth, finding material so prepared and ready at hand as was that of the pure heart of Mary, produced such effects, as only the Lord Himself, who was the Author of them, could properly estimate. There is but one thing, which I wish to record, having received an understanding thereof, that in the outward demonstration of his love for his most holy Mother, He guided Himself not by the natural affections and inclinations of a Son, but by her capability of meriting as a pilgrim in mortal life; for He well knew that, if in these demonstrations He would allow his filial love for such a Mother to have full sway, He would impede her merits by forcing upon Her the continual enjoyment of the delights of her Beloved. On this account the Lord restrained to a certain extent the human activity of his love and permitted his Mother, though She had reached the pinnacle of sanctity, to engage in meritorious labor and suffering by stopping now and then the flow of visible favors from his divine humanity. In his daily intercourse the divine Child therefore maintained a certain reserve and moderation. Hence, though the most assiduous Lady was so solicitous in serving and ministering to Him in all his wants, her most holy Son indulged in no such outward tokens of his filial love as would have been an adequate return for her loving service.

Words of the Queen

THE VIRGIN MARY SPEAKS TO SISTER MARY OF AGREDA

62. My daughter, all the works of my most holy Son and my own actions are full of mysterious instruction and doctrine for the mortals who contemplate them diligently and reverently. The Lord absented Himself from me in order that, seeking Him in sorrow and tears, I might find Him again in joy and with abundant fruits for my soul. I desire that thou imitate me in this mystery and seek Him with such earnestness, as to be consumed with a continual longing without ever in thy whole life coming to any rest until thou holdst Him and canst lose Him no more (Cant. S, 4). In order that thou mayest understand better this sacrament of the Lord, remember, that the infinite Wisdom made men capable of his eternal felicity and placed them on the way to this happiness, but left them in doubt of its attainment, as long as they have not yet acquired it, and thus filled them with joyful hope and sorrowful fear of its final acquisition. This anxiety engenders in men a lifelong fear and abhorrence of sin, by which alone they can be deprived of beatitude, and thus prevent them from being ensnared and misled by the corporeal and visible things of this earth. This anxiety the Creator assists by adding to the natural reasoning powers, faith and hope, which are the spurs of their love toward seeking and finding their last end. Besides these virtues and others infused at Baptism, He sends his inspirations and helps to keep awake the soul in the absence of its Lord and to prevent forgetfulness of Him and of itself while deprived of his amiable presence. Thus it pursues the right course until it finds the great goal, where all its inclinations and longing shall be satiated.

63. Hence thou canst estimate the listless ignorance of mortals and how few stop to consider the mysterious order of

the creation and justification and all the works of the Almighty tending toward this exalted end. From this forgetfulness flow so many evils endured by men while they appropriate so many earthly goods and deceitful delights, as if they could ever find in them their ultimate end. The height of perversity opposed to the order of the Creator, is that mortals in this transitory and short life rejoice in visible things as if they were their last end, while they ought, on the contrary, to make use of creatures to gain, not to lose, the highest Good. Do thou, therefore, my dearest, be mindful of this dangerous human folly. Consider all delights and joys of the world as insanity, its laughing as sorrow, sensible enjoyment as self deceit, as the source of foolishness, which intoxicates the heart and hinders and destroys all true wisdom. Live in constant and holy fear of losing eternal life and rejoice in nothing except in the Lord until thou obtainest full possession of Him. Fly from conversation with men and dread its dangers. If sometimes God places thee in the way of human intercourse for his glory and by obedience, although thou must trust in his protection, yet never be remiss or careless in guarding thyself from contamination. Do not trust thy natural disposition when there is question of friendship and close intercourse with others; in this consists for thee a greater danger; for the Lord has given thee a pleasing and mild disposition, so that thou mayest naturally incline toward Him, resist none of his intentions and make a proper return for the blessings bestowed upon thee. But as soon as thou givest entrance to creatures into thy heart thou wilt certainly be carried away and alienated by them from the highest Good, and thou wilt pervert the intentions and operations of his infinite wisdom in thy behalf. It would certainly be most unworthy of thee to divert that which is most noble in thy nature toward an unseemly end. Raise thyself above all created things, and above thyself (Thren. 3,

28). Perfect the operations of thy faculties and set before them the exalted perfections of thy God, of my beloved Son and thy Spouse, who is beautiful among the sons of men (Ps. 44, 3). Love Him with all the powers of thy heart and soul.

Chapter VI

CONCERNING A VISION WHICH WAS GRANTED TO MOST
HOLY MARY WHEN THE CHILD JESUS WAS TWELVE YEARS
OLD, AND WHICH WAS TO ASSIST IN PRODUCING WITHIN
HER THE PERFECT COPY AND IMAGE OF THE EVANGELICAL
LAW.

64. In the first and second chapters of this book I began what
I must now complete in the following chapters: but I do it
not without misgivings as to my halting and inadequate
powers of expression and with much more hesitation on
account of the lukewarmness of my heart, all of which make
me unfit to speak of the hidden intercourse of the incarnate
Word with his most blessed Mother. And especially do they
make me unworthy of treating about that heavenly intercourse of the Son and the Mother at Nazareth during the
eighteen years intervening between his dispute with the
doctors at Jerusalem and the beginning of his public preaching in his thirtieth year. On the shores of this vast ocean of
mysteries I stand full of confusion and doubt, asking the
most high Lord from the bottom of my soul, to transfer my
pen to the hands of an angel, in order that no injustice may
be done to the subject of the discourse; or that He himself,
the most powerful and wise God, speak for me, enlighten my
faculties, so that governed by his divine light, they may be fit

instruments of his will and truth and be free from the human
frailty of an ignorant woman.

65. I have already said in former chapters, that our great
Lady was the first and specially privileged Disciple of her
most holy Son, chosen among all creatures as the model of
the new evangelical law and its Author, according to which
He was to mould all the saints of the new law and judge of
all the results of the Redemption. In regard to Her the incarnate Word proceeded like a most skillful artist, who under-
stands the art of painting and all that pertains to it most
thoroughly; who, throwing all his powers into one chosen
work, seeks to gain from it alone renown and fame as from
the full exposition of his art. It is certain that all the holiness
and glory of the saints was the result of the love and merits of
Christ: (Eph. 2, 3) but in comparison with the excellence of
Mary, they seem insignificant and as it were only rough
sketches; for in all the saints are found defects (I John 1, 8).
But this living image of the Onlybegotten was free from all
imperfections; and the first strokes of his pencil in Her were
of greater beauty than the last touches in the highest angels
and saints. She is the model for all the perfection of holiness
and virtues of all his elect, and the utmost limit to which the
love of Christ can proceed in mere creatures. No one received
any grace or glory that most holy Mary could not receive,
and She received all that others were incapable of receiving:
and her most blessed Son gave to Her all that She could
receive and that He could communicate.

66. The multitude and variety of the saints silently enhance the Artificer of their great sanctity, and the greatness of
the highest is made more conspicuous by the beauty of the
lowest: but all of them together are a glorification of most
holy Mary. For by her incomparable holiness they are all
surpassed and they all partake of so much the greater felicity
as they imitate Her, whose holiness redounds over all. If the

most pure Mary has reached the highest pinnacle in the ranks of the just She may also on this very account be considered as the instrument or the motive power through which the saints themselves have reached their station. As we must judge of her excellence (even if only from afar), by the labor which Christ the Lord applied for her formation, let us consider what labor He spent upon Her and how much upon the whole Church. To establish and to enrich his Church He deemed it sufficient to spend only three years in preaching, selecting the Apostles, teaching the people, and inculcating the evangelical law by his public life; and this was amply sufficient to accomplish the work enjoined upon Him by the eternal Father and to justify and sanctify all the true believers. But in order to stamp upon his most holy Mother the image of his holiness, He consumed not three years, but ten times three years, engaging in this work with all the power of his divine love, without ever ceasing hour after hour to add grace to grace, gifts to gifts, blessings to blessings, and holiness to holiness. And at the end of all this He still left Her in a state, in which He could continue to add excellence after his Ascension to his eternal Father as I will describe in the third part. Our reason is unbalanced, our words fail at the greatness of this incomparable Lady; for She is elect as the sun (Cant. 6, 9) ; and her effulgence cannot be borne by terrestrial eyes, nor comprehended by any earthly creatures.

67. Christ our Redeemer began to manifest his designs in regard to his heavenly Mother after they had come back from Egypt to Nazareth, as I have already mentioned; and from that time on He continued to follow up his purpose in his quality as Teacher and as the divine Enlightener in all the mysteries of the Incarnation and Redemption. After they returned from Jerusalem in his twelfth year, the great Queen had a vision of the Divinity, not an intuitive vision, but one consisting of intellectual images; one very exalted and full of

the new influences of the Divinity and of the secrets of the Most High. She was especially enlightened in regard to the decrees of the divine Will concerning the law of grace, which was now to be established by the incarnate Word, and concerning the power, which was given to Him in the consistory of the most blessed Trinity. At the same time She saw how for this purpose the eternal Father consigned to His Son the seven sealed book, of which saint John speaks (Apoc. 5, 1), and how none could be found either in heaven or on earth, who could unseal and open it, until the Lamb broke its seals by his Passion and Death and by his doctrines and merits. For in this figure God wished to intimate, that the secret of this book was nothing else than the new law of the Gospel and the Church founded upon it in this world.

68. Then the heavenly Queen saw in spirit, that, by the decree of the most blessed Trinity, She was to be the first one to read and understand this book; that her Onlybegotten was to open it for Her and manifest it all to Her, while She was to put it perfectly into practice; that She was the first one, who was to accompany the Word, and who was to occupy the first place next to Him on the way to heaven, which He had opened up for mortals and traced out in this book. In Her, as his true Mother, was to be deposited this new Testament. She saw how the Son of the eternal Father and of Herself accepted this decree with great pleasure; and how his sacred humanity obeyed it with ineffable joy on her account. Then the eternal Father turned to the most pure Lady and said:

69. "My Spouse and my Dove, prepare thy heart for the plenitude of knowledge and for receiving the new Testament and Law of my Only begotten in thy soul. Excite thy desires and apply thy mind to the knowledge and practice of our teachings and precepts. Receive from Us the gifts of our liberality and of our love for thee. In order that thou mayest

give Us fitting thanks, consider, that by the disposition of our infinite wisdom, We have resolved to make thee, a mere creature, the closest image and likeness of my Onlybegotten, and thus produce in thee effects and fruits worthy of his merits. Therein shall his most holy name be magnified and honored in a fitting degree. Be mindful, therefore, my beloved and chosen Daughter, that a great preparation is required of thee."

70. And the most humble Lady answered: "Eternal Lord and immense God, in thy real and divine presence I lie prostrate, acknowledging at the sight of thy infinite Being my own insignificance, which is mere nothingness. I perceive thy greatness and my littleness. I know that I am unworthy to be thy slave; and for the kindness with which Thou hast looked upon me, I offer to Thee the fruit of my womb and thy Onlybegotten and I beseech Him to answer for his unworthy Mother and his handmaid. My heart is prepared and it is overwhelmed with gratitude for thy mercies and consumed with affection, as long as it cannot satisfy its vehement longings. But if I shall find grace in thy eyes, I will speak, 0 my Lord and Master, in thy presence, asking only this, that Thou do with thy slave whatever Thou wishest and commandest; for no one is able to execute it unless Thou thyself assist him, 0 Lord and most high King. If Thou desirest from me a heart free and devoted, I now offer it to Thee, ready to obey Thee and suffer for Thee until death." Immediately the heavenly Princess felt new influences of the Divinity, being enlightened, purified and spiritualized with such plenitude of the Holy Ghost as to exceed all that had happened to Her until that day; for this blessing was one of the most memorable ones for the peerless and sovereign Lady. Although all of them were exalted and without equal in any of the rest of creatures, reaching the highest perfection; yet in the participation of the divine perfections there is no measure, as long

as the capacity of the creature to receive them does not fail. As this power of participation was so vast in this Queen and increased with each participation, the great gifts merely disposed Her for still greater ones. The divine power, therefore, not finding in Her any obstacle, set all its treasures in motion and laid them up in the secure and most faithful depository of the most holy Mary our Queen.

71. She issued from this ecstatic vision and betook Herself to her most holy Son, prostrating Herself at his feet and saying: "My Lord, my Light and my Teacher, behold thy unworthy Mother prepared for the fulfillment of thy wishes: admit me anew as thy disciple and servant and make use of me as the instrument of thy wisdom and power. Execute in me thy pleasure and that of thy eternal Father." Her most holy Son received Her with the majesty and authority of a divine Teacher and instructed Her in most exalted mysteries. In most persuasive and powerful words He explained to Her the profoundest meanings of the works enjoined upon Him by the eternal Father in regard to the Redemption of man, the founding of the Church and the establishment of the new evangelical law. He declared and reaffirmed, that in the execution of these high and hidden mysteries She was to be his Companion and Coadjutrix, receiving and enjoying the first fruits of grace; and that therefore She, the most pure Lady, was to follow Him in his labors until his death on the Cross with a magnanimous and well prepared heart in invincible and unhesitating constancy. He added heavenly instruction such as enabled Her to prepare for the reception of the whole evangelical Law, the understanding and practice of all its precepts and counsels in their highest perfection. Other sacramental secrets concerning his works in this world the Child Jesus manifested to his most blessed Mother on this occasion. And the heavenly Lady met all his words and

intentions with profound humility, obedience, reverence, thanksgiving and most ardent love.

Words of the Queen

THE VIRGIN MARY SPEAKS TO SISTER MARY OF AGREDA

72. My daughter, many times in the course of thy life, and especially while thou art writing this history of my own life, I have called upon thee and invited thee to follow me by the closest imitation possible to thee. I now renew this invitation and demand, for now thou hast by the condescension of the Most High received light and intelligence in this sacrament of his powerful arm in my heart: how He wrote therein the whole law of grace and all the doctrine of the Gospel, what effects this favor wrought in me, and how I corresponded by the closest and most perfect imitation of my most holy Son and Teacher. The knowledge of all this thou must consider as one of the greatest favors ever bestowed upon thee by the Lord. For in it thou wilt find the sum total and essence of the most exalted sanctity and perfection, reflected as in the clearest mirror. The paths of divine light will therein be revealed to thee, whereon thou canst walk secure from the darkness of ignorance enveloping other mortals.

73. Come then, my daughter, come and follow me. And in order that thou mayest imitate me as I desire and that thy understanding may be properly enlightened, thy spirit sufficiently ennobled and prepared, and thy will inflamed, separate thyself from all earthly things as thy Spouse wishes; withdraw thyself from what is visible, forsake all the creatures, deny thyself, close thy senses to the deceits and fabulations of the world (Ps. 39, 5). And in thy temptations I exhort thee not to be troubled or afflicted very much; for if they cause thee to halt in thy course, they will already have gained a great advantage over thee and they will prevent thee

from becoming strong in the practice of perfection. Listen therefore to the Lord alone, who is desirous of the beauty of thy soul (Ps. 44, 12); who is liberal in bestowing his gifts upon it, powerful to deposit therein the treasures of his wisdom, and anxious to see thee prepare thyself to receive them. Allow Him to write into thy heart the evangelical Law. Let that be thy continual study, thy meditation day and night, the sweet nourishment of thy memory, the life of thy soul and the sweet nectar for thy spiritual taste. Thus wilt thou obtain what the Most High and I require of thee, and what thou thyself desirest.

Chapter VII

THE EXALTING PURPOSE OF THE INSTRUCTION OF MOST
HOLY MARY ARE EXPLAINED MORE AT LARGE; AND HOW
SHE PUT THESE INSTRUCTIONS INTO PRACTICE.

74. All free and voluntary causes must have some reasonable
end or purpose, which move them to act, and having obtained a clear view of this end, they proceed to choose the
means for obtaining it. This is certainly true of the works of
God, who is the first and primary Cause, and who is infinite
Wisdom itself, disposing and executing all things and reaching from end to end in sweetness and power, as the wise man
says. Nor does He seek the destruction and annihilation of
any creature, but all of them He has made in order that they
may enjoy life and existence (Wis. 8, 1). The more wonderful
and excellent the works of the Most High, so much the more
admirable and exalted are the ends to which they tend.
Although the ultimate end of all things is the manifestation
of his own glory; yet all are ordained according to infinite
knowledge and are connected one with each other like the
links of a chain. Thus all creatures succeed each other from
the lowest to the highest and nearest to God, the Author of
all.

75. All the excellence and sanctity of our great Lady is included in her having been molded by God as the image or
living stamp of his own Son; being so well adjusted and

refined in grace that She seemed another Christ by communication and privilege (Gal. 4, 4). Thus was established a singular and divine intercourse between Her and her Son. She had given Him the form and existence of man, while the Lord gave Her that other highest spiritual existence of grace, so that there was a mutual correspondence and similarity of gifts. The ends which the Most High had in view, were proportionate to this rare wonder and to this, the greatest of all his operations in mere creatures. In the second and sixth chapter I have said something concerning the honor of Christ and its being bound up with the efficacy of his doctrines and merits: that his honor required their power to be made known in his most holy Mother, and that all the effects of the evangelical Law and the fruits of his Redemption should redound to his glory by being exhibited in Her. More than in all the rest of his holy Church and in all the predestined, was this to be found in the sovereign Lady, his Mother.

76. The second end, which the Lord had in view in this work, concerned likewise the ministry of the Redeemer; for the work of our Redemption was to correspond with those of the Creation of the world, and the remedy of sin was to be correlative with its entrance among men. Therefore, it was befitting that, just as the first Adam had as a companion in sin our mother Eve, and was moved and abetted therein by her, causing the loss of the whole human race, so also, in the reparation of this great ruin, the second and heavenly Adam, Christ our Lord, was to have as a companion and helper his most pure Mother. She was to concur and cooperate in the Redemption; although in Christ alone, who is our Head, existed the full power and adequate cause of the general Redemption. In order that this mystery might not want the proper dignity and correspondence, it was necessary that what was said by the Most High in the first formation of

man, be also fulfilled in regard to Christ and his Mother: "It is not good for man to be alone: let us make him a help like unto himself" (Gen 2, 18). This the Lord in his Omnipotence did, so that, speaking of the second Adam, Christ, He could say: "This now is bone of my bones, and flesh of my flesh; She shall be called Woman because She was taken out of man" (Gen. 2, 23). I shall not detain myself in further explanation of this sacrament; for it is clearly seen by reason enlightened by divine faith, and the resemblance between Christ and his most holy Mother is clearly manifest.

77. Another motive for this mystery, though here mentioned in the third place, is first in regard to the intention; for it concerns the eternal predestination of Christ our Lord, which I have described in the first part of this history. The primary intention of the eternal Word in assuming flesh and becoming the Teacher of men, correspond with the greatness of that very work, which was to be performed. This was the greatest of all his works and it was really the end for which all the rest were to be executed. Hence the divine wisdom so arranged matters, that among mere creatures there should be One, which fully met his desire of being our Teacher and adopting us as his children by his grace. If the Creator had not thus formed the most holy Mary and furnished Her with a degree of sanctity like to that of his divine Son (according to our coarse way of speaking), the adequate motive for his Incarnation, so far as it is manifest to us, would have been wanting. Compare with this what is said of Moses, when he received the tablets of the Law written by the finger of God: he broke them as soon as he saw the people in their idolatry, judging them too faithless to be worthy of such great benefit. Afterwards the Law was written on other tablets made by the hands

of man, and these were preserved in the world. The first tablets, made by the hands of God and having written upon them Law of the Lord, were broken by the first sin; and we would not have had any evangelical Law, if there had not been other tablets, Christ and Mary, formed in another way; She in the ordinary and natural way, He by the consent and of the substance of Mary. If this great Lady had not concurred and cooperated as a worthy instrument, we other mortals would be now without this evangelical Law.

78. In the plenitude of this divine science and grace Christ our Lord attained all these sublime ends by teaching the most blessed Mother the mysteries of the evangelical Law. In order that She might be proficient in all of them and at the same time understand them in their different aspects; in order that She might afterwards be Herself the consummate Teacher and Mother of wisdom, the Lord used different means of enlightening Her. Sometimes by abstractive visions of the Divinity, with which during this part of her life She was more frequently favored; at other times by intellectual visions, which were more habitual though less clear. In the one as well as in the other She saw the whole militant Church, with all its history from the beginning of the world until the Incarnation; and what was to be its lot afterwards until the end of the world, and later on in eternal beatitude. This knowledge was so clear, distinct and comprehensive, that She knew all the just and the saints, and those who were to distinguish themselves afterwards in the Church: the Apostles, Martyrs, Patriarchs of the religious orders, the Doctors, Confessors and Virgins. All these our Queen knew in particular with all their merits and graces and the rewards apportioned to them.

79. She was acquainted also with the Sacraments, which her divine Son was to establish in the Church; their efficacy, the results in those that receive them, varying according to the different dispositions of the recipients, and all their strength flowing from the sanctity and merits of her most

holy Son, our Redeemer. She was also furnished with a clear understanding of all the doctrines, which He was to preach and teach; of the new and old Testament, and of all mysteries hidden under its four different ways of interpreting them, the literal, moral, allegoric and anagogic; and all that the interpreters of the Scriptures were to write in explanation. But her understanding of all these was much more extensive and profound than theirs. She was aware that all this knowledge was given to Her in order that She might be the Teacher of the whole Church; for this was her office in the absence of her most holy Son, after his Ascension into heaven. In Her the new children of the Church and the faithful engendered by grace were to have a loving Mother, who carefully nourished them at the breasts of her doctrines as with sweetest milk, the proper food of infant children. Thus the most blessed Lady during these eighteen years of her hidden intercourse with her most holy Son fed upon and digested the substance of the evangelical doctrines, receiving them from their Author, Christ, the Redeemer. Having tasted and well understood the scope and efficacy of this law, She drew forth from it sweet nourishment for the primitive Church, whose members were yet in their tender years and unfit for the solid and strong food of the Scriptures and the perfect imitation of their Master and Redeemer. But since I am to speak of this part of her history in its proper place, I do not expatiate farther upon this matter.

80. Besides these visions and instructions concerning her divine Son and his human nature, the great Lady had also two other sources of information which I have already mentioned. The one was the reflection of his most holy Soul and its interior operation, which She saw as in a mirror and in which was included at the same time a reflex image of all his knowledge of things created; so that She was informed of all the counsels of the Redeemer and Artificer of sanctity and

also of all the works, which He intended to undertake and execute either by Himself or by his ministers. The other source of information was his own spoken word; for the Lord conversed with his most worthy Mother about all things concerning his Church, from the greatest to smallest, including also all the happenings contemporary with and bearing upon the different phases of the history of the Church. On this account the heavenly Disciple and our Instructress was so imbued with his doctrine and so proficient in the most perfect practice of it, that the perfection of her works corresponded with her immense wisdom and science. Her knowledge was so clear and deep, that it comprehended everything and was never equaled by any creature, nor can it be conceived in its full extent either in thought or words. Neither was there anything wanting that is necessary, nor was there anything added that was superfluous, nor did She ever mistake one thing for another, nor was She in need of discourse or inquiry in order to be able to explain the most hidden mysteries of the Scriptures, whenever such explanation was necessary in the primitive Church.

Words of the Queen

THE VIRGIN MARY SPEAKS TO SISTER MARY OF AGREDA

81. The Most High, who in sheer goodness and bounty has given existence to all creatures and denies his providential care to none, faithfully supplies all souls with light, by which they can enter into the knowledge of Him and of eternal life, provided they do not of their own free will prevent and obscure this light by sin or give up the quest of the kingdom of heaven. To the souls, whom, according to his secret judgments, He calls to his Church, He shows himself still more liberal. For with the grace of Baptism He infuses into them not only those virtues, which are called essentially infused

and which the creature cannot merit by its own efforts; but also those, which are accidentally infused and which it can merit by its own labors and efforts. These the Lord gives freely beforehand, in order that the soul may be more prepared and zealous in the observance of his holy Law. In other souls, in addition to the common light of faith, the Lord in his clemency grants supernatural gifts of knowledge and virtue for the better understanding of the evangelical mysteries and for the more zealous practice of good works. In this kind of gifts He has been more liberal with thee than with many generations; obliging thee thereby to distinguish thyself in loving correspondence due to Him and to humble thyself before Him to the very dust.

82. In order that thou mayest be well instructed and informed, I wish to warn thee as a solicitous and loving Mother, of the cunning of satan for the destruction of these works of the Lord. From the very moment in which mortals begin to have the use of their reason, each one of them is followed by many watchful and relentless demons. For as soon as the souls are in a position to raise their thoughts to the knowledge of their God and commence the practice of the virtues infused by Baptism, these demons, with incredible fury and astuteness, seek to root out the divine seed; and if they cannot succeed in this, they try to hinder its growth, and prevent it from bringing forth fruit by engaging men in vicious, useless, or trifling things. Thus they divert their thoughts from faith and hope, and from the pursuit of other virtues, leading them to forget that they are Christians and diverting their attention from the knowledge of God and from the mysteries of the Redemption and of life eternal. Moreover the same enemy instills into the parents a base neglectfulness and carnal love for their offspring; and he incites the teachers to carelessness, so that the children find no support against evil in their education, but become de-

praved and spoiled by many bad habits, losing sight of virtue and of their good inclinations and going the way of perdition.

83. But the most kind Lord does not forget them in this danger and He renews in them his holy inspirations and special helps. He supplies them with the holy teachings of the Church by his preachers and ministers. He holds out to them the aid of the Sacraments and many other inducements to keep them on the path of life. That those who walk in the way of salvation are the smaller number, is due to the vice and depraved habits imbibed in youth and nourished in childhood. For that saying of Deuteronomy is very true : "As the days of thy youth, so also shall thy old age be" (Deut. 33, 25). Hence the demons gain courage and increase their tyrannical influence over souls in the early years of man's life, hoping that they will be able to induce men to commit so much the greater and the more frequent sins in later years, the more they have succedeed in drawing them into small and insignificant faults in their childhood. By these they draw them on to a state of blind presumption; for with each sin the soul loses more and more the power of resistance, subjects itself to the demon, and falls under the sway of its tyrannical enemies. The miserable yoke of wickedness is more and more firmly fastened upon it; the same is trodden underfoot by its own iniquity and urged onward under the sway of the devil from one precipice to another, from abyss to abyss (Ps. 41, 8) : a chastisement merited by all those, that allow themselves to be overcome by evildoing in the beginning. By these means Lucifer has hurled into hell so great a number of souls and continues so to hurl them every day, rising up in his pride against the Almighty. In this manner has he been able to introduce into the world his tyrannical power, spreading among men forgetfulness of death, judgment, heaven and hell, and casting so many nations from

abyss to abyss of darkness and bestial errors, such as are contained in the heresies and false sects of the infidels. Do thou therefore beware of this terrible danger, my daughter, and let not the memory of the law of thy God, his precepts and commands, and the truths of the Catholic Church and the doctrines of the Gospels ever fail in thy mind. Let not a day pass in which thou dost not spend much time in meditating upon all these; and exhort thy religious and all those who listen to thee to do the same. For thy enemy and adversary is laboring with ceaseless vigilance to obscure thy understanding in forgetfulness of the divine law, seeking to withdraw thy will, which is a blind faculty, from the practice of justification. This, thou knowest, consists in acts of living faith, trustful hope, ardent love, all coming from a contrite and humble heart (Ps. SO, 19).

Chapter VIII

HOW OUR GREAT QUEEN PRACTICED THE TEACHINGS OF
THE GOSPEL AS TAUGHT HER BY HER MOST HOLY SON.

84. Our Redeemer advanced in age and divine activity,
leaving behind Him the years of his boyhood and fulfilling
the task imposed upon Him by his eternal Father for the
benefit of mankind. He did not engage in the work of
preaching, nor did He perform at that time such open miracles as afterwards in Galilee, or before, in Egypt. But under
cover of secrecy He produced great effects in the souls and
bodies of men. He visited the poor and infirm; He consoled
the afflicted and sorrowful. By special enlightenment and
holy inspirations He led many souls to the way of salvation,
inducing them to turn to their Creator and to withdraw from
the devil and the works of death. These labors were continu-
ous and He was frequently absent from the house of the
blessed Virgin. Although the persons thus assisted were
aware, that they were moved and converted by the words and
the presence of Jesus, yet, as they were left in ignorance of the
mystery of his assistance and could ascribe it only to the
agency of God himself, they did not speak about it. The great
Lady learned of these wonders by seeing them reflected in the
most holy soul of her Son and by other means; and She

adored Him and gave Him thanks for them prostrate at his feet.

85. The rest of the time her most holy Son passed with his Mother, instructing Her and engaging with Her in prayer. He spoke to Her of his solicitude for his cherished flock, of the merits which He wished to accumulate for the benefit of souls, and of the means to be applied for their salvation. The most prudent Mother listened to all his words and cooperated with his divine love and wisdom, assisting Him in his office of Father, Brother, Friend, Teacher, Advocate, Protector and Redeemer of the human race. These conferences They held either by conversation or by interior communications, for in both ways the Son and the Mother could hold converse with each other. Her most holy Son would say: "My Mother, the fruit of my works and the foundation upon which I wish to build the Church, is to be a doctrine founded in holy science, which if believed and followed, shall be the life and salvation of men: an efficacious and holy law, which shall be capable of destroying the deathly poison of Lucifer, instilled by the first sin. I wish that men, by means of my precepts and counsels, become spiritualized and exalted to a participation and likeness of Myself, and that they, in their mortal flesh, become depositaries of my riches and afterwards participators of my eternal glory. I wish to give them the law of Moses, so renewed and improved, that it shall contain also the precepts and counsels."

86. All these intentions of the Master of life his heavenly Mother understood with profoundest insight and accepted with ardent love, reverencing and thanking Him in the name of all the human race. And as the Lord proceeded in all his instructions, She understood more and more fully the efficacy of all these sacraments, the powerful influence of the evangelical Law and doctrine in obedient souls, and the rewards attached to it; and She labored in its practical ful-

fillment as if She were the representative of each one of the creatures. She knew all the four Gospels word for word as they were to be written, and all the mysteries, which were to be contained therein. She of Herself understood all the teachings of the Gospels; for her knowledge was greater than that of its authors. She could have explained them without having seen the text. She knew also that her knowledge was to be copied from that of Christ, engraved on her soul as was the Law of the old Testament on the tablets in the ark. Her knowledge was to serve as the original, legitimate and veracious manuscript of the new Law of grace for the guidance of the saints and the just; for all of them were to copy the virtues and the holiness contained in this archive of grace, most holy Mary.

87. Her divine Teacher also instructed Her in her obligation of practicing this holy doctrine in its entirety, so that the high purposes, which He had in view in making Her partake in such exalted blessings and favors, might be attained. If we were to relate here, how fully and exquisitely the great Queen corresponded with his designs, it would be necessary to describe her whole life in this chapter; for it was a complete summary of the Gospel, copied from her own Son and Teacher. All that this holy doctrine has effected in the Apostles, Martyrs, Confessors, Virgins and in all the just and the saints, which have lived and shall live to the end of the world, could not be described, much less understood, except by the Lord himself. Yet we must consider, that all the saints and the just were conceived in sin and all of them placed some hindrance to grace; all of them could have attained higher grace and holiness and fell short in their correspondence with grace. But our heavenly Lady had no such defects or failings; She alone was material adequately disposed and adapted for the powerful activity of God and his blessings. She was the one who, without embarrassment and without opposition,

received the impetuous torrent of the Divinity communicated to Her by her own Son and God. From all this we may understand, that only in the beatific vision and in eternal felicity we shall be able to estimate, how much was due to this wonder of his Omnipotence.

88. Whenever I wish to explain some of the more important things manifested to me in this matter, I am at a loss what terms to use. For our great Queen and Lady observed the precept and doctrines of the Gospel according to the measure of her profound understanding of them and no creature is capable of reaching the limits of the science and intelligence of the Mother of wisdom in these teachings of Christ. Moreover, that which is understood of it exceeds the capacity of human words and speech. Let us take for an example the doctrine of that first sermon, which the Teacher of life gave on the mountain to his disciples, and which is recorded by saint Matthew (Matth. 5, 1). In it is contained the sum of Christian perfection, on which the Church is founded and which makes those blessed that observe them.

89. "Blessed are the poor in spirit," says our Lord and Teacher, "for theirs is the kingdom of heaven." This was the first and solid foundation of all evangelical life. Although the Apostles and our holy Father saint Francis understood it in a most exalted manner, yet Mary alone penetrated and fully weighed the greatness of this poverty in spirit; and just as She understood it, so She practiced it to its last limits. Into her heart the image of temporal riches found no entrance, nor did She feel the inclination toward them; but, while loving created things as the handiwork of the Lord, She at the same time detested them in so far as they were a hindrance or a burden to the love of God. She made use of them in moderation and only in so far as they were useful toward divine love. This admirable and most perfect poverty entitled Her to possess all things as Queen of heaven and earth. What I have

said here in regard to poverty, though strictly true, is but little in comparison to what our great Lady really understood and practiced in regard to this poverty of spirit, the first beatitude.

90. The second beatitude is: "Blessed are the meek, for they shall possess the earth." By her sweetest meekness the most holy Mary excelled in the practice of this beatitude not only over all mortals, just as Moses excelled all men of his time, but She surpassed the angels and seraphim themselves; for this sincerest Dove, being yet in mortal flesh, was interiorly and exteriorly no more exposed to disturbance and excitement of her faculties, than these pure spirits, who are not endowed with senses. In such an unlimited degree was She Mistress of all her bodily faculties and powers, as well as of the hearts of all with whom She had intercourse, that She possessed the earth in every day and reduced it to peaceful subjection. The third beatitude is: "Blessed are they that mourn, for they shall be comforted." The most holy Mary understood, more than any tongue can explain, the value and excellence of tears, and at the same time the foolishness and danger of laughter and human enjoyment. For, while all the children of Adam, though they are conceived in original sin and afterwards incur many other actual sins, give themselves over to laughter and gaiety, this heavenly Mother, being without sin at her Conception and ever after, was aware, that this mortal life should be consumed in weeping over the absence of the supreme Good and over the sins, which have been and are committed against God. For the sake of all men She wept over their sins, and merited by her most innocent tears the great consolations and favors of the Lord. Her most pure heart was in continual distress at the sight of the offenses committed against her Beloved and her God; her eyes distilled incessant tears (Jer. 9, 1), and her bread day and night was to weep over the ingratitude of sinners toward their

Creator and Redeemer (Ps. 41, 4). No creatures, not all of them together, wept more than the Queen of angels, though for men, on account of their sins, there is abundant cause of wailing and weeping, while in Her there was cause only for joy and delight on account of her treasures of grace.

91. The fourth beatitude, "Blessed are they that hunger and thirst after justice, for they shall have their fill," helped our heavenly Lady to enter into the understanding of this mysterious hunger and thirst. In Her this hunger and thirst for justice was greater than all the disgust ever entertained against it by the enemies of God. Having arrived at the pinnacle of justice and sanctity, her desire for it increased in proportion; while the plenitude of graces, poured out upon Her in a continual stream from the treasury of the Divinity, satiated her longing desires. As for the fifth beatitude: "Blessed are the merciful for they shall obtain mercy," She possessed it in such a high degree, that She alone deserved to be called the Mother of mercy, just as the Lord alone is called the Father of mercies (II Cor. 1, 3). She, who was most innocent and without any fault in the eyes of God, exercised mercy in its highest degree for the benefit and for the salvation of the human race. As She knew by her exalted science the excellence of this virtue, She never denied and never will deny mercy to anyone, whoever may ask; nor will She ever cease to seek out and hasten to the relief of the poor and needy, in order to offer them her assistance.

92. Without compeer was She also in the exercise of the sixth beatitude: "Blessed are the clean of heart, for they shall see God." For She was elect as the sun (Cant. 6, 9), a true imitation of the real Sun of justice and an image of our material sun, which is not defiled by things beneath it. Into the heart and mind of our most pure Princess no touch of defilement has ever found entrance; on the contrary, defilement was made impossible in Her on account of the exquis-

ite purity of her thoughts and because, from the first moment
of her existence and many times afterwards, She was favored
with the vision of the Divinity, although, being yet in a state
of pilgrimage, these visions were not continual. The seventh
beatitude: "Blessed are the peacemakers, for they shall be
called the children of God," was conferred upon Her in
admirable measure. She stood in need of this blessing in
order to preserve the peace of her heart and of her faculties in
the trials and tribulations of her life and in the passion and
death of her most holy Son. Never was She inordinately
disturbed, and She knew how to accept the greatest sufferings
with supreme peace of mind, being in all things a perfect
Daughter of the heavenly Father. Yea, it was especially by the
exercise of this beatitude, that She deserved to be called the
Daughter of the eternal Father. In the eighth beatitude:
"Blessed are they that suffer persecution for justice sake, for
theirs is the kingdom of heaven," Mary reached the pinnacle
of perfection. For She alone besides God was capable of
bearing with equanimity the sacrifice of the life and honor of
Christ our Lord, and the atrociousness with which it was
consummated. For we must remember that She was the true
Mother, as God was the true Father of his Onlybegotten.
This Lady alone imitated the Lord in his Passion and understood fully, that to such extremes must be executed the law of
her divine Teacher in the Gospels.

93. In this manner I am able to explain part of what I
have understood of the knowledge of the Gospel possessed
and put into practice by this great Lady. In the same way She
comprehended the evangelical precepts, counsels and parables of the Gospel; as for instance, the precepts of loving
enemies, pardoning injuries, doing good works in secret and
without vainglory, avoiding hypocrisy; the counsels of perfection and the teachings contained in the parables of the
recovered treasures, the lost pearl, the virgins, the seed scat-

tered on the ground, the talents and all other parables of the four Gospels. All of them She understood, together with the doctrines which they inculcate, and the high ends which the Master had in view. She knew all things in the most holy and perfect manner, and thus She also accomplished them to the last point. Of this Lady we can say what Christ said of Himself: that She came not to abrogate the law, but to fulfill it.

Words of the Queen

THE VIRGIN MARY SPEAKS TO SISTER MARY OF AGREDA

94. My daughter, it was proper that the Teacher of virtue should make known to us what He did, and that He should fulfill what He taught. For both word and action belong to the office of teaching. The words should instruct, while the example should move and give witness to the teaching, in order that it may be accepted and practiced. All this was fulfilled by my most holy Son, and by me in imitation of Him (Matth. 5, 9). As neither He nor I was to remain always upon this earth, He wished to leave behind Him the holy Gospels as a summary of his life and of mine, in order that the children of the light, by believing and practicing its teachings, might regulate their lives in imitation of his. For in it the practical results of the teachings of Christ are exhibited, such as they brought forth in me by imitating Him. Of great value are the sacred Gospels, and for this reason thou must look upon them with utmost veneration. I call thy attention to the fact, that my most holy Son and I are much honored and pleased to see the divine sayings and the doings of his life properly esteemed and respected among men. On the other hand, the Lord considers the forgetting and the neglecting of the doctrines contained in the Gospels a great injury done to Him by the children of the Church in our times. For there are many who do not listen or attend to them, who give no

thanks for this blessing, and who make no more of them than if they were pagan writings, or as if they did not contain in them the light of faith.

95. Thy debt is great in this regard; for thou hast received insight into the veneration and esteem in which I held the evangelical doctrines, and thou wast made aware, how I labored in order to put them into practice. Thou hast not been able to learn all of what I practiced and understood, as thy capacity is too limited; yet remember at least, that with no entire nation have I been so condescending as with thee alone in lavishing this blessing. Therefore, be very careful how thou correspond with it, lest thou render fruitless the love which has been instilled into thee for the divine Scriptures, and particularly for the Gospels and their exalted doctrines. They are to serve thee as a shining beaconlight, and my life should be thy model for forming thy own. Take heed how important and necessary it is for thy welfare to attend to this with all diligence; how much pleasure thou canst thereby give to my Son and Lord, and how I shall consider myself obliged anew to treat with thee as a Mother and as a Teacher. Fear the danger of not attending to the divine calls, for that is the cause of the loss of innumerable souls. Since thou receivest so many and so wonderful calls from thy merciful and omnipotent God, how reprehensible will be thy rudeness, how abominable thou wilt make thyself to the Lord, to me and the saints, if thou fail to correspond with them!

Chapter IX

HOW THE MOST HOLY MARY WAS INSTRUCTED IN THE ARTICLES OF FAITH AND WHAT USE SHE MADE OF THIS KNOWLEDGE.

96. The unshakable foundation of our justification, and the beginning of all holiness in men, is the belief in the truths, which have been revealed by God in his holy Church. Like a most skillful architect, the Lord has built his Church on a firm rock, in order that the storms and floods of her earthly course of existence might find Her altogether immovable (Luke 6, 48). Thus wisely provided with a firm foundation in her articles of faith, the evangelical Church is invincibly established as the only true one, the Roman Catholic Church. She is one in the unity of faith, hope and charity, to be found only in Her; one without the division or contradiction which reigns in the synagogues of satan. The sects and heresies are full of darkness and errors and are at war not only with each other and with right reason, but each one is at war with itself by maintaining contradictory and erroneous doctrines at the same or different times. Against all these our holy faith shall ever remain victorious and the portals of hell shall never prevail against it in the least of its points (Matth 16, 18); though, according to the prophecy of the Master of Life, the powers of hell incessantly winnow and sift it like wheat, as has happened to saint Peter and his successors.

97. In order that our Queen and Lady, this wonderful ocean of grace and knowledge, might receive adequate information concerning the evangelical law, it was necessary that She come into possession also of all the truths of the Catholic faith, which would in all times be believed by the faithful. She must be especially well instructed in the first principles of all Christian belief. For all truths, down to the very dogmas, which were to be defined and believed concerning her own Self, were within the capacity of most holy Mary and could be entrusted to her admirable wisdom. Hence, as I shall describe afterwards, She was informed of all tenets of the Catholic faith together with the circumstances of time, place and manner of their publication as they became opportune and necessary in the course of the history of the Church. In order to instruct the blessed Virgin especially in these articles, the Lord sent upon Her an abstractive vision of the Divinity, such as I have described on other occasions. In this vision were manifested to her most hidden mysteries of his inscrutable Judgment and Providence. She became aware of the infinite bounty, whereby He established the blessing of infused faith and enabled man deprived of the vision of the Divinity, easily and quickly to come to the knowledge of God, without hesitation and without waiting or searching for this knowledge by limited and shortsighted investigation of natural science. For from the first dawn of reason, our Catholic faith raises us immediately to the certain knowledge, not only of the Divinity in three Persons, but of the humanity of Christ our Lord and of the means of gaining eternal life. All this is not attained by the fruitless and sterile human science, unless the mind is impregnated with the force and virtue of divine faith.

98. In this vision then, our great Queen clearly perceived all these mysteries and all that is contained in them. She saw how the holy Church propounded fourteen special articles of

Catholic belief from the very beginning, and how She afterwards, in diverse times, defined many truths and dogmas, which are contained in them and in the holy Scriptures as in roots ready to be cultivated and to bring forth fruit. After seeing all this in her vision, She saw it reflected also in the most holy soul of Christ, where the whole fabric of divine teachings originated. Thereupon the celestial Princess entered into conference with her Lord concerning the practical application of these articles of faith to her life. He informed Her, that She was to be the first One, who should, in a singular and most perfect manner, believe and practically exhibit each of the articles of divine faith. In regard to the first of those seven articles that pertain to the Divinity, She understood that there is but one true God, independent, necessary, infinite, immense in his attributes and perfections, unchangeable and eternal. She understood also how just and necessary it is for creatures to believe and confess this truth. She gave thanks for the revelation of this first article and begged her most holy Son to continue to favor the human race by conferring upon men the grace of believing and accepting this truth. By this infallible, though obscure, light, She saw the wickedness of idolatry and wept with indescribable sorrow and bitterness over such aberration. In reparation She ardently exercised Herself in faith and worship of God, and performed many other acts inspired by her intimate sense of this obligation.

99. Then proceeding to the second article, that God is the Father, She learned how it was to lead on men to the belief of the Trinity and other doctrines, which explain the three persons in one God, and how men are to come to the full knowledge of their last end, its proper attainment and enjoyment. She understood how the person of the Father could not be born or proceed from the Others, and how He is, as it were, the origin of all else; hence She clearly saw how He

created heaven and earth and all creatures and how He is without beginning and at the same time the beginning of all things. For this truth our heavenly Lady gave thanks and in the name of the whole human race, began to shape her actions in correspondence with this new knowledge. The third article, that there is a Son, the Mother of grace believed with particular clearness of comprehension, especially as regards the processions of the Deity ad intra. The first and most important of these acts ad intra is none other than the eternal generation of the Son. This takes place from all eternity by the operation of the divine intellect through which the Son is engendered of the Father, being not inferior, but equal in Divinity, eternity, and infinite attributes. She believed and comprehended also in the fourth article, that there is a Holy Ghost, the third Person, proceeding from the Father and the Son as from one principle, by an act of the will, equal to the other Persons in all things and having only these personal distinctions, which result from the emanations and processions of the infinite intellect and will. Although, concerning these mysteries, most holy Mary possessed the knowledge, which She had already attained in her former visions, it was supplemented in this vision by the knowledge of the circumstances and qualifications attached to these truths and articles of the Catholic faith, and by the discernment of the heresies, which Lucifer concocted and sowed in opposition to these articles ever since he fell from heaven and knew of the Incarnation of the Word. In satisfaction for all these errors the most blessed Lady excited acts of supreme faith, in the manner already described.

100. Also the fifth article, that the Lord is the Creator, most holy Mary believed and understood. She perceived that the creation of all things, though it is attributed to the Father, is common to the three Persons, in as far as they are one only God, infinite, omnipotent and the first cause of the

existence and preservation of all creatures; that no other being has the power to create or produce out of nothing any other being, even if there were question of an angel creating the lowest worm. For only He, who is independent of any inferior or superior cause can create. She understood the necessity of this article of the holy faith for counteracting the errors of Lucifer, in order that God might be known and acknowledged as the Author of all things. In the sixth article She understood anew all the mysteries of predestination, vocation and final justification; how the reprobate, because they did not profit by the means offered to them by divine mercy, lose eternal happiness. The most faithful Lady perceived also how the work of salvation is common to the three persons; and how it pertains especially to the Word in as far as He is man; because He was to be the price of the rescue, which would be accepted by God in satisfaction for original and actual sins. The great Queen took notice of all the Sacraments and mysteries accepted and believed by the holy Church; and She accompanied the understanding of each of them with heroic acts of many virtues. In the seventh article which contains the doctrine of God's activity in bringing about the eternal happiness of man, She understood all that pertains to the eternal felicity of mortal creatures in the fruition of the beatific vision; how important it is for them to believe in this truth in order to attain eternal happiness and how they should consider themselves not a progeny of this earth, but citizens of heaven, who are only making a pilgrimage and ought, therefore, be much consoled in this faith and hope of heaven.

101. Of the seven articles which pertain to the divine humanity, our great Queen had a similar knowledge, yet accompanied by new affections of her purest and humblest heart. That He was conceived as man by the operation of the Holy Ghost She had experienced in Herself and She knew

that this would be an article of the holy faith. Indescribable were the effects which this knowledge wrought in the most prudent Lady. She humbled Herself below the most insignificant of creatures and to the very dust of the earth. She was profoundly penetrated by the consciousness of having been created out of nothing. She completed the deep trenches and built the strong foundations of humility, upon which the Almighty was to erect the high and exquisite edifice of infused science and exalted perfection. She extolled the Almighty and gave thanks to Him for Herself and for the whole human race, because He had chosen such an excellent way of drawing toward Him the hearts of men by his human presence and by the intimate relations established with them by the Christian faith. The same effects were produced in Her by the second of these articles, that Christ our Lord was born of Mary, a Virgin. She had full understanding of the mysteries contained in this dogma: that She was the One chosen by God to retain intact her Virginity and yet be also selected among all creatures as the Mother of the Lord; that as well the Almighty as She herself should share in the dignity and excellence of such divine handiwork; and that the holy Church should believe and hold such a doctrine as one of her certain tenets. Enraptured by the consideration of these and many other truths, the heavenly Lady excited within Herself such acts of exalted virtue as cannot be expressed by any human terms. She spent Herself in returning a full measure of praise, worship, and thankful acknowledgment for each of them, humbling Herself in proportion as She was exalted and annihilating Herself to the dust.

102. The third of these articles is, that Christ our Lord underwent suffering and death; the fourth, that He descended into hell and freed the souls of the just, who were in limbo awaiting his coming; the fifth, that He rose from the dead; the sixth, that He ascended into heaven and is seated at the

right hand of the eternal Father; the seventh, that thence He is to come to judge the living and the dead in the general judgment in order to give to each according to his works. These truths, just as the others, the most holy Mary believed and understood profoundly as well in themselves as in regard to the order, sequence and necessity with which they are to be held and believed by mortals. She alone made up for the faults of those who have not or will not believe in these truths and for the deficiencies caused by our slowness in believing them and by our want of proper esteem, veneration and thankfulness due to these divine teachings. The whole Church calls our Queen most fortunate and blessed, not only because She gave belief to the messenger of heaven (Luke 1, 45), but because She unswervingly trusted in the fulfillment of the mysteries wrought and accomplished in her virginal womb; and She believed them both for Herself and for all the children of Adam. She was the Champion of the divine faith, who, in the sight of the heavenly court, unfurled the banner of holy faith to all the faithful on earth. She was the first Queen of the Catholic faith in this world and was to have no equal. In Her all Catholics have a true Mother; and on this account, those that call upon Her, are especially her children; for without a doubt this kind Mother and Commandress of the Catholic faith looks with an especial love upon those who follow Her in this great virtue of faith and who exert themselves in its spread and defense.

103. My discourse would be too prolix, if I were to say all that I have learned of the faith of our great Lady, of all her penetration into. the circumstances and secrets of these articles of faith, and into all the truths connected with these Catholic doctrines. Certainly I have not words enough to rehearse the mysteries revealed to Her in her conferences with her divine Teacher, Jesus, in her humble and prudent inquiries, in the answers of her most sweet Son, in the pro-

found secrets laid bare before her eyes, and in the sacraments manifest only to Mother and Son. Moreover, I was informed that it is not proper to reveal all of them to men in this mortal life. But in most holy Mary the whole of this new and divine Testament was deposited and She alone preserved it most faithfully, in order that She might in proper time dispense whatever the necessities of the holy Church might demand. 0 most fortunate and happy Mother! For if a wise son is the delight of his father (Prov. 10, 1), who can describe the joy of this great Queen, when She saw the glory resulting to the Eternal Father through the work I of his Onlybegotten, who was also her Son, and when She fully penetrated the vast mysteries contained in the doctrines of the holy Catholic faith?

Words of the Queen

THE VIRGIN MARY SPEAKS TO SISTER MARY OF AGREDA

104. My daughter, mortal mind is not capable of comprehending what I was made to feel through the infused knowledge and faith of the articles established by my most holy Son as those of the holy Church, and what were the effects wrought thereby upon my faculties. Necessarily, therefore, thy words fail thee in seeking to declare what thou hast understood concerning them; for all the concepts of the mind fall short of comprehending and expressing these mysteries. But what I desire and command, is this; that thou preserve with all reverence and solicitude the precious knowledge and understanding of these venerable sacraments. For as Mother I remind and warn thee of the cruel and cunning efforts of thy enemies to rob thee of them. Be thou ever on thy guard, that they may find thee full of strength, and that thy domestics, which are the faculties of thy body and mind, be clothed with the double vestments of interior

and exterior watchfulness in order to be able to resist the onslaught of their temptation (Prov. 31, 17). The powerful arms for battling against those who make war on thee, must be the doctrines of the Catholic faith (Rom. 1, 17), for the firm belief in them and the continual exercise of them, the incessant meditation and remembrance of them, illumine the souls, drives away errors, disclose the deceits of satan and disperse his falsehoods just as the rays of the sun dispel the dark clouds. Moreover, all these exercises serve as substantial nourishment of the spirit to strengthen the soul for the battles of the Lord.

105. If the faithful do not feel these and even more wonderful effects of faith, it is not because faith has not the strength and efficacy to produce them, but it is because some of the faithful are so forgetting and negligent, while others give themselves up so much to a carnal and bestial life and thereby counteract the blessing of faith. They think so rarely of it, that they might as well not have received it at all. As they live like the infidels who have never enjoyed its advantages and as they gradually become conscious of their unhappy infidelity, they fall into greater wickedness than the unbelievers. For such is the result of their abominable ingratitude and contempt for this exalted and sovereign gift. I ask of thee, my dearest daughter, that thou give thanks for the blessings of holy faith with profound humility and fervent love; that thou practice it with unceasing and heroic acts; that thou continually meditate on its mysteries. Thus shalt thou enjoy without hindrance its sweet and godlike effects. The more vivid and penetrating thy knowledge of the mysteries of faith, so much the greater and more powerful will be its effects upon thee. If thou concurrest with proper diligence, thou wilt grow in the understanding of the exalted and wonderful mysteries and sacraments pertaining to the essence of the triune God, to the hypostatical union of the

divine and human nature, to the life, death and resurrection of my most holy Son, and to the other activities of the God-man. Thus wilt thou taste of his sweetness and gather plentiful fruits of peace and of eternal life.

Chapter X

HOW MOST HOLY MARY RECEIVED ENLIGHTENMENT ON
THE TEN COMMANDMENTS, AND HOW SHE APPLIED IT.

106. Just as the doctrines of the Catholic faith pertain to the
activity of the intellect, so the commandments pertain to the
activity of the will. Although all free acts, as well those required by the practice of the infused, as those of the acquired
virtues, depend upon the activity of the willpower, yet they
do not all depend upon it in the same way; for the acts of
faith proceed immediately from the intellect, and depend
upon the will only in so far as they are embraced by it with a
sincere, pious and reverential affection. The obscure acts and
truths of faith do not force their acceptance upon the intellect without cooperation of the will, and therefore the intellect waits upon the decision of the will. But in the exercise of
virtues founded upon faith, the will acts for itself and relies
upon the intellect only for guidance toward the accomplishment of that which was resolved upon. The will is so free and
independent that it permits no commands of the intellect,
nor any kind of violence. This is the order established by the
Lord, so that no one might be forced to serve Him unwillingly, through necessity, by compulsion or violence; but that,
according to the Apostle, each one may serve God with
unrestricted liberty and joyfulness.

107. After the blessed Virgin had been so divinely instructed in the articles and dogmas of our holy faith, She was favored by another vision of the Divinity, similar to that mentioned in the last chapter. It was vouchsafed to Her for the purpose of renewing in Her the understanding of the ten commandments of the Decalogue. In it were manifested to Her, with great clearness and fullness, all the mysteries of the Commandments as they were propounded by the divine clemency for the guidance of men to eternal life and as they had been given to Moses on the two tablets. On the first of these tablets were written the three precepts concerning the honor and worship of God, on the second, the seven pertaining to our intercourse with our neighbors. The Redeemer of the world, her most holy Son, was to rewrite all of them in the hearts of men (I Pet. 1, 4), while our Queen and Lady was to commence the practice of all that each one contained. She also understood their relation to each other, and how necessary they were to men in order to attain to the participation of the Divinity. She had a clear comprehension of the equity, justice and wisdom with which they were established by the divine will; and that they were a holy, immaculate, sweet, lightsome, pure, unerring and convenient law for the creatures. She saw how welladjusted and conformable they were to human nature, how well they can and ought to be embraced with joy and appreciation, and how their Author proffered the help of his grace for their observance. Our great Queen perceived in this vision many other exalted mysteries and secrets concerning the holy Church, concerning those who, in it, would observe the divine commands, and those who would despise and transgress them.

108. The blessed Lady issued from this vision transformed by an ardent and zealous love for the divine law. Immediately She betook Herself to her most holy Son, in whose soul She saw the divine laws clearly

mirrored, to reproduce them in her own self according to the order of grace. At the same time, by abundant enlightenment, She was made aware how it pleased the Lord to make Her a living model of the observance of all these commandments. It is true, as I have said several times, that our great Lady possessed a habitual infused knowledge of all these mysteries for her continual guidance; yet this habitual knowledge was renewed and intensified day by day. As the extent and depth of mysteries was so to say infinite, there always remained a measureless field of new secrets open for her interior vision. On this occasion many new points were explained to Her by the divine Teacher, and He propounded to Her the new law and precepts in their bearing upon each other and in the sequence, which they were to hold in the militant Church of his Gospel. Also concerning each one of them separately, She obtained new and special enlightenments. Although our limited capacity and understanding cannot comprehend such high and sovereign sacraments, none of them were concealed from the heavenly Lady. For we must not measure her profound knowledge with the capacity of our shortsighted understanding.

109. With a most humble and ready heart She subjected Herself to the observance of all his commandments, and petitioned God to instruct Her and grant Her this divine grace to execute all that He had commanded. The Lord answered Her as follows: "My Mother, thou art the one whom I have eternally chosen and predestined for the greater pleasure of my Father, one in Divinity with Me. Our eternal love, which urges Us to communicate the blessings of our Divinity to creatures and thus raise them to the participation of our glory and felicity, has established this holy and pure law, by which mortals may attain the end for which they were created. This our wish shall be fulfilled perfectly in thee, my beloved Dove, for in thy heart our divine law shall be

written so clearly and deeply, that from the very beginning of thy existence to all eternity it shall not be effaced; and in no wise shall it remain unfulfilled or ineffectual in thee, as is the case with other children of Adam. Take notice, dearest Sulamite, that this law is entirely pure and immaculate; and that therefore, We wish to deposit it in thee, who art also pure and immaculate and in whom all our intentions and operations are glorified."

110. These words, which were realized in the heavenly Mother without any hindrance, enriched and deified Her with the full understanding and acceptance of the ten Commandments and the mysteries contained therein. Directing her intellect by the celestial light and conforming her will to that of the divine Teacher, She entered into the meaning of the first and most noble of all the commandments: "Thou shalt love the Lord thy God with thy whole heart, and with thy whole soul, and with thy whole mind" (Matth. 22, 37), for in these words it was given afterwards by the Evangelists and long before by Moses in Deuteronomy. Her mind grasped it with all the qualifications added thereto by the Lord: that men should preserve it in their hearts, that the fathers should teach it to their children, and that they should meditate upon it in their houses and outside of them, on their journeys, during sleep and in their watching, and that they should incessantly have it before the eyes of their soul. Just as deep as was her understanding of this commandment, so great was her zeal in fulfilling all that the Lord wished to command thereby. Though no other child of Adam has succeeded in fulfilling it perfectly during mortal life, yet most holy Mary succeeded, and more completely than the highest and most ardent Seraphim, than all the saints and the blessed of heaven. I will not tarry in explaining this more fully, for in the first part of this history, when speaking of her virtues, I have sufficiently discoursed upon the love of the blessed

Virgin. On this occasion particularly She shed the most bitter tears because of the sins which were to be committed against this great Commandment; and She took it upon Herself to satisfy by her love for the defects and faults of mortals.

111. Upon the first precept follow the two others; not to dishonor the name of God by false and vain swearing, and to honor Him by observing and sanctifying his feasts. These Commandments the Mother of wisdom understood and penetrated, engraving them in her pious and humble heart and resolving to render supreme veneration and worship to the Deity. Deeply she pondered on the injuries committed by creatures against the immutable being of God and his infinite goodness by false and vain oaths, or by blasphemies against God and against his saints. In her sorrow on account of the presumptuous transgression of these commandments by the rational creatures She conjured her attending angels in her name to charge the guardian spirits of all men to prevent the committance of this outrage against God; to restrain men, by holy inspirations and by the fear of God, from perjuring or blaspheming his holy name. Moreover, She besought the Almighty to shower his benedictions of sweetness on those, who abstained from vain oaths and who reverenced his holy name.

112. In regard to the keeping of the holidays, which is the third Commandment the great Queen was made acquainted by her guardian angel with all the feasts, which were to be instituted by the Church, and with the manner of their celebration and observance. As I have mentioned in its place, She had commenced to celebrate those which commemorate the already consummated mysteries of her life, such as that of the most holy Trinity, and those pertaining to her most holy Son and the angels. To celebrate these and other mysteries, afterwards solemnized by the Church, She invited the heavenly court, and, in union with them, She sang hymns of

praise and thanksgiving to the Lord. The days which are
especially assigned for the worship of God, She spent entirely
therein; not that her exterior activity ever interfered with her
interior attention, or hindered the flights of her soul, but
because She wished to sanctify the feasts of the Lord in such
a manner as was required by the new law of grace; and all this
as the first disciple of the Redeemer of the world, She eagerly
strove to fulfill.

113. The same understanding and knowledge most holy
Mary possessed in regard to the seven Commandments,
which concern our duties toward our neighbor. Regarding
the fourth Commandment, to honor father and mother, She
understood well who were to be included under the name of
parents; how, after the honor due to God, that due to parents
comes next; and how children are to render them this honor
in all reverence; also what are the obligations of parents
toward their children. She saw the justice of the fifth commandment, forbidding murder, since the Lord is the Master
of life and being of man, and withheld power over it even
from its owner, and therefore much more from any of his
fellow beings. As life is the very first of the natural goods and
the foundation of grace, She gave thanks to the Lord for
having by his Commandment so bountifully protected it.
She looked upon all men as creatures of his hand, capable of
his grace and glory, and purchased by the blood of her Son;
and therefore She earnestly prayed for the faithful observance
of this commandment in the Church of God. Our most pure
Lady understood the nature of the sixth Commandment in
the same manner as the blessed, who need no precaution
against human passions and can look upon it without being
touched by it. The most blessed Lady, altogether preserved
from the taint of sin, understood the nature of this Commandment even from a higher standpoint of grace than the
saints. Such were the sentiments awakened in this great

Paragon of chastity while She excited love for it and sorrow for the impurities committed by men, that She wounded anew the heart of the Almighty (Cant. 4, 9); and, according to our way of speaking, consoled her divine Son for the offenses of mankind against this precept. Since She knew that in the new law of the Gospel the observance of this Commandment was to be carried so far as to make possible congregations of virgins and men, who would promise inviolate chastity by vow, She besought the Lord to guarantee them his unbroken blessings. The Lord granted this request of his purest Mother and He assured Her that, as a reward of virginal purity, its devotees should have the privilege of being the followers of Her, who was the Virgin Mother of the Lamb (Ps. 44, 15). With incomparable joy She gave thanks to the Lord for thus extending the practice of virginity, which She herself had inaugurated in the new law. I will not stop to descant upon the priceless value of this virtue, since I have already spoken of it in the first part and in other places.

114. Equally remarkable was Mary's understanding of the other Commandments, of the seventh: "Thou shalt not steal"; of the eighth, "Thou shalt not give false testimony"; of the ninth, "Thou shalt not covet thy neighbor's wife"; of the tenth, "Thou shalt not covet thy neighbor's goods and possessions." In regard to each of them She excited great acts of interior compliance with them and for each of them She praised and thanked the Lord, that He should have provided for men such wise and effectual means of attaining their eternal happiness through these beneficent and well adapted laws. For She saw, that by their observance, men would not only secure eternal reward due to them, but could also enjoy true peace and tranquillity adapted to each one's state and circumstances. For if all rational creatures would submit to the just requirements of God's law, and would resolve to follow and observe his Commandments, they would enjoy

that most delightful and exquisite happiness, which is produced by the testimony of a good conscience. All the human
delight cannot be compared to the consolation of having
been faithful to the divine law in all things, great and small
(Matth. 25, 21). This blessing we owe mostly to Christ, our
Redeemer, who confirmed us in doing good and thus secures
for us sweet rest, and peace, and consolation, and many other
blessings in this life. If all of us do not attain them, it is
because we do not observe his Commandments. The labors,
misfortunes, and unhappiness of the people are the inseparable effects of the transgressions of mortals, and, though each
one contributes his share in causing our misfortunes, yet we
are so senseless, that as soon as we are overtaken by any
adversity, we begin to lay the blame on others, while we
should lay it only on ourselves.

115. Who can estimate the evils of this life springing from
dishonest dealings, forbidden by the seventh commandment,
or from the want of contentment with one's own lot in
reliance on the help of the Lord, who forgets not the birds of
the air, or the smallest worm of the earth? What miseries and
afflictions do not Christian nations suffer merely because
their rulers are not satisfied with the territories given into
their charge by the highest King? Seeking to extend their
sway and influence they have left in the world neither peace,
nor quiet possession, nor any souls for the service of their
Creator. No less evil and discord is caused by false testimony
and lies, which offend the infinite truth and hinder human
intercourse, sowing the seed of strife, destroying peace and
tranquillity in the human hearts. Both the one as well as the
other prevent the Creator to dwell in them as is his wish.
Coveting another's wife and adultery violate the holy law of
matrimony, confirmed and sanctified by the Sacrament, and
how many hidden and open evils have they not caused, and
do they not cause, among Catholics? If we consider how

many transgressions are manifest to the eyes of the world, and how many more remain hidden to men, while they are not hidden to God, the exact and just judge, who punishes them even now, shall we not be convinced that He will be so much the severer in his punishments, the more He has overlooked our sins at present and the longer He has patiently allowed the Christian commonwealths to continue in existence?

116. All these truths our great Queen perceived in the Lord. Although She was aware of the wickedness of men in thus lightly throwing aside the respect and reverence due to their God after He had so kindly provided for them such necessary laws and precepts; yet the most prudent Lady was neither scandalized at human frailty, nor did She wonder at man's ingratitude; but like a kind Mother, She pitied the mortals, and with most ardent love She thanked the Almighty for his benefits trying to satisfy for the transgressions against the evangelical law and asking for the grace to observe them perfectly. The summary of all these Commandments: to love God above all and our neighbor as ourselves, the most holy Mary comprehended perfectly; also the truth, that the proper understanding and practice of these two Commandments is the perfection of true virtue. He that practices them is not far from the kingdom of God, and the observance of them is to be preferred to the offering of holocausts, as the Lord himself teaches us in the Gospel (Mark 12, 34, 33). In the proportion as our Queen understood these precepts, so She put them into practice, fulfilling them as they are contained in the Gospel, without the omission of the least of its precepts or counsels. This heavenly Princess put the teachings of the Redeemer more perfectly into practice than all the saints and faithful of the holy Church.

Words of the Queen

THE VIRGIN MARY SPEAKS TO SISTER MARY OF AGREDA

117. My daughter, when the Word of the eternal Father issued forth from his bosom and assumed humanity in my womb, He came to enlighten those that walk in the darkness and in the shadow of death (Luke 1, 79), and to restore them to their lost happiness. Hence, in order to be their light, their way, their truth and their life, it was necessary that He should give them a law so holy, that it would justify them; so clear that it would enlighten them; so secure, that it would encourage them; so powerful, that it would move them; so efficacious, that it would help them; so truthful, that it would bring joy and delight to all that would observe it. The immaculate law of the Gospel has in it the power to produce all these and other more wonderful effects; and God has created and constituted rational creatures in such a way, that all their happiness, corporal and spiritual, temporal and eternal, depends entirely upon observing this law. Hence thou canst judge of the blind ignorance with which their deadly enemies have fascinated mortals (Gal. 3, 1), since all men, in the inordinate desire and pursuit of happiness, neglect the divine law, where alone it can be found; and hence few really attain happiness.

118. Knowing this, prepare thy heart so that the Lord may write in it his holy law. Forget and put away from thee all that is visible and earthly, so that all thy faculties may be free and unencumbered of any images except of those which are fixed there by the finger of God and are contained in the doctrine and precepts of the gospel truths. In order that thy desires may not be frustrated beseech the Lord day and night, to make thee worthy of the blessings and promises of my most holy Son. Remember that the negligence is more abominable in thee than in all the other mortals; for no one else

has his divine love so urgently called, or assisted with the like blessings and helps. In the days of abundance as well as in the days of affliction and temptation remember thy debt to the Lord and his jealous zeal, so that neither favors may exalt thee nor sufferings and pain oppress thee. If in the one as in the other state do thou turn to the divine law written in thy heart, observing it inviolably and incessantly with all attention and perfection. In regard to the love of the neighbors apply always the first law of doing unto others as thou wishest done to thyself, which is the standard of all intercourse with men. If thou desirest them to think and act well toward thee, thou thyself must do the same with thy brethren. If thou feel that they offend thee in little things, avoid thou giving them any such offense. If thou see others doing what seems evil and disagreeable to their neighbor, avoid it thyself; for thou knowest how much it offends against the law established by the Most High. Weep over thy faults and those of thy fellowmen; because they are against the law of God; this is true charity toward the Lord and toward thy neighbor. Sorrow over the afflictions of others as over thy own, for thus wilt thou imitate me.

Chapter XI

THE DEEP KNOWLEDGE OF THE MOST HOLY MARY CON-
CERNING THE SEVEN SACRAMENTS WHICH WERE TO BE
INSTITUTED BY CHRIST THE LORD, AND CONCERNING THE
FIVE PRECEPTS OF THE CHURCH.

119. In order to complete the beauty and the riches of the
holy Church, it was proper that her Founder, Christ our
Redeemer, should institute the seven sacraments, which were
to serve as the common treasury of all his merits. Yea, the
Creator of all these blessings himself was to remain really
present in one of them as the nourishment and consolation
of the faithful and as a pledge of their enjoying Him eternally
face to face. For the perfection of the knowledge and grace of
the most holy Mary it was necessary that the fulness of these
sacramental blessings be transplanted into her dilated and
ardent soul, in order that to its full extent and in the same
manner as it existed in the heart of her holiest Son, the law of
grace might be written and recorded in the tablets of her
mind. In his absence She was to be the Teacher of the
Church and She was to instruct the primitive Christians to
venerate and enjoy these Sacraments with all the perfection
possible.

120. By a new enlightenment, each of these mysteries in
particular were accordingly made manifest to the blessed
Mother in the interior of her most holy Son. In regard to the

first of these Sacraments She saw, that the ancient law of circumcision was to be honorably laid aside and to be replaced by the admirable and sweet sacrament of Baptism. She was informed that the matter of this Sacrament was to be pure natural water and that its form was to contain the names of the three Persons, the Father, the Son and the Holy Ghost, thus implicitly including faith in the most holy Trinity. She understood how Christ, its Author, was to impart to this Sacrament the power of taking away all sins and of perfectly sanctifying its recipient. She saw the admirable effects it was to cause in men, regenerating them so as to constitute them adoptive sons of God and heirs of heaven; infusing into them the virtues of faith, hope and charity with many other virtues, and impressing upon their souls the character of children of the holy Church. This and all other effects of this holy Sacrament were made manifest to most holy Mary. Thereupon She sought her divine Son with burning desire to be allowed to receive it in proper time; which He promised Her, and as I shall describe later on, afterwards really fulfilled.

121. A like understanding the great Lady also received concerning the second Sacrament, that of Confirmation. This is given in the second place, because Baptism is intended to engender the children of the Church, while Confirmation is to make them strong and courageous in confessing the faith received in Baptism, augmenting the first graces and adding thereto the graces suited to each one's state. She understood the form, matter, minister and effects of this Sacrament, and the character it impresses upon the soul; and how, by the holy oil and chrism, which form the matter of this Sacrament, is typified the odor of the good works of Christ in which the faithful participate by faith, while the same only in a different way, is also indicated by the form of the Sacrament, namely, by the words used in its administra-

tion. Corresponding with these enlightenments, our great Queen elicited heroic acts of praise, thanksgiving and fervent petition, desiring that all men draw from these fountains of the Lord and enjoy these incomparable treasures, while acknowledging and confessing Him as the true God and Redeemer. She wept bitterly over the lamentable loss of so many, who, in spite of the preaching of the Gospel, feel not its healing powers.

122. In regard to the third Sacrament, that of Penance, the heavenly Lady saw the usefulness and necessity of this means of restoring souls to the grace and friendship of God, since by their frailty they lose it so often. She understood its requirements and the power of its ministers and the ease with which the faithful can secure to themselves its blessings. As the true Mother of mercy She gave special thanks to the Almighty for providing such a powerful medicine against the repeated and daily faults of her children. She prostrated Herself upon the ground and, in the name of the holy Church, She reverently acknowledged the sacred tribunal of Confession, where the Lord, with ineffable kindness, relieved and solved all doubts of the souls in regard to their justification or condemnation, leaving it to the judgment of the priests, whether they should grant or deny absolution.

123. Especially deep was the intelligence of the most prudent Lady in regard to the sovereign sacramental mystery of the most holy Eucharist. Her penetration of its secrets surpassed that of the most exalted seraphim. For to Her was manifested the supernatural manner of the presence of the humanity and Divinity of her Son under the appearances of bread and wine, the power of the words of consecration, by which the substance of the bread and wine is changed into the substance of his body and blood, while the appearances remained; how He could be present at the same time in so many diverse parts; how the sacred mystery of the Mass was

to be instituted, in order that He may be consecrated and offered to the eternal Father to the end of times; how He should be reverenced and adored in the holy Sacrament in so many temples of the Catholic Church throughout the world; what effects of grace He would produce in those, who were to receive Him more or less well prepared, and what punishments would come to those who receive Him unworthily. She was informed also of the faith of the believers and the errors of the heretics in regard to this mystery, and especially of the immense love of her Son in thus resolving to give Himself as food and nourishment of eternal life to each one of the mortals.

124. By these and other enlightenments concerning the most holy Eucharist, her most chaste bosom was visited with new conflagrations of love beyond the conception of human intellect. Although She had invented new canticles of praise and worship at the enlightenments, which She had received concerning each article of faith and each mystery; yet in considering this great Sacrament her heart expanded more than ever before, and, prostrate on the ground, She spent Herself in new demonstrations of love, worship, praise, thanksgiving and humility; in sentiments of deepest sorrow for those, who were to abuse it for their own damnation. She burned with the desire of seeing this Sacrament instituted, and if She had not been sustained by the power of the Almighty, the force of her affection would have bereft Her of natural life. Moreover the presence of her most holy Son was also calculated to moderate the excess of her longings and enabled Her to abide the time of its institution. Even from that time on She wished to prepare Herself for its reception, and asked Her Son to be allowed to receive Him in the holy Sacrament as soon as it should be instituted. She said to Him: "Supreme Lord and life of my soul, shall I, who am such an insignificant worm and the most despicable among

men, be allowed to receive Thee? Shall I be so fortunate as to bear Thee once more within my body and soul? Shall my heart be thy dwelling and tabernacle, where Thou shalt take thy rest and shall I thus delight in thy close embrace and Thou, my Beloved, in mine?"

125. The divine Master answered: "My beloved Mother, many times shalt thou receive Me in the holy Sacrament, and after my Death and Ascension into heaven that shall be thy consolation; for I shall choose thy most sincere and loving heart as my most delightful and pleasant resting place." At this promise of the Lord the great Queen humbled Herself anew and, prostrate in the dust, She gave Him thanks, exciting the admiration of heaven itself. From that hour She began to dispose all her thoughts and actions with the object of preparing Herself for the time when She would be allowed to receive her most holy Son in the holy Sacrament; and during all the years She never forgot, or interrupted these acts of her will. Her memory, as I have already said, was more tenacious and constant than that of an angel, and her intelligence was greater than that of all the angels; therefore, as She always bore in mind this and other mysteries, her actions corresponded to her great knowledge. From that time on also, She continually and fervently besought the Lord, that He give light to mortals in order that they might know and revere this, the greatest of all the Sacraments, and that they might receive it worthily. Whenever we receive this holy Sacrament in proper disposition (and so it should be always), we owe it, next to the influence of the Redeemer, to the tears and prayers of this heavenly Mother, who merited this grace for us. If anyone of us audaciously receives it in the state of sin, let him know that, besides the sacrilegious insult offered to his Lord and God, he also offends the most holy Mother; since he despises and abuses her love, her pious desires, her

prayers, tears and sighs. Let us exert ourselves to avoid such horrible crimes.

126. In regard to the fifth Sacrament, that of Extreme Unction, most holy Mary understood the object for which it was instituted, its matter and form and the part borne by its minister. She saw that its matter must be the blessed oil of olives, serving as a symbol of mercy; that its form should be the words of supplication, spoken while the senses, with which we have sinned are anointed, and that none other than a priest could be its minister. She knew its object and results, which are the help afforded to the faithful in the danger of death, and strengthening them against the temptations and assaults of the devil, so frequent and terrible in the last hour. Thus he that receives this sacrament worthily recovers the strength of soul, which has been lost by the sins previously committed, and also, if it is useful, health of the body. At the same time the sick are moved to sentiments of devotion and to a desire of seeing God, while venial sins are forgiven together with some of the effects of mortal sin; it stamps upon the body the seal of heaven (though not an indelible one), so that the demon dares not approach where, by grace and by his Sacraments, the Lord has taken up his habitation. By the power of this Sacrament Lucifer loses the authority and right acquired over man through original and actual sin, so that the body of the just, which is to rise and, with the soul, is to enjoy its God, may be properly marked for its union with its soul. All this the most faithful Mother and Lady knew and for it She gave thanks in the name of the faithful.

127. Concerning the sixth Sacrament, Holy Orders, She understood how her most blessed Son, the provident Founder of grace and of the Church, thereby constituted apt ministers of his Sacraments for the sanctification of his mystical body and for the consecration of his body and blood; giving

them a dignity above that of all men and of the angels themselves. This caused in Her such an extreme reverence for the dignity of priests, that She began from that moment to revere and honor them. She asked the Almighty to make them worthy and efficient ministers of his graces and to inspire the faithful with a high veneration for the priesthood. She wept over the faults as well of the priests as of the people in regard to their duties toward each other. But since I have already spoken of the great respect due to the priests, I will not now expatiate upon this subject. All the rest which pertains to this Sacrament, its matter and form, its effects and ministry, was likewise made known to the most blessed Mother.

128. She was also instructed in the great object of Matrimony, the seventh and last of the Sacraments; namely, to sanctify and bless the propagation of the faithful in the evangelical law and to typify the mystery of the spiritual marriage and close union of Christ with his Church (Ephes. 5, 32). She understood how this Sacrament was to be perpetuated, what is its matter and form; what great benefits resulted from it for the faithful children of the Church, and all the other mysteries concerning its effects, necessity and power. For all this She composed hymns of praise and thanksgiving in the name of the faithful, who were to share in its blessings. At the same time She was informed of the rites and ceremonies to be instituted by the Church in future times for the ministration of the Sacraments and for the well ordering of divine worship among the faithful: also of the laws of the holy Church for the government of the faithful, especially of the five precepts of the Church: namely, to hear Mass on feast days; to confess and partake of the most sacred body of Christ at stated times; to fast on the appointed days; to give tithes and firstfruits of our earthly goods to the Lord.

129. In all these precepts of the Church the most blessed Lady perceived the mysteries of our justification, the object

of their establishment, the effects caused by them in the faithful, and the necessity of their existence in the new Church of God. She saw how necessary for the faithful was the first of these commandments, establishing days consecrated to the Lord, that men might seek their God, assist at the sacred and mysterious sacrifice of the Mass, which was to be offered for the living and the dead; that they might renew the profession of faith and the memory of the divine Passion and Death, by which we were redeemed; that they might, as much as possible, cooperate in the offering of this great sacrifice and partake of the blessings and fruits gained by the Church in the most sacred mystery of the Mass. She saw also the necessity of stirring up our loyalty and fervor by sacramental Confession and holy Communion, in order to restore to us the friendship and love of the Almighty. For besides the danger incurred by forgetting or neglecting the use of these two Sacraments, men commit another injury by frustrating the loving desires of their God in establishing such Sacraments for our benefit; since such neglect cannot exist without great contempt of the divine goodness, either tacit or expressed, it is a very serious insult to God in the guilty ones.

130. She had the same understanding of the last two precepts: to fast and to pay tithes. She saw how necessary it was for men to vanquish their enemies by restraint and mortification of the passions, which cause so many unhappy and negligent Christians to lose eternal happiness. It is the disorder of the flesh, which foments these passions, and the flesh is subdued by fasting. Herein the Teacher of life himself has given us an example, although He had no need to conquer the disorders of sin. The paying of tithes most holy Mary recognized as specially ordained by the Lord, in order that thereby the faithful might acknowledge Him as the supreme Creator and Lord of all, paying tribute to Him of their temporal goods and thanking Him for the gifts of his Provi-

dence in the preservation of life. He wished also that these offerings be appropriated for the sustenance and comfort of his priests. For, seeing that their sustenance is secured by the sweat of the people, they were to be thankful to the Lord for so abundantly supplying their needs and mindful of their obligation to seek the spiritual welfare of souls and to devote their whole life to the worship of God and the advance of his holy Church.

131. I have tried to be very succinct in my explanations of these great mysteries, which secretly transpired in the inflamed and magnanimous heart of the Queen of heaven, when She was instructed by the Almighty in the laws and precepts of the new Church of the Gospel. The fear of being too prolix, and much more that of committing an error, has prevented me from manifesting all that has interiorly been made known to me and all that I have understood in this matter; the light of our holy faith, assisted by Christian piety and prudence, will teach Catholics the greatest venerations for these high mysteries; it will lead them to contemplate with lively faith the wonderful harmony of the Sacraments, laws, doctrines and mysteries contained in the Catholic Church, and how she has governed herself steadily from the beginning and will govern herself to the end of the world. All this was treasured up admirably in the soul of the blessed Lady and Queen; in Her, according to our way of speaking, Christ brought his Church to the highest purity and perfection; in Her He deposited all the riches of the new law in order that She might be the first to enjoy them to their full extent and that She might fructify, love, increase them and render thanks for them in the name of all the other mortals. She was also to weep over their sins, in order that the flood of mercy for the human race might not be impeded. The soul of Mary was to serve as the public record of all that God was to do for the Redemption of man, and the document, which

was to bind Him to complete his Redemption. She was to be both the Coadjutrix and the everlasting memorial of all the wonders He intended to work among us.

Words of the Queen

THE VIRGIN MARY SPEAKS TO SISTER MARY OF AGREDA

132. My daughter, many times I have reminded thee how injurious to the Almighty and how dangerous to mortals is the forgetfulness and the neglect of the mysterious and wonderful works of his divine clemency toward men. My maternal solicitude urges me to renew in thee the memory and the sorrow for this lamentable tendency. Where is the judgment and good sense of men, that they should forget their eternal welfare and the glory of their Redeemer and Creator? The gates of grace and of glory are open; and yet they not only do not enter, but they fly from light and life, and they shut them out from hearts darkened by the shadows of death. O more than inhuman cruelty of the sinner toward himself! Overtaken by the most dangerous and deathly sickness, He does not wish to accept the remedy so graciously offered to him! Who would not willingly be snatched from death and restored to life? What sick person would not be grateful to the physician for curing him of his sickness? If men know how to be thankful for the restoration of health, which is so soon to be again taken from them by death and only serves them to endure new labors and dangers, why are they so foolish and hard of heart as not to be thankful for or even recognize the blessings of Him, who gives them eternal life and happiness, who rescues them from pains without end and inconceivably great?

133. O my dearest daughter, how can I receive as children and be a Mother to those who thus despise my dearest Son and Lord and all his clemency? The angels and saints of

heaven understand his kindness, and they are astounded at the gross and dangerous ingratitude of mortals, and they see how the rectitude of divine judgments shall become manifest before the whole world. Already in previous parts of this history I have declared to thee many of these secrets; and now I have made known to thee still more, in order that thou mayest imitate me so much the more closely and weep with me over this unhappy state of mortals, by which God has been, and is, so greatly offended. Weep thou over their sins and at the same time try to make up for them. I wish that thou let no day pass without having given most humble thanks to his greatness; since He had instituted the great Sacraments and receives only abuse in return. Do thou receive them with profound reverence, faith and firm hope. Especially must thou be filled with highest esteem for the sacrament of Penance and try to excite in thee the dispositions and fulfill the requirements, which the holy Church and its teachers point out as necessary for its worthy reception. Approach it with an humble and thankful heart day after day; and whenever thou art conscious of any fault, do not postpone the remedy afforded by this Sacrament. Wash and cleanse thy soul; for it is the most abominable carelessness to know oneself stained with sin, and to remain in such disgrace for a long time, yea even for one instant.

134. Particularly do I wish thee to understand the wrath of the Almighty against those who dare to receive the Sacraments unworthily, especially the august Sacrament of the Altar. 0 soul! How dreadful is this sin in the eyes of the Lord and his saints! Yea, not only the receiving of Him unworthily, but the irreverence committed in his real presence on the altar! How can they be called children of the Church, who, claiming to believe and respect this mystery, not only neglect to visit Him in the many places where He is sacramentally present, but also dare to indulge in such disrespect toward

Him as even the heathens are not guilty of against their false idols? This is a matter which could not be deplored sufficiently in many discourses; and I tell thee, my daughter, that the men of the present age have so outraged the justice of the Lord, that I cannot even manifest to them, what in my kindness I desire as a remedy of this evil. But let them know at present that his sentence shall be dreadful and without mercy, rendered against those wicked and faithless servants who are condemned by the words of their own mouth (Luke 19, 22). This thou canst announce to all that will hear thee; and counsel them to come at least once a day to the churches in which their God is sacramentally present, in order to adore and worship Him; and let them assist at the sacrifice of the Mass, for men do not know how much they lose by their negligence in this regard.

Chapter XII

THE INCESSANT PRAYERS AND PETITIONS OF CHRIST, THE
REDEEMER, FOR OUR WELFARE; AND HOW OUR MOST HOLY
MOTHER JOINED HIM THEREIN AND RECEIVED MANY NEW
ENLIGHTENMENTS.

135. The more our limited discourse seeks to make clear and
extol the mysterious works of Christ, our Redeemer, and of
his most holy Mother, the more evident it becomes, that
mere human words are far from being able to compass the
greatness of these sacraments; for, as Ecclesiasticus says, they
surpass all our words of praise (Ecclus. 43, 33). Nor can we
ever fathom or compass them, and there will always remain
many greater secrets than those we have sought to explain.
For those which we do explain are very insignificant, and we
do not deserve to comprehend, nor to speak about the few,
which we attempt to fathom. Inadequate is the intellect of
the highest seraphim to weigh and pierce the secrets that
passed between Jesus and Mary during the years in which
They lived together. Especially is this true of the years, of
which I am now speaking, during which the Teacher of life
instructed Her in everything that was to happen in the law of
grace; namely, how much this new law was to accomplish in
this the sixth age of the world, which includes these sixteen
hundred and fifty seven years and all the unknown future
until the end of the World. In all this the most blessed Lady

was instructed in the school of her divine Son; for He foretold Her all by word of mouth, pointing out the time and place of each event, the kingdoms and provinces of their history during the existence of the Church. This was shown Her so dearly that if She had lived through our centuries in mortal flesh, She would have known all the individual members of the holy Church with their features and names. This happened in regard to the persons, whom She afterwards saw and conversed with during her life; for when they came into her presence for the first time, She already knew them by her interior faculties and merely began to know them by the experience of the senses.

136. Still, while the most holy Mother of wisdom so clearly understood these mysteries in the soul of her Son and in the operations of his faculties, She did not penetrate so deeply into these secrets as the most holy Soul of Christ, which was beatifically united to the Divinity; for the heavenly Lady was a creature and as yet did not continually enjoy the beatific vision. Nor did She always comprehend the image conceived in the beatific vision of this divine Soul of Christ, for this happened only when She herself was enjoying the intuitive vision of the Divinity. But She beheld the imaginary species of the interior faculties of Christ concerning the mysteries of the militant Church, and She understood also how they depended upon his most holy will: that He decreed and controlled all its developments according to their proper time, place and occasion. She was made aware in like manner, how the human will of the Redeemer conformed itself to the divine, and was governed by it in all its decrees and dispositions. The divine harmony overflowed in the will and faculties of the blessed Lady, leading Her to cooperate with the will of her Son, and through it, with the divine. Hence there existed an ineffable similarity between

Christ and holy Mary and She was the helpmate of Christ in
the building up of the new Law.

137. All these hidden sacraments ordinarily transpired in
that humble oratory of the Queen, where the greatest of all
mysteries, the Incarnation of the divine Word in her virginal
womb, had taken place. Though it was such a narrow and
poorly furnished room, consisting merely of the bare and
rude walls, yet it enclosed the grandeur of Him who is immense and shed forth all the majesty and sacredness, which
since then is attached to the rich temples and innumerable
sanctuaries of the world. In this holy of holies the Highpriest
of the new Law ordinarily performed his prayers, which
always concluded with fervent intercessions for men. At these
times also He spoke to his Virgin Mother about all the works
of the Redemption and communicated to Her the rich gifts
and treasures of grace, which He had come to shower upon
the children of light in the new Testament and in his holy
Church. Many times did He beseech his eternal Father not to
allow the sins and the ingratitude of men to hinder their
Redemption. As Christ in his foreknowledge was always
conscious of the sins of the human race and of the damnation of so many thankless souls, the thought of dying for
them caused Him to sweat blood many times on these occasions. Although the Evangelists, because they never intended
to relate all the events of his life, mention this sweating of
blood but once before his Passion, it is certain that this
happened many times and in the presence of his most holy
Mother; and this has been intimated to me several times.

138. During prayer our blessed Master sometimes assumed a kneeling posture, sometimes He was prostrate in the
form of a cross or at other times raised in the air in this same
position which He loved so much. In the presence of his
Mother He was wont to pray: "0 most blessed Cross! When
shall thy arms receive mine, when shall I rest on thee and

when shall my arms, nailed to thine, be spread to welcome all sinners? (Matth. 9, 13). But as I came from heaven for no other purpose than to invite them to imitate Me and associate with Me, they are even now and forever open to embrace and enrich all men. Come then, all ye that are blind, to the light. Come ye poor, to the treasures of my grace. Come, ye little ones, to the caresses and delights of your true Father. Come, ye afflicted and worn out ones, for I will relieve and refresh you (Matth. 11, 28). Come, ye just, since you are my possession and inheritance. Come all ye children of Adam, for I call upon you all. I am the way, the truth and the life (13, 6), and I will deny nothing that you desire to receive. My eternal Father, they are the works of thy hands, do not despise them; for I will offer Myself as a sacrifice on the Cross, in order to restore them to justice and freedom. If they be but willing I will lead them back to the bosom of thy elect and to their heavenly kingdom, where thy name shall be glorified."

139. At all these prayers the beloved Mother was present, and in her purest soul, as in the purest crystal, the light of the Onlybegotten was reflected. His interior and exterior prayers reechoed in Her, causing Her to imitate his petitions and prayers in the same postures. When the great Lady for the first time saw Him sweat blood, her maternal heart was transfixed with sorrow and filled with astonishment at the effects caused in Christ, our Lord, by the sins and ingratitudes committed by men, foreseen by the Lord and known to Her. In the anguish of her heart She turned to her fellow mortals and exclaimed: "0 children of men! Little do ye understand how highly the Lord esteems his image and likeness in you! For, as the price of your salvation, He offers his own blood and deems it little to shed all of it for you. 0 could I but unite your wills with mine, in order that I might bring you to love and obey Him! Blessed by his right hand be

the grateful and the just among men, who will be faithful children of their Father! Let those be filled with light and with the treasures of grace, who will respond to the ardent desires of my Lord in regard to their salvation. Would that I could be the insignificant slave of the children of Adam and thereby induce and assist them to put an end to their sins and their own damnation! Lord and Master! Life and light of my soul! Who can be so hard of heart and so hostile to himself, that he should not feel himself urged on by thy blessings? Who can be so ungrateful and so unheedful, as to ignore thy most burning love? How can my heart bear with men, who, being so favored by thy bounty, are so coarse and rebellious? 0 children of Adam! Turn your inhuman cruelty upon me. Afflict and insult me as much as you will, only pay my beloved Lord the reverence and love which you owe to his endearments. Thou, my Son and Lord, art Light of light, Son of the eternal Father, figure of his substance (Heb. 1, 3), as everlasting, as immense, as infinite as He, equal to Him in essence and attributes, being with Him one God and one supreme Majesty (John 10, 30). Thou art chosen among thousands (Cant. 5, 10), beautiful above all the sons of men, holy, innocent and without defect of any kind. How then, eternal God, can mortals ignore the object of their most noble love? the Principle, which gives them existence? the End wherein consists their eternal true happiness? 0 that I could give my life in order that all might escape their error!"

140. Many other sentiments of burning love, far beyond the powers of my heart and tongue, this heavenly Lady uttered in her dovelike sincerity; and in this love, and in profoundest reverence, She wiped the sweat from the face of her sweetest Son. At other times She found Him in quite a different condition, shining with glory and transfigured as afterwards on mount Tabor (Matth. 17, 2), in the midst of a great multitude of angels, who adored Him and in the sweet

harmony of their voices gave praise and thanksgiving to the Onlybegotten of the Father made man. These celestial voices our blessed Lady heard and She joined hers with them. At other times this happened while He was not transfigured; for the divine will ordained that the sensitive part of the divine humanity of the Word should sometimes have this solace, while at other times it should enjoy also the transfiguring overflow of the glory of the soul into the body; yet this only at great intervals. But whenever the heavenly Mother found Him in this state and beheld his glorified body, or when She heard the hymns of the angels, She participated in these delights to such an extent, that, if her spirit had not been so strong, and if her Lord and Son had not fortified Her, She would have lost all her natural powers; and even as it was, the holy angels had to support the failing strength of her body on those occasions.

141. Many times, when her divine Son was in one of these states of suffering or joy, and was praying to the eternal Father or, as it were, conferring with Him concerning the highest mysteries of the Redemption, the Person of the Father approved or conceded his petitions for the relief of men, or showed to the most holy humanity of Christ the secret decrees of predestination, reprobation or condemnation of some souls. All this our blessed Lady heard, humbling Herself to the dust. With unequaled reverence and fear She adored the Omnipotent, and accompanied her Son in his prayers, petitions and thanksgivings, offered up to the eternal Father for mankind in praise of all his inscrutable judgments. Such secrets and mysteries the most prudent Virgin conferred in her heart, and stored them up in her memory, converting them into the material and nourishment of her fiery love. None of these blessings and secret favors were in her unprofitable or fruitless. To all of them She corresponded according to the inmost desires of her Lord. In all of them She fulfilled

the highest intentions of the Almighty, and all his works found due response from Her as far as was possible from a mere creature.

THE VIRGIN MARY SPEAKS TO SISTER MARY OF AGREDA

142. My daughter, one of the reasons why men should call me Mother of mercy, is the knowledge of my loving desire, that all be satiated with the flood of grace and taste the sweetness of the Lord as I myself. I call and invite all to come with me to the fountain of the Divinity. Let the most poor and afflicted approach, for if they respond and follow me, I will offer them my protection and help, and I will intercede for them with my Son and obtain for them the hidden manna, which will give to them nourishment and life (Apoc. 2, 17). Deny thyself and put off all the works of human weakness, and, by the true light, which thou hast received concerning the works of my Son and my own, contemplate and study thyself in this mirror, in order to arrive at that beauty, which the highest King seeks in thee.

143. Since this is the most powerful means for perfection in thy works, I wish that thou write this advice into thy heart. Whenever thou must perform any interior or exterior work, consider beforehand whether what thou art going to say or do corresponds with the doings of thy Lord, and whether thou hast the intention thereby to honor thy Lord and benefit thy neighbor. As soon as thou art sure that this is thy motive, execute thy undertaking in union with Him and in imitation of Him; but if thou findest not this motive let the undertaking rest. This was my invariable course in pursuing the imitation of my Lord and Teacher; though in me there was no reluctance toward the good, but only the desire of imitating Him perfectly. In this imitation consists the fruit

of his holy teaching, in which He urges us to do, what is most pleasing and acceptable to the eternal God. Moreover from this day on be mindful not to undertake any work, not to speak or even think any of anything, without first asking my permission and consulting with me as thy Mother and Teacher. And as soon as I answer thee give thanks to the Lord; if I do not answer after continued inquiry, I promise and assure thee on the part of the Lord, that He will, nevertheless, give thee light as to what will be according to his most perfect will. In all things, however, subject thyself to the guidance of thy spiritual director, and never forget this practice!

Chapter XIII

MOST HOLY MARY PASSES HER THIRTY-THIRD YEAR, EVER
AFTER REMAINING UNCHANGED AS TO HER VIRGINAL
BODY; SHE PLANS TO SUPPORT HER MOST HOLY SON AND
SAINT JOSEPH BY THE LABOR OF HER HANDS.

144. After Jesus had reached his twelfth year our great Queen
and Lady occupied Herself particularly in the exercises and
the mysteries, which I have pointed out but could not fully
describe in the foregoing chapters. In the course of time our
Savior passed the period of his adolescence at eighteen and
his blessed Mother (according to the dates given in Vol. II P.
138 and 475), reached her perfect growth in her thirtythird
year. I call it that, because according to the division of man's
life commonly accepted, the age of thirtythree years is that of
full bodily growth and perfection, being the end of youthful
vigor, or, as others would have it, the beginning of it. Whatever opinion is accepted, that is the end of natural perfection
of the body and it lasts only a short time; for immediately
corrupted nature, never remaining in the same state, begins
to decline. Like the moon, which begins to lessen as soon as
it has reached fullness, it never remains in the same state.
From that time on the body does not grow in length, nor can
the increase in bulk be called a perfection, being rather a
defect of nature. On this account our Lord Christ died at the
completion of his thirty-third year; for his most ardent love

induced Him to wait only until his body should have attained its perfect growth and vigor and was in all respects most capable of bringing the perfect gifts of nature and grace to this sacrifice. Not because divine grace was in need of any growth in Him, but in order that his human nature might correspond with the perfection of grace and that nothing might be wanting even exteriorly to the completeness of his sacrifice for mankind. In accordance with this it is said, that the Almighty created Adam and Eve in the condition of a man and woman at the age of thirtythree years. It is true, of course, that in the first and second age of the world the life of man was much longer and, by dividing the periods of human life at that time, many more years would have to be counted for each period before the time of David than after that time, when old age begins at seventy years.

145. When therefore the Queen of heaven arrived at her thirtythird year, her virginal body had attained full natural growth, so well proportioned and beautiful, that She was the admiration not only of human beings, but of the angelic spirits themselves. She had grown in size and stature to the most perfect proportion in all the parts of her body and most strikingly resembled her divine Son in features and complexion, when later on He arrived at that age; always, of course, taking into account, that Christ was the most perfect Man, while his Mother was the most perfect Woman. Other mortals, on account of the decline of the natural humors and temperature, ordinarily begin to deteriorate and gradually approach decay as far as their body is concerned; the exquisite balance of bodily humors is disturbed and the earthly ones begin to predominate more and more; the hair begins to whiten, the countenance to wrinkle, the blood to cool, some of the strength to weaken; and the whole human frame, in spite of the greatest care, commences to decline toward old age and corruption. But in the most holy Mary it was not so;

for the wonderful beauty and strength, which She had attained at the age of thirty-three years, remained unchanged; and when She had reached her seventieth year, as I shall relate later on, She still retained the same beauty and entirety of her virginal body as at the age of thirty-three.

146. The blessed Lady was well aware of this special privilege conceded to Her by the Most High and She rendered Him most humble thanks. She understood also that it was granted to Her in order that the likeness of her most holy Son might always be preserved in Her, though with the differences consequent upon her different nature and longer life; for the Lord attained full bodily growth at thirty-three years, while She retained it during her much longer life. Saint Joseph, although he was not so very old at the time when our blessed Lady reached her thirtythird year, was much broken and worn out as far as his body was concerned; for his continual cares, his journeys and his incessant labors for the sustenance of his Spouse and of the Lord had weakened him much more than his years. This was so ordained by the Lord, who, wishing to lead him on to the practice of patience and of other virtues, permitted him to suffer sickness and pain (as I will relate in the following chapter). His most prudent Spouse, knowing that he was much weakened and always having loved and served him better than any wife ever did her husband, spoke to him and said: "My spouse and my master, I am deeply obliged to you for the faithful labors, watchfulness and care thou hast bestowed on my welfare. For in the sweat of thy brow thou hast until now supported me, thy servant, and my most holy Son, the true God, and in this thy solicitude, thou hast spent thy strength and the best part of thy health and of thy life in protecting me and attending upon my welfare. From the hands of the Almighty thou shalt receive the reward of thy works and the blessings of sweetness which thou deservest (Ps, 20, 4). But now I beseech thee, my

master, rest henceforth from thy labors since thy impaired strength is not any more equal to them. I wish from now on to show my gratitude by laboring in thy service and provide for such sustenance as the Lord wishes us to have."

147. The saint listened to the words of his sweetest Spouse with abundant tears of humblest acknowledgment and consolation. Although he at first earnestly entreated Her to be allowed to continue forever in his labors, yet at last he yielded to her request and obeyed his Spouse, the Mistress of the world. From that time on he rested from the hard labor of his hands, by which he had earned a livelihood for all three. They gave away the carpenter tools as an alms, not wishing to have anything superfluous or useless in their house and family. Being thus at leisure, saint Joseph occupied himself entirely in the contemplation of the mysteries of which he was the guardian and in the exercise of virtues. As He had the happiness and good fortune of continually enjoying the sight and the intercourse of the divine Wisdom incarnate, and of Her, who was the Mother of It, this man of God reached such a height of sanctity, that, his heavenly Spouse excepted, no one ever surpassed Him and he far outstripped all other creatures. The blessed Lady, and also her most holy Son, attended upon him and nursed him in his sickness, consoling and sustaining him with the greatest assiduity; and hence there are no words sufficiently expressive of the humility, reverence and love which all this caused in the simple and grateful heart of this man of God. He thus became the admiration and joy of the angels and the pleasure and delight of the Most High.

148. Thenceforth the Mistress of the world took upon Herself the task of supporting by her work her most holy Son and her husband, for such was the will of the eternal Wisdom in order to raise Mary to the very pinnacle of all virtues and perfections and in order to furnish an example for the confu-

sion of the daughters and the sons of Adam and Eve. The
Lord set up for us as a model this strong Woman, clothed
with beauty and fortitude. For at this age of thirtythree years
She was to show Herself girded with strength and ready to
extend her hands to the poor, purchasing the field and
cultivating the vineyard by her own labor to bring forth its
fruits. The heart of her husband confided in Her, and not
only that of her husband, Saint Joseph, but also that of her
Son, the true Godman, the Teacher of the poor and the Poor
of the poor: and they were not deceived (Prov. 31, 10). The
great Queen began to busy Herself much more in spinning
and weaving linen and wool, thus mysteriously fulfilling all
that Solomon says about Her in the Proverbs. But as I have
explained this chapter of Scripture at the end of the first part,
I shall not repeat it here, although much of what I said then
pertains to this period of her life when both interiorly and
exteriorly She executed it in action.

149. The Lord was not wanting in ability to provide for
his bodily living, that of his blessed Mother and of saint
Joseph; for not in bread alone does man live and is sustained
(Matth. 4, 4) ; He could have created it by his mere word, as
He himself assures us. He could have each day created the
necessary food; but then the world would have been deprived
of this spectacle of his holy Mother, Lady of the whole world,
laboring for their sustenance; and the Virgin herself would
have been deprived of the reward due to these meritorious
works. All was arranged by the Teacher of our salvation with
admirable providence for the glory of our Queen and for our
instruction. Her diligence and care in these employments
cannot be expressed in words. She labored much: and because She always lived in retirement, She was assisted by that
most fortunate woman, of whom I have spoken before (Vol.
11227,423). This woman assumed some of the labor of the
great Queen and performed the necessary errands. But Mary

never used any command when in want of her assistance, but spoke to her in humble request and with the utmost consideration, always seeking to find out her wishes by asking her whether she would not like to do this or that. Her blessed Son, like his heavenly Mother, ate no meat; their nourishment was only fish, fruit and herbs, and these only in the greatest moderation. For saint Joseph She procured flesh meat, and, although their poverty and want was apparent also in this, yet it was seasoned by the good will and loving kindness with which She served it to her spouse. The blessed Lady slept but little, and often She spent the greater part of the night in work; for the Lord now permitted her to spend more time in such employment than in Egypt. Sometimes it happened that with all her diligence and labor She could not earn what was necessary; for saint Joseph now had need of more expensive nourishment and clothes than formerly. At such times Christ our Lord made use of his almighty power in multiplying what was in their possession, or in commanding the angels to bring the necessaries from elsewhere. But more frequently He miraculously enabled his most holy Mother to accomplish much in a short time by the labor of her hands and thus multiply its results.

Words of the Queen

THE VIRGIN MARY SPEAKS TO SISTER MARY OF AGREDA

150. My daughter, in what thou hast written of my labors, thou shouldst have received a most exalted doctrine for thy imitation and direction; but in order that thou mayest not forget I will now give thee a summary of it. I wish that thou imitate me in three virtues which thou wilt find in what thou hast written: they are the virtues of prudence, charity and justice, so little taken notice of by mortals. Prudence should teach thee to provide for the wants of thy neighbor as far as

possible in thy state. Charity should make thee diligent and
zealous in coming to their assistance. Justice should oblige
thee to fulfill the obligations of charity, as necessity and love
itself point them out to thee. Thou shouldst be an eye to the
blind, an ear to the deaf, and thy hands should labor for
those that are maimed (Job 29, 15). Although, on account of
thy state of life, thou must practice this doctrine principally
and continually in a spiritual way, yet I desire that thou take
it to the heart also as far as the temporal and bodily wants of
thy neighbor demand, always striving to be most faithful in
imitating me. For I also provided for the necessities of my
spouse, and held Myself ready to serve and support him,
deeming myself obliged thereto; and I fulfilled this obligation
with ardent charity until he died. Although the Lord had
given him to me for my support, I faithfully provided for
him by my labors as long as he was unable to perform this
task himself. I judged it to be my duty thus to use the
strength given to me by the Lord and would have considered
it a great fault not to do so with great assiduity.

151. The children of the Church pay no attention to this
example and therefore they have fallen into a perverseness
which greatly exasperates the just Judge. For, though all
mortals, not only since the first sin by which all incurred
work as a punishment, but also from the very first beginning,
were created in order to work (Gen. 2, 15), nevertheless,
work is not evenly distributed among men. The powerful
and the rich and those whom the world calls lords and nobles
all try to exempt themselves from this common law and try
to throw this burden upon the humble and the poor of
human society. The rich keep up their pride and ostentation
by the labor and sweat of the poor, and the powerful draw
their strength from the weakness and helplessness of the
lowly. In many of the proud, by their haughtiness, this
perversity reaches such extremes that they begin to think all

this is due to them and they despise, oppress and trod under foot the poor (James 2, 6). They falsely suppose that others are created only in order that they themselves might enjoy leisure and delight and all the world's goods; and in addition to this, they do not even pay the small wages for these services. In this matter of not paying proper wages to the poor and to the servants and in matters of like sort thou wilt find great crimes against the order and will of the Almighty. But let it be known that just as the rich pervert justice and reason and refuse to take their share in human labor, so also will mercy be inverted for them, and be showered upon the despised and lowly (Wis. 6, 7). Those who in their pride gave themselves up to contemptible idleness, shall be chastised by the demons whom they have imitated.

152. Thou, dearest, take heed against such deception; let the advantages of earnest labor be always before thy eyes according to my example; separate thyself from the children of Belial, who so idly seek vain applause, and thus labor for naught. Do not deem thyself above others, because thou art a superior, but deem thyself more lowly and humble, a slave of all the rest; diligently serving them all without distinction. If necessary, be ready to labor for their sustenance and be convinced that this is incumbent upon thee not only as their superior, but also because the religious are thy sisters, daughters of the heavenly Father and creatures of the Lord thy Spouse. Since thou hast received more than all the rest at his liberal hand, thou art also obliged to labor more than they. The weak and ailing relieve of bodily labor and do their work thyself. I wish that thou not only avoid charging others with work which thou canst perform thyself and which belongs to thee, but that thou assume, as much as possible, that of all the rest, deeming thyself their inferior and their servant as I wish thee always to consider thyself. Since thou canst not do all thyself, and since it is necessary that thou distribute bodily

labor among thy subjects, I exhort thee to observe good order and equity, not putting more labor upon those who are too humble or weak to object; but I wish that thou humiliate those who are of a haughty and proud spirit and are unwilling to occupy themselves in hard work. However, this must be done without exasperating them and with a gentle firmness, helping them to suppress their lukewarmness and want of subjection by placing upon them the yoke of holy obedience in accordance with their profession. In doing this thou conferrest upon them the greatest blessing and thou only fulfillest thy own obligation; therefore, thou shouldst see to it that they understand thee in that way. All this thou wilt attain if thou make no personal distinctions and assign to each one the work which she can do, and what is appropriate to her; obliging and compelling each one with equity and justice to abhor idleness and laxity, and let them see thee engaged in the hardest and most difficult work. Thereby thou wilt gain an humble liberty of commanding them; but what thou canst do thyself, command no one, in order that thou mayest enjoy the fruit and the reward of labor in imitation of me and in obeying all that I advise and remind thee of.

Chapter XIV

THE SUFFERINGS AND INFIRMITIES OF SAINT JOSEPH IN THE
LAST YEARS OF HIS LIFE AND HOW THE QUEEN OF HEAVEN,
HIS SPOUSE, NURSED HIM DURING THAT TIME.

153. A common defect in all of us that are called to the light
and to the profession of holy faith in the school of Christ,
our Lord, is that of looking upon Him too much as our
Redeemer and not sufficiently as our Teacher in our sufferings (Luke 24, 26). We all desire to reap the fruit of salvation
and enter the portals of grace and glory; but we do not with
like zeal seek to follow Him on the way of the Cross by
which He entered and upon which He invites us to attain
eternal glory (Matth. 16, 24). Although, as Catholics, we do
not fall into such insane errors as the heretics; for we know
and profess that without exertion and labor there can be no
reward or crown (II Tim. 2, 5) ; and that it is a sacrilegious
blasphemy to avail oneself of the salvation of Christ in order
to sin without remorse or restraint. Nevertheless, as far as
really practicing the works inculcated by faith, some of the
children of the Church differ little from the children of
darkness; for they look upon difficult and painful works as
unnecessary for the following of Christ and for participation
in his glory.

154. Let us throw off this error in our practice and let us
understand well that suffering was not only for Christ, our

Lord, but also for us; that if He suffered labors and death as the Redeemer of the World, He suffered them also as our Teacher, thereby inviting us as his friends to enter upon the way of his Cross; so much so, that his nearest friends receive the greatest share of suffering, and no one can merit heaven without the price of personal exertions. In imitation of his most holy Mother, the Apostles, Martyrs, Confessors and Virgins and all his followers have won their crown by labors and those that have been most prepared for suffering have obtained so much the more abundant reward and the higher crown. It might be objected that our Lord was at the same time God and man, and that if He has given us the most conspicuous and wonderful example of suffering, He did it more in order to be admired than to be imitated. But this is only a bold and daring pretense on our part; for He can meet this objection with the example of his Mother, our most pure and innocent Queen, with that of her blessed spouse, and of so many men and women, weak and deficient as we ourselves, who were less guilty, but who have imitated Him and followed Him on the way of the Cross. The Lord did not suffer only in order to excite our admiration, but in order that we imitate his example, and He did not let even his Divinity stand in the way of labor and suffering, but allowed sorrow and suffering to overwhelm Him in proportion to his innocence and sinlessness.

155. Along this royal highway of the Cross the Lord led the spouse of his blessed Mother, saint Joseph, whom He loved above all the sons of men. In order to increase his merits and crown before the time of his meriting should come to an end, He visited him in the last years of his life with certain sicknesses, such as fever, violent headaches and very painful rheumatisms, which greatly afflicted and weakened him. In the midst of these infirmities, he was suffering from another source, more sweet, but extremely painful,

namely, from the fire of his ardent love which was so vehement, that the flights and ecstasies of his most pure soul would often have burst the bounds of his body if the Lord, who vouchsafed them, had not strengthened and comforted him against these agonies of love. In these sweet excesses the Lord allowed him to suffer until his death and on account of the natural weakness of his extenuated body, this exercise was the source of ineffable merits for the fortunate saint, not only because of the sufferings occasioned, but because of the love by which these sufferings were brought about.

156. Our great Queen, his Spouse, was a witness to all these mysteries; and, as I have already stated (Vol. II 368, 381, 394, 404), She knew the whole interior of the soul of saint Joseph, being thus rejoiced by the knowledge of having for her spouse a man so holy and so beloved of the Lord. She beheld and comprehended the sincerity and purity of his soul; his burning love; his exalted and heavenly thoughts; his dovelike patience and meekness in his grievous ailments and exquisite sufferings. She knew that he never complained either of these nor of any of the other trials, nor ever asked for any relief in his wants and necessities; for he bore all with incomparable equanimity and greatness of soul. As his most prudent Spouse contemplated and weighed all these heroic virtues of saint Joseph, She grew to look upon him with such a veneration as cannot ever be properly estimated by anyone. She labored with incredible joy for his support and comfort; and the greatest of his comforts was that She should prepare and administer his victuals with her own virginal hands. But as all her service seemed little in the eyes of the heavenly Lady compared to the necessities of her spouse, She sometimes, in her love for him, made use of her power as Queen and Mistress of all creation and commanded that the food which She administered to him impart special strength and supply new life to this holy and just man of God.

157. This command of the great Lady, whom all creatures obeyed, was fulfilled; and when saint Joseph tasted of the victuals, which bore these blessings of sweetness, and when he perceived their effects, he was wont to say to the Queen: "My Lady and Spouse, what celestial food is this which vivifies me, rejoices my senses, restores my strength and fills my soul and spirit with new delight?" The Empress of heaven served him his meals on bended knees; and when he was much disabled and suffering, She took off his shoes in the same posture. At other times She supported him in her arms. Although the humble saint sought to rouse himself in order to forestall some of these ministrations of his Spouse, he could not altogether prevent them, for She was intimately aware of all his sufferings and weaknesses and of the circumstances and occasions when he needed her assistance. At such times the heavenly Nurse always hastened to assist him in his wants. Often also, as the Mistress of wisdom and of virtue, She comforted him by words of sweetest consolation. In the last three years of his life, when his infirmities increased, our Queen attended upon him day and night and her only other employment was the service and ministration due to her most holy Son. Jesus sometimes joined and assisted Her in the care of her holy spouse whenever he was not engaged in other necessary works. There was never a sick person, nor will there ever be one, who was so well nursed and comforted. Great was the happiness and worth of this man of God, saint Joseph, for he alone deserved to have for his Spouse Her, who was the Spouse of the Holy Ghost.

158. But the heavenly Lady was not satisfied with these proofs of her devotion toward holy Joseph: She made use of other means for his relief and comfort. Several times She asked the Lord in her ardent charity to impose upon Her the pains suffered by her spouse and release him therefrom. To gain her point, She, the Mother and Mistress of all sanctity,

pleaded before the Most High, alleging that her debt was greater than that of all the earthborn and that since She had not given the proper return, She was inferior to them, deserving all their sufferings and offered her heart for all manner of pain and suffering. She pleaded also the sanctity of saint Joseph, his purity, innocence, and the delight of the Lord in this heart made according to that of his Son. She asked for many blessings for him and gave most heartfelt thanks for having created a man so worthy of his favors, so full of justice and holiness. She invited the holy angels to give thanks to God for him; and in contemplating the glory and wisdom of the Lord as shown in this man, She sang new hymns of praise. For on the one hand She saw the pains and sufferings of her beloved spouse, which excited her pity and condolence, and on the other hand She was aware of his merits and the delight of the Lord in this man, and how the saint pleased and glorified his God by his patience. The heavenly Lady exercised different virtues suitable to the occasion, and of so exalted a degree, that She excited the admiration of the angelic spirits. Yet greater should be the admiration of us ignorant men to see that a mere Creature so perfectly fulfilled so many different duties and that in Her the anxiety of Martha should not interfere with the contemplation of Mary. She imitated in this the activity of the supernal spirits, who guard and assist us without losing sight of the Most High (Matth. 18, 10). But Mary far excelled them in her attention to God, while engaged in bodily labor, of which they were incapable. Though She was a child of Adam, She lived like a heavenly spirit, occupying the superior part of her being in the exalted exercises of her divine love and employing her inferior faculties in works of charity toward her spouse.

159. Sometimes, when the merciful Queen perceived the bitterness and severity of the sufferings of saint Joseph, She was moved to tender pity; and then She would humbly ask

permission of her most holy Son to be allowed to command the natural sources and occasions of these pains to disappear and thus put a stop to the sufferings of this just and beloved man of God. As all creatures obeyed the command of their great Mistress, her holy spouse was then immediately relieved and rested from his pains, sometimes for a day, sometimes longer, until his ailments, according to the decree of the Almighty, again assumed sway for the increase of his merits. At other times She ordered the holy angels, as their Queen (though not in the form of a command, but of a request), to console saint Joseph and comfort him in his sorrows and labors, as the frail condition of his body demanded. Thereupon the angelic spirits would appear to saint Joseph in human forms, most beautiful and shining, and begin to speak to him of the Divinity and its infinite perfections. Then they would raise their voices in sweetest harmony of celestial music, singing hymns of divine canticles, by which they restored his drooping strength and inflamed the love of his purest soul. To rejoice him the more he was specially informed, not only of the source of these blessings and divine favors, but of the great holiness of his virginal Spouse, of her singular love and charity in conversing with him and serving him, and of many other excellences and privileges of the great Mistress of the world. All this together caused such effects in saint Joseph, and so raised his merits before God, as no tongue can express, nor any human understanding in this life can comprehend.

Words of the Queen

THE VIRGIN MARY SPEAKS TO SISTER MARY OF AGREDA

160. My daughter, one of the virtuous works most pleasing to the Lord and most fruitful for souls, is the loving care of the sick. By it is fulfilled to a great extent that natural law

which requires us to do to our neighbors what we wish them to do to us. In the Gospel this is adduced as one of the works for which the Lord shall give eternal reward to the just (Matth. 25, 34); and the failure to exercise this duty is alleged as one of the causes of the eternal damnation of the wicked. In the same place the justice of this retribution is also explained; namely, as men are the children of the eternal Father, the Lord accounts any good or ill done to our neighbor as done to his own children, whose part He takes; for so it is customary among human parents. With regard to thyself thou must moreover consider that thou art the mother of thy religious and that they, just as thou thyself, are the spouses of my blessed Son. The fact that they have received of Him less blessings should so much the more oblige thee to serve and nurse them in their sickness. On this account I have on another occasion told thee that thou must consider thyself the infirmarian of all of them, as being inferior to them because of thy great obligations. I assign to thee thereby an office which is great in the house of the Lord. In order to fulfill its obligations do not charge others with the work which thou canst do thyself in the service of the sick; and whatever, on account of the duties of thy office thou canst not compass, be thou careful in commending to the special care of those who are appointed to discharge these duties by obedience. Besides common charity, there are other reasons why the religious should be attended to in their ailments with the greatest care and solicitude; namely, in order that their afflictions and necessities may not cause them to long for return to their parental homes and to the world. Be sure, that in this way much harm enters the cloister; for human nature is so adverse to suffering, that, rather than feel the want of necessities, it will again face the greatest dangers of the soul.

161. In order to stir thee on toward proficiency in the exercise of this doctrine, the charity which I showed toward my spouse, Joseph, in his ailments should serve thee as a spur and encouragement. Very tardy is that charity (and even the politeness), which waits until the needy one asks for help. I did not wait, but hastened to assist before I was asked. My charity and attention anticipated the requests of my spouse and thus I consoled him not only by my services but by my loving solicitude and attention. I shared his sufferings and hardships with heartfelt compassion; but at the same time I praised the Most High and thanked Him for the blessings of affliction conferred on his servant. If sometimes I sought to relieve his pains, it was not in order to deprive him of the occasion of meriting, but that he might by this aid excite himself to glorify so much the more the Author of all goodness and holiness; and to these virtues I exhorted and encouraged him. With similar perfection shouldst thou exercise this noble virtue, providing for the needs of the sick and weak, comforting them by thy compassion and words of advice, doing them all kinds of good service, without wishing them to lose the reward of suffering. Let not thy carnal love disturb thee when thy sisters fall sick, although they be those thou lovest or needest most; for thereby many souls, both in the world and in religion, lose the merit of their labors. The sorrow occasioned by the sight of sickness or danger in their friends, disturbs their equanimity and under the pretense of compassion, they begin to complain and refuse to submit themselves to the dispositions of divine Providence. In all these things I have given thee an example and I demand of thee to imitate it perfectly by following my footsteps.

Chapter XV

OF THE HAPPY DEATH OF SAINT JOSEPH AND WHAT FOL-
LOWED UPON IT : HOW JESUS, OUR REDEEMER, AND
BLESSED MARY, OUR LADY ASSISTED AT HIS PASSING AWAY.

162. Already eight years saint Joseph had been exercised by
his infirmities and sufferings, and his noble soul had been
purified more and more each day in the crucible of affliction
and of divine love. As the time passed his bodily strength
gradually diminished and he approached the unavoidable
end, in which the stipend of death is paid by all of us children of Adam (Heb. 9, 27). In like manner also increased the
care and solicitude of his heavenly Spouse, our Queen,
assisting and serving him with unbroken punctuality. Perceiving, in her exalted wisdom, that the day and hour for his
departure from this cumbrous earth was very near, the loving
Lady betook Herself to her blessed Son and said to Him:
"Lord God Most High, Son of the eternal Father and Savior
of the world, by thy divine light I see the hour approaching
which thou hast decreed for the death of thy servant Joseph. I
beseech Thee, by thy ancient mercies and by thy infinite
bounty, to assist him in that hour by thy almighty power. Let
his death be as precious in thy eyes, as the uprightness of his
life was pleasing to Thee, so that he may depart in peace and
in the certain hope of the eternal reward to be given to him
on the day in which Thou shalt open the gates of heaven for

all the faithful. Be mindful, my Son, of the humility and love of thy servant; of his exceeding great merits and virtues; of the fidelity and solicitude by which this just man has supported Thee and me, thy humble handmaid, in the sweat of his brow."

163. Our Savior answered: "My Mother, thy request is pleasing to me, and the merits of Joseph are acceptable in my eyes. I will now assist him and will assign him a place among the princes of my people (Ps. 115, 15), so high that he will be the admiration of the angels and will cause them and all men to break forth in highest praise. With none of the human born shall I do as with thy spouse." The great Lady gave thanks to her sweetest Son for this promise; and, for nine days and nights before the death of saint Joseph he uninterruptedly enjoyed the company and attendance of Mary or her divine Son. By command of the Lord the holy angels, three times on each of the nine days, furnished celestial music, mixing their hymns of praise with the benedictions of the sick man. Moreover, their humble but most precious dwelling was filled with the sweetest fragrance and odors so wonderful that they comforted not only saint Joseph, but invigorated all the numerous persons who happened to come near the house.

164. One day before he died, being wholly inflamed with divine love on account of these blessings, he was wrapped in an ecstasy which lasted twenty-four hours. The Lord himself supplied strength for this miraculous intercourse. In this ecstasy he saw clearly the divine Essence, and, manifested therein, all that he had believed by faith: the incomprehensible Divinity, the mystery of the Incarnation and Redemption, the militant Church with all its Sacraments and mysteries. The blessed Trinity commissioned and assigned him as the messenger of our Savior to the holy Patriarchs and Prophets of limbo; and commanded him to prepare them for

their issuing forth from this bosom of Abraham to eternal rest and happiness. All this most holy Mary saw reflected in the soul of her divine Son together with all the other mysteries, just as they had been made known to her beloved spouse, and She offered her sincerest thanks for all this to her Lord.

165. When Saint Joseph issued from this ecstasy his face shone with wonderful splendor and his soul was entirely transformed by his vision of the essence of God. He asked his blessed Spouse to give him her benediction; but She requested her divine Son to bless him in her stead, which He did. Then the great Queen of humility, falling on her knees, besought saint Joseph to bless Her, as being her husband and head. Not without divine impulse the man of God fulfilled this request for the consolation of his most prudent Spouse. She kissed the hand with which he blessed Her and asked him to salute the just ones of limbo in her name. The most humble Joseph, sealing his life with an act of self-abasement, asked pardon of his heavenly Spouse for all his deficiencies in her service and love and begged Her to grant him her assistance and intercession in this hour of his passing away. The holy man also rendered humblest thanks to her Son for all the blessings of his life and especially for those received during this sickness. The last words which saint Joseph spoke to his Spouse were: "Blessed art Thou among all women and elect of all the creatures. Let angels and men praise Thee; let all the generations know, praise and exalt thy dignity; and may in Thee be known, adored and exalted the name of the Most High through all the coming ages; may He be eternally praised for having created Thee so pleasing in his eyes and in the sight of all the blessed spirits. I hope to enjoy thy sight in the heavenly fatherland."

166. Then this man of God, turning toward Christ, our Lord, in profoundest reverence, wished to kneel before Him. But the sweetest Jesus, coming near, received him in his

arms, where, reclining his head upon them, Joseph said: "My highest Lord and God, Son of the eternal Father, Creator and Redeemer of the World, give thy blessing to thy servant and the work of thy hand; pardon, 0 most merciful King, the faults which I have committed in thy service and intercourse. I extol and magnify Thee and render eternal and heartfelt thanks to Thee for having, in thy ineffable condescension, chosen me to be the spouse of thy true Mother; let thy greatness and glory be my thanksgiving for all eternity." The Redeemer of the world gave him his benediction, saying: "My father, rest in peace and in the grace of my eternal Father and mine; and to the Prophets and Saints, who await thee in limbo, bring the joyful news of the approach of their redemption." At these words of Jesus, and reclining in his arms, the most fortunate saint Joseph expired and the Lord himself closed his eyes. At the same time the multitude of the angels, who attended upon their King and Queen, intoned hymns of praise in loud and harmonious voices. By command of the Lord they carried his most holy soul to the gathering place of the Patriarchs and Prophets, where it was immediately recognized by all as clothed in the splendors of incomparable grace, as the putative father and the intimate friend of the Redeemer, worthy of highest veneration. Conformably to the will and mandate of the Lord, his arrival spread inutterable joy in this countless gathering of the saints by the announcement of their speedy rescue.

167. It is necessary to mention that the long sickness and sufferings which preceded the death of saint Joseph was not the sole cause and occasion of his passing away; for with all his infirmities he could have extended the term of his life, if to them he had not joined the fire of the intense love within his bosom. In order that his death might be more the triumph of his love than of the effects of original sin, the Lord suspended the special and miraculous assistance by which his

natural forces were enabled to withstand the violence of his love during his lifetime. As soon as this divine assistance was withdrawn, nature was overcome by his love and the bonds and chains, by which this most holy soul was detained in its mortal body, were at once dissolved and the separation of the soul from the body in which death consists took place. Love was then the real cause of the death of saint Joseph, as I have said above. This was at the same time the greatest and most glorious of all his infirmities for in it death is but a sleep of the body and the beginning of real life.

168. Her spouse having thus passed away, the great Lady began to prepare his body for burial according to Jewish custom. No other hands touched him than her own and those of the holy angels, who assisted Her in visible human forms. In order that the utmost propriety might be observed by the Virgin Mother, God enveloped the body of saint Joseph in a wonderful light, which hid all except his countenance; and thus his purest Spouse, although She clothed him for burial, saw only his face. Sweetest fragrance exhaled from his body and it remained so beautiful and lifelike, that the neighboring people eagerly came to see it and were filled with admiration. Accompanied by the Redeemer of the world, his most blessed Mother and a great multitude of angels, and escorted by their friends and many others, the sacred body of the most glorious saint Joseph was borne to the common burying place. But on all these occasions and in these occupations, the most prudent Queen preserved her composure and gravity, without allowing her countenance to exhibit any unwomanly or disorderly excitement; nor did her sorrow prevent Her from attending to all that belonged to the service of her deceased spouse or her divine Son. In everyone of her movements was visible the royal and magnanimous behavior of the Queen of the human race. She reiterated her thankful acknowledgment of the great favors done to her spouse by

the son of God and, prostrate at his feet in new abasement of humility, She said to Him: "Lord and Master of my whole being, my true Son, the holiness of my spouse Joseph might until now have detained Thee in my company; though unworthy of it, I beseech Thee by thy own goodness not to forsake me now; receive me anew as thy servant and look upon the humble desires and longings of my heart." The Savior of the world accepted this new offering of his most holy Mother and He promised not to leave Her until the time when obedience to his eternal Father would oblige Him to begin his life of public preaching.

Words of the Queen

THE VIRGIN MARY SPEAKS TO SISTER MARY OF AGREDA

169. My dearest daughter, it was not without special reason that thy heart was moved to great compassion and pity toward those who are at the point of death and that thou art inspired with a desire to help them in that hour; for it is true, as thou hast perceived, that then the souls of men incur the most incredible and dangerous attacks from the demons, as well as from their own frailty and from the creatures around them. That hour is the great trial of life, upon which depends the last sentence of eternal death or eternal life, of eternal suffering or eternal glory. As the Most High has condescendingly vouchsafed to fill thee with these sentiments, I exhort thee to exert all thy powers and faculties to act accordingly. Remember, then, my friend, that when Lucifer and his satellites of darkness perceive, by the course of natural events, that anyone falls a prey to a dangerous and mortal disease, they immediately prepare to assail the poor and un-bewaring soul with all their malice and astuteness in order to vanquish them if possible by various temptations. Whenever they see

an opening for attacking the souls, they try to supply in fury and malice the shortness of time.

170. At such times they gather like bloodthirsty wolves and search out the natural and acquired failings in his nature, taking into account his inclinations, habits and customs, and where his passions cause him greater weakness, in order to direct toward this part the strongest battery and engines of war. Those that have a disorderly love of earthly life, they persuade that there is not such great danger and they prevent others from undeceiving them. Those that have been negligent in the reception of the Sacraments, they try to make still more careless and they place obstacles and difficulties in the way in order that they may die without them, or in order that they may receive them without fruit and with a bad disposition. Others they fill with false suggestions and shame in order that they may not confess their sins and open their conscience. Others they confuse and try to prevent from making proper restitution and thus unburdening their consciences. Others, who love vanity, they entangle, even at that last hour, in many vain and proud desires with regard to what is to be done for them after death. Those that have been avaricious or sensual, they seek to excite violently toward what they loved so blindly during life. In short, of all the bad habits and customs this cruel enemy avails himself in order to fill their minds with images of creatures and draw them away from their salvation or make them incapable of it. All the sinful actions and vicious habits of their previous life have become, as it were, pledges in the hands of the common enemy for the possession of the sinner and weapons for assault and battery in this tremendous hour of death. Every appetite, which has been inordinately indulged, is an avenue or bypath by which he enters into the citadel of the soul. Once in, he breathes forth his pestilential fumes, and raises the clouds of darkness, his proper work, so that the soul may

not give heed to the divine inspirations, have no true sorrow for its sins, and do no penance for its wicked life.

171. Generally these enemies cause a great damage to the souls in that hour by exciting the vain hope of a longer life and being able to execute later on what God suggests to them by means of the holy angels. Giving way to this deceit, they find themselves afterwards betrayed and lost. Just as great is the danger of those who have shown little esteem for the saving graces of the Sacraments: for this contempt is very offensive to the Lord and to the saints, and divine justice is wont to punish it by leaving these souls to their own wicked counsels. This leads them to great neglect in profiting by this help. Thus they are themselves forsaken by the Lord in their last hour, in which they expected to provide for their salvation. There are few among the just whom this ancient serpent does not furiously attack in their last agony. And if satan boasts of having ruined even saints at such times, what hope have the wicked, the negligent and sinful, who have spent their whole lives in making themselves unworthy of divine favor and grace, and who are devoid of meritorious works to offset the assaults of their enemies? My holy Spouse, saint Joseph, was one of those who enjoyed the privilege of neither seeing nor feeling the presence of the demon in his last hour; for as soon as they approached to deal with him as they do with the rest of men, they felt a powerful force, which kept them at a distance and the holy angels hurled them back into their abyss. Seeing themselves thus oppressed and crushed, they were seized with great uneasiness and confusion. Almost stupefied, Lucifer called a meeting of his followers in hell, in order to consult about this surprising event and in order to have them once more search the earth for the Messias; and then happened what thou shalt relate later on in its place.

172. Hence thou wilt understand the great danger in the hour of death, when both the good works and the bad will begin to show their effects. I will not tell thee how many are thus lost, in order that thy sincere love of God may not cause thee to die of sorrow at this loss. But the general rule is: a good life gives hope of a good end; all other reliance is doubtful, and salvation resting upon it is very rare and merely accidental. The best precaution is to take a good start from afar; and therefore I admonish thee, that, at the dawning of each day, when thou lookest upon the light, thou seriously consider whether it may not be the last of thy life, and, if it should be the last (for thou dost not know), that thou place thy soul in such a state as to be able to meet death with a smiling face. Do not delay even for one instant sorrow for thy sins and a firm purpose of confessing them as soon as thou findest thyself guilty of any and of amending the least of thy imperfections. In all this be so careful that thou leave not upon thy conscience the smallest defect without being sorry for it and without cleansing thyself by the blood of my most holy Son. Place thyself in such a condition that thou art ready to appear before the just Judge, who is to examine and judge thy least thoughts and all thy movements.

173. In order that according to thy pious wishes, thou mayest help those who are in danger of death, thou shouldst give to others the same counsels that I have now given thee. Exhort them to lead a careful life in order to secure a happy death. Moreover, say some prayers for this intention every day of thy life, fervently asking the Almighty to disperse the deceits of the devils, to destroy the snares prepared against those who are in the throes of death, and that his right hand confound all the demons. Know that I have directed my prayers to that end for mortals and in this I wish thee to imitate me. That thou mayest help them so much the more, I wish thee to order and command the demons to depart from

the sick and stop their persecutions; and thou canst very efficaciously use this power, even when thou art absent from the sick, for thou art to command them in the name of the Lord, and thou art to compel them to obey thee for his greater honor and glory.

174. When thy own religious are in danger of death do thou, without exciting them, instruct them in what they are to do. Admonish them and help them to receive the holy Sacraments, and see that they receive them frequently during life in preparation for a good end. Seek to encourage and console them, speaking to them of the things of God and his mysteries contained in the holy Scriptures. Exhort them to awaken their good intentions and desires and to prepare themselves to receive the light and the graces of the Most High. Excite them to hope, strengthen them against temptations and teach them how they are to resist and overcome them, seeking to divine them before they themselves manifest them to thee. The Almighty will give thee an understanding of them so that thou mayest apply the right medicine to each; for the infirmities of the soul are hard to diagnose and cure. All that I now tell thee thou must execute as the most beloved daughter of the Lord and in his service, and I will procure for thee certain privileges for thyself and for those thou desirest to aid in that terrible hour. Do not stint thy charity in these works for thou shalt work not by thy own strength alone, but by the power which God wishes to exercise in thee for his own glory.

Chapter XVI

THE AGE OF THE QUEEN OF HEAVEN AT THE DEATH OF
SAINT JOSEPH, AND SOME OF THE PRIVILEGES OF HER HOLY
SPOUSE.

175. The most fortunate of men, saint Joseph, reached an age
of sixty years and a few days. For at the age of thirty-three he
espoused the blessed Virgin and he lived with Her a little
longer than twenty-seven years as her husband. When saint
Joseph died, She had completed the half of her forty-second
year; for She was espoused to saint Joseph at the age of
fourteen (as stated in the first part, book second, chapter
twenty-second). The twenty-seven years of her married life
completed her forty-first year, to which must be added the
time from the eighth of September until the death of her
blessed spouse. The Queen of heaven still remained in the
same disposition of natural perfection as in her thirty-third
year; for, as already stated in the thirteenth chapter of this
book, She showed no signs of decline, or of more advanced
age, or of weakness, but always remained in that same most
perfect state of womanhood. She felt the natural sorrow due
to the death of saint Joseph; for She loved him as her spouse,
as a man preeminent in perfection and holiness, as her protector and benefactor. This sorrow in the most prudent Lady
was well-ordered and most perfect, but it was far from being
therefore less deep; for her love was great, yea so much the

greater as She was well informed of the high rank he held among the saints, who are written in the book of eternal life and in the eternal mind of the Most High. We do not lose without sorrow what we love in an ordinary manner; so much the greater will be our sorrow for losing what we love much.

176. It is not the purpose of this history to describe at length the perfections and excellences of saint Joseph, nor have I any commission to do so, except in so far as will suffice to point out his dignity and that of our Queen, to whose merits (next to those of her divine Son) must be ascribed the gifts and graces conferred by the Almighty upon this glorious Patriarch. The heavenly Lady was either the instrumental or meritorious cause of the holiness of her spouse, or at least the final object or purpose of this holiness. For all the vast Perfection of his virtues and graces were conferred upon saint Joseph for the purpose of making of him a worthy protector and spouse of Her, whom God selected as his Mother. According to this standard and according to the love of God for his most holy Mother is to be measured the holiness of saint Joseph; and from my understanding of this matter, if there had been in the world another man more perfect and more worthy, the Lord would have chosen this other one for the spouse of his Mother. Since he was chosen by God, saint Joseph was no doubt the most perfect man upon earth. Having created and destined him for such a high end, it is certain that God, in his almighty power, prepared and perfected him in proportion to the exaltedness of his end. That is (according to our way of thinking), his holiness, virtues, gifts, graces and infused and natural habits were made to correspond by divine influence with the end for which he was selected.

177. I perceive a certain difference in the graces given to this great Patriarch and those vouchsafed to other saints; for

many saints were endowed with graces and gifts that are intended not for the increase of their own sanctity, but for the advance of the service of the Most High in other souls; they were, so to say, gifts and graces freely given and not dependent upon the holiness of the receiver. But in our blessed Patriarch all the divine favors were productive of personal virtue and perfection; for the mysterious purpose, toward which they tended and helped along, was closely connected with the holiness of his own life. The more angelic and holy he grew to be, so much the more worthy was he to be the spouse of most holy Mary, the depository and treasurehouse of heavenly sacraments. He was to be a miracle of holiness, as he really was. This marvelous holiness commenced with the formation of his body in the womb of his Mother. In this the providence of God himself interfered, regulating the composition of the four radical humors of his body with extreme nicety of proportion and securing for him that evenly tempered disposition which made his body a blessed earth fit for the abode of an exquisite soul and well-balanced mind (Wisdom 8, 19). He was sanctified in the womb of his mother seven months after his conception, and the leaven of sin was destroyed in him for the whole course of his life, never having felt any impure or disorderly movement. Although he did not receive the use of his reason together with this first sanctification, which consisted principally in justification from original sin, yet his mother at the time felt a wonderful joy of the Holy Ghost. Without understanding entirely the mystery she elicited great acts of virtue and believed that her Son, or whomever she bore in her womb, would be wonderful in the sight of God and men.

178. The holy child Joseph was born most beautiful and perfect of body and caused in his parents and in his relations an extraordinary delight, something like that caused by the birth of saint John the Baptist, though the cause of it was

more hidden. The Lord hastened in him the use of his reason, perfecting it in his third year, endowing it with infused science and augmenting his soul with new graces and virtues. From that time the child began to know God by faith, and also by natural reasoning and science, as the cause and Author of all things. He eagerly listened and understood profoundly all that was taught him in regard to God and his works. At this premature age he already practiced the highest kinds of prayer and contemplation and eagerly engaged in the exercise of the virtues proper to his youth; so that, at the time when others come to the use of reason, at the age of seven years or more, saint Joseph was already a perfect man in the use of it and in holiness. He was of a kind disposition, loving, affable, sincere, showing inclinations not only holy but angelic, growing in virtue and perfection and advancing toward his espousal with most holy Mary by an altogether irreproachable life.

179. For the confirmation and increase of his good qualities was then added the intercession of the blessed Lady; for as soon as She was informed that the Lord wished Her to enter the married state with him, She earnestly besought the Lord to sanctify saint Joseph and inspire him with most chaste thoughts and desires in conformity with her own. The Lord listened to her prayer and permitted Her to see what great effects his right hand wrought in the mind and spirit of the patriarch saint Joseph. They were so copious, that they cannot be described in human words. He infused into his soul the most perfect habits of all the virtues and gifts. He balanced anew all his faculties and filled him with grace, confirming it in an admirable manner. In the virtue and perfection of chastity the holy spouse was elevated higher than the seraphim; for the purity, which they possessed without body, saint Joseph possessed in his earthly body and in mortal flesh; never did an image of the impurities of the

animal and sensible nature engage, even for one moment, any of his faculties. This freedom from all such imaginations and his angelic simplicity fitted him for the companionship and presence of the most Pure among all creatures, and without this excellence he would not have been worthy of so great a dignity and rare excellence.

180. Also in the other virtues he was wonderfully distinguished, especially in charity; for he dwelt at the fountainhead of that living water, which flows on to eternal life (John 4, 14); he was in close proximity to that sphere of fire and was consumed without resistance. The best that can be said of the charity of our saint is what I have already said in the preceding chapter; namely, that his love of God was really the cause of his mortal sickness and of his death. The manner of his death was a privilege of his singular love, for his sweet sighs of love surpassed and finally put an end to those of his sickness, being far more powerful. As the objects of his love, Christ and his Mother, were present with him always and as both of Them were more closely bound to him than to any of the womanborn, his most pure and faithful heart was unavoidably consumed by the loving effects of such a close union. Blessed be the Author of such great wonders and blessed be the most fortunate of mortals, saint Joseph, who so worthily corresponded to their love. He deserves to be known and extolled by all the generations of men and all nations, since the Lord has wrought such things with no other man and to none has He shown such love.

181. The divine visions and revelations vouchsafed to saint Joseph, I have particularly mentioned in the course of this history (Vol. II 422, 423, 471); but there were many more than can be described, and the greatest of them all was his having known the mysteries of the relation between Christ and his Mother and his having lived in their company for so many years as the putative father of the Lord and as the

true spouse of the Queen of heaven. But I have been informed concerning certain other privileges conferred upon saint Joseph by the Most High on account of his great holiness, which are especially important to those who ask his intercession in a proper manner. In virtue of these special privileges the intercession of saint Joseph is most powerful: first, for attaining the virtue of purity and overcoming the sensual inclinations of the flesh; secondly, for procuring powerful help to escape sin and return to the friendship of God; thirdly, for increasing the love and devotion to most holy Mary; fourthly, for securing the grace of a happy death and protection against the demons in that hour; fifthly, for inspiring the demons with terror at the mere mention of his name by his clients; sixthly, for gaining health of body and assistance in all kinds of difficulties; seventhly, for securing issue of children in families. These and many other favors God confers upon those who properly and with good disposition seek the intercession of the spouse of our Queen, saint Joseph. I beseech all the faithful children of the Church to be very devout to him and they will experience these favors in reality, if they dispose themselves as they should in order to receive and merit them.

Words of the Queen

THE VIRGIN MARY SPEAKS TO SISTER MARY OF AGREDA

182. My daughter, although thou hast described my spouse, saint Joseph, as the most noble among the princes and saints of the heavenly Jerusalem; yet neither canst thou properly manifest his eminent sanctity, nor can any of the mortals know it fully before they arrive at the vision of the Divinity. Then all of them will be filled with wonder and praise as the Lord will make them capable of understanding this sacrament. On the last day, when all men shall be judged, the

damned will bitterly bewail their sins, which prevented them from appreciating this powerful means of their salvation, and availing themselves, as they easily could have, of this intercessor to gain the friendship of the just Judge. The whole human race has much undervalued the privileges and prerogatives conceded to my blessed spouse and they know not what his intercession with God is able to do. I assure thee, my dearest, that he is one of the greatly favored personages in the divine presence and has immense power to stay the arms of divine vengeance.

183. I desire that thou be very thankful to the divine condescension for vouchsafing thee so much light and knowledge regarding this mystery, and also for the favor which I am doing thee therein. From now on, during the rest of thy mortal life, see that thou advance in devotion and in hearty love toward my spouse, and that thou bless the Lord for thus having favored him with such high privileges and for having rejoiced me so much in the knowledge of all his excellences. In all thy necessities thou must avail thyself of his intercession. Thou shouldst induce many to venerate him and see that thy own religious distinguish themselves in their devotion to him. That which my spouse asks of the Lord in heaven is granted upon the earth and on his intercession depend many and extraordinary favors for men, if they do not make themselves unworthy of receiving them. All these privileges were to be a reward for the amiable perfection of this wonderful saint and for his great virtues; for divine clemency is favorably drawn forth by them and looks upon saint Joseph with generous liberality, ready to shower down its marvelous mercies upon all those who avail themselves of his intercession.

Chapter XVII

THE DOINGS OF MOST HOLY MARY AFTER THE DEATH OF
SAINT JOSEPH AND SOME OF HER DEALINGS WITH THE
HOLY ANGELS.

184. Christian perfection is all included in the two states of
life known to the Church: the active and the contemplative
life. To the active life belong all the operations of the body
and the senses, practiced in our intercourse with our neighbor in temporal affairs. They embrace a wide field and include the practice of the moral virtues, which constitute the
perfection of our active life. To the contemplative life belong
the interior activities of the understanding and will, aiming at
the most noble and the spiritual objects proper to the rational
creature. Therefore, the contemplative life is more excellent
than the active, and, as it is more quiet, more delightful and
beautiful, it is also more desirable in itself. It tends more
directly toward the highest end, that is God, since it consists
in the deepest know ledge and love of God, and thus partici-
pates of the qualities of eternal life, which is entirely contemplative. These two lives, the two sisters Martha and Mary
(Luke 10, 41), the one quiet and thoughtful, the other
solicitous and bustling; or those other two sisters and wives,
Lia and Rachel: the one, fruitful, but ugly and with sore eyes,
the other beautiful and gracious, but sterile in the beginning.
For the active life is more productive, though in it the soul is

taken up with numerous and various occupations, during which it is kept in disturb deserts and solitudes, which are more favorable to that kind of life; and the other, that pursued the active life, and the care of souls by teaching and exhortation, set aside some of their time for retirement from exterior activity, and divided their days between contemplation and active life. By thus attending to both with perfection, they attained the merits and reward of the two kinds of life, founded on love and grace as their principal support.

186. The most blessed Mary alone joined these two lives in a perfect manner: the highest and most ardent contemplation was not hindered by her occupations in the active life. In Her was the solicitude of Martha without its excitement, and the quiet and rest of Mary without idleness of the body; She possessed the beauty of Rachel and the fruitfulness of Lia; and only this great and prudent Queen truly exemplified what these sisters mysteriously typified. Although She attended upon her ailing spouse, and supported him and her most holy Son by her labor, She did not on that account interrupt or curtail her heavenly contemplations, nor was She under any necessity of seeking solitude or retirement, in order to restore the quiet and peace of her heart and raise it beyond the seraphic regions. Yet, when She found Herself alone and deprived of the company of saint Joseph, She so arranged her exercises, as to spend her time entirely in the interior activity of divine love. She immediately perceived, by her insight into the interior of her most holy Son, that such was his will, that She should relax her labors by which She had attended to the wants of saint Joseph through night and day, and that instead of this hard labor, She should now join his Majesty in his prayers and exalted works.

187. The Lord also reminded Her that for the moderate nourishment necessary to Them it would be sufficient to engage in labor only for a short time each day; for from that

time on they were to eat only once a day at eventide, having until now followed another custom out of regard to saint Joseph and in order to keep him consoling company at mealtimes. Thenceforward Jesus and Mary ate but once a day at about six o'clock in the evening; many times their meal consisted merely of bread, at other times the blessed Lady added fruits or herbs, or perhaps fish; and this formed the only refreshment of the Sovereigns of the heaven and earth. Although their frugality and abstinence had always been great, yet it was greater after they were left alone, and They never dispensed Themselves except in regard to the kind of food and in regard to the time of taking it. When They were invited they ate a little of what was offered to Them, without abstaining entirely, commencing to practice the advice which Jesus was afterwards to give to his disciples for their conduct while preaching the Gospel. The simple food used by the heavenly Sovereigns was served by the great Lady to her divine Son on her knees, having asked permission thus to serve it. Sometimes She also prepared it in that posture, moved thereto by the thought that it was to serve as nourishment of the true Son of God.

188. The presence of saint Joseph was no hindrance to the most blessed Mother in treating her Son with all due reverence, not missing the least point of what this reverence toward Him demanded. But after the death of saint Joseph the great Lady practiced prostrations and genuflections much more frequently; for there was always more freedom for such actions in the presence of her holy angels, than in the presence of her spouse who was man. Many times She remained prostrate upon the ground until the Lord commanded Her to rise; very often She kissed his feet, at other times his hand, usually She was filled with tears of the profoundest humility and reverence. She always stood in the presence of her divine Son in posture of adoration and most ardent love, awaiting

his divine pleasure and intent upon imitating his interior virtues. Although She had no faults, and was not guilty of even the least imperfection or negligence in the service and love of her most holy Son, her eyes (like those of the servant and of the anxious handmaid mentioned by the Prophet, only more devotedly) were continually upon the hands of her Master, in order to obtain the graces She desired for assisting Her to greater perfection. It cannot enter into human thought what divine science aided Her in understanding and performing so many and so great works in union with the incarnate Word during the time They both lived alone together, without any other company than that of the holy angels of their guard and service. They alone were the eye-witnesses and were moved to admiration and to highest praises, to see themselves so inferior in wisdom and purity to a mere Creature who was worthy of such holiness: for She alone made a full return for the graces She received.

189. With the holy angels the Queen of heaven entered into a sweet emulation and strife in regard to the ordinary and humble services which were necessary for the comfort of the Word of God and the well-ordering of their little dwelling, for there was no one to attend to these things except the heavenly Lady and those most noble and faithful vassals and ministers, who, for this purpose assisted in human forms ready and anxious to attend to all the work. The great Queen wished to perform all the humble work Herself and with her own hands to scrub the house and arrange its poor furnishings, wash the dishes and cooking utensils, and set the rooms in order; but these courtiers of the Most High, being truly courteous and more expeditious, though not more humble in their operations, usually anticipated these services before the Queen could find time to perform them. Sometimes, and at certain periods, often, She would find them thus at the work which She was about to perform, the holy angels having

begun it beforehand; but at her word they desisted and allowed Her to satisfy her humility and devotion in completing it Herself. In order that they might not interfere with her affectionate desires, She said to the holy angels: "Ministers of the Most High, you are such pure spirits that you reflect the light of the Divinity for my illumination, and, therefore, these low and servile occupations are not suitable to your state, your nature and condition. These pertain to me, who, besides being only of earth, am the lowest of the mortals and the least of the servants of my Lord and Son. Permit me, my friends, to perform the service to which I am bound, since I can thereby gain merits which, on account of your station and dignity, you do not need. I know the value of these servile works which the world despises, and the Lord has given me this knowledge not in order that I may allow them to be done by others, but that I may perform them myself."

190. "Our Queen and Lady," answered the angels, "it is true that in thy eyes and in the estimation of the Lord these works are as valuable as Thou knowest them to be; but if Thou dost thereby earn the precious rewards of thy humility, take notice that we would be deficient in obedience to the Lord if we would knowingly omit any of these works permitted us by the Most High. The merits which Thou losest in not performing this service, Thou, O Lady, canst easily make up by the mortification of denying thyself the desire of executing them." The most prudent Virgin answered these arguments by saying: "No, my masters and sovereign spirits, you must not look upon these works in such a light; for if you consider yourselves bound to serve me as the Mother of your great Lord, whose creatures you are, remember that He has raised me from the dust to this great dignity and that therefore my debt of gratitude for this benefit is greater than yours. As my obligation is so much the greater, my return must also be greater than yours. If you desire to serve my Son

as his creatures, I likewise must serve Him on this account, and I am more bound to do so because I am the Mother of such a Son. Thus you will always find me more obliged than yourselves to be humble, thankful and annihilated to the very dust in his presence."

191. These and similar sweet and admirable contentions were going on between most holy Mary and her angels; and the palm of humility always remained in the hands of their Queen and Mistress. The world is justly ignorant of these mysteries, being unworthy of knowing them on account of its vanity and pride. Its foolish arrogance deems insignificant and contemptible these humble and servile occupations, while the courtiers of heaven who know their value appreciate them, and the Queen of creation eagerly sought after them as very precious. But let us leave the world to its intentional or unconscious ignorance. Humility is not for the proud of heart, nor lowly service for purple and fine linen, nor scrubbing and washing for costly gems and silks, nor are the precious jewels of these virtues intended indiscriminately for all men. But if the contagion of worldly pride enters into the schools of humility and contempt of the world, namely, into religious communities, and if this kind of humiliation is looked upon by them as a disgrace, we cannot deny that such sentiments are nothing but a most shameful and reprehensible pride. If we religious men and women despise the benefits of such humble occupations and count them a degradation like worldly people, how can we appear before the angels and our Queen, who esteemed as greatest honors those very works which we look upon as contemptible and dishonorable?

192. My sisters, daughters of this great Queen and Lady, to you I speak, who are called and transported to the bridal chamber of the great King to true joy and exaltation (Ps. 44, 16)! Do not allow yourselves to be robbed of your right to be

called children of such a Mother! If She, who was the Queen of angels and men, humbled Herself by engaging in such lowly and trivial occupations, in scrubbing and busying Herself in the most common handiwork, what presumption shall the haughtiness, vain pride and want of humility of mere slaves appear to be in her sight and in the sight of the Lord God himself? Far from our community be such treason, fit only for Babylon and its inhabitants. Let us feel honored by that which the exalted Queen esteemed as a crown of merit, and let it be for us a subject of most shameful confusion and a cause for dreadful reprehension to be found wanting in the same zealous contention of humility which She entertained with the holy angels. Let us eagerly seek after humble and servile occupation and let us cause in the angels and heavenly companions the same emulation, which was so pleasing to our Queen, and to her most holy Son and our Spouse.

193. We must understand that without real and solid humility, it is audacious to seek the reward of uncertain spiritual or sensible consolations, and to strive after them is daring foolishness. Let us rather look upon our heavenly Teacher who is the perfect example of a holy and perfect life. In the great Queen the favors and delights of heaven alternated with her humble and servile occupations for it happened many times when She was engaged in prayer with her Son, that the holy angels in sweet, harmonious voices sang the hymns and canticles composed by Mary herself in praise of the infinite Being of God and of the hypostatical union of the Word with human nature in the second Person of the Trinity. The Blessed Lady often asked the angels to repeat these hymns to her Lord and Creator and, alternating the verses with them, She added new hymns. They obeyed Her, lost in admiration at the profound wisdom manifested in what She thus said and composed for them. Then, whenever

her most holy Son retired to rest, or during his meals, She commanded them, as the Mother of their Creator, solicitous to entertain Him, that they furnish sweet music in her name and the Lord permitted it whenever She so ordered, therein yielding to the ardour of her love and veneration, with which She served Him in his last years. In order to narrate all that has been revealed to me in this regard, a much longer discourse were necessary and much greater ability than mine. From what I have insinuated one can judge to some extent of other deep mysteries of this intercourse and find motive and occasion to magnify and extol the great Lady and Queen whom may all nations know and praise as blessed among creatures, as the Mother of the Creator and Redeemer of the world.

Words of the Queen

THE VIRGIN MARY SPEAKS TO SISTER MARY OF AGREDA

194. My daughter, I wish that, before proceeding to narrate other mysteries, thou understand well all that the Lord commanded in regard to my intercourse with my holy spouse, saint Joseph. When I espoused myself to him, God commanded me to change the order of my meals and other exterior duties in order to accommodate myself to his circumstances; for he was the head of the family, and, according to the common rule, I was the inferior. The same conduct was also followed by my most holy Son, though He was true God, yet He subjected Himself before the eyes of the world to him who was thought to be his father. As soon as We were alone after the death of my spouse, who was the occasion of this change in our lives, we returned to our former way of living. The Lord did not expect saint Joseph to accommodate himself to us, but that We should accommodate ourselves to him as the common order among men required. Nor did the

Lord resort to miracles in order to escape the necessity of taking food or of following ordinary human occupations; for in all things, He acted as the Teacher of all virtues, and of all perfection, being an example to parents and children, to prelates, superiors and superioresses, to subjects and inferiors; to parents, in order that they may learn to love their children, help them, nourish them, exhort them, correct them and lead them on in the way of salvation without remissness or carelessness; to children, in order that they may learn to esteem, love and honor their parents as the instruments of their existence, diligently obey them according to the natural law, which requires and teaches obedience and repudiates the opposite as monstrous and horrible; to prelates and superiors, in order that they may love their subjects and direct them as their children; to inferiors, that they obey without resistance, even if they should in other respects be of higher and better condition in life; for in so far as the superior represents God, the prelate is always superior in dignity; but real charity must always teach both to be of one spirit.

195. In order that thou mayest acquire this great virtue, I desire that thou conform and accommodate thyself to thy sisters and inferiors without affection of formality, and that thou treat them with dovelike meekness and sincerity. Do thou pray when they pray, work and eat, and take thy recreation with them. For real perfection in a convent consists in conforming with the common spirit, and if thou act thus, thou wilt be guided by the holy Spirit, who governs all well regulated communities. Following this order thou canst make progress in abstinence, eating less than the others, though the same amount of food is placed before thee. Without being singular thou canst, with a little discretion, abstain from what thou desirest for the love of thy Spouse and of me. If thou art not hindered by some grave infirmity, never absent thyself from the common exercises unless

perhaps obedience to thy superiors sometimes prevent thee. Be present at all common exercises with special reverence, attention and devotion, for at such times thou wilt most frequently be visited by the Lord.

196. I wish also that thou learn from this chapter to conceal carefully the special works thou undertakest in imitation of my own; for, although I had no need of refraining from any work in the presence of saint Joseph, yet I was careful to add retirement as an additional observance of perfection and prudence, since retirement of itself makes good works more praiseworthy. But this is not to be understood of ordinary and obligatory works, since thou must give a good example and let thy light shine, avoiding any danger of scandal or cause for cavil. There are many works which can be done in secret and unobserved by the eyes of creatures, and which are not lightly to be exposed to the danger of publicity and ostentation. In thy retirement thou canst make many genuflections; prostrate in the dust, thou canst humiliate thyself, adoring the supreme Majesty of the Most High and offering thy mortal body, which oppresses thy soul, as a sacrifice for the disorderly inclinations against justice and reason. Thus thou wilt not reserve any part of thy being from the service of thy Creator and Spouse, and thou wilt force thy body to make up the loss which it causes to the soul by its passions and earthly affections.

197. With this object in view seek to keep it always in strict subjection, allowing it to partake only of those comforts which serve to keep it in proper condition for the activity of the soul and not to pander to its passions and appetites. Mortify and crush it until it is dead to all that is delightful to the senses, so that even the common actions necessary for life shall appear to thee more painful than agreeable, taste more of bitterness than of dangerous enjoyment. Although I have already on other occasions spoken to thee of the value of this

mortification and humiliation, thou shouldst now, by this example which I have given thee, be still more convinced of their great value. I now command thee not to despise any of these acts or deem them of little consequence, but esteem all of them as precious treasures to be gained for thyself. In this thou must be covetous and avaricious, eagerly grasping the occasions of doing servile work, such as scrubbing, cleaning the house, engaging in the most menial services, and attending upon the sick and infirm as I have said before. In all of these works place me before thy eyes as an example in order that my carefulness and humility may urge thee on, full of joy to be able to imitate me, and shame for any negligence therein. If I, who never had displeased or offended the Lord since the beginning of my existence, judged this virtue of humility so necessary in order to find grace in his eyes and be raised up by his right hand, how much more is it necessary for thee to humble thyself to the dust and annihilate thyself in his sight, who wast conceived in sin and hast so often offended Him? (Ps. 50, 7) . Humiliate thyself to nothingness, and acknowledge that what being the Most High has given thee, thou hast but ill employed, and that, therefore, thy very existence should be a subject of humiliation to thee. Thus wilt thou at last find the treasure of grace.

Chapter XVIII

OTHER MYSTERIES AND OCCUPATIONS OF THE GREAT
QUEEN AND LADY AND HER MOST HOLY SON, WHILE THEY
LIVED ALONE TOGETHER.

198. As I have already said in other places the knowledge of
many of the sacramental mysteries of Jesus and Mary are
reserved for the increase of the accidental beatitude of the
predestined in eternal life. The highest and most ineffable of
these mysteries took place during the four years in which
they lived together after the death of saint Joseph and after
the public preaching of our Lord. It is impossible for any
mortal worthily to understand such profound secrets: how
much less can I, rude and untutored as I am, manifest
properly what I have been made to understand concerning
them. But in that which I do manifest, will be seen the cause
of my inability. The soul of Christ our Lord was a most
transparent and flawless mirror, in which the blessed Mother
saw reflected all the mysteries and sacraments which the
Lord, as the Head and Artificer of the holy Church, the
Restorer of the human race, the Teacher of eternal salvation
and the angel of the great council, wrought and accomplished according to eternal decrees of the most blessed
Trinity.

199. In the execution of this work consigned to Him by
the eternal Father, Christ our Lord consumed his whole

earthly life and lent to it all the perfection possible to a God man. In the measure as He approached its consummation and the full accomplishment of its sacraments, so also the force of His divine Wisdom and Omnipotence became more evident. Of all these mysteries our great Queen and Lady was the eyewitness and her purest heart was their depository. In all things She cooperated with her divine Son, as his helpmate in the works of the reparation of mankind. Accordingly, in order to understand entirely the designs of eternal Providence and the process of dispensing all the mysteries of salvation, it was necessary that She comprehend also the things hidden in the science of Christ our Redeemer, the works of his love and prudence by which He prepared the efficient means of attaining his high purposes. In the little which I can say of the works of most holy Mary, I must always presuppose the works of her most Holy Son; for She cooperated with Him and imitated Him as her pattern and model.

200. The Savior of the world was already twentysix years of age; and in the measure as his most holy humanity approached its perfect growth and its earthly end, Christ proceeded to manifest it by permitting his operations to show more and more openly the purpose of the Redemption. All these mysteries the evangelist Luke includes in those few words, with which he closes the second chapter: "And Jesus advanced in wisdom, and age, and grace with God and man." Among men his blessed Mother cooperated and grew in knowledge with the increase and progress of her Son, without remaining ignorant of anything that the Son of God and man could ever communicate to a mere creature. Among these hidden and divine mysteries the great Lady also perceived during these years, how her Son and true God began more and more to extend his plans, not only those of his uncreated Divinity, but of his humanity, so as to include all

the mortals in his Redemption as a whole; how He weighed its value in the eyes of the eternal Father, and how, in order to close the gates of hell and call men to eternal happiness, He had come down from heaven to suffer the bitterest torments and death; and how, in spite of all this, the folly and wickedness of those that were to be born after He had thus annihilated Himself on the Cross, would rather urge Him to widen the portals and open the lowest abysses of hell, consigning them to those horrible and dreadful torments, which their blind ignorance continued to disregard.

201. The knowledge and contemplation of this sad fate caused great affliction and sorrow to the human nature of Christ our Lord, and sometimes pressed forth a bloody sweat. In these agonies the divine Teacher persevered in his petitions for all that were to be redeemed. In conformity with the will of his eternal Father He desired with the most ardent love to be sacrificed for the rescue of men. For, as not all were to be saved by his merits and sacrifices, He knew, that at all events the divine justice must be satisfied and the offenses to the Divinity be made good by the punishment, which divine equity and justice had prepared from all eternity for the infidels and the thankless sinners on the day of retribution. Entering into these profound secrets by her deep wisdom the great Lady joined her most holy Son in the sorrowful contemplation and sighs for those unfortunates, while at the same time her heart was torn by grief at the heavy affliction of the blessed fruit of her womb. Many times the meekest Dove shed ensanguined tears, when She saw her Son sweat blood in the agonies of his sorrow. For only this most prudent Lady and her Son, the true God and man, could ever justly weigh, as in the scales of the sanctuary, what it meant, on the one hand to see a God dying upon a cross in order to seal up the infernal regions, and, on the other hand,

the hardness and blindness of mortal hearts in casting themselves headlong into the jaws of eternal death.

202. In these great sorrows it sometimes happened, that the most loving Mother was overcome by deathly weaknesses, and they would no doubt have ended her life, if She had not been preserved by divine intervention. Her sweetest Son, in return for her most faithful and loving compassion, sometimes commanded the angels to console Her and take Her into their arms, at other times, to sing her own heavenly canticles of praise in honor of the Divinity and humanity. At other times the Lord himself took Her into his arms and gave Her new celestial understanding of her exemption from this iniquitous law of sin and its effects. Sometimes, thus reclining in his arms, the angels sang to Her in admiration, while She, transformed and enraptured in heavenly ecstasies, experienced new and exquisite influences of the Divinity. At such times this chosen One, this perfect and only One, was truly reclining on the left hand of the humanity, while rejoiced and caressed by the right hand of the Divinity (Cant. 2, 6) ; her most loving Son and Spouse conjured the daughters of Jerusalem not to wake his Beloved from his sleep, which cured the sorrows and infirmities of her love, until She herself desired to be thus waked; and the supernal spirits broke forth in wonder, to see Her raised above them all, resting on her beloved Son, clothed in varicolored garment at his right hand, and they blessed and extolled Her above all creatures (Ps. 44, 10).

203. The great Queen was made acquainted with the deepest secrets concerning the predestination of the elect in virtue of the Redemption, and She saw them as they were written in the eternal memory of her Son. She was enabled to see how He applied to them his merits and efficaciously interceded for their salvation; how his love and grace, of which the reprobate made themselves unworthy, were award-

ed to the predestined according to their different dispositions. Among the predestined She also saw those, whom the
Lord in his wisdom and solicitude was to call to his apostolate and imitation, and how by means of his hidden and
foreordained decrees, He began to enlist them to the standard of his Cross, which they themselves afterwards were to
unfold before the world; and how He pursued the policy of a
good general, who, planning a great battle or conquest,
assigns the different duties to different parts of his army,
chooses the most courageous and welldisposed for the most
arduous positions. Thus Christ our Redeemer, in order to
enter upon the conquest of the world and despoil the demon
of his tyrannical possession by the power of his Godhead as
the Word, disposed of this new army to be enlisted, assigned
the dignities and offices of his courageous and strong captains
and predestined them for their posts of duty. All the preparations and apparatus of this war were prearranged in the
divine wisdom of his most holy will just in the order in
which all was to take place.

204. All this was also open and manifest to the most prudent Mother; and to Her was given, by infused species, to see
and personally to know many of the predestined, especially
the Apostles and disciples, and a great number of those, who
were called to the holy Church in the primitive and later
ages. On account of this supernatural knowledge given to
Her by God, She knew the Apostles and others before coming in contact with them, and just as the divine Master had
prayed and obtained for them their vocation before He called
them, so also the heavenly Lady had made them the object of
her prayers. Hence, in the favors and graces, which the
Apostles received before hearing or seeing their Master, and
which disposed and prepared them to accept their vocation
to the apostolate, the Mother of grace had likewise cooperated. In proportion as the time of his public preaching drew

nearer, the Lord redoubled his prayers and petitions for them and sent them greater and more efficacious inspirations. In like manner the prayers of the heavenly Lady grew to be more fervent and efficacious; and when afterwards they attached themselves to the Lord and saw Her face to face, She was wont to say of them as well as of many others, to her Son: "These, my Son and Master, are the fruits of thy prayers and of thy holy desires." And She sang songs of praise and thanksgiving, because She saw his wishes fulfilled, and because She saw those, who were called from the beginning of the world, drawn to his following.

205. In the prudent contemplation of those wonders our great Queen was wont to be absorbed and to break out in matchless hymns of admiration and praise, performing heroic acts of love and adoring the secret judgments of the Most High. Entirely transformed and penetrated by this fire, which issued from the Lord in order to consume the world, She was accustomed, some times in the secret of her heart, at others in a loud voice, to exclaim: "O infinite love! O manifestation of goodness ineffable and immense! Why do mortals not know Thee? Why should thy tenderness be so ill repaid? O ye labors, sufferings, sighs, petitions and desires of my Beloved, altogether more precious than pearls, than all the treasures of the world! Who shall be so unhappy and so ungrateful as to despise Thee? O children of Adam, whom can you find to die for you many times, in order that your ignorance might be undeceived, your hardness be softened and your misfortunes relieved?" After these ardent exclamations, the blessed Mother conversed with her Son mouth to mouth, and the highest King consoled and dilated her heart reminding Her, how pleasing She herself was to the Most High, how great a grace and glory were to be merited for the predestined in comparison with the ingratitude and hardness of the reprobate. Especially He showed Her the love of

Himself toward Her, that of the blessed Trinity, and how much God was pleased with her faithful correspondence and immaculate purity.

206. At other times the Lord showed Her, what He was to do in his public preaching; how She was to cooperate with Him and help Him in the affairs and in the government of the new Church. She was informed of the denial of saint Peter, the unbelief of Thomas, the treachery of Judas, and other events of the future. From that moment on the dutiful Lady resolved to labor zealously in order to save that treasonous disciple, and She followed her resolve, as I shall relate in its place. The perdition of Judas began by his despising her good will and by conceiving against the Mother of Grace a sort of ill will and impiety. Of these great mysteries and sacraments the heavenly Lady was informed by her most holy Son. So great was the wisdom and science deposited in Her, that all attempts at fully explaining them is vain; for only the knowledge of the Lord could exceed that of Mary, which far excelled that of all the seraphim and cherubim. But if our Lord and Redeemer Jesus, and Mary, his most holy Mother, employed all these gifts of grace and science in the service of mortals; and if a single sigh of Christ our Lord was of incalculable value for all creatures, and if those of his Mother, though they had not the same value as his, being those of a mere creature, were worth more in the eyes of God than the doings of all creation taken together, to what an immense value will both their united merits swell, when we add together what Son and Mother did for us, in their petitions, tears, bloody sweat, fearful torment and death of the Cross and all the other actions, in which the Mother joined the divine Son as his helpmate and partaker of all his acts! O ingratitude of men! O hardness of our carnal heart, more than adamantine! Where is our insight? Where our reason? Where is even the most common compassion or gratitude of

human nature? Is it not moved to pity and compassion by the sensible objects, the causes of its eternal damnation? Why then does it so completely forget to be moved by the life and sufferings of the Lord, the cause of everlasting happiness and peace in the life to come?

Words of the Queen

THE VIRGIN MARY SPEAKS TO SISTER MARY OF AGREDA

207. My daughter, it is certain, that even if thou or any of the mortals were able to speak in the language of the angels, they would not on that account be able to describe the blessings and favors, which the right hand of the Most High showered upon me in those last years of the life of my Son with me. These works of the Lord are of an order, far above thy capacity and that of the rest of the mortals. But since thou hast received such special enlightenment concerning these sacraments, I wish that thou praise and extol the Almighty for all that He did for me and for raising me out of the dust by such exalted favors. Although thy love of the Lord must be spontaneous as that of a devoted daughter and of a most loving spouse, not selfish or forced; yet I wish, that, for the support of thy human weakness and the strengthening of thy hope, thou fondly remember, how delightful the Lord is in his charity toward those who love Him with filial fear. 0 my dearest Daughter, if men would place no hindrance by their sins, and if they would not resist this infinite bounty, how measureless would be the favors and blessings upon them! According to thy way of understanding thou must look upon Him as being outraged and made sorrowful by the opposition of mortals to his boundless desires of doing them good. And they carry their opposition so far, that they accustom themselves not only to be unworthy of tasting of his sweetness, but also not to believe, that others ever partici-

pate in his sweetness and blessings, which He desires so much to communicate to all.

208. Be careful also to give thanks for the incessant labors of my most holy Son for all men, and for what I have done in union with Him, as has been shown thee. Catholics should bear in mind more constantly the passion and death of the Lord, because the Church so often recalls it to their remembrance, although few show themselves grateful. But there are still fewer who take thought of the other works of my Son and of mine. For the Lord allowed not one hour, yea not a moment, to pass, in which He did not employ in gaining gifts and graces for rescuing all men from eternal damnation and making them participants of his glory. These works of the Lord God incarnate will be witnesses against the forgetfulness and hardheartedness of the faithful, especially on the day of judgment. If thou, who possessest the light and the doctrine of the Most High and my teachings, wilt not be grateful, thy confusion will be even greater than that of others, since thy guilt is more heinous. Thou must not only correspond to the many general blessings, but also to the special and particular ones, which thou experiencest every day. Guard against the danger of forgetfulness and conduct thyself as my daughter and disciple. Do not delay for one moment to apply thyself to a good life in the best way possible to thee. For this purpose attend well to the interior lights and to the instructions of thy spiritual guides, the ministers of the Lord. Be assured, if thou correspond to some of the graces and favors, the Most High will open up his almighty hands and fill thee with riches and treasures.

Chapter XIX

CHRIST OUR LORD BEGINS TO PREPARE FOR HIS PUBLIC
PREACHING BY ANNOUNCING TO SOME THE PRESENCE OF
THE REDEEMER INTO THE WORLD; HIS :MOST HOLY
MOTHER ASSISTS HIM THEREIN AND THE POWERS OF HELL
BEGIN TO GET UNEASY.

209. The fire of divine charity burned in the bosom of our
Redeemer and Master as in a closed furnace until the opportune time destined for its manifestation. For in due time He
was to lay bare the burning love of his bosom by means of his
public preaching and miracles, and at last even to break the
vase of his humanity in order to pour forth his charity.
Although it is true, as Solomon says, that fire cannot be
concealed in the bosom without burning the vestments
(Prov. 6, 27), and although the Lord always manifested his
love, sending forth from Him its sparks and flames in all his
doings since the moment of his Incarnation; yet, in comparison to what He was to accomplish in his chosen time and in
comparison to the conflagration of his interior love, we may
say that the flames of his love had until then remained covered and enclosed. The Lord had now reached perfect adolescence, attaining his twentyseventh year. According to our
way of speaking, it seemed as if He could not any more
restrain the impetus of his love and of his desire to fulfill the
will of the eternal Father in accomplishing the salvation of

men. He was filled with sorrowing love, prayed and fasted much, and began to mingle with the people and communicate with mortals. Many times He passed the nights in prayer on the mountains, and began to absent Himself two or three days from the house and from his most holy Mother.

210. The most prudent Lady, by these absences and excursions of her Son, foresaw the approach of his labors and sufferings. She already felt the sword, prepared for her devout and affectionate love, piercing her heart and soul, and was entirely consumed in most tender acts of love for her Beloved. During these absences of her Son her heavenly courtiers and vassals, the holy angels, attended upon Her in visible forms, and the great Lady spoke to them of her sorrows, and sent them as messengers to her Son and Lord in order that they might bring Her news of his occupations and exercises. The holy angels obeyed their Queen and by their frequent messages She was enabled, in her retirement, to follow the highest King Christ in all his prayers, supplications and exercises. Whenever the Lord returned She received Him prostrate upon the ground, adoring Him and thanking Him for the blessings, which He had gained for the sinners. She served Him as a loving Mother and sought to procure for Him the poor refreshment, of which She knew He stood in need as a true man subject to suffering; for often it happened that He had passed two or three days without rest, or food or sleep. As already described the most blessed Mother was well aware of the labors and cares weighing down the soul of the Redeemer. The Lord always informed Her of them, and of his new undertakings, of the hidden blessings communicated to many souls by new light concerning the Divinity and concerning the Redemption.

211. Full of this knowledge the great Queen was wont to say to her most holy Son: "My Lord, highest and true happiness of souls! I see, Light of my eyes, that thy most ardent

love for men will not rest or be appeased until it has secured eternal salvation for them; this is the proper occupation of thy charity and the work assigned to Thee by the eternal Father. Thy words and precious works must necessarily draw toward Thee many hearts; but, 0 my sweetest Love, I desire that all the mortals be attracted and that all of them correspond to thy solicitude and exceeding great charity. Behold me, thy slave, 0 Lord, with a heart prepared to fulfill all thy wishes and to offer her life, if necessary, in order that all creatures may submit to the longings of thy most ardent love, which so completely devotes itself to drawing them to thy grace and friendship." To this offering the Mother of mercy was urged by her ardent desire to see the teaching and labors of our Redeemer and Master bring forth their proper fruit. As the most prudent Lady fully estimated their value and dignity, She wished that they be lost for none of the souls, nor that proper thanks for them should be wanting in men. In her charity She wished to assist the Lord, or rather to assist her fellowmen, who heard his words and witnessed his works, in corresponding to these favors and lose not their chances of salvation. She was consumed with a desire to render worthy thanks and praise to the Lord for his wonderful bounty toward souls, seeking to repay the debt of acknowledgment and gratitude, not only for those mercies that were efficacious, but for those which the guilt of men made inactive. In this thanksgiving the thanks of our great Lady were as hidden as they were admirable. For in all the works of Christ our Lord She participated in a most exalted degree, not only in so far as She cooperated as the cause, but in as far as the effects are concerned. She so labored for each soul, as if She herself were the one to be benefited. Of this I will say more in the third part.

212. To this offering of the most loving Mother her most holy Son answered: "My dearest Mother! already the time is

come in which I must, conformably to the will of my eternal Father, commence to prepare some hearts for the reception of my light and doctrine and for giving them notice of the opportune and foreordained time of the salvation of men. In this work I wish thee to follow and assist Me. Beseech thou my Father to send his light into the hearts of the mortals and awaken their souls, that they may with an upright intention receive the message of the presence of their Savior and Teacher in the world." From that day on his Mother, according to his own desire, accompanied Him in all his excursions from the town of Nazareth.

213. Our Lord began to make these excursions more frequently in the three years preceding his public preaching and Baptism; in the company of our great Queen He made many journeys in the neighborhood of Nazareth and to the province of Nephthali, as was prophesied by Isaias (Is. 5,2), or other parts. In his conversation with men He began to announce to them the coming of the Messias, assuring them, that He was already in the world and in the territory of Israel. He told them of it without intimating that He himself was the one they thus expected; for the first testimony of his being Son of God, was given publicly by the eternal Father, when the voice from heaven was heard at the Jordan: "This is my beloved Son in whom I am well pleased" (Matth. 3, 17). Without especially announcing his true dignity, the Onlybegotten spoke of it in general terms, as one who knows with certainty. Without performing any public miracles or using other outward demonstration, He secretly accompanied his teachings and testimonies by interior inspirations and helps, which He conferred on the hearts of those with whom He conversed and treated. Thus disposing their souls by faith, He prepared them to receive Him afterwards so much the more readily in person.

214. He made acquaintance with such, as, by his divine
wisdom, He knew to be prepared and capable (or rather, less
unsuited) to accept the seed of truth. To the more ignorant
He spoke of the signs of the coming of the Redeemer known
to all, such as the coming of the three Kings and the slaughter of the Innocents, and of similar events. With the more
enlightened He adduced the testimonies of the Prophets,
already fulfilled, and He explained to them these truths with
the power and force of a divine Teacher. He proved to them,
that the Messias had already come to Israel, and He pointed
out to them the kingdom of God and the way to reach it. As
He exhibited in his outward appearance so much beauty,
grace, peace, sweetness and gentleness of manner and of
speech, and as all his discourse, though veiled, was nevertheless so vivid and strong, and as He added thereto also his
interior help of grace, the fruit of this wonderful mode of
teaching was very great. Many souls forsook the path of sin,
others began a virtuous life, all of them were instructed and
made capable of understanding the great mysteries, and
especially of believing, that the Messias had already begun his
reign.

215. To these works of mercy the divine Teacher added
many others; for He consoled the sorrowful, relieved the
oppressed, visited the sick and grief-stricken, encouraged the
disheartened, gave salutary counsel to the ignorant, assisted
those in the agony of death, secretly gave health of body to
many, helped those in great distress, and at the same time led
them on to the path of life and of true peace. All those that
trustfully came to Him, or heard Him with devout and
upright mind, were filled with light and with the powerful
gifts of his Divinity. It is not possible to enumerate or estimate the admirable works of the Redeemer during these
three years of public preaching after his Baptism. All was
done in a mysterious manner so that without manifesting

Himself as the Author of salvation, He communicated it to a vast number of souls. In nearly all these wonderful operations our great Lady was present as a most faithful witness and coworker. As all of them were manifest to Her, She assisted and gave thanks for them in the name of the creatures and the mortals who were thus favored by divine bounty. She composed hymns of praise to the Almighty, prayed for the souls as one knowing all their interior necessities, and by her prayers gained for them new blessings and favors. She herself also undertook to exhort and counsel them, drawing them to the sweet teachings of her Son and giving them intimation of the coming of the Messias. Yet She practiced these works of mercy more among women, imitating among them the works of mercy which her most holy Son performed for men.

216. Few persons accompanied or followed the Savior and his most blessed Mother in those first years; for it was not yet time to call them to a close following of his doctrines. He permitted them to remain in their homes, simply instructing and urging them to a more perfect life by his divine enlightenment. The ordinary companions of the heavenly Teachers were the holy angels, who served them as most faithful vassals and servants. Although they often returned from these excursions to their home in Nazareth, yet on their journeys They stood more in need of the ministry of these courtiers of heaven. Some of the nights they passed in prayer without any other shelter than that of the sky, and on these occasions the angels protected them and sheltered Them from the in clemency of the weather, and sometimes they brought food. At other times the Lord and his Mother begged food, refusing to accept any money, or other gifts not necessary for their present nourishment. When at times They separated, the Lord Jesus visiting the sick in hospitals and his Mother other sick persons, innumerable angels accompanied Mary in visible forms. Through their mediation She per-

formed some of her works of charity and was kept informed
of the doings of her most holy Son. I do not dilate in particular upon the wonders performed by Them during this time;
nor upon the labors and difficulties encountered on these
excursions, in the taverns, and from the obstacles which the
common enemy placed in their way: it is enough to know
that the Teacher of life and his most holy Mother were
looked upon as poor pilgrims, and that they preferred the
way of suffering, without evading any labor deemed advisable
for our salvation.

217. In this hidden manner the divine Master and his
Mother spread the knowledge of his coming to all sorts of
persons; yet the poor were more especially the objects of his
blessed solicitude. They ordinarily are more capable of God's
truths, because they are less burdened with sin and endowed
with more light, and because their minds are more free and
unhampered by vain anxieties. They are likewise more humble and diligent in subjecting their will and understanding,
and in applying themselves to an upright and virtuous life.
Moreover, as during these three years Jesus did not preach
openly, nor with manifest authority confirmed by miracles,
He addressed Himself rather to the humble and poor, who
are led to the truth with less show of authority. Nevertheless
the attention of the ancient serpent was much aroused by
many of the doings of Jesus and his Mother; for not all of his
miracles remained concealed, though the power by which
they were done was hidden. Satan saw that through his words
and exhortations many sinners were brought to penance,
amended their life and escaped his tyranny; others advanced
in virtue, and in all who listened to the Teacher of life, the
common enemy noticed a great and unheard of change.

218. What enraged him most, was that he could not succeed in his attempts with those that were in the throes of
death. Though he multiplied his cunning and malice in these

last hours of the souls in this life, it often happened that this bloodthirsty dragon, having approached the sick in order to exert his malice, was interrupted by the entrance of Jesus or Mary and felt a powerful force, which hurled him and his demons to the deepest caverns of hell. If Jesus or Mary had previously come to the sickroom, the demons could not enter and could exert no influence upon the sick person, who thus died in the powerful protection of the Lord. As the dragon felt this divine power without being able to account for it, he conceived an insane rage, and anxiously sought means of counteracting the damage. Then happened what I shall relate in the next chapter, as I do not wish to enlarge this present one.

Words of the Queen

THE VIRGIN MARY SPEAKS TO SISTER MARY OF AGREDA

219. My daughter, I see thee astonished at the information, which I give thee concerning the mysterious works of my most holy Son and concerning my own share in them. For thou seest on the one hand, how powerful they are for making an impression on human hearts, and on the other, that many of them have remained hidden until now. Thy wonder should not be that men have not known these mysteries, but that, having been informed of so many others concerning the life and activity of their own and my Lord, they have held them in such contempt and forgetfulness. If they were not so ignoble of heart, and would lovingly contemplate the divine truths, they would find in my Son's and in my own life, as far as it is known to them, most powerful motives for thankfulness. By the articles of faith and by the many other truths taught and preached in the holy Church, many worlds could be converted. For these truths exhibit clearly, that the Onlybegotten of the eternal Father clothed Himself in the

mortal flesh of sinful man in order to redeem the human race by the frightful death of the Cross (Philip 2, 7), acquiring for them eternal life by the loss of his own, and recalling and liberating them from everlasting death. If this blessing were taken at its true value and mortals were not so ungrateful to their God and Savior and so cruel toward themselves, none would lose their chance of salvation or bring upon themselves eternal damnation. In thy amazement then, my dearest, weep ceaselessly over the terrible loss sustained by so many insane and thankless souls, who are forgetful of God, of their duty and of their own selves.

220. On former occasions I have already told thee, that the number of those foreknown as doomed, is so great, and of those that save themselves is so small, that it is not expedient to say more in particular. For if thou hast the sentiments of a true daughter of the Church, the spouse of Christ, my Son and Lord, thou wouldst die at seeing such misfortune. What thou mayest know, is, that all the loss and misfortune apparent in Christian nations and governments, as well among chiefs as among subjects of the Church and of the secular state, all originate and flow from the forgetfulness and contempt of the works of Christ and of the works of his Redemption. If there were a way of rousing them to a sense of thankfulness and to a sense of their duty as faithful and acknowledged children of their Creator and Redeemer, and of me, who am their Intercessor, the wrath of the divine Judge would be appeased, and there would be some diminution of the widespread ruin and Perdition among Catholics. The eternal Father, who is justly zealous for the honor of his Son and rigorously chastises the servants, who know the will of their Lord and refuse to fulfill it, would again be reconciled.

221. The faithful in the Church make much of the sin of the infidel Jews in taking away the life of their God and

Master. They are right in doing so, for it was a most heinous crime and merited the punishments decreed against that people. But Catholics forget, that their own sins are rendered heinous by other elements of guilt surpassing that of the Jews; for although their error was culpable, they esteemed it as truth in the end; then also the Lord delivered Himself up to them, allowing them to follow the counsels of hell, by which they were oppressed for their sins (Luke 22, 53). In our days the Catholics are not in ignorance, but in the fullness of the light, by which they know and understand the divine mysteries of the Incarnation and Redemption. The holy Church has been founded, spread out, made illustrious by miracles, by saints, by holy writings, by the knowledge and proclamation of truths unknown to the Jews. In spite of all these multiplied advantages, blessings, truths and enlightenments, many live like infidels and as if they had not before their eyes so many inducements to draw them on and oblige them, nor so many chastisements to fill them with dread. How can Catholics then, under these circumstances, imagine that the sins of others were greater or more grievous than their own? How can they presume that their punishment shall not be more lamentable? O my daughter, ponder well this doctrine, and be filled with a holy fear! Humiliate thyself to the dust and confess thyself the lowest of the creatures before the Most High. Look upon the works of thy Redeemer and Master. Imitate them and apply them sorrowfully to satisfy for thy own faults in sorrow and penance. Do thou imitate and follow me in my ways, as far as thou art enlightened from on high. And I wish that thou labor not only for thy own salvation, but also for the salvation of thy brethren. This thou must do by praying and suffering for them, charitably admonishing those thou canst, and eagerly doing for them more than is thy duty. Show thyself even more anxious to benefit those who have offended thee, be patient with all, and humiliate thyself below the most abject. According to the directions given thee before, be thou solicitous to assist, with fervent charity and firm assurance, those that are in the dangers of death.

Chapter XX

LUCIFER CALLS A MEETING IN HELL IN ORDER TO HINDER
THE WORKS OF CHRIST OUR REDEEMER AND OF HIS MOST
HOLY MOTHER.

222. The tyrannical sway of Lucifer over this world was not
any more so unobstructed as it had been in the ages preceding the Incarnation of the divine Word; for from the hour in
which the Son of the eternal Father descended from heaven
and assumed flesh in the bridal chamber of his virginal
Mother, this strongly armed one felt a superior force, which
oppressed and crushed him, as I have related in its place
(Luke 11, 21). After the birth of Christ he felt this power,
when the Infant Jesus entered into Egypt (Vol. II 130, 643),
and on many occasions afterward this dragon was routed and
overcome by the force of divine truth issuing from the great
Queen. Comparing and connecting these past happenings
with all the new experiences related in the foregoing chapter,
the ancient serpent was beginning to be much troubled by
his fears and suspicions, lest a new and vast force had established itself on the earth. But as the sacrament of the Incarnation was deeply hidden from him, he lived on in his blind
fury without suspicion of the truth, although, since his fall
from heaven, he had most anxiously tried to ascertain when
and how the divine Word would leave heaven and assume
human flesh; for this wonderful work of God was what his

arrogance and pride feared most of all. This anxiety induced him to convoke the many council meetings, of which I have spoken in this history, and also the one of which I now speak.

223. Finding himself then full of uncertainty concerning the experiences of the demons and of Himself with Jesus and Mary, this enemy of the human race questioned himself by what power he had been vanquished and put to flight in his attempts to ruin the dangerously sick and the dying and in his other encounters with the Queen of heaven. As he could not clear the mystery for himself, he resolved to consult those of his associates who excelled in malice and astuteness. He gave forth a roar or tremendous howl in hell, using the language understood by the demons, and called together those who were subject to him. All of them having been gathered together, he made them a speech, saying: "My ministers and companions, who have always followed me in my just opposition, you well know that in the first state in which we were placed by the Creator of all things, we acknowledged Him as the universal source of all our being and thus also respected Him. But as soon as, to the detriment of our beauty and preeminence, so close to the Deity, He imposed upon us the command, that we adore and serve the person of the Word, in the human form, which He intended to assume, we resisted his will. For although I knew, that this reverence was due Him as God, yet as He chose to unite Himself to the nature of man, so ignoble and inferior to mine, I could not bear to be subject to Him, nor could I bear to see, that He did not favor me rather than the creature man. He not only commanded us to adore Him, but also to recognize as our superior a Woman, his Mother, a mere earthly creature. To these grievances I took exception and you with me. We objected to them and resolved to deny Him obedience. On account of our behavior at that time we

are punished and made to suffer the pains of our present condition. Although we are aware of these truths and acknowledge them with terror among ourselves, it will not do to confess them before men (Jas. 2, 19). And this I put as a command upon you all, in order that they may not know of our present difficulty and weakness."

224. "But if this Godman and his Mother are really to come, it is clear, that their coming into this world shall be the beginning of our greatest ruin and torment, and that, for this reason, I must seek with all my strength to prevent it and to destroy Them, even at the cost of overturning and destroying all the world. You all know how invincible has been my strength until now, since such a great portion of the world obeyed my command and is subject to my will and cunning. But in the last few years I have noticed on many occasions, that your powers seemed to have decreased and weakened, that you were oppressed and overcome, and I myself feel a superior force, which restrains and intimidates me. Several times I have searched with you through the whole world, trying to find some clue for this loss and oppression which we feel. If this Messias, who is promised to the chosen people of God, is already in the world, we not only fail to discover Him on the whole face of the earth, but we see no certain signs of his coming and we perceive none of the pomp and outward show naturally attendant upon such a person. Nevertheless I have my misgivings, lest the time of his coming from heaven onto this earth be already near. Therefore we ought all be eager to destroy Him and the Woman whom He shall choose for His Mother. Whoever shall distinguish himself in this work, shall not complain of my thankfulness and reward. Until now I have found guilt and the effects of guilt in all men, and I have seen no such majesty and grand magnificence as would induce the Word to become man and which would oblige mortals to adore Him and offer Him

sacrifice, for by this homage we shall be able to recognize Him. The certain indication of his coming and the distinguishing mark of the Messias will no doubt be, that neither sin nor its consequences, common to other children of Adam, will ever be able to touch Him."

225. "So much the greater therefore," continued Lucifer, "is my confusion at present; for, if the eternal Word has not yet come into the world, I cannot understand these new experiences, nor whence comes this strong opposition which overpowers us. Who drove us out and hurled us from Egypt? Who destroyed the temples and crushed the idols of that country in which we were adored by all the inhabitants? Who oppresses us now in the land of Galilee and its neighborhood, and prevents us from perverting many of the persons in danger of death? Who keeps away from sin so many souls as if they were withdrawn from our jurisdiction, and who causes so many to better their lives and begin to seek the kingdom of God? If this damaging influence is allowed to continue, great misfortune and torment may arise for all of us from this secret force, which we do not comprehend. It is necessary to put a stop to it and search anew all over the world, whether it does not contain a great prophet or saint, who seeks our destruction; I have not been able to discover anyone to whom I could ascribe such a power. Only I have a great hatred against that Woman, our enemy, especially since we persecuted Her in the temple and later on in her house at Nazareth. For we have always been vanquished and terrified by the virtue which shields Her and resists our malice. Never have I been able to search her interior or come near her person. She has a Son, and, when Both of Them attended at his father's death, all of us were unable to approach the place where They were. They are poor and neglected people; She is an unknown and helpless little woman: but I presume without a doubt, that both Son and Mother must be counted

among the just. For I have continually sought to draw them into the failings common to men, and yet I have never succeeded in causing them to commit the least of the disorderly or reprehensible of actions, which are so common and natural with other people. I know that the Almighty conceals from me the state of these souls; and this doubtlessly argues some hidden danger for us. Although the interior condition of some other souls has been concealed from us on certain occasions, yet this was but rarely and not in the manner as with these Two. Even if this Man is not the Messias, it is certain that they are just and our enemies, which is sufficient reason for persecuting Them and ruining Them, and especially for seeking to find out who They are. Do you all follow me in the enterprise with all diligence, for I shall be your leader in our fight against Them."

226. With this exhortation Lucifer concluded his long speech, in which he gave to the demon much other information and malicious counsel. But I need not mention them here, since this history will contain other references to the hellish plots to make us understand the cunning of that venomous serpent. Immediately the prince of darkness, together with countless legions of evil spirits, issued forth from hell and spread over the whole world. They persisted in roaming through it many times, searching out in their malice and cunning all the just, tempting those they recognized as such and provoking them and other men to commit the evil deeds hatched out in their own infernal minds. But Christ our Lord in his wisdom concealed his own person and that of his Mother for many days from the haughty Lucifer. He did not permit him to see or recognize Him, until He betook Himself to the desert, where He allowed and wished the devil to tempt Him after his long fast; and Lucifer did tempt Him, as I shall relate in its place.

227. When this meeting was held in the infernal regions, Christ, to whom as our divine Master all was known, betook Himself to prayer against the malice of the dragon and among other petitions He prayed as follows:

"Eternal and most high God and Father, I adore Thee and exalt thy infinite and immutable Essence; I confess Thee as the highest and boundless Good and I offer Myself in sacrifice to thy divine will for the vanquishing and crushing of the infernal powers and of their malicious counsels against my creatures. I shall battle for them against my and their enemies, and by my own works and victories I shall leave them an encouragement and example of what they must do, so that those who serve Me from their heart, may prevail against Lucifer's malice. Defend, my Father, the souls from the snares and cruelty of the serpent and its followers, and grant to the just the power of thy right hand, in order that through my intercession and Death they may gain victory over their temptations and dangers." Our great Queen and Lady had a like knowledge of the evil counsels of Lucifer and saw all that passed in her divine Son and the prayer He offered. As the Coadjutrix of his triumphs She joined in the prayers and petitions of her Son to the eternal Father. The Most High granted all of them, and on this occasion Jesus and Mary obtained immense assistance and rewards from the Father for those that battle against the demons in the name of Jesus and Mary. So great was the efficacy of their prayers, that all those who pronounce these names in reverence and faith, overcome their hellish enemies and precipitously repel them in virtue of the prayers, triumphs and victories of our Savior and of his most holy Mother. On account of the protection thereby offered to us against the arrogant giants of hell, and on account of all the other helps furnished us in the holy Church of our Lord, no excuse is left us for not battling legitimately and valiantly, or for not overcoming and vanquishing the demon, as the enemy of the eternal God and our own. For in this we should follow the example of our Savior according to our ability.

Words of the Queen

THE VIRGIN MARY SPEAKS TO SISTER MARY OF AGREDA

228. My daughter, weep with bitterest sorrow over the stubbornness and blindness of mortals in not understanding and acknowledging the loving protection, which they have in my divine Son and in me as a relief from all their troubles and necessities. My Lord spared Himself no exertion and left no means unemployed in order to gain for them inestimable treasures of heaven. He garnered up his infinite merits in the holy Church, the most important fruit of his Passion and Death; He left the secure pledges of his glorious love; and procured for them most easy and efficacious means in order that all of them might enjoy and apply them for their use and for their eternal salvation. He offers them moreover his protection and mine; He loves them as children; He cherishes them as his chosen friends; He calls them by his inspirations; He invites them by his blessings and graces; He awaits them as a most kind Father; He seeks them as their Pastor; He helps them as the most Powerful; He rewards them as One possessing infinite riches, and governs them as a mighty King. All these and innumerable other favors, which are pointed out by faith, offered by the Church and presented before their very eyes, men forget and despise; as if blind, they love the darkness and deliver themselves up to the fury and rage of those cruel enemies. They listen to his lies, obey his wicked suggestions and confide in his snares; they trust and give themselves up to the unquenchable fire of his wrath. He seeks to destroy them and consign them to eternal death,

only because they are creatures of the Most High, who vanquished and crushed this most cruel foe.

229. Guard thyself, therefore, my dearest, against this deplorable error of the children of men and disengage thy faculties in order that thou mayest clearly see the difference between the service of Christ and that of Belial. Greater is that difference than the distance between heaven and earth. Christ is eternal life, the true light and the pathway to eternal life; those who follow Him He loves with imperishable love, and He offers them his life and his company; with it, an eternal happiness, such as neither eyes have seen, nor ears have heard, nor ever can enter into the mind of man (John 14, 6). Lucifer is darkness itself, error, deceit, unhappiness and death; he hates his followers and forces them into evil as far as possible, and at the end inflicts upon them eternal fire and horrid torments. Let mortals give testimony, whether they are ignorant of these truths, since the holy Church propounds them and calls them to their minds every day. If men believe these truths, where is their good sense? Who has made them insane? Who drives from their remembrance the love, which they ought to have for themselves? Who makes them so cruel to themselves? 0 insanity never sufficiently to be bewailed and so little considered by the children of Adam! All their life they labor and exert themselves to become more and more entangled in the snares of their passions, to be consumed in deceitful vanities and to deliver themselves over to an inextinguishable fire, death and everlasting perdition, as if all were a mere joke and as if Christ had not come down from heaven to die on a Cross for their rescue! Let them but look upon the price, and consider how much God himself paid for this happiness, who knew the full value of it.

230. The idolaters and heathens are much less to blame for falling into this error; nor does the wrath of the Most High enkindle so much against them as against the faithful of

his Church, who have such a clear knowledge of this truth. If the minds of men, in our present age, have grown forgetful of it, let them understand that this happened by their own fault, because they have given a free hand to their enemy Lucifer. He with tireless malice labors to overthrow the barriers of restraint, so that, forgetful of the last things and of eternal torment, men may give themselves over, like brute beasts, to sensual pleasures, and unmindful of themselves consume their lives in the pursuit of apparent good, until, as Job says (Job 21, 13), they suddenly fall a prey to eternal perdition. Such is in reality the fate of innumerable foolish men, who abhor the restraint imposed upon them by this truth. Do thou, my daughter, allow me to instruct thee, and keep thyself free from such harmful deceit and from this forgetfulness of the worldly people. Let the despairing groans of the damned, which begin at the end of their lives and at the beginning of their eternal damnation, ever resound in thy ears: O we fools, who esteemed the life of the just as madness! O how are they counted among the sons of God, and their lot is among the saints ! We have erred then from the path of truth and of justice. The sun has not arisen for us. We have wearied ourselves in the ways of iniquity and destruction, we have sought difficult paths and erred by our own fault from the way of the Lord. What has pride profited us? What advantage has the boasting of riches brought us? All has passed away from us like a shadow. O had we but never been born! This, my daughter, thou must fear and ponder in thy heart, so that, before thou goest to that land of darkness and of eternal dungeons from whence there is no return, thou mayest provide against evil and avoid it by doing the good. During thy mortal life and out of love do thou now perform that of which the damned in their despair are forced to warn thee by the excess of their punishment.

Chapter XXI

SAINT JOHN, HAVING OBTAINED GREAT FAVORS FROM THE
MOST HOLY MARY, IS ORDERED BY THE HOLY GHOST TO
GO FORTH ON HIS PUBLIC PREACHING. HE FIRST SENDS TO
THE HEAVENLY LADY HIS CROSS.

231. I have already spoken of some of the favors conferred on
saint John by the blessed Mary during her sOjourn in Egypt;
also of her solicitude for her cousin Elisabeth and saint John,
when Herod resolved to take away the lives of the holy
Innocents. I have also mentioned, that the future Precursor
of Christ, after the death of his mother, remained altogether
in the desert until the time appointed by the divine wisdom,
and that he lived there more the life of a seraph than of a
man. His conversation was with the holy angels and with the
Lord of all creation; this was his sole occupation and never
was he idle in the exercise of his love and of the heroic virtues, which he began in the womb of his mother. Not for
one moment was grace in him unprofitable, nor did he fail in
the least point of perfection possible. His senses, being
altogether withdrawn from earthly things, did not in any way
hinder him; for they did not serve him as windows, through
which the images of the deceitful vanities of the creatures are
wont to bring death to the souls. Since this saint was so
fortunate as to be visited by the divine light before he saw the
light of created sun of this world, he overlooked all that is

seen by eyes of flesh, and fixed his interior gaze immovably upon the being of God and his infinite perfections.

232. The divine favors received by saint John exceed all human intelligence, capacity and thought; his holiness and exalted merits we shall understand in the beatific vision and not before. As it does not pertain to the object of this history to relate what I have seen of these mysteries, and what the holy doctors and other authors have written of his prerogatives, I must confine myself to relate that which is necessary for my present purpose; namely, what refers to the share of the heavenly Lady in his exaltation; for through Her saint John received most inestimable favors. Among them not the least was her sending food to him every day until he reached the age of seven years, which She did by the ministry of the holy angels, as I mentioned above. From his seventh year until he reached the ninth, She sent him only bread; but after that year she ceased to send him any food. For She understood that during the rest of his stay in the desert, it was the will of heaven and of himself, that he nourish himself by roots, wild honey and locusts, which he accordingly did until he came forth to preach. Yet, though Mary did not any more send him food, She continued to send to him her holy angels in order to console him and inform him of the doings and mysteries of the incarnate Word; but these visits happened no oftener than once a week.

233. These great favors, besides serving other ends, encouraged saint John to bear with his solitude: not that the desolation of his abode and the severity of his penance caused him any discouragement; 'to make these desirable and sweet to him, his own wonderful holiness and grace were sufficient. But these tokens of love served to counteract the vehemence of his love, which drew him toward Christ and his Mother and to make their absence and the want of their intercourse bearable to him. For there is no doubt, that restraining his

desire for this intercourse was a far greater pain and suffering to his loving soul, than all the inclemencies of his habitation, his fasting and penances, and the horrors of the lonely mountains, and would have been impossible if his heavenly Lady and aunt had not assisted him by continually sending her holy angels to bring messages from his Beloved. The great Hermit inquired into all the particulars of the Son and Mother with the anxious solicitude of a loving bridegroom (Cant. 1, 6). He transmitted to them the messages of his ardent love and of the sighs, that came from his inmost heart wounded by the absence of the Objects of his love. He besought the celestial Princess through her messengers to send him their blessing and he asked the angels to adore and humbly reverence the Lord in his name. He himself ceased not to adore Him in spirit and in truth from his solitude. He asked also the holy angels, who visited him and the others that attended upon him, to do the same. These were the ordinary occupations of the Precursor until he arrived at the perfect age of thirty years and in this manner he was prepared by divine Providence for his appointed task.

234. The destined and acceptable time decreed by the eternal wisdom for sending forth saint John, the Harbinger of the incarnate Word, the Voice resounding in the desert, had now come (Is. 40, 3). As related by the Evangelists, in the fifteenth year of the reign of Tiberius Caesar, under the high priests Annas and Caiphas, the command of God came to John, the son of Zacharias in the desert (Luke 3, 1). And he came to the banks of the Jordan, preaching the baptism of penance for the remission of sins and preparing the hearts for the reception of the promised Messias, pointing Himself with his finger, who had been expected for so many ages. This command of the Lord saint John heard in an ecstasy, in which, by an especial operation of the Divinity, he was enlightened and prepared by the plenitude of the light and

grace of the holy Spirit. In this rapture he obtained a deep insight into the mysteries of the Redemption, and he was favored with an abstractive vision of the Divinity, so wonderful that he was transformed and changed to a new existence of sanctity and grace. . The Lord commanded him to issue forth from the desert in order to prepare the way for the preaching of the incarnate Word by his own, thus exercising the office of a Precursor and all that pertained to it; for he was now instructed and filled with most abundant grace for his work.

235. The new preacher saint John came from the desert clothed in camel skin, girded with a cincture or cord made likewise of leather. His feet were bare, his features thin and emaciated, his appearance wonderfully graceful, modest and humble, his soul was filled with invincible and magnanimous courage, his heart inflamed with the love of God and man, his words rang forth strong and forceful, piercing to the souls of his hearers like the sparks from the immutable and divine essence of the Almighty. He was gentle toward the meek, loving toward the humble, wonderful in the sight of angels and men, terrible to the proud, dreadful to the sinners, and an object of horror to the demons. He was a Preacher fit to be the instrument of the incarnate Word and such as was needed for this people of the Hebrews, who were so hardhearted, thankless and stubborn, and who were now cursed with heathen governors, avaricious and proud priests, without enlightenment, without prophets, without piety, without fear of God, though they had been visited by so many calamities and chastisements for their sins. He was now sent to open the eyes of his people to their miserable state and prepare their hearts to know and receive their Savior and Teacher.

236. The anchoret John, many years before, had made for himself a large cross, which he had placed at the head of his

couch: with it he performed some exercises of penance and
he was accustomed to place himself upon it in the form of
one crucified, when he was engaged in prayer. He did not
wish to leave this treasure in the desert; therefore, before
issuing forth, he sent it by the hands of the holy angels to the
Queen of heaven and earth and requested them to tell Her
that the cross had been his greatest and most beloved companion in his long banishment; that he sent it to Her as a
precious treasure, because he knew what was to be wrought
upon it by the Son of God, and also because the holy angels
had told him, that her most holy Son and Redeemer of the
world often made use of a cross like this, when performing
his prayers in his oratory. The angels had made this cross
fashioning it from a tree in the desert at his request; for the
saint had neither the necessary strength nor the instruments
for this kind of work, whereas the holy angels wanted not the
skill and needed no instruments on account of the power
they have over material creation. With this present and
message of saint John the holy princes returned to their
Queen, and She received this token from their hands with
innermost emotions of sorrow and consolation, at the
thought of what mysteries were in so short a time to be
enacted upon the hard wood of the Cross. She addressed it in
words of tenderness and placed it in her oratory, where She
kept it ever afterwards together with the other cross which
had been used by her Son. At her death the most prudent
Lady left these crosses, with other remembrances, to the
Apostles as a priceless heritage, and by them they were carried
through different countries where they preached.

237. In regard to this matter I had some doubts, which I
proposed to the Mother of wisdom, saying to Her:

"Queen of heaven and my Mistress, most holy among the
saints and chosen among creatures as the Mother of God
himself: being an ignorant and dull woman, I find a difficul-

ty in what I have here written; if Thou give me permission, I would like to mention it to Thee, for Thou, o Lady, art the Mistress of wisdom and hast deigned to be my Teacher in the doctrine of eternal life and salvation. My difficulty is this: I see not only saint John but also Thee, my Queen, reverence the Cross before thy most holy Son had died upon it; whereas I have always believed, that until the hour in which He wrought our salvation upon sacred wood of the Cross, it had served as a gibbet of shame for the punishment of criminals and that therefore it was considered as a token of contempt and ignominy; and even the holy Church teaches us, that all its value and dignity came to the Cross by its contact with the body of the Redeemer and through its connection with mystery of man's Redemption."

Words of the Queen

THE VIRGIN MARY SPEAKS TO SISTER MARY OF AGREDA

238. My daughter, gladly will I satisfy thy desire and answer thy doubt. What thou sayest is true: the Cross was ignominious before my Son and Lord honored and sanctified it by his Passion and Death and solely on account of this Passion and Death the adoration and reverence shown to it by the Church is now due to it. If anyone, who was ignorant of the mysteries, which were connected with it and which were so well known to me and saint John, would have given it such worship and honor as I have before the Redemption, he would have been guilty of error and idolatry; for he would have worshipped a creature of which he did not know that it was worthy of such honor. But we showed this veneration to the Cross for several reasons : We knew for certain, that the Redeemer was to accomplish his work upon the Cross; we knew also that, before dying upon it, He had begun to sanctify this sacred emblem by his contact in placing Himself

upon it during his prayers and in offering Himself freely to die upon it. The eternal Father moreover had accepted these foreseen works of the Cross from his divine Son by an unalterable decree. All the actions and the contacts of the incarnate Word were of infinite value and thus sanctified the sacred wood, making it worthy of the highest veneration. Whenever I or saint John showed this reverence to the Cross, we had before our minds these mysteries and truths: we did not adore the Cross in itself, nor the material of which it was made; for the divine worship was not due to it until the works of the Redemption should have been completed upon it; but we waited for the formal execution of the work intended to be performed upon it by the incarnate Word. This was the real object of our reverence and worship of the Cross. And this is also now the meaning and intent of the practice of the adoration of the Cross in the holy Church.

239. Accordingly thou must ponder well thy obligation and that of all the mortals in regard to the reverence and esteem due to the holy Cross; for if I and the holy Precursor, even before the Death of my divine Son upon it, so eagerly imitated Him in his love and reverence of it and in the exercises which He performed in connection therewith, what should not the faithful children of the Church do after they have seen their Creator and their Redeemer crucified upon it, and when they have the image of the Crucified before their very eyes? I desire, then, my daughter, that thou embrace the Cross with boundless esteem, that thou use it as the priceless jewel of thy Spouse, and that thou accustom thyself to perform those exercises upon it, which are known and practiced by thee, without ever of thy own will forgetting or neglecting them as long as obedience will permit thee. Whenever thou approachest such sacred exercises, let it be with a profound reverence and with a deep pondering of the Passion and Death of the Lord, thy Beloved. Try to introduce the same

custom among thy religious, zealously exhorting them thereto; for no exercise is more proper to the spouses of Christ, and if performed with devotion and reverence, it will be most pleasing to their Lord. In addition to this, I wish that thou, in imitation of saint John the Baptist prepare thy heart for all that the holy Spirit wishes to work in thee for his own glory and for the benefit of souls. As far as depends upon thee, love solitude and withdraw thy soul from the confusion of created things. Whenever thy duty to God forces thee to deal with creatures, seek always thy own sanctification and the edification of thy neighbor, so that in thy outward conversation and intercourse the zeal of thy spirit may shine forth. His exalted virtues now known to thee and those resplendent in the lives of other saints, should serve thee as a spur and as an example: seek, like a busy bee, to build up the sweet honeycomb of sanctity and innocence so much desired in thee by my divine Son. Distinguish well between the labors of the bee and of the spider: the one converts her nourishment into sweetness useful for the living and the dead, while the other changes it into snare and venom. Do thou gather the flowers of virtue from the saints in the garden of the Church, as far as thy weak endeavors with the aid of grace will permit; imitate them eagerly and incite others by thy eloquence, thus drawing blessings upon the living and the dead while thou anxiously flyest from the harm and damage of sinful deeds.

Chapter XXII

MOST HOLY MARY ORDERS HER ONLYBEGOTTEN SON FOR THE REDEMPTION OF THE HUMAN RACE TO THE ETERNAL FATHER; IN RETURN FOR THIS SACRIFICE HE GRANTS HER A CLEAR VISION OF THE DIVINITY; SHE TAKES LEAVE OF HER SON AS HE DEPARTS FOR THE DESERT.

240. The love of our great Queen and Lady for her divine Son must always remain the standard by which we must measure as well her actions as all her emotions either of joy or sorrow during her earthly life. But we cannot measure the greatness of her love itself, nor can the holy angels measure it, except by the love which they see in God by the intuitive vision. All that can ever be expressed by our inadequate words, similes and analogies, is but the least portion of what this heavenly furnace of love really contained. For She loved Jesus as the Son of the eternal Father, equal to Him in essence and in all the divine attributes and perfections; She loved Him as her own natural Son, Son to Her in as far as He was man, formed of her own flesh and blood; She loved Him because as man He was the Saint of saints and the meritorious cause of all other holiness (Dan. 9, 24). He was the most beautiful among the sons of men (Ps. 44, 3). He was the most dutiful Son of his Mother, her most magnificent Benefactor; since it was He, that by his sonship, had raised Her to the highest dignity possible among creatures.

He had exalted Her among all and above all by the treasures of his Divinity and by conferring upon Her the dominion over all creation together with favors, blessings and graces, such as were never to be conferred upon any other being.

241. These motives and foundations of her love were established and as it were, all comprehended in the wisdom of the heavenly Lady, together with many others, which only her exalted knowledge could appreciate. In her heart there was no hindrance of love, since it was the most innocent and pure; She was not ungrateful, because her profoundest humility urged Her to a most faithful correspondence; She was not remiss, because in Her the most abundant grace wrought with all its efficacy; She was not slow or careless, since She was filled with most zealous and diligent fervor; not forgetful, since her most faithful memory was constantly fixed upon the blessings received and upon the reasons and the precepts of deepest love. She moved in the sphere of the divine love itself, since She remained in his visible presence and attended the school of divine love of her Son, copying his works and his doings in his very company. Nothing was wanting to this peerless One among lovers for entertaining love without limitation of measure or manner. This most beautiful Moon then, being at its fullness, and looking into this Sun of justice just as it had risen like a divine aurora from height to height and reached the noontide splendor of the most clear light of grace; this Moon, Mary, detached from all material creatures and entirely transformed by the light of this Sun, having experienced on her part all the effects of his reciprocal love, favors and gifts, in the height of her blessedness, at a time when the loss of all these blessings in her Son made it most arduous, heard the voice of the eternal Father, calling Her as once He had called upon her prototype, Abraham, and demanding the deposit of all her love and hope, her beloved Isaac (Gen. 22, 1).

242. The most prudent Mother was not unaware, that the time of her sacrifice was approaching; for her sweetest Son had already entered the thirtieth year of his life and the time and place for satisfying the debt He had assumed was at hand. But in the full possession of the Treasure, which represented all her happiness, Mary was still considering its loss as far off, not having as yet had its experience. The hour therefore drawing near, She was wrapt in a most exalted vision and felt that She was being called and placed in the presence of throne of the most blessed Trinity. From it issued a voice of wonderful power saying to Her: "Mary, my Daughter and Spouse, offer to Me thy Onlybegotten Son in sacrifice." By the living power of these words came to Her the light and intelligence of the Almighty's will, and in it the most blessed Mother understood the decree of the Redemption of man through the Passion and Death of her most holy Son, together with all that from now on would happen in the preaching and public life of the Savior. As this knowledge was renewed and perfected in Her, She felt her soul overpowered by sentiments of subjection, humility, love of God and man, compassion and tenderest sorrow for all that her Son was to suffer.

243. But with an undismayed and magnanimous heart She gave answer to the Most High: "Eternal King and omnipotent God of infinite wisdom and goodness, all that has being outside of Thee exists solely for thy mercy and greatness, and Thou art undiminished Lord of all. How then dost Thou command me, an insignificant wormlet of the earth, to sacrifice and deliver over to thy will the Son, whom thy condescension has given me? He is thine, eternal Father, since from all eternity before the morning star Thou hast engendered Him (Ps. 109, 3), and Thou begettest Him and shalt beget Him through all the eternities; and if I have clothed Him in the form of servant (Philip 2, 7) in my womb

and from my own blood, and if I have nourished his humanity at my breast and ministered to it as a Mother: this most
holy humanity is also thy property, and so am I, since I have
received from Thee all that I am and that I could give Him.
What then can I offer to Thee, that is not more thine than
mine? I confess, most high King, that thy magnificence and
beneficence are so liberal in heaping upon thy creatures thy
infinite treasures, that in order to bind Thyself to them Thou
wishest to receive from them as a free gift, even thy own
Onlybegotten Son, Him whom Thou begettest from thy
own substance and from the light of thy Divinity. With Him
came to me all blessings together and from his hands I received immense gifts and graces (Wis. 7, 11) ; He is the
Virtue of my virtue, the Substance of my spirit, Life of my
soul and Soul of my life, the Sustenance of all my joy of
living. It would be a sweet sacrifice, indeed, to yield Him up
to Thee who alone knowest his value; but to yield Him for
the satisfaction of thy justice into the hands of his cruel
enemies at the cost of his life, more precious than all the
works of creation; this indeed, most high Lord, is a great
sacrifice which Thou askest of his Mother. However let not
my will but thine be done. Let the freedom of the human
race be thus bought; let thy justice and equity be satisfied; let
thy infinite love become manifest; let thy name be known
and magnified before all creatures. I deliver Him over into
thy hands before all creatures. I deliver over into thy hands
my beloved Isaac, that He may be truly sacrificed; I offer my
Son, the Fruit of my womb, in order that, according to the
unchangeable decree of thy will, He may pay the debt contracted not by his fault, but by the children of Adam, and in
order that in his Death He may fulfill all that thy holy
Prophets, inspired by Thee, have written and foretold."

244. This sacrifice with all that pertained to it, was the
greatest and the most acceptable that ever had been made to

the eternal Father since the creation of the world, or ever will be made to the end, outside of that made by his own Son, the Redeemer; and hers was most intimately connected with and like to that, which He offered. If the greatest charity consists in offering one's life for the beloved, without a doubt most holy Mary far surpassed this highest degree of love toward men, as She loved Her Son much more than her own life. For in order to preserve the life of her Son, She would have given the lives of all men, if She had possessed them, yea and countless more. Among men there is no measure by which to estimate the love of that heavenly Lady, and it can be estimated only by the love of the eternal Father for his Son. As Christ says to Nikodemus (John 15, 13): so God loved the world, that He gave his only Son in order that none of those who believed in Him might perish; so this might also be said in its degree of the love of the Mother of mercy and in the same way do we owe to Her proportionately our salvation. For She also loved us so much, that She gave her only Son for our salvation; and if She had not given it in this manner, when it was asked of Her by the eternal Father on this occasion, the salvation of men could not have been executed by this same decree, since this decree was to be fulfilled on condition, that the Mother's will should coincide with that of the eternal Father. Such is the obligation which the children of Adam owe to most holy Mary.

245. Having accepted the offering of the great Lady, it was fitting that the most Blessed Trinity should reward and immediately pay Her by some favor, which would comfort Her in her sorrow and manifest more clearly the will of the eternal Father and the reasons for his command. Therefore the heavenly Lady, still wrapped in the same vision and raised to a more exalted ecstasy, in which She was prepared and enlightened in the manner elsewhere described (I, 623), the Divinity manifested Itself to Her by an intuitive and direct

vision. In this vision, by the clear light of the essence of God, She comprehended the inclination of the infinite Good to communicate his fathomless treasures to the rational creatures by means of the works of the incarnate Word, and She saw the glory, that would result from these wonders to the name of the Most High. Filled with jubilation of her soul at the prospect of all these sacramental mysteries, the heavenly Mother renewed the offering of her divine Son to the Father; and God comforted Her with the life-giving bread of heavenly understanding, in order that She might with invincible fortitude assist the incarnate Word in the work of Redemption as his Coadjutrix and Helper, according to the disposition of infinite Wisdom and according as it really happened afterwards in the rest of her life.

246. Then most holy Mary issued forth from this exalted rapture in the description of which I will not further detain myself; for it was accompanied by the same circumstances as the other intuitive visions already mentioned. But by its effects and the strength imparted through it, She was now prepared to separate from her divine Son, who had already resolved to enter upon his fast in the desert in view of receiving his Baptism. He therefore called his Mother and, speaking to Her with the tokens of sweetest love and compassion, He said: "My Mother, my existence as man I derive entirely from thy substance and blood, of which I have taken the form of a servant in thy virginal womb (Phil. 2, 7). Thou also hast nursed Me at thy breast and taken care of Me by thy labors and sweat. For this reason I account Me more thine own and as thy Son, than any other ever acknowledged, or more than any ever will acknowledge himself as the son of his mother. Give Me thy permission and consent toward accomplishing the will of my eternal Father. Already the time has arrived, in which I must leave thy sweet intercourse and company and begin the work of the Redemption of man.

The time of rest has come to an end and the hour of suffering for the rescue of the sons of Adam has arrived. But I wish to perform this work of my Father with thy assistance, and Thou art to be my companion and helper in preparing for my Passion and Death of the Cross. Although I must now leave Thee alone, my blessing shall remain with Thee, and my loving and powerful protection. I shall afterwards return to claim thy assistance and company in my labors; for I am to undergo them in the form of man, which Thou hast given Me."

247. With these words, while both Mother and Son were overflowing with abundant tears, the Lord placed his hands around the neck of the most tender Mother, yet Both maintaining a majestic composure such as befitted these Masters in the art of suffering. The heavenly Lady fell at the feet of her divine Son and, with ineffable sorrow and reverence, answered: "My Lord and eternal God: Thou art indeed my Son and in Thee is fulfilled all the force of love, which I have received of Thee: my inmost soul is laid open to the eyes of thy divine wisdom. My life I would account but little, if I could thereby save thy own, or if I could die for Thee many times. But the will of the eternal Father and thy own must be fulfilled and I offer my own will as a sacrifice for this fulfillment. Receive it, my Son, and as Master of all my being, let it be an acceptable offering, and let thy divine protection never be wanting to me. It would be a much greater torment for me, not to be allowed to accompany Thee in thy labors and in thy Cross. May I merit this favor, my Son, and I ask it of Thee as thy true Mother in return for the human form, which Thou hast received of me." The most loving Mother also besought Him to take along some food from the house, or that He allow it to be sent to where He was to go. But the Savior would not consent to anything of the sort, at the same time enlightening his Mother of what was befitting for the

occasion. They went together to the door of their poor house, where She again fell at his feet to ask his blessing and kiss his feet. The divine Master gave Her his benediction and then began his journey to the Jordan, issuing forth as the good Shepherd to seek his lost sheep and bring them back on his shoulders to the way of eternal life, from which they had been decoyed by deceit (Luke 15, 5).

248. When our Redeemer sought saint John in order to be baptized, He had already entered his thirtieth year, although not much of it had yet passed; for He betook Himself directly to the banks of the Jordan, where saint John was baptizing (Matth. 3, 13), and He received Baptism at his hands about thirty days after He had finished the twenty-ninth year of his life on the same day as is set aside for its celebration by the Church. I cannot worthily describe the sorrow of most holy Mary at his departure, nor the compassion of the Savior for Her. All words and description are far too inadequate to manifest what passed in the heart of the Son and Mother. As this was to be part of their meritorious sufferings, it was not befitting that the natural effects of their mutual loves should be diminished. God permitted these effects to work in Them to their full extent, and as far as was compatible with the holiness of both Mother and Son. Our divine Teacher found no relief in hastening his steps toward the goal of our Redemption, to which He was drawn by the force of his immense charity; nor was the thought of what He intended, a lessening of the sense of loss, which She sustained at his departure; for all this only made more certain and more conspicuous the torments which He was to undergo. 0 my dearest Love! Why does not our ingratitude and hardness of heart allow us to meet Thee with a responsive love? Why does not the perfect uselessness of man, and still more, his ingratitude, influence Thee to desist? Without us, 0 my eternal Goodness and Life, Thou wilt be just as happy

without us as with us, just as infinite in perfections, holiness and glory; we can add nothing to that which Thou hast in Thyself, since Thou art entirely independent of creatures. Why then, 0 my Love, dost Thou so anxiously seek us out and care for us? Why dost Thou, at the cost of thy Passion and the Cross, purchase our happiness? Without doubt, because thy incomprehensible love and goodness esteems it as thy own, and we alone insist in treating our own happiness as alien to Thee and to ourselves.

Words of the Queen

THE VIRGIN MARY SPEAKS TO SISTER MARY OF AGREDA

249. My daughter, I wish that thou ponder and penetrate more and more this mystery of which thou hast written, so fixing it in thy soul, that thou wilt be drawn to imitate my example at least in some part of it. Consider then, that in the vision of the Divinity which I had on this occasion, I was made to comprehend the high value which the Lord sets upon the labors, the Passion and Death of my Son, and upon all those who were to imitate and follow Jesus in the way of the Cross. Knowing this, I not only offered to deliver my Son over to Passion and Death, but I asked Him to make me his companion and partaker of all his sorrows, sufferings and torments, which request the eternal Father granted. Then, in order to begin following in the footsteps of his bitterness, I besought my Son and Lord to deprive me of interior delights; and this petition was inspired in me by the Lord himself, because He wished it so, and because my own love taught me and urged me thereto. This desire for suffering and the wishes of my divine Son led me on in the way of suffering. He himself, because He loved me so tenderly, granted me my desires; for those whom He loves, He chastises and afflicts (Prov. 3, 12). I as his Mother was not to be deprived of this

blessed distinction of being entirely like unto Him, which alone makes this life most estimable. Immediately this will of the Most High, this my earnest petition, began to be fulfilled: I began to feel the want of his delightful caresses and He began to treat me with greater reserve. That was one of the reasons, why He did not call me Mother, but Woman, at the marriagefeast at Cana and at the foot of the Cross (John 2, 4, 19, 26) ; and also on other occasions, when He abstained from words of tenderness. So far was this from being a sign of a diminution of his love, that it was rather an exquisite refinement of his affection to assimilate me to Him in the sufferings which He chose for Himself as his precious treasure and inheritance.

250. Hence thou wilt understand the ignorance and error of mortals, and how far they drift from the way of light, when, as a rule, nearly all of them strive to avoid labor and suffering and are frightened by the royal and secure road of mortification and the Cross. Full of this deceitful ignorance, they do not only abhor resemblance to Christ's suffering and my own, and deprive themselves of the true and highest blessing of this life; but they make their recovery impossible, since all of them are weak and afflicted by many sins, for which the only remedy is suffering. Sin is committed by base indulgence and is repugnant to suffering sorrow, while tribulation earns the pardon of the just judge. By the bitterness of sorrow and affliction the vapors of sin are allayed; the excesses of the concupiscible and irascible passions are crushed; pride and haughtiness are humiliated; the flesh is subdued; the inclination to evil, to the sensible and earthly creatures, is repressed; the judgment is cleared; the will is brought within bounds and its desultory movements at the call of the passions, are corrected; and, above all, divine love and pity are drawn down upon the afflicted, who embrace suffering with patience, or who seek it to imitate my most

holy Son. In this science of suffering are renewed all the blessed riches of the creatures; those that fly from them are insane, those that know nothing of this science are foolish.

251. Exert thyself then, my dearest daughter, to advance in this knowledge, welcome labors and suffering, and give up ever desiring human consolations. Remember also that in the spiritual consolations the demon conceals his pitfalls for thy ruin and destruction, for thou shouldst know his continual attempts to ruin the spiritually inclined. The pleasures of contemplating and looking upon the Lord, and his caresses great or small, are so enticing, that delight and consolation overflow in the faculties of the mind and cause some souls to accustom themselves to the sensible pleasures of this intercourse. In consequence thereof they make themselves unfit for other duties belonging to reasonable life of human creatures; and when it is necessary to attend to them they are annoyed, lose their interior peace and control, become morose, intractable, full of impatience toward their neighbors, forgetting all humility and charity. When they then perceive their own restlessness and its consequences, they blame all to their exterior occupations, in which the Lord has placed them for the exercise of their obedience and charity, failing to see or acknowledge that all their troubles arise from their want of mortification and subjection to providence and from their attachment to their own selfish inclinations. The demon tries to beguile them by mere desires for quiet and solitude and the secret communications of the Lord in solitude; for they imagine, that in retirement all is good and holy, and that all their trouble arises from inability to follow their pious desires in solitude.

252. In these very faults thou hast fallen sometimes, and from now on I wish that thou guard against them especially. For all things there is a time, as the Wise man says (Eccles. 3, 5), both for enjoying delightful embraces and for abstaining

therefrom. To seek to prescribe to the Lord a time for his intimate embraces is the error of souls only beginning imperfectly to serve the Lord and to strive after virtue; and similar is the fault of feeling too deeply the want of these consolations. I do not tell thee therefore purposely to seek distraction and exterior occupations, nor to find thy pleasure in them, for this is nothing short of dangerous; but to obey with peace of mind whenever thy superiors command, and willingly to leave the delights of the Lord in order to find Him again in useful labor and in the service of thy neighbor. This thou must prefer to retirement and to private consolations, and on this account thou must not love them too much; for in the anxious cares of a superior thou must learn to believe, hope and love so much the more deeply. In this manner thou must find thy Lord at all times, in all places and occupations, as thou hast already experienced. I desire that thou never consider thyself deprived of his sweetest vision and presence, or of his most loving intercourse, or that thou doubt with pusillanimity, whether thou canst find and enjoy God outside of thy retirement. All creation is full of his glory (Eccli. 42, 16), and there is no void, and thou livest and movest and hast thy being in God (17, 28). Enjoy thou thy solitude whenever He does not oblige thee to these exterior occupations.

253. All this thou wilt still more fully understand in the nobility of the love, which I require of thee for the imitation of my Son and of me. With Him thou must rejoice sometimes in his youth; sometimes accompany Him in his labors for the salvation of men; sometimes retire with Him to solitude; sometimes be transfigured with Him to a new creature; sometimes embrace with Him tribulations and the cross, following up the divine lessons which He taught thereby; in short, I wish thee to understand well, that in me there was a continual desire to imitate, or an actual imitation,

of all that was most perfect in his works. In this consisted my greatest perfection and holiness, and therein I wish thee to follow me, so far as thy weak strength, assisted by grace, will allow. For this purpose thou must first die to all the inclinations of a daughter of Adam, without reserving in thee any choice of desires, any self constituted judgment as to admitting or rejecting the good; for thou knowest not what is befitting, and thy Lord and Spouse, who knows it and who loves thee more than thou dost thyself, will decide all this for thee, if thou resignest thyself entirely to his will. He gives thee a free hand only in regard to thy love of Him and in thy desire to suffer for Him, while in all the rest thy desires will only make thee drift away from his will and mine. This will surely be the result of following thy own will and inclinations, desires and appetites. Deny and sacrifice them all, raising thyself above thyself, up to the high and exalted habitation of the Lord and Master; attend to his interior lights and to the truth of his words of eternal life (John 6, 69), and in order that thou mayest follow them, take up the Cross (Matth. 16, 24), tread in his footsteps, walk in the odor of his ointments (Cant. 1,3), and be anxious to reach thy Lord; and having obtained possession of Him, do not leave Him (Cant. 3, 4).

Chapter XXIII

THE OCCUPATIONS OF THE VIRGIN MOTHER DURING THE ABSENCE OF HER MOST HOLY SON AND HER INTERCOURSE WITH HER GUARDIAN ANGELS.

254. When the Redeemer of the world had left the bodily presence of his most loving Mother, She felt Herself as it were in an eclipse or under a shadow, caused by the transposition of the clear Sun of justice, which had illumined and rejoiced Her; yet, though this might be true of her senses, her soul lost nothing of the light in which it bathed and in which it was raised above the burning love of the seraphim. As all the operations of her faculties, during the absence of the human personality of her Son, concerned themselves with the Deity, She so ordered all her doings, that, retired within her dwelling and separated from all human intercourse, She might apply Herself to the contemplation and praise of the Lord. She wanted to give Herself up entirely to the exercise of prayer and petition in order that the seed of the divine word and doctrine, which the Lord was to plant into the hearts of men, might not be lost on account of their hardness and ingratitude and not fail to give abundant fruit of eternal life and salvation of souls. By means of her infused knowledge She knew the intentions of the incarnate Word and therefore the most prudent Lady resolved not to converse with any human creature, in order to imitate Him in his

fasting and retirement of the desert, as I will relate farther on; for She was a living image and faithful reproduction of Christ, whether He was absent or present.

255. Shut up in her house during all the days in which her divine Son was absent, our blessed Lady spent her time in exercise of devotion. Her prayers were so ardent, that She shed tears of blood in weeping over the sins of men. She genuflected and prostrated Herself upon the ground more than two hundred times each day; and this was an exercise, which She practiced with especial earnestness during all her life, as an exterior manifestation of her humility, charity, reverence and worship of God. Of it I shall speak many times in the course of this history. Thus cooperating with her absent Son and Redeemer, She interceded so powerfully and efficaciously with the eternal Father, that on account of her merits and on account of her presence here upon this earth, (according to our way of speaking) He forgot the sins of all the mortals, who were then making themselves unworthy of the preaching and doctrine of his most holy Son. Mary then, cleared away this hindrance by the clamors of her burning charity. She was the Mediatrix, who merited and gained for us the blessing of being taught by our Lord himself and of receiving the law of his holy Gospel from his own lips.

256. What time still remained after her prolonged contemplations and exalted prayers, the great Queen spent in conversation and intercourse with her holy angels; for the Lord had commanded them anew to attend upon their Mistress in bodily forms during all the time in which her Son was to be absent. It is in this form that they were to serve his Tabernacle and guard the holy City of his habitation. The ministers of God obeyed most diligently and served their Queen with admirable and befitting reverence. As love is so active and so impatient of the absence and privation of the object beloved, it finds its greatest comfort in speaking of its

sorrow and rehearsing the cause of it, in renewing ever again the memory and discussing the excellences and conditions of the beloved; by such discourse it beguiles its sorrow, diverts its grief, and recalls to memory the images of her well beloved. Such was also the course pursued by the most loving Mother of our truest and highest Good; for while her faculties were overwhelmed by the immense ocean of the Divinity She felt not the bodily absence of her Son and Lord; but as soon as She again recovered the use of her senses, which had been accustomed to his amiable intercourse, and now found Herself deprived of it, She immediately felt the irresistible force of her most intense, chaste and sincere love, unfathomed by any creature. It would have been impossible for nature to suffer such pain and still retain life, had it not in Her been divinely supported and strengthened.

257. In order to afford some relief to her sorrow laden heart, She therefore returned to her holy angels and complained to them as follows: "Ye diligent ministers of the Most High, fashioned by the hands of my Beloved, my friends and companions, give me intelligence of my cherished Son and Master; tell me where He tarries, and inform Him that I am dying on account of the want of his life-giving presence. 0 sweet and bounteous love of my soul! Where art Thou, more beautiful than all the sons of men? Where dost Thou lay thy head? Where rests thy most delicate and most holy body from its fatigues? Who is there to attend upon Thee, light of my eyes? How can my tears ever cease to flow, deprived of the clear light of the Sun, which illumined mine? Where, 0 my Son, canst Thou find repose? Where shall this thy lonely and poor little bee find Thee? What course shall this thy little bark pursue in the vast billows of this ocean of love? Where shall I find peace? 0 Beloved of my desires, to forget thy presence is not possible to me! How then can it be possible to live in mere memory of Thee without actual intercourse?

What shall I do? 0 who shall console me and lend me his company in this bitter solitude, whom shall I seek among creatures, as long as Thou art absent, who art the only One and all that my heart yearns after in its love? Sovereign spirits, tell me, what does my Lord and my Beloved? Inform me of his exterior movements, and omit nothing of his interior doings, as far as in the light of his Divinity is made clear to you. Point out to me all his footsteps in order that I may follow and imitate Him."

258. The holy angels obeyed their Queen, consoling Her in the sorrows of her mournful love, speaking of the Most High and repeating to Her most exalted praises of the most sacred humanity of her son and of all his perfections. They informed Her of all his occupations and undertakings, and of the places in which He wandered. This they did by enlightening her understanding in the same way a higher angel is wont to enlighten those of an inferior order: for this was her manner of intercourse with the angels, unhindered by her body and the senses. The heavenly Spirits communicated to Her the prayers of the incarnate Word, his teachings, his visits to the poor and the sick, and other actions, so that the heavenly Lady was enabled to imitate Him in all these proceedings according to her condition. She thus engaged in most excellent and magnanimous undertake which illumined mine? Where, 0 my Son, canst Thou find repose? Where shall this thy lonely and poor little bee find Thee? What course shall this thy little bark pursue in the vast billows of this ocean of love? Where shall I find peace? 0 Beloved of my desires, to forget thy presence is not possible to me! How then can it be possible to live in mere memory of Thee without actual intercourse? What shall I do? 0 who shall console me and lend me his company in this bitter solitude, whom shall I seek among creatures, as long as Thou art absent, who art the only One and all that my heart yearns

after in its love? Sovereign spirits, tell me, what does my Lord and my Beloved? Inform me of his exterior movements, and omit nothing of his interior doings, as far as in the light of his Divinity is made clear to you. Point out to me all his footsteps in order that I may follow and imitate Him."

258. The holy angels obeyed their Queen, consoling Her in the sorrows of her mournful love, speaking of the Most High and repeating to Her most exalted praises of the most sacred humanity of her son and of all his perfections. They informed Her of all his occupations and undertakings, and of the places in which He wandered. This they did by enlightening her understanding in the same way a higher angel is wont to enlighten those of an inferior order: for this was her manner of intercourse with the angels, unhindered by her body and the senses. The heavenly Spirits communicated to Her the prayers of the incarnate Word, his teachings, his visits to the poor and the sick, and other actions, so that the heavenly Lady was enabled to imitate Him in all these proceedings according to her condition. She thus engaged in most excellent and magnanimous undertakings, as I shall yet describe, and by this means She was eased in her sorrow and grief.

259. She also several times sent the holy angels to visit in her name her sweetest Son. On such occasions She gave them most prudent instructions, full of deep and reverential love: also supplying them with linen cloths and towels, prepared by her own hands, in order that they might wipe the divine visage of the Savior, when they saw him exhausted and covered with a bloody sweat; for the blessed Mother knew, that He was thus overcome more and more often, as He approached the fulfillment of all the works of the Redemption. The holy angels obeyed their Queen therein with incredible reverence and holy fear, because they knew that the Lord himself permitted it in order to yield to the ardent

desires of his most holy Mother. At other times, informed by the angels or by a special vision or revelation of the Lord, She knew of his prayers and petitions for mankind in the mountains: then She would perform the same prayers in her house in the same posture and with the same words. Sometimes, when She saw that the Lord of all creation was in want of food, She also sent Him, by the hands of the angels, some nourishment, although this happened but seldom; for the Lord, as I have indicated in the foregoing chapter, did not always permit his Mother to act according to the promptings of her love; therefore, during the forty days of his fast, She did not send any food, because She understood such to be his will.

260. At other times the heavenly Lady occupied Herself in composing hymns of praise and thanksgiving to the Most High; this She did by Herself or in company and alternating songs with the angels. All these canticles were most exalted in style and contained the deepest mysteries. At other times She hastened to the assistance of her neighbor in imitation of her most holy Son. She visited the sick, consoled the sorrowful and afflicted, enlightened the ignorant, brought relief to them and enriched them with divine grace and bounty. Only during the time of the great fast of our Lord She retired and remained in her house, as I have already mentioned. During this retirement, our Queen and Lady separated Herself from all human company and She was favored by almost continually recurring ecstasies, in which She received peerless gifts and treasures of the Divinity; for the hand of the God imprinted and painted, as upon an admirably prepared canvas, the outlines and images of his infinite perfections. All these new graces and gifts She employed in working for the salvation of men, and all her occupations and thoughts followed closely the doings of the Savior, as becoming the Coadjutrix of the Lord in his labors for the Redemption of mortals.

Although these benefits and close intercourse with the Lord could not but bring Her a great and ever new joy and exultation of soul in the Holy Spirit, yet in the inferior and sensible parts of her being She experienced the pains, which She had sought and asked of the Savior in union with Him and in imitation of his sufferings. In this desire of following Him in his sufferings, She was insatiable, and She besought the eternal Father for this privilege with incessant and burning love. She renewed that most pleasing sacrifice of the life of her Son and her own, which She had made in accordance with the will of God, and She was consumed with the desire of suffering with her Beloved, enduring the greatest pains precisely because of the want of such suffering.

Words of the Queen

THE VIRGIN MARY SPEAKS TO SISTER MARY OF AGREDA

261. My dearest daughter, the wisdom of the flesh has made men ignorant, foolish and hostile to God, because it is of the devil, deceitful, earthly and rebellious to the divine laws (Rom. 8, 7). The more the children of Adam study and exert themselves to reach the evil objects of their carnal and animal passions, and to attain the means of indulging them, so much the more will they fall into ignorance of divine things, by which alone they can come to their true ultimate end. This ignorance and worldly prudence is still more abominable and still more hateful in the eyes of God, when it occurs in the children of the Church. By what right can the children of this world call themselves sons of God, brethren of Christ and inheritors of his possessions? The adopted son must be, in all that is possible, like unto the natural son. A brother is not of different blood or position from that of his brother. One is not called an heir merely because he is in some way concerned with the possessions of his father, but because he

has the full enjoyment and comes into the possession of the principal property of the testator. How then are those heirs of Christ, who love, desire and seek only earthly goods and are perfectly satisfied with them? How can those be his brothers, who so widely depart from his position, his teachings and his holy rule of life? How can they be similar to Him and claim to be his image and likeness, when they so often destroy in themselves all likeness of Him and allow themselves to be so often sealed with the image of the infernal beast? (Apoc. 16, 2).

262. By divine light thou knowest, my daughter, these truths, and how much I exerted myself to make myself the image of the Most High, namely, my Son and Lord. Do not think, that I have given thee such deep insight into my works without some purpose; for it is my wish that this remain written in thy heart and be forever before thy eyes, serving thee as a rule for all thy conduct during the remainder of thy life, which cannot be of very long duration now. Do not allow thyself to be retarded and snared away from my following by intercourse with creatures; let them alone, avoid them, despise them in so far as they can hinder thee on thy way. In order that thou mayest advance in my school, I wish to see thee poor, humble, despised, abased yet always with a cheerful heart and countenance. Do not try to repay thyself with the applause or the love of any creature, nor allow human sentiment to rule thee; for the Most High has not destined thee for such useless entanglements, or for occupations so lowly and adverse to the religious state to which He has called thee. Think attentively and humbly of the tokens of his love received at his hands; and of the treasures of his grace, which He has showered upon thee. Neither Lucifer nor any of his ministers and followers are ignorant of them: they are filled with wrath against thee and in their cunning they will let no stone unturned for thy destruction. His

greatest efforts will be directed against thy interior, where he has planted his battery of cunning and deceit. Do thou live well prepared and watchful against all his attacks, close the portals of thy senses and preserve the authority of thy will, without allowing it to be spent on human undertakings no matter how good and upright they may appear to thee: for if in the least point thou curtail the love which God requires of thee, this very point will be seized upon by thy enemies as a portal of entrance. All the kingdom of God is within thee (Luke 17, 21), keep it there, and there wilt thou find it, and in it all the good thou desirest. Forget not my teachings and discipline, lock it up in thy bosom and remember how great is the danger and damage from which I thereby wish to preserve thee. That thou art called to imitate and follow me, is the greatest blessing, which thou canst ever desire. I am ready in my extreme clemency to grant thee this blessing, if thou dispose thyself to high resolves, holy words and perfect works, which alone can raise thee to the state which the Almighty and I desire thee to attain.

Chapter XXIV

OUR SAVIOR JESUS GOES TO THE BANKS OF THE JORDAN, WHERE HE IS BAPTIZED BY SAINT JOHN. SAINT JOHN HIMSELF THEN ASKS TO BE BAPTIZED BY THE SAVIOR.

263. Leaving his beloved Mother in the poor dwelling at Nazareth, our Redeemer, without accompaniment of any human creature, but altogether taken up with the exercise of his most ardent charity, pursued his journey to the Jordan, where, in the neighborhood of a town called Bethany, otherwise called Betharaba, on the farther side of the river, his Precursor was preaching and baptizing. At the first steps from the house, our Redeemer, raising his eyes to the eternal Father, offered up to Him anew with an infinite love, whatever He was now about to begin for the salvation of mankind: his labors, sorrows, passion and death of the Cross, assumed for them in obedience to the eternal Will, the natural grief at parting as a true and loving Son from his Mother and at leaving her sweet company, which for twenty-nine years He had now enjoyed. The Lord of all creation walked alone, without show and ostentation of human retinue. The supreme King of kings and Lord of lords (Apoc. 19, 16), was unknown and despised by his own vassals, vassals so much his own, that they owed their life and preservation entirely to Him. His royal outfit was nothing but the utmost poverty and destitution.

264. As the Evangelists have passed over in silence the do-ings of our Savior during his early years, and so many other circumstances of his life, which were most real and most worthy of our attention, and since our gross forgetfulness is so much accustomed to pass over unnoticed what has not been written, therefore we examine and consider so little the immensity of his blessings and of his measureless love, by which He has enriched us so much and has sought us to bind us to Him with so many bonds of charity (Oseas. 11, 4). O eternal love of the Onlybegotten of the Father! O delight and life of my soul How little known, and much less acknowl-edged, is thy most burning love? Why, O Lord and sweet love of my soul, why dost Thou exhibit so many artifices of love, so many watchings and sufferings for those whom Thou needest not and who will neither correspond nor attend to thy favors, not any more than if they had been offered but deceit or buffoonery? O hearts of men, more rude and fierce than that of wild beasts! What has hardened you so? What detains you? What oppresses you and makes you so sluggish that you will not follow thankfully in the ways of your Bene-factor? O lamentable illusion and aberration of the human understanding! What mortal lethargy has come over it? Who has blotted out from its memory such infallible truths and such memorable benefits, and even thy own true happiness? Are we of flesh and have we our senses? Who has made us more hard and insensible than are the rocks and stony moun-tain heights? Why do we not wake up and recover some of our sensibility at sight of the benefits of our Redemption? At the words of a Prophet the dead bones came to life and moved about (Ezechiel 37, 10), but we resist the words and exertions of Him who gives life and being to all. So defective is our earthly love; so great our forgetfulness!

265. Accept me then, 0 my Lord, and light of my soul, accept this vile wormlet of the earth, which creeps along in

order to meet thy beautiful footsteps now begun in search of me! By them thou raisest me to the certain hope of finding in Thee the truth, the way and the delights of eternal life. I possess nothing wherewith to repay Thee, my Beloved, except thy own goodness and love and the being which through them Thou hast given me. Less than thy own Self cannot be paid for the infinite bounty Thou hast shown to me. Thirsting after thy love I go to meet Thee on the way: do not, O my Lord and Master, take away or deprive her of the vision of thy clemency, whom in her poverty Thou hast sought so diligently and lovingly. Life of my soul and Soul of my life, as I have not been so fortunate as to merit to see Thee bodily in this life and in that blessed age of thy earthly life, let me at least be a daughter of thy holy Church, let me be a part of this thy mystical body and the congregation of thy faithful. In this life, so full of dangers, in this frail flesh, in these times of calamity and tribulations, do I live; but I cry out from its profound depths, I sigh from the bottom of my heart for thy infinite merits. That I shall share them, I have the assurance of faith, the spur of hope, and the claims of holy charity. Look down then upon thy humble slave in order to make me thankful for such great blessings, meek of heart, constant in love, and entirely comfortable and pleasing to thy holy will.

266. While proceeding on his way to the Jordan, our Savior dispensed his ancient mercies by relieving the necessities of body and soul in many of those whom He encountered at different places. Yet this was always done in secret; for before his Baptism He gave no public token of his divine power and his exalted office. Before appearing at the Jordan, He filled the heart of saint John with new light and joy, which changed and elevated his soul. Perceiving these new workings of grace within himself, he reflected upon them full of wonder, saying: "What mystery is this? What presentiments of

happiness? From the moment when I recognized the presence of my Lord in the womb of my mother, I have not felt such stirring of my soul as now! Is it possible that He is now happily come, or that the Savior of the world is now near me?" Upon this enlightenment of the Baptist followed an intellectual vision, wherein he perceived with greater clearness the mystery of the hypostatic union of the person of the Word with the humanity and other mysteries of the Redemption. In the fulness of this intellectual light he gave the testimonies, which are recorded by saint John in his Gospel and which occurred while the Lord was in the desert and afterwards, when He returned to the banks of the Jordan. The Evangelist mentions one of these public testimonies as happening at the interpellation of the Jews, and the other when the Precursor exclaimed: "Behold the lamb of God," as I shall narrate later on (John 1,36). Although the Baptist had been instructed in great mysteries, when he was commanded to go forth to preach and baptize; yet all of them were manifested to him anew and with greater clearness and abundance on this occasion, and he was then notified that the Savior of the world was coming to be baptized.

267. The Lord then joined the multitude and asked Baptism of saint John as one of the rest. The Baptist knew Him and, falling at his feet, hesitated, saying: "I have need of being baptized, and Thou, Lord, askest Baptism of me?" as is recorded by saint Matthew. But the Savior answered: "Suffer it to be so now. For so it becometh us to fulfill all justice" (Matth. 3, 14). By thus hesitating to baptize Christ his Lord and asking Him for Baptism instead, he gave evidence that he recognized Him as the true Redeemer and there is no contradiction between this and what saint John records of the Baptist as saying to the Jews: "And I knew Him not; but He who sent me to baptize with water said to me : "He, upon whom thou shalt see the Spirit descending, and re-

maining, He it is that baptizeth with the Holy Ghost. And I saw, and I gave testimony that this is the Son of God" (John 1, 33, 34). There is also no contradiction between these words of saint John and those of saint Matthew; for the testimony of heaven and the voice of the eternal Father over Christ on the banks of the Jordan happened when the Precursor had the vision mentioned in the preceding paragraph. Hence he had not seen Christ bodily until then and could, therefore, deny having known Christ, at least in the same way as he then knew Him; for just because he knew Christ then both by sight and by intellectual vision, he prostrated himself at the feet of the Savior.

268. When saint John had finished baptizing our Lord, the heavens opened and the Holy Ghost descended visibly in the form of a dove upon his head and the voice of his Father was heard: "This is my beloved Son, in whom I am well pleased" (Matth. 3, 17). Many of the bystanders heard this voice, namely, those who were not unworthy of such a wonderful favor; they also saw the Holy Ghost descending upon the Savior. This was the most convincing proof which could ever be given of the Divinity of the Savior, as well on the part of the Father, who acknowledged Him his Son, as also in regard to the nature of the testimony given; for without any reserve was Christ manifested as the true God, equal to his eternal Father in substance and in perfection. The Father himself wished to be the first to testify to the Divinity of Christ in order that by virtue of his testimony all the other witnesses might be ratified. There was also another mystery in this voice of the eternal Father: it was as it were a restoration of the honor of his Son before the world and a recompense for his having thus humiliated Himself by receiving the Baptism of the remission of sins, though He was entirely free from fault and never could have upon Him the guilt of sin (Heb. 7, 26).

269. This act of humiliation in receiving Baptism in the company of those who were sinners, Christ our Redeemer offered up to the eternal Father as an act of acknowledgment of the inferiority of his human nature, which, in common with all the rest of the children of men, He had derived from Adam. By it He also instituted the sacrament of Baptism, which was to wash away the sins of the world through his merits. By thus humiliating Himself in this baptism of sins, He sought and obtained from the eternal Father a general pardon for all those who were to receive it; He freed them from the power of the demon and of sin, and regenerated them to a new existence, spiritual and supernatural as adopted sons of the Most High, brethren of their Redeemer and Lord. The past, present and future sins of men always remaining in the sight of the eternal Father, had prevented the effects of this Baptism; but Christ our Lord merited the application of this so easy and delightful remedy, so that the eternal Father was obliged to accept it in justice as a complete satisfaction according to all the requirements of his equity. Christ was also not deterred from thus securing this remedy by his foreknowledge of the abuse of holy Baptism by so many mortals in all ages and of its neglect by innumerable others. All these impediments and hindrances Christ our Lord removed by satisfying for their offenses, humiliating Himself and assuming the form of a sinner in his Baptism (Rom. 8, 3). This is the meaning of the words: suffer it to be so now for so it becometh us to fulfill all justice. Then in order to honor the incarnate Word and in recompense for his humiliation, and in order to approve of Baptism and establish its wonderful efficacy, the eternal Father gave forth his voice and the Holy Ghost descended. Thus was Christ proclaimed as the true Son of God, and all three Persons of the Holy Trinity ratified the sacramental rite of Baptism.

270. The great Baptist was the one who reaped the greatest fruit from these wonders of holy Baptism; for he not only baptized his Redeemer and Master, saw the Holy Ghost and the celestial light descending upon the Lord together with innumerable angels, heard the voice of the Father and saw many other mysteries by divine revelation: but besides all this, he himself was baptized by the Redeemer. The Gospel indeed says no more than that he asked for it, but at the same time it also does not say that it was denied him; for, without a doubt, Christ after his own Baptism, conferred it also on his Precursor and Baptist. It was He that instituted this Sacrament afterwards as He made it a general law and enjoined the public ministration of it upon the Apostles after the Resurrection. As I shall relate later on, it was also the Lord who baptized his most holy Mother before its general promulgation, and He, on that occasion, established the form in which Baptism was to be administered. These facts were made known to me, and also that saint John was the first fruit of the Baptism of Christ our Lord and of the new Chrrch, which He founded in this Sacrament. Through it the Baptist received the character of a Christian together with a great plenitude of grace, since he had not upon him original sin; for he had been justified by the Redeemer before he was born, as was said in its place. By the answer of the Savior: "Suffer it to be so now, that all justice be fulfilled," He did not refuse, but He deferred saint John's Baptism until He himself should have been baptized and have fulfilled the requirements of God's justice. Immediately after his own Baptism He baptized saint John, gave him his blessing, and betook Himself to the desert.

271. Let us return now to the main subject of this history, namely, to the occupations of our great Queen and Lady. As soon as her most holy Son was baptized, although She knew by the divine light of his movements, the holy angels who

had attended upon their Lord brought Her intelligence of all that had happened at the Jordan; they were those that carried the ensigns or shields of the passion of the Savior, as described in the first part. To celebrate all these mysteries of Christ's Baptism and the public proclamation of his Divinity, the most prudent Mother composed new hymns and canticles of praise and of incomparable thanksgiving to the Most High and to the incarnate Word. All his actions of humility and prayers She imitated, exerting Herself by many acts of her own to accompany and follow Him in all of them. With ardent charity She interceded for men, that they might profit by the sacrament of Baptism and that it might be administered all over the world. In addition to these prayers and hymns of thanksgiving, She asked the heavenly courtiers to help Her in magnifying her most holy Son for having thus humiliated Himself in receiving Baptism at the hands of one of his creatures.

Words of the Queen

THE VIRGIN MARY SPEAKS TO SISTER MARY OF AGREDA

272. My daughter, since in recounting to thee the works of my most holy Son I so often remind thee how thankfully I appreciated them, thou canst understand how pleasing to the Most High is the faithful correspondence on thy part, and the great mysteries of his blessings connected with it. Thou art poor in the house of the Lord, a sinner, insignificant and useless as dust; yet I ask thee to assume the duty of rendering ceaseless thanks for all that the incarnate Word has done for the sons of Adam and for establishing the holy and immaculate, the powerful and perfect law for their salvation. Especially shouldst thou be thankful for the institution of Baptism by which He frees men from the tyranny of the devil, fills them with grace, clothes them with justice and assists

them to sin no more. This is indeed a duty incumbent upon all men in common; but since creatures neglect it almost entirely, I enjoin thee to give thanks for all of them, as if thou alone wert responsible for them. Thou art bound to the Lord for other things to special thankfulness, because He has shown Himself so generous to none among other nations as He has with thee. In the foundation of his holy law and of his Sacraments thou wert present in his memory; He called and chose thee as a daughter of his Church, proposing to nourish thee by his own blood with infinite love.

273. And if the Author of grace, my most holy Son, as a prudent and wise Artificer, in order to found his evangelical Church and lay its first foundations in the sacrament of Baptism, humiliated Himself, prayed and fulfilled all justice, acknowledging the inferiority of his human nature; and if, though at the same time God and man, He hesitated not to lower Himself to the nothingness of which his purest soul was created and his human being formed: how much must thou humiliate thyself, who hast committed sins and art less than the dust and despicable ashes? Confess that in justice thou meritest only punishment, the persecution and wrath of all the creatures; that none of the mortals who has offended his Creator and Redeemer can say in truth that any injustice or offense is done to them if all the tribulations and afflictions of the world from its beginning to its end were to fall upon them. Since all sinned in Adam (I Cor. 15, 22), how deeply should they humiliate themselves when the hand of the Lord visits them? (Job 19, 21). If thou shouldst suffer all the afflictions of men with the utmost resignation and at the same time wouldst fulfill all that I enjoin upon thee by my teachings and exhortations with the greatest fidelity, thou nevertheless must esteem thyself as a useless and unprofitable servant (Luke 17, 10). How much then must thou humiliate thyself when thou failest so much in thy duty and in the

return due to all the blessings received from God? As I desire thee to make a proper return both for thyself and for others, think well how much thou art obliged to annihilate thyself to the very dust, not offering any resistance, nor ever being satisfied until the Most High receive thee as his daughter and accept thee as such in his own presence and in the celestial vision of the triumphant Jerusalem.

Chapter XXV

OUR REDEEMER, AFTER HIS BAPTISM, WALKS TO THE DE-
SERT WHERE, BY THE PRACTICE OF HEROIC VIRTUES, HE
GAINS GREAT VICTORIES OVER OUR VICES; HIS MOST HOLY
MOTHER KNOWS OF ALL HIS DOINGS AND IMITATES HIM
MOST PERFECTLY.

274. By the testimony which the eternal Truth had vouchsafed to give of the Divinity of Christ our Savior, his Person
and his teachings were so fully accredited before men that He
could have immediately begun his public life and his divine
activity and miracles, so that all should have recognized Him
as the natural Son of the eternal Father, as the Messias of the
Jews, and the Savior of men. Nevertheless the divine Teacher
of all holiness did not wish to commence his preaching nor
to be known as our Redeemer without having first triumphed over our enemies, over the world, the demon and
the flesh, in order that afterwards He might so much the
more easily overcome the hellish deceits continually spread
about by satan. By his heroic exercises of virtue He wished to
give us the first lesson of a Christian and spiritual life and to
teach us by these triumphs of Christian perfection, how we
are to strengthen our weakness and discourage our common
enemies by continued battle and victories, lest we be otherwise delivered over to them by the fluctuations of our own
wills. Although the Lord, as being God, was infinitely above

the demon and, as man without deceit of sin, supremely holy and the Master over all creation (1 Pet. 2, 22); He nevertheless wished to overcome in his human nature, by his personal justice and holiness, all the vices and their author; and, therefore, He offered his most holy humanity to the buffetings of temptation, concealing his superiority from his invisible enemies.

275. By his retirement Christ our Lord began to conquer and taught us to conquer the world; for it is an established fact that the world is accustomed to forsake those whom it does not need for its earthly purposes, that it does not seek those who themselves do not seek it. Therefore, he who really despises the world must show his contempt by ceasing to have any connection with it in his affections and aspirations. The Lord vanquished also the flesh, teaching us to overcome it by imposing upon his most innocent body such a severe and prolonged fast; though his body showed no rebellion toward the good nor any inclinations to evil. The devil He vanquished by the preaching of the truth, as I shall explain more fully afterward; for all the temptations of the father of lies are wont to come cloaked and veiled in deceitful snares. That the Lord should not enter upon his public teaching and make Himself known to the world before He had gained his triumphs over the body is another warning and admonition against the weakness of our flesh. He wished to caution us against the honors of this world, even those that accrue to us from supernatural favors, as long as our passions are not conquered and as long as we have not vanquished our common enemies. For if the applause of men finds us unfortified and still living under the influence of the enemies within our own selves, the favors and blessings of the Lord offer us little security and the wind of vainglory may overturn even the towering mountains of virtues. It imports much to all men to remember that we carry the treasures of heaven in most

fragile vases (II Cor. 4, 7); and that, if God wishes to glorify his name by our weakness, He will know by what means He shall draw his doings to light. Avoidance of the enemy alone is incumbent upon us and most suitable.

276. Without delay Christ our Lord pursued his journey from the Jordan to the desert after his Baptism. Only his holy angels attended and accompanied Him serving and worshipping Him, singing the divine praises on account of what He was now about to undertake for the salvation of mankind. He came to the place chosen by Him for his fast: a desert spot among bare and beetling rocks, where there was also a cavern much concealed. Here He halted, choosing it for his habitation during the days of his fast (Matth. 4, 1). In deepest humility He prostrated Himself upon the ground which was always the prelude of his prayer and that of his most blessed Mother. He praised the eternal Father and gave Him thanks for the works of his divine right hand and for having according to his pleasure afforded Him this retirement. In a suitable manner He thanked even this desert for accepting his presence and keeping Him hidden from the world during the time He was to spend there. He continued his prayers prostrate in the form of a cross, and this was his most frequent occupation in the desert; for in this manner He often prayed to the eternal Father for the salvation of men. During these prayers, for reasons which I shall explain when I come to the prayer in the garden, He sometimes sweated blood.

277. Many of the wild beasts of the desert came to the neighborhood now inhabited by their Creator; for He sometimes walked about in these regions. With an admirable instinct they recognized Him and gave forth their voices, moving about as if in testimony of his Divinity. But the birds of heaven of which great multitudes gathered around the Savior, were especially eager in their demonstrations, mani-

festing their joy at the blessed presence of their divine King and Lord by their sweet and loud singing and in divers other ways. After the Savior had begun his fast He persevered therein without eating anything for forty days, offering up his fast to the eternal Father as a satisfaction for the disorder and sins to which men are drawn by the so vile and debasing, yet so common and even so much esteemed vice of gluttony. Just as our Lord overcame this vice so He also vanquished all the rest, and He made recompense to the eternal Judge and supreme Legislator for the injuries perpetrated through these vices by men. According to the enlightenment vouchsafed to me, our Savior, in order to assume the office of Preacher and Teacher and to become our Mediator and Redeemer before the Father, thus vanquished all the vices of mortals and He satisfied the offenses committed through them by the exercises of the virtues contrary to them, just as He did in regard to gluttony. Although He continued this exercise during all his life with the most ardent charity, yet during his fast He directed in a special manner all his efforts toward this purpose.

278. A loving Father, whose sons have committed great crimes for which they are to endure the most horrible punishment, sacrifices all his possessions in order to ward off their impending fate: so our most loving Father and Brother, Jesus Christ, wished to pay our debts. In satisfaction for our pride He offered his profound humility; for our avarice, his voluntary poverty and total privation of all that was his; for our base and lustful inclinations, his penance and austerity; for our hastiness and vengeful anger, his meekness and charity toward his enemies; for our negligence and laziness, his ceaseless labors; for our deceitfulness and our envy, his candid and upright sincerity and truthfulness and the sweetness of his loving intercourse. In this manner He continued to appease the just Judge and solicited pardon for us disobe-

dient and bastard children; and He not only obtained this pardon for them, but He merited for them new graces and favors, so that they might make themselves worthy of his company and of the vision of his Father and his own inheritance for all eternity. Though He could have obtained all this for us by the most insignificant of his works; yet He acted not like we. He demonstrated his love so abundantly, that our ingratitude and hardness of heart will have no excuse.

279. In order to keep informed of the doings of our Savior the most blessed Mary needed no other assistance than her continual visions and revelations; but in addition to all these, She made use of the service of her holy angels, whom She sent to her divine Son. The Lord himself thus ordered it, in order that, by means of these faithful messengers, both He and She might rejoice in the sentiments and thoughts of their inmost hearts faithfully rehearsed by these celestial messengers; and thus They each heard the very same words as uttered by Each, although both Son and Mother already knew them in another way. As soon as the great Lady understood that our Redeemer was on the way to the desert to fulfill his intention, She locked the doors of her dwelling, without letting anyone know of her presence; and her retirement during the time of our Lord's fast was so complete, that her neighbors thought that She had left with her divine Son. She entered into her oratory and remained there for forty days and nights without ever leaving it and without eating anything, just as She knew was done by her most holy Son. Both of them observed the same course of rigorous fasting. In all his prayers and exercises, his prostrations and genuflections She followed our Savior, not omitting any of them; moreover She performed them just at the same time; for, leaving aside all other occupations, She thus profited by the information obtained from the angels and by that other

knowledge, which I have already described. Whether He was present or not, She knew the interior operations of the soul of Christ. All his bodily movements, which She had been wont to perceive with her own senses, She now knew by intellectual vision or through her holy angels.

280. While the Savior was in the desert He made every day three hundred genuflections, which also was done by our Queen Mary in her oratory; the other portions of her time She spent in composing hymns with the angels, as I have said in the last chapter. Thus imitating Christ the Lord, the Holy Queen cooperated with Him in all his prayers and petitions, gaining the same victories over the vices, and on her part proportionately satisfying for them by her virtues and her exertions. Thus it happened, that, while Christ as our Redeemer gained for us so many blessings and abundantly paid all our debts, most holy Mary, as his Helper and our Mother, lent us her merciful intercession and became our Mediatrix to the fullest extent possible to a mere creature.

Words of the Queen

THE VIRGIN MARY SPEAKS TO SISTER MARY OF AGREDA

281. My daughter, corporal penances are so appropriate and fitted to mortal creatures, that the ignorance of this truth and the neglect and contempt of bodily mortification cause the loss of many souls and bring many more into the danger of eternal loss. The first reason why men should afflict their body and mortify their flesh is their having been conceived in sin (Ps. 50, 7). By this original sin human nature is depraved, filled with passions, rebellious to reason, inclined to evil and adverse to the spirit (Rom. 7, 23). If the soul allows itself to be carried away by them, it will be precipitated by the first vice into many others. But if this beastly flesh is curbed by mortification and penance, it loses its strength and acknowl-

edges the authority of the spirit and the light of truth. The second reason is that none of the mortals have altogether avoided sinning against God; and the punishment and retribution must inevitably correspond to the guilt, either in this life or the next; therefore, as the soul commits sin in union with the body, it follows that both of them must be punished. The interior sorrow is not sufficient for atonement, if the flesh seeks to evade the punishment corresponding to the guilt. Moreover, the debt is so great and the satisfaction that can be given by the creature so limited and scanty that there remains continual uncertainty whether the Judge is satisfied even after the exertions of a whole lifetime: hence, the soul should find no rest to the end of life.

282. Even though divine clemency is so liberal with men, that, if they try to satisfy for their sins by penance as far as their limited capacity goes, God remits their offenses and in addition thereto has promised the guilty ones new gifts and graces and eternal rewards: yet his faithful and prudent servants, who really love their Lord, are constrained voluntarily to add other penances; for the debtor who merely wishes to do what he is obliged to and adds nothing of his own freewill, certainly pays his debts, but will remain poor and destitute, if after payment of his debts nothing remains. What then are those to expect, who neither pay nor make any efforts towards paying? The third reason for bodily mortification, and the most urgent one, is the duty of Christians to imitate their divine Teacher and Master. Moreover, my divine Son and I, without being guilty of any faults, or bad inclinations, devoted ourselves to labors and made our lives a continual practice of penance and mortification of the flesh. It was thus that the Lord saw fit to attain the glory of his body and of his holy name, and He wished me to follow Him in all things. If We then pursued such a course of life because it was reasonable, what must be thought of mortals

that seek nought but sweetness and delight, and abhor all penances, affronts, ignominies, fasting and mortification? Shall then only Christ, our Lord, and I suffer all these hardships while the guiltladen debtors and deservers of all these punishments throw themselves head over heels into the filth of their carnal inclinations? Shall they employ their faculties, given to them for the service of Christ, my Lord, and for his following, merely in dancing attendance on their lusts and the devil, who has introduced evil into the world? This absurd position, maintained by the children of Adam, is the cause of great indignation in the just Judge.

283. It is true, my daughter, that by the bodily afflictions and mortifications of my most blessed Son, the defects and deficiencies of human merits have been atoned for; and that He wished me, as a mere creature and as one taking the place of other creatures, to cooperate with Him most perfectly and exactly all in his penances and exercises. But this was not in order to exempt men from the practice of penance, but in order to encourage them to it; for in order merely to save them, it was not necessary to suffer so much. Our blessed Savior, as a true Father and Brother, wished also to enhance the labors and penances of those who were to follow in his footsteps; for the efforts of creatures are of little value in the eyes of God unless they are made precious by the merits of Christ. If this is true of works which are entirely virtuous and perfect, how much more is it true of those which are infected with so many faults and deficiencies, even in the greatest acts of virtue, as ordinarily performed by the children of Adam? For in the works of even the most spiritual and virtuous persons many deficiencies occur. These deficiencies are made good by the merits of Christ, our Lord, so that the works of men may become acceptable to the eternal Father. But those who neglect good works and remain altogether idle can by no means expect to apply to themselves the good works of

Christ; for they have in themselves nothing that can be perfected by the works of Christ, but only such things as deserve condemnation. I do not sneak now, my daughter, of the damnable error of some of the faithful, who have introduced into the works of penance the sensuality and vanity of the world, so that they merit greater punishment for their penance than for their sins, since they foster in their penances vain and imperfect purposes and forget the supernatural ends of penance, which alone give value to penance and life to the soul. On some other occasion, if necessary, I will speak of this error; do thou now deplore this blindness and labor with great zeal; for if thy labors were even as great as that of the Apostles, Martyrs, Confessors, they would be no greater than they should be. Chastise thy body with ever greater severity, and remember that thou art deficient in many things, while thou hast but a short life and art so weak and incapable of repaying thy debts.

Chapter XXVI

AFTER HIS FAST THE LORD ALLOWS HIMSELF TO BE TEMPT-
ED BY LUCIFER; CHRIST VANQUISHES HIM, AND HIS MOST
HOLY MOTHER IS KEPT INFORMED OF ALL THAT HAPPENS.

284. In the twentieth chapter I have related how Lucifer
came forth from the infernal caverns in order to find and
tempt the divine Master. I mentioned also that the Lord
concealed Himself in the desert, where, after a fast of about
forty days, He permitted the tempter to approach Him, as
told by the Evangelists (Matth. 4, 2). Coming to the desert
and finding the object of his search alone, Lucifer was highly
rejoiced; for he found Jesus separated from his Mother,
whom he and his satellites esteemed their Enemy on account
of the defeats they had suffered at her hands. As he never had
entered into any contest with the Lord, and as Mary was
absent, the dragon in his pride accounted his victory secure.
But when Lucifer and the other demons observed their
Opponent more closely, they began to feel great fear and
discouragement. Not because they recognized his Divinity,
for of this they had no suspicions as long as they saw Him so
despised; nor because of any previous experience with Him,
for as yet they had measured their forces only with the heavenly Queen; but because they saw manifested in his exterior
so much reserve and so much majesty, and because his
actions were so perfect and heroic, that they inspired great

fear and dread. His behavior and his condition were totally different from those of other men, whom they had tempted and easily overcome. Lucifer conferred about these matters with his demons, saying: "What manner of man is this, who is so adverse to the vices by which we assail other men? If He is so forgetful of the world and has his flesh in such entire subjection and control, how shall we find any opening for our temptations? How shall we hope for victory, if He has deprived us of the weapons, by which we make warfare among men? I have many misgivings about this contest." So great is the value and power of contempt of the world and subjection of the flesh, that they fill with terror the devil and all hell; and the demons would not rise up against us in such pride, if they would not find men subject to these tyrants before he comes to tempt them.

285. Christ the Savior permitted Lucifer to remain under the false impression, that He was a mere human creature though very holy and just; He wished to raise his courage and malice for the contest, for such is the effect of any advantages espied by the devil in his attacks upon the victims of his temptations. Rousing his courage by his own arrogance, he began this battle in the wilderness with greater prowess and fierceness than the demons ever exhibited in their battles with men. Lucifer and his satellites strained all their power and malice, lashing themselves into fury against the superior strength which they soon found in Christ our Lord. Yet our Savior tempered all his actions with divine wisdom and goodness, and in justice and equity concealed the secret source of his infinite power, exhibiting just so much as would suffice to prove Him to be a man so far advanced in holiness as to be able to gain these victories against the infernal foes. In order to begin the battle as man, He directed a prayer to the eternal Father from his inmost soul, to which the intelligence of the demon could not penetrate, saying: "My Father

and eternal God, I now enter into battle with the enemy in order to crush his power and humble his pride and his malice against my beloved souls. For thy glory and for the benefit of souls I submit to the daring presumption of Lucifer. I wish thereby to crush his head in order that when mortals are attacked by his temptations without their fault, they may find his arrogance already broken. I beseech Thee, my Father, to remember my battle and victory in favor of mortals assailed by the common enemy. Strengthen their weakness through my triumph, let them obtain victory; let them be encouraged by my example, and let them learn from Me how to resist and overcome their enemies."

286. During this battle the holy angels that attended upon Christ were hidden from the sight of Lucifer, in order that he might not begin to understand and suspect the divine power of our Savior. The holy spirits gave glory and praise to the Father and the Holy Ghost, who rejoiced in the works of the incarnate Word. The most blessed Virgin also from her oratory witnessed the battle in the manner to be described below. The temptation of Christ began on the thirtyfifth day of his fast in the desert, and lasted to the end of the fast, as related by the Evangelists. Lucifer assumed the shape of a man and presented himself before the Lord as a stranger, who had never seen or known Him before. He clothed himself in refulgent light, like that of an angel, and, conjecturing that the Lord after his long fast must be suffering great hunger, he said to Him: If Thou be the Son of God, command that these stones be made bread" (Matth. 4, 3). By thus cunningly resting his advice on the supposition of his being the Son of God, the demon sought some information on what was giving him the greatest concern. But the Savior of the world answered only in these few words: "Not in bread alone doth man live, but in every word that proceedeth from the mouth of God." Christ took the words from the eighth chapter of

Deuteronomy. But the devil did not penetrate into the meaning given to these words by Christ for Lucifer understood Him to mean, that God could sustain the life of man without bread or any other nourishment. But though this was also the true signification of these words, yet our divine Master included a much deeper meaning; desiring by these words to say to the devil: This Man, with whom thou speakest, lives in the word of God, which is the divine Word, hypostatically united to his humanity. Though that was precisely what the Lucifer desired so much to know, he did not deserve to understand the words of the Godman, because He did not wish to adore Him as true God.

287. Lucifer found himself repulsed by the force of this answer and by the hidden power which accompanied it; but he wished to show no weakness, nor desist from the contest. The Lord allowed the demon to continue in his temptation and for this purpose permitted Himself to be carried by the devil bodily to Jerusalem and to be placed on the pinnacle of the temple. Here the Lord could see multitudes of people, though He himself was not seen by anybody. Lucifer tried to arouse in the Lord the vain desire of casting Himself down from this high place, so that the crowds of men, seeing Him unhurt, might proclaim Him as a great and wonderful man of God. Again using the words of the holy Scriptures, he said to Him: "If Thou be the Son of God, cast Thyself down, for it is written (Ps. 90, 11): that He hath given his angels charge over Thee, and in their hands they shall bear Thee up, lest perhaps Thou dash thy foot against a stone" (Matth. 4, 6). The heavenly spirits who accompanied their King, were full of wonder, that He should permit Lucifer to carry Him bodily in his hands, solely for the benefit of mortal man. With the prince of darkness were gathered innumerable demons; for on that occasion hell was almost emptied of its inhabitants in order to furnish assistance for this enterprise.

The Author of wisdom answered: "It is also written: Thou shalt not tempt the Lord thy God" (Deut. 6, 16). While giving these answers the Redeemer of the world exhibited a matchless meekness, profoundest humility, and a majesty so superior to all the attempts of satan, as was of itself alone sufficient to crush Lucifer's arrogance and to cause him torments and confusion never felt before.

288. Being thus foiled, he attacked our Lord in still another way, seeking to rouse his ambition by offering Him some share in his dominion. For this purpose he took the Lord upon a high mount, from whence could be seen many lands, and said to Him with perfidious daring: "All these will I give to Thee, if falling down, Thou wilt adore me" (Matth. 4, 9). Exorbitant boldness, and more than insane madness and perfidy! Offering to the Lord what he did not possess, nor ever could give, since the earth, the stars, the kingdoms, principalities, riches and treasures, all belong to the Lord, and He alone can give or withhold them when it serves and pleases Him! Never can Lucifer give anything, even not of the things of the earth, and therefore all his promises are false. The King and Lord answered with imperial majesty: "Begone, satan, for it is written: The Lord thy God thou shalt adore, and Him only shalt thou serve." By this command, "Begone satan," Christ the Redeemer took away from Lucifer permission further to tempt Him, and hurled him and all his legions into the deepest abysses of hell. There they found themselves entirely crushed and buried in its deepest caverns, unable to move for three days. When they were permitted again to rise, seeing themselves thus vanquished and annihilated, they began to doubt whether He, who had so overwhelmed them, might not be the incarnate Son of God. In this doubt and uncertainty they remained, without ever being able to come to certain conviction until the death

of the Savior. Lucifer was overcome by hellish wrath at his defeat and was almost consumed in his fury.

289. Our divine Conqueror Christ then sang hymns of praise and thanks to the eternal Father for having given Him this triumph over the common enemy of God and man; and amid the triumphal songs of a multitude of angels, He was borne back to the desert. They carried Him in their hands, although He had not need of their help, since He could make use of his own divine power; but this service of the angels was due to Him in recompense for enduring the audacity of Lucifer in carrying to the pinnacle of the temple and to the mountain top the sacred humanity of Christ, in which dwelt substantially and truly the Divinity itself. It would never have entered into the thoughts of man, that the Lord should give such a permission to satan, if it had not been made known to us in the Gospels. But I do not know which deserves the greater astonishment: that He should consent to be carried about from one place to another by Lucifer, who did not know Him; or that He should allow Himself to be sold by Judas, or to be received in the holy Sacrament by this treacherous disciple and by so many sinful members of the Church, who do know Him to be their God and yet receive Him unworthily. What we certainly must wonder at, is that He permitted as well the one as the other and that He continues to permit it for our benefit and in order to draw us to Him by his meekness and by his patient love. O sweetest master of my soul! How sweet, and kind, and merciful art Thou not toward the souls! (Joel 2, 13). Out of purest love Thou didst descend from heaven to earth for them, Thou didst suffer and give away thy life for their salvation. Mercifully Thou waitest for them and bearest with them, Thou callest and seekest after them; Thou receivest them and dost enter into their bosom; Thou yieldest Thyself entirely to them and anxiously desirest them to be thine. What transfixes and

bursts my heart, is that, while Thou seekest to draw us to Thee out of pure love, we fly from Thee and respond to all Thy excesses of love only by ingratitude. O immense love of my God, so badly repaid and so little acknowledged! Give me, O Lord, fountains of tears to weep over this wrong, which is so deeply to be deplored, and let all the just of the earth help me. When the Lord had been carried back to the desert, the angels, according to the Gospel, ministered unto Him (Matth. 4, 11); for at the end of his temptation and fast they served Him with a celestial food, in order that his sacred body might again be invigorated. Not only were the angels present to rejoice at this divine banquet, but also the birds of the desert came in order to contribute to the recreation of their Creator by their harmonious songs and graceful movements; and in their own way the wild animals of the desert joined them, throwing off their native wildness and producing their joyful antics and sounds in acknowledgment of the victory of their Lord.

290. Let us return to Nazareth, where, in her oratory, the Princess of the angels had witnessed the battles of her most holy Son. She had seen them all by the divine light already described and by the uninterrupted messages of her angels, who brought them back and forth between the Savior and the blessed Queen. She repeated the same prayers as the Lord and at the same time. She entered likewise into the conflict with the dragon, although invisibly and spiritually. From her retreat She anathemized and crushed Lucifer and his followers, cooperating in all the doings of Christ in our favor. When She perceived that the demon carried the Lord from place to place, She wept bitterly, because the malice of sin reduced the King of kings to such misusage. In honor of all the victories, which He gained over the devil, She composed hymns of praise to the Divinity and the most holy humanity of Christ, while the angels set them to music and were sent

with them to congratulate Him for the blessings won for the human race. Christ on his part sent back the angels with words of sweet consolation and rejoicing on account of his triumphs over Lucifer.

291. And since She had been his faithful companion and sharer in his labors and fasts of the desert, the Lord sent Her some of the celestial food and commanded the angels to present and minister it to Her. Wonderful to record, the great multitudes of the birds that had gathered around the Savior, flew after these angels with a heavier, yet an exceedingly swift flight, and entered the dwelling of the Queen of heaven and earth; and while the blessed Lady partook of the food sent to her by her Son, they sang and chirped before our Lady in the same way as they had done in the presence of the Savior. The most holy Virgin tasted the heavenly food, now even more precious to Her, since it came from and was blessed by the hands of her Son; and by it She was again rejoiced and strengthened after her long and rigorous fast. She gave thanks to the Almighty and humiliated Herself to the very earth; and the acts of her virtue were so heroic and excellent, that our words and conceptions are not able to encompass them. We shall see them in their true light, when we shall rejoice with the Lord; then we shall give glory and praise for these ineffable blessings, as is due Him from all the human race.

QUESTION WHICH I ASKED THE QUEEN OF HEAVEN, MOST HOLY MARY

292. Queen of all the heavens and Mistress of the universe, thy kind condescension emboldens me to ask Thee, as my Teacher and Mother, for information concerning a certain doubt raised in my mind by the mention of the celestial food, which the angels served to the Savior in the desert. I

understood it to be of the same quality as that served to Thee and to the Lord on other occasions, when the ordinary food was wanting. I have called it celestial food, because I had no other name for it; yet I do not know if that name is appropriate. For I am uncertain whence this food was procured and what was its nature. In heaven I understand, there is no need of bodily food, for there the earthly mode of sustaining life is not continued. Although the blessed enjoy also sensible delight from created objects, and also the taste must have its proper function in heaven just as the other senses, I suspect that its pleasures are not derived from the eating of food, but from some overflow of the soul's glory into the body and its senses. Thus the grossness and imperfection of the senses in mortal life have no share in their heavenly activity and in its objects. Of all this, I, being so ignorant, desire to be informed by thy motherly kindness and condescension.

Words of the Queen

THE VIRGIN MARY SPEAKS TO SISTER MARY OF AGREDA

293. My daughter, thou hast well doubted: for it is true, that in heaven no material food or nourishment is used, as thou hast already understood and declared. The food which the angels brought to my holy Son and to me, was truly a heavenly food, and I myself have suggested this name to thee, because the strength of this food is heavenly and not earthly, where everything is gross, very material and limited. It will help thee to understand something of the quality of this food, and the manner of its creation, when I tell thee, that the Lord, to supply our wants, made use of some created material, most ordinarily water, on account of its clearness and simple composition; for the Lord does not require complicated matter for his miracles. At other times it was bread or some kinds of fruit. These materials He furnished

with such a power and such qualities of taste, that they exceeded, as heaven does the earth, all the delicacies here below. There is nothing in the world which can be compared to them; for all other food is insipid and strength less in comparison to this celestial food. To understand this the better, consider the examples mentioned in holy Scripture: for instance the food given to Elias, by the strength of which he walked for forty days and nights to mount Horeb; the manna, which was called the bread of the angels, because they prepared it by condensing the vapors of the earth (Exod. 16, 14) and thus condensed and shaped like grain, they showered it upon the earth. It possessed a great variety of tastes, as Scripture tells us, and it was very nourishing to the body. Also the water converted into wine by the most holy Son at the nuptials of Cana was of such good taste and strength, that it excited the admiration of the guests (John 2, 10).

294. In the same way as the Lord gave a supernatural excellence to the water and turned it into a most sweet and delicate liquor, so He also gave a spiritual strength to the bread or the fruit. Such nourishment restored the waste of bodily strength and delighted the senses in an admirable manner, renewing their vigor and fitting them for labors and difficulties without causing the least loathing or inconvenience. This kind of food was ministered by the holy angels to my most holy Son after his fast, and this I and my spouse Joseph received on different occasions. The Almighty showed the same favor also to some of his friends and servants, rejoicing them with heavenly food, although not so frequently and in so wonderful a manner as He did Us. Thy doubt is then answered; but now listen to the instruction pertaining to this chapter.

295. In order to understand better what thou hast written, thou must keep in mind three motives of our Lord in

entering upon this battle with Lucifer, and this understanding will furnish thee great light and strength against Satan and his followers. His first motive was to destroy sin and the seeds of sin, sown in the human nature by satan in the first transgression of Adam. These seeds are the seven capital vices: pride, avarice, lust and the others, being the seven heads of the dragon. Lucifer appointed an infernal chieftain over each one of these vices in the battle of hell against the human race, and the evil spirits were distributed into squadrons under these leaders in order to maintain the sort of orderly confusion, which I have described in the first part of this heavenly history (Part I, No. 103). Accordingly my divine Son entered into conflict with each one of these princes of darkness, vanquishing them and destroying their power. In the Gospels only three temptations are mentioned, being those which are more manifest to the senses; but the conflict and the triumph was far more extensive, for Christ our Lord overcame all these princes and their vices. Pride He overcame by his humility; anger, by his meekness; avarice, by his contempt for riches; and all the other vices, by their corresponding virtues. The greatest defeat and consternation, however, overtook these enemies at the foot of the Cross, when they became certain that it was the incarnate Word who had conquered and crushed them. Since that time they are timid in entering into conflict with those men, who rely on the power and triumph of my Son.

296. The second motive for engaging in this conflict was obedience to the command of the eternal Father, who not only wished Him to die for men, and redeem them by his Passion and Death, but also to enter into battle with the demons and vanquish them by the force of his incomparable virtues. The third motive, and the one that was consequent upon the second, was to furnish mankind an example and a model for triumphing over their enemies and to take away

from all men any cause of wonder or surprise at being tempted and persecuted by the devils. He wished that all should
have this consolation in their temptations and conflicts, that
their Redeemer and Teacher first suffered them in his own
Person (Heb. 4, 15); for, though in some respects his temptations were different from ours, yet in substance, they were
entirely the same, only of greater satanic force and malice.
My Lord permitted Lucifer to strain all his powers in his
battle with Him, in order that by his divine power He might
crush and enfeeble hell in its battles against mankind, making
it more easy for us to overcome them, if we wish to avail
ourselves of the advantages gained by this very conflict of our
Redeemer.

297. All mortals have need of this instruction, if they are
to vanquish the demon; but thou, my daughter, needest it
more than many generations on account of the wrath of this
dragon against thee and on account of thy natural weakness
in battle, when not assisted by my teaching and this example.
Before all see that thou keep in subjection thy flesh and the
influences of the world. Mortifying thy flesh and flying the
world by retiring from creatures to the interior of thy soul,
thus conquering both these enemies and preserving the
blessed light of grace, which thou there receivest, and loving
nothing except in as far as well ordered charity permits. For
this purpose renew in thyself the memory of the narrow path
pointed out to thee; for the Lord has given thee a natural
faculty of ardent love, and We wish that thou consecrate this
faculty entirely to the love of God. Consent not to any
movement of thy appetites, no matter in how small a matter;
and allow thy senses no liberty, except for the exaltation of
the Most High, or for suffering or doing something for the
benefit and love of thy neighbor. If thou obey me in all
things, I will see that thou art protected and strengthened
against this cruel dragon for the battles of the Lord (I King

25, 28). A thousand shields will surround thee both for defense and offense against the demon. Accustom thyself always to use against him the words of holy Writ, not deigning to exchange many words with such an astute enemy. Weak creatures should not indulge in conferences or arguments with their mortal enemy and the master of lies; since even my divine Son, who was Allpowerful and infinitely wise, did not do so. In this He gave the souls an example how circumspectly they are to act with the devil. Arm thyself with living faith, unwavering hope and love of humility, for these are the virtues by which the dragon is crushed and vanquished and against which he dares not make a stand. He flies from them because they are powerful weapons against his pride and arrogance.

Chapter XXVII

CHRIST OUR REDEEMER LEAVES THE DESERT AND RETURNS
TO THE PLACE WHERE SAINT JOHN WAS BAPTIZING. HIS
OCCUPATION UNTIL HE CALLS THE FIRST DISCIPLES. THE
BLESSED VIRGIN KNOWS OF ALL HIS DOINGS AND IMITATES
THEM.

298. Christ our Redeemer, having triumphed over the devil
and all his vices and having attained the high and mysterious
ends of his retirement and fast in the desert, now resolved to
leave his solitude in order to pursue the further works enjoined upon Him by the eternal Father for the Redemption
of man. In taking leave of the desert, He prostrated Himself
upon the ground, praising the eternal Father and giving Him
thanks for all that He had done through his sacred humanity
for the glory of the Divinity and for the benefit of the human
race. He added also a fervent prayer for all those who would,
in imitation of Him, retire either for their whole life or for
some time, into solitude, and far from the world and its
allurements follow Him in contemplation and holy exercises
for their spiritual advancement. The Father in heaven promised his favors and his words of eternal life as well as his
special helps and his blessings of sweetness to all those, who
on their part dispose themselves properly to receive and
correspond with them. Having said this prayer the Savior, as

true man, asked permission to leave the desert and attended by the holy angels He departed.

299. The Master directed his most faithful steps toward the Jordan, where his great Precursor saint John was still preaching and baptizing. By his presence and appearance there He wished to secure new testimony of his mission and Divinity through the mouth of saint John. Moreover He was drawn by his own love to see and speak with him, for during his Baptism the heart of the Precursor had become inflamed and wounded by the divine love of the Savior, which so resistlessly attracted all creatures. In the hearts which were well disposed, as was that of saint John, the fire of love burned with so much the greater ardor and violence. When the Baptist saw the Savior coming to him the second time, his first words were those recorded by the Evangelist: "Behold the Lamb of God, behold Him who taketh away the sin of the world." Saint John gave this testimony while pointing out the Lord with his finger to those who were listening to his instructions and were receiving Baptism at his hands. He added: "This is He of whom I said: after me there cometh a Man, who is preferred before me; because He was before me. And I knew Him not; but that He may be made manifest in Israel, therefore I am come baptizing with water."

300. These words the Baptist spoke, because before Jesus had come to be baptized, he had not seen Him, nor received any revelations concerning his coming, as was the case on this occasion and as I have said in chapter the twenty-fourth. He continued to speak of Christ, telling the bystanders how he had seen the Holy Ghost descend upon the Lord in Baptism, and how he had given testimony of his being Christ the Son of God (John 1, 2932). For while Jesus was in the desert the Jews had sent to Him the embassy from Jerusalem, which is spoken of in the first chapter of the Gospel of saint John, asking him, who he was and the other questions there rec-

orded. The Baptist answered that he was baptizing in water, but that in their midst had been One whom they knew not (for Christ had been among them at the Jordan). This One, saint John said, was to come later, whose shoelatches he was not worthy to loosen. Hence, when saint John again saw the Savior returning from the desert, he called Him the Lamb of God and referred to the testimony, which shortly before he had given to the Pharisees, at the same time adding, that he had seen the Holy Ghost descending upon his head, as had been promised him by revelation beforehand. Both saint Matthew and saint Luke also mention, that the voice of the Father was heard at his Baptism, whereas saint John the Apostle mentions only the appearance of the Holy Ghost in the form of a dove; for he wished to record merely the words of saint John to the Jews in regard to Christ.

301. The Queen of heaven, in her retirement, knew of this faithful testimony of the Precursor in denying, that he himself was the Christ and in asserting the Divinity of her Son. In return She begged the Lord to reward his faithful servant John. The Almighty granted her prayer, for the holy Baptist was raised above all the womanborn in the esteem of the Most High. Because saint John refused the honors offered to him, the Lord conferred upon him the highest honor that is possible to give to a man next to the Redeemer. On this occasion, when the Baptist saw the Savior the second time, he was filled with new and vast graces of the Holy Ghost. Some of the bystanders, when they heard him say: "Behold the Lamb of God," were strongly moved and asked him many questions; but, the Savior, permitting him to inform his hearers of the truth as explained above, turned away and left this place to go to Jerusalem. Jesus was but a very short time near the Precursor. He did not go directly to the holy city; but for many days He tarried in smaller towns, teaching the people and in a veiled manner telling them, that

the Messias was already in the world. He directed them on the way of salvation, and induced many to seek the Baptism of John, in order to prepare themselves by penance for the coming Redemption.

302. The Evangelists say nothing of the time and of the doings of Christ immediately after his fast. But I have been informed, that the Savior remained about ten months in Judea before He returned to Nazareth in order to see his blessed Mother. Nor did He enter Galilee until He had again allowed Himself to be seen by saint John, who for the second time proclaimed Him as the Lamb of God. This time it was done in the hearing of Andrew and the first Apostles; and immediately afterward He called Philip, as related by John the Evangelist (John I, 3643). These ten months the Savior spent in enlightening the souls and preparing them by his helps, his teaching and admirable blessings, stirring them up from their stupor, so that afterwards, when He should begin to work miracles, He might find them more ready to believe and follow Him as their Redeemer. Many of those whom He had during this time catechized and instructed, really became his followers. He did not speak with the pharisees and scribes during this time; for they were not so well disposed to believe that the Messias had come. They did not admit such belief even afterwards, when this truth had been confirmed by his preaching and when his miracles and other testimonies had so clearly given witness to Christ our Lord (Matth. 11, 5). To the humble and the poor, who on account of their station of life merited to be the first to be evangelized and instructed (Luke 4, 18), the Savior preached during these ten months in the kingdom of Judea; to them He showed his merciful liberality not only by individual instruction, but by his hidden favors and private miracles. Hence they received Him as a great Prophet and a holy Man. He stirred the hearts of

innumerable persons to forsake sin and to seek the kingdom of God, which was now approaching.

303. Our blessed Lady remained during all this time in Nazareth, knowing of all the doings of her Son; She was kept informed of them not only by the divine light, of which I have spoken, but also by the messages brought to Her by her thousand angels, who, during the absence of the Redeemer, always appeared to Her in bodily forms. In order to imitate Him perfectly, She left her solitude at the same time as the Savior. Though She could not grow in love, yet, after the overthrow of the demons through our Lord's fasting and other virtues, She manifested it by greater fervor. The heavenly Mother having received new increase of grace, ardently set about imitating all the works of her Son for the benefit of the human race and acting as his messenger in the manifestation of his office as Redeemer of mankind. Accompanied by her angels, filled with the plenitude of wisdom and furnished with the power of Mistress of the universe, She went forth from her house in Nazareth to the neighboring places and performed great miracles, although in a hidden manner, just as the incarnate Word was doing in Judea. She spoke of the advent of the Messias without revealing who He was; She instructed many in the way of life, drew them from their sins, put to flight the demons, enlightened the erring and the ignorant and prepared them for the Redemption by inducing them to believe in its Author. To these spiritual works of mercy She added many bodily blessings, healing the sick, consoling the afflicted, visiting the poor. Though She labored mostly among the women, yet She benefited also many of the men, who, if they were despised and poor, were not deprived of her aid and of the happiness of being visited by the Sovereign of the angels and of all the universe.

304. In imitation of all that the Lord was doing in Judea, She also went about on foot spending nearly all this time on

her excursions, yet She returned a few times to her dwelling in Nazareth. During these ten months She ate very little; for, as I have indicated in the preceding chapter, She had been so satiated and strengthened by the celestial food sent to Her by her Son from the desert, that She was enabled not only to travel afoot to many places and over great distances, but also to abstain from other nourishment. The blessed Lady likewise knew of the doings of saint John while preaching and baptizing on the banks of the Jordan. Several times She sent him a multitude of her angels in order to encourage him and thank him for the loyalty he had shown to her Lord and Son. In the midst of all these occupations the loving Mother suffered great agonies of desire to enjoy the sight and the presence of her most holy Son; while the heart of Jesus in return was wounded by the clamors of her chaste and heavenly love. Before returning to visit Her and before beginning his public preaching and miracles, happened what I shall relate in the following chapter.

Words of the Queen

THE VIRGIN MARY SPEAKS TO SISTER MARY OF AGREDA

305. I will give thee two important lessons deducted from this chapter. First, love solitude and seek it with particular affection in order that thou mayest partake of the blessings promised and merited by my divine Son for those who imitate Him therein. As far as possible, when thou art not obliged to converse with thy neighbor in virtue of obedience always try to be alone; and when thou art obliged to come out of thy retirement and solitude, carry it with thee in the secret of thy heart in such a manner that thy senses and thy occupations shall not deprive thee of it. Attend to thy outward employments as if they were to be done only in passing, and consider thy retirement as something which is to be

permanent; for this purpose thou must not allow the images of creatures to enter thy mind, for, very often, they occupy the mind more completely than the objects themselves, and they always embarrass the soul and take away from it the liberty of the heart. It is unworthy of thee to let thy heart be interested in anything or be taken up by any creature. My divine Son wishes to be in it all alone and this is also what I desire. My second lesson is that thou learn to set a proper value on thy soul, in order to preserve it in its purity and innocence. Over and above this, however, although it is my will that thou labor for the justification of all men, I wish that thou, in imitation of my Son and of me, busy thyself especially with the poor and despised of this world. These little ones often beg for the bread of counsel and instruction (Thren. 4, 4), and they find none to give it to them, as do the rich and powerful of the earth who have many to advise them. Of these poor and despised ones many come to thee; admit them with true compassion; console them kindly, so that, in their simplicity, they may follow enlightened counsel; for counsel is to be administered to the better instructed in a different way. Seek to gain those souls, who, on account of their temporal necessities, are so much the more precious in the eyes of God; I wish that thou labor incessantly, that they and all others may not waste the fruit of Redemption; nor do thou ever rest from this labor; be ready even to die, if necessary, to advance this enterprise.

Chapter XXVIII

CHRIST, OUR REDEEMER, BEGINS TO CALL AND SELECT HIS DISCIPLES IN THE PRESENCE OF THE BAPTIST, AND COMMENCES TO PREACH. THE MOST HIGH COMMANDS HIS BLESSED MOTHER TO FOLLOW HIM.

306. Our Savior, having visited the villages in Judea for ten months after his fast, now resolved to manifest Himself to the world; not that He had spoken exclusively only in private of the truths of eternal life ; but He had not until then proclaimed Himself publicly as the Messias and the Master of life, whereas now the time for doing so, according to the decrees of infinite Wisdom, had arrived. Hence the Lord sought again the presence of his Precursor John, in order that through his testimony (since such was his office in the world), the light might be manifested in the darkness (John 1, 5). By divine revelation the Baptist knew of this visit of the Savior and of his intention to make Himself known to the world as the Redeemer and the true Son of the eternal Father. When, therefore, saint John saw Him coming he exclaimed in wonderful joy of his spirit to his disciples: "Ecce Agnus Dei," "Behold the Lamb of God." This testimony referred not only to his previous identical words in regard to Christ, but also presupposed the more particular instructions which he had given to his close disciples. It was as if he said to them: Here now you see the Lamb of God, of whom I

have spoken to you, who has come to redeem the world and open the way to heaven. This was the last time that the Baptist saw the Savior in the natural way; but Christ appeared to him just before his death, as I shall relate farther on.

307. The two first disciples of Christ who were with saint John at the time, heard this testimony and, moved by it and by the light and grace interiorly imparted to them, they began to follow the Lord. Benignantly turning to them the Lord asked them, what they sought (John, 1, 38). They answered that they wished to know where He lived; and the Lord bade them follow. They were with Him that day as saint John tells us. One of them, he says, was saint Andrew, the brother of saint Peter; the other he does not mention. But I was made to understand that it was saint John himself, who, in his great modesty, did not wish to give his name. These two, then, saint John and saint Andrew, were the first fruits of the Baptist's apostolate, being the first of the disciples of the Baptist who followed the Savior in consequence of his express testimony and without being outwardly called by the Lord. Saint Andrew immediately sought his brother Simon and took him along, saying that he had found the Messias, who called Himself Christ. Looking upon Peter He said: "Thou art Simon the son of Jona: thou shalt be called Cephas, which is interpreted Peter." All this happened within the confines of Judea and on the next day the Lord entered Galilee. There He found saint Philip and called him to his following. Philip immediately sought Nathanael and brought him to Jesus, telling him what had happened and that they had found the Messias in the Person of Jesus of Nazareth, Nathanael, having spoken with the Lord as recorded in the first chapter of saint John's Gospel, joined as the fifth of the disciples of Christ.

308. With these five disciples, the first stones in the foundation of the new Church, Christ, the Savior, entered Galilee for the purpose of beginning his public preaching and baptizing. In the Apostles thus called He enkindled, from the moment of their joining the Master, a new light and fire of divine love and showered upon them the sweetness of his blessings (Ps, 20, 4). It is not possible worthily to describe the labors undergone by the divine Teacher in the vocation and education of these and of the other disciples, in order to found upon them the Church. He sought them out with great diligence and solicitude; He urged them on frequently by the powerful and efficacious help of his grace; He enlightened their hearts and enriched them with incomparable gifts and blessings; He received them with admirable kindness; He nourished them with the sweetest milk of his doctrines; He bore with them with invincible patience; He caressed them as a most loving Father caresses his tender and darling sons. As our nature is base and uncouth material for the exalted and exquisite aspirations of the Spirit, and as they were to be not only perfect disciples, but consummate masters of perfection in the world and in the Church, the work of transforming and raising them from their rough natural state into such a heavenly and divine position by his instructions and example, necessarily was a vast enterprise. In the performance of this work the Lord has left a most exalted example of patience, meekness and charity for all the prelates, princes and whoever is charged with the guidance of subjects. Not less significant for us sinners are the proofs of his fatherly kindness: for He was not satisfied with simply bearing with their faults and defects, their natural inclinations and passions: but He allowed his tender kindness to overflow thus wonderfully toward them, in order that we might be cheered on to trust Him and not permit ourselves to be dismayed amidst the

countless imperfections and weaknesses natural to our earthly existence.

309. By the means already mentioned the Queen of heaven was informed of all the wonderful doings of our Savior in the vocation of the Apostles and disciples and in his public preaching. She gave thanks to the eternal Father for these the first disciples, acknowledging and admitting them in imitation of her Son as her spiritual children, and offering them to the divine Majesty with new songs of praise and joy. On this occasion of the choice of the first disciples She was favored by a new revelation of the Most High in which She was informed again of his holy and eternal decree concerning the Redemption of man and of the manner in which it was to be executed in the preaching of his most holy Son. He said to Her: "My Daughter and my Dove, chosen out of thousands, it is necessary that Thou accompany and assist my Onlybegotten and thine in the labors which He is about to undertake in the work of the Redemption. The time of his suffering is come and I am about to open up the stores of wisdom and goodness in order to enrich men by my treasures. Through their Redeemer and Teacher I wish to free them from the slavery of sin and of the devil and to pour out the abundance of my grace upon the hearts of all the mortals who prepare themselves to know my incarnate Son and to follow Him as their Head and Guide upon the way of eternal salvation. I wish to raise from the dust and enrich the poor, cast down the proud, exalt the humble and enlighten the blind in the darkness of death (Is. 9, 2). I wish to set up my friends and chosen ones and make known the greatness of my name. In the execution of this, my holy and eternal will, I wish that Thou my cherished and chosen One, cooperate with my Son, that thou accompany Him, follow and imitate Him, and I will be with Thee in all that Thou shalt do."

310. "Supreme King of the universe," most holy Mary answered, "from whom all creatures receive their being and preservation, although I am but vile dust and ashes, I will speak in thy presence according to thy condescension (Gen. 18, 27). Accept, 0 most high Lord and God, the heart of thy handmaid, which is prepared to sacrifice itself for the accomplishment of thy pleasure. Receive the holocaust, not only of my lips, but of my inmost soul in obedience to the orders of thy wisdom manifested unto thy slave. Behold me prostrate before thy presence and supreme Majesty: fulfill in me entirely thy will and pleasure. I desire, 0 almighty God, if it is possible, to suffer and to die either with or instead of thy and my Son. This would be the fulfillment of all my desires and the excess of my joy, that the sword of thy justice strike rather me, since I am closer to guilt. He is sinless as well by nature as also by the prerogatives of the Divinity. All creatures are infinitely distant from his dignity; yet it is also true that any of the acts of thy Onlybegotten is abundantly sufficient for the Redemption, and that He has done much for men. If on account of this it is possible for me to die in order to save his priceless life, I am prepared to die. But if thy decree is unchangeable, grant me, highest God and Father, if possible, that I pour out my life with his. But in this also will I submit to thy will, just as I am ready to obey Thee in following Him and in sharing his labors. Do Thou assist me with the power of thy right hand in order that I may hasten to imitate Him and fulfill thy pleasure and my own longings."

311. I cannot further describe in words what I understood concerning the heroic and wonderful acts performed by our Queen and Lady on this occasion; how fervently She desired to die and suffer on receiving this command of the Most High, either in order to exempt her most holy Son from death or at least to share his Death with Him. Hence, if

fervent acts of love, even when they are directed toward things impossible, so highly oblige God, that if they arise from a true and upright heart, He accepts them as really effective and as worthy of full reward: what must have been the merits of the Mother of grace and love in thus offering her life as a sacrifice of her love? Neither human nor angelic intellect shall ever reach this exalted sacrament of love. It would have been sweet to Her to suffer and die; but it occasioned Her much more pain not to be permitted to die with her Son, or to be alive while She saw Him suffer and die, as I shall record later on. Hence, one can form some estimate how closely allied in glory Mary must be with Christ and how similar her grace and sanctity was to that of her model, Christ; for in all things She corresponded to his love and rose to the highest point imaginable in a mere creature. In these sentiments our Queen issued forth from her vision, and the Most High again commanded her angels to assist and serve Her in what She was to do. They, as the most faithful ministers of the Lord, obeyed, ordinarily accompanied Her in visible forms and served Her wherever She went.

Words of the Queen

THE VIRGIN MARY SPEAKS TO SISTER MARY OF AGREDA

312. My daughter, all the doings of my most holy Son prove his divine love toward men and how different this love is from that which they have among themselves. Mortals are ordinarily so small-minded, niggardly, avaricious and sluggish, that they are usually not moved to love anyone unless they see some advantage in the objects of their love. Hence the love of creatures is founded upon the good thought to be in that which they love. But divine love, having its fountain within itself, and being capable of effecting its own wishes, does not seek the creature because it is worthy, but it loves

creatures in order to make them worthy of love. Therefore, no soul must despair of the divine goodness. Yet no one must on that account have a vain and presumptuous trust, expecting divine love to work in it effects of grace of which he is altogether unworthy; for in these gifts of his love the Most High follows a course of equity most mysterious to the creature. Although God loves them all and wishes all to be saved, yet in the distribution of these gifts and effects of his love He undeniably applies a certain measure and weight of his sanctuary, by which He dispenses them. Now, as man cannot penetrate or comprehend this secret, he must take care not to forfeit or lose the first grace and first vocation; for he does not know whether he will not lose the second by his ingratitude, and he can be certain of not losing the second only by making use of the first grace. The soul can know for certain only this: that grace will not be denied if the soul does not make itself unworthy. These workings of divine love in the soul are accompanied by interior enlightenment, so that in the presence of this light, men are reproved for their sins and convinced of their evil state and of the danger of eternal death. But human pride makes many of them so foolish and base of heart that they resist this light; others are hard to move and never fail to have some vain excuse for their negligence; whence they counteract the first effects of the love of God and make themselves unfit for future graces. Now, without the help of grace, men cannot avoid evil, nor can they do the good, or even know it; thus many cast themselves from abyss to abyss. For, since they counteract and repel grace, and thus are unworthy of further help, they inevitably draw upon themselves ruin by falling from sin to sin.

313. Be attentive, therefore, my dearest, to the light which has excited thy heart to the love of the Most High; for by the enlightenment which thou hast received in the history of my life, even if thou hadst no other light, thou art placed

under such great obligations that if thou dost not correspond with them in the holiness of thy life, thou shalt be more reprehensible in the eyes of God and in mine, and in the presence of angels and men, than all the other humanborn. Let also the conduct of the first disciples of my most holy Son, and the promptitude with which they followed Him, serve thee as an example. Although his forbearance and kind instruction were a special grace, they faithfully corresponded to it and followed the teachings of their Master. Their human nature was weak, yet they did not make themselves incapable of receiving further blessings of God's right hand and they set their desires toward much higher aims than their weak strength would be able to attain. In order to bring this faithful love in thee to its greatest perfection, I wish that thou imitate me in all the works which I have performed on this occasion, and in the desire to die for my divine Son or with Him, if it had been permitted. Prepare thy heart for what I shall yet reveal to thee of the Death of the Lord and of my own life in order that thou mayest in all things do what is perfect and holy. Consider, my daughter, that I have a complaint against the human race, of which I have spoken to thee at other times, and which applies to nearly all men: that they neglect and forget to inform themselves of what I and my most holy Son have done for them; that they do not weigh gratefully the blessings of each hour, nor seek to make a proper return. See that thou do not thus offend me, since I have made thee a sharer in these exalted secrets and sacraments, wherein thou findest so much light and instruction and the practice of the highest and most excellent virtues. Raise thyself above thyself, labor diligently in order that thou mayest receive more and more grace, and, by corresponding with it, gather much merit and eternal rewards. All the works which I have performed on this occasion, and in the desire to die for my divine Son or with Him, if it had been permitted.

Prepare thy heart for what I shall yet reveal to thee of the Death of the Lord and of my own life in order that thou mayest in all things do what is perfect and holy. Consider, my daughter, that I have a complaint against the human race, of which I have spoken to thee at other times, and which applies to nearly all men: that they neglect and forget to inform themselves of what I and my most holy Son have done for them; that they do not weigh gratefully the blessings of each hour, nor seek to make a proper return. See that thou do not thus offend me, since I have made thee a sharer in these exalted secrets and sacraments, wherein thou findest so much light and instruction and the practice of the highest and most excellent virtues. Raise thyself above thyself, labor diligently in order that thou mayest receive more and more grace, and, by corresponding with it, gather much merit and eternal rewards.

Chapter XXIX

CHRIST RETURNS WITH THE FIVE FIRST DISCIPLES TO
NAZARETH; HE BAPTIZES HIS MOST HOLY MOTHER; OTHER
INCIDENTS DURING THIS TIME.

314. The mystic edifice of the militant Church which aspires
to the most exalted mysteries of the Divinity, is founded
entirely upon the holy Catholic faith, established by our
Redeemer and Master, its wise and prudent Architect. To
insure this firmness in the first foundation stones, his disciples, He began immediately to imbue them with the truths
and mysteries relating to his Divinity and humanity. In order
to make Himself known as the Messias and the Redeemer of
the world, who had descended from the bosom of his eternal
Father to assume human flesh, it was urgently necessary to
explain to them the manner of his Incarnation in the womb
of his most blessed Mother. It behooved Him, therefore, in
order that they might know and venerate Her as a true
Mother and Virgin, to speak to them of this heavenly mystery together with what relates to the hypostatic union and
the Redemption. With this heavenly doctrine, then, were
nourished the firstborn sons of the Savior and, before the
Apostles came into the presence of the great Queen and
Lady, they had already conceived most exalted ideas of her
celestial excellences. They had been informed that She was a
Virgin before, during and after her parturition, and they had

been inspired by Christ with the profoundest reverence and love and filled with the desire of immediately seeing and knowing such a heavenly Creature. Christ thus aimed not only to satisfy his own zeal in extending the honor of his holy Mother, but also to excite in his Apostles the highest veneration and reverence toward Her. Although all of them were divinely enlightened, yet saint John began to distinguish himself in this love of Mary before all the rest; from the very first words of the Master concerning the dignity and excellence of his purest Mother, he grew in the loving esteem of her holiness; for he was selected and prepared for greater privileges in the service of his Queen, as I shall relate and as is recorded in the Gospels.

315. The five disciples of the Lord begged Him to grant them the consolation of seeing and reverencing his Mother. In accordance with their petition, He journeyed directly to Nazareth through Galilee, continuing to preach and teach publicly on the way and proclaiming Himself as the Master of truth and eternal life. Many, carried away by the force of his doctrines and by the light and grace overflowing into their hearts, began to listen to Him and to follow Him; though He did not, for the present, call any more to be his disciples. It is worthy of notice that though the five disciples had conceived such an ardent devotion to the heavenly Lady and though they saw with their own eyes how worthy She was of her eminent position among creatures, yet they all maintained strict silence about their thoughts. By the disposition of heaven they seemed as if mute and ignorant in all that concerned the publication of what they thought and felt in regard to her excellences; for it was not befitting that these mysteries of our holy faith should be proclaimed to all men indiscriminately. The Sun of justice was now dawning upon souls (Mal. 4, 2), and it was necessary that its own splendor should shine forth to illumine all the nations; and although

its resplendent moon, his Mother, was now in the fullness of her sanctity, it behooved Her to reserve her light for the night, in which the Church should deplore the absence of that Sun in the bosom of his eternal Father. And this office She fulfilled, as I shall relate in the third part; for then the splendor of the great Lady broke forth, while before that time her holiness and excellence were manifested only to the Apostles, in order that they might know and reverence Her, and that they might listen to Her as the worthy Mother of the Redeemer of the world and as the Teacher of all virtue and perfection.

316. The Savior then pursued his way to Nazareth, instructing his new children and disciples not only in the mysteries of faith, but in all virtues by word and example, as He continued to do during the whole period of his evangelical preaching. With this in view He searched out the poor and afflicted, consoled the sick and sorrowful, visited the infirmaries and prisons, performing miracles of mercy as well for body as for soul. Yet He did not profess Himself as the Author of any miracles until he attended the marriage feast at Cana, as I shall relate in the next chapter. While the Savior proceeded on his journey his most holy Mother prepared to receive Him and his disciples at Nazareth; for She was aware of all that happened, and therefore hospitably set her poor dwelling in order and solicitously procured the necessary victuals beforehand for their entertainment.

317. When the Savior of the world approached the house, his blessed Mother awaited Him at the door, and, as He entered, prostrated Herself on the ground, adoring Him and kissing his hands and feet, while She asked for his blessing: Then She sounded the praise of the most holy Trinity in exalted and wonderful words, and also of his humanity in the presence and hearing of the new disciples. This She did not without mysterious purpose on her part; for, besides showing

to her divine Son the honor and adoration due to Him as the true Godman. She wished also to make a return for the praise with which her Son had exalted Her in the eyes of his disciples. Thus, just as the Son had in her absence instilled into their minds the reverence for the dignity of his Mother, so the most prudent and faithful Mother, in the presence of her Son, wished to instruct them in regard to the worship due to their divine Master, as to their God and Redeemer. The profound humility and worship with which the great Lady received Christ the Savior filled the disciples with new devotion and reverential fear for their divine Master; henceforth She served them as an example and model of true devotion, entering at once into her office as Instructress and spiritual Mother of the disciples of Christ by showing them how to converse with their God and Redeemer. They were immediately drawn toward their Queen and cast themselves on their knees before Her, asking to be received as her sons and servants. The first to do this was saint John, who from that time on distinguished himself in exalting and reverencing Mary before all the Apostles, while She on her part received him with an especial love; for, besides his excelling in virginal chastity, he was of a meek and humble disposition.

318. The great Lady received them all as her guests, serving them their meals and combining the solicitude of a Mother with the modesty and majesty of a Queen, so that She caused admiration even in the holy angels. She served her divine Son on her knees in deepest reverence, At the same time She spoke of the Majesty of their Teacher and Redeemer to the Apostles instructing them in the great doctrines of the Christian faith. During that night, when the Apostles had retired, the Savior betook himself to the oratory of his purest Mother as He had been wont to do, and She, the most Humble among the humble, placed Herself at his feet as in the years gone by. In regard to the practice of humility, all

that She could do seemed little to the great Queen, and
much less than She ought to in view of his infinite love and
the immense gifts received at his hands. She confessed Herself as useless as the dust of the earth. The Lord lifted Her
from the ground and spoke to Her words of life and eternal
salvation, yet quietly and serenely. For at this period He
began to treat Her with greater reserve in order to afford Her
a chance of merit, as I have mentioned when I spoke of this
departure for the desert and for his Baptism.

319. The most blessed Lady also asked Him for the Sacrament of Baptism, which He had now instituted, and which
He had promised Her before. In order that this might be
administered with a dignity becoming as well the Son as the
Mother, an innumerable host of angelic spirits descended
from heaven in visible forms. Attended by them, Christ
himself baptized his purest Mother. Immediately the voice of
the eternal Father was heard saying: "This is my beloved
Daughter, in whom I take delight." The incarnate Word
said: "This is my Mother, much beloved, whom I have
chosen and who will assist Me in all my works." And the
Holy Ghost added: "This is my Spouse, chosen among
thousands." The purest Lady felt and received such great and
numerous effects of grace in her soul, that no human words
can describe them; for She was exalted to new heights of
grace and her holy soul was made resplendent with new and
exquisite beauty of heaven. She received the characteristic
token impressed by this Sacrament, namely, that of the
children of Christ in his holy Church. In addition to the
ordinary effects of this Sacrament (outside of the remission of
sins, of which She stood in no need), She merited especial
graces on account of the humility with which She submitted
to this Sacrament of purification. By it She accumulated
blessings like to those of her divine Son, with only this
difference: that She received an increase of grace, which was

not possible in Christ. Thereupon the humble Mother broke out in .a canticle of praise with the holy angels, and prostrate before her divine Son, She thanked Him for the most efficacious graces She had received in this Sacrament.

Words of the Queen

THE VIRGIN MARY SPEAKS TO SISTER MARY OF AGREDA

320. My daughter, I see thee much moved to emulation and desire by the great happiness of the disciples of my most holy Son, and especially that of saint John, my favored servant. It is certain that I loved him in a special manner; because he was most pure and candid as a dove; and in the eyes of the Lord he was very pleasing, both on account of his purity and on account of his love toward me. His example should serve thee as a spur to do that which my Son and I expect of thee. Thou art aware, my dearest, that I am the most pure Mother and that I receive with maternal affection all those who fervently and devoutly desire to be my children and servants in the Lord. By the love which He has given me, I shall embrace them with open arms and shall be their Intercessor and Advocate. Thy poverty, uselessness and weakness shall be for me only a more urgent motive for manifesting toward thee my most liberal kindness. Therefore, I call upon thee to become my chosen and beloved daughter in the holy Church.

321. I shall, however, make the fulfillment of my promise depend upon a service on thy part: namely, that thou have a true and holy emulation of the love with which I loved saint John, and of all the blessings flowing from it, by imitating him as perfectly as thy powers will allow. Hence, thou must promise to fulfill all that I now command thee, without failing in the least point. I desire, then, that thou labor until all love of self die within thee, that thou suppress all the

effects of the first sin until all the earthly inclinations consequent upon it are totally extinguished; that thou seek to
restore within thee that dovelike sincerity and simplicity
which destroys all malice and duplicity. In all thy doings
thou must be an angel, since the condescension of the Most
High with thee was so great as to furnish thee with the light
and intelligence more of an angel than that of a human
creature. I have procured for thee these great blessings and,
therefore, it is but reasonable on my part to expect thee to
correspond with them in thy works and in thy thoughts. In
regard to me thou must cherish a continual affection and
loving desire of pleasing and serving me, being always attentive to my counsels and having thy eyes fixed upon me in
order to know and execute what I command. Then shalt
thou be my true daughter, and I shall be thy Protectress and
loving Mother.

CITY OF GOD PART II

THE TRANSFIXION

BOOK VI

The Marriage at Cana; How Most Holy Mary Accompanied the Redeemer of the World In His Preaching; the Humility shown by the Heavenly Queen in regard to the Miracles Wrought by Her Divine Son; the Transfiguration of the Lord; His Entrance Into Jerusalem; His Passion and Death; His Triumph over Lucifer and his Demons by His Death on the Cross; the Most Sacred Resurrection Of the Savior and His Wonderful Ascension Into Heaven

Chapter I

AT THE REQUEST OF HIS MOST BLESSED MOTHER, CHRIST, OUR SAVIOR, BEGINS TO MANIFEST HIMSELF TO THE WORLD BY HIS FIRST MIRACLE.

322. The evangelist, saint John, who in his first chapter mentions the calling of Nathanael, the fifth disciple of the Lord, begins his second chapter with the words: "And the third day, there was a marriage at Cana of Galilee; and the Mother of Jesus was there. And Jesus also was invited and his disciples to the marriage" (John 2, 1). Hence it appears that the blessed Lady was in Cana before her most holy Son was invited to the wedding. I was ordered by my superiors to inquire how this harmonizes with what I have said in the preceding chapter and to ascertain what day was meant. Then I was informed that, notwithstanding, the different opinions of the commentators, this history of the Queen and that of the Gospels coincided with each other, and that the course of events was as follows: Christ the Lord, with the five Apostles or disciples on entering Galilee, betook themselves directly to Nazareth, preaching and teaching on the way. On this journey He tarried only a short time, but at least three days. Having arrived at Nazareth He baptized his blessed Mother, as I have related, and thereupon immediately went forth to preach with his disciples in some of the neighboring places. In the meanwhile the blessed Lady, being invited to

the marriage mentioned by the Evangelist, went to Cana; for
it was the marriage of some of her relatives in the fourth
degree on her mother's, Saint Anne's, side. While the great
Queen was in Cana, the news of the coming of the Redeemer
into the world and of his having chosen some disciples had
already spread. By the disposition of the Lord, who secretly
ordained it for his own high ends, and through the manage-
ment of his Mother, He was called and invited to the wedding with his disciples.

323. The third day mentioned by the Evangelist as the
wedding day of Cana is the third day of the week, and,
although he does not say this expressly, yet likewise he does
not say that it was the third day after the calling of the disciples or his entrance into Galilee. If he had meant this he
certainly would have been more explicit. According to the
ordinary course, it was impossible that Jesus should be present at a wedding on the third day after his entering Galilee
from Judea at the place where He chose his first disciples; for
Cana lay within the limits of the tribe of Zabulon, near the
boundary of Phoenicia, far northward from Judea and adjoining the tribe of Aser, a considerable distance from the
place where the Savior entered from Judea into Galilee. If the
wedding at Cana had been on the third day after the calling
of the first disciples, then only two days intervened, whereas
the journey from Judea to Cana required three days; moreover, He would first have to be near Cana in order to receive
such an invitation, which would likewise require some time.
Then, also, in order to journey from Judea to Cana, He
would have to pass through Nazareth, for Cana is nearer to
the Mediterranean sea and to the tribe of Aser, as I have said;
hence his Mother would certainly have known of his coming,
and therefore would have awaited his arrival instead of going
on her visit to Cana. That the Evangelist does not mention
the visit of the Lord to Nazareth, nor the Baptism of the

blessed Lady, was not because it did not really happen, but because He and the other writers confine themselves to that which pertains to their purpose. Saint John himself says that they omit the mention of many miracles performed by the Lord (John 20, 30), since it was not necessary to describe all of them. From this explanation it will be seen that this history is confirmed by the Gospels themselves and by the very passage in question.

324. While, therefore, the Queen of the world was in Cana, her most holy Son with his disciples was invited to the marriage; and as in his condescension He had brought about this invitation, He accepted it. He betook himself to this wedding in order to sanctify and confirm the state of Matrimony and in order to begin to establish the authenticity of his doctrine by the miracle which He was to perform and of which He was to declare Himself openly as the Author. As He had already proclaimed Himself as the Teacher by admitting his disciples, it was necessary to confirm their calling and give authority to his doctrine in order that they might receive and believe it. Hence, though He had performed other wonders in private, He had not made Himself known as the Author of them in public, as on this occasion. On this account the Evangelist says: "This beginning of miracles did Jesus in Cana of Galilee" (John 2, 11). This miracle took place on the same day on which a year ago had happened the Baptism of Jesus by saint John. This day was also the anniversary of the adoration of the Kings, and, therefore, the holy Roman Church celebrates the three mysteries on one and the same day, the sixth of January. Our Lord had now completed the thirtieth year of his life and had begun his thirty-first year thirteen days before, being those from the Nativity to Epiphany.

325. The Master of life entered the house of the marriage feast saluting those present with the words:

"The peace of the Lord and his light be with you," literally fulfilling them by his arrival. Thereupon He began to exhort and instruct the bridegroom concerning the perfection and holiness of his state of life. In the meanwhile the Queen of heaven instructed the bride in a similar manner, admonishing her in sweetest and yet most powerful words concerning her obligations. Both of the marriage couple afterwards fulfilled most perfectly the duties of their state, into which they were ushered and for which they were strengthened by the Sovereigns of heaven and earth. I will not detain myself in declaring that this bridegroom was not saint John the Evangelist. It is enough to know (as I have stated in the last chapter), that saint John had come with the Savior as his disciple. The Lord had not come to this wedding in order to disapprove of matrimony, but in order to establish it anew and give it credit, sanctifying and constituting it a Sacrament by his presence. Hence He could not have had the intention of separating the two married people immediately after they had entered into this union. Nor did the Evangelist ever have any intention of marrying. On the contrary, our Savior, having exhorted the bridegroom and bride, added a fervent prayer addressed to the eternal Father, in which He besought Him to pour his blessings upon the institution for the propagation of the human race in the new Law and to vest this state with sacramental power to sanctify all those who would receive it worthily in his holy Church.

326. The blessed Virgin, cooperating in this work and in all others for the benefit of the human race, knew of the wishes and the prayer of her divine Son and joined Him therein; and as She took upon Herself the duty of making a proper return, which is so much neglected by other men, She broke out in canticles of praise and thanksgiving to the Lord for this benefit, and the angels, at her invitation, joined Her in the praise of God. This, however, was known only to the

Lord and Savior, who rejoiced in the wise behavior of his purest Mother as much as She rejoiced in his. Then They spoke and conversed with those that came to the wedding; but always with a wisdom and gravity worthy of Themselves and with a view of enlightening the hearts of all that were present. The most prudent Lady spoke very few words and only when She was asked or when it was very necessary; for She always listened and attended without interruption to the doings and sayings of the Lord, treasuring them up and meditating upon them in her most pure heart. All the words and behavior of this great Queen during her life furnish an exquisite example of retirement and modesty; and on this occasion She was an example not only for the religious, but especially for women in the secular state, if they could only keep it before their mind in similar circumstances (such, for instance, as this marriage feast afforded), thus learning to keep silence, to restrain themselves, compose their interior and allow no levity or looseness to creep into their exterior deportment. For never is moderation more necessary than in times of danger; and in women the most precious adornment and the most charming beauty is silence, restraint and modesty by which many vices are shut out and by which all virtues of a chaste and respectable woman receive their crowning grace.

327. At table the Lord and his most holy Mother ate of some of the food, but with the greatest moderation; yet also without showing outwardly their great abstinence. Although when They were alone They did not eat of such food, as I have already recorded, yet these Teachers of perfection, who wished not to disapprove of the common life of men, but wished to perfect it, accommodated Themselves to all circumstances without any extremes or noticeable singularity wherever it was possible to do so without blame and without imperfection. The Lord not only inculcated this by his

example, but He commanded his disciples and Apostles to eat of what was placed before them on their evangelical tours of preaching and not to show any singularity in their way of life, such as is indulged in by the imperfect and those little versed in the paths of virtue; for the truly poor and humble must not presume to have a choice in their victuals. By divine arrangement and in order to give occasion to the miracle, the wine gave out during the meal and the kind Lady said to her Son: "They have no wine." And the Lord answered: "Woman, what is that to Me and to thee? My hour is not yet come." This answer of Christ was not intended as a reproach, but contained a mystery; for the most prudent Queen had not asked for a miracle by mere accident, but by divine light. She knew that the opportune time for the manifestation of the divine power of her Son was at hand. She, who was full of wisdom and knowledge concerning the works of the Redemption and was well informed at what time and on what occasions the Lord was to perform them; therefore, She could not be ignorant of the proper moment for the beginning of this public manifestation of Christ's power. It must also be remembered that Jesus did not pronounce these words with any signs of disapproval, but with a quiet and loving majesty. It is true that He did not address the blessed Virgin by the name of Mother, but Woman; however, this was because, as I have said before, He had begun to treat Her with greater reserve.

328. The mysterious purpose hidden in this answer of Christ was to confirm the disciples in their belief of his Divinity and to show Himself to all as the true God, independent of his Mother in his being and in his power of working miracles. On this account, also, He suppressed the tender appellation of Mother and called Her Woman, saying: What does it concern thee or what part have We, thou and I, in this? As if He wanted to say: The power of performing

miracles I have not received from thee, although thou hast given Me the human nature in which I am to perform them. My Divinity alone is to perform them and for It the hour is not yet come. He wished to give Her to understand that the time for working miracles was not to be determined by his most holy Mother, but by the will of God, even though the most prudent Lady should ask for them at an opportune and befitting time. The Lord wished to have it understood that the working of miracles depended upon a higher than the human will, on a will divine and above that of his Mother and altogether beyond it; that the will of his Mother was to be subject to that which was his as the true God. Hence Christ infused into the minds of the Apostles a new light by which they understood the hypostatic union of his two natures, and the derivation of the human nature from his Mother and of the divine by generation from his eternal Father.

329. The blessed Lady well understood this mystery and She said with quiet modesty to the servants, "Whatsoever He shall say to you, do ye." In these words, showing her wise insight into the will of her Son, She spoke as the Mistress of the whole human race, teaching us mortals, that, in order to supply all our necessities and wants, it was required and sufficient on our part to do all that the Savior and those taking his place shall command. Such a lesson could not but come from such a Mother and Advocate, who is so desirous of our welfare and who, since She so well knew what hindrance we place in the way of his great and numerous miracles for our benefits, wishes to instruct us to meet properly the beneficent intentions of the Most High. The Redeemer of the world ordered the servants to fill the jars or water pots, which according to the Hebrew custom had been provided for the occasion. All having been filled, the Lord bade them draw some of the wine into which the water had been

changed, and bring it to the chief steward of the feast, who was at the head of the table and was one of the priests of the Law. When this one had tasted of the wine, he called the bridegroom in surprise and said to him: "Every man at first setteth forth good wine, and when men have well drunk, then that which is worse, but thou hast kept the good wine until now."

330. The steward knew nothing of the miracle when he tasted of the wine; because he sat at the head of the table, while Christ and his Mother with his disciples occupied the lower end of the table, practicing the doctrine which He was afterwards to teach us; namely, that in being invited to a feast we should not seek to occupy the better places, but be satisfied with the lowest. Then the miracle of changing the water into wine and the dignity of the Redeemer was revealed. The disciples believed anew as the Evangelist says, and their faith in Him was confirmed. Not only they, but many of the others that were present, believed that He was the true Messias and they followed Him to the City of Capernaum, whither the Evangelist tells us He, with his Mother and disciples went from Cana. There, according to saint Matthew, He began to preach, declaring Himself the Teacher of men. What saint John says of his manifesting His glory by this sign or miracle does not contradict his having wrought miracles before, but supposes them to have been wrought in secret. Nor does he assert that his glory was not shown also in other miracles; but infers merely that Jesus did not wish to be known as their Author, because the right time determined by divine wisdom had not come. It is certain that He performed many and admirable wonders in Egypt; such as the destruction of the temples and their idols. To all these miracles most holy Mary responded with heroic acts of virtue in praise and thanksgiving to the Most High, that his Holy name was thus gloriously manifested. She was intent on encouraging the

new believers and in the service of her divine Son, fulfilling these duties with peerless wisdom and charity. With burning love She cried to the eternal Father, asking Him to dispose the hearts and souls of men for the enlightening words of the incarnate Word and drive from them the darkness of their ignorance.

Words of the Queen

THE VIRGIN MARY SPEAKS TO SISTER MARY OF AGREDA

331. My daughter, without any excuse is the forgetfulness and negligence shown by each and everyone of the children of the Church in regard to the spread and manifestation of the glory of their God by making known his holy name to all rational creatures. This negligence is much more blamable now, since the eternal Word became man in my womb, taught the world and redeemed it for this very purpose. With this end in view the Lord founded his Church, enriched it with blessings and spiritual treasures, assigned to it ministers and endowed it with temporal riches. All these gifts are intended not only to preserve the Church in its present state, but to extend it and draw others to the regeneration of the Catholic faith. All should help along to spread the fruits of the Death of their Redeemer. Some can do it by prayer and urgent desires for the exaltation of his holy name; others by almsgiving, others by diligent preaching, others by fervent works of charity. But if this remissness is perhaps less culpable in the ignorant and the poor, who have none to exhort them; it is very reprehensible in the rich and the powerful, and especially in the ministers and prelates of the Church, whose particular duty is the advancement of the Church of God. Many of them, forgetting the terrible account which they will have to render, seek only their own vain honor instead of Christ's. They waste the patrimony of the blood of

the Redeemer in undertakings and aims not even fit to mention; and through their fault allow innumerable souls to perish, who by proper exertions could have been gained for the holy Church; or at least they lose the merit of such exertions and deprive Christ of the glory of having such faithful ministers in his Church. The same responsibility rests upon the princes and the powerful of the world, who receive from the hands of God, honors, riches and temporal blessings for advancing the glory of the Deity, and yet think less of this obligation than of any other.

332. Do thou grieve for all these evils and labor, as far as thy strength will allow, that the glory of the Most High be manifest, that He be known in all nations, and that from the very stones may be generated sons of Abraham (Matth. 3, 9), since of all this thou art capable. Beseech Him to send able workers and worthy ministers to his Church in order to draw men to the sweet yoke of the Gospel; for great and plentiful is the harvest, and few are the faithful laborers and zealous helpers for harvesting it. Let what I have told thee of my maternal and loving solicitude in gaining followers for my Son and in preserving them in his doctrine and companionship, be to thee a living example for thy own conduct. Never let the flame of this charity die out in thy breast. Let also my silence and modesty at the wedding feast be an inviolable rule for thee and thy religious in all exterior actions, in retirement, moderation and discretion of words, especially in the presence of men; for these virtues are the court dress, with which the spouses of Christ must adorn themselves in order to find grace in his divine eyes.

Chapter II

MOST HOLY :MARY ACCOMPANIES THE SAVIOR IN HIS PREACHING TOURS; SHE BEARS :MANY HARDSHIPS AND TAKES CARE OF THE WOMEN THAT FOLLOW HIM, CONDUCTING HERSELF IN ALL THINGS WITH THE HIGHEST PERFECTION.

333. It would not be foreign to the purpose of this history to describe the miracles and the heroic works of Christ, our Redeemer and Master; for in almost all of them his most blessed and holy Mother concurred and took a part. But I cannot presume to undertake a work so arduous and so far above human strength and capacity. For the Evangelist saint John, after having described many miracles of Christ, says at the end of his Gospel, that Jesus did many other things, which, if they were all described, could not be contained in all the books of the world (John 21, 25). If such a task seemed so impossible to the Evangelist, how much more to an ignorant woman, more useless than the dust of the earth? All that is necessary and proper, and abundantly sufficient for founding and preserving the Church has been written by the four Evangelists; and it is not necessary to repeat it in this history. Yet in order to compose this history and in order not to pass over in silence so many great works of the exalted Queen, which have not been mentioned, it is necessary to touch on a few particulars. Moreover, I think, that to write of

them and thus fasten them in my memory will be both consoling and useful for my advancement. The others, which the Evangelists recorded in their Gospels and of which I have not been commanded to write, are better preserved for the beatific vision, where the saints shall see them manifested to them by the Lord and where they will eternally praise Him for such magnificent works.

334. From Cana in Galilee Christ, the Redeemer, walked to Capernaum, a large and populous city near the sea of Tiberias. Here, according to saint John (John 2, 12), He remained some days, though not many; for as the time of the Pasch was approaching. He gradually drew nigh to Jerusalem in order to celebrate this feast on the fourteenth of the moon of March. His most blessed Mother, having rid Herself of her house in Nazareth, accompanied Him thenceforth in his tours of preaching and of teaching to the very foot of the Cross. She was absent from Him only a few times, as when the Lord absented Himself on Mount Tabor (Matth. 17, 1), or on some particular conversions, as for instance that of the Samaritan woman, or when the heavenly Lady herself remained behind with certain persons in order to instruct and catechize them. But always after a short time, She returned to her Lord and Master, following the Sun of justice until it sank into the abyss of Death. During these journeys the Queen of heaven proceeded on foot, just as her divine Son. If even the Lord was fatigued on the way, as saint John says (John 4, 6), how much more fatigued was this purest Lady? What hardships did She not endure on such arduous journeys in all sorts of weather? Such is the rigorous treatment accorded by the Mother of mercy to her most delicate body! What She endured in these labors alone is so great that not all the mortals together can ever satisfy their obligations to Her in this regard. Sometimes by permission of the Lord, She suffered such great weakness and pains that He was con-

strained to relieve Her miraculously. At other times He commanded Her to rest Herself at some stopping place for a few days; while again on certain occasions, He gave such lightness to her body, that She could move about without difficulty as if on wings.

335. As I have already mentioned, the heavenly Lady had the whole doctrine of the evangelical law written in her heart. Nevertheless She was as solicitous and attentive as a new disciple to the preaching and doctrine of her divine Son, and She had instructed her angels to report to Her, if necessary, the sermons of the Master whenever She was absent. To the sermons of her Son She always listened on her knees, thus according to the utmost of her powers showing the reverence and worship due to his Person and doctrine. As She was aware at each moment, of the interior operations of the Soul of Christ, and of his continual prayers to the eternal Father for the proper disposition of the hearts of his hearers and for the growth of the seed of his doctrine into eternal life, the most loving Mother joined the divine Master in his petitions and prayers and in securing for them the blessings of her most ardent and tearful charity. By her attention and reverence She taught and moved others to appreciate duly the teaching and instructions of the Savior of the world. She also knew the interior of those that listened to the preaching of the Lord, their state of grace or sin, their vices and virtues. This various and hidden knowledge, so far above the capacity of men, caused in the heavenly Mother many wonderful effects of highest charity and other virtues; it inflamed Her with zeal for the Honor of the Lord and with ardent desires, that the fruits of the Redemption be not lost to the souls, while at the same time, the danger of their loss to the souls through sin moved Her to exert Herself in the most fervent prayer for their welfare. She felt in her heart a piercing and cruel sorrow, that God should not be known. adored and

served by all his creatures: and this sorrow was in proportion to the unequaled knowledge and understanding She had of all these mysteries. For the souls, that would not give entrance to divine grace and virtue, She sorrowed with ineffable grief, and was wont to shed tears of blood at the thought of their misfortune. What the great Queen suffered in this her solicitude and in her labors exceeds beyond all measure the pains endured by all the martyrs of the world.

336. All the followers of the Savior, and whomever He received into his ministry, She treated with incomparable prudence and wisdom, especially those whom She held in such high veneration and esteem as the Apostles of Christ. As a Mother She took care of all, and as a powerful Queen She procured necessaries for their bodily nourishment and comforts. Sometimes, when She had no other resources, She commanded the holy angels to bring provisions for them and for the women in their company. In order to assist them toward advancing in the spiritual life, the great Queen labored beyond possibility of human understanding; not only by her continual and fervent prayers for them but by her precious example and by her counsels, with which She nourished and strengthened them as a most prudent Mother and Teacher. When the Apostles or disciples were assailed by any doubts, which frequently happened in the beginning, or when they were attacked by some secret temptation, the great Lady immediately hastened to their assistance in order to enlighten and encourage them by the peerless light and charity shining forth in Her; and by the sweetness of her words they were exquisitely consoled and rejoiced. They were enlightened by her wisdom, chastened by her humility, quieted by her modesty, enriched by all the blessings that flowed from this storehouse of all the gifts of the Holy Ghost. For all these benefits, for the calling of the disciples, for the conversion and perseverance of the just, and for all

the works of grace and virtue, She made a proper return to God, celebrating these events in festive hymns.

337. As the Evangelists tell us, some of the women of Galilee followed Christ the Redeemer on his journeys. Saint Matthew, saint Mark and saint Luke tell us that some of those whom He had cured of demoniacal possession and of other infirmities, accompanied and served Him (Matth. 27; Mark 15; Luke 8); for the Master of eternal life excluded no sex from his following, imitation and doctrine. Hence some of the women attended upon Him and served Him from the very beginning of his preaching. The divine wisdom so ordered it for certain purposes, among which was also the desire to provide proper companions for his blessed Mother during these travels. Our Queen interested Herself in a special manner in these pious and holy women, gathering them around Her, teaching and catechising them and bringing them as listeners to the sermons of her divine Son. Although She herself was fully enlightened and instructed in the evangelical doctrine and abundantly able to teach them the way of eternal life, nevertheless, partly in order to conceal this secret of her heart, She always availed Herself of the sayings of Christ in his public preaching as a text for her instructions and exhortations, whenever She taught these and many other women who came to Her either before or after hearing the Savior of the world. Not all of them followed Christ, but through the efforts of the heavenly Lady all of them received sufficient knowledge of the sacred mysteries for their conversion. Thus She drew innumerable women to the knowledge of Christ, to the way of eternal salvation and evangelical perfection; though the Evangelists say no more of them than that some of them followed Christ. It was not necessary for the Evangelists to go into these particulars in their histories. The admirable works of the blessed Lady among the women stopped not short with merely teaching

them divine faith and virtues by word of mouth, but She also taught them to practice the most ardent charity by visiting the sick in the infirmaries, the poor, the imprisoned and afflicted; nursing with her own hands the wounded; consoling the sorrowful and giving aid to those in necessity. If I were to mention all these works, it would be necessary to fill the greater part of this history with discourse on them, or to make it much more extensive.

338. Nor are the innumerable and vast miracles of the great Queen during the public preaching of Christ our Lord recorded in the Gospels or in other histories; for the Evangelists spoke only of the wonders wrought by Christ and in so far as was useful to establish the faith of the Church. It was necessary that men should first be well established and confirmed in this faith, before the great deeds of the most holy Mother should become manifest. According to what has been given me to understand, it is certain that She brought about not only many miraculous conversions, but She cured the blind and the sick, and called the dead to life. That this should be so was proper for many reasons: on the one hand, She was the Assistant in the principal work for which the incarnate Word came into the world, namely in his preaching and his Redemption; for thereby the eternal Father opened up the treasures of his Omnipotence and infinite Goodness, manifesting them in the divine Word and in the heavenly Mother. On the other hand, She as his Mother was to resemble her Son in the working of miracles, increasing the glory of Both; for in this way She accredited the dignity and doctrine of her Son and eminently and most efficaciously assisted Him in his ministry. That these miracles should remain concealed, was due both to the disposition of divine Providence and to the earnest request of Mary herself; hence She performed them with such a wise secrecy, that all the glory redounded to the exaltation of the Redeemer in whose

name and virtue they were wrought. The same course She
also maintained in her instructions; for She did not preach in
public, nor at any prearranged place or time, nor to those
who were attended to by the appointed teachers and ministers of the divine word. The blessed Lady knew that this kind
of work was not incumbent upon women (I Cor. 14, 34).
She contented Herself with the assistance She could render
by private instruction and conversation, which She did with
celestial wisdom and efficacy. By this assistance and by her
prayers, She secured more conversions than all the preachers
of the world.

339. This will be better understood if we remember that,
besides the heavenly influence of her words, She possessed a
most intimate knowledge of the nature, disposition, inclinations and bad habits of all men, of the time and occasion best
suited to bring all to the way of eternal life, and that to this
knowledge were added the most fervent prayers and the
exquisite sweetness of her conversation. All these gifts were
animated by her most ardent charity and the desire to bring
souls to salvation and to the friendship of the Lord, and,
therefore, the results of her labors were exceedingly great: She
rescued innumerable souls, drawing them on and enlightening them. None of her petitions were denied Her and none
of her efforts failed of the holy effects which She asked for
them. As, then, the work of salvation was the principal object
of all her endeavors, She without a doubt performed greater
deeds than can ever be understood by men in this mortal life.
In all these labors the heavenly Lady proceeded with the
greatest gentleness, like the simplest dove, with extreme
patience and forbearance, overlooking the imperfections and
rudeness of the new faithful; enlightening the ignorance of
the vast number of those that came to subject themselves to
the doctrines of the Redeemer. On all occasions She preserved the quiet high-mindedness of a Queen; yet at the same

time only She, in imitation of the Savior, could ever have joined with it such perfection of humility and sweetness. Between Themselves They treated all with such great kindness and fullness of charity, that no one could ever be excused from humble subjection to such Teachers. They spoke and conversed and ate with the disciples and with the women that followed them (Matth. 9, 10; John 12, 2; Luke 5, 29; 7,36), observing all due moderation and reserve, so that no one found it strange, or doubted that the Savior was a true man, the natural and legitimate Son of the most holy Mary. It was for this purpose also, that the Lord treated other guests with such affability, as is recorded in the holy Gospels.

Words of the Queen

THE VIRGIN MARY SPEAKS TO SISTER MARY OF AGREDA

340. My daughter, it is true that I labored more than is known or imagined by mortals in following and accompanying my divine Son to the foot of the Cross; nor were my anxieties for their welfare any less after his death, as thou wilt be made to understand in writing the third part of this history. Amidst all my labors and hardships I was ineffably rejoiced in spirit to see the incarnate Word working for the salvation of men and opening the book sealed by the seven mysteries of his Divinity and sacred humanity. The human race owes me no less for my rejoicing at the welfare of each one, than for my solicitude in procuring it, because both sprang from the same love. In this I wish thee to imitate me, as I have so often exhorted thee. Although thou dost not hear with thy bodily ears the sermons of my divine Son, nor his own voice in preaching, thou canst yet imitate me in the reverence with which I listened to Him; for it is the same One that speaks to thy heart, and who teaches thee the same doctrine. Therefore, I exhort thee whenever thou recognizest

the enlightening voice of thy Spouse and Pastor, to kneel down in reverence and listen to his words, adoring Him full of thankfulness and writing his counsel in thy heart. If thou happenest to be in a public place, where thou canst not show this external reverence, do it interiorly and obey Him in all things as if thou wert present at his very preaching; for, just as hearing Him then without obeying Him would not have made thee happy, so thou canst now make thyself blessed by executing that which Thou hearest Him say to thee interiorly, even though thou dost not hear Him with thy bodily ears. Great is thy obligation, since most extraordinary is the kindness and mercy shown to thee by the Most High and by me. Be thou not dull of heart, lest thou remain poor amidst such riches of the divine enlightenment.

341. But not only to the interior voice of the Lord must thou listen reverently, but also to the voice of his ministers, preachers and priests, whose words are the echoes of the Most High and the aqueducts through which the blessed doctrine of life and the perennial fountains of divine truth flow to the souls. In them God speaks and the voice of his divine law resounds; hear them with such reverence, that thou art unwilling to look for any error, nor presume to pass judgment on what they say. For thee all must appear wise and eloquent, and in everyone of them hear only the voice of Christ, my Son and Lord. Be warned not to fall into the foolish presumption of the worldly, who with very reprehensible vanity and pride, most hateful in the sight of God, despise his ministers and preachers, because they do not speak in accordance with their depraved taste. When they go to hear the divine truth, they judge only of the expression and style, as if the word of God were not simple and strong (Heb. 4, 12), depending not on oratorical and artful arrangement of words, adjusted merely to the weakness of those that listen. Do not count this as an unimportant ad-

vice; listen to all that I say to thee in this history, since, as a careful Teacher, I wish to inform thee of little things as well as of great, of unimportant as well as of important points. Remember, that to perform anything with perfection is always great. I also exhort thee to treat affably the rich as the poor, without the acceptation of persons so common among the children of Adam. My divine Son and I rejected and condemned all such distinction, showing ourselves equally kind to all, and even more so to those who were most despised, indigent and afflicted (James 2, 2). Worldly wisdom looks upon the person, not at the state of the souls, nor at virtue, but at outward ostentation; but heavenly prudence considers the image of God in all. Just as little shouldst thou wonder that thy sisters and neighbors perceive thy defects of nature, such as are derived from the first sin, thy infirmities, fatigues, thy appetites and other shortcomings. Sometimes the hiding of these defects is hypocrisy and want of humility; the friends of God should fear only sin and should desire to die rather than commit it: all the other defects do not sully the conscience and it is not necessary to conceal them.

Chapter III

THE HUMILITY OF THE BLESSED MARY NOTWITHSTANDING
THE MIRACLES WROUGHT BY THE LORD; THE INSTRUC-
TION ON HUMILITY WHICH SHE GAVE TO THE APOSTLES IN
REGARD TO THE WONDERS WHICH THEY THEMSELVES
WERE TO PERFORM; OTHER REFLECTIONS.

342. The principal lesson to be learned from the history of
the most holy Mary (if it is attentively studied), is a clear
demonstration of the profound humility of the Queen and
Mistress of the humble. This virtue in Her is so ineffable,
that it can never be sufficiently extolled or duly appreciated;
for it will never be understood in all its perfection either by
angels or men. But just as the sweetness of sugar is added to
confections and medicines in order to relieve the bitterness of
taste, thus humility was mingled in all the virtues and doings
of the most holy Mary, perfecting them and rendering them
agreeable to the wishes of the Most High and pleasing to
men; so that on account of her humility the Almighty looked
upon Her with pleasure and all the nations call Her blessed
(Luke 1, 48). The most prudent Lady lost not a single
chance, occasion, time or place during her whole life for
performing all the acts of virtue possible to Her; but it is a
greater marvel that none of her actions or virtues ever was
found wanting in the least point of humility. This virtue
raised Her above all that was not God; and just as by humili-

ty Mary conquered all creatures, SO, in a certain sense, by the same virtue, She also overcame God himself, causing Him to find such complaisance in Her that no grace which She chose to ask either for Herself or for others was ever denied Her. She subdued all creatures to her wishes by her humility: for in the house of her parents, as I have related in the first part, She won over her mother, saint Anne, and the servants to permit Her to practice humility; in the temple, the maiden and her companions at last yielded to her self-abasement; in matrimony, saint Joseph allowed Her to perform the humblest services; the angels gave way to her desire for lowly occupations; and the Apostles and Evangelists obeyed Her in not proclaiming her praises to the world. By her humility She moved the Father and the Holy Spirit, and even her most holy Son, to ordain that her dignity should remain concealed to the world, and that She should be treated in such a way as not to cause men to praise Her for being the Mother of Him who wrought such great miracles and holy doctrines.

343. Such profound and exquisite humility could be practiced only by the most Humble among the humble; for neither the other children of Adam, nor the angels themselves could ever be placed in similar positions for practicing it, even if they should not fall short on account of the inferiority of nature. We will understand this better when we consider how the poison has so deeply entered the rest of the mortals by the first bite of the ancient serpent, that, in order to counteract it, the divine Wisdom has appointed the bad effects of sin itself as a remedy. For our own and proper defects, brought home to each one's consciousness, are intended to make sensible of the inherent degradation of our present state of existence, which we would otherwise continue to ignore. It is manifest that we have a spiritual soul, but it belongs to the lowest order of spiritual beings, while God

occupies the highest and the angels an intermediate degree; and as regards the body, we are made not only of the lowest elements, that is of earth, but also of its most unclean constituents, that is of its slime (Gen. 2, 7). All this was arranged not in vain by the eternal Wisdom and Power, but with a great purpose, intending that the slime of the earth should always take its proper place and be satisfied with the lowest position, no matter how much it might find itself embellished and adorned with grace. For it must bear all these graces in a vessel of clay and dust (II Cor. 4, 7). We all lose sight of this truth and of our lowliness, so inherent in our human nature; and in order to keep alive the sense of our vileness and degradation, it is necessary that we experience the attacks of our passions and the disorder of our doings. And even our daily experience in this regard is sufficient to bring us to our senses and to make us confess our perversity: we still lay claim to the full excellence and distinction of a noble humanity, while we are but dust and slime of the earth, and, moreover, by our actions prove ourselves unworthy even of this lowly and earthly existence.

344. The most holy Mary alone not having on Her the touch of Adam's guilt nor experiencing any of its foul and dangerous consequences, was proficient in the art of true humility and carried it to its highest perfection; and just because She understood to its fullest extent the position occupied by a mere creature, She humiliated Herself more than all the children of Adam, though they are burdened not only with terrestrial origin, but with their own sins. Other men, if they become humble, were first humiliated and must confess with David: "Before I was humbled, I offended;" and "It is good for me that thou hast humbled me, that I may learn thy justification" (Ps. 118, 67, 71). But the Mother of humility did not enter into her humility by being humbled; She was humble without ever being humiliated. She was

never degraded by guilt or passion, but always generously humble of her own accord. Though the angels cannot be properly compared with men, being of a superior hierarchy and nature, and free from passions or guilt of sin; yet these sovereign spirits could not attain the humility of most holy Mary, even if they did humble themselves before their Creator as his creatures. That the blessed Lady was of terrestrial and human make was for Her a motive and a means of excelling the angels in self-abasement, since they could not make their higher spiritual nature serve as a reason for abasing themselves as much as the blessed Queen. Moreover, She possessed the dignity of being the Mother of God and the Mistress of the angels and of all creation, and none of them could ever claim such a dignity and excellence, which enhanced any act of humility on the part of the blessed Virgin and made her humility surpass all perfection of this virtue ever attained by any other created being.

345. There was in Mary an excellence of humility altogether singular and peculiar to Her; for neither the full knowledge that She was the Mother of God, nor the consideration of all the wonders that She wrought, or that were wrought by her divine Son, nor her position as the Keeper and Dispenser of all the divine treasures, as the most immaculate among all creatures and as the most powerful and most favored of all God's creatures, could ever cause her heart to forsake the place She had chosen in estimating Herself as the lowest of all the handiwork of the Most High. O rare humility! O fidelity never experienced among mortals! 0 wisdom which even the angels themselves cannot aspire to! Who that is acknowledged by all as the most highly exalted of all creation, can ever in his own mind belittle himself and count himself as the most insignificant? Who, like She, can conceal from himself the praise which all unite in giving? Who, in imitation of Her, can be so contemptible in his own eyes,

while for the rest he is so admirable? Who, singled out for high distinction, does not lose sight of lowliness, and who, invited to a like position, can thus select the most lowly, not by necessity or in sadness, nor with impatient protest, but with all his heart and with the sincerest content! O children of Adam, how slow and dull we all are in this divine science! How necessary it is that the Lord conceal from us our own blessings, or accompany them with some burden or counterweight, lest we frustrate all his goodness toward us and lest we be prevented from scheming some robbery of the glory due to Him as the Author of all good in us! Let us then understand what a dastardly humility ours is, and how precarious, if we ever have it at all; for the Lord (let us so express it), must use much circumspection and care in entrusting us with any advantage or virtue on account of the weakness of our humility and seldom does our ignorance fail to indulge itself with some petty theft on such occasions, or at least with a vain complacency or inconsiderate joy.

346. The humility in the conduct of the most holy Mary in regard to the miracles of Christ our Lord was a source of great admiration to her holy angels; for they were not accustomed to behold in the children of Adam, and not even among themselves, such self-abasement united to such great perfection and magnificence of activity. Nor did the miracles of the Savior, in whom the holy angels expected and had already experienced proofs of his Omnipotence, excite their admiration so much as the peerless fidelity with which the most blessed Virgin referred all miraculous works to the glory of God and by which She esteemed Herself so unworthy of them, that She deemed his not omitting them on account of her demerits, an especial favor of her divine Son. Such humility She practiced in spite of the fact that She, by her constant prayer, was precisely the instrumental cause of nearly all the miracles wrought by the Lord; not to mention

this other fact that if the heavenly Mother had not intervened between Christ and the human race, the world would never have come into the possession of the Gospel, nor ever merited to experience any of its effects.

347. The miracles and doings of Christ our Lord and Savior were so new and unheard of in the world that great admiration and honor could not but have been the result for his most holy Mother; for She was not only known to the Apostles and disciples, who acknowledged Her as the true Mother of the Redeemer, but by the new faithful, who all came to acknowledge Her as the true Mother of the Messias and many times congratulated Her on account of the wonders wrought by her Son. All this, however, was for Her a new occasion of humility; for She always humbled Herself to the dust and debased Herself in her own mind beyond all conception of created mind. Yet with all her humility She did not show Herself slow and ungrateful in the acknowledgment of all the favors lavished upon Her; for in humiliating Herself at sight of all the great works of Christ, She rendered worthy thanks to the eternal Father for each one of them and thus filled out the great void of ingratitude of the human race. And by means of the secret communication of her purest soul with that of the Savior, She sought to divert toward God, her Son, the honor attributed to Her by his hearers. This happened on some occasions which even the Evangelists mention. For instance, when the Jews attributed the healing of the deaf-mute to the devil, the Lord incited a woman to exclaim: "Blessed is the womb that bore Thee, and the paps that gave Thee suck!' the humble and attentive Mother, hearing these words of praise, begged her divine Son to divert this praise from Her, and the Lord acceded to her request in such a way, that He turned these words into a still greater, yet, at that time a hidden, praise. For the Lord answered:

"Yea rather, blessed are they who hear the word of God and keep it" (Luke 11, 27). By these words He neutralized the praise given to Her as Mother, but enhanced it in application to Her as a saint; directing the attention of his hearers to the essential of all virtue, in which his Mother was distinguished above all others and most wonderful, though at the same time none of his hearers adverted to this hidden signification.

348. Another instance of this kind is mentioned by saint Luke, when he says that some one interrupted the preaching of the Lord by the message that his Mother and his brethren had arrived, and that they could not come near to Him on account of the press of the multitude. The most prudent Virgin, fearing lest those within hearing would break out in applause at seeing the Mother of the Savior, asked her Son to prevent such an event. The Lord again yielded, and said: "My mother and my brethren are they who hear the word of God and do it" (Luke 8, 21). In these words likewise the Lord did not deprive his Mother of the honor due to Her on account of her holiness; but referred it to Her above all others; yet in such a way that the attention of the bystanders was diverted from Her, and She, on her part, gained her object of seeing the Lord alone praised and acknowledged for his works. I wish to mention that these events, as I have been made to understand, happened on different occasions and at different places. Accordingly saint Luke records them in two different chapters, eight and nine, though saint Matthew refers to the wonderful cure of the possessed mute in chapter the twelfth, and immediately adds that the Savior was notified of the presence of his Mother and his brethren, who wished to speak to the Lord. On this account and on account of what else is said there, some commentators have thought that both the abovementioned incidents took place at one and the same time. But having again been ordered to ask by

my superiors, I was told that they were separate events, happening at different times; which can also be deduced from the balance of the context of these chapters; for saint Luke mentions the incident of the exclaiming woman after having related the healing of the possessed deafmute. The other incident he relates in the eighth chapter, after the Lord had preached the parable of the seed; and both of them followed immediately after what the Evangelist had said before that.

349. In order to understand more fully the perfect accord of the Evangelists and the reason why the blessed Queen came to her Son on those occasions, I wish to state that the Virgin Mother frequented the sermons of Christ our Savior for two reasons. Sometimes She wished to hear Him, as I have stated above; at other times She sought Him in order to ask some favor for the souls, either regarding their conversion or the cure of the sick or afflicted; for the kindest Lady took the remedy of all such evils into her own hand, just as She had done at the marriage feast of Cana. Being made aware of these and other pressing necessities either by the angels or by her interior light, She was accustomed to approach the Lord; and such was also the object of seeking the Master on the occasions mentioned by the Evangelists. As this happened not only once but many times, and since the crowds attending the sermon of the Lord were often very great, He was notified on these and many other occasions not mentioned, that his Mother and his brethren were seeking Him, and on these two occasions He spoke the words recorded by saint Luke and saint Matthew. There is nothing strange in his having repeated the same words on two different occasions; for He also repeated on several occasions this other saying of his: "Because every one that exalteth himself shall be humbled; and he that humbleth himself shall be exalted" (Luke 14, 11; 18, 14), which the Lord used in the parable of the

publican and the pharisee, as also in that of the guests invited
to the marriage, as can be seen in the fourteenth and eight-
eenth chapters of saint Luke and the twenty-third chapter of
saint Matthew.

350. The blessed Mary practiced humility not only Herself, but She was the great Teacher of humility for the Apostles and disciples; for it was necessary that they be well
founded and rooted in this virtue in order to receive the gifts
and to work the wonders, not only later on in the foundation
of the Church, but even now, in the first beginnings of their
duties as preachers of the word (Mark 3, 14). The holy
Evangelists tell us that the Lord sent before Him the Apostles
(Luke 9, 2), and afterwards, the seventy-two disciples, and
that He gave them power to expel the demons from the
possessed and to cure the sick. The great Mistress of the
humble counseled and exhorted them with words of eternal
life, how they were to govern themselves in performing these
miracles. By her teaching and, intercession the spirit of
wisdom and humility was deeply planted into their hearts, so
that they well understood how entirely these miracles are
wrought by divine power and that all the glory of these works
belonged to the Lord alone. They understood that they
themselves were merely the instruments; that, just as the
brush does not deserve the glory attached to a work of art,
nor the sword that of victory, but all belongs to the artist or
to the wielder of the sword; so all the honor and praise due to
their miracles belonged to the Lord and Master, in whose
name they performed them. It is worthy of notice that none
of these lessons given to the Apostles before being sent to
preach are mentioned in the holy Gospels; but this was
intentional, because all these instructions were given to them
by the blessed Lady. Yet when the disciples returned to their
Master, and full of exultation told Him that they had subjected to themselves the demons in his name (Luke 10, 17),

He reminded them that He had given them this power and that they should not be elated except in having their names recorded in heaven. So feeble is our humility, that the Savior was obliged to apply such corrections and antidotes in order to preserve it in his own disciples.

351. But afterwards, in order that they might be worthy founders of the holy Church, the science of humility, taught them by Christ the Lord and his holy Mother, was still more necessary; for then they were to perform still greater miracles in the name of Christ and in confirmation of the faith and of their evangelical preaching. The heathens, being accustomed blindly to give divine honors to anything great or strange, and seeing the miracles wrought by the Apostles, were only too ready to adore them as gods. Thus when they saw saint Paul and saint Barnaby in Lycaonia cure the man crippled from his birth (Acts 14,9), they proclaimed the one as Mercury and the other as Jupiter. Later on, when saint Paul survived the bite of a viper while all the others had been bitten and died thereof, he was called a god (Acts 28, 6). All these miraculous events and occasions most holy Mary foresaw in the fullness of her knowledge and as the Assistant of her divine Son in the establishment of the law of grace. During the time of his preaching, which lasted three years, Christ went to celebrate the Pash three times. and the blessed Lady accompanied Him each time, being present when in the first year He used the whip to drive the sellers of sheep, pigeons and cattle from the house of God. In all the doings of the Savior in the city and in his sufferings, the great Lady accompanied Him with admirable affection and heroic acts of virtue according to her condition and circumstances; and She conducted Herself with sublime perfection, especially in regard to the practice of her most ardent charity, which She derived from the Lord Himself. Since She lived only in God, and God in Her, the charity of Christ burned in her bosom

and left Her to seek the good of her fellowmen with all the powers of her body and soul.

Words of the Queen

THE VIRGIN MARY SPEAKS TO SISTER MARY OF AGREDA

352. In his malice and astuteness, the ancient serpent strains all his powers to destroy in the human heart the science of humility, sowed by the Redeemer as a seed of holiness in the human heart; and in its place he seeks to sow the cockle of pride (Matth. 13, 25). In order to root out these and allow free growth to the blessing of humility, it is necessary that the soul consent and seek to be humiliated by its fellow creatures and that it ask the Lord incessantly and in all sincerity of heart for this virtue and for the means to attain it. Very scarce are the souls that apply themselves to this science and reach the perfection of this virtue; for it requires entire conquest of one's whole self to which few attain, even among those who profess to be virtuous. This contagion of pride has so deeply penetrated into the human faculties, that it is communicated to nearly all of men's doings and there is scarcely one among men who is without pride, just as the rose never grows without thorns or the grain without husks. On this account the Most High makes so much of the truly humble; and those who entirely triumph over pride, He exalts and places with the princes of his people, esteeming them as his favored children and exempting them from the jurisdiction of the demon. Thus it comes that the devil dares scarcely approach them, because he fears the humble and their victories over him more than the fires of hell.

353. I desire, my dearest, that thou attain the inestimable treasure of humility in all its fullness, and that thou offer to the Most High a docile and yielding heart, in order that He may impress upon it, like on soft wax, the image of my own

most humble activity. As thou hast been informed of such deeply hidden secrets concerning this sacrament, thou art under great obligations to correspond to my wishes, not losing the least occasion of humiliation and advancing in this virtue. Neglect none of them, since thou knowest how much I sought after them, who was the Mother of God himself, most pure and full of grace. The greater my prerogatives, so much the greater was my humility, because in my estimation they far exceeded my merits and only increased my obligations. All you children of Adam (Ps. 50, 7), were conceived in sin, and there is none who has not sinned on his own account. If none can deny this infection of his nature, why should not all humiliate themselves before God and before men? Lowering themselves to the very dust and placing themselves in the last place is not such a great humiliation for those who have sinned, for even then they will always be more honored than they deserve. The truly humble must lower themselves beneath that which they have deserved. If all the creatures would despise and abhor them, or offend them; if they would consider themselves worthy of hellfire, they would only fulfill justice, but not the requirement of humility, since that would only be admitting their deserts. But real, deep humility goes to the length of desiring a greater humiliation than that due to one's self in justice. On this account there is no mortal who can attain to the kind of humility which I practiced, such as thou hast understood and described; but the Most High will be satisfied with and ready to reward the efforts of those who humble themselves as far as they can and as they deserve in justice.

354. Let then the sinners admit their baseness and understand how they make of themselves monsters of hell by imitating Lucifer in his pride. For pride found him beauteous and endowed with great gifts of grace and nature; and although he dissipated these blessings, he had nevertheless

possessed them as his own. But man, who is mere slime, and moreover has sinned and is full of ugliness and baseness, is a monster, if he bloats himself up in vain pride. By such absurdity he surpasses even the demon; since man possesses a nature neither so noble, nor was ever gifted with such grace and beauty as Lucifer. He and his hellish followers despise and laugh over men, who in such inferiority swell up in pride; for they can well understand this vain and contemptible madness and delirium. Mind well therefore, my daughter, this lesson, and humiliate thyself lower than the earth, showing just as little sense of injury as the dust, whenever the Lord, either himself or through others, sends thee humiliation. Never judge thyself injured by anyone nor consider thyself offended; if thou abhor pretense and lying, remember, that the greatest offense is to aspire after honor or high position. Do not attribute to creatures that which God brings about in order to humiliate thee or others by affliction and tribulations; for this is protesting against mere instruments, while it is divine mercy which inflicts punishment on men for their humiliation. This, if they would only understand, is really what is happening by the disposition of the Lord to the kingdoms of our day. Humiliate thyself in the divine presence for thyself and for all thy fellowmen, in order to placate his wrath, just as if thou alone wert guilty; and as if thou never hadst made any satisfaction; since during mortal life no one can ever know whether he has satisfied for his transgressions. Seek to appease Him as if thou alone hadst offended Him; and in regard to the gifts and favors which thou hast received and dost receive, show thyself grateful as one who deserves much less and owes much more. By these considerations humiliate thyself more than all others, and labor without ceasing to correspond to the divine clemency, which has shown itself so liberal toward thee.

Chapter IV

THE DEVIL IS MUCH DISTURBED AND DISCONCERTED ON
ACCOUNT OF THE MIRACLES OF CHRIST AND OF SAINT
JOHN THE BAPTIST. HEROD SEIZES AND BEHEADS SAINT
JOHN; SOME PARTICULARS OF HIS DEATH.

355. The Redeemer of the world, departing from Jerusalem
and traveling about in Judea for some time, pursued the
work of preaching and performing miracles. While He was
baptizing and at the same time commissioning his disciples
to baptize, as is recorded in the third and fourth chapter of
Saint John's Gospel, his Precursor also continued to baptize
in Ainon on the banks of the Jordan near the city of Salem.
But the Baptisms of the Lord and those of saint John were
not of the same kind: for saint John continued to give only
the baptism of water and of penance, while our Lord administered his own Baptism, that of real pardon of sins and
justification, such as it is now in the Church, accompanied
by the infusion of grace and of the virtues. To the mysterious
power and effects of the Baptism of Christ was moreover
added the efficacy of his words and instructions confirmed by
the wonder of his miracles. On this account more disciples
and followers soon gathered around Christ than around saint
John, in fulfillment of the words of the Baptist, that Christ
must grow, while he must be diminished (John 3, 22). At the
Baptisms of the Lord his most holy Mother ordinarily was

present and She beheld all the great results of this regeneration in the favored souls. With the same gratitude as if She herself were receiving the benefits of the Sacrament, She gave thanks for them, breaking forth in canticles of praise and exercising heroic virtues as a thank offering to the Author of them. Thus in all these wonderful activities She gained for Herself incomparable and unheard of merits.

356. When by divine permission Lucifer and his followers arose from the ruinous defeat which they had experienced at the triumph of Christ in the desert, and when they returned and saw the works of the most sacred humanity, divine Providence ordained, that, though always remaining ignorant of the principal mystery connected with Christ they should nevertheless see enough to lead to their entire discomfiture. Lucifer therefore perceived the great results of the preaching, the miracles, the Baptism of Christ our Lord, and how by these means innumerable souls were withdrawn from his jurisdiction and from the shackles of sin in the reformation of their life. The same effects he recognized also in the preaching of saint John and in his baptism. He remained ignorant of the essential difference between these two preachers and their baptisms and at the same time had no doubts about the final overthrow of his dominion, if their activity should continue. Hence, Lucifer could not but be full of fear and unrest. He knew well that he was too weak to resist the power of heaven, which he felt was exerted against him in these new Preachers and their doctrines. These considerations filled his proud mind with great apprehension, and therefore he called another meeting of the princes of darkness and said to them: "Strange things happen in the world during these years, and every day do they multiply, so that my fears lest the divine Word has come into the world according to the promise are growing more and more harrowing. I have searched the face of the whole earth and cannot find Him.

But these two Men, who are preaching and deprive me every day of many souls, excite within me great misgivings; the one I could never overcome in the desert, and the other vanquished all of us, so that even now we are disheartened and crushed. If They continue as They have begun, all our triumphs will turn to confusion. They cannot Both be the Messias, and I cannot as yet be sure that either one of them is He; but to draw so many souls from a life of sin, is a work not equalled by any to this day. It supposes a new power, which we must investigate and trace to its source; and we must destroy these two Men. Follow me and assist me with all your strength, astuteness and sagacity; because otherwise they will frustrate our intentions."

357. These ministers of evil therefore came to the determination of persecuting anew our Savior Christ and his Precursor saint John; but as they had no knowledge of the mysteries of the divine Wisdom, all their great projects and resolves were vain and without firmness. They were sadly misled and confused on the one hand, by so many miracles, and on the other hand by outward appearances entirely different from those which they had attributed to the incarnate Word at his coming into the world. In order that his malice might find some enlightenment, and in order that his companions, who were to spy out and discover what secret power had so discomfited them, might be more successful in assisting him, Lucifer ordered meetings of the demons to be held, in which they were to communicate to each other what they had seen and understood concerning recent events; and he offered them great rewards and preferments in his hellish dominions for good service. For the purpose of throwing them into a still greater doubt and confusion, the Lord permitted the hellish fiends to imagine greater holiness in the life of saint John the Baptist. He did not perform the same wonders as Christ; but the outward signs of his holiness were

very remarkable and his exterior virtues were wonderful. God also concealed some of the more extraordinary wonders performed by Jesus from the dragon, and there was a great similarity between Christ and saint John in regard to certain particulars which came to the knowledge of the devil, so that he remained in doubt and could not come to a certain decision as to which of Them really deserved to hold the office and dignity of Messias. "Both," (he said to himself) "are great Saints and Prophets; the life of the One is that of the common people, but yet extraordinary and strange in some respects; the other performs many miracles and his doctrine is nearly the same. Both cannot be the Messias: but let Them be whoever They may, I recognize Them as my great Enemies and as Saints, and must persecute Them until I have undone Them."

358. These suspicions of the demons began from the time when he saw saint John in the desert leading such a wonderful and unheard of life even from his childhood, and at the time he thought that his virtues were greater than that of a mere man could be. On the other hand, he also learned of some of the doings and of the heroic virtues of the life of Christ our Lord, which were not less wonderful, and the dragon compared them with those of John. Yet as the Savior lived a life more of the common order among men, Lucifer was more anxious to find out who this John could be. With this desire he incited the Jews and the pharisees of Jerusalem to send the priests and Levites to saint John in order to ascertain who he was (John 1, 19) whether he was Christ, as through Lucifer they were led to suspect. And the devil's suggestions must have been very persistent, since they knew that the Baptist was of the tribe of Levi, and hence, as was well known, could not be the Messias ; for according to the Scriptures and according to their knowledge of the law and of revealed truth, the Messias was to be of the tribe of Juda

(Ps. 81, 11). But the devil troubled their minds so much, that yielding to his astute malice, they asked this question. The devil pursued a double object; for if John was the Messias, he wanted him to reveal it; if not, he wanted to diminish his influence with the people, who believed him to be the Messias; or he wished saint John to fall into a vain complaisance or at least usurp, either wholly or in part, the honor thus held out to him. Hence the demon eagerly listened to every word of the answer given by saint John.

359. But the holy Precursor answered with heavenly wisdom, confessing the truth in such a way that the astuteness of the enemy was foiled and his uncertainty was greater than before. He answered, that he was not Christ. Then they asked again, whether he was Elias. Since it was written of Elias, that he was to come before Christ and as the Jews were so dull as not to know how to distinguish between the first and second coming, they asked him, whether he was Elias. He answered: "I am not," adding: "I am the voice of one crying in the wilderness, make straight the way of the Lord," as said the prophet Isaias (John 1, 20, 21). All these questions were put by the messengers through instigation of the devil; for he expected that if saint John was a holy man, he would tell the truth, and therefore reveal clearly who he was. When he heard saint John call himself a "voice," he was much taken aback, suspecting in his ignorance that he meant to call himself the eternal Word. His restlessness was augmented the more, when he reflected on the apparent unwillingness of saint John to reveal himself to the Jews. Hence he suspected, that his having called himself a "voice" was only a covered way of speaking. The devil argued, that if saint John had called himself openly the Word of God he would have thereby revealed his Divinity; hence, in order not to discover himself, he had assumed the name "voice" instead of "word." Into such confusion of mind did Lucifer fall concerning the

mystery of the Incarnation; and, while he believed the Jews had been deluded and misled, he himself was cast into a much greater error by his false theology.

360. Thus deceived, his fury against the Baptist outgrew all bounds. But remembering his defeats in the battles against the Savior, and conscious of having had just as little success in leading saint John into any grave fault, he resolved to make war upon him by another channel. And he found such a channel already prepared. The Baptist had reprehended Herod for his disgraceful and adulterous connection with Herodias, who had openly left her husband, Philip, his brother, as is related by the Evangelists (Marc. 6, 17). Herod was aware of the holiness of saint John and of his sayings; he held him in fear and veneration and listened to him with pleasure. But whatever force the truth and the light of reason exerted in Herod, it was readily perverted to evil by the malicious and boundless hatred of the wicked Herodias and her daughter, who was like her mother in morals. The adulterous woman was deeply degraded by her passions and sensuality, and therefore lent herself readily as an instrument of demoniac malice. This woman, having been previously instigated by the devil to procure the death of saint John in different ways, now incited the king to condemn him to death. He that had called himself the voice of God and who was the greatest of womanborn, was therefore taken prisoner. The anniversary of the unfortunate birthday of Herod was to be celebrated by a banquet and ball, given by him to the magistrates and nobles of Galilee, of which he was king. The degraded Herodias brought her daughter to the feast, in order to dance before the guests. The blinded and adulterous king was so taken in by the dancing girl, that he promised her any gift or favor she desired, even if it were the half of his kingdom. She, directed by her mother (and both of them by the devil), asked for more than a kingdom, yea, more than

many kingdoms, namely, the head of John the Baptist, and that it be given to her immediately on a plate. The king commanded it to be done on account of the oath he had taken and because he had subjected himself to the influence of a vile and degraded woman. Men are accustomed to consider it an unbearable offense to be called a woman, because they think it denies them the superiority deemed peculiar to manhood; but it is a greater disgrace to be governed and led about by women's whims; for he that obeys, is inferior to the one that commands. And yet many are thus degraded without adverting thereto, and so much the greater is their degradation, the more immodest the woman they follow; for, having lost the virtue of modesty, nothing remains in a woman, which is not most despicable and abominable in the sight of God and man.

361. During the imprisonment of saint John brought about by Herodias, he was much favored by our Savior and by his Mother. The Lady comforted him many times by sending her holy angels, sometimes also ordering them to prepare and bring him nourishment. The Lord also conferred on him many interior graces and favors. But the demon who wished to destroy him, gave no rest to Herodias until he should see him dead. He eagerly seized the occasion of the banquet, inciting Herod to utter that foolish promise and oath for the sake of Herodias' daughter and confusing his mind so that he impiously looked upon a failure to fulfill his sworn promise as a sin and as a dishonor, and thus in his blindness he delivered the head of the Baptist to the dancing girl, as is related in the Gospel. At the same time the Queen of the world was, in the usual manner, made aware of the interior will of her most holy Son, that the hour of martyrdom had arrived for the Baptist and that he should give his life in testimony of the truths he had preached. The most pure Mother prostrated Herself at the feet of Christ our Lord

and tearfully implored Him to assist his servant and Precursor in that hour, to comfort and console him, and that his death might be so much the more precious in his eyes in view of his suffering for the honor and defense of the truth.

362. The Savior responded to her petition with much pleasure, saying that He would fulfill it entirely and bidding Her immediately to accompany Him on a visit to saint John, Then Christ and his holy Mother were miraculously and invisibly borne to the dungeon cell where saint John lay fettered in chains and wounded in many parts of his body; for the wicked adulteress, wishing to do away with him, had ordered some of her servants, (six on three different occasions), to scourge and maltreat him, which they actually did in order to please their mistress. By these means this tigress had attempted to murder the Baptist before the banquet at which Herod commanded him to be beheaded. The devil incited these cruel henchmen to assail saint John with vilest insults and bodily ill-treatment for they were most wicked men, fit servants of such an accursed and infamous adulteress. The presence of Christ and his blessed Mother filled that foul prison of the Baptist with celestial light. While the other parts of the palace of Herod were infested by innumerable demons and sycophants more criminal than the state prisoners in their dungeons below, the cell of saint John was entirely sanctified by the presence of the Sovereigns of heaven, who were accompanied by a great host of angels.

363. As soon as the Precursor beheld before him the Redeemer and his Mother in the midst of the angelic hosts, his chains fell from him and his wounds were healed. With ineffable joy he prostrated himself on the ground and in deepest humility and admiration asked the blessing of the incarnate Word and his blessed Mother. Having fulfilled his request, They remained for some time holding divine converse with their friend and servant, which I cannot all repeat

here, though I will mention some of what impressed itself more vividly on my dull mind. In kindest tone and manner the Savior said: "John, my servant, how eagerly thou pressest on to be persecuted, imprisoned and scourged, and to offer thy life for the glory of my Father even before I myself enter upon my sufferings! Thy desires are quickly approaching their fulfillment, since thou art soon to enjoy thy reward in suffering tribulations such as I myself have in view for my humanity; but it is thus the eternal Father rewards the zeal with which thou hast fulfilled the office of being my Precursor. Let thy loving anxieties now cease and offer thy neck to the axe; for such is my wish, and thus shalt thou enjoy the happiness of suffering and dying for my name. I offer to the eternal Father thy life, in order that mine be yet prolonged."

364. The sweetness and power of these words penetrated the heart of the Baptist and filled it with such delights of divine love, that for a time he could not give any answer. But being reenforced by divine grace and dissolved in tears, he thanked his Lord and Master for the ineffable favor of this visit, which was now added to so many other great ones he had received at his hands; and with sighs of love from his inmost soul he said:

"My eternal God and Lord, I cannot ever merit pains or sufferings worthy of such a great consolation and privilege as that of enjoying thy divine presence and that of thy exalted Mother, my Mistress; altogether unworthy am I of this new blessing. In order that thy boundless mercy may be exalted, permit me, Lord, to die before Thee, so that thy holy name may be made more widely known; and look with favor on my desire of enduring the most painful and lingering death. Let Herod and sin, and hell itself, triumph over me in my death, for I offer my life for Thee, my Beloved, in the joy of my heart. Receive it, my God, as a pleasing sacrifice. And thou, Mother of my Savior and my Mistress, turn thy most loving eyes in clemency upon thy servant and continue to show him thy favor as a Mother and as the cause of all blessing. During all my life I have despised vanities and loved the Cross, which is to be sanctified by my Redeemer; I have desired to sow in tears; but never could I have merited the delight of such a visit, which has sweetened all my sufferings, gladdened my bondage and makes death itself more pleasing and acceptable than life."

365. While They were yet engaged in this conversation, three servants of Herod entered his prison with a hangman ready to execute upon him the implacable fury of the cruel adultress. Saint John presented his neck and the executioner fulfilled the impious order of Herod by cutting off his head. The High Priest Christ at the Same moment received in his arms the body of the Saint, while his blessed Mother held his head in her hands, both of Them offering this victim to the eternal Father on the altar of their sacred hands. This was possible not only because the two Sovereigns of the world were invisible, but also because the servants of Herod had begun to quarrel as to which of them should flatter the infamous dancer and her mother by bringing them the head of saint John. In their dispute one of them, without paying attention to any other circumstance, snatched the head from the hands of the Queen of heaven and the rest of them followed in order to offer it on a plate to the daughter of Herodias. The sacred soul of the Baptist, in the company of a multitude of angels, was sent to limbo, and its arrival renewed the joy of the holy souls there imprisoned. The Sovereigns of heaven returned to the place, whence they had come. Of the holiness and excellence of the great Precursor many things are written in the Church, and although I have been informed of several other mysteries concerning him, which I could relate, I cannot depart from my original purpose or extend this history in writing of them. I wish only to say, that

the fortunate and blessed Precursor of Christ received great favors at the hands of Christ the Redeemer and his holy Mother during the whole course of his life: in his happy birth, his stay in the desert, his preaching and in his holy death. Such wonders were wrought for no other man by the right hand of God.

Words of the Queen

THE VIRGIN MARY SPEAKS TO SISTER MARY OF AGREDA

366. My daughter, thou hast been very short in describing the mysteries of this chapter; yet a great lesson is contained therein for thee and all the children of light. Write it in thy heart and notice well the great difference between the innocence and holiness of the Baptist, who was poor, afflicted, persecuted and imprisoned, and the abominable wickedness of Herod, the powerful king, who was flattered and served in the midst of his riches and base pleasures. Both were of the same human nature, but entirely different in the sight of God, according as they used ill or well their free will and the created things around them. The penance, poverty, humility, contempt, tribulations of saint John, and his zeal for the glory of my divine Son, merited for him the singular favor of dying in our arms. Herod, on the contrary, by his hollow pomp, his pride, vanity, tyranny and wickedness was struck down by the minister of God in order to be punished in the eternal flames. Remember that the same happens now and always in the world; although men do not pay attention to it or fear it. They fear the vain strength of the world, not reflecting that it is but fleeting shadow and withering grass.

367. Just as little do men think of the ultimate end, and of the abyss, into which vices draw them even in this world. Although the demon cannot take away man's liberty, nor ever completely sway his free will, yet, by leading them into

so many and grievous sins, he obtains such an influence over it, that he is enabled to use it as an instrument of the evil he proposes. In spite of witnessing so many and such terrible examples, men remain callous to the fearful danger to which they expose themselves by their sins in imitation of Herod and his adulterous concubine. In order to cast souls into this abyss of wickedness Lucifer meets them with the vain pride and honor of this world and with its base pleasures, representing them as alone important and desirable. Thus the ignorant children of perdition loosen the bonds of reason in order to follow the degrading pleasures of their flesh and be enslaved by their mortal enemy. My daughter, the Savior and I have taught the way of humility, of contempt, and tribulation. This is the royal road, on which we first walked, and of which We have set Ourselves up as Teachers. We are the Protectors of all the afflicted and illused, ready to assist by miraculous and especial favors all those who call upon Us in their necessities. Of this assistance and protection the followers of this world and its vain pleasures deprive themselves, since they hate the way of the Cross. To the Cross thou wast called and invited, and on account of it thou art favored with the sweetness of my loving guidance. Follow me and labor to imitate me, since thou hast found the secret treasure (Matth. 12, 44) and the precious pearl, for the possession of which thou must despise all that is earthly and give up all human freedom in so far as it is contrary to the pleasure of my most exalted Lord.

Chapter V

THE FAVORS BESTOWED UPON THE APOSTLES BY CHRIST, THE SAVIOR, ON ACCOUNT OF THEIR DEVOTION TO HIS MOST HOLY MOTHER, AND THE SAD PERDITION OF JUDAS ON ACCOUNT OF NEGLECT OF THIS DEVOTION.

368. One of the great miracles of divine omnipotence and a wonder of wonders was the conduct of the most holy Mary toward the Apostles and disciples of her Son and Savior Christ. A full account of her wisdom is impossible to human tongue, and if I would wish to describe no more than what I have been made to understand concerning this matter, I would be obliged to write a large volume. I will touch upon it in this chapter and as occasion requires in the rest of this history. All that I can say is very little, yet from it the faithful can infer enough for their instruction. All those whom the Savior received into his divine school, were to see and treat familiarly his most blessed Mother. Hence He infused into their hearts an especial reverence and devotion toward that blessed Lady. But though this infused reverence was common to all, it was not equal in all the disciples; for the Lord distributed his gifts according to his free will in reference to their dispositions and in accordance with the duties and offices for which each one was destined. By conversation and familiar intercourse with their great Queen and Lady their reverential love and devotion was to grow and increase; for

the blessed Lady spoke to all, loved them, consoled them, instructed and assisted them in their necessities, without ever permitting them to leave her conversation and presence unreplenished by interior joy and consolation greater than they had asked for. Yet the measure of good fruit derived from them was dependent upon the disposition of the heart of those that received these favors.

369. They were all enabled to begin their intercourse with the Mother of God in high admiration of her prudence, wisdom, purity, holiness and great majesty, and were made sensible of a sweetness in Her inexpressibly humble and pleasing. This was so ordained by the Most High, because as I have said in the fifth book, chapter twentysecond, it was not yet time to reveal this mystic Ark of the new Testament to the world. Thus, just as the Lord, however much He wished to break forth in her praise, could not manifest it in words and concentrated it within his heart; so the holy Apostles, sweetly constrained into silence, found a vent for their fervent feelings in a so much the more intense love of most holy Mary and praise of her Maker. As the great Lady, on account of her peerless insight knew the natural disposition of each of the disciples, his measure of grace, his present condition and future office, She proceeded according to this knowledge in her petitions and prayers, in her instructions and conversings with them, and in the favors She obtained for each in support of his vocation. Such a loving zeal in the conduct of a mere Creature so entirely pleasing to the wishes of his Lord, excited a new and boundless admiration in the holy angels. Of no less admiration was the hidden providence of the Almighty by which the Apostles were made to correspond to the blessings and favors received by them at the intercession of the most holy Mother. All this caused a divine harmony of action, hidden to men and manifest only to the heavenly spirits.

370. Especially signalized for the reception of these sacramental favors were saint Peter and saint John; the former
because he was destined to be the vicar of Christ and head of
the militant Church and because he therefore deserved the
special reverence and love of the holy Mother; the latter
because he was to take the place of the Lord after his Passion
in attending upon and conversing with the heavenly Lady
upon earth. As therefore the government and custody of the
mystic Church. namely of Mary immaculate and of the
visible militant Church, namely the faithful on earth, was to
be divided between these two Apostles, it was no wonder,
that they should be singularly favored by the great Queen of
the world. But as saint John was chosen to serve Mary and
attain the dignity of an adopted son of the Mistress of heav-
en, he at once began to experience special urgings of grace
and signalize himself in the service of the most holy Mary.
Although all the Apostles excelled in devotion to the Queen
beyond our power of understanding or conception, the
evangelist saint John penetrated deeper into the mysteries of
this City of God and received through Her such divine
enlightenment as to excel all the other Apostles. This is also
evident from his Gospel (John 21, 20) ; all the divine insight
therein manifested he received through the Queen of heaven,
and the distinction of being called the beloved disciple of
Jesus, he gained by his love toward the most blessed Mother.
As this love was reciprocated by the heavenly Lady, he became the most beloved disciple both of Jesus and Mary.

371. The Evangelist, besides chastity and virginal purity,
possessed some other virtues which were especially pleasing
to the Queen; among them were a dovelike simplicity, as is
manifest from his writings, and a great gentleness and humility, which made him most meek and tractable. The heavenly
Mother always looked upon the peaceful and the humble as
the most faithful imitators of her divine Son. On this ac-

count the blessed Queen favored saint John above all the other Apostles and he himself became more and more anxious to serve Her with ever increasing reverential love and affection. From the very first moment of his vocation saint John commenced to excel all the rest in piety toward the Mother Mary and to fulfill the least of her wishes as her most humble slave. He attended upon Her more assiduously than the rest; and whenever it was possible he sought to be in her company and take upon himself some of the bodily labors connected with her present life. Sometimes it happened that the fortunate Apostle competed with the holy angels in his zeal for thus assisting the great Queen; while She still more eagerly sought to perform these works of humility Herself; for in this virtue She triumphed over all other creatures and none of them could ever hope in the least to surpass or equal Her in acts of humility. The beloved disciple was very diligent in reporting to the heavenly Lady the works and miracles wrought by the Savior, whenever She herself could not be present, and in informing Her of the new disciples converted by his teaching. He was constantly alert and studious to serve Her in the least of her wishes, fulfilling each one of them with a loving eagerness.

372. Saint John also distinguished himself by the reverence with which he spoke to Mary, for in her presence he always called Her "Lady," or "my Mistress;" and in Her absence he entitled Her "Mother of our Master Jesus." After the Ascension of the Lord when speaking of Her, he was the first to call Her "Mother of God and of the Redeemer of the world;" and when speaking to Her he addressed Her "Mother" and "Mistress." In her honor he invented also the other titles calling Her "The propitiation for sin" and "the Mistress of Nations." In particular saint John invented the title "Mary of Jesus," as She was often called in the primitive Church; and he gave Her that name, because he knew that the sound

of these words awoke the sweetest memories in the heart of the blessed Virgin. I also desire to give joyful thanks to the Lord, that without my merits He has called me to the light of holy faith and to the religious life, which I profess under this very name of Mary of Jesus. The other Apostles were well aware of the favor in which he stood with most holy Mary, and they often asked him to be their messenger in their behalf for what they desired to say or ask of their Queen. The gentle intercession of this holy Apostle often procured for them tokens of the loving kindness of the sweetest Mother. Concerning this intercourse of saint John with the Mother of grace, I will say more in the third part and it would be easy to write an extensive history in merely mentioning the favors and blessings obtained by saint John from this Mistress and Queen of the world.

373. Next to saint Peter and saint John, saint James was most beloved by the blessed Mother. He was the brother of saint John, and, as we shall see from some instances to be related in the third part of this history, he obtained admirable favors at the hands of the great Lady. Also saint Andrew was among those especially favored by the Queen; because She knew of his great devotion to the passion and cross of Christ and of his being destined to die on it like his divine Master. I will not stop to speak of her love toward the other Apostles, for She regarded them all with great affection, some on account of one virtue, some on account of another, and all of them because of their connection with her most holy Son. This affection toward them She showed with rarest prudence, humility and charity. Magdalen also had a share in her special love; for Mary knew that the love of this woman for her Son was most ardent and that this great penitent was eminently chosen for the manifestation of the magnificence of God's mercy toward men. Most holy Mary distinguished her before the other women in her familiar intercourse and

enlightened her in regard to most exalted mysteries, by which
She inflamed still more the love of Magdalen toward Jesus
and toward Herself. The holy penitent consulted the heavenly Lady in regard to her desire of retreating into solitude in
order to live in continual contemplation and penance; and
the sweetest Mother instructed her in the deep mysteries of
solitary life. This life She afterwards embraced with the
consent and blessing of the Queen. Later on Mary visited her
in her retreat in person and by means of the angels often
encouraged and consoled Magdalen in the horrors of the
desert. The other women, who were in the company of Jesus,
were much favored by the most blessed Mother; all of them
and all the disciples of the Lord experienced her incomparable kindness and they were filled with an intense devotion
and affection toward the Mistress and Mother of grace. They
drew of the treasures of grace from Her as from a storehouse,
where God had laid up his gifts for the whole human race. I
do not dwell longer on this doctrine, for, aside of its being
unnecessary since it is expounded by our holy Church, it
would consume much time to do it justice.

374. I will, however, say something of that which has
been made known to me concerning the wicked Apostle
Judas; for it belongs to this history and less is known of him.
It will at the same time be a warning to the obstinate and an
admonition for those little devoted to the most blessed Mary;
for it is a sad truth that there should be any mortals who
entertain little love toward a Creature so lovable, and One
whom the infinite God himself loves without bound or
measure; whom the angels love with all their heavenly powers, the Apostles and saints from their inmost souls, whom all
creatures should eagerly strive to love, and who never can be
loved according to her merits. Yet this unhappy Apostle
strayed from the royal road of divine love and its blessings.
The understanding, which has been given me concerning this

defection for the purpose of making it known in this history, is contained in the following paragraphs.

375. Judas was attracted to the school of Christ our Teacher by his forceful doctrines, and was filled with the same good intentions which moved the others. Powerfully drawn by these motives, he asked the Savior to admit him among his disciples, and the Savior received him with the bowels of a loving Father, who rejects none that come to Him in search of truth. In the beginning Judas merited special favors and forged ahead of some of the other disciples, deserving to be numbered among the twelve Apostles; for the Savior loved his soul according to its present state of grace and his good works, just as He did the others. The Mother of grace and mercy observed the same course with him, although by her infused knowledge She immediately became aware of the perfidious treachery with which he was to end his apostolate. She did not, on this account, deny him her intercession and maternal love; but she applied Herself even more zealously to justify as far as possible the cause of her divine Son against this perfidious and unfortunate man, in order that his wickedness, as soon as it should be put into action, might not have the shadow of an excuse before men. Well knowing that such a character as his could not be overcome by rigor, but would only be driven by it to so much the greater obstinacy, the most prudent Lady took care, that none of the wants or the comforts of Judas should be ignored and She began to treat him, speak and listen to him more gently and lovingly than to all the rest. This She carried so far, that Judas, when the disciples once disputed among themselves concerning their standing with the Queen (as, according to the Evangelist [Luke 22, 24], it happened also concerning the Redeemer), never experienced the least jealousy or doubt in this matter; for the blessed Lady in the beginning always distinguished him by tokens of special love

and he, at that time, also showed himself thankful for these favors.

376. But as Judas found little support in his natural disposition, and as the disciples, not being as yet confirmed in virtue and not as yet even in grace, were guilty of some human failings, the imprudent man began to compliment himself on his perfection and to take more notice of the faults of his brethren than of his own (Luke 6,41). He permitted himself thus to be deceived, making no effort to amend or repent, he allowed the beam in his own eyes to grow while watching the splinters in the eyes of others. Complaining of their little faults and seeking, with more presumption than zeal, to correct the weaknesses of his brethren, he committed greater sins himself. Among the other Apostles he singled out saint John, looking upon him as an intermeddler and accusing him in his heart of ingratiating himself with the Master and his blessed Mother. The fact that he received so many special favors from Them was of no avail to deter him from this false assumption. Yet so far Judas had committed only venial sins and had not lost sanctifying grace. But they argued a very bad disposition, in which he willfully persevered. He had freely entertained a certain vain complacency in himself; this at once called into existence a certain amount of envy, which brought on a calumnious spirit and harshness in judging of the faults of his brethren. These sins opened the way for greater sins; for immediately the fervor of his devotion decreased, his charity toward God and men grew cold, and his interior light was lost and extinguished; he began to look upon the Apostles and upon the most holy Mother with a certain disgust and find little pleasure in their intercourse and their heavenly activity.

377. The most prudent Lady perceived the growth of this defection in Judas. Eagerly seeking his recovery and salvation before he should cast himself entirely into the death of sin,

She spoke to him and exhorted him as her beloved child and with extreme sweetness and force of reasoning. Although at times this storm of tormenting thoughts, which had begun to rise in the breast of Judas, was allayed; yet it was only for a short time, and soon it arose and disturbed him anew. Giving entrance to the devil into his heart, he permitted a furious rage against the most meek Dove to take possession of him. With insidious hypocrisy he sought to deny his sins or palliate them by alleging other reasons for his conduct: as if he could ever deceive Jesus and Mary and hide from Them the secrets of his heart. Thereby he lost his interior reverence for the Mother of mercy, despising her exhortations and openly reproaching Her for her gentle words and reasoning. This ungrateful presumption threw him from the state of grace, the Lord was highly incensed and deservedly left him to his own evil counsels. By thus designedly rejecting the kindness and the intercession of most holy Mary, he closed against himself the gates of mercy and of his only salvation. His disgust with the sweetest Mother soon engendered in him an abhorrence of his Master; he grew dissatisfied with his doctrines and began to look upon the life of an Apostle and intercourse with the disciples as too burdensome.

378. Nevertheless divine Providence did not abandon him immediately, but continued to send him interior assistance, although in comparison with former helps they were of a kind more common and ordinary. They were, however, in themselves sufficient for his salvation, if he would have made use of them. To these graces were added the gentle exhortations of the kindest Mistress, urging him to restrain himself and to humble himself and ask pardon of his divine Master. She offered him mercy in his name and her own kind assistance in obtaining it, promising to do penance for him, if he would consent to be sorry for his sins and amend his life. All these advances did the Mother of grace make in

order to prevent the fall of Judas. She was well aware, that
not seeking to arise from a fall and to persevere in sin was a
much greater evil than to have fallen. The conscience of this
proud disciple could not but reproach him with his wickedness; but becoming hardened in his heart, he began to dread
the humiliation, which would have been to his credit, and he
fell into still greater sins. In his pride he rejected the salutary
counsels of the Mother of Christ and chose rather to deny his
guilt, protesting with a lying tongue, that he loved his Master
and all the rest, and that there was no occasion for amending
his conduct in this regard.

379. It was indeed an admirable example of patience and
charity which Christ, our Savior, and his most blessed Mother gave us in their conduct toward Judas after his fall into sin;
for as long as he remained in their company, They never
showed exteriorly any change or irritation in their behavior
toward him, nor did They cease to treat him with the same
kindness and gentleness as all the rest. This was the reason
why the wickedness of Judas, who necessarily showed signs of
his evil state in his daily conversation and intercourse, remained so long concealed to the Apostles. For it is not easy,
and perhaps not possible, continually to cover up or hide the
tendencies of one's mind. In matters not depending upon
deliberation we always act according to our character and our
habits, and thus we disclose them at least to the watchful eyes
of those with whom we have much intercourse. But as all of
the disciples witnessed the constant affability and love of
Christ our Redeemer and his most blessed Mother toward
Judas, they suppressed their suspicions and ignored the
exterior proofs of his wickedness. Hence all of them were
much disturbed and agitated, when at the last Supper the
Lord told them, that one of them was to betray Him (Matth.
24); and each one searched his soul, whether the accusation
could refer to his own self. Saint John, on account of his

greater intimacy, had some suspicion of the wicked doings of Judas and he was made more restless by his love; therefore Jesus pointed out the traitor, but only by a sign, as is related in the Gospel (John 13, 26). Before that time the Lord had not given the least intimation of what was passing in the heart of Judas. This forbearance was yet more wonderful in the most blessed Mary, who, though the Mother of Christ and a mere Creature, saw his perfidious betrayal close at hand and about to cause the death of her own Son, whom She loved so tenderly as a Mother and as a Handmaid.

380. O ignorance and folly of men! How differently do we behave, if we are slightly affronted, though we deserve it so much! How unwillingly do we bear with the weaknesses of others, though expecting all men to bear with ours! How grudgingly we pardon an offense, though daily and hourly asking the Lord to pardon us our own! (Matth.6. 12). How prompt and cruel are we in making known the faults of our brethren, yet how resentful and angry at any word of criticism against us! None do we measure with the same measure with which we desire to be measured, and we do not wish to be judged by the same standard as we judge others (Matth. 7, 1, 2). All this is perversity and darkness, a breath from the mouth of the hellish dragon, who wishes to stem the flow of the most precious virtue of charity and disconcert the order of human and divine reasonableness; for God is charity, and he who exercises it perfectly is in God and God is in him. Lucifer is wrath and vengeance and all those that yield to these vices follow the devil, who is leading them on to all the vices opposed to the good of the neighbor. Though the beauty of this virtue of charity has always filled my heart with the desire of possessing it fully, nevertheless I see, as in a clear mirror, that I have arrived not even at a beginning of this most noble virtue as exhibited in these wonders of divine charity toward the most ungrateful disciple Judas.

381. In order that I may not incur the blame of concealing what belongs to this chapter, I will mention another cause of the ruin of Judas. When the number of the Apostles and disciples increased, the Lord resolved to appoint one of them to take charge of the alms received; thus to supply the common needs and pay the imperial tribute. Jesus made known his wishes to all indiscriminately without addressing Himself to anyone in particular. While all of them feared such an office and sought to evade it, Judas immediately strove to obtain it. In order to secure his appointment he humbled himself so far as to ask saint John to speak to the most holy Queen and induce Her to arrange this matter for him with her Son. Saint John yielded to the request of Judas and spoke to the most prudent Mother; but She, knowing that this request of Judas was not proper or just, but proceeded from ambition and avarice, did not wish to propose it to the divine Master. The same kind of influence Judas sought to bring into play through saint Peter and other Apostles, without success; for the Lord in his goodness wished to stay his ruin, and justify his cause before men, if He should grant the request. At this resistance the heart of Judas, already corrupted by avarice, instead of quietly yielding, was consumed with unhappy desires for the office, and the devil stirred up thoughts of vilest ambition, such as would have been most improper and wicked in anyone, and hence were much more culpable in Judas, who had been a disciple in the school of highest perfection and who had lived in the light of the Sun of justice and its beautiful Moon, Mary! Neither in the day of abundant graces, when the Sun Jesus lighted his paths, nor in the night of temptations, when the Moon Mary disclosed to him the wiles of the poisonous serpent, could he have failed to become aware of the wickedness of such suggestions. But, as he flew from the light and cast himself willfully into darkness, he presumed to ask most

holy Mary in a direct manner for her influence in obtaining his object. He had lost all fear and hid his avarice in the cloak of virtue. Approaching Her, he said that he had made his request through saint Peter and saint John, with the sole desire of diligently serving Her and his divine Master, since not all would attend to the duties of this office with proper solicitude; and that, therefore, he now asked Her to obtain the position of purser for him from the Master.

382. The great Lady answered him with extreme gentleness: "Consider well, my dearest, what thou askest, and examine whether thy intentions are upright. Ponder well, whether it is good for thee to seek that which all thy brethren fear and refuse to accept, unless they shall be compelled thereto by the command of their Lord and Master. He loves thee more than thou lovest thyself and without doubt knows what will benefit thee; resign thyself to his most holy will, change thy purpose, and seek to grow rich in humility and poverty. Rise from thy fall, for I will extend thee a helpful hand and my Son will show thee his loving mercy." Who would not have yielded to these sweetest words and such urgent advice, spoken by such an amiable and heavenly Creature as was most holy Mary? But this fierce and adamantine heart was not softened or moved. On the contrary, the soul of Judas was offended and enraged against the heavenly Lady for thus offering him a means of escaping from his dreadful danger. Boundless ambition and avarice roused his fury against Her who seemed to hinder him in his projects and he considered her well-meant advice as an insult. But the most meek and loving Dove pretended not to notice his obstinacy and said nothing more to him at that time.

383. After his interview with most holy Mary, the avarice of Judas would not allow him to rest; casting off all modesty and natural shame (and the least spark of faith), Judas now resolved to apply to his divine Master and Savior. Clothing

himself like a consummate hypocrite in the garb of a sheep, he went to his Master and said: "Master, I wish to fulfill thy wishes and serve Thee as thy purser and as the dispenser of the alms which we receive; I will look to the interests of the poor, fulfilling thy doctrine that we should do unto others as we wish them to do unto us, and I will see to it that alms are distributed according to thy wishes, more profitably and orderly than hitherto." Such reasoning the specious hypocrite boldly used, committing many enormous sins in one and the same act. For, first of all he lied, concealing his real intention. Then, being ambitious of an honor which he did not merit, he neither wished to appear in his true light nor did he wish to be in truth what he merely pretended to be. He also blamed his brethren, discrediting them and praising himself: the ordinary course of those who are ambitious. What is especially to be noticed in this conduct of Judas is that he showed his loss of infused faith; for he attempted to deceive Christ, his divine Master, by wearing the cloak of hypocrisy. For, if he had firmly believed that Christ was true God and man who penetrated into the secrets of the heart, he could not have hoped to be able to deceive Him; nor would he have attempted such double dealing, not only because he would have known Christ as the omniscient God, but because he would not have hoped to impose upon the infused and beatific science of Christ as man. Hence Judas had lost belief in all these prerogatives, and to his other sins, added the sin of heresy.

384. What the Apostle says in his first letter to Timothy was literally fulfilled in this treacherous disciple: "For they that will become rich, fall into temptation and into the snares of the devil and into many unprofitable and hurtful desires, which drown men into destruction and perdition. For the desire of money is the root of all evils; which some coveting have erred from the faith and have entangled themselves in

many sorrows" (I Tim. 6,9). All this happened to the perfidious and avaricious disciple, and his avarice was so much the more blamable, since he had the striking and admirable example of Christ and of his Mother and that of the whole apostolic company before his eyes; and they all accepted only very moderate alms. But the wicked disciple imagined that on account of the great miracles of his Master and the multitudes which followed and gathered around Him, the alms and offerings would increase and he could have at his disposal large amounts. Seeing that his expectations were not realized, he was much disappointed, as he plainly showed on the occasion of the anointing of the Lord by Mary Magdalen (Mark 14, 4) ; his desire of gathering in alms induced him to estimate the value of the ointment at three hundred pence and to complain that this money was withheld from the poor, among whom it could have been distributed. He was moved to say this because he regretted very much not to lay hands on it himself; little cared he for the poor. He was highly incensed against the Mother of mercy because She distributed such generous alms among the poor; against the Lord because He would not accept large donations, and against the Apostles and disciples because they did not ask for them. All this vexed him sorely because his purse was thereby kept empty. Some months before the Death of the Savior, he began frequently to avoid the other Apostles, absenting himself from their company and from the Redeemer; for the intercourse with them was getting irksome to him, and he joined them only in order to collect what donations he could. During these times of absence the demon inspired him with the thought of breaking entirely with the Master and of delivering Him over to the Jews.

385. But let us return to the answer given to Judas by the Master, whom he asked to make him purser. We shall see how hidden and terrible are the judgments of the Most High.

The Redeemer wished to ward off from him the danger which lay behind this request and which threatened the avaricious Apostle with final perdition. In order that Judas might not excuse himself under plea of ignorance, the Lord answered him: "Dost thou know, Judas, what thou seekest and what thou askest? Be not so cruel toward thy own self as to solicit and seek to obtain the poison and the arms which may cause thy death." Judas replied: "Master I desire to serve Thee by employing my strength in the service of thy faithful followers and in this way I can do it better than in any other; for I offer to fulfill all the duties of this office without fail." This daring presumption of Judas in seeking and coveting danger, justified the cause of God in allowing him to enter and perish in the danger thus sought and coveted. He resisted the light (Eccli. 15, 17), and hardened himself against it, water and fire was shown him, life and death: he stretched forth his hand and chose perdition. The justice of the Most High was made clear and his mercy was exalted, since He had so often presented Himself at the portals of this hardened heart, whence He had been spurned in order to make way for the devil. Later on I will mention further particulars of the wickedness of Judas as a warning to mortals; for I do not wish to prolong this chapter too much and they will fit better into other parts of this history. What mortal, subject to sin, will not be seized with great fear when he thus sees one of his fellow beings, who belonged to the school of Christ and of his blessed Mother, who was reared in the light of his doctrines and miracles, who performed the same wonders as the rest, in so short a time pass from the condition of an Apostle into that of a demon? transform himself from an innocent sheep into a ravening and bloodthirsty wolf? From venial sins, Judas proceeded to most grievous and horrible crimes. He yielded himself to the devil, who already suspected that Christ was God and who began to exercise the wrath he had against the Lord upon this unfortunate disciple strayed from the little flock. If then the fury of Lucifer is just as great and much greater after having learnt to his cost that Christ is the true God and Redeemer, what hope has the soul of escaping this inhuman and cruel enemy who so vehemently and furiously seeks our eternal damnation?

Words of the Queen

THE VIRGIN MARY SPEAKS TO SISTER MARY OF AGREDA

386. My daughter, all that thou hast written in this chapter is a most important warning for all those that live in the flesh and in the imminent danger of losing their eternal happiness. It should teach them to seek my most kind and powerful intercession and to fear the judgments of the Most High; for in this lies an efficacious means of salvation and of meriting higher reward for the Lord. I wish to remind thee once more, that among the secrets revealed to the beloved John at the last Supper, was also this, that he had become the beloved disciple of Christ on account of his love toward me, and that Judas fell because he despised the mercy and kindness which I had shown him. At that time, also, the Evangelist understood other great mysteries communicated and wrought in me; that I should take part in the labor and suffering of the Passion and that he should have special charge of me. My dearest, the purity which I require of thee must be greater than that of an angel; and if thou strive after it thou wilt become my dearest child, as saint John, and a most beloved and favored spouse of my Son and Lord. His example and the ruin of Judas should continually serve thee as a stimulus and as a warning, to seek only after my love and to be sincerely thankful for the love shown thee without thy merit.

387. I wish thee also to understand another secret hidden from the world: namely, that one of the most vile and horri-

ble sins before the Lord is the little esteem in which the just and the friends of the Church are held, and especially the little veneration shown toward me, who was chosen for his Mother and am the cause of the happiness of all men. If the failure to love the enemies and contempt of them is so displeasing to the Lord and to the saints of heaven (Matth. 18, 35), how shall He bear with such treatment of his most dear friends, whom He holds as the apple of his eye and in deepest affection? (Ps. 33, 16). This counsel thou canst never bear in mind too much in this mortal life, and it is one of the signs of reprobation to hold in abhorrence the just. Beware of this danger and judge no one, especially those that reprehend and admonish thee (Matth. 7, 1). Do not allow thyself to desire worldly things, least of all any office of superiority; a desire which allures the human sense, disturbs the judgment and obscures reason. Envy no one his honor, nor the possession of any earthly thing, nor seek to obtain from the Lord anything else than his love and friendship. Man is full of blindest inclinations, and if he does not restrain them, he will begin to ask for that which will cause his eternal perdition. Sometimes the Lord, according to hidden judgments, grants these petitions in punishment for wicked desires and of other sins, as it happened with Judas. Such souls receive earthly reward for any good actions which they may have performed during mortal life. If thou wilt look into the deceptive course of the lovers of this world, thou wilt see that they consider themselves fortunate, whenever they attain all that they desire according to their earthly inclinations. This only hastens their greater misfortune; for they, having received their reward, cannot expect any in the eternal life. But the just, who despise the world and meet with many adversities, are withdrawn and shielded from danger, because the Lord denies them the temporal goods, which they desire and ask for. In order that thou mayest not fall into such danger, I exhort and command thee never to hanker after nor to seek earthly possession. Separate thyself from all; preserve thy will free and independent; never desire for anything beyond what is God's pleasure, for He will assume charge of all those that resign themselves to his divine Providence.

Chapter VI

CHRIST IS TRANSFIGURED ON MOUNT TABOR IN THE
PRESENCE OF HIS MOST HOLY MOTHER; THEY GO FROM
GALILEE TO JERUSALEM PREPARATORY TO THE PASSION;
AND THE SAVIOR IS ANOINTED BY MAGDALEN IN BETHANY.

388. Our Redeemer and Master Jesus had already consumed
more than two years and a half in preaching and performing
wonders, and He was approaching the time predestined by
the eternal wisdom for satisfying divine justice, for redeeming
the human race through his Passion and Death and thus to
return to his eternal Father. Since all his works were ordered
with the highest wisdom for our instruction and salvation,
the Lord resolved to prepare and strengthen some of his
Apostles for the scandal of his Passion by manifesting to
them beforehand in its glory that same body, which He was
so soon to exhibit in the disfigurement of the Cross. Thus
would they be reassured by the thought, that they had seen it
transfigured in glory before they looked upon it disfigured by
his sufferings. This he had promised a short time before in
the presence of all, although not to all, but only to some of
his disciples, as is recorded by saint Matthew (Matth. 16,
28). For his Transfiguration He selected a high mountain in
the center of Galilee, two leagues east of Nazareth and called
Mount Tabor. Ascending to its highest summit with the
three Apostles, Peter, and the two brothers James and John,

He was transfigured before them (Matth. 17, 1; Mark 9, 1; Luke 9, 28). The three Evangelists tell us that besides these Apostles, were present also the two prophets, Moses and Elias, discoursing with Jesus about his Passion, and that, while He was thus transfigured, a voice resounded from heaven in the name of the eternal Father, saying: "This is my beloved Son, in whom I am well pleased: hear ye Him."

389. The Evangelists do not say that most holy Mary was present at this Transfiguration, nor do they say that She was not there; this did not fall within their purpose, and they did not think it proper to speak of the hidden miracle by which She was enabled to be there. For the purpose of recording this event here, I was given to understand that at the same time in which some of the holy angels were commissioned to bring the soul of Moses and Elias from their abode, others of her own guard carried the heavenly Lady to Mount Tabor, in order to witness the Transfiguration of her divine Son, for without a doubt She really witnessed it. There was no necessity of confirming the most holy Mother in her faith, as was necessary with the Apostles; for She was invincibly confirmed in faith. But the Lord had many different objects in view at his Transfiguration; and there were special reasons for his not wishing to celebrate this great event without the presence of his most holy Mother. What for the Apostles was a gratuitous favor, was a duty in regard to the Queen and Mother, since She was his Companion and Copartner in the works of the Redemption even to the foot of the Cross. It was proper to fortify Her by this favor against the torments in store for her most holy soul. Moreover, She was to remain on earth as the Teacher of the holy Church, therefore it was proper that She should be one of the eyewitnesses of this great mystery. To grant such a favor was easily within the power of her divine Son, since He was wont to lay open to Her all the workings of his divine soul. Nor would the love of such a

Son permit Him to withhold that favor from his Mother; for He otherwise omitted nothing whereby He could in any way demonstrate his tender love for Her, and this certainly would be a token of highest esteem for her excellence and dignity. I have, therefore, been informed that for these reasons and for many others not necessary to mention here, most holy Mary assisted at the Transfiguration of her divine Son, our Redeemer.

390. During this Transfiguration the blessed Mary saw not only the humanity of Christ our Lord transformed in glory, but She was favored by an intuitive and clear vision of the Divinity itself; for the Lord wished Her to partake of the privilege implied in being present at this event in a more abundant and distinguished manner than the Apostles. Moreover, there was a great difference between her insight and that of the Apostles into the glory of the transfigured body; for the Apostles, as saint Luke tells us (Luke 9, 32), were not only asleep when Jesus at the beginning of this mysterious glorification retired to pray, but they were also seized with such fear at the voice resounding from heaven, that they fell with their faces to the earth and rose not until the Lord himself spoke to them and raised them up (Matth. 17, 6). The blessed Mother, on the other hand, witnessed and heard all these events without undue excitement; for, besides being accustomed to such great manifestations of glory, She was divinely fortified and enlightened for looking upon the Divinity. Hence She was enabled to look fixedly upon the glorified body, without experiencing the terror and weakness of the senses which overtook the Apostles. The most blessed Mother had already on other occasions seen the body of her divine Son glorified, as was related in other parts of this history (Nos. 695, 851); but on this occasion She looked upon Him with much greater enlightenment and with a mind much more alert to all the wonders therein

hidden. Hence, also, the effects caused in Her by this vision were such that She was totally renewed and inflamed by this communication with the Divinity. As long as She lived She never lost the impression caused by the sight of such glory manifested in the humanity of Christ. The memory of it greatly consoled Her in the absence of her divine Son, whenever his glorious presence was not otherwise felt by Her, as we shall see in the third part of this history. Yet on the other hand the memory of this glorious Transfiguration of Christ also made Her feel so much the more deeply the maltreatment experienced by Christ in his Passion and Death.

391. But no human ingenuity can suffice fully to describe the effects of this glorious vision of her Son on her most holy soul. With inmost gratitude and deepest penetration She began to ponder upon what She had seen and heard; exalted praise of the omnipotent God welled forth from her lips, when She considered how her eyes had seen refulgent in glory that same bodily substance, which had been formed of her blood, carried in her womb and nursed at her breast; how She had with her own ears heard the voice of the eternal Father acknowledge her Son as his own and appoint Him as the Teacher of all the human race. With her holy angels She composed new canticles to celebrate an event so full of festive joy for her soul and for the most sacred humanity of her Son. I will not expatiate upon this mystery, nor discuss in what the Transfiguration of the body of Jesus really consisted. It is enough to know that his countenance began to shine like the sun and his garments became whiter than the snow (Matth. 17, 2). This outward splendor was merely the effect of the glory of his Divinity always united to his beatified soul. At his Incarnation, the glory which would naturally have been communicated permanently to his sacred body, was miraculously suspended for the time of his natural life: now, this suspension of his divine glory ceased and the body, for a

short time, was allowed to share the glory of his soul. This is the splendor which became visible to those who were present. Immediately after the miraculous suspense, the divine glory was again confined only to his soul. As his soul was always in the beatified state, so also his body, according to the common order, should have continually shared in this glory, and therefore this transient glorification of his body was likewise a miracle.

392. After the Transfiguration the most blessed Mother was brought back to her house in Nazareth; her divine Son descended the mountain and immediately came to visit her in order to take final leave of his parental province and set out for Jerusalem. There, on the following Pasch, which was to be for Him the last upon earth, He was to enter upon his Passion. Having spent only a few days at Nazareth, He departed with his Mother, his disciples and Apostles and some of the holy women, traveling about through Galilee and Samaria before entering Judea and Jerusalem. The Evangelist saint Luke writes of this journey where he says, that He set his face toward Jerusalem (Luke 9,51); for He journeyed to Jerusalem with a joyous countenance and full of desire to enter upon his sufferings, in order thereby, according to his own most ardent and generous desire, to sacrifice Himself for the human race. He was not to return to Galilee, where He had wrought so many miracles. Knowing this at his departure from Nazareth, He glorified his eternal Father and, in the name of his sacred humanity, gave thanks for having, in that house and neighborhood, received the human form and existence which He was now to deliver over to suffering and death. Of the prayers of Christ our Lord on this occasion I will record as far as I can the following one:

393. "My eternal Father, in compliance with thy will I gladly haste to satisfy thy justice by suffering even unto death. Thus shall I reconcile to Thee all the children of

Adam, paying their debts and opening to them the gates of heaven which have been closed against them. I shall seek those who have turned away and lost themselves, so that they may be restored by the force of my love. I shall find and gather together the lost of the house of Jacob (Is. 56,8), raise up the fallen, enrich the poor, refresh the thirsty, cast down the haughty and exalt the humble. I wish to vanquish hell and enhance the glories of the triumph over Lucifer (I John 3, 8), and over the vices which he has sown into the world. I wish to raise up the standard of the Cross, beneath which virtue, and all those that put themselves under its protection, are to fight their battles. I wish to satiate my heart with insults and affronts, which are so estimable in thy eyes. I wish to humiliate Myself even to death at the hands of mv enemies, in order that our chosen friends may be consoled in their tribulations and that they may be honored by high rewards, whenever they choose to humiliate themselves in suffering the same persecutions. 0 beloved Cross! When shalt thou receive Me in thy arrns? 0 sweet ignominies and affronts! When shalt thou bear Me on to overcome death through the sufferings of my entirely guiltless flesh? Ye pains, affronts, ignominies, scourges, thorns, torments, death, come to Me, who wish to embrace you, yield yourselves to my welcome, since I well understand your value. If the world abhors you, I long for you. If the world, in its ignorance, despises you, I, who am truth and wisdom, love and embrace you. Come then to Me, for in welcoming you as man, I exalt you as the true God and am ready to efface the touch of sin from you and from all that will embrace you. Come to Me, ye pains, and disappoint Me not; heed not my Omnipotence, for I shall permit you to exert your full force upon my humanity. You shall not be rejected and abhorred by Me as you are by mortals. The deceitful fascination of the children of Adam in vainly judging the poor and the afflicted of this world as unhappy, shall now disappear; for if they see their true God, their Creator, Master and Father, suffering horrible insults, scourgings, the ignominious torment and destitution of the Cross, they will understand their error and esteem it as an honor to follow their crucified God."

394. These are some of the sentiments which I have been made to perceive in the heart of the Master of life, our Savior. The sufferings of his Death on the Cross show (as my words cannot express), how great was the love with which He sought and underwent them. Notwithstanding all this, our hearts are weighed down by sin entangled in vanities (Ps. 4, 3). Though we have life and truth before our eyes, we are nevertheless carried away by our pride and repelled by humility, ravished by what is pleasurable and full of abhorrence for what is painful. 0 lamentable error! To labor much in order to avoid laboring a little, to exhaust our selves entirely, merely in order to avoid a small inconvenience, to foolishly resolve on suffering eternal shame and confusion, just in order to evade a slight dishonor, or in order not to forego one hour of vain and apparent honor! Who that claims the use of his reason, can say that he loves himself by following such a course? No mortal enemy of his can ever do him a greater harm than he does himself by doing what is displeasing to God. we hold those as our enemies who flatter and entertain us while they have treason in their hearts; and we would call those foolish who would allow themselves to be betrayed by an insignificant pleasure and delight. If we judge right in this, as we really do, what shall we say of the judgment of those who are devotees of the world? Who has intoxicated them? Who has thus deprived them of their reason? 0 how great is the number of fools!

395. Most holy Mary alone of all the children of Adam adjusted her whole life according to the will and conduct of her Son, without departing in the least from the closest

imitation of his life and fulfillment of his doctrine. She was that most prudent Creature, full of knowledge and wisdom, who could make up for our ignorance and foolishness and gain for us eternal truth in the midst of our darkness. This happened also on the occasion of which I have spoken, for the heavenly Lady, being the mirror of her Son's soul, saw all the affection and love actuating his interior. Since this was also the guide of her activity, She entirely conformed to them and with Him addressed her prayers to the eternal Father as follows: "Most High God and Father of mercies, I confess thy infinite and immutable essence. Eternally do I praise and exalt Thee, for in this place, after Thou hadst created me, Thou hast deigned to glorify the power of thy arm by raising me to the dignity of Mother of thy Onlybegotten and magnified the out flowing of thy ancient mercies with me, thy humble slave, and because thy and my Onlybegotten in the flesh which He assumed from my substance, has condescended to retain me in his most delightful company for thirty-three years, permitting me to enjoy his graces, his teachings and his guidance for the enlightenment of the soul of thy handmaid. Today, my Lord and eternal Father, I leave my country and I joyfully follow my Son and Master in order to be present at the sacrifice of his life and of his human existence for mankind. There is no sorrow like unto my sorrow at seeing the Lamb, which taketh away the sins of the world, delivered over to bloodthirsty wolves; at seeing that One subjected to suffering, torment, and death, who is the living image and figure of thy substance (Heb. 1,3) ; who is engendered of Thee from all eternity, and equal to Thee through all the ages; at seeing that One subjected to insult and death of the Cross, whom I have given life in my womb, and at seeing the beauty of that countenance obscured by filth and wounds, which is the joy of my eyes and the delight of all the angels. 0 would it were possible, that I receive the pains and sorrows which await Him, and that I might suffer death in order to save his life! Accept, heavenly Father, the sacrifice of my sorrowing affection, which I offer in union with Him, in order that thy holy will and pleasure may be fulfilled. 0 how quickly flee the days and hours, which shall end in the night of my sorrow and bitterness! It will be a fortunate day for the children of men, but a night of affliction for my sorrow laden heart, so soon to be deprived of its illuminating Sun. O children of Adam, so deeply lost in error and so forgetful of yourselves! Awake at last from your heavy slumber and recognize the weight of your sins in the devastation they are about to cause in your God and Creator! See their dire effects in my mortal sorrow and bitterness of my soul! Begin at last to take heed of the damage wrought by sin!"

396. I cannot worthily express all the thoughts and affections of the Mistress of the world in this her departure from Nazareth, her prayers and petitions to the eternal Father, her most sweet and sorrowful conversations with her divine Son, the greatness of her grief and the vastness of her merits. For, on account of the conflict between the love of a true Mother, by which She naturally desired to preserve Him from the terrible torments, and the conformity of her will with that of Jesus and of his eternal Father, her heart was pierced by the sword of sorrow, prophesied by Simeon (Luke 2, 35). In her affliction She complained to her divine Son in words of deepest prudence and wisdom, yet also of sweetest sorrow, that She should be unable to prevent his sufferings, or at least die with Him. These sorrows of the Mother of God exceeded the sufferings of all the martyrs who have died or will die for love of God to the end of the world. In such a state of mind and affection the Sovereigns of the world pursued their way from Nazareth toward Jerusalem through Galilee, which the Savior was not to revisit in this life. As the end of his labors for the salvation of men drew to a close, his miraculous works

increased in number, and, as the sacred writers of the Gospels relate, they became especially numerous in the last months intervening between his departure from Galilee and the day of his entrance into Jerusalem. Until that day, after having celebrated the feast or the Pasch of the Tabernacles, the Savior traveled about and labored in Judea, awaiting the appointed time, when, according to his will, He was to offer Himself in sacrifice.

397. During these journeying his most holy Mother accompanied Him, except on a few occasions, when They separated in order to attend to the welfare of souls in different localities. On such errands saint John was deputed to accompany Her and administer to her wants. From that time on saint John received most exalted enlightenments in regard to the great mysteries and hidden sacraments of the most pure Virgin and Mother. Among the wonders wrought by the most prudent and powerful Queen at this time, were those of most exalted flights of charity in procuring by her petitions and prayers the justification of souls; for also She, just as her most holy Son, now began to be more lavish in her blessed benefactions to mankind, bringing many to the path of eternal life, curing the sick, visiting the poor and the afflicted, the destitute and the infirm, assisting the dying with her own hands, especially those that were most forsaken and afflicted with greater suffering and pain. Of all these works in his special office of attending upon the blessed Mother, the beloved disciple was a witness. But as the force of her love, at the prospect of seeing her divine Son leave Her to return to his eternal Father, had now increased a thousand fold, the blessed Mother had such a yearning desire of being in his presence, that She often swooned away in ecstasies of love and affection, whenever She was obliged to endure his absence for any length of time. The divine Master on his part, who as God knew all that passed in the heart of his

beloved Mother, faithfully corresponded with her feelings. Speaking to Her those words, which were now fulfilled to the letter: "Thou hast wounded my heart, my Sister, my Spouse, thou hast wounded my heart with one of thy eyes;" for, as if wounded and overcome by his own love, He was drawn again to her presence. According to what has been made known to me, Christ our Lord, in as far as He was man, could not ever have left the presence of his Mother, if He had given full sway to his love for a Mother who loved Him so much. Hence it was natural that He should hasten to relieve and console Her by his presence and intercourse. The beauty of the most pure soul of his Mother refreshed Him and made all his labors and hardships appear sweet to Him. He looked upon Her as the choice and only fruit of all his exertions, and the mere presence of Mary repaid Him for all his bodily sufferings.

398. Our Savior continued to perform his miracles in Judea. Among them was also the resurrection of Lazarus in Bethany, whither He had been called by the two sisters, Martha and Mary. As this miracle took place so near to Jerusalem, the report of it was soon spread throughout the city. The priests and Pharisees, being irritated by this miracle, held a council (John 9, 17), in which they resolved upon the death of the Redeemer and commanded all those that had any knowledge of his whereabouts, to make it known; for after the resurrection of Lazarus, Jesus retired to the town of Ephrem, until the proximate feast of the Pasch should arrive. As the time of celebrating it by his own Death drew nigh, He showed Himself more openly with his twelve disciples, the Apostles; and He told them privately that they should now get themselves ready to go to Jerusalem, where the Son of man, He himself, should be delivered over to the chiefs of the Pharisees, bound as a prisoner, scourged, and illtreated unto the death of the Cross (Matth. 20, 18). In the meanwhile the

priests kept a sharp watch to find Him among those who came to celebrate the Pasch. Six days previous He again visited Bethania, where He had called Lazarus to life, and where He was entertained by the two sisters. They arranged a banquet for the Lord and his Mother, and for all of his company. Among those that were at table with Them, was also Lazarus, whom He had brought back to life a few days before.

399. While our Savior, according to the custom of the Jews, was reclining at this banquet, Magdalen, filled with divine enlightening and most magnanimous sentiments, entered the banquet hall. As an outward token of her ardent love toward Christ, her divine Master, she anointed his feet and poured out over them and over his head an alabaster vase filled with a most fragrant and precious liquor, composed of spikenard and other aromatic ingredients. Then She wiped his feet with her hair just as she had done at another occasion in the house of the Pharisee, related by saint Luke (Luke 7, 38). Although the other three Evangelists in relating this second anointment, apparently differ as to some of the circumstances; yet I was not informed that they refer to different anointments or speak of more than one woman, but that they refer only to Magdalen, who was moved to these acts of devotion by inspiration of the Holy Ghost and by her own burning love toward Christ the Redeemer. The fragrance of this ointment filled the whole house, for She had procured a large quantity, and of the most precious kind; nor did she stint it in any way, but broke the vessel in token of her generous love and devotion to the Master. The avaricious Apostle Judas, who wished to get possession of the ointment in order to sell it for the increase of his purse, began to criticize this mysterious anointing of his Master and also to stir up some of the other Apostles under pretext of poverty and of charity toward the poor (John 12, 5). These, he said,

are defrauded of their alms by this lavish expense and waste of so costly an article. At the same time all this had been ordained by divine Providence, while Judas acted only as an avaricious and disgruntled hypocrite.

400. The Teacher of truth and life defended Magdalen against this accusation of inconsiderate prodigality. He commanded Judas and the others not to molest her (Matth. 24, 10), since her action had not been vain or without good cause. He told them the poor would not on that account lose the alms, which they should receive each day, whereas such opportunity of showing honor to his Person would not be afforded every day; that the anointment had been performed by this generous and loving woman through enlightenment of the holy Spirit and as a prophetic announcement of the mysterious unction the Savior was so soon to undergo in the torments of his Death and at his burial. Nothing of all this the perfidious disciple took to heart, but on the contrary he conceived a furious wrath against his Master on account of his thus justifying the action of Magdalen. Lucifer, profiting by the disposition of this depraved heart, incited it to new upwellings of avarice, anger, and mortal hate against the Author of life. Thenceforth Judas schemed to bring about his Death, and resolved, as soon as he should come to Jerusalem, to betray Him to the Pharisees and help to discredit Him in their eyes, as he afterwards did. After this banquet he betook himself secretly to Jerusalem and told them that his Master taught new laws contrary to those of Moses and of the emperors; that He was addicted to banqueting, a friend of depraved and profane company; that He had admitted as his followers many of a wicked life, both men and women; that without delay they should see such conduct stopped lest ruin overtake them when it was too late to secure relief. As the pharisees were already of the same mind and were instigated by the same prince of darkness, they gladly accepted his

advice. With them therefore he agreed on a price for the betrayal of Christ our Savior.

401. All the thoughts of Judas lay open not only to his divine Master, but also to his most blessed Mother. The Lord said nothing to Judas in regard to this matter, but continued to deal with him as a kind Father and to enlighten his obstinate heart. His Mother, however, redoubled her admonitions and gentle endeavors to withdraw Judas from the precipice; and on this night of the banquet, which was that preceding Palm Sunday, She called him aside to speak to him alone, representing to him amid a flood of tears and with most sweet and persuasive words, what terrible danger threatened him if he should persist in his intentions. She asked him to give up his designs and, if he was offended at his Master, to take vengeance on Her. For this was a smaller evil, since She was only a creature, while He was his Master and the true God. In order to satisfy the avarice of this insatiable heart, She offered him some presents, which She had received for this purpose from Magdalen. But none of her efforts were of any avail with this hardened soul, nor did any of these sweet and living words soften this more than adamantine heart. On the contrary, as he did not find an answer and the exhortations of the most prudent Queen were so urgent, he lashed himself into greater fury, showing his wrath by a sullen silence. He was, however, not ashamed to take what she offered to him; for his avarice was equal to his perfidy. The most blessed Mary then left him and betook Herself to her Son and Master. Full of the bitterest sorrow She cast Herself weeping at his feet. In her exquisite grief and compassion She wished to bring some consolation to the sacred humanity of Christ her Son, whom She now beheld suffering of the sorrow unto death, which He afterwards manifested in the presence of his disciples (Matth. 24, 38). Of this kind were

the sufferings of Christ for the sins of those men who were to misapply his Passion and Death, as I shall relate farther on.

Words of the Queen

THE VIRGIN MARY SPEAKS TO SISTER MARY OF AGREDA

402. My daughter, thou daily understandest and declarest more fully in this history, that my Son, and I with Him, in our ardent love, embraced the way of the Cross and suffering for the whole course of our natural life. Thou receivest this knowledge more fully and hearest this doctrine repeated so often, that thou must strive to follow it closely in thy daily life. This duty grows upon thee from the day in which my Son has chosen thee as bride, and will oblige thee more and more, so that thou canst not evade the duty of embracing and loving hardships to such an extent, that thy greatest pain shall be to be without them. Renew every day this desire in thy heart, for I wish thee to be very proficient in this science, which the world abhors so much. But remember, at the same time, that God does not afflict creatures merely for the sake of afflicting them, but in order to make them more capable and worthy of receiving the blessings and treasures prepared for them beyond all human conception (1 Cor. 2, 9). For the confirmation of this truth and as a pledge of his promises He permitted the Transfiguration of Himself on Mount Tabor in my presence and that of some of the disciples. In the prayer which He then made to the eternal Father and which I alone knew of and understood, He humbled Himself before his Father confessing Him (as He always did in his prayers) as the true God, infinite in his perfections and attributes, and besought Him to concede a share of the glory of his own body to all those, who in their mortal bodies should afflict themselves and bear hardships for his love and in imitation of his own, and to grant this glory in the measure proper to

each after the resurrection of their bodies in the final judgment. Since the eternal Father granted this request, there is a certain contract between God and man. The glory which was given to the body of Christ the Savior was a pledge of that which Christ was to secure for all his followers. Great, therefore, is the value of the momentary hardships endured in the privation of earthly delights and in mortifications and sufferings for the sake of Christ (II Cor. 4, 17).

403. On account of the merits of this prayer of Christ, this glory which belongs to Him is due to the creatures in justice, since men are the members of Christ's mystical body (II Tim. 4, 8) . Yet this union with Christ, by which man merits such reward, must be brought about by grace and by imitation of the same suffering which merited it for the Redeemer. If all bodily suffering merits its crown, a much greater crown is merited by the patient endurance and pardoning of injuries, and by returning good for them, as We acted in regard to Judas; for the Lord did not only not take away from Judas his apostolate, or show Himself in any way irritated against him, but He patiently bore with him to the very end, when Judas had already made himself altogether unfit for any graces by giving himself up to the devil. During our mortal life the Lord is very slow in visiting his vengeance upon us; but He will make up for his slowness in the severity of his punishments after death. If then God suffers and bears with us so much, how much must one poor worm of the earth bear with another, since both are of the same nature and condition? By the light of this truth and by the charity of the Lord and Spouse, thou must regulate the amount of thy patience and long suffering with others and the zeal for their salvation. I do not say that thou must therefore permit what is against the honor of God, for that would not be a true zeal for the good of thy neighbor; but thou must love them as creatures of the Lord and abhor sin; thou must suffer and

ignore whatever is done against thee, always seeking, as far as in thee lies, the salvation of others. Do not lose heart, when thou seest no immediate fruit, but continue to present to the eternal Father the merits of my most holy Son, my intercession and that of the saints and angels; for as God is charity and as they are the ministers of the Most High, they will gladly make use of this same charity for the benefit of those who are still on their pilgrimage.

Chapter VII

THE SACRAMENTAL MYSTERY PRECEDING THE TRIUMPHAL ENTRY OF CHRIST INTO JERUSALEM; HOW HE ENTERED INTO THE CITY AND HOW HE WAS RECEIVED BY ITS INHABITANTS.

404. Among the works of God, which, because they are performed outside of his own essence, are called ad extra, the greatest was that of assuming flesh, suffering and dying for the salvation of men. This sacrament human wisdom could never have perceived, if its Author had not demonstrated it to us by so many proofs and testimonies. In spite of all these proofs, many who are wise only according to the flesh, find it difficult to believe that which is so much to their own salvation and benefit. Others, though they believe it, do not believe all the circumstances connected with it. But the true Catholics believe and confess this sacrament such as the holy Church proposes it to them. By explicitly professing our faith in the mysteries thus revealed, we at the same time explicitly profess our faith in the mysteries, which are there under included, and which it was not necessary to define more particularly, because they are not especially necessary for salvation. Some of these God reserves for their proper time, while others will be reserved for the last day, when all of them shall be manifest to men in the presence of the just Judge (I Cor. 4, 5). The intention of the Lord in command-

ing me to write this history (as I have often said and yet oftener understood), was to manifest many of these hidden mysteries without admixture of mere human opinion and conjecture; many of them I have therefore recorded, just as they have been made known to me, while I am aware at the same time, that many other wonderful and venerable sacraments will still remain hidden. Toward these mysteries I wish to prepare the pious faith of Catholics. To believe what is accessory, should not be hard for those who believe the principal mysteries of the Catholic faith. For upon these principal mysteries of the faith rests all that I have written and all that I shall yet write, especially in regard to the Passion of our Redeemer.

405. On the sabbath following the anointment of Magdalen in Bethany and after the banquet mentioned in the preceding chapter, our divine Master sought retirement. The most blessed Mother, leaving Judas to his hardheartedness, betook Herself to her divine Son, and, as was her wont, joined Him in his prayers and sacred exercises. Our Lord was now about to enter upon the greatest conflict in his career as man, having, as David says (Ps. 18, 7), reached out from highest heaven in order to engage in this battle and by it to vanquish the demon, sin and death. As this most Obedient of sons accepted freely the torments of the Cross, He now, at their approach, offered Himself anew to the eternal Father. Prostrate, with his face touching the ground, He confessed Him and adored Him, with deepest resignation beseeching Him to accept the insults and pains, ignominies and death of the Cross for his own glory and for the rescue of the human race. The most blessed Mother had retired to one side of the oratory, accompanying her beloved Son and Lord in his prayers and shedding with Him tears of inmost affection.

406. On this occasion, before the hour of midnight, the eternal Father and the Holy Ghost appeared in visible form

with multitudes of angels as witnesses. The eternal Father accepted the sacrifice of Christ, his most blessed Son, and formally consented that the rigor of his justice should be satisfied upon his Person for the pardon of the world. Then the eternal Father, addressing the blessed Mother herself, said: "Mary, our Daughter and Spouse, I desire that thou now again ratify this sacrifice of thy Son, since I on my part am willing to deliver Him up for the Redemption of man." And the humble and sincerest Dove replied: "Behold, o Lord, I am but dust and ashes, unworthy that thy Onlybegotten and the Redeemer of the world should also be my Son. But I hold myself entirely subject to thy ineffable condescension, which has given Him being in my womb, and I offer Him and myself entirely as a sacrifice to thy divine pleasure, I beseech Thee, 0 Lord God and Father, to permit me to suffer with thy and my Son." The eternal Father received this subjection of most holy Mary as a pleasing sacrifice. Raising up from the ground both the Son and the Mother, He said: "This is the fruit of the blessed earth, which I have desired." Immediately thereupon He exalted the Humanity of Christ to the throne of his Majesty, and placed Him on his right hand equal in authority and preeminence with Himself.

407. The blessed Mother remained in the place where She was, but entirely transformed and exalted in wonderful splendor and jubilee of soul. On seeing her Onlybegotten seated at the right hand of the eternal Father, She pronounced those first words of the one hundred and ninth psalm, in which David had mysteriously prophesied this event: "The Lord said unto my Lord: Sit thou at my right hand." Expatiating upon these words the heavenly Queen composed a mysterious hymn of praise in honor of the eternal Father and of the incarnate Word. When She had finished, the Father added all the rest of the psalm, decreeing

then and there by his immutable will, that all the import of
these mysterious and profound words should now be executed and fulfilled. It is very difficult for me to mould into the
inadequate words which are within my power, the intelligence which was given me of this high mystery; but I will
make an attempt to do so, as far as the Lord will empower
me. Let something of this hidden and wonderful sacrament,
and of that which most holy Mary and the angelic spirits
understood, be felt also by ourselves.

408. The eternal Father then proceeded and said: "Until I
make thy enemies thy footstool." Since Thou hast humiliated
Thyself in accordance with my eternal will, Thou hast merited that Thou be exalted above all the creatures; and that, in
the very nature of man which Thou hast received from Me,
Thou reign at my right hand forever and ever without end.
For all eternity I place thy enemies under thy feet and dominion, subject to thy humanity as their God and Redeemer;
so that those who will not obey Thee or acknowledge Thee,
shall see thy humanity exalted and glorified. Although I do
not put this decree into full execution until the Redemption
of man shall have been accomplished, I desire that even now
my courtiers shall witness what both the demons and mankind shall see afterwards; I place Thee in possession at my
right hand at the very moment in which Thou hast humiliated Thyself to the ignominious death of the Cross. If I now
deliver Thee over to thy enemies and to the workings of their
malice, it is done for my glory and good pleasure, and in
order that afterwards they may be placed beneath thy feet to
their entire confusion. "The Lord will send forth the sceptre
of thy power out of Sion: rule Thou in the midst of thy
enemies." For I, the omnipotent God, who am He that is
truly and indeed, control and send forth the invincible
scepter of my power; so that afterwards, when Thou shalt
have triumphed over death by completing the Redemption of

the human race, they may recognize Thee as their Savior, their Guide, their Leader and as the Lord of all; but I desire even now, before Thou sufferest death, and at the very moment when men are plotting thy ruin in their contempt of Thee, that Thou triumph in a wonderful manner. I ordain that Thou triumph both over their malice and over their death; and that by the very power of thy virtue they be compelled to honor Thee, confess Thee, adore and worship Thee of their own free will; that the demons be vanquished and confounded by the strength of thy own virtue, that the Prophets and the Just, who are waiting for Thee in limbo, together with my heavenly spirits, recognize thy wonderful exaltation according to my good will and pleasure. "With Thee is the principality in the day of thy strength: in the brightness of the saints: from the womb before the daystar I begot Thee." On the day of this thy strength and power, by which Thou triumphest over thy enemies, I am in Thee and with Thee as the Beginning. From this Source, by the eternal fecundity of my intellect, Thou didst issue forth before the light of grace by which We decreed to manifest Ourselves to creatures, and from this Beginning didst thou come forth, clothed in the light of glory, by which the saints are rejoiced and beatified. And also in as far as Thou art man, thy beginning is with Thee and Thou was engendered in the day of thy virtue; for from the instant in which Thou hast received human existence by temporal generation from thy Mother, Thou didst possess the merit of the works, which is with Thee now, and Thou didst deserve the glory and honor by which thy virtue is to crown Thee on this day and in the days of my eternity. "The Lord hath sworn, and He will not repent: Thou art a priest forever according to the order of Melchisedech." I, who am the Lord God Almighty, able to fulfill all my promises, absolutely decree, as by an immutable oath, that Thou be the Highpriest of the new Church and of the evangelical law, according to the order of Melchisedech of old; for Thou shalt be the true Priest, who shall offer the bread and wine prefigured by the oblation of Melchisedech (Gen. 14, 18). And I shall not regret this decree; for this oblation shall be pure and acceptable, and a sacrifice of praise in my honor. "The Lord at thy right hand hath broken kings in the day of his wrath." This shalt Thou do by the works of thy humanity, assisted by the right hand of thy Divinity in the fullness of its strength. By thy humanity, I who am one God with Thee, shall crush the tyranny of the princes of darkness and of this world, as well the apostate angels as also wicked men, who will not acknowledge, serve and adore Thee as their Lord and God. This chastisement I will inflict at a time when neither Lucifer nor his followers shall yet know Thee, and it shall be for them the day of my wrath. Afterwards that day will also come for those men who have not received Thee nor followed thy holy law. All of them shall I crush and humiliate in my just indignation. "He shall judge among nations, He shall fill with ruins; He shall crush the heads in the land of many." Having then justified my cause with all the children of Adam, who have not profited of thy mercy in graciously redeeming them from sin and from eternal death, I, the Lord, shall judge according to my equity and justice all the nations; and choosing the just from the midst of the sinners and the reprobate, I shall fill up the ruined places of the apostate angels, who have not preserved for themselves their habitations in the reign of grace. At the same time I shall crush upon earth the multitudes of those men who, by their own obstinate and depraved will, persist in their pride. "He shall drink of the torrent in the way: therefore He shall lift up his head." Thy head shall be raised up by the Lord God of vengeance himself, in order that thou mayest judge the earth and justly deal with the proud. As if Thou hadst drunk of the torrent of his wrath, Thou shalt dip thy arrows in the blood of thy enemies and, with the sword of his chastisement, Thou shalt confound them in their expectation of happiness. Thus shall thy head be lifted up and exalted above all thy enemies, who are disobedient to the law and faithless to thy doctrines and teachings. For this shall be thy just reward for thy having drunk of the torrent of reproaches and affronts even to the death of the Cross for their Redemption.

409. Such and much deeper understanding was given to most holy Mary concerning this mysterious psalm, which the eternal Father repeated on this occasion. Although some of the verses are quoted as of another person, yet they all referred to Himself and to the incarnate Word. The mysteries contained therein may be reduced to two principal heads: threats against sinners, infidels, and wicked Christians, because they do not acknowledge the Redeemer of the world or observe his laws; and promises of the eternal Father to his incarnate Son, that He will glorify his name and exalt it in spite of and above all his enemies. As if in pledge or advance payment of the universal exaltation of Christ after his Ascension, and especially at the final judgment, the Father decreed that the inhabitants of Jerusalem should meet Him with great applause and honor at his entrance into Jerusalem on the day following this mysterious vision. Thereupon the Father and the Holy Ghost, with the holy angels, that wonderingly had assisted at this great sacrament, disappeared, while Christ and his blessed Mother remained to spend the rest of that blessed night in divine colloquies.

410. On the morning of the next day, which corresponds to our Palm Sunday, the Lord proceeded with his disciples toward Jerusalem, being accompanied by many angels, who sang hymns of praise at seeing Him so enamored of men and so solicitous for their eternal salvation. Having walked more or less of two miles and arrived in the village of Bethphage,

He sent two disciples to an influential man of that neighborhood. From him they brought two beasts of burden, one of
which had not yet been used or ridden by anyone. The Lord
progressed on his way to Jerusalem while they spread some of
their cloaks and other garments both upon the ass and her
colt. The Lord was to make use of both of them according to
the prophecies of Isaias (Is. 62, 11), and Zacharias (Zach. 9,
9), who had foretold these particulars many ages before, in
order that the priests and scribes should not be able to allege
ignorance as an excuse. All the four Evangelists describe this
wonderful triumph of Christ and relate what was seen by the
bodily eyes of those present. As they proceeded on their way
the disciples, and with them all the people, the infants as well
as the grown persons, hailed Jesus as the true Messias, the
Son of David, the Savior of the world and as their legitimate
King. Some of them exclaimed: "Peace be in heaven and
glory in the highest: blessed be He that cometh as the King
in the name of the Lord," others: "Hosanna to the Son of
David: save us, Son of David: blessed be the kingdom which
now has arrived, the kingdom of our forefather David."
Some others lopped branches from palms and other trees in
sign of triumph and joy, and spread their garments upon the
ground to prepare a way for the triumphant Conqueror,
Christ our Lord.

411. All these demonstrations of worship and admiration,
which these men gave to the divine and incarnate Word,
were calculated to manifest the power of his Divinity, especially at this time, when the priests and pharisees were watching Him and seeking to put an end to his life in that very
city. For if they had not been moved interiorly by a divine
power, above and beyond that of their admiration for the
miracles wrought by Him, it would have been impossible to
draw such a gathering. Many of them were heathens and his
declared enemies, who nevertheless hailed Him as the true

Messias, Savior and King, and subjected themselves to a poor, despised and persecuted Man, who came not in triumphal chariots, or in the prancing of steeds and ostentation of riches, but without any show of arms or outward human power. Outwardly all this was wanting, as He thus entered seated on a beast contemptible in the sight of human vanity and pretension. The only signs of his dignity were in his countenance, which showed forth the gravity and serene majesty of his soul; while all the rest fell far short and was opposed to what the world is wont to applaud and celebrate. Hence the outward happenings of this day proclaimed his divine power, which directly moved the hearts of men to acknowledge Him as their Christ and Redeemer.

412. In order that the promise of the eternal Father might be entirely fulfilled, He not only moved the hearts of men in the city of Jerusalem by his divine light, to acknowledge Him as Redeemer, but He caused his triumph to be felt among all creatures especially those who were capable of reasoning (No. 408). For the entry of Jesus into Jerusalem was announced by the archangel Michael to the holy Fathers and Prophets in limbo; and moreover, by a special vision, they were made to see whatever happened on this occasion. From those cavernous abodes they acknowledged, confessed and adored Christ, our Lord and Master, as their true God and as the Redeemer of the world. They composed new hymns of praise in honor of his admirable triumph over death, sin, and hell. The divine influence was also active in the hearts of many of those yet living in the world. For those that had faith or knowledge of Christ our Lord, not only in Palestine and its surroundings, but in Egypt and in other countries, were moved to adore the Redeemer in spirit; and this they did with unwonted joy, caused in them by the divine visitation of grace, although they did not expressly know the cause or the object of this movement in their hearts. But it came to them not

without profit for their souls: for they were confirmed in their faith and in their welldoing. In order that the triumph of our Savior over death might be more glorious, the Most High ordained, that on that day death should have no power over any of the mortals, so that, although in the natural course many would have died, not one of the human race died within those twenty-four hours.

413. To this triumph over death was added the triumph over hell, which, though it was more hidden, was even more glorious. For as soon as the people began to proclaim and invoke Christ as their Savior and King who came in the name of the Lord, the demons felt the power of the right hand of God, and all of them, in whatever place they lurked throughout the world, were hurled into the dark caverns of the infernal abyss. During the short space of time in which Christ proceeded on his triumphal march, not a demon remained upon the earth, but all of them were trembling with wrath and terror in the depths of hell. Hence they began to be filled with a still greater dread, lest the Messias be already in the world, and they immediately communicated their suspicions to each other, as I shall relate in the next chapter. The Savior proceeded on his triumphal way to the gates of Jerusalem, while the angels, who witnessed and followed his march, chanted new hymns of praise and glory in wonderful harmony. Having entered the city amid the jubilee of all its inhabitants, Jesus dismounted from the foal, and directed his divinely beautiful footsteps toward the temple, where He roused the admiration of all the multitudes by the wonders, which, according to the Evangelists, He wrought on that occasion (Matth. 21, 12; Luke 19, 4S). Burning with zeal for the house of his Father, He overthrew the tables of those that bought and sold within the sacred precincts and cast forth those who made it a place of business and a den of thieves. Yet with the triumphal march the Lord

suspended also the divine influence, which had disposed so well the hearts of the inhabitants of Jerusalem. Although the just had been much benefited, and many others had been justified, others returned to their vices and imperfections, because they did not profit by the light and inspiration sent to them from on high. Though so many had hailed and acknowledged Christ our Savior as King of Jerusalem, not one tendered Him hospitality or received Him in his house (Mark 11,11).

414. The Lord remained in the temple teaching and preaching until nightfall. Wishing by his own example to confirm his teaching in regard to the veneration and worship due to that place, He would not permit even a glass of water to be brought to Him, and without having partaken either of this or any other refreshment, He returned that evening to Bethany (Matth. 21; 17, 18), whence He daily made his way to the city until the day of his Passion. The heavenly Mother and Mistress, most holy Mary, remained that day in Bethany, where from her retirement She saw by a supernatural vision all that happened in the wonderful triumph of her Son and Master. She witnessed all the doings of the sovereign spirits of heaven and of the mortals upon earth, and what befell the demons in hell; and how in all this the eternal Father merely fulfilled the promises, which He had made to his incarnate Son in giving Him command and power over all his enemies. She saw also all that the Savior did on this occasion and in the temple. She heard the heavenly Father's voice answering the prayer of Christ, our Redeemer: "I have glorified, and will glorify again." By these words He gave men to understand that besides the glory and triumph conceded to the incarnate Word on that day and on other occasions, as described in this history, He would glorify and exalt Him after his Death, for such was the meaning of the words of the eternal Father; in this sense also it was understood and fully

comprehended by the most blessed Mother in wonderful exultation of her spirit.

Words of the Queen

THE VIRGIN MARY SPEAKS TO SISTER MARY OF AGREDA

415. My daughter, thou hast partly described, and hast understood much more concerning the mysterious triumph of my most holy Son on his entrance into Jerusalem and its preparations; but thou wilt understand much more of it, when thou shalt come face to face with the Lord, for as pilgrims, mortals cannot penetrate into such secrets. Nevertheless thou canst learn and understand enough from what thou hast written to perceive how exalted are the judgments of the Lord and how far removed from all the thoughts of men (Is. 55,9). The Most High looks into the hearts of men and at the interior, where is hidden the beauty of the King's daughter (Ps, 44, 14); while men look only at the exterior and at what is perceived by the senses. On this account the just and the chosen ones are highly esteemed by the Lord in their humiliation and self-abasement; while the proud are cast down and rejected by Him in their self-sufficiency. This truth, my daughter, is understood by few, and therefore the children of darkness know not how to strive after any other honor or exaltation than that of the world. Sad to say, also the children of the Church, although well knowing and confessing that this worldly honor is vain and without substance, and that it does not have any more stability than the flowers or herbs of the field, do not live up to this knowledge. As their conscience does not give them witness of faithful cooperation with the light of grace and the practice of virtue, they seek after the false and deceitful applause and commendation of men; whereas God alone can truly honor and exalt those, who merit his regard. The world ordinarily

and fraudulently misjudges true merit, lavishing its honors upon those who least deserve it, or upon those who know how to solicit and strive after it most cunningly and inconsiderately.

416. Fly from this deceit, my daughter, and let the praise of men make no impression upon thee; repel its flatteries and compliments. Give to each the importance and consideration due to it; for the children of the world are very much blinded in their judgments. None of the mortals could ever merit the honor and applause of men so much as my most holy Son; yet He readily yielded it up and judged at its true worth that which the people gave Him at his entrance into Jerusalem. He permitted it merely in order that the divine power might be manifested and in order that his Passion might afterwards be so much the more ignominious. He wished to teach men, that no one should accept honors for their own value, but in order that the higher end, that is the glory of God and the exaltation of the Most High, might thereby be advanced; that without this object in view they are altogether vain and useless, void of profit or advantage of any kind; for they can never procure the true happiness of a creature capable of eternal glory. Since I see thee desirous of knowing why I was not present at this triumph of my most holy Son, I shall fulfill thy desire, and I refer thee to what thou hast often related in this history about the clear vision of the interior of my Son, which was always present to me. By this vision I was enabled to perceive, when and why He wished me to absent myself from Him. On such occasions I would throw myself at his feet, beseeching Him to declare his will and pleasure in regard to what I should do. Then the Lord would sometimes give his orders plainly and in express commands; at others He would leave it to my own discretion and choice, permitting me to act according to my prudence and divine enlightenment. This was the course He pursued at the time, when

He resolved to enter in triumph the gates of Jerusalem. He left it altogether to my own judgment, whether I should accompany Him or remain in Bethany. Thereupon I asked his permission to absent myself from this mysterious event, begging Him to take me with Him to his Passion and Death. I thought it more befitting and more pleasing in his eyes to offer myself as participant in the ignominies and sorrows of his Passion, than to share in the outward honor given to Him by men. For, as I was his Mother, some of this honor would certainly have devolved upon me, if I had shown myself to those who were praising and blessing Him. I knew that this triumph, beside its not being desired by me, was ordained by the Lord for the manifestation of his infinite power and Divinity, and therefore in no wise pertaining to me; nor would the honor, which they would have extended to me, augment that which was due to Him as the Savior of the human race. At the same time, in order that I might properly rejoice in this mystery and duly glorify the Almighty for these wonders, I was made to see by divine enlightenment and especial vision all that thou has already written concerning this event. This behavior should instruct thee and teach thee to imitate me; follow thou my humble footsteps, withdraw thy affections from all that is earthly, lift thy aspirations on high, despising and fleeing all human honors and in divine enlightenment esteeming them as vanity of vanities and affliction of spirit (Eccles. 1, 14).

Chapter VIII

THE DEMONS MEET IN HELL TO DISCUSS THE TRIUMPH OF
CHRIST OUR LORD IN JERUSALEM; THE RESULTS OF THIS
CONFERENCE, AND MEASURES RESOLVED UPON BY THE
PRIESTS AND PHARISEES OF JERUSALEM.

417. All the mysteries connected with the triumph of our
Savior were great and admirable; but not the least wonderful
were the hidden effects of the divine power on the hellish
fiends, when, at the entrance of Jesus into Jerusalem, they
were cast into the infernal abysses. Two entire days, from
Sunday until Tuesday of that week, the demons lay shattered
by the right hand of the Almighty, manifesting their furious
torment to the damned souls of those hellish caverns by their
horrid and confused howls of despair. The whole infernal
dominion was filled on that occasion with unwonted confusion and pain. The prince of this darkness, Lucifer, more
confounded than all the rest, called to his presence all the
devilish hosts, and stationing himself on an eminence, spoke
to them as their chief.

418. "It cannot be otherwise than that this Man, who
thus persecutes us and destroys our influence, and who thus
crushes my power, is more than a Prophet. For Moses, Elias
and Eliseus and others of our enemies among the ancients
never vanquished us so completely, although they performed
miracles; nor did they ever succeed in hiding from me so

many of their doings as this One; for especially of his interior
works I can obtain little information. How can a mere man
perform such works and manifest such supreme power over
all creation, as are publicly ascribed to Him? Without any
change or inflation of mind He received the praise and
glorification for these works from the mouths of men. In
celebrating this triumphal entry into Jerusalem He has shown
new power over us and over all the world; for even now I
find my strength for visiting destruction upon Him and
blotting out his name from the land of the living vanishing
away (Jer. 11, 19). In his present triumph not only his own
friends have extolled Him and proclaimed Him as blessed,
but even many of those who were subject to me have done
the same and have called Him the Messias promised in their
law; He has drawn them all to venerate and adore Him. This
certainly seems to exceed mere human power; and if He is no
more than man, there never was one who partook of the
divine power in such a degree, and He is doing and will do
us great damage. Since the time when we were cast from
heaven we have never experienced such ruinous defeat, nor
have I ever encountered such overwhelming power before
this man came into the world. If He should be the incarnate
Word (as we suspect) there is necessity for thorough deliberation; for if we permit Him to live, He will by his example
and teaching draw after Him all mankind. In my hate I have
several times sought to bring about his death; but without
success. In his own country, when I instigated his country-
men to cast Him from the precipice, He contemptuously
took his way through the midst of those who were to execute
the sentence (Luke 4, 30). On another occasion He simply
made Himself invisible to the pharisees, whom I had incited
to stone Him."

419. "But now, with the help of his disciple and our
friend Judas, matters seem to promise better success. I have

so wrought upon the mind of Judas, that he is willing to sell and betray his Master to the pharisees, whom I have likewise incited to furious envy. They are anxious to inflict upon Him a most cruel death, and will no doubt do so. They are only waiting for an occasion, which I will try my utmost to procure for them; for Judas and the priests and the pharisees are ready to do anything I suggest. Nevertheless I see in this a great danger, which demands our closest attention; for if this Man is the Messias expected by his people, He will offer his Death and all his sufferings for the Redemption of men and thereby satisfy for their misdeeds and gain infinite merits for all of them. He will open the heavens and pave the way for mortals to the enjoyment of those rewards of which God has deprived us. Such an issue, if we do not prevent it, shall indeed be a terrible torment for us. Moreover this Man will leave to the world a new example of patience in suffering and show its merit to all the rest of mankind; for He is most meek and humble of heart, and was never seen impatient or excited. These same virtues He will teach all men, which even to think of is an abomination to me, since these are the virtues most offensive to me and to all those who follow my guidance or are imbued with my sentiments. Hence it is necessary to unite on a course of action in regard to persecuting this strange Man, Christ, and that you let me know what is your understanding of this matter."

420. Then the princes of darkness, lashing themselves to incredible fury against our Redeemer held long consultations concerning this enterprise. They deeply deplored their having been probably led into great error, by plotting his death with so much cunning and malice. They concluded henceforth to make use of redoubled astuteness and cunning to repair the damage done and hinder his death, for they were by this time confirmed in their suspicion, that He was the Messias, although they did not reach altogether definite conclusions in

this matter. This suspicion was for Lucifer the cause of so much anxiety and torment, that he approved of the new determination to hinder the death of the Savior and he closed the meeting by saying: "Believe me, friends, that if this Man is at the same time true God, He will, by his Passion and Death, save all men; our dominion will be overthrown and mortals will be raised to new happiness and dominion over us. We were greatly mistaken in seeking his death. Let us immediately proceed to repair our damage."

421. With this intention Lucifer and all his ministers betook themselves to the city and neighborhood of Jerusalem, and there, as is referred in the Gospels, they exerted their influence with Pilate and his wife to prevent the death of the Lord (Matth. 27, 19), and to place other hindrances, which certainly arose, but are not recorded in the Gospels. For before all others they beset Judas with new suggestions, dissuading him from his intended treachery toward his divine Master. When by their suggestions they failed to change his mind or make him desist from his purpose, Lucifer appeared to him in visible and corporeal form and reasoned with him not to procure the death of Christ through the help of the pharisees. Being aware of the unbounded avarice of the disciple, the demon offered him great riches, if he would not deliver Him over to his enemies. Lucifer now tried much more· earnestly to deter Judas than formerly to persuade him to sell his most meek and divine Master.

422. But, 0 woe and misery of human aberration! Judas had given himself up to the leading of satan's malice, but would not now follow his guidance away from it. For the enemy could not call to aid the force of divine grace, and vain are all other motives and influences to prevent man from falling into sin and to make him follow his true good. It was not impossible for God to convert the heart of this perfidious disciple; but the persuasion of the demon, who had torn him

from grace, was of no avail for this purpose. The Lord however was justified in not supplying Judas with further help, since he had cast himself into his exceeding great obstinacy while in the very school of his divine Master, continuing to resist his teaching, inspirations and vast favors; disregarding, in dreadful presumption, the counsels of the Lord and those of his most holy Mother; despising the living example of their lives, the intercourse with them and with all the Apostles. Against all these influences for good the impious disciple had hardened himself with more than demoniacal obstinacy and beyond all the malice of a man free to follow the right. Having run such a course of evil, he arrived at a state, in which his hatred of Christ and of his Mother made him incapable of seeking any of their mercy, unworthy of any light to recognize it and blind to all reason and natural law, which could have made him hesitate to injure the guiltless Originator of so many blessings conferred upon him. This is indeed an astounding example and dreadful warning for the foolish weakness and malice of men, all of whom, if they have no fear, may be drawn into similar dangers and destruction, and bring upon themselves a like unhappy and lamentable ruin.

423. The demons, in despair of ever being able to influence Judas, betook themselves to the pharisees. By many suggestions and arguments they sought to dissuade them from persecuting Christ, our Lord and Savior. But the same happened with them as with Judas and for the same reasons; they could not be diverted from their purpose nor from the wicked deed which they had planned. Although some of the scribes, from motives of human prudence, were led to reconsider whether what they had resolved was advisable; yet, as they were not assisted by divine grace, they were soon again overcome by their hate and envy of the Savior. Hence resulted the further efforts of Lucifer with the wife of Pilate and

with Pilate himself. The former, as is recorded in the Gospels, they incited to womanly pity in order that she might urge Pilate to beware of condemning that just Man (Matth. 27, 19). By these suggestions and by others, which they themselves made to Pilate, they induced him to resort to so many different shifts in order to evade passing sentence of death upon the innocent Savior. Of these I will speak in their proper place. As Lucifer and his satellites were entirely discomfited in their efforts, they again changed their purpose and in their fury now resolved to induce the pharisees, the executioners and their helpers, to heap the most atrocious cruelties upon the Lord and, by the excess of torment, to overcome the invincible patience of the Redeemer, All these machinations of the devil the Lord permitted in order that the high ends of the Redemption might be attained; yet He did not allow the executioners to execute on the sacred person of the Savior some of the more indecent atrocities, to which they were incited by the demons.

424. On the Wednesday following his triumphal entry into Jerusalem Christ our Lord remained at Bethany without going to Jerusalem, and on this day the scribes and pharisees met at the house of Caiphas in order to plan the death of the Savior of the world (Mark 14, 1). The welcome, which the Redeemer had met with among the inhabitants of Jerusalem, and which had followed so shortly upon the resurrection of Lazarus and the many other miracles of those days, had excited their envy to the highest pitch. Besides they had already resolved to take away his life under the false pretext of the public good, as Caiphas had prophesied so contrary to his intention (John 11, 49). The demon, who saw them thus determined, suggested to some of them not to execute their design on the feast of the Pasch lest the people who venerated Christ as the Messias or a great prophet, should cause a disturbance. Lucifer sought by this delay an opportunity to

hinder the death of the Lord altogether. But as Judas was now entirely in the clutches of his avarice and hate, and altogether deprived of any saving grace, he came to the meeting of the priests in great disturbance and terror of mind, and began to treat with them concerning the betrayal of his Master. He closed the deal by accepting thirty pieces of silver, contenting himself with such a price for Him who contained within Himself all the treasures of heaven. In order not to lose their opportunity the priests put up with the inconvenience of its being so near the Pasch. All this was so disposed by divine Providence directing these events.

425. At the same time happened what our Savior is recorded as saying in saint Matthew: "You know that after two days shall be the Pasch, and the Son of man shall be delivered up to be crucified" (Matth. 26, 2). Judas was not present when these words were uttered by Christ; but in the same furious spirit in which he had sold Jesus, he returned to the Apostles and perfidiously began to inquire of his companions, and even of the Lord and his blessed Mother, whither They were to go from Bethany and what the Master was to do on the following few days. All this was merely a treacherous preparation of the perfidious disciple for the betrayal of his Master to the chief pharisees. Like a consummate hypocrite, Judas sought to palliate his treachery by a pretended interest and anxiety. But both the Savior and his most blessed Mother well understood the purpose of feverish activity; for the holy angels immediately reported to Them his shameful contract to which he had bound himself for thirty pieces of silver. On that very day, when the traitor approached the great Lady to ask Her, where the Lord proposed to partake of the Pasch, She, with ineffable meekness, answered him: "Who can penetrate, 0 Judas, the secret judgments of the Most High?" Thenceforward She ceased to warn him against committing the sin; but both She and the Lord tolerated his

presence, until he himself despaired of remedy and eternal
salvation. But this meekest Dove, now certain of the irreparable ruin of Judas and of the delivery of her most holy Son
into the hands of his enemies, broke out in tenderest lamentations in the presence of the angels, for they were the only
ones with whom She could confer about her heartrending
sorrow. In their presence She permitted the sea of her sorrow
to overflow and gave expression of words of greatest wisdom
and affection. She excited the wonder of these holy angels,
who saw such an exalted and new perfection practiced by a
mere Creature in the midst of bitterest sorrows and tribulations.

Words of the Queen

THE VIRGIN MARY SPEAKS TO SISTER MARY OF AGREDA

426. My daughter, all that thou hast understood and written
in this chapter contains great and instructive mysteries for the
mortals who will meditate upon it. Prudently consider first of
all, how my most holy Son, though He, in order to foil and
overcome the devil, and in order to weaken his power against
men, permitted him to retain the nature and the penetrating
knowledge of an angel, nevertheless concealed many things
from him, as thou hast already recorded in other places. In
withholding them from his knowledge the Almighty foiled
the malice of this dragon in a manner most befitting his
sweet and irresistible Providence. On this account was the
hypostatic union of the divine and the human natures concealed, and the devil was allowed to fall into so great confusion regarding this mystery and to be driven into so many
cross purposes, until the Lord revealed himself and convinced
him of the divine glory of his soul even from the moment of
his conception. Likewise He permitted the devil to witness
some of the miracles of his most holy life, and concealed

from him many others. In a similar manner the Lord provides for the welfare of souls in our days, for, although the devil can by his natural powers inform himself of all the doings of each soul, God will not permit it and hides much from him for reasons of his own Providence. Afterwards He allows him to find them out for his greater humiliation. Thus after the work of the Redemption, He permitted the demon for his greater torment and confusion to become aware of so many unheeded mysteries. The infernal dragon is continually lurking about to search into the doings of souls, not only into the exterior, but into the interior activities of each soul. But my most holy Son exerts a most loving care over them ever since He was born and died for them.

427. This blessed care would be much more general and continual with many, if they themselves did not make themselves unworthy by delivering themselves over to the enemy and listening to his deceits and his malicious and cunning advice. Just as the virtuous and the friends of God gradually become instruments in the hands of the Lord and resign themselves entirely to his divine disposition, so that He alone governs and directs them and does not allow them to be moved by other agencies; so, in like manner, many of the reprobate and of those who are forgetful of their Creator and Redeemer and who deliver themselves over to the devil by repeated sins, are moved and drawn into all kinds of wickedness and are mere tools of his depraved malice. An example of this we have in the perfidious disciple and in the murderous pharisees persecuting their Redeemer. None of the mortals are blameless in this respect: for, just as Judas and the priests by the use of their own free will, refused to follow the good advice of the demon and desist from persecuting Christ our Savior, so they could much more easily have refused to join him in persecuting Christ, when they were first tempted. For then they were assisted by grace, if only they wished to

use it, while afterwards they were assisted only by their own free choice and led by their bad habits. That they were in the second instance deprived of grace and help of the Holy Ghost, was only just, because they had given themselves up and subjected themselves to the demon. They had made up their minds to follow him in all his malice and allow themselves to be governed entirely by his perversity, without ever considering the goodness and power of their Creator.

428. Hence you will understand that this infernal serpent can have no power to lead anyone toward the good. but very much toward leading those souls into sin, who are neglectful in issuing from their evil state. Truly I say to thee, my daughter, that if mortals would thoroughly understand this danger, they would be struck with great terror; for there is no created power, which can prevent a soul that has once yielded to sin from casting itself from abyss to abyss. Since the sin of Adam, the weight of human nature, burdened with the concupiscible and irascible passions, is drawn toward sin as the stone toward its center. Joined to this tendency are the bad habits and customs, the power of satan over those who have sinned, and his unceasing tyranny. Who is there, that is so much an enemy of his own welfare as to despise these dangers? The Almighty alone can free him and to his right hand is reserved the remedy. In spite of all this mortals live as secure and forgetful of their ruin as if each one had it in his own power to prevent and repair it at his pleasure. Though many know and openly confess that they cannot rise from their own ruin without the help of God; yet they allow this consciousness to become a mere habit and a vague sentiment and instead of lovingly seeking his aid, they offend and irritate God, expecting Him to wait upon them with his grace until they are tired of sinning or until they are unable to continue their abominable wickedness and ingratitude.

429. Do thou fear, my dearest, this dreadful danger and beware of the first sin, for after the first sin thou wilt be still less able to resist the second, and thou increasest the power of the devil over thee. Remember that thy treasure is most valuable and the vase, in which thou carriest it, fragile: by one fall thou canst lose it all (II Cor. 4, 7). Great is the cunning and sagacity which the serpent uses against thee, and thy insight is but small. Therefore thou must collect thy senses and close them to all outward things; thou must withdraw thy interior within the wall of protection and refuge raised for thee by the Almighty, whence thou canst repel all the inhuman assaults of thy enemies. To excite this fear in thee, it will be sufficient to consider the punishment of Judas which has been made clear to thy understanding. In regard to thy imitation of my behavior in other matters: how thou shouldst act toward those who hate and persecute thee, how thou shouldst love them and bear with them in charity and patience, and how thou shouldst pray for them to the Lord with true zeal for their salvation, as I have done for the traitor Judas: in all this I have before this often exhorted thee. I desire that thou excel and distinguish thyself therein, and that thou instruct thy religious and all those with whom thou dealest in this manner of acting. For in view of the patience and meekness of my most holy Son and my own example, the wicked and all mortals shall be covered with unutterable confusion because they have not pardoned each other with fraternal charity. The sins of hate and vengeance shall be punished with greater severity than other sins on the judgment day; and in this life these vices will soonest drive away the infinite mercy of God and cause eternal punishment of men, unless they amend in sorrow. Those that are kind and sweet toward their enemies and persecutors, and who forget injuries, resemble on that account more particularly the incarnate Word: for Christ always went about seeking to

pardon and to load with blessings those who were in sin. By imitating the charity and the meekness of the Lamb, the soul disposes itself to receive and maintain that noble spirit of charity and love of God and the neighbor, which makes it apt for all the influences of divine grace and benevolence.

Chapter IX

CHRIST OUR SAVIOR PARTS FROM HIS MOST HOLY MOTHER
IN BETHANY IN ORDER TO ENTER UPON HIS SUFFERINGS
ON THE THURSDAY OF HIS LAST SUPPER; THE GREAT LADY
ASKS TO PARTAKE OF HOLY COMMUNION WITH THE REST,
AND AFTERWARDS FOLLOWS WITH MAGDALEN AND OTHER
HOLY WOMEN.

430. Let us now proceed in our history and return to our
Savior in Bethany, whither, after his triumphal entry into
Jerusalem, He had returned with his Apostles. In the last
chapter we anticipated the course of events in relating what
was undertaken by the demons before the betrayal of Christ
and what resulted from the infernal consultation, the treachery of Judas and the council of the pharisees. We will now
take up the thread of events in Bethany, where the great
Queen attended upon and served her divine Son during the
three days intervening between the Palm Sunday and Maun-
dy Thursday. All this time, except what was consumed on
Monday and Tuesday in going to Jerusalem and teaching in
the temple, the Author of life spent with his blessed Mother;
for on Wednesday He did not go to Jerusalem, as I have
already said. On these last journeys He instructed his disciples more clearly and fully concerning the mysteries of his
Passion and of human Redemption. Nevertheless, although
they listened to the teachings and forewarnings of their God

and Master, each one was affected thereby only in so far as his disposition allowed and according to the motives and sentiments of his heart. They were always tardy in their response and in the weakness they fell short of their protestations of zealous love, as the events afterwards showed and as we shall see later on.

431. But to the most blessed Mother our Savior, during the day immediately preceding his Passion, communicated such exalted sacraments and mysteries of the Redemption and of the new law of grace, that many of them will remain hidden until they shall be revealed in the beatific vision. Of those which I have understood I can say very little: but into the heart of the great Queen her Son deposited all that David calls uncertain and hidden of his divine wisdom (Ps. SO, 8). Namely the greater part of the secrets of his works ad extra; such as our salvation, the glorification of the predestined and the consequent exaltation of his holy name. The Lord instructed Mary in all that She was to do during his Passion and Death and enlightened Her anew with divine light. In all these conferences her most holy Son spoke to Her with a new and kingly reserve, such as was in harmony with the greatness of the matter treated of; for now the tenderness and caresses of a Son and Spouse had entirely ceased. But as the natural love of the sweetest Mother and the burning charity of her purest soul had now reached a degree above all comprehension of the human mind, and as the conversation and intercourse with her divine Son was now drawing to a close, no created tongue can describe the tender and mournful affections of that purest of hearts and the sighs of her inmost soul. She was as the mysterious turtledove, that already began to feel the approach of that solitude, which the company of no creature in heaven or on earth could ever relieve or compensate.

432. Thursday, the eve of the Passion and Death of the Savior, had arrived; at earliest dawn the Lord called to Him his most beloved Mother and She, hastening to prostrate Herself at his feet, responded; "Speak, my Lord and Master, for thy servant heareth." Raising Her up from the ground, He spoke to Her in words of soothing and tenderest love: "My Mother, the hour decreed by the eternal wisdom of my Father for accomplishing the salvation and restoration of the human race and imposed upon Me by his most holy and acceptable will, has now arrived; it is proper that now We subject to Him our own will, as We have so often offered to do. Give Me thy permission to enter upon my suffering and death, and, as my true Mother, consent that I deliver Myself over to my enemies in obedience to my eternal Father. In this manner do Thou also willingly cooperate with Me in this work of eternal salvation, since I have received from Thee in thy virginal womb the form of a suffering and mortal man in which I am to redeem the world and satisfy the divine justice. Just as thou, of thy own free will, didst consent to my Incarnation, so I now desire thee to give consent also to my passion and death of the Cross. To sacrifice Me now of thy own free will to the decree of my eternal Father, this shall be the return which I ask of thee for having made thee my Mother; for He has sent Me in order that by the sufferings of my flesh I might recover the lost sheep of his house, the children of Adam" (Matth. 18, 11).

433. These and other words of the Savior, spoken on that occasion, pierced the most loving heart of Mary and cast Her into the throes of a sorrow greater than She had ever endured before. For now had arrived that dreadful hour, whence there was no issue for her pains, neither in an appeal to the swiftfleeting time nor to any other tribunal against the inevitable decree of the eternal Father, that had fixed the term of her beloved Son's life. When now the most prudent

Mother looked upon Him as her God, infinite in his attributes and perfections, and as the true Godman in hypostatical union with the person of the Word, and beheld Him sanctified and ineffably exalted by this union with the Godhead: She remembered the obedience He had shown Her as his Mother during so many years and the blessings He had conferred upon Her during his long intercourse with Her; She realized that soon She was to be deprived of this blessed intercourse and of the beauty of his countenance, of the vivifying sweetness of his words; that She was not only to lose all this at once, but moreover that She was to deliver Him over into the hands of such wicked enemies, to ignominies and torments and to the bloody sacrifice of a death on the Cross. How deeply must all these considerations and circumstances, now so clearly before Her mind, have penetrated into her tender and loving heart and filled it with a sorrow unmeasurable! But with the magnanimity of a Queen, vanquishing this invincible pain, She prostrated Herself at the feet of Her divine Son and Master, and, in deepest reverence, kissing his feet, answered:

434. "Lord and highest God, Author of all that has being, though Thou art the Son of my womb, I am thy handmaid; the condescension of thy ineffable love alone has raised me from the dust to the dignity of being thy Mother. It is altogether becoming that I, vile wormlet, acknowledge and thank thy most liberal clemency by obeying the will of the eternal Father and thy own. I offer myself and resign myself to his divine pleasure, in order that in Me, just as in Thee, my Son and Lord, his eternal and adorable will be fulfilled. The greatest sacrifice which I can make, is that I shall not be able to die with Thee, and that our lot should not be inverted; for to suffer in imitation of Thee and in thy company would be a great relief for my pains, and all torments would be sweet, if undergone in union with thine. That Thou shouldst

endure all these torments for the salvation of mankind shall be my only relief in my pains. Receive, O my God, this sacrifice of my desire to die with Thee, and of my still continuing to live, while thou, the most innocent Lamb and figure of the substance of thy eternal Father undergoest Death (Heb. 1, 3). Receive also the agonies of my sorrow to see the inhuman cruelty of thy enemies executed on thy exalted Person because of the wickedness of the human kind. O ye heavens and elements and all creatures within them, ye sovereign spirits, ye Patriarchs and Prophets, assist me to deplore the death of my Beloved, who gave you being, and bewail with me the misery of men, who are the cause of this Death, and who, failing to profit of such great blessings, shall lose that eternal life so dearly bought! O unhappy you, that are foreknown as doomed! and O ye happy predestined, who shall wash your stoles in the blood of the Lamb (Apoc, 7, 14), you, who knew how to profit by this blessed sacrifice, praise ye the Lord Almighty! O my Son and infinite delight of my soul, give fortitude and strength to thy afflicted Mother; admit Her as thy disciple and companion, in order that she may participate in thy Passion and Cross, and in order that the eternal Father may receive the sacrifice of thy Mother in union with thine."

435. With these and other expressions of her sentiments, which I cannot all record in words, the Queen of heaven answered her most holy Son, and offered Herself as a companion and a coadjutrix in his Passion. Thereupon, thoroughly instructed and prepared by divine light for all the mysteries to be wrought by the Master of life towards accomplishing all his great ends, the most pure Mother, having the Lord's permission, added another request in the following words: "Beloved of my soul and light of my eyes. my Son, I am not worthy to ask Thee what I desire from my inmost soul; but Thou, 0 Lord, art the life of my hope, and

in this my trust I beseech Thee, if such be thy pleasure, to make me a participant in the ineffable Sacrament of thy body and blood. Thou hast resolved to institute it as a pledge of thy glory and I desire in receiving Thee sacramentally in my heart to share the effects of this new and admirable Sacrament. Well do I know, 0 Lord, that no creature can ever merit such an exquisite blessing, which Thou hast resolved to set above all the works of thy magnificence; and in order to induce Thee to confer it upon me, I have nothing else to offer except thy own self and all thy infinite merits. If by perpetuating these merits through the same humanity which thou hast received from my womb, creates for me a certain right, let this right consist not so much in giving Thyself to me in this Sacrament, as in making me thine by this new possession, which restores to me thy sweetest companionship. All my desires and exertions I have devoted to the worthy reception of this holy Communion from the moment in which Thou gavest me knowledge of it and ever since it was thy fixed decree to remain in the holy Church under the species of consecrated bread and wine. Do Thou then, my Lord and God, return to thy first habitation which Thou didst find in thy beloved Mother and thy slave, whom Thou hast prepared for thy reception by exempting Her from the common touch of sin. Then shall I receive within me the humanity, which I have communicated to Thee from my own blood, and thus shall we be united in a renewed and close embrace. This prospect enkindles my heart with most ardent love, and may I never be separated from Thee, who art the infinite Good and the Love of my soul."

436. Many words of incomparable love and reverence were spoken on that occasion by the Queen and Lady; for in the wonderful love of her heart She sought of her most holy Son the privilege of participating in his sacred body and blood. The Lord on his part answered Her with great tender-

ness and granted her request, promising Her the blessing of holy Communion at the hour of its institution. The purest Mother, in deepest devotion, broke out in heroic acts of humility, thankfulness, reverence and living faith in expectation of the desired participation in the most holy Eucharist. Then happened what I shall relate next.

437. The Savior commanded the holy angels of her guard to attend upon Her in visible forms and to serve and console Her in her sorrow and loneliness. With this command they complied most faithfully. The Lord also expressed his desire, that after his departure for Jerusalem with his disciples, She should follow shortly after in company with the holy women who had accompanied them from Galilee, and that She should instruct and encourage them, in order that they might not be scandalized in seeing Him suffer the great ignominies and torments of the frightful death of the Cross. At the close of this interview the Son of the eternal Father gave his blessing to his beloved Mother and prepared to enter upon that last journey, which led to his suffering and Death. The sorrow which filled the hearts of both Son and Mother passes all conception of man; for it was proportioned to the love They had for each other, and this love again was proportioned to the dignity and greatness of the persons concerned. But, although we can so little describe it in words, we are not free to exempt ourselves from meditating upon it and following Them on their sorrowful journey with the deepest compassion. For if we neglect to do so as far as our strength and ability permits, we cannot avoid being reprehended as hardhearted ingrates.

438. Our Savior, having thus parted with his most beloved Mother and sorrowful Spouse, and taking along with Him all his Apostles, a little before midday of the Thursday of the last Supper, departed on his last journey from Bethany to Jerusalem. At the very outset He raised his eyes to the

eternal Father, and, confessing Him in words of thankfulness and praise, again professed his most ardent love and most lovingly and obediently offered to suffer and die for the Redemption of the human race. This prayer and sacrifice of our Savior and Master sprang from such ineffable love and ardor of his spirit, that it cannot be described; all that I say of it seems to me rather a gainsaying of the truth and of what I desire to say. "Eternal Father and my God," said Christ our Lord, "in compliance with thy holy will I now go to suffer and die for the liberation of men, my brethren and the creatures of thy hands. I deliver Myself up for their salvation and to gather those who have been scattered and divided by the sin of Adam (John 11, 52). I go to prepare the treasures, by which the creatures, made according to thy image and likeness, are to be enriched and adorned, so that they may be restored to the height of thy friendship and to eternal happiness, and in order that thy holy name may be known and exalted among all creatures. As far as shall depend upon Thee and Me, no soul shall be deprived of a salvation most abundant; and thy inviolate equity shall stand justified in all those who despise this copious Redemption. "

439. Then following the Author of life, the most blessed Mother, in the company of Magdalen and of the other holy women who had attended upon the Savior and had followed Him from Galilee, took leave of Bethany. In the same manner as the divine Master instructed his Apostles and prepared them for his Passion, in order that they might not desert Him on account of the ignominies they were to witness and on account of the temptations of satan: so also the Queen and Mistress of all virtues exerted Herself in preparing the devoted band of her disciples for witnessing courageously the Death and the frightful scourging and torments of their divine Master. Although, on account of their feminine nature, these women naturally were more frail and weak than

the Apostles, yet some of them showed much more fortitude in adhering to the teachings and in relying on the previous exhortations and examples of their great Mistress and Queen. Among them all, as the Evangelists relate, Mary Magdalen distinguished herself, for she was entirely consumed in the flames of her love; and even naturally She was of a magnanimous, courageous and energetic disposition, well educated and full of a noble fidelity. She, before all others of the apostolate, had taken it upon herself to accompany the Mother of Jesus and attend upon Her during the entire Passion and this her resolve she fulfilled as the most faithful friend of the blessed Mother.

440. The most holy Mother imitated and joined the Savior in his prayer and the offering which He made at this time; for, as I have often said, in the clear mirror furnished Her by the divine light, She was made to see all the works of her divine Son in order that She might imitate them as closely as possible. The holy angels of her guard, obeying the orders of the Savior, accompanied and attended upon Her in visible forms. With these heavenly spirits She conversed about the great sacrament of the Passion, which was yet hidden to her companions and to all the human creatures. They well perceived and deeply pondered the measureless conflagration of love in the pure and candid heart of the Mother and the force with which they saw Her drawn after the sweet ointments of mutual love between Her and Christ, her Son, Spouse and Redeemer. They presented to the eternal Father the sacrifice of praise and expiation offered to Him by his firstborn and only Daughter among the creatures. Since all the mortals were insensible of this benefit and of the indebtedness, in which they were placed by the love of Christ their Lord and his blessed Mother, She ordered the holy angels to give benediction, glory and honor to the

Father, the Son and the Holy Ghost; and they eagerly fulfilled the wish of their great Princess and Queen.

441. Words fail me, and worthy sentiments of sorrow, for expressing properly what I understood on this occasion concerning the amazement of the holy angels, when on the one hand they saw the incarnate Word and his most holy Mother wending their way in most ardent love of mankind toward the accomplishment of man's Redemption, and on the other beheld the vileness, ingratitude, and hardhearted neglect of men concerning their obligations consequent upon this blessing; a blessing which would have moved to recognition even the demons, if they had been the objects of such a benefit. The amazement of the angels arose not from any ignorance on their part, but from indignation at our unbearable in gratitude. I am but a weak woman and less than a wormlet of the earth; but in the light which has been given me concerning this matter, I wish to raise up my voice, so that it may be heard through all the world and rouse up the children of vanity and lovers of deceit (Cant. 1, 3), to a sense of their obligation toward Christ and his holy Mother. Prostrate on the ground, I wish to implore all men, not to be so dull of heart and hostile to themselves as not to rise from this stupor of forgetfulness, which keeps us in constant danger of eternal death and deprives us of the celestial life and happiness merited for us by the Redeemer and Lord by the bitterness of the Cross.

Words of the Queen

THE VIRGIN MARY SPEAKS TO SISTER MARY OF AGREDA

442. My daughter, as thy soul has been furnished with special gifts of enlightenment, I call and invite thee anew to cast thyself into the sea of mysteries contained in the passion and death of my divine Son. Direct all thy faculties and

strain all the powers of thy heart and soul, to make thyself at least somewnat worthy of understanding and meditating upon the ignominies and sorrows of the Son of the eternal Father in his death on the Cross for the salvation of men; and also of considering my doings and sufferings in connection with his bitterest Passion. This science, so much neglected by men, I desire that thou, my daughter, study and learn, so as to be able to follow thy Spouse and imitate me, who am thy Mother and Teacher. Writing down and feeling deeply all that I shall teach thee of these mysteries, thou shouldst detach thyself entirely of human and earthly affections and of thy own self, so as freely to follow our footsteps in destitution and poverty. And since I do thee the special favor of calling thee aside to instruct thee in fulfillment of the will of my holy Son and since We seek through thee to teach others; thou shouldst correspond to this copious Redemption as if it was solely for thy benefit and as if all of it would be lost, if thou dost not profit by its blessings. So much must thou esteem it; for in the love which caused my most holy Son to die for thee, He looked upon thee with as great an affection, as if thou hadst been the only one that needed the remedy of his Passion and Death.

443. This is the standard by which thou must measure thy obligations and thy gratitude. Since thou then both seest the base and dangerous forgetfulness of men in regard to this benefit, and knowest that for these very men their God and Creator had died, it should be thy earnest endeavor to compensate Him for their neglect by thy ardent love, as if the proper return for his benefits was left entirely to thy fidelity and gratitude alone. At the same time grieve over the blind folly of men in despising eternal felicity and in treasuring up for themselves the wrath of the Lord by frustrating the boundless effects of his love for the world. This is the purpose for which I make known to Thee so many secrets and

my unparalleled sorrow in the hour of his parting from me to go to his sacred sufferings unto death. There are no words which can describe the bitterness of my soul on that occasion; but the contemplation of it should cause thee to esteem no hardship great, to seek no rest or consolation on earth, except to suffer and die for Christ. Do thou sorrow with me; for this faithful correspondence is due to me, who favor thee with these graces.

444. I wish thee also to ponder, what a horrible crime it is in the eyes of the Lord, in mine, and in those of all the saints, that men should despise and neglect the frequent reception of the holy Communion, and that they should approach it without preparation and fervent devotion. Principally in order that thou mayest understand and record this warning, I have manifested to thee, what I did on that occasion and how I prepared myself so many years for receiving my most blessed Son in the holy Sacrament and also the rest, which thou art yet to write for the instruction and confusion of men. For if I, who was innocent of any hindering sin and filled with all graces, sought to increase my fitness for this favor by such fervent acts of love, humility and gratitude, consider what efforts thou and the other children of the Church, who every day and hour incur new guilt and blame, must make in order to fit yourselves for the beauty of the Divinity and humanity of my most holy Son? What excuse can those men give in the last judgment, who have despised this ineffable love and blessing, which they had always present in the holy Church, ready to fill them with the plenitude of his gifts, and who rather sought diversion in worldly pleasures and attended upon the outward and deceitful vanities of this earthly life? Be thou amazed at this insanity as were the holy angels, and guard thyself against falling into the same error.

Chapter X

CHRIST OUR SAVIOR CELEBRATES THE LAST SUPPER WITH HIS DISCIPLES ACCORDING TO THE LAW AND HE WASHES THEIR FEET; HIS MOST HOLY MOTHER OBTAINS A FULL KNOWLEDGE AND UNDERSTANDING OF ALL THESE MYSTERIES.

445. Our Redeemer proceeded on his way to Jerusalem on the evening of the Thursday preceding his Passion and Death. During their conversation on the way, while he instructed them in the approaching mysteries, the Apostles proposed their doubts and difficulties, and He, as the Teacher of wisdom and as a loving Father answered them in words which sweetly penetrated into their very hearts. For, having always loved them, He, like a divine Swan, in these last hours of his life, manifested his love with so much the greater force of amiable sweetness in his voice and manner. The knowledge of his impending Passion and the prospect of his great torments, not only did not hinder Him in the manifestations of his love, but, just as fire is more concentrated by the frost, so his love broke forth with so much the greater force at the prospect of these sufferings. The conflagration of the love which burned in the heart of Jesus, issued forth to overpower by its penetrating activity, first those who were nearest about Him and then also those, who sought to extinguish it forever. Excepting Christ and His blessed Mother,

the rest of us mortals are ordinarily roused to resentment by injury, or dismayed and disgusted by adversity, and we deem it a great thing not to revenge ourselves on those who offend us; but the love of the divine Master was not daunted by the impending ignominies of his Passion, nor dampened by the ignorance of his Apostles and the disloyalty, which He was so soon to experience on their part.

446. The Apostle asked Him where He wished to celebrate the paschal supper (Matth. 26); for on that Thursday night the Jews were to partake of the lamb of the Pasch, a most notable and solemn national feast. Though of all their feasts, this eating of the paschal lamb was most prophetic and significant of the Messiah and of the mysteries connected with Him and his work, the Apostles were as yet scarcely aware of its intimate connection with Christ. The divine Master answered by sending saint Peter and saint John to Jerusalem to make arrangements for the paschal lamb. This was to be in a house, where they would see a servant enter with a jug of water, and whose master they were to request in Christ's name to prepare a room for his last Supper with his disciples. This man lived near to Jerusalem; rich and influential, he was at the same time devoted to the Savior and was one of those who had witnessed and had believed in his miracles and teachings. The Author of life rewarded his piety and devotion by choosing his house for the celebration of the great mystery, and thus consecrate it as a temple for the faithful of future times. The two Apostles immediately departed on their commission and following the instructions, they asked the owner of this house to entertain the Master of life for the solemn celebration of this feast of the unleavened bread.

447. The heart of this householder was enlightened by special grace and he readily offered his dwelling with all the necessary furniture for celebrating the supper according to

the law. He assigned to them a very large hall, appropriate tapestries and adorned for the mysteries which, unbeknown to him and the Apostles, the Lord was to celebrate therein. After due preparation had thus been made the Savior and the other Apostles arrived at this apartment. His most blessed Mother and the holy women in her company came soon after. Upon entering, the most humble Queen prostrated Herself on the floor and adored her divine Son as usual, asking his blessing and begging Him to let Her know what She was to do. He bade Her go to another room, where She would be able to see all that was done on this night according to the decrees of Providence, and where She was to console and instruct, as far as was proper, the holy women of her company. The great Lady obeyed and retired with her companions. She exhorted them to persevere in faith and prayer, while She, knowing that the hour of her holy Communion was at hand, continued to keep her interior vision riveted on the doings of her most holy Son and to prepare Herself for the worthy reception of his body and blood.

448. His most holy Mother having retired, our Lord and Master, Jesus, with his Apostles and disciples, took their places to celebrate the feast of the lamb. He observed all the ceremonies of the Law (Exodus 12, 3), as prescribed by Himself through Moses. During this last Supper He gave to the Apostles an understanding of all the ceremonies of the figurative law, as observed by the Patriarchs and Prophets. He showed them how beneath it was hidden the real truth, namely, all that He himself was to accomplish as Redeemer of the world. He made them understand, that now the law of Moses and its figurative meaning was evacuated by its real fulfillment; that, as the light of the new law of grace had begun to shine, the shadows were dispelled and the natural law, which had been reconfirmed by the precepts of Moses, was now placed permanently upon its real foundation,

ennobled and perfected by his own teachings; that the efficacy of the Sacraments of the new Law abrogated those of the
old as being merely figurative and ineffectual. He told them
that, by celebrating this Supper, He set an end to the rites
and obligations of the old Law, which was only a preparation
and a representation of what He was now about to accomplish, and hence having attained its end, had now become
useless.

449. This instruction enlightened the Apostles concerning
the deep mysteries of this last Supper. The other disciples
that were present, did not understand these mysteries as
thoroughly as the Apostles. Judas attended to and understood
them least of all, yea, not at all; for he was completely under
the spell of his avarice, thinking only of his prearranged
treason and how he could execute it most secretly. The Lord
revealed none of his secret treachery; for so it best served the
designs and equity of his most high Providence. He did not
wish to exclude him from the Supper and from the other
mysteries, leaving it to his own wickedness to bring about his
exclusion. The divine Master always treated him as his
disciple, apostle and minister, and was careful of his honor.
Thus He taught the children of the Church by his own
example, with what veneration they should treat his ministers
and priests, how they must guard their honor and avoid
speaking of their sins and weaknesses still adhering to frail
human nature in spite of their high office. None of them will
ever be worse than Judas, as we can well assume; and not one
of the faithful will ever be like Christ, our Lord and Savior,
nor, as our faith teaches us, will anyone ever have his divine
authority and power. Hence, as all men are of infinitely
smaller consideration than our Savior, let them accord to his
ministers, who though wicked will ever be better than Judas,
the same treatment as He condescended to accord to this
most wicked disciple and Apostle. This duty toward priests is

not less urgent even in superiors; for also Christ our Lord who bore with Judas and was so careful of his reputation was infinitely his superior.

450. On this occasion the Redeemer composed a new canticle by which He exalted the eternal Father for having in his Son fulfilled the figures of the old Law and for thus advancing the glory of his holy name. Prostrate upon the earth, He humiliated Himself in his humanity before God, confessing, adoring and praising the Divinity as infinitely superior to his humanity. Then addressing the eternal Father, He gave vent to the burning affection of his heart in the following sublime prayer.

451. "My eternal Father and infinite God, thy divine and eternal will resolved to create this my human nature in order that I may be the Head of all those that are predestined for thy glory and happiness and who are to attain their true blessedness by availing themselves of my works. For this purpose, and in order to redeem them from the fall of Adam, I have lived with them thirty-three years. Now, my Lord and Father, the opportune and acceptable hour for fulfilling thy eternal will has arrived, the greatness of thy holy name is about to be revealed to men and thy incomprehensible Divinity, through holy faith, is to be made known and exalted among all nations. It is time that the seven sealed book be opened as Thou hast commissioned Me to do, and that the figures of old come to a happy solution (Apoc. 5, 7). The ancient sacrifices of animals, which prefigured the one I am now voluntarily to make of Myself for the children of Adam, for the members of my mystical body, for the sheep of thy flock, must now come to an end, and I beseech Thee in this hour to look down with an eye of mercy. If in the past thy anger has been placated by these ancient figures and sacrifices which I am now about to abrogate, let it now, my Father, be entirely extinguished, since I am ready to offer

Myself in voluntary sacrifice to die for men on the Cross and give Myself as a holocaust of my love (Eph. 5,2). Therefore, Lord, let the rigor of thy justice be relaxed and look upon the human race with eyes of mercy. Let Us institute a new law for men, by which they may throw down the bars of their disobedience and open for themselves the gates of heaven. Let them now find a free road and open portals for entering with Me upon the vision of thy Divinity, as many of them as will follow my footsteps and obey my law."

452. The eternal Father graciously received this prayer of our Redeemer and sent innumerable hosts of his angelic courtiers to assist at the wonderful works, which Christ was to perform in that place. While this happened in the Cenacle, most holy Mary in her retreat was raised to highest contemplation, in which She witnessed all that passed as if She were present. Thus She was enabled to co-operate and correspond as a most faithful Helpmate, enlightened by the highest wisdom. By heroic and celestial acts of virtue She imitated the doings of Christ, our Savior; for all of them awakened fitting resonance in her bosom and caused a mysterious and divine echo of like petitions and prayers in the sweetest Virgin. Moreover She composed new and admirable canticles of praise for all that the sacred humanity of Christ was now about to accomplish in obedience to the divine will and in accordance and in fulfillment of the figures of the old Law.

453. Very wonderful and worthy of all admiration would it be for us, as it was for the holy angels and as it will be for all the blessed, if we could understand the divine harmony of the works and virtues in the heart of our great Queen, which like a heavenly chorus neither confused nor hindered each other in their superabundance on this occasion. Being filled with the intelligence of which I have spoken, She was sensible of the mysterious fulfillment and accomplishment of the

ceremonies and figures of the old Law through the most noble and efficacious Sacraments of the new. She realized the vast fruits of the Redemption in the predestined; the ruin of the reprobate; the exaltation of the name of God and of the sacred humanity of Christ; the widespread knowledge and faith in the true God now beginning throughout the world. She fully understood, how the heavens had been closed for so many ages in order that now the children of Adam might enter through the establishment and progress of the new evangelical Church and its ministers; and how her divine Son was the most wonderful and skillful Artificer of all these blessings, exciting the admiration and praise of all the courtiers of heaven. For these magnificent results, without forgetting the least of them, She now blessed the eternal Father and gave Him ineffable thanks in the consolation and jubilee of her soul.

454. But also She reflected, that all these admirable works were to cost her divine Son the sorrow, ignominies, affronts and torments of his Passion, and at last the bitter death of the Cross, all of which He was to endure in the very humanity that He had received from Her; while at the same time, such a number of the children of Adam, for whom He suffered, would ungratefully waste the copious fruit of the Redemption. This knowledge filled with bitterest sorrow the purest heart of the loving Mother. But as She was a living and faithful reproduction of her most holy Son, all these sentiments and operations found room in her magnanimous and expanded heart, and therefore She was not disturbed nor dismayed, nor did She fail to console and instruct her companions; but, without losing touch of her high intelligences, She descended to their level of thought in her words of consolation and of eternal life for their instruction. O admirable Instructress and superhuman example entirely to be followed and imitated! It is true, that in comparison with this

sea of grace and light, our prerogatives dwindle into insignificance; but it is also true, that our sufferings and trials in comparison with hers are so to say only imaginary and not worthy to be even noticed, since She suffered more than all the children of Adam together. Yet neither in order to imitate Her, nor for our eternal welfare, can we be induced to suffer with patience even the least adversity. All of them excite and dismay us and take away our composure; we give vent to our passions, we angrily resist and are consumed with restless sorrow; in our stubbornness we lose our reason, give free reign to evil movements and hasten on toward the precipice. Even good fortune lures us to destruction, and so no reliance can be placed in our infected and spoiled nature. Let us be mindful of our heavenly Mistress on such occasions, in order that we may set ourselves right.

455. Having completed the Supper and fully instructed his disciples, Christ our Savior, as saint John tells us (John 13, 4), arose from the table in order to wash their feet. He first prostrated Himself before his eternal Father and addressed to Him another prayer of the same kind as that before the supper. It was not uttered in words, but was conceived interiorly, as follows: "Eternal Father, Creator of the universe, I am thy image and the figure of thy substance, engendered by thy intellect (Heb. 1,3). Having offered Myself for the Redemption of the world through my Passion and Death according to thy will, I now desire to enter upon these sacraments and mysteries by humiliating Myself to the dust, so that the pride of Lucifer may be confounded by the humility of thy Onlybegotten. In order to leave an example of humility to my Apostles and to my Church, which must be built up on the secure foundation of this virtue, I desire, my Father, to wash the feet of my disciples, including the least of all of them, Judas, steeped in his own malice. I shall prostrate Myself before him in deepest and sincerest self-

abasement to offer him my friendship and salvation. Though he is my greatest enemy among the mortals, I shall not refuse him pardon for his treachery, nor deny him kindest treatment, so that, if he shall decline to accept it, all the world may know, that I have opened up to him the arms of my mercy, and that he repelled my advances with obstinate contempt."

456. Such was the prayer of the Savior in preparing to wash the feet of his disciples. There are not words or similitudes in all creation which could properly express the divine impetus of the love with which He undertook and accomplished these works of mercy; for in comparison to it the activity of fire is but slow, the inflowing of the tide but weak, the tendency of a stone toward its center but tardy, and all the forces of the elements in the world that we can imagine in their united activity, but inadequate representations of the power of his love. But we cannot fail to perceive, that divine love and wisdom alone could ever conceive a humiliation, by which both the Divinity and his sacred humanity lowered themselves beneath the feet of mere creatures, and beneath the feet of the worst of them, Judas, that He who is the Word of the eternal Father, the Holy of the holy, the essential Goodness, the Lord of lords and the King of kings, should prostrate Himself before the most wicked of men and touch the feet of this most impure and degraded of his creatures with his lips, and that He should do all this merely for the chance of justifying his wayward disciple and securing for him immeasurable blessings.

457. The Master arose from his prayer and, his countenance beaming with peace and serenity, commanded his disciples to seat themselves like persons of superior station, while He himself remained standing as if He were their servant. Then He laid aside the mantle, which He wore over the seamless garment and which covered all his Person except

the feet. He wore sandals, which however He sometimes had dispensed with on his preaching tours, though at other times He had worn them ever since his most holy Mother had put them on his feet in Egypt. They grew in size with his feet as He advanced in age, as I have already remarked (Vol. II, 691). Having laid aside this mantle, which was the garment spoken of by the Evangelist (John 13, 4), He girded his body with one end of a large towel, permitting the other part to hang down free. Then He poured water into a basin for washing the feet of the Apostles, who were wonderingly observing the proceedings of their divine Master.

458. He first approached the head of the Apostle, saint Peter. But when this excitable Apostle saw prostrate at his feet the Lord, whom he had acknowledged and proclaimed as the Son of God, being again renewed and enlightened in his faith and overcome by humiliation at his own insignificance, he said: "Thou shalt never wash my feet!" The Author of life answered him with some earnestness: "Thou dost not know at present what I am doing, but later on thou wilt understand it." This was the same as to say to him: obey now first my command and will, and do not prefer thy will unto mine, disturbing and perverting the order of virtues. Before all thou must yield captive thy understanding and believe that what I do is proper; then, having believed and obeyed, thou wilt understand the hidden mysteries of my doings, into the knowledge of which thou must enter by obedience. Without obedience thou canst not be truly humble, but only presumptuous. Nor can thy humility take preference of mine; I humiliated Myself unto the Death; and in order to thus humiliate Me, I sought the way of obedience; but thou, who art my disciple, dost not follow my doctrine. Under color of humility thou art disobedient, by thus perverting the right order thou stripst thyself as well of humility as of obedience, following thy own presumptuous judgment.

459. Saint Peter did not understand this doctrine contained in the first answer of our Lord; for though he belonged to his school, he had not yet experienced the divine effects of this washing and contact. Floundering in the errors of his indiscreet humility, he answered the Lord: "I will never consent that Thou wash my feet!" But the Lord of life answered with greater severity: "If I wash thee not, thou shalt have no part with Me." By this threatening answer the Lord sanctioned obedience forever as the secure way. According to human insight, saint Peter certainly had some excuse for being slow in permitting God to prostrate Himself before an earthly and sinful man as he was and to allow Him, whom he had so recently acknowledged and adored as his Creator, to perform such an unheard of act of self-abasement. But his opposition was not excusable in the eyes of the divine Master, who could not err in what He wished to do. For whenever there is not an evident error in what is commanded, obedience must be blind and without evasion. In this mystery the Lord wished to repair the disobedience of our first parents, Adam and Eve, by which sin entered into the world; and because of the similarity and relation between it and the disobedience of saint Peter, our Lord threatened him with a similar punishment, telling him, that if he did not obey, he should have no part in Him; namely, that he should be excluded from the merits and fruits of the Redemption, by which alone we become worthy of his friendship and glory. He also threatened to deprive him of participation in his body and blood, which He was now about to perpetuate in the sacramental species of bread and wine. The Savior gave him to understand, that how ardently so ever He desired to communicate Himself not only in part but in entirety, yet disobedience would certainly deprive even the Apostle of this blessing.

460. By this threat of our Lord Christ saint Peter was so chastened and instructed, that he immediately submitted from his whole heart and said: "Lord, not only my feet, but also my hands and my head." He wished to say: I offer my feet in order to walk in obedience, my hands in order to exercise it, and my head in order to surrender all of my own judgment, that may be contrary to its dictates. The Lord accepted this submission of saint Peter and said: "He that is washed, needs not but to wash his feet, but is clean wholly. And you are clean, but not all," for among them was seated the most unclean Judas. This Christ said, because the disciples (all except Judas), had been justified and cleaned by his doctrines; and they needed only to be cleansed from imperfections and venial sins, so that they might approach holy Communion with so much the more worthiness and better preparation, such as is required in order to participate fully in its divine effects and receive its abundant graces with so much the greater efficacy and plenitude. For venial sins, distractions and lukewarmness hinder all these benefits very much. Thereupon the feet of saint Peter were washed, as also those of the other disciples, who permitted it in great astonishment and bathed in tears; for all of them were filled with new enlightenment and gifts of grace.

461. The divine Master then proceeded to wash also the feet of Judas, whose perfidious treason could not prevent the charity of Christ from secretly bestowing upon him tokens of even greater charity than upon the other Apostles. Without permitting it to be noticed by the others, He manifested his special love toward Judas in two ways. On the one hand, in the kind and caressing manner in which He approached Him, knelt at his feet, washed them, kissed them and pressed them to his bosom. On the other hand, by seeking to move his soul with inspirations proportionate to the dire depravity of his conscience; for the assistance offered to Judas was in

itself much greater than that offered to the other Apostles. But as the disposition of this Apostle was most wicked, his vices deeply ingrown upon him, his understanding and his faculties much disturbed and weakened; as he had entirely forsaken God and given himself over to the devil, and, as he had enthroned the evil spirit in his heart; he resisted all the divine advances and inspirations connected with this washing of his feet. He was moreover harassed by the fear of breaking his contract with the scribes and pharisees. As the bodily presence of Christ and the interior urgency of his inspirations both bestormed his sense of right, there arose within his darkened soul a dreadful hurricane of conflicting thoughts, filling him with dismay and bitterness, and fiercest anger, whirling him still farther away from his Savior and turning the divine balsam applied to his soul into deadly poison of hellish malice and total depravity.

462. Thus it came that the malice of Judas resisted the saving contact of those divine hands, in which the eternal Father had placed miraculous power to enrich all creatures with his blessings. Even if he had not received any other assistance except that naturally flowing from the visible and personal presence of the Author of life, the wickedness of this unhappy disciple would have been beyond all bounds. The outward aspect of Christ our Lord was most exquisitely charming and attractive; his countenance, serenely dignified, yet sweetly expressive and beautiful, was framed in abundant waves of golden chestnut hair, freely growing after the manner of the Nazarenes; his frank and open eyes beamed forth grace and majesty; his mouth, nose and all the features of his face exhibited the most perfect proportion and his whole Person was clothed in such entrancing loveliness, that He drew upon Himself the loving veneration of all who beheld Him without malice in their hearts. Over and above all this, the mere sight of Him caused in the beholders an interior joy

and enlightenment, engendering heavenly thoughts and
sentiments in the soul. This divine Personage, so lovable and
venerable, Judas now saw at his feet, striving to please him by
new tokens of affection and seeking to gain him by new
impulses of love. But so great was the perversity of Judas,
that nothing could move or soften his hardened heart; on the
contrary, he was irritated by the gentleness of the Savior, and
he refused to look upon his face or take notice of his actions;
for from the time in which he had lost faith and grace, he
was filled with hatred toward his Master and toward his
heavenly Mother and never looked Them in the face. Greater, in a certain respect, was the terror of Lucifer at the presence of Christ our Savior: for this demon, having established
himself in the heart of Judas, could not bear the humility of
the divine Master toward his disciples and sought to escape
from Judas and from the Cenacle. But the Lord detained him
by his almighty power in order that his pride might be
crushed. Yet later on he was cast out from that place, filled
with fury, and with the suspicion, that Christ might after all
be the true God.

463. The Lord completed the washing of the feet, and
again assuming the upper garment, seated Himself in the
midst of his Apostles and began the discourse recorded by
saint John: "Know you what I have done to you? You call me
Master, and Lord; and you say well; if then I, being your
Lord and Master, have washed your feet; you also ought to
wash one another's feet. For I have given you an example,
that as I have done to you, so you do also. Amen, Amen, I
say to you: The servant is not greater than his lord; neither is
the Apostle greater than He that sent him" (John 13, 13).
Then the Lord proceeded to propound great mysteries and
truths, which I will not expatiate upon, but for which I refer
the reader to the Gospels. This discourse still further enlightened the Apostles in the mysteries of the most blessed Trinity

and of the Incarnation, and prepared them by new graces for the holy Eucharist, confirming them in their understanding of the vast significance of his doctrines and miracles. Among them all saint Peter and saint John were most fully enlightened; but each of the Apostles received more or less insight according to his disposition and according to the divine ordainment. What saint John says about his questioning the Lord concerning the traitor who was to sell Him, and the answer of the Lord, all happened before at the Supper itself, when the beloved disciple reclined on the bosom of his divine Master. For saint Peter, in his fervent attachment to his Master and his outspoken love, was anxious to know who was the traitor, in order that he might avenge or prevent the treason. But saint John, though he recognized the traitor by the bread dipped into the sauce and handed to Judas, would not inform saint Peter. He alone knew the secret, but taught by the charity which he had acquired in the school of his divine Master, he buried the secret in his bosom.

464. While he thus reclined on the bosom of Jesus our Savior, saint John was privileged in many other ways; for there he was made to see many most exalted mysteries of the divine humanity and of the Queen of heaven, his most holy Mother. On this occasion also he was commissioned to take charge of Her; for on the Cross Christ did not say to him: She shall be thy Mother, nor, thou shalt be her son; but, behold thy Mother, because this was not a matter resolved upon at that time, but one which was then to be made manifest publicly as having been ordained and decreed beforehand. Of all these sacraments connected with the washing of the feet, of the words and discourses of her Son, his most pure Mother was minutely informed by interior vision, as I have stated at other times, and for all of them She gave thanks and glory to the Most High. And when afterwards the wonderful works of the Lord were accomplished,

She beheld them not as one ignorant of them; but as one who saw fulfilled, what She had known before and what had been recorded in her heart like the law recorded on the tablets of Moses. She enlightened also her companions of all that was proper, reserving whatever they were not capable of understanding.

Words of the Queen

THE VIRGIN MARY SPEAKS TO SISTER MARY OF AGREDA

465. My daughter, in three virtues mentioned by thee in the foregoing chapter as especially practiced by my Son and Lord, I wish that thou be particularly zealous as his spouse and my beloved disciple. They are the virtues of charity, humility and obedience in which Jesus desired to signalize Himself toward the end of his life. Without doubt He manifested his love for men during his whole life, since He performed for them such admirable works from the very first instant of his conception in my womb. But towards the end of his life, when He established the evangelical law of the New Testament, the fire of ardent love, that burned in his bosom, burst out in more consuming flames. On this last occasion the charity of the Savior for the children of Adam exerted its full force, since it was urged on by the sorrows of death that encompassed Him, and was spurred on from the outside by the dislike of men for suffering, their self chosen misfortunes and their boundless ingratitude and perversity in seeking to destroy the honor and the life of Him, who was ready to sacrifice all for their eternal happiness. By this conflict his love was inflamed to the point at which it could not be extinguished (Cant. 8, 7) ; and thus being now about to leave the earth, He was driven to exercise all his ingenuity in attempting to prolong his benefactions and his intercourse with men, leaving among them, by his teachings, works and

examples, the sure means of participating in the effects of his divine charity.

466. In this art of loving thy neighbor for God's sake I wish that thou be very expert and zealous. This thou wilt be, if the very injuries and sufferings with which they afflict thee, shall waken in thee a greater love. Thou must remember, that then alone wilt thou be secure and unwavering, when neither benefits nor flatteries of men have any effect on thee. For to love those who do thee good, is a duty; but if thou art heedless, thou canst not know, whether in that case thou lovest them for God's sake, or for the sake of the benefits they confer, which would be loving thy own advantage or thyself rather than thy neighbor for God's sake. He who loves for other than God's sake or for vain complaisance merely, has not yet learned true charity; since he is yet taken up with the blind love of his own ease. But if thou love those who do not satisfy any of these cravings, thou art led on to love them for the Lord's sake as the principal motive and object of thy love, loving Him in his creatures, whoever they be. Thou must exercise thyself in both the corporal and the spiritual works of mercy; but as thou hast fewer occasions to exercise those of the body than those of the spirit, thou must continually extend thy spiritual works of charity, multiplying, according to the will of thy Savior, thy prayers, petitions, pious practices, accompanying them with prudent and holy admonitions and thus advancing the spiritual welfare of souls. Remember that my Lord and Son conferred no bodily blessings on anyone, without accompanying them with spiritual, and it would have been derogatory to the divine perfection of his works, to perform them without this plenitude of goodness. From this thou wilt understand how much we must prefer the benefits of soul to those of the body; hence thou must always seek them in the first place, although earthlyminded men blindly prefer temporal blessings, forgetting the eternal

ones and those tending toward the friendship and grace of the Most High.

467. The virtues of humility and obedience were highly exalted by the conduct of my most holy Son in washing the feet of his Apostles. If by thy interior enlightenment concerning this extraordinary example thou dost not humble thyself to the dust, thy heart is indeed hardened and thou art very obtuse in the knowledge of the Lord. Let it then be understood henceforth, that thou never canst consider or profess thyself sufficiently humbled, even when thou findest thyself despised and trodden under foot by all men, sinners as they are; for they never can be as bad as Judas, or thou as good as thy Lord and Master. But to merit and to be honored by this virtue of humility, will give thee such perfection and worthiness, that thou wilt deserve the name of a spouse of Christ and make thyself somewhat like unto Him. Without this humility no soul can be raised to excellence and communication with the Lord; for the exalted must first be humbled and only the lowly ones can and should be exalted (Matth. 23, 12) ; and souls are always raised up by the Lord in proportion as they have humiliated themselves.

468. In order that thou mayest not lose this pearl of humility just at the time when thou thinkest thyself secure of it, remember that the exercise of it is not to be preferred to obedience, nor must thou practice it merely at thy own will, but in subjection to thy superiors; for if thou prefer thy own judgment to that of thy superiors even if thou do it under color of humility, thou art guilty of pride; for that would be not only refusing to seek the lowest place, but placing thyself above thy superior. Hence thou mayest understand the error of shrinking back, like saint Peter, from the favors and blessings of the Lord, depriving thee thereby not only of the gifts and treasures offered thee, but of the advantage of humility, which thou seekest and which is much preferable.

Thou failest also in gratefully acknowledging the high ends and in striving after the exaltation of his holy name, which the Lord seeks in such works. It is not thy business to enter into the examination of his secret and exalted judgments, nor to correct them by thy reasonings and thy objections on account of which thou mightst think thyself unworthy of his favors or incapable of performing the works enjoined. All this is a seed of Lucifer's pride, covered up by apparent humility as he thus seeks to hinder the communications of the Lord, his gifts and his friendship, which thou desirest so much. Let it then be to thee an inviolable rule, that as soon as thy confessors and superiors approve of certain favors and blessings as coming from the Lord, thou accept them as such with due thanks and reverence. Do not allow thyself to be led into new doubts and vacillating fears, but correspond with the favors of the Lord in humble fear and tranquil obedience.

Chapter XI

CHRIST OUR SAVIOR CELEBRATES THE SACRAMENTAL SUPPER, CONSECRATING HIS TRUE AND SACRED BODY AND BLOOD IN THE HOLY EUCHARIST; HIS PRAYERS AND PETITIONS; THE COMMUNION OF HIS BLESSED MOTHER AND OTHER MYSTERIES OF THIS OCCASION.

469. With great diffidence do I enter upon the treatment of the ineffable mystery of the holy Eucharist and of what happened at its institution; for, raising the eyes of my soul toward the light which encompasses and governs me in the performance of this work, the high intelligence given me of these vast wonders and sacraments reproaches me with my littleness in comparison with the greatness therein manifested. My faculties are disturbed and I cannot find words to explain what I see and conceive, although all these conceptions are far from the reality that is shown to my understanding. But, though ignorant of the terms and though very unfit for such discourse, I must speak, in order that I may continue this history and relate what part the great Lady of the world had in these wonders. If I do not speak as appropriately as the matter demands, let my amazement and my lowly condition be my excuse; for it is not easy to yield to the exactions of spoken words, when the will is so intent on supplying the defects of the understanding and on enjoying that, which it is hopeless and even unbecoming to manifest.

470. Christ had partaken of the prescribed supper with his disciples reclining on the floor around a table, which was elevated from it little more than the distance of six or seven fingers; for such was the custom of the Jews. But after the washing of the feet He ordered another, higher table to be prepared, such as we now use for our meals. By this arrangement He wished to put an end to the legal suppers and to the lower and figurative law and establish the new Supper of the law of grace. From that time on He wished the sacred mysteries to be performed on the tables or altars, which are in use in the Catholic Church. The table was covered with a very rich cloth and upon it was placed a plate or salver and a large cup in the form of a chalice, capacious enough to hold the wine. All this was done in pursuance of the will of Christ our Savior, who by his divine power and wisdom directed all these particulars. The master of the house was inspired to offer these rich vessels, which were made of what seemed a precious stone like emerald. The Apostles often used it afterwards in consecrating, whenever the occasion permitted it. The Lord seated himself at this table with the Apostles and some of the other disciples, and then ordered some unleavened bread to be placed on the table and some wine to be brought, of which He took sufficient to prepare the chalice.

471. Then the Master of life spoke words of most endearing love to his Apostles, and, though his sayings were wont to penetrate to the inmost heart at all times, yet on this occasion they were like the flames of a great fire of charity, which consumed the souls of his hearers. He manifested to them anew the most exalted mysteries of his Divinity, humanity and of the works of the Redemption. He enjoined upon them peace and charity, of which He was now to leave a pledge in the mysteries about to be celebrated. He reminded them, that in loving one another, they would be loved by the eternal Father with the same love in which He was beloved.

He gave them an understanding of the fulfillment of this promise in having chosen them to found the new Church and the law of grace. He renewed in them the light concerning the supreme dignity, excellence and prerogatives of his most pure Virgin Mother. Among all the Apostles, saint John was most deeply enlightened in these mysteries on account of the office imposed upon him. The great Lady, from her retreat, beheld in divine contemplation all these doings of her Son in the Cenacle; and in her profound intelligence She entered more deeply into their meaning than the Apostles and the angels, who also were present in bodily forms, adoring their true Lord, Creator and King. By the hands of these angels Enoch and Elias were brought to the Cenacle from their place of abode; for the Lord wished that these Fathers of the natural and of the written Laws should be present at the establishment of the law of the Gospel, and that they should participate in its mysteries.

472. All these being present, awaiting full of wonder what the Author of life intended to do, there appeared also in the hall the person of the eternal Father and of the Holy Ghost as they had appeared at the baptism of Christ at the Jordan and at the Transfiguration on mount Tabor. Although all the Apostles and disciples felt this divine presence, yet only some of them really were favored with a vision of it; among these was especially saint John the evangelist, who was always gifted with eagle sight into the divine mysteries. The entire heaven was transplanted to the Cenacle of Jerusalem; for of such great importance was the magnificence of this work, by which the new Church was founded, the law of grace established and eternal salvation made secure. For a better understanding of the doings of the incarnate Word, I must remind the reader, that He possessed two natures in one Person, the divine and the human nature united in one divine Person of the Word; hence the proper activities of both natures are

rightly attributed to one and the same Person, just as the same Person is called both God and man. Consequently, when I say that the incarnate Work spoke and prayed to the eternal Father, it must not be interpreted as meaning, that He prayed or spoke in as far as He was divine, since in Divinity He was equal to the Father; but in as far as He was human, inferior and composed of body and soul as we ourselves are. In this sense therefore Christ confessed and extolled the immensity and infinitude of the eternal Father, praying for the whole human race.

473. "My Father and eternal God, I confess, praise and exalt thy infinite essence and incomprehensible Deity, in which I am one with Thee and the Holy Ghost, engendered from all eternity by thy intellect, as the figure of thy substance and the image of thy individual nature (John 10, 30; Ps. 119, 3; Heb. 1, 3). In the same nature, which I have assumed in the virginal womb of my Mother, I wish to accomplish the Redemption of the human race with which Thou hast charged Me. I wish to restore to this human nature the highest perfection and the plenitude of thy divine complaisance; and then I wish to pass from this world to thy right hand, bearing with Me all those whom Thou hast given Me without losing a single one of them for want of willingness on our part to help them (John 17, 12). My delight is to be with the children of men (Prov. 8, 31) and as, in my absence, they will be left orphans, if I do not give them assistance, I wish, my Father, to furnish them with a sure and unfailing token of my inextinguishable love and a pledge of the eternal rewards, which Thou holdest in reserve for them. I desire that they find in my merits an easy and powerful remedy for the effects of sin, to which they are subject on account of the disobedience of the first man, and I wish to restore copiously their right to the eternal happiness for which they are created."

474. "But since there will be few who will preserve themselves in this justice, they will need other assistance, so that they may reinstate themselves and strengthen themselves in the way of justification and sanctification by being continually furnished with new and exalted gifts and favors of thy clemency in their dangerous pilgrimage through life. It was our eternal decree, that they should have created existence and participate in our divine perfections and happiness for all eternity; and thy love, which caused Me to assume a nature able to suffer and welcome the humiliation of the cross (Philip 2, 8), would not rest satisfied, until it invented new means of communicating itself to men according to their capacity and our wisdom and power. These means shall consist in visible and sensible signs adapted to their condition as sentient beings and causing invisible effects in the spiritual and immaterial part of their natures."

475. "To advance these high ends for thy exaltation and glory, eternal Lord and Father, in my name and in that of all the poor and afflicted children of Adam, I ask the fiat of thy eternal will. If their sins call out for thy justice, their neediness and misery appeal to thy infinite mercy. At the same time I, on my part, interpose all the works of my humanity, which is indissolubly bound to my Divinity. I offer my obedience in accepting suffering unto death; my humility, in subjecting Myself to the depraved judgment of men; the poverty and labors of my life, the insults of my Passion and Death, and the love, which urges Me to undergo all this for the advance of thy glory and for the spreading of thy knowledge and adoration among all creatures capable of thy grace and happiness. Thou, O eternal Lord and my Father, hast made Me the Brother and the Chief of men, and hast destined them to partake eternally of the joys of our Divinity (Colos. 1, 18). As thy children, they are to be heirs with Me of thy everlasting blessings (Rom. 8, 17), and as members of

my body, they are to participate in the effects of my brotherly love (I Cor. 6,15). Therefore, as far as depends upon Me, I desire to draw them on toward my friendship and to see them share in the goods of the Divinity, to which they were destined in their origin from their natural head, the first man."

476. "Impelled by this boundless love, Lord and Father, I ordain, that from now on men may reenter into thy full friendship and grace through the sacrament of Baptism, and that they may do so as soon as they shall be born to daylight; and their desire of renascence into grace, which they cannot in their infancy manifest on their own account, shall, with thy permission, be manifested for them by their elders. Let them become immediate heirs of thy glory; let them be interiorly and indelibly marked as children of my Church; let them be freed from the stain of original sin; let them receive the gifts of faith, hope and charity, by which they may perform the works of thy children: knowing Thee, trusting in Thee, and loving Thee for thy own Self. Let them also receive the virtues by which they restrain and govern disorderly inclinations and be able to distinguish, without fail, the good from the evil. Let this Sacrament be the portal of my Church, and the one which makes men capable of receiving all the other favors and disposes them to new gifts and blessings of grace. I ordain also, that besides this Sacrament, they may receive another, in which they shall be confirmed and rooted in the holy faith they have accepted, and become courageous in its defense as soon as they shall arrive at the use of reason. And because human frailty easily falls away from the observance of my law and since my charity will not permit Me to leave them without an easy and opportune remedy, I wish to provide the sacrament of Penance. Through it men, by acknowledging their faults and confessing them with sorrow, may be reinstated in justice and in the merits of glory prom-

ised to them. Thus shall Lucifer and his followers be prevented from boasting of having so soon deprived them of advantages of Baptism."

477. "By the justification of these Sacraments men shall become fit to share in the highest token of my love in the exile of this their mortal life; namely, to receive Me sacramentally under the species of bread and wine in an ineffable manner. Under the species of bread I shall leave my body, and under the species of wine, my blood. In each one of them I shall be present really and truly and I institute this mysterious sacrament of the Eucharist as a heavenly nourishment proportioned to their condition as wayfaring men; for their sake shall I work these miracles and remain with them until the end of the coming ages (Matth. 28, 20). For the strengthening and defense of those, who approach the end of their lives, I moreover appoint the sacrament of Extreme Unction, which shall at the same time be a certain pledge of the bodily resurrection of those thus anointed. In order that all may contribute proportionately to the sanctification of the members of the mystical body of the Church, in which by the most harmonious and orderly cooperation all must have their proper position, I Institute the sacrament of Ordination to distinguish and mark some of its members by a special degree of holiness and place them above the other faithful as fit ministers of the Sacraments and as my chosen priests. Although they derive all their powers from Me, I nevertheless wish that it should flow from Me through one of their number, who shall be my Vicar and the Chief, representing my Person and act as my high priest. Into his keeping I deposit the keys of heaven and him all upon earth shall obey. For the further perfection of my Church I also establish the last of the Sacraments, Matrimony, to sanctify the natural union of man and wife for the propagation of the human race. Thus shall all the grades of my Church be enriched and

adorned by my infinite merits. This, eternal Father, is my last will, whereby I make all the mortals inheritors of my merits in the great storehouse of grace, my new Church."

478. This prayer Christ our Redeemer made in the presence of the Apostles, but without any exterior manifestation. The most blessed Mother, who from her retreat observed and followed Him, prostrated Herself upon the floor and, as his Mother, offered to the eternal Father the same petitions as her Son. Although She could not add anything to the merits of the works of her divine Son, nevertheless, as on other occasions, She, as his Helpmate, united her petitions with his, in order that by her faithful companionship She might move the eternal Father to so much the greater mercy. And the Father looked upon Them both, graciously accepting the prayers respectively of the Son and Mother for the salvation of men. Besides prayer, her divine Son left the performance of yet another work in her charge. In order to understand what this was, it must be remembered (as I mentioned in the preceding chapter) that Lucifer was present at the washing of the Apostles' feet, and that, being forced to remain and witness the doings of Christ in the Cenacle, he astutely conjectured some great blessings to be intended for the Apostles. Although the dragon felt his forces much diminished and altogether unavailing against the Redeemer, he nevertheless sought with implacable fury and pride to spy out these mysteries for the concoction of future malicious plans. The great Lady perceived these intentions of Lucifer and knew that the foiling of them was to be left in her hands. Therefore, inflamed by zeal and love for the Most High, She, as sovereign Queen, commanded the dragon and all his squadrons to leave the hall and descend to tire depths of hell.

479. To accomplish this the arm of the Almighty gave new power to the Blessed Virgin, so that neither the rebellious Lucifer nor all his hosts could resist. They were hurled

into the infernal abysses, there to remain until they should again be permitted to issue as witnesses to the passion and death of the Savior in order to be finally convinced of his being the Messias and Redeemer, true God and man. Let it then be understood, that Lucifer and his demons were present at the legal supper and washing of the feet, and also afterwards at the entire passion of Christ! But that they were not present at this institution of the holy Eucharist, nor at the Communion of the disciples. Then the great Queen was raised to a most sublime state of contemplation of the mysteries about to be enacted, and the holy angels, as to another valorous Judith, sang to Her of this glorious triumph over the dragon. At the same time Christ our Lord offered up to the eternal Father exalted thanksgiving and praise for the blessings conceded to the human race in consequence of his petition.

480. Thereupon Christ our Lord took into his venerable hands the bread, which lay upon the plate, and interiorly asked the permission and cooperation of the eternal Father, that now and ever afterwards in virtue of the words about to be uttered by Him, and later to be repeated in his holy Church, He should really and truly become present in the host, Himself to yield obedience to these sacred words. While making this petition He raised his eyes toward heaven with an expression of such sublime majesty that He inspired the Apostles, the angels and his Virgin Mother with new and deepest reverence. Then He pronounced the words of consecration over the bread, changing its substance into the substance of his true body and immediately thereupon He uttered the words of consecration also over the wine, changing it into his true blood. As an answer to these words of consecration was heard the voice of the eternal Father, saying: "This is my beloved Son, in whom I delight, and shall take my delight to the end of the world; and He shall be with

men during all the time of their banishment." In like manner was this confirmed by the Holy Ghost. The most sacred humanity of Christ, in the Person of the Word, gave tokens of profoundest veneration to the Divinity contained in the Sacrament of his body and blood. The Virgin Mother, in her retreat, prostrated Herself on the ground and adored her Son in the blessed Sacrament with incomparable reverence. Then also the angels of her guard, all the angels of heaven, and among them likewise the souls of Enoch and Elias, in their own name and in the name of the holy Patriarchs and Prophets of the old law, fell down in adoration of their Lord in the holy Sacrament.

481. All the Apostles and disciples, who, with the exception of the traitor, believed in this holy Sacrament, adored it with great humility and reverence according to each one's disposition. The great high priest Christ raised up his own consecrated body and blood in order that all who were present at this first Mass might adore it in a special manner, as they also did. During this elevation his most pure Mother, saint John, Enoch and Elias, were favored with an especial insight into the mystery of his presence in the sacred species. They understood more profoundly, how, in the species of the bread, was contained his body and in those of the wine, his blood; how in both, on account of the inseparable union of his soul with his body and blood, was present the living and true Christ; how with the Person of the Word, was also therein united the Person of the Father and of the Holy Ghost; and how therefore, on account of the inseparable existence and union of the Father, Son and Holy Ghost, the holy Eucharist contained the perfect humanity of the Lord with the three divine Persons of the Godhead. All this was understood most profoundly by the heavenly Lady and by the others according to their degree. They understood also the efficacy of the words of the consecration, now endowed

with such divine virtue, that as soon as they are pronounced with the intention of doing what Christ did at that time, by any priest since that time over the proper material, they would change the bread into his body and the wine into his blood, leaving the accidents to subsist in a new way and without their proper subject. They saw, that this change would take place so certainly and infallibly, that heaven and earth would sooner fall to pieces, than that the effect of these words of consecration, when pronounced in the proper manner by the sacerdotal minister of Christ, should ever fail.

482. The heavenly Queen understood also by a special vision how the most sacred body of Christ is hidden beneath the accidents of bread and wine without change in them or alteration of the sacred humanity; for neither can the Body be the subject of the accidents, nor can the accidents be the form of the body. The accidents retain the same extension and qualities as before, and each of their parts retain the same position after the host has been consecrated; and the sacred body is present in an invisible form, also retaining the same size without intermingling of parts. It remains in the whole host, and all of it in every particle of the host, without being strained by the host, or the host by the body. For neither is the extension of his body correlative with the accidental species, nor do they depend upon the sacred body for their existence. They therefore have a totally different mode of existence and the body interpenetrates the accidents without hindrance. Although naturally the head would demand a different place than the hands, or these a different one from the breast or any other part of the body; yet by the divine power the consecrated body places itself unimpaired in its extent in one and the same place, because it bears no relation to the space which it would naturally occupy, having thrown aside all these relations though still remaining a quantitative body. Moreover it need not necessarily remain in one deter-

mined place only, or in only one host, but at the same time it can be present in many innumerable consecrated hosts.

483. She understood likewise, that the sacred body, although not naturally depending upon the accidents as above declared, yet does not continue to exist sacramentally in these accidents after the corruption of the species of the bread and wine; and this for no other reason than because it was so willed by Christ the Author of these wonders. The coexistence of the sacred body and blood of our Lord with the incorrupted species of bread and wine therefore rests upon the arbitrary and voluntary disposition of the Creator of this Sacrament. As soon as they deteriorate and disappear on account of the natural process destructive of these species (for instance, as happens in holy Communion with the sacramental host, which is changed and corrupted by the heat of the stomach, or when this is effected by other causes) then God, in the last instant, when the species are ready for their last transformation, again creates another substance. This new substance, being now devoid of the Divinity, nourishes the human body and finally coalesces with the human form of existence, which is the soul. This wonderful creation of a new substance for the assumption of the changed and corrupted species is consequent upon the will of the Lord, who wishes not to continue the existence of his body in the corrupted accidents, and this process is demanded also by the laws of nature; for the substance of man cannot grow except by some other substance, which, being newly added, prevents the accidents from continuing to exist.

484. All these and other wonders the right hand of the Almighty perpetuated in this most august sacrament of the holy Eucharist. All of them the Mistress of heaven and earth understood and comprehended profoundly. In like manner saint John, the Fathers of the ancient Law, and the Apostles who were present, perceived these mysteries each in their

degree. Aware of the great blessing contained therein for all men, Mary foresaw also the ingratitude of mortals in regard to this ineffable Sacrament, established for their benefit, and She resolved to atone, with all the powers of her being, for our shameless and ungrateful behavior. She took upon Herself the duty of rendering thanks to the eternal Father and to his divine Son for this extraordinary and wonderful benefit to the human race. This earnest desire dwelled in her soul during her whole life and many times did She shed tears of blood welling forth from her purest heart in order to satisfy for. our shameful and torpid forgetfulness.

485. Still greater was my admiration when Jesus our God, having raised the most holy Sacrament, as I said before, for their adoration, divided it by his own sacred hands, first partook of it Himself as being the First and Chief of all the priests. Recognizing Himself, as man, inferior to the Divinity, which He was now to receive in this his own consecrated body and blood. He humiliated and, as it were, with a trembling of the inferior part of his being, shrank within Himself before that Divinity, thereby not only teaching us the reverence with which holy Communion is to be received; but also showing us what was his sorrow at the temerity and presumption of many men during the reception and handling of this exalted and sublime Sacrament. The effects of holy Communion in the body of Christ were altogether miraculous and divine; for during a short space of time the gifts of glory flowed over in his body just as on mount Tabor, though the effects of this transfiguration were manifest only to his blessed Mother, and partly also to saint John, Enoch and Elias. This was the last consolation He permitted his humanity to enjoy as to its inferior part during his earthly life, and from that moment until his Death He rejected all such alleviation. The Virgin Mother, by a special vision, also understood how Christ her divine Son received Himself in

the blessed Sacrament and what was the manner of its presence in his divine Heart. All this caused inestimable affection in our Queen and Lady.

486. While receiving his own body and blood Christ our Lord composed a canticle of praise to the eternal Father and offered Himself in the blessed Sacrament as a sacrifice for the salvation of man. He took another particle of the consecrated bread and handed it to the archangel Gabriel who brought and communicated it to the most holy Mary. By having such a privilege conferred on one of their number, the holy angels considered themselves sufficiently recompensed for being excluded from the sacerdotal dignity and for yielding it to man. The privilege of merely having even one of their number hold the sacramental body of their Lord and true God filled them with a new and immense joy. In abundant tears of consolation the great Queen awaited holy Communion. When saint Gabriel with innumerable other angels approached, She received it, the first after her Son, imitating his self-abasement, reverence and holy fear. The most blessed Sacrament was deposited in the breast and above the heart of the most holy Virgin Mother, as in the most legitimate shrine and tabernacle of the Most High. There the ineffable sacrament of the holy Eucharist remained deposited from that hour until after the Resurrection, when saint Peter said the first Mass and consecrated anew, as I shall relate in its place. The Almighty wished to have it so for the consolation of the great Queen and in order to fulfill his promise, that He would remain with the children of men until the consummation of the ages (Matth. 28, 20); for after his death his most holy humanity could not remain in his Church any other way than by his consecrated body and blood. This true manna was then deposited in the most pure Mary as in the living ark together with the whole evangelical law, just as formerly its prophetic figures were deposited in the ark of

Moses (Heb. 9, 4). The sacramental species were not consumed or altered in the heart of the Lady and Queen of heaven until the next consecration. Having received holy Communion, the blessed Mother gave thanks to the eternal Father and to her divine Son in new canticles similar to the ones the incarnate Word had rendered to his Father.

487. After having thus favored the heavenly Princess, our Savior distributed the sacramental bread to the Apostles (Luke 22, 17), commanding them to divide it among themselves and partake of it. By this commandment He conferred upon them the sacerdotal dignity and they began to exercise it by giving Communion each to Himself. This they did with the greatest reverence, shedding copious tears and adoring the body and blood of our Lord, whom they were receiving. They were established in the power of the priesthood, as being founders of the holy Church and enjoying the distinction of priority over all others (Ephes. 2, 20). Then saint Peter, at the command of Christ the Lord, administered two of the particles of holy Communion to the two patriarchs, Enoch and Elias. This holy Communion so rejoiced these two holy men, that they were encouraged anew in their hope of the beatific vision, which for them was to be deferred for so many ages, and they were strengthened to live on in this hope until the end of the world. Having given most fervent and humble thanks to the Almighty for this blessing, they were brought back to their abiding place by the hands of the holy angels. The Lord desired to work this miracle in order to pledge Himself to include the ancient natural and written laws in the benefits of the Incarnation, Redemption and general resurrection; since all these mysteries were contained in the most holy Eucharist. By thus communicating Himself to the two holy men, Enoch and Elias, who were still in their mortal flesh, these blessings were extended over the human race such as it existed under the natural and the written laws,

while all the succeeding generations were to be included in the new law of grace, the Apostles at the head. This was all well understood by Enoch and Elias, and, returning to the midst of their contemporaries, they gave thanks to their and our Redeemer for this mysterious blessing.

488. Another very wonderful miracle happened at the Communion of the Apostles. The perfidious and treacherous Judas, hearing the command of his Master to partake of holy Communion, resolved in his unbelief not to comply, but if he could do so without being observed, determined to secrete the sacred body and bring it to the priests and pharisees in order to afford them a chance of incriminating Jesus by showing them what He had called his own body; or if he should not succeed therein, to consummate some other vile act of malice with the divine Sacrament. The Mistress and Queen of heaven, who by a clear vision was observing all that passed and knew the interior and exterior effects and affections in the Apostles at holy Communion, saw also the accursed intentions of the obstinate Judas. All the zeal for the glory of her Lord, existing in Her as his Mother, Spouse and Daughter, was aroused in her purest heart. Knowing that it was the divine will, that She should make use of her power as Mother and Queen, She commanded the holy angels to extract from the mouth of Judas the consecrated particles as well of the bread as of the wine and replace them from whence they had been taken. It well befitted Her on this occasion to defend the honor of her divine Son and prevent Judas from heaping such an ignominious injury upon Christ the Lord. The holy angels obeyed their Queen, and when it was the turn of Judas to communicate, they withdrew the consecrated species one after the other, and, purifying them from their contact with Judas, the most wicked of living men, they restored them to their place, altogether unobserved by the disciples. Thus the Lord shielded the honor of his

malicious and obstinate Apostle to the end. This was attended to by the angels in the shortest space of time and the
others then received holy Communion, for Judas was neither
the first nor the last to communicate. Then our Savior offered thanks to the eternal Father and therewith ended both
the legal and the sacramental Supper in order to begin the
mysteries of his Passion, which I will relate in the subsequent
chapters. The Queen of heaven attended to all full of wonder
and joyful praise, magnifying the Most High.

THE VIRGIN MARY SPEAKS TO SISTER MARY OF AGREDA

489. O my daughter! Would that the believers in the holy
Catholic faith opened their hardened and stony hearts in
order to attain to a true understanding of the sacred and
mysterious blessing of the holy Eucharist! If they would only
detach themselves, root out and reject their earthly inclinations, and, restraining their passions, apply themselves with
living faith to study by the divine light their great happiness
in thus possessing their eternal God in the holy Sacrament
and in being able, by its reception and constant intercourse,
to participate in the full effects of this heavenly manna! If
they would only worthily esteem this precious gift, begin to
taste its sweetness, and share in the hidden power of their
omnipotent God! Then nothing would ever be wanting to
them in their exile. In this, the happy age of the law of grace,
mortals have no reason to complain of their weakness and
their passions; since in this bread of heaven they have at hand
strength and health. It matters not that they are tempted and
persecuted by the demon; for by receiving this Sacrament
frequently they are enabled to overcome him gloriously. The
faithful are themselves to blame for all their poverty and
labors, since they pay no attention to this divine mystery, nor

avail themselves of the divine powers, thus placed at their disposal by my most holy Son. I tell thee truly, my dearest, that Lucifer and his demons have such a fear of the most holy Eucharist, that to approach it, causes them more torments than to remain in hell itself. Although they do enter churches in order to tempt souls, they enter them with aversion, forcing themselves to endure cruel pains in the hope of destroying a soul and drawing it into sin, especially in the holy places and in the presence of the holy Eucharist. Their wrath against the Lord and against the souls alone could induce them to expose themselves to the torment of his real sacramental presence.

490. Whenever He is carried through the streets they usually fly and disperse in all haste; and they would not dare to approach those that accompany Him, if by their long experience they did not know, that they will induce some to forget the reverence due to their Lord. Therefore they make special efforts to tempt the faithful in the churches; for they know what great injury they can thereby do to the Lord himself, who in his sacramental love is there waiting to sanctify men and to receive the return of his sweetest and untiring love. Hence thou canst also understand the strength of those who prepare themselves to partake of this bread of the angels and how the demons fear the souls, who receive the Lord worthily and devoutly and who strive to preserve themselves in this purity until the next Communion. But there are very few who live with this intention, and the enemy is ceaselessly alert in striving to throw them back into their forgetfulness, distraction and indifference, so that he may not be obliged to encounter such powerful weapons in the hands of men. Write this admonition in thy heart; and since without thy merit the Almighty has ordained, that thou receive holy Communion daily, seek by all possible means to preserve thyself in the good dispositions from one Communion to the

other. It is the will of the Lord and my own, that with this sword thou fight the battles of the Almighty in the name of the holy Church against the invisible enemies. For in our days they are heaping affliction and sorrow upon the mistress of nations, while there is none to console her or to take it to heart (Thren. 1, 1). Do thou thyself weep for the same reason and let thy heart be torn in sorrow. But while the omnipotent and just Judge who is so greatly incensed against the Catholics for having outraged his justice by their unmeasurable and continual transgressions even under the aegis of their grand faith, none are found to consider and weigh the fearful damage, nor to approach the easy remedy of receiving the holy Eucharist with a contrite and humble heart; nor does any one ask for my intercession.

491. Though all the children of the Church largely incur this fault, yet more to be blamed are the unworthy and wicked priests; for by the irreverence with which they treat the blessed Sacrament the other Catholics have been drawn to undervalue it. If the people see that their priests approach the divine mysteries with holy fear and trembling, they learn to treat and receive their God in like manner. Those that so honor Him shall shine in heaven like the sun among the stars; for the glory of my divine Son's humanity will redound in a special measure in those who have behaved well toward Him in the blessed Sacrament and have received Him with all reverence; whereas this will not happen to those who have not frequented this holy table with devotion. Moreover the devout will bear on their breast, where they have so often harbored the holy Eucharist, most beautiful and resplendent inscriptions, showing that they were most worthy tabernacles of the holy Sacrament. This will be a great accidental reward for them and a source of jubilation and admiration for the holy angels and all the rest of the blessed. They will also enjoy the special favor of being able to penetrate deeper into

the mystery of the presence of the Lord in the sacrament and to understand all the rest of the wonders hidden therein. This will be such a privilege, that it alone would suffice for their eternal happiness, even if there were no other enjoyment in heaven. Moreover the essential glory of those, who have worthily and devoutly received the holy Eucharist, will in several respects exceed the glory of many martyrs who have not received the body and blood of the Lord.

492. I wish thee also to hear, my dearest daughter, from my own mouth, what were my sentiments when in mortal life I was about to receive holy Communion. In order that thou mayest better understand what I say, reflect on all I have commanded thee to write about my gifts, merits and labors in life. I was preserved from original sin and, at the instant of my Conception, I received the knowledge and vision of the Divinity, as thou hast often recorded. I knew more than all the saints; I surpassed the highest seraphim in love; I never committed any fault; I constantly practiced all the virtues in a heroic degree and in the least of them I was greater than all the saints in their highest perfection; the intention and object of my actions were most exalted and my habits and gifts were noble without measure; I imitated my most holy Son most closely; I labored most faithfully; I suffered with eagerness and cooperated with the doings of the Lord exactly as was becoming to me; I ceased not to exercise my love and gain new and super-eminent merits of grace. Yet I thought myself to have been fully repaid by being allowed to receive Him even once in the holy Eucharist; yea, I did not consider myself worthy of this one favor. Reflect then what should be thy sentiments, and those of the rest of the children of Adam, on being admitted to the reception of this admirable Sacrament. And if for the greatest of saints one holy Communion is a superabundant reward, what must the priests and the faithful think, when they are allowed to

receive it so frequently? Open thy eyes in the deep darkness and blindness which overwhelm men around thee, and raise them up to the divine brightness in order to understand these mysteries. Look upon all thy works as insufficient, all thy sufferings as most insignificant, all thy thanksgiving as falling far short of what thou owest for such an exquisite blessing as that of possessing in the holy Church, Christ my divine Son, present in the holy Sacrament in order to enrich all the faithful. If thou hast not wherewith to show thy thanks for this and the other blessings which thou receivest, at least humiliate thyself to the dust and remain prostrate upon it; confess thyself unworthy in all the sincerity of thy heart. Magnify the Most High, bless and praise Him, preserving thyself at all times worthy to receive Him and to suffer many martyrdoms in return for such a favor.

Chapter XII

THE PRAYER OF OUR LORD IN THE GARDEN AND ITS MYS-
TERIES. WHAT HIS MOST BLESSED MOTHER KNEW OF IT.

493. By the wonderful mysteries, which our Savior Jesus had
celebrated in the Cenacle, the reign which, according to his
inscrutable decree, his eternal Father had consigned to Him,
was well established; and the Thursday night of his last
Supper having already advanced some hours, He chose to go
forth to that dreadful battle of his suffering and death by
which the Redemption was to be accomplished. The Lord
then rose to depart from the hall of the miraculous feast and
also most holy Mary left her retreat in order to meet Him on
the way. At this face to face meeting of the Prince of eternity
and of the Queen, a sword of sorrow pierced the heart of Son
and Mother, inflicting a pang of grief beyond all human and
angelic thought. The sorrowful Mother threw Herself at the
feet of Jesus, adoring Him as her true God and Redeemer.
The Lord, looking upon Her with a majesty divine and at the
same time with the overflowing love of a Son, spoke to Her
only these words: "My Mother, I shall be with thee in tribulation; let Us accomplish the will of the eternal Father and
the salvation of men." The great Queen offered Herself as a
sacrifice with her whole heart and asked his blessing. Having
received this She returned to her retirement, where, by a

special favor of the Lord, She was enabled to see all that passed in connection with her divine Son. Thus She was enabled to accompany Him and cooperate with Him in his activity as far as devolved upon Her. The owner of the house, who was present at this meeting, moved by a divine impulse, offered his house and all that it contained to the Mistress of heaven, asking Her to make use of all that was his during her stay in Jerusalem; and the Queen accepted his offer with humble thanks. The thousand angels of her guard, in forms visible to Her, together with some of the pious women of her company, remained with the Lady.

494. Our Redeemer and Master left the house of the Cenacle with all the men, who had been present at the celebration of the mysterious Supper; and soon many of them dispersed in the different streets in order to attend to their own affairs. Followed by his twelve Apostles, the Lord directed his steps toward mount Olivet outside and close to the eastern walls of Jerusalem. Judas, alert in his treacherous solicitude for the betrayal of his divine Master, conjectured that Jesus intended to pass the night in prayer as was his custom. This appeared to him a most opportune occasion for delivering his Master into the hands of his confederates, the scribes and the pharisees. Having taken this dire resolve, he lagged behind and permitted the Master and his Apostles to proceed. Unnoticed by the latter he lost them from view and departed in all haste to his own ruin and destruction. Within him was the turmoil of sudden fear and anxiety, interior witnesses of the wicked deed he was about to commit. Driven on in the stormy hurricane of thoughts raised by his bad conscience, he arrived breathless at the house of the high priests. On the way it happened, that Lucifer, perceiving the haste of Judas in procuring the death of Jesus Christ, and (as I have related in chapter the tenth), fearing that after all Jesus might be the true Messias, came toward him in the shape of a

very wicked man, a friend of Judas acquainted with the intended betrayal. In this shape Lucifer could speak to Judas without being recognized. He tried to persuade him that this project of selling his Master did at first seem advisable on account of the wicked deeds attributed to Jesus; but that, having more maturely considered the matter, he did not now deem it advisable to deliver Him over to the priests and pharisees; for Jesus was not so bad as Judas might imagine; nor did He deserve death; and besides He might free Himself by some miracles and involve his betrayer into great difficulties.

495. Thus Lucifer, seized by new fear, sought to counteract the suggestions with which he had previously filled the heart of the perfidious disciple against his Author. He hoped to confuse his victim; but his new villainy was in vain. For Judas, having voluntarily lost his faith and not being troubled by any such strong suspicions as Lucifer, preferred to take his Master's life rather than to encounter the wrath of the pharisees for permitting Him to live unmolested. Filled with this fear and his abominable avarice, he took no account of the counsel of Lucifer, although he had no suspicion of his not being the friend, whose shape the devil had assumed; Being stripped of grace he neither desired, nor could be persuaded by anyone, to turn back in his malice. The priests, having heard that the Author of life was in Jerusalem, had gathered to consult about the promised betrayal. Judas entered and told them that he had left his Master with the other disciples on their way to mount Olivet; that this seemed to be the most favorable occasion for his arrest, since on this night they had already made sufficient preparation and taken enough precaution to prevent his escaping their hands by his artifices and cunning tricks. The sacrilegious priests were much rejoiced and began to busy themselves to procure an armed force for the arrest of the most innocent Lamb.

496. In the meanwhile our divine Lord with the eleven
Apostles was engaged in the work of our salvation and the
salvation of those who were scheming his death. Unheard of
and wonderful contest between the deepest malice of man
and the immeasurable goodness and charity of God! If this
stupendous struggle between good and evil began with the
first man, it certainly reached its highest point in the death of
the Repairer; for then good and evil stood face to face and
exerted their highest powers: human malice in taking away
the life and honor of the Creator and Redeemer, and his
immense charity freely sacrificing both for men. According to
our way of reasoning, it was as it were necessary that the most
holy soul of Christ, yea that even his Divinity, should revert
to his blessed Mother, in order that He might find some
object in creation, in which his love should be recompensed
and some excuse for disregarding the dictates of his justice.
For in this Creature alone could He expect to see his Passion
and Death bring forth full fruit; in her immeasurable holiness
did his justice find some compensation for human malice;
and in the humility and constant charity of this great Lady
could be deposited the treasures of his merits, so that afterwards, as the new Phoenix from the rekindled ashes, his
Church might arise from his sacrifice. The consolation which
the humanity of Christ drew from the certainty of his blessed
Mother's holiness gave Him strength and, as it were, new
courage to conquer the malice of mortals; and He counted
Himself well recompensed for suffering such atrocious pains
by the fact that to mankind belonged also his most beloved
Mother.

497. All that happened the great Lady observed from her
retreat. She perceived the sinister thoughts of the obstinate
Judas, how he separated himself from the rest of the Apostles,
how Lucifer spoke to him in the shape of his acquaintance,
and all the rest that passed when he reached the priests and

helped them to arrange with so much haste the capture of the Lord. The sorrow which then penetrated the chaste heart of the Virgin Mother, the acts of virtue which She elicited at the sight of such wickedness, and what else She then did, cannot be properly explained by us; we can only say that in all She acted with the plenitude of wisdom and holiness, and with the approbation of the most holy Trinity. She pitied Judas and wept over the loss of that perfidious disciple. She sought to make recompense for his malice by adoring, confessing, praising and loving the Lord, whom he delivered by such fiendish and insulting treachery. She offered Herself with eagerness to die in her Son's stead, if necessary. She prayed for those who were plotting the capture and death of her divine Lamb, for She regarded them as prizes to be estimated according to the infinite value of his precious lifeblood for which this most prudent Lady foresaw they would be bought.

498. Our Savior pursued his way across the torrent of Cedron (John 18, 1) to mount Olivet and entered the garden of Gethsemane. Then He said to all the Apostles: "Wait for Me, and seat yourselves here while I go a short distance from here to pray (Matth. 26, 36) ; do you also pray, in order that you may not enter into temptation" (Luke 22, 40). The divine Master gave them this advice, in order that they might be firm in the temptations, of which He had spoken to them at the Supper: that all of them should be scandalized on account of what they should see Him suffer that night, that Satan would assail them to sift and stir them up by his false suggestions; for the Pastor (as prophesied) was to be ill treated and wounded and the sheep were to be dispersed (Zach. 13, 7). Then the Master of life, leaving the band of eight Apostles at that place and taking with Him saint Peter, saint John, and saint James, retired to another place, where they could neither be seen nor heard by the rest (Mark 14, 33). Being with the three Apostles He raised his eyes up to

the eternal Father confessing and praising Him as was his custom; while interiorly He prayed in fulfillment of the prophecy of Zacharias, permitting death to approach the most innocent of men and commanding the sword of divine justice to be unsheathed over the Shepherd and descend upon the Godman with all its deathly force. In this prayer Christ our Lord offered Himself anew to the eternal Father in satisfaction of his justice for the rescue of the human race; and He gave consent, that all the torments of his Passion and Death be let loose over that part of his human being, which was capable of suffering. From that moment He suspended and restrained whatever consolation or relief would otherwise overflow from the impassible to the passible part of his being, so that in this dereliction his passion and sufferings might reach the highest degree possible. The eternal Father granted these petitions and approved this total sacrifice of the sacred humanity.

499. This prayer was as it were the floodgate through which the rivers of his suffering were to find entrance like the resistless onslaught of the ocean, as was foretold by David (Ps. 68, 2). And immediately He began to be sorrowful and feel the anguish of his soul and therefore said to the Apostles: "My soul is sorrowful unto death" (Mark 14,34). As these words and the sorrow of Christ our Lord contain such great mysteries for our instruction, I will say something of what has been shown me and as far as I can understand concerning them. The Lord permitted this sorrow to reach the highest degree both naturally and miraculously possible in his sacred humanity. This sorrow penetrated not only all the lower faculties of his human life in so far as his natural appetites were concerned; but also all the highest faculties of his body and soul, by which He perceived the inscrutable judgments and decrees of the divine justice, and the reprobation of so many, for whom He was to die. This was indeed by far the

greater source of his sorrow, as we shall see farther on. He did not say that He was sorrowful on account of his death, but unto death; for the sorrow naturally arising from the repugnance to the death He was about to undergo, was a minor fear. The sacrifice of his natural life, besides being necessary for our Redemption, was also demanded as a return for the joy of having in his human body experienced the glory of the Transfiguration. On account of the glory then communicated to his sacred body He held Himself bound to subject it to suffering, deeming that a recompense of what He had received. This we see verified also in the three Apostles, who were witnesses as well of the glorious as of the sorrowful mystery. This they themselves now understood, being informed thereof by an especial enlightenment.

500. Moreover the immense love of our Savior for us demanded that full sway be given to this mysterious sorrow. For if He had caused it to stop short of the highest which that sorrow was capable of, his love would not have rested satisfied, nor would it have been so evident that his love was not to be extinguished by the multitude of tribulations (Cant. 8, 7). At the same time He showed thereby his charity toward the Apostles, who were with Him and were now much disturbed by perceiving, that his hour of suffering and death, which He had so often and in so many ways foretold them, was now at hand. This interior disturbance and fear confounded and confused them without their daring to speak of it. Therefore the most loving Savior sought to put them more at rest by manifesting to them his own sorrow unto death. By the sight of his own affliction and anxiety they were to take heart at the fears and anxieties of their own souls. There was still another mystery contained in this sorrow of the Lord, which referred especially to the three Apostles, saint Peter, John and James. For, more than all the rest, they were imbued with an exalted conception of the

greatness and Divinity of their Master as far as the excellence
of his doctrine, the holiness of his works, and the power of
his miracles were concerned. They realized more completely
and wondered more deeply at his dominion over all creation.
In order that they might be confirmed in their belief of his
being a man capable of suffering, it was befitting that they
should know as eyewitnesses his truly human sorrow and
affliction. By the testimony of these three Apostles who were
distinguished by such favors, the holy Church was afterwards
to be well fortified against the errors, which the devil would
try to spread against the belief in the humanity of Christ our
Savior. Thus would the rest of the faithful have the consolation of this firmly established belief in their own affliction
and sorrow.

501. Interiorly enlightened in this truth, the three Apostles were exhorted by the Author of life by the words: "Wait
for Me, watch and pray with Me." He wished to inculcate
the practice of all that He had taught them and to make
them constant in their belief. He thereby reminded them of
the danger of backsliding and of the duty of watchfulness and
prayer in order to recognize and resist the enemy, remaining
always firm in the hope of seeing his name exalted after the
ignominy of his Passion. With this exhortation the Lord
separated Himself a short distance from the three Apostles.
He threw himself with his divine face upon the ground and
prayed to the eternal Father: "Father, if it is possible, let this
chalice pass from Me" (Matth. 26, 38). This prayer Christ
our Lord uttered, though He had come down from heaven
with the express purpose of really suffering and dying for
men; though He had counted as naught the shame of his
Passion, had willingly embraced it and rejected all human
consolation; though He was hastening with most ardent love
into the jaws of death, to affronts, sorrows and afflictions;
though He had set such a high price upon men, that He

determined to redeem them at the shedding of his lifeblood. Since by virtue of his divine and human wisdom and his inextinguishable love He had shown Himself so superior to the natural fear of death, that it seems this petition did not arise from any motive solely coming from Himself. That this was so in fact, was made known to me in the light which was vouchsafed me concerning the mysteries contained in this prayer of the Savior.

502. In order to explain what I mean, I must state, that on this occasion Jesus treated with the eternal Father about an affair, which was by far the most important of all, namely, in how far the Redemption gained by his Passion and Death should affect the hidden predestination of the saints. In this prayer Christ offered, on his part, to the eternal Father his torments, his precious blood and his Death for all men as an abundant price for all the mortals and for each one of the human born till that time and yet to be born to the end of the world; and, on the part of mankind, He presented the infidelity, ingratitude and contempt with which sinful man was to respond to his frightful Passion and Death; He presented also the loss which He was to sustain from those who would not profit by his clemency and condemn themselves to eternal woe. Though to die for his friends and for the predestined was pleasing to Him and longingly desired by our Savior; yet to die for the reprobate was indeed bitter and painful; for with regard to them the impelling motive for accepting the pains of death was wanting. This sorrow was what the Lord called a chalice, for the Hebrews were accustomed to use this word for signifying anything that implied great labor and pain. The Savior himself had already used this word on another occasion, when in speaking to the sons of Zebedee He asked them: whether they could drink the chalice, which the Son of man was to drink (Matth 20, 22). This chalice then was so bitter for Christ our Lord, because

He knew that his drinking it would not only be without fruit for the reprobate, but would be a scandal to them and redound to their greater chastisement and pain on account of their despising it (I Cor. 1, 23).

503. I understood therefore that in this prayer Christ besought his Father to let this chalice of dying for the reprobate pass from Him. Since now his Death was not to be evaded, He asked that none, if possible, should be lost; He pleaded, that as his Redemption would be superabundant for all, that therefore it should be applied to all in such a way as to make all, if possible, profit by it in an efficacious manner; and if this was not possible, He would resign Himself to the will of his eternal Father. Our Savior repeated this prayer three times at different intervals (Matth. 26, 44), pleading the longer in his agony in view of the importance and immensity of the object in question (Luke 22, 43). According to our way of understanding, there was a contention or altercation between the most sacred humanity and the Divinity of Christ. For this humanity, in its intense love for men who were of his own nature, desired that all should attain eternal salvation through his Passion; while his Divinity, in its secret and high judgments, had fixed the number of the predestined and in its divine equity could not concede its blessings to those who so much despised them, and who, of their own free will, made themselves unworthy of eternal life by repelling the kind intentions of Him who procured and offered it to them. From this conflict arose the agony of Christ, in which He prayed so long and in which He appealed so earnestly to the power and majesty of his omnipotent and eternal Father.

504. This agony of Christ our Savior grew in proportion to the greatness of his charity and the certainty of his knowledge, that men would persist in neglecting to profit by his Passion and Death (Luke 22, 44). His agony increased to

such an extent, that great drops of bloody sweat were pressed from Him, which flowed to the very earth. Although this prayer was uttered subject to a condition and failed in regard to the reprobate who fell under this condition; yet He gained thereby a greater abundance and secured a greater frequency of favors for mortals. Through it the blessings were multiplied for those who placed no obstacles, the fruits of the Redemption were applied to the saints and to the just more abundantly, and many gifts and graces, of which the reprobates made themselves unworthy, were diverted to the elect. The human will of Christ, conforming itself to that of the Divinity, then accepted suffering for each respectively: for the reprobate, as sufficient to procure them the necessary help, if they would make use of its merits, and for the predestined, as an efficacious means, of which they would avail themselves to secure their salvation by cooperating with grace. Thus was set in order, and as it were realized, the salvation of the mystical body of his holy Church, of which Christ the Lord was the Creator and Head.

505. As a ratification of this divine decree, while yet our Master was in his agony, the eternal Father for the third time sent the archangel Michael to the earth in order to comfort Him by a sensible message and confirmation of what He already knew by the infused science of his most holy soul; for the angel could not tell our Lord anything He did not know, nor could he produce any additional effect on his interior consciousness for this purpose. But, as I related above (No. 498), Christ had suspended the consolation, which He could have derived from his human nature from this knowledge and love, leaving it to its full capacity for suffering, as He afterwards also expressed Himself on the Cross (No. 684). In lieu of this alleviation and comfort, which He had denied Himself, He was recompensed to a certain extent, as far as his human senses were concerned, by this embassy of the arch-

angel. He received an experimental knowledge of what He had before known by interior consciousness; for the actual experience is something superadded and new and is calculated to move the sensible and bodily faculties. Saint Michael, in the name of the eternal Father, intimated and represented to Him in audible words, what He already knew, that it was not possible for those to be saved who were unwilling; that the complaisance of the eternal Father in the number of the just, although smaller than the number of the reprobate was great; that among the former was his most holy Mother, a worthy fruit of his Redemption; that his Redemption would also bear its fruits in the Patriarchs, Prophets, Apostles, Martyrs, Virgins and Confessors, who should signalize themselves in his love and perform admirable works for the exaltation of the name of the Most High. Among these the angel moreover mentioned some of the founders of religious orders and the deeds of each one. Many other great and hidden sacraments were touched upon by the archangel, which it is not necessary to mention here, nor have I any command to do so; and therefore what I have already said, will suffice for continuing the thread of this history.

506. During the intervals of Christ's prayer, the Evangelists say, He returned to visit the Apostles and exhort them to watch and pray lest they enter into temptation (Matth. 14, 41; Mark 14, 38; Luke 22, 42). This the most vigilant Pastor did in order to show the dignitaries of his Church what care and supervision they were to exercise over their flocks. For if Christ, on account of his solicitude for them interrupted his prayer, which was so important, it was in order to teach them, how they must postpone other enterprises and interests to the salvation of their subjects. In order to understand the need of the Apostles, I must mention, that the infernal dragon, after having been routed from the Cenacle and forced into the infernal caverns, was permitted by the Savior

again to come forth, in order that he might, by his malicious attempts, help to fulfill the decrees of the Lord. At one fell swoop many of these demons rushed to meet Judas and, in the manner already described, to hinder him, if possible, from consummating the treacherous bargain. As they could not dissuade him, they turned their attention to the other Apostles, suspecting that they had received some great favor at the hands of the Lord in the Cenacle. What this favor was Lucifer sought to find out, in order to counteract it. Our Savior saw this cruelty and wrath of the prince of darkness and his ministers; therefore as a most loving Father and vigilant Superior He hastened to the assistance of his little children and newly acquired subjects, his Apostles. He roused them and exhorted them to watch and pray against their enemies, in order that they might not enter unawares and unprovided into the threatening temptation.

507. He returned therefore to the three Apostles, who, having been more favored, also had more reasons for watchfulness in imitation of their Master. But He found them asleep; for they had allowed themselves to be overcome by insidious disgust and sorrow and in it had been seized by such a remissness and lukewarmness, that they fell asleep. Before speaking to them or waking them, the Lord looked at them for a moment and wept over them. For He saw them oppressed and buried in this deathly shade by their own sloth and negligence. He spoke to Peter and said to him: "Simon, sleepest thou? couldst not thou watch one hour?" And immediately He gave him and the others the answer: "Watch ye, and pray that you enter not into temptation (Mark 14, 37); for my enemies and your enemies sleep not as you do." That He reprehended Peter especially was not only because he was placed as head of the rest, and not only because he had most loudly protested that he would not deny Him and was ready to die for Him, though all the others should be

scandalized in Him and leave Him; but also because Peter, having from his whole heart made freely these protests, deserved to be corrected and admonished before all the rest. For no doubt the Lord chastises those whom He loves and is always pleased by our good resolutions, even when we afterwards fall short in their execution, as happened with the most fervent of all the Apostles, saint Peter. When the Lord came the third time and woke up all the twelve, Judas was already approaching in order to deliver Him into the hands of his enemies, as I shall relate in the next chapter.

508. Let us now return to the Cenacle, where the Queen of heaven had retired with the holy women of her company. From her retreat, by divine enlightenment, She saw most clearly all the mysteries and doings of her most holy Son in the garden. At the moment when the Savior separated Himself with the three Apostles Peter, John and James, the heavenly Queen separated Herself from the other women and went into another room. Upon leaving them She exhorted them to pray and watch lest they enter into temptation, but She took with Her the three Marys, treating Mary Magdalen as the superior of the rest. Secluding Herself with these three as her more intimate companions, She begged the eternal Father to suspend in Her all human alleviation and comfort, both in the sensitive and in the spiritual part of her being, so that nothing might hinder Her from suffering to the highest degree in union with her divine Son. She prayed that She might be permitted to feel and participate in her virginal body all the pains of the wounds and tortures about to be undergone by Jesus. This petition was granted by the blessed Trinity and the Mother in consequence suffered all the torments of her most holy Son in exact duplication, as I shall relate later. Although they were such, that, if the right hand of the Almighty had not preserved Her, they would have caused her death many times over; yet, on the other hand,

these sufferings, inflicted by God himself, were like a pledge and a new lease of life. For in her most ardent love She would have considered it incomparably more painful to see her divine Son suffer and die without being allowed to share in his torments.

509. The three Marys were instructed by the Queen to accompany and assist Her in her affliction, and for this purpose they were endowed with greater light and grace than the other women. In retiring with them the most pure Mother began to feel unwonted sorrow and anguish and She said to them: "My soul is sorrowful, because my beloved Son is about to suffer and die, and it is not permitted me to suffer and die of his torments. Pray, my friends, in order that you may not be overcome by temptation." Having said this She went apart a short distance from them, and following the Lord in his supplications. She, as far as was possible to Her and as far as She knew it to be conformable to the human will of her Son, continued her prayers and petitions, feeling the same agony as that of the Savior in the garden. She also returned at the same intervals to her companions to exhort them, because She knew of the wrath of the demon against them. She wept at the perdition of the foreknown; for She was highly enlightened in the mysteries of eternal predestination and reprobation. In order to imitate and cooperate in all things with the Redeemer of the world, the great Lady also suffered a bloody sweat, similar to that of Jesus in the garden, and by divine intervention She was visited by the archangel saint Gabriel, as Christ her Son was visited by the archangel Michael. The holy prince expounded to Her the will of the Most High in the same manner as saint Michael had expounded it to Christ the Lord. In both of Them the prayer offered and the cause of sorrow was the same; and therefore They were also proportionally alike to one another in their actions and in their knowledge. I was made to understand

that the most prudent Lady was provided with some cloths for what was to happen in the Passion of her most beloved Son; and on this occasion She sent some of her angels with a towel to the garden in which her Son was then perspiring blood, in order to wipe off and dry his venerable countenance. The Lord, for love of his Mother and for her greater merit, permitted these ministers of the Most High to fulfill her pious and tender wishes. When the moment for the capture of our Savior had arrived, it was announced to the three Marys by the sorrowful Mother. All three bewailed this indignity with most bitter tears, especially Mary Magdalen, who signalized herself in tenderest love and piety for her Master.

Words of the Queen

THE VIRGIN MARY SPEAKS TO SISTER MARY OF AGREDA

510. My daughter, all that thou hast understood and written in this chapter will serve as a most potent incentive to thee and to all the mortals who will consider it carefully. Estimate then, and weigh within thy soul, how important is the eternal predestination or reprobation of the souls, since my most holy Son looked upon it with such great anxiety, that the difficulty or impossibility of saving all men added such immense bitterness to the Death, which He was about to suffer for all. By this conflict He manifests to us the importance and gravity of the matter under consideration, He prolonged his supplications and prayers to his eternal Father and his love for men caused his most precious blood to ooze forth from his body on perceiving, that the malice of men would make them unworthy of participation in the benefits of his Death. The Lord my Son has indeed justified his cause in thus having lavished his love and his merits without measure for the purchase of man's salvation; and likewise, the

eternal Father has justified Himself in presenting to the world such a remedy and in having made it possible for each one freely to reach out for such widely different lots, as death and life, fire and water (Eccli. 15, 71).

511. But what pretense or excuse will men advance for having forgotten their own eternal salvation, when my divine Son and I have desired and sought to procure it for them with such sacrifices and untiring watchfulness? None of the mortals will have any excuse for their foolish negligence, and much less will the children of the holy Church have an excuse, since they have received the faith of these admirable sacraments and yet show in their lives little difference from that of infidels and pagans. Do not think, my daughter, that it is written in vain: "Many are called, but few are chosen" (Matth. 20, 16): fear this sentence and renew in thy heart the care and zeal for thy salvation, conformable to the sense of obligation arising from the knowledge of such high mysteries. Even if it were not a question of eternal salvation for thee, thou shouldst correspond to the loving kindness with which I manifest to thee such great and divine secrets. That I call thee my daughter and a spouse of my Lord, should cause thee to pay no attention to any visible thing and embrace only love and suffering for his sake. This I have shown thee by my example, since I applied all my faculties continually to these two things with the highest perfection. In order that thou mayest attain this, I wish that thy prayer be without intermission and that thou watch one hour with me, that is during the whole of thy life; for, compared with eternity, life is less than one hour, yea less than one moment. With such sentiments I wish that thou follow up the mysteries of the Passion, writing them, feeling them and imprinting them upon thy heart.

Chapter XIII

OUR SAVIOR IS DELIVERED INTO THE HANDS OF HIS ENE-
MIES BY THE TREASON OF JUDAS AND IS TAKEN PRISONER;
THE BEHAVIOR OF THE MOST HOLY MARY ON THIS OCCA-
SION AND SOME OF THE MYSTERIES OF THIS EVENT.

512. While our Savior occupied Himself in praying to his
Father for the spiritual salvation of the human race, the
perfidious disciple Judas sought to hasten the delivery of
Christ into the hands of the priests and pharisees. At the
same time Lucifer and his demons, not being able to divert
the perverse will of Judas and of the other enemies of Christ
from their designs on the life of Christ their Creator and
Master, changed the tactics of their satanic malice and began
to incite the Jews to greater cruelty and effrontery in their
dealings with the Savior. As I have already said several times,
the devil was filled with great suspicions lest this most extraordinary Man be the Messias and the true God. He now
resolved to ascertain whether his misgivings were well founded or not by instigating the Jews and their ministers to the
most atrocious injuries against the Savior. He imparted to
them his own dreadful envy and pride, and thus literally
fulfilled the prophecy of Solomon (Wis. 2, 7). For it seemed
to the demon, that if Christ was not God and only a man,
He certainly must weaken and be conquered in these persecutions and torments. If on the other hand He was God, He

would manifest it by freeing Himself and performing new miracles.

513. Similar motives urged on the priests and pharisees. At the instigation of Judas they hastily gathered together a large band of people, composed of pagan soldiers, a tribune, and many Jews. Having consigned to them Judas as a hostage, they sent this band on its way to apprehend the most innocent Lamb, who was awaiting them and who was aware of all the thoughts and schemes of the sacrilegious priests, as foretold expressly by Jeremias (Jer. 11, 19). All these servants of malice, bearing arms and provided with ropes and chains, in the glaring torch and lantern light, issued from the city in the direction of mount Olivet. The prime mover of the treachery, Judas, had insisted upon so much precaution; for, in his perfidy and treachery, he feared that the meekest Master, whom he believed to be a magician and sorcerer, would perform some miracle for his escape. As if arms and human precautions could ever have availed if Jesus should have decided to make use of his divine power! As if He could not have brought this power into play in the same way as He had done on other occasions, should He now choose not to deliver Himself to suffering and to the ignominies of the Cross!

514. While they were approaching, the Lord returned the third time to his Apostles and finding them asleep spoke to them: "Sleep ye now, and take your rest. It is enough: the hour is come; behold the Son of man shall be betrayed into the hands of sinners. Rise up, let us go. Behold he that will betray Me is at hand" (Mark 14, 41). Such were the words of the Master of holiness to the three most privileged Apostles; He was unwilling to reprehend them more severely than in this most meek and loving manner. Being oppressed, they did not know what to answer their Lord, as Scripture says (Mark 14, 40). They arose and Jesus went with them to join

the other eight disciples. He found them likewise overcome
and oppressed by their great sorrow and fallen asleep. The
Master then gave orders, that all of them together, mystically
forming one body with Him their Head, should advance
toward the enemies, thereby teaching them the power of
mutual and perfect unity for overcoming the demons and
their followers and for avoiding defeat by them. For a triple
cord is hard to tear, as says Ecclesiastes (4, 12), and he that is
mighty against one, may be overcome by two, that being the
effect of union. The Lord again exhorted all the Apostles and
forewarned them of what was to happen. Already the confused noise of the advancing band of soldiers and their
helpmates began to be heard. Our Savior then proceeded to
meet them on the way, and, with incomparable love, magnanimous courage and tender piety prayed interiorly: "O
sufferings longingly desired from my inmost soul, ye pains,
wounds, affronts, labors, afflictions and ignominious death,
come, come, come quickly, for the fire of love, which burns
for the salvation of men, is anxious to see you meet the
Innocent one of all creatures. Well do I know your value, I
have sought, desired, and solicited you and I meet you
joyously of my own free will; I have purchased you by my
anxiety in searching for you and I esteem you for your merits.
I desire to remedy and enhance your value and raise you to
highest dignity. Let death come, in order that by my accepting it without having deserved it I may triumph over it and
gain life for those who have been punished by death for their
sins (Osee 13, 14). I give permission to my friends to forsake
Me; for I alone desire and am able to enter into this battle
and gain for them triumph and victory" (Is. 53, 3).

515. During these words and prayers of the Author of
life, Judas advanced in order to give the signal upon which he
had agreed with his companions (Matth. 26, 48), namely the
customary, but now feigned kiss of peace, by which they

were to distinguish Jesus as the One whom they should single out from the rest and immediately seize. These precautions the unhappy disciple had taken, not only out of avarice for the money and hatred against his Master, but also, on account of the fear with which he was filled. For he dreaded the inevitable necessity of meeting Him and encountering Him in the future, if Christ was not put to death on this occasion. Such a confusion he feared more than the death of his soul, or the death of his divine Master and, in order to forestall it, he hastened to complete his treachery and desired to see the Author of life die at the hands of his enemies. The traitor then ran up to the meekest Lord, and, as a consummate hypocrite, hiding his hatred, he imprinted on his countenance the kiss of peace, saying: "God save Thee, Master." By this so treacherous act the perdition of Judas was matured and God was justified in withholding his grace and help. On the part of the unfaithful disciple, malice and temerity reached their highest degree; for, interiorly denying or disbelieving the uncreated and created wisdom by which Christ must know of his treason, and ignoring his power to destroy him, he sought to hide his malice under the cloak of the friendship of a true disciple; and all this for the purpose of delivering over to such a frightful and cruel death his Creator and Master, to whom he was bound by so many obligations. In this one act of treason he committed so many and such formidable sins, that it is impossible to fathom their immensity; for he was treacherous, murderous, sacrilegious, ungrateful, inhuman, disobedient, false, lying, impious and unequalled in hypocrisy; and all this was included in one and the same crime perpetrated against the person of God made man.

516. On the part of the Lord shone forth his ineffable mercy and equity, since those words of David were fulfilled in an eminent manner: "With them that hated peace I was peaceable; when I spoke to them they fought against Me

without cause" (Ps. 119, 7). So completely did the Lord fulfill this prophecy, that when, in answer to the kiss of Judas, He said: "Friend, whereto art thou come ?" He sent into the heart of the traitorous disciple a new and most clear light, by which Judas saw the atrocious malice of his treason, the punishment to follow, if he should not make it good by true penitence, and the merciful pardon still to be obtained from the divine clemency. What Judas clearly read in those few words of Christ was: "Friend, take heed lest thou cause thy perdition and abuse my meekness by this treason. If thou seek my friendship, I will not refuse it to thee on account of this deed, as soon as thou art sorry for thy sin. Consider well thy temerity in delivering Me by false friendship and under cover of a false peace and a kiss of reverence and love. Remember the benefits thou hast received of my charity, and that I am the Son of the Virgin, by whom thou hast been so often favored and rejoiced with motherly advice and counsel during thy apostolate. Even if it were only for her sake, thou shouldst not commit such a treason as to sell and deliver her Son. In no wise does her loving meekness deserve such an outrageous wrong, for She has never been unkind to thee. But although thou hast now committed this wrong, do not despise her intercession, for She alone will be powerful with Me and for her sake I offer thee pardon and life, since She has many times besought Me to do so. I assure thee, that We love thee; for thou art yet in life, where there is hope and where we will not deny thee our friendship, if thou seek it. But if thou refuse it, thou wilt merit our abhorrence and eternal chastisement and pain." The seed of the divine words took no root in the heart of that unhappy reprobate. It was harder than adamant and more inhuman than that of a wild beast. Resisting the divine clemency he finally fell into despair, as I shall relate in the next chapter.

517. The signal of the kiss having been given by Judas, the Lord with his disciples and the soldiers, who had come to capture Him, came face to face, forming two squadrons the most opposed and hostile that ever the world saw. For on the one side was Christ our Lord, true God and man, as the Captain of all the just, supported by his eleven Apostles the chieftains and champions of his Church with innumerable hosts of angelic spirits full of adoring wonder at this spectacle. On the other side were Judas, the originator of the treason, filled with hypocrisy and hatred, and many Jews and gentiles, bent on venting their malice with the greatest cruelty. Surrounding these were Lucifer and a multitude of demons, inciting and assisting Judas and his helpers boldly to lay their sacrilegious hands upon their Creator. With unfathomable love for suffering and great force and authority the Lord then spoke to the soldiers, saying: "Whom seek ye ?" (John 18, 45). They answered: "Jesus of Nazareth." Jesus said to them: "I am He." By these inestimably precious and blessed words Christ declared Himself as our Redeemer and Savior; for only by his offering Himself freely to redeem us by his Passion and Death, could our hope of eternal life ever rest on firm foundation.

518. His enemies could not understand or fathom the true meaning of these words: I am He. But his most blessed Mother and the angels understood them, as did also, to a great extent, the Apostles. It was as if He had said: "I am who am" (Exod. 3, 14), as I have said to my prophet Moses; for I am of Myself, and all creatures have their being and existence from Me: I am eternal, immense, infinite, one in substance and attributes; and I have made Myself man hiding my glory, in order that, by means of my Passion and Death, to which you wish to condemn Me, I might save the world. As the Lord spoke with divine power, his enemies could not resist and when his words struck their ears, they all fell backwards

to the ground (John 18, 6). This happened not only to the
soldiers, but to the dogs, which they had brought with them,
and to the horses on which some of them rode: all of them
fell to the ground and remained motionless like stones.
Lucifer and his demons were hurled down with them, deprived of motion and suffering new confusion and torture.
Thus they remained for some seven or eight minutes, showing no more signs of life than if they had died. O word of a
God, so mysterious in meaning and more than invincible in
power! Let not the wise glory before Thee in their wisdom
and astuteness; nor the powerful in their valor (Jer. 9, 23); let
the vanity and arrogance of the children of Babylon be
humbled, since one word from the mouth of the Lord,
spoken with so much meekness and humility, confounds,
destroys and annihilates all the pride and power of man and
hell. Let us children of the Church also learn, that the victories of Christ are gained by confessing the truth, by giving
place unto wrath (Rom. 12, 19), by showing meekness and
humility of heart (Matth. 11, 29), by overcoming and being
overcome with dovelike simplicity, by the peacefulness and
resignment of sheep free from resistance of furious and
ravenous wolves.

519. Sadly our divine Lord contemplated the picture of
eternal damnation exhibited in them and listened to the
prayer of his most holy Mother to let them rise, for upon her
intercession his divine will had made that dependent. When
it was time for them to come to themselves, He prayed to the
eternal Father, saying:

"My Father and eternal God, in my hands Thou hast
placed all things (John 13, 3), and hast consigned to Me the
Redemption required by thy justice. I wish to satisfy it and
give Myself over to death with all my heart, in order to merit
for my brethren participation in thy treasures and the eternal
happiness held out to them." By this expression of his effica-

cious will the Lord gave permission to that whole miserable band of men, demons and animals to arise and be restored to the same condition as before their falling down. A second time the Savior said to them: "Whom seek ye?" and they again answered: "Jesus of Nazareth." The Lord answered most meekly: "I have already told you, that I am He. If therefore you seek Me, let these go their way" (John 18, 8). With these words He gave permission to the servants and the soldiers to take Him prisoner and execute their designs, which, without their understanding it, meant nothing else than to draw upon his divine Person all our sorrows and infirmities (Is. 53, 4).

520. The first one who hastened to approach in order to lay hands upon the Master of life, was a servant of the highpriests named Malchus. In spite of the fear and consternation of all the Apostles, saint Peter, more than all the rest, was roused with zeal for the defense of the honor and life of the divine Master. Drawing a cutlass which he had with him, he made a pass at Malchus and cut off one of his ears, severing it entirely from the head (John 18, 10). The stroke would have resulted in a much more serious wound, if the divine providence of the Master of patience and meekness had not diverted it. The Lord would not permit that any other death than his own should occur at his capture; his wounds, his blood and suffering alone should rescue to eternal life the human race, as many of it as are willing. Nor was it his will, or according to his teaching, that his Person be defended by the use of arms, and He did not wish to leave such an example in his Church as one to be principally imitated for her defense. In order to confirm this doctrine, which He had always inculcated, He picked up the severed ear and restored it to its place, perfectly healing the wound and making Malchus more sound and whole than he was before. But He first turned to saint Peter and reprehended him, saying: "Put

up thy sword into the scabbard, for all that shall take it to kill with it, shall perish. Dost thou not wish that I drink the chalice, which my Father hath given Me? Thinkst thou that I cannot ask my Father, and He will give me presently many legions of angels for my defense? But how then shall the Scriptures and the Prophets be fulfilled?" (John 18, 11; Matth. 26, 53).

521. Thus saint Peter, the head of the Church, by this loving exhortation had been taught and enlightened, that his arms for the establishment and defense of the Church were to be spiritual and that the law of the Gospel does not inculcate battles and conquests with material weapons, but conquests of humility, patience, meekness and perfect charity, which overcome the demon, the world, and the flesh; that divine virtue would triumph over its enemies and over the power and intrigues of this world; that arms for attack and defense were not for the followers of Christ our Savior, but for the princes of the earth to safeguard their earthly possessions; while the sword of the Church was to be spiritual, reaching rather the soul than the body. Then Christ our Lord, turning toward his enemies and the servants of the Jews, spoke to them with great majesty and grandeur: "You are come as it were to a robber with swords and clubs to apprehend Me. I sat daily with you, teaching in the temple, and you laid not hands on Me. But this is your hour and the power of darkness" (Matth. 26, 55; Luke 22, 53). All the words of our Savior contained the profoundest mysteries, and it is impossible to comprehend them all or explain them, especially those which He spoke at his Passion and Death.

522. Well might those ministers have been softened and made ashamed of their wickedness by this reprehension of the divine Master; but they were far from it, because they were of the cursed and sterile earth, drained of the dew of virtue and human kindness. Nevertheless the Author of life

wished to admonish them of the truth to that extent. Thereby their malice would be so much the more inexcusable and this sin and all the others, committed in the very presence of the highest holiness and justice, would have its due correction and they themselves a powerful help for conversion, if they should desire it; moreover it would thereby become evident that He knew all that was to happen, that He delivered Himself into their hands and over to this Death of his own free will. For these, and for many other sublime reasons, the Lord spoke the above words, penetrating their inmost mind. For He knew and fully understood the cause of their malice, hatred and envy: namely, because He had publicly reprehended the vices of the priests and pharisees; because He had taught the truth and the way of life to the people; because He had, by his example and his miracles, captured the good will of the humble and the pious and brought many sinners to his friendship and grace. He reminded them, that one who had power to bring about all these results in public, and who could not be apprehended in the temple or in the city in which He taught, could certainly not be captured in the open field without his consent. He clearly made them sensible, that the reason of their failing to do so before, was because He himself had not given his permission to men or demons until the hour chosen by Himself. In order to signify to them, that the hour of his being captured, ill-treated and afflicted had come He said: "This is your hour and the power of darkness." As if He had said to them: Until now it was necessary for Me to be with you as your Master for your instruction, therefore I did not permit you to take my life. But I desire to consummate by my death the work of the Redemption consigned to Me by my eternal Father; and therefore I now permit you to take Me prisoner and to execute your will upon my Person. Thereupon they fell upon the most meek Lamb like fierce tigers, binding Him securely with ropes and chains in order thus to lead Him to the house of the high priest, as I shall presently relate.

523. The most pure Mother of Christ our Lord was most attentive to all that passed in his capture, and by means of her clear visions saw it more clearly than if She had been present in person; for by means of her supernatural visions She penetrated into all the mysteries of his words and actions. When She beheld the band of soldiers and servants issuing from the house of the high priest, the prudent Lady foresaw the irreverence and insults with which they would treat their Creator and Redeemer; and in order to do what was within her power, She invited the holy angels and many others in union with Her to render adoration and praise to the Lord of creation as an offset to the injuries and affronts He would sustain at the hands of those ministers of darkness. The same request She made to the holy women who were praying with Her. She told them, that her most holy Son had now given permission to his enemies to take him prisoner and ill-treat him, and that they were about to make use of this permission in a most impious and cruel manner. Assisted by the holy angels and the pious women the faithful Queen engaged in interior and exterior acts of devoted faith and love, confessing, adoring, praising and magnifying the infinite Deity and the most holy humanity of her Creator and Lord. The holy women imitated Her in the genuflections and prostrations, and the angelic princes responded to the canticles with which She magnified, celebrated and glorified the Divinity and humanity of Christ. In the measure in which the children of malice increased their irreverence and injuries, She sought to compensate them by her praise and veneration. Thus She continued to placate the divine justice, lest it should be roused against his persecutors and destroy them; for only most holy Mary was capable of staying the punishment of such great offenses.

524. And the great Lady not only placated the just Judge, but even obtained favors and blessings from the divine clemency for the very persons who irritated Him and thus secured a return of good for those who were heaping wrongs upon Christ the Lord for his doctrine and benefits. This mercy attained its highest point in the disloyal and obstinate Judas; for the tender Mother, seeing him deliver Jesus by the kiss of feigned friendship, and considering how shortly before his mouth had contained the sacramental body of the Lord, with whose sacred countenance so soon after those same foul lips were permitted to come in contact, was transfixed with sorrow and entranced by charity. She asked the Lord to grant new graces, whereby this man, who had enjoyed the privilege of touching the face whereon angels desire to look, might, if he chose to use them, save himself from perdition. In response to this prayer of most holy Mary, her Son and Lord granted Judas powerful graces in the very consummation of his treacherous delivery. If the unfortunate man had given heed and had commenced to respond to them, the Mother of mercy would have obtained for him many others and at last also pardon for his sin. She has done so with many other great sinners, who were willing to give that glory to Her, and thus obtain eternal glory for themselves. But Judas failed to realize this and thus lost all chance of salvation, as I shall relate in the next chapter.

525. Likewise, when the great Lady saw all the servants and soldiers who had come to take Him, fall to the ground at his divine word, She, in company with the angels, broke out in a song of praise of his infinite power and of the virtue of his humanity, which thereby renewed the victory of the Most High over Pharaoh and his troops in the Red sea (Exod. 15, 4). She exalted the Lord of hosts, because He was about to deliver Himself in an admirable manner to suffering and death in order to save the human race from the captivity of

Lucifer. Then She besought the Lord to permit all these dumbfounded and vanquished enemies to regain their senses and to arise. She was moved to the petition by her most generous kindness and deep compassion for these men created by the Lord according to his own image and likeness; on the other hand, She wanted to fulfill in an eminent degree the law of loving our enemies and doing good to those who persecute us, inculcated and practiced by her own Son and Master (Matth. 5, 44), and finally because She knew that the prophecies of holy Scripture were to be fulfilled in the Redemption of man. Although all these were infallible, this did not hinder the most holy Mary from giving voice to her prayer and thereby moving the Most High to grant these favors; for in the infinite wisdom and in the decrees of his eternal will all these means were foreseen as producing these effects in the manner most conformable to the foreknowledge and foresight of the Lord. But it is not necessary to enter into further explanation of such mysteries at present. When the servants of the high priest laid hands on and bound the Savior, the most blessed Mother felt on her own hands the pains caused by the ropes and chains, as if She Herself was being bound and fettered; in the same manner She felt in her body the blows and torments further inflicted upon the Lord, for, I have already said, this favor was granted to his Mother, as we shall see in the course of the Passion. Thus her sensible participation in his sufferings was some kind of relief of the pain, which She would have suffered in her loving soul at the thought of not being with Him in his torments.

Words of the Queen

THE VIRGIN MARY SPEAKS TO SISTER MARY OF AGREDA

526. My daughter, in all that thou art made to understand and write concerning these mysteries, thou drawest upon thyself (and upon mortals) a severe judgment, if thou dost not overcome thy pusillanimity, ingratitude and baseness by meditating day and night on the Passion and Death of Jesus crucified. This is the great science of the saints, so little heeded by the worldly; it is the bread of life and the spiritual food of the little ones, which gives wisdom to them and the want of which starves the lovers of this proud world (Wis. 15, 3). In this science I wish thee to be studious and wise, for with it thou canst buy thyself all good things (Wis. 7, 11). My Son and Lord taught us this science when He said: "I am the way, the truth and the life: no one cometh to my Father except through Me" (John 14, 6). Tell me then, my daughter: if my Lord and Master has made Himself the life and the way for men through his Passion and Death, is it not evident that in order to go that way and live up to this truth, they must follow Christ crucified, afflicted, scourged and affronted? Consider the ignorance of men who wish to come to the Father without following Christ, since they expect to reign with God without suffering or imitating his Passion, yea without even a thought of accepting any part of his suffering and Death, or of thanking Him for it. They want it to procure for them the pleasures of this life as well as of eternal life, while Christ their Creator has suffered the most bitter pains and torments in order to enter heaven and to show them by his example how they are to find the way of light.

527. Eternal rest is incompatible with the shame of not having duly labored for its attainment. He is not a true son of his father, who does not imitate him, nor he a good disciple, who does not follow his Master, nor he a good servant,

who does not accompany his lord; nor do I count him a devoted child, who does not suffer with me and my divine Son. But our love for the eternal salvation of men obliges us, who see them forgetful of this truth and so adverse to suffering, to send them labors and punishments, so that if they do not freely welcome them, they may at least be forced to undergo them and so be enabled to enter upon the way of salvation. And yet even all this is insufficient, since their inclinations and their blind love of visible things detains them and makes them hard and heavy of heart; they rob them of remembrance and affection toward these higher things, which might raise them above themselves and above created things. Hence it comes, that men do not find joy in their tribulations, nor rest in their labors, nor consolation in their sorrows, nor any peace in adversities. For, altogether different from the saints who glory in tribulation as the fulfillment of their most earnest desires, they desire none of it and abhor all that is painful. In many of the faithful this ignorance goes still farther; for some of them expect to be distinguished by God's most intimate love, others, to be pardoned without penance, others, to be highly favored. Nothing of all this will they attain, because they do not ask in the name of Christ the Lord and because they do not wish to imitate Him and follow Him in his Passion.

528. Therefore, my daughter, embrace the Cross and do not admit any consolation outside of it in this mortal life. By contemplating and feeling within thyself the sacred Passion thou wilt attain the summit of perfection and attain the love of a spouse. Bless and magnify my most holy Son for the love with which He delivered Himself up for the salvation of mankind. Little do mortals heed this mystery; but I, as an Eyewitness, assure thee, next to ascending to the right hand of his eternal Father, nothing was so highly estimated and so earnestly desired by Him, as to offer Himself for suffering

and death and to deliver Himself up entirely to his enemies. I wish also that thou lament with great sorrow the fact that Judas, in his malice and treachery, has many more followers than Christ. Many are the infidels, many the bad Catholics, many the hypocrites, who under the name of a Christian, sell and deliver Him and wish to crucify Him anew. Bewail all these evils, which thou understandest and knowest, in order that thou mayest imitate and follow me in this matter.

Chapter XIV

THE FLIGHT AND DISPERSION OF THE APOSTLES AFTER THE
CAPTURE OF THEIR MASTER; HOW HIS MOST BLESSED
MOTHER WAS AWARE OF ALL THAT HAPPENED AND HOW
SHE ACTED IN CONSEQUENCE; THE PERDITION OF JUDAS
AND THE WORRY OF THE DEMONS OVER WHAT THEY WERE
OBLIGED TO EXPERIENCE.

529. After the seizure of our Savior Jesus, his prophecy at the
Supper, that all of the Apostles would be greatly scandalized
in his Person (Matth. 26, 31) and that satan would attack
them in order to sift them like wheat, was fulfilled. For when
they saw their divine Master taken prisoner and when they
perceived, that neither his meekness, nor his words so full of
sweetness and power, nor his miracles, nor his doctrine
exemplified by such an unblamable life, could appease the
envy of the priests and pharisees, they fell into great trouble
and affliction. Naturally the fear of personal danger diminished their courage and confidence in the counsels of their
Master, and beginning to wander in their faith, each one
became possessed with anxious thoughts as to how he could
escape the threatening persecutions foreshadowed by what
had happened to their Captain and Master. The Apostles,
availing themselves of the preoccupation of the soldiers and
servants in binding and fettering the meek Lamb of God,
betook themselves to flight unnoticed. Certainly their ene-

mies, if they had been permitted by the Author of life, would have captured all the Apostles, especially if they had seen them fly like cowards or criminals (Matth. 26, 56). But it was not proper that they should be taken and made to suffer at that time. This was clearly indicated as the will of the Lord, when He said: that if they sought Him, they should let his companions go free; these words had the force of a divine decree and were verified in the event. For the hatred of the priests and pharisees extended to the Apostles, and was deep enough to make them desire the death of all of them. That is the reason why the high priest Annas asked the divine Master about his disciples and his doctrine (John 18,8).

530. At the flight of the Apostles, Lucifer, already troubled and vaguely perplexed, betook himself off hesitating between different projects of his redoubled malice. He certainly wished to see the doctrine of the Savior and all his disciples blotted out from the world, so that not even the memory of them be left. Hence he would have been well satisfied, if the Jews had imprisoned and killed them all. But he had no hope of easily attaining this wish, and therefore he busied himself in disquieting the Apostles by various suggestions and inciting them to flight, in order that they might not witness the patience and virtues of their Master in his sufferings. The astute dragon feared, that by this new proof of his doctrine in his living example the Apostles might be confirmed and fortified in their faith and thus resist the temptations which he planned for them; therefore it seemed to him, that if he could weaken them now, he could more easily cause them to fall away entirely by subsequent persecutions easily to be raised against them among the only too ready enemies of their Master. Thus the demon deceived himself by his own malicious calculations. When therefore he saw the Apostles filled with cowardly fear and much disturbed by the sorrow of their hearts, he rejoiced in their evil

plight and considered it the best time to begin his temptations. He assailed them with rabid fury, filling them with strong doubts and suspicions against the Master of life and urging them to give Him up and betake themselves to flight. They easily yielded to his suggestions of flight; but they resisted many of the doubts against faith, although some failed more, some less, not all of the Apostles being equally disturbed or scandalized.

531. They separated from each other, scattering in different directions; for it would have been difficult for all of them to hide as they wished, if they remained together. Only saint Peter and saint John kept each other company to follow their God and Master and see the end of his misfortune (Matth. 26, 58). But in the soul of each one of the eleven Apostles raged a battle of sorrow and grief, which wrung their hearts and left them without consolation or the least rest. On the one side battled reason, grace, faith, love and truth; on the other temptation, suspicion, fear, cowardice and sorrow. Reason and truth reproached them with their inconstancy and disloyalty in having forsaken their Master by cowardly flying from danger, after having been warned of it and after having offered themselves so shortly before to die for Him if necessary. They remembered their disobedience in neglecting to pray and strengthen themselves against temptations, as the Lord had commanded them. Their love for his sweet conversation and company, for his teaching and miraculous power, and their conviction that He was true God, urged them to return and seek Him, and to offer themselves to danger and death like faithful servants and disciples. To all this was joined the memory of his most sweet Mother, the consideration of her intense sorrow, and the desire to seek Her and attend upon Her in her trouble. But on the other hand was their timidity, exaggerating their fears of the Jews, their dread of death, of shame and confusion. In regard to seeking the

company of the sorrowful Mother, they feared lest She would oblige them to return to their Master, and lest they should be more easily found if they stayed with Her in the same house. Dreadful above all were the impious and horrible suggestions of the demons. For the dragon filled them with harassing doubts, whether it would not be suicide to thus deliver themselves to a certain death; that, if their Master could not free Himself, much less could He free them from the hands of the priests; that He would now certainly be put to death, and that therefore all ties between Him and them were dissolved, since they would not see Him any more; that, although his life seemed to be blameless, yet He had taught some very hard doctrines, some of them unheard of until that time, whence He had incurred the hatred of those learned in the law and of the priests, as well as the indignation of all the people. Moreover it was a serious matter to follow a Man, who was to be condemned to an infamous and frightful death.

532. Such was the interior contention and strife in the hearts of the Apostles. Satan under cover of this excitement, continually sought to instill into their minds doubts concerning the teachings of Christ and concerning the prophecies, that treated of the mysteries of his Passion. As in their sad interior conflict they failed to see the least assurance of seeing their Master escape the hands of the priests alive, their fears settled into a profound sorrow and melancholy, in which they decided to fly from the danger and save their own lives. And they were seized with such timidity and cowardice, that during this night they felt nowhere safe, and every shadow or noise made them tremble with fear. The consideration of the treachery of Judas added still more to their fear; for, as he had not been seen in the company of any of the eleven after his treacherous delivery of the Lord, they dreaded lest he should excite against them the hatred of the priests. Saint

Peter and saint John, being more fervent in the love of their Master, made a greater show of resistance to fear and to the demon; and the two together resolved to follow their Master at a distance. In taking this resolve, they relied much upon the acquaintance of saint John with the high priest Annas, who with Caiphas alternated in the office of high priest. In that year it was held by Caiphas, who in the meeting had given the prophetic counsel, asking whether one man had not better die in order that the whole world might not perish (John 18, 15, 49). This acquaintance had arisen from the fact, that saint John was esteemed as a man, distinguished and of noble lineage, of affable and courteous manners and amiable in person. Trusting to these favorable circumstances the two Apostles followed the Lord with less fear. The thought of their heavenly Queen was deep in their hearts, and they reflected on her bitter sorrow and desired to bring relief and console Her if possible. In this pious and loving desire especially saint John excelled all the others.

533. The heavenly Princess, from the Cenacle, clearly understood and saw all; not only her most holy Son in captivity and suffering, but all that happened inwardly and outwardly to the Apostles. She observed their tribulation and temptations, their thoughts and resolves, where each one was and what he did. But although all was known to the most gentle Dove, She allowed Herself no feeling of indignation against the Apostles, nor did She ever in the least reproach them for their disloyalty; on the contrary, She was the One, who was principally instrumental in restoring them to a better mind, as I shall show later on (746, 747). From that hour on She commenced to pray for them. In sweetest charity and with the compassion of a Mother, She interiorly addressed them: "0 ye simple sheep, chosen by the Lord, do ye forsake your most loving Pastor, who cares for you and feeds you on the pastures of eternal life ? Why, being disciples of such a truth-

ful doctrine, do you leave your Benefactor and Master? How can you forget the sweet and loving intercourse, which so attracted your hearts? Why do you listen to the master of lies and follow the ravenous wolf, who seeks your ruin? O most patient and sweetest Lord, how meek, and kind and merciful does the love of men make Thee! Extend thy gentle love to this little flock, which is now troubled and dispersed by the fury of the serpent. Do not deliver over to the beasts those souls, who have confessed thy name (Ps. 73, 19). Great hopes hast thou set in those, whom Thou hast chosen as thy servants and through whom Thou hast already accomplished great things. Let not such graces be in vain, nor reject those whom Thou hast freely chosen for the foundations of thy Church. Let not Lucifer glory in having, beneath thy very eyes, vanquished the best of thy family and household. My Son and Lord, look upon thy beloved disciples John, Peter and James, so much favored by thy love and good will. Turn an eye of clemency also upon the rest, crush the pride of the dragon, which now pursues them with implacable fury."

534. In all that most holy Mary did on this occasion and in the pleasure She caused the Almighty by her holiness, She exceeded in grandeur all that was ever possible in men and angels. Over and above the sensible and spiritual sorrows caused by the torments of her divine Son and the affronts perpetrated against his divine Person (for which the blessed Mother entertained the highest veneration attainable by a creature), She was overwhelmed with the sorrow caused by the fall of the Apostles, the greatness of which She alone could properly estimate. She was obliged to witness their weakness and forgetfulness in the face of his divine favors, his doctrines and exhortations, and in so short a time after the last Supper, when He had warned them so lovingly, given them holy Communion and elevated them to such a high dignity as the priesthood. She saw also the danger of their

falling into even greater sins on account of the astute and furious attacks of Lucifer and his demons, and on account of the heedlessness of the Apostles in their greater or less confusion and fear. Yet notwithstanding this great sea of sorrow She multiplied and intensified her petitions in order to merit for them sufficient assistance and speedy pardon from her Son, so that they might again return to their faith and to his friendship in grace. She alone was the powerful and efficacious instrument of these results. During these hours the great Lady united within Herself all the faith, all the holiness, all the worship and divine cult of the Church; for in Her was preserved and enclosed as in the living and incorruptible ark and as in the temple and sanctuary, the evangelical law and sacrifice. She by Herself alone then constituted the entire Church, because She alone preserved full faith, hope and love, complete worship and adoration for the great object of our faith, not only supplying her full share for Herself, but for the Apostles and for the whole human race. She it was who compensated, as far as was possible to a creature, for the deficiencies and faults in the rest of the mystical members of the Church. She performed heroic acts of faith, hope, love toward Her Son and true God, She venerated and adored Him by her prostrations and genuflections, She blessed Him with wonderful songs of praise, not allowing her deep and bitter sorrow to interfere with the beautiful and harmonious disposition and the full operation of all her faculties, as preordained by the Almighty. What Ecclesiasticus says of music: that it is inopportune in time of sorrow (Eccli. 22, 6), does not apply to Her; for only the blessed Mary was able and knew how to augment the beautiful harmony of virtues in the midst of sorrow.

535. Leaving the twelve Apostles in the sad state above mentioned, I now proceed to relate the most unhappy end of the traitor Judas, somewhat anticipating the course of events,

in order to have done with his lamentable and unfortunate lot and continue the narrative of the Passion. With the band that had taken the Lord prisoner, the sacrilegious disciple arrived at the house of the high priest, that of Annas first, and then at that of Caiphas, who, with the scribes and pharisees were awaiting results. When the perfidious disciple saw his divine Master overwhelmed with blasphemies and injuries and how He suffered all with such admirable silence, meekness and patience, he began to reflect upon his own treachery and that it alone caused such cruel injustice to be heaped upon an innocent Man and his Benefactor. He recalled the miracles he had witnessed, the doctrines he had heard, and the benefits enjoyed at his hands, and he remembered the kindness and meekness of the most holy Mary, the charity with which She had solicited his conversion, and the malice with which he had offended the Son and the Mother for such insignificant gain. All the sins he had committed piled themselves up before his interior gaze like a dark and chaotic, impenetrable mountain.

536. As I have stated above, Judas was forsaken by divine grace at the time when he consummated his treachery by his perfidious kiss and by his contact with Christ our Savior. According to the hidden judgments of the Most High, although he was now left to his own counsels, the divine justice and equity, ingrained in the natural reason, permitted these reflections to arise and to be supplemented by many suggestions of Lucifer who possessed him. But though Judas thus reasoned correctly in these matters, it was the devil who awakened these truths and added many other false and deceitful suggestions, in order to deduct from them not the salutary hope of remedy, but to convince him of the impossibility of repairing the damage and to lead him to the despair to which he at last yielded. Lucifer roused in him a keen sorrow for his misdeeds; not however for a good purpose, nor

founded upon having offended the divine Truth, but upon
his disgrace among men and upon the fear of retribution
from his Master, whom he knew to be miraculously powerful
and One whom he would be able to escape nowhere in the
whole world. Everywhere the blood of the just One would
forever cry for vengeance against him. Filled with these
thoughts and others aroused by the demon, he was involved
in confusion, darkness and rabid rage against himself. Fleeing
from all human beings he essayed to throw himself from the
highest roof of the priests' house without being able to
execute his design. Gnawing like a wild beast at the flesh of
his arms and hands, striking fearful blows at his head, tearing
out his hair and raving in his talk, he rushed away and showered maledictions and execrations upon himself as the most
unfortunate and miserable of men.

537. Seeing him thus beside himself Lucifer inspired him
with the thought of hunting up the priests, returning to them
the money and confessing his sin. This Judas hastened to do,
and he loudly shouted at them those words: "I have sinned,
betraying innocent blood!" (Matth. 27,4). But they, not less
hardened, answered that he should have seen to that before.
The intention of the demon was to hinder the death of
Christ if possible, for reasons already given and yet to be
given (No. 419). This repulse of the priests, so full of impious cruelty, took away all hope from Judas and he persuaded
himself that it was impossible to hinder the death of his
Master. So thought also the demon, although later on he
made more efforts to forestall it through Pilate. But as Judas
could be of no more use to him for his purpose, he augmented his distress and despair, persuading him that in order to
avoid severer punishments he must end his life. Judas yielded
to this terrible deceit, and rushing forth from the city, hung
himself on a dried out fig tree (Matth. 27, 5). Thus he that
was the murderer of his Creator, became also his own mur-

derer. This happened on Friday at twelve o'clock, three hours before our Savior died. It was not becoming that his death and the consummation of our Redemption should coincide too closely with the execrable end of the traitorous disciple, who hated him with fiercest malice.

538. The demons at once took possession of the soul of Judas and brought it down to hell. His entrails burst from the body hanging upon the tree (Acts 1, 18). All that saw this stupendous punishment of the perfidious and malicious disciple for his treason, were filled with astonishment and dread. The body remained hanging by the neck for three days, exposed to the view of the public. During that time the Jews attempted to take it down from the tree and to bury it in secret, for it was a sight apt to cause great confusion to the pharisees and priests, who could not refute such a testimony of his wickedness. But no efforts of theirs sufficed to drag or separate the body from its position on the tree until three days had passed, when, according to the dispensation of divine justice, the demons themselves snatched the body from the tree and brought it to his soul, in order that both might suffer eternal punishment in the profoundest abyss of hell. Since what I have been made to know of the pains and chastisements of Judas, is worthy of fear inspiring attention, I will according to command reveal what has been shown me concerning it. Among the obscure caverns of the infernal prisons was a very large one, arranged for more horrible chastisements than the others, and which was still unoccupied; for the demons had been unable to cast any soul into it, although their cruelty had induced them to attempt it many times from the time of Cain unto that day. All hell had remained astonished at the failure of these attempts, being entirely ignorant of the mystery, until the arrival of the soul of Judas, which they readily succeeded in hurling and burying in this prison never before occupied by any of the

damned. The secret of it was, that this cavern of greater torments and fiercer fires of hell, from the creation of the world, had been destined for those, who, after having received Baptism, would damn themselves by the neglect of the Sacraments, the doctrines, the Passion and Death of the Savior, and the intercession of his most holy Mother. As Judas had been the first one who had so signally participated in these blessings, and as he had so fearfully misused them, he was also the first to suffer the torments of this place, prepared for him and his imitators and followers.

539. This mystery I was commanded to reveal more particularly for a dreadful warning to all Christians, and especially to the priests, prelates and religious, who are accustomed to treat with more familiarity the body and blood of Christ our Lord, and who, by their office and state are his closer friends. In order to avoid blame I would like to find words and expressions sufficiently strong to make an impression on our unfeeling obduracy, so that we all may take a salutary warning and be filled with the fear of the punishments awaiting all bad Christians according to the station each one of us occupies. The demons torment Judas with inexpressible cruelty, because he persisted in the betrayal of his Master, by whose Passion and Death they were vanquished and despoiled of the possession of the world. The wrath which they had conceived against the Savior and his blessed Mother, they wreck, as far as is allowed them, on all those who imitate the traitorous disciple and who follow him in his contempt of the evangelical law, of the Sacraments and of the fruits of the Redemption. And in this the demons are but executing just punishment on those members of the mystical body of Christ, who have severed their connection with its head Christ, and who have voluntarily drifted away and delivered themselves over to the accursed hate and implacable fury of his enemies. As the instruments of divine

justice they chastise the redeemed for their ingratitude toward their Redeemer. Let the children of the Church consider well this truth, for it cannot fail to move their hearts and induce them to evade such a lamentable fate.

540. During the whole course of the Passion Lucifer with his demons moved about, eagerly spying out all the circumstances of each event in order to ascertain whether Christ the Lord was really the Messias and Redeemer of the world. On the one hand the miracles seemed to argue the truth of his suspicions, on the other very often the doings and the sufferings, so much like those of weak human nature, argued the contrary. The strongest argument for the truth of his suspicions was Lucifer's personal experience of the power of the Redeemer, when He said "I am He," which caused him and all his associates to fall prostrate, annihilated in the presence of the Lord; and this had happened only a short time after he had been permitted to issue from hell, whither the demons had been hurled from the Cenacle. It was true, Mary had routed them from the hall of the last Supper; yet Lucifer with his ministers connected it with the power exercised by Jesus and they could not but admit, that this power of both Mother and Son was something altogether new and unexperienced by them. When he had received permission to rise from his fall in the garden, he conferred with the rest and expressed his opinion, that this could not be merely human power, but without doubt the power of One, who is God and at the same time man. "If He shall die, as we have planned, He will accomplish the Redemption of man and satisfy the justice of God; then our sway will cease and all our intentions will be frustrated. We have erred in seeking his death. If now we cannot prevent his death, let us see how far his endurance will go and excite his enemies to torture Him with most impious cruelty. Let us stir up their fury against Him; let us suggest to their minds new insults, affronts, ignominies and

torments to be inflicted upon his Person; let us drive them to vent upon Him all their wrath in order to exhaust his patience, and let us carefully study the results." These proposals the demons sought to realize, although, on account of the hidden mysteries alluded to above (and to be mentioned later, No. 579, 627, 631), they found that not all of their plans succeeded. Whenever they incited the executioners to inflict tortures unbecoming his royal and divine Person, the Lord would not permit such indignities farther than was becoming, while He gave free scope to their inhuman barbarities and savage fury in all the rest.

541. The great Lady of heaven, Mary, likewise interfered in order to curb the insolent malice of Lucifer; for She was well aware of all the designs of the infernal dragon. At times She would make use of her sovereign power as Queen to prevent some of the hellish suggestion to reach the ministers of the Passion; at others She prevented their execution by her prayers, or She enlisted the service of her holy angels to drive away and confuse the persecutors of her Son. Those sufferings, which by her great wisdom She knew, that her Son wished to undergo, She permitted, fulfilling in all things the divine will. She knew all about the unhappy death of Judas, his torments and place of imprisonment in hell; the bed of fire, which He was to occupy for all eternity, as the master of hypocrisy and the leader of all those who were to deny Christ our Redeemer, as well in thought as in their works, who, according to Jeremias (17, 3), leave the veins of living waters, that is Christ, and whose names are written and sealed upon the earth, far from heaven, where are written the names of the predestined. All this the Mother of mercy knew and She wept over his fate most bitterly, praying for the welfare of men and for their salvation from such great blindness and ruinous destruction. Yet in all this She conformed Herself to the just and hidden decrees of divine Providence.

Words of the Queen

THE VIRGIN MARY SPEAKS TO SISTER MARY OF AGREDA

542. My daughter, thou art astonished, not without cause, at what thou hast learned and recorded of the unhappy fate of Judas and of the fall of the Apostles, who were all disciples in the school of Christ, nursed at his breast by his doctrine, by the example of his life, and by his miracles, enjoying his sweetest and gentlest intercourse, and many other benefits of my assistance and intercession. But I truly say to thee, if all the children of the Church would attentively consider this example, they would find a salutary exhortation and warning in this mortal state of life against the danger surrounding them even in the midst of the favors and blessings they continually receive at the hands of the Lord. All of them cannot be equal to seeing Him with bodily eyes and having intercourse with Him as the living image of all sanctity. The Apostles received from me personal exhortations and they were eyewitnesses of my blameless and holy conduct; they received great tokens of my kindness and my charity flowed directly from God through me upon them. If they, in the very act of receiving such favors and in the very presence of their God and Savior, forgot all of them and all of their obligation of corresponding to them: who then shall be so presumptuous in this mortal life as not to fear the danger of eternal ruin, no matter how many favors he has received from the Almighty? They were Apostles chosen by their divine Master, their true God; yet one of them fell lower than any other individual of the human race; and the others failed in faith, the foundation of all virtue. Yet all this was conformable to the just judgments of the Most High. Why then should those who are not Apostles, be without fear, who have not so labored in the school of Christ and who have not so merited my intercession?

543. Concerning the perdition of Judas and of his most just punishment thou hast written enough in order to set forth to what extremes a man can be brought by yielding to vices and to the devil, and by refusing to hear and follow the pleading of grace. I moreover inform thee, that not only the torments of the traitorous disciple Judas, but also those of many other Christians, who condemn themselves and shall be sent to the same place of punishment, which was assigned to them and Judas from the beginning of the world, are greater than the torments of many demons. For my most holy Son did not die for the angels, but for men; nor were the fruits and results of the Redemption for the demon, but entirely at the disposal of the children of the Church in the holy Sacraments. The contempt for these incomparable benefits is not properly the sin of the devils, but of the Christians; and therefore they must expect a special and appropriate punishment for this contempt. The mistake of not having recognized Christ as the true God causes the deepest and most tormenting regret to Lucifer and his evil spirits for all eternity. Hence, on account of this error, they are filled with special wrath against those that were redeemed, particularly against the Christians, who derived the greatest benefits from the Redemption and the blood of the Lamb. That is why the devils are so eager to cause forgetfulness and misuse of these graces in them and why afterwards in hell, they are permitted to vent so much the greater fury and wrath upon the wicked Christians. If it were not for the equitable dispositions of divine justice by which the pains are proportioned to the guilt, they would wreck still fiercer vengeance upon them. But the goodness of the Lord extends even to this place and restrains the malice of the demons by his infinite power and wisdom.

544. In the fall of the other eleven Apostles, I wish, my dearest, that thou learn the frailty of human nature, since

even in such great blessings and favors received of the Lord, it easily falls into the habit of gross negligence and ingratitude, such as the Apostles manifested in flying from their heavenly Master and leaving Him in a spirit of doubt. Men incur this danger from their earthly and sensuous inclinations, the result of past sins and of the habits formed by a terrestrial, carnal and sensuous life, void of spirituality. On account of it they desire and love the divine favors and benefits only in a carnal manner. As soon as they fail to find that kind of enjoyment in them, they turn to other sensible enjoyments, are moved by them and lose the true conception of a spiritual life; for they treat it and estimate it according to the low standard of mere sensuality. Hence the Apostles, though they were so greatly favored by my most holy Son, fell into such gross heedlessness and sins; for the miracles, the teachings and the examples affected them only in a sensible manner; and as they, in spite of their being raised to justice and perfection, permitted themselves to be affected by them only outwardly, they were presently disturbed by temptation and yielded to it. They acted like men who had done little to penetrate into the mysteries and into the spirit of what they had seen and heard in the school of their Master. By this example, my daughter, and by my teachings thou oughtest to be well instructed, a spiritual disciple of mine, and not a terrestrial, accustoming thyself to despise mere outwardness, even in favors bestowed upon thee by the Lord or myself. When thou receivest them, do not attach thyself merely to the material or sensible in them, but raise thy mind to the exalted and the spiritual contained therein; to that which is perceived by the interior and spiritual, and not by the animal senses (I Cor. 2, 14). If even the merely sensible can hinder the spiritual life, how much is this true of that which pertains altogether to earthly, animal and carnal life? Clearly I desire of thee to forget and blot out of thy faculties all images and

remembrances of mere creatures in order that thou mayest be
fit to receive my salutary teaching and be capable of imitating
me.

Chapter XV

JESUS THE SAVIOR, BOUND AS A PRISONER, IS DRAGGED TO THE HOUSE OF ANNAS; WHAT HAPPENED IN CONNECTION THEREWITH AND WHAT THE MOST BLESSED MOTHER SUFFERED DURING THAT TIME.

545. Fit were it to speak of the suffering, the affronts and the Death of our Savior Jesus in such vivid and efficacious words, that they enter into the soul like a two-edged sword, piercing with deepest sorrow our inmost hearts (Heb. 4, 13). Not of an ordinary kind were the pains He suffered and there is no sorrow like unto his sorrow (Thren. 1, 12). For his body was not like the bodies of the rest of men, nor did the Lord suffer for Himself, nor for his own sins, but for us and for our sins (I Pet. 2, 21). Hence the words and expressions, by which we describe his torments and sorrows, should not be of the common or ordinary kind. But, woe is me, who cannot give sufficient force to my words, and cannot find those my soul seeks in order to manifest this mystery! I will speak according to my capacity and as far as is given me, although my powers constrain and limit the greatness of what I understand, and my inadequate words cannot reach the secret concepts of the heart. Let then the vividness and force of the faith, which we profess as children of the Church, supply what is defective in my words. If our words are but of the ordinary kind, let our compassion and our sorrow be extraordinary; let our

thoughts be of the loftiest, our comprehension most real, our consideration of the deepest, our thankfulness heartfelt, and our love most fervent; for all that we can do shall fall short of what the reality demands, of what we owe as servants, as friends, and as children adopted through his most sacred Passion and Death.

546. Having been taken prisoner and firmly bound, the most meek Lamb Jesus was dragged from the garden to the house of the high priests, first to the house of Annas (John 18, 13). The turbulent band of soldiers and servants, having been advised by the traitorous disciple that his Master was a sorcerer and could easily escape their hands, if they did not carefully bind and chain Him securely before starting on their way, took all precautions inspired by such a mistrust (Mark 14, 44). Lucifer and his compeers of darkness secretly irritated and provoked them to increase their impious and sacrilegious ill-treatment of the Lord beyond any bounds of humanity and decency. As they were willing accomplices of Lucifer's malice, they omitted no outrage against the person of their Creator within the limits set them by the Almighty. They bound Him with a heavy iron chain with such ingenuity, that it encircled as well the waist as the neck. The two ends of the chain, which remained free, were attached to large rings or handcuffs, with which they manacled the hands of the Lord, who created the heavens, the angels and the whole universe. The hands thus secured and bound, they fastened not in front, but behind. This chain they had brought from the house of Annas the high priest, where it had served to raise the portcullis of a dungeon. They had wrenched it from its place and provided it with padlock handcuffs. But they were not satisfied with this unheard of way of securing a prisoner; for in their distrust they added two pieces of strong rope: the one they wound around the throat of Jesus and, crossing it at the breast, bound it in

heavy knots all about the body, leaving two long ends free in front, in order that the servants and soldiers might jerk Him in different directions along the way. The second rope served to tie his arms, being bound likewise around his waist. The two ends of this rope were left hanging free to be used by two other executioners for jerking Him from behind.

547. In this manner the almighty and holy One permitted Himself to be bound and made helpless, as if He were the most criminal of men and the weakest of the womanborn; for He had taken upon Himself all the iniquities and weaknesses of our sins (Is. 53, 6). They bound Him in the garden, adding to the chains and ropes insulting blows and vilest language; for like venomous serpents they shot forth their sacrilegious poison in abuse and blasphemy against Him who is adored by angels and men, and who is magnified in heaven and on earth. They left the garden of Olives in great tumult and uproar, guarding the Savior in their midst. Some of them dragged Him along by the ropes in front and others retarded his steps by the ropes hanging from the handcuffs behind. In this manner, with a violence unheard of, they sometimes forced Him to run forward in haste, frequently causing Him to fall; at others they jerked Him backwards; and then again they pulled Him from one side to the other, according to their diabolical whims. Many times they violently threw Him to the ground and as his hands were tied behind He fell upon it with his divine countenance and was severely wounded and lacerated. In his falls they pounced upon Him, inflicting blows and kicks, trampling upon his body and upon his head and face. All these deviltries they accompanied with festive shouts and opprobrious insults, as was foretold by Jeremias (3, 30) .

548. During all this time Lucifer, while inciting these ministers of evil, watched all the actions and movements of our Savior. His patience he thus put to the test in order to

find out, whether Jesus was only a man; for this doubt and perplexity tormented his wicked pride above all others. As he was obliged to acknowledge the meekness, patience and sweetness of Christ, his serene majesty without change or disturbance amid all these injuries and sufferings, the infernal dragon was enraged only so much the more and at one time, like one crazed by fury, he attempted to seize the ropes in order that he and his fellow demons might pull at them more violently than his human foes and thus perhaps overcome the meekness of the Savior. But he was withheld by the most holy Mary, who, from her retreat by a clear vision saw all that happened to her divine Son. When She noticed this attempt of Lucifer, She made use of her power as sovereign Queen and commanded him to desist. All strength immediately left Lucifer and he could not proceed in his presumptuous intent. It was not becoming that his malice should add to the sufferings and death of the Redeemer in such a manner. He was however given permission to excite all his fellow demons against the Lord, and these again were left a free hand to incite his mortal enemies among the Jews ; since the latter had liberty of will to consent or not. Lucifer used this freedom to its full extent, and therefore said to the other evil spirits: "What kind of a man is this, now born into the world, who by his patience and by his works so torments us and annihilates us? None ever maintained such equanimity and such longsuffering in tribulations since the time of Adam until now. Never have we found among mortals such humility and meekness. How can we rest, when we see in the world such a rare and powerful example, drawing others after Him? If this is the Messias, He will certainly open heaven and close up the highway, by which we have so far led men into our eternal torments; we shall be vanquished and all our plans will be frustrated. Even if He is but a mere man, I cannot permit such an example for the rest of mankind. Haste then, ministers of my exalted power, let us persecute Him through his human foes, who, obedient to my sway, have conceived of me some of our own furious envy."

549. The Author of our salvation, hiding his power of annihilating his enemies in order that our Redemption might be the more abundant, submitted to all the consequences of the impious fury which Lucifer and his hellish squadron fomented in the Jews. They dragged Him bound and chained under continued ill-treatment to the house of Annas, before whom they presented Him as a malefactor worthy of death. It was the custom of the Jews to present thus bound those criminals who merited capital punishment; and they now made use of this custom in regard to Jesus, in order to intimate his sentence even before the trial. The sacrilegious priest Annas seated himself in proud and arrogant state on the platform or tribunal of a great hall. Immediately Lucifer placed himself at his side with a multitude of evil spirits. The servants and soldiers brought before Him Jesus, bound and fettered, and said: "At last we bring hither this wicked Man, who by his sorceries and evil deeds has disturbed all Jerusalem and Judea. This time his magic art has not availed Him to escape our hands and power."

550. Our Savior Jesus was attended by innumerable angels, who confessed and adored Him, full of admiration for the incomprehensible judgments of his wisdom (Rom. 11, 33) by which the Lord consented to be held as a sinner and a criminal. The iniquitous high priest pretended to be just and zealous for the honor of the Lord, whose life he was seeking. The most meek Lamb was silent and opened not his mouth, as Isaias prophesied (53, 7). Imperiously and haughtily the high priest asked Him about his disciples (John 18, 19), and what doctrine He was preaching and teaching. This question was put merely for the purpose of misinterpreting his answer, if Jesus should utter any word that afforded such a chance.

But the Master of holiness, who is the Guide and the Correc-
tor of the most wise (Wis. 7, 15), offered to the eternal
Father the humiliation of being presented as a criminal
before the high priest and of being questioned by him as a
prevaricator and author of a false doctrine. Our Redeemer
with an humble and cheerful countenance answered the
question as to his doctrines: "I have spoken openly to the
world: I have always taught in the synagogue and in the
temple, whither all the Jews resort: and in secret I have
spoken nothing. Why askest thou Me? ask those, who have
heard what I have spoken unto them: behold they know what
I have said." As the doctrine of Christ our Lord came from
his eternal Father, He spoke for it and defended its honor.
He referred them to his hearers, both because those by whom
He was now surrounded, would not believe Him and wished
to distort all He should say, and because the truth and force
of his teachings recommended and forced themselves upon
the minds of his greatest enemies by their own excellence.

551. Concerning the Apostles He said nothing, because it
was not necessary on this occasion and because they were not
reflecting much credit upon their Master by their present
conduct. Though his answer was so full of wisdom and so
well suited to the question, yet one of the servants of the high
priest rushed up with raised hand and audaciously struck the
venerable and sacred face of Jesus, saying: "Answerest Thou
the high priest so?" The Lord accepted this boundless injury,
praying for the one who had inflicted it; and holding Himself
ready, if necessary, to turn and offer the other cheek for a
second stroke, according to the doctrine He had himself
inculcated (Matth. 5,39). But in order that the atrocious and
daring offender might not shamelessly boast of his wickedness, the Lord replied with great tranquility and meekness:
"If I have spoken evil, give testimony of the evil; if well, why
strikest thou Me ?"O sight most astounding to the supernal

spirits! Since this is He, at the mere sound of whose voice the foundations of the heavens tremble and ought to tremble and the whole firmament is shaken! This is the Lord of whom Job says, He is wise of heart and mighty in strength; who hath resisted Him and hath peace? Who hath removed mountains, and they, whom He overthrew in his wrath, knew it not; He who moveth the earth out of its place; who commandeth the sun, and it riseth not; and shutteth up the stars as it were under a seal; who doth things great and incomprehensible, whose wrath no man can resist, and under whom they stoop, that bear up the world (Job 9, 4, etc.); this is the One, who for the love of men patiently suffers a servant to strike and wound Him in the face by a buffet!

552. By the humble and appropriate reply of the Lord, the wickedness of the sacrilegious servant stood reprimanded. Yet neither the shame of this reprimand, nor the shameful negligence of the high priest, which permitted such a criminal unfairness in his very presence, moved either him or the other Jews to moderate their conduct toward the Author of life. While this ill-treatment of the Lord was going on, saint Peter and the other disciple, who was none other than saint John, arrived at the house of Annas. Saint John, as being well known there, readily obtained entrance, while saint Peter remained outside. Afterwards the servant maid, who was an acquaintance of saint John, allowed also him to enter and see what would happen to the Lord (John 18, 16). The two disciples remained in the portico adjoining the court hall of the priest, and saint Peter approached the fire, which the soldiers, on account of the coldness of the night, had built in the enclosure near the portico. The servant maid, on closer inspection, noticed the depressed bearing of saint Peter. Coming up to him she recognized him as a disciple of Jesus, and said: "Art thou not perhaps one of the disciples of this Man?" This question was asked by the maid with an air of

contempt and reproach. Peter in his great weakness and hesitancy yielded to a sense of shame. Overcome also by his fear he answered: "I am not his disciple." Having given this answer, he slipped away to avoid further conversation, and left the premises. But he soon afterwards followed his Master to the house of Caiphas, where he denied Him again at two different times, as I shall relate farther on.

553. The denial of Peter caused greater pain to the Lord than the buffet which He had received; for this sin was directly opposed and abhorrent to his immense charity, while pains and sufferings were sweet and welcome to Him, since He could thereby atone for our sins. After this first denial of Peter, Christ prayed for him to his eternal Father and ordained that through the intercession of the blessed Mary he should obtain pardon even after the third denial. The great Lady witnessed all that passed from her oratory, as I have said. As She contained in her own breast the propitiatory and sacrifice of her Son and Lord in sacramental form, She directed her petitions and loving aspirations to Him, eliciting most heroic acts of compassion, thanksgiving, adoration and worship. She bitterly wept over the denial of saint Peter, and ceased not, until She perceived that the Lord would not refuse him the necessary helps for effectually rising from his fall. The purest Mother also felt all the wounds and torments of her Son in the same portions of her virginal body as the Savior. When the Lord was bound with the chains and ropes, She felt on her wrists such pains, that the blood oozed from her fingernails, as if they had been really bound and crushed: in the same manner also the other wounds affected her body. As to these tortures were added the sorrows of her heart in seeing Christ our Lord suffer, She shed miraculous tears of blood. She felt also the buffet in the same way, as if that sacrilegious hand had struck at the same time her Son and Herself. At this wicked affront and at the blasphemous insult

offered to the Lord, She called out to her holy angels to join Her in magnifying and adoring their Creator in compensation for the injuries offered Him by sinners, and in many most sorrowful lamentations She conferred with the angels concerning the cause of her affliction and mourning.

Words of the Queen

THE VIRGIN MARY SPEAKS TO SISTER MARY OF AGREDA

554. My daughter, to great deeds art thou called and invited on account of the divine enlightenment thou receivest concerning the mysteries of the sufferings of my most holy Son and of myself for the human race, and on account of the knowledge which thou hast obtained concerning the small return made by heartless and ungrateful men for all our pains. Thou livest yet in mortal flesh and art thyself subject to this ignorance and weakness; but by the force of truth thou art now roused to great wonder, sorrow and compassion at the want of attention displayed by mortals toward these great sacraments and at the losses sustained by them through their lukewarmness and negligence. What then are the thoughts of the angels and saints, and what are my thoughts in beholding this world and all the faithful in such a dangerous and dreadful state of carelessness, when they have the Passion and Death of my divine Son before their eyes, and when they have me, for their Mother and Intercessor and his most pure life and mine for an example? I tell thee truly, my dearest, only my intercession and the merits of his Son, which I offer to the eternal Father, can delay the punishment and placate his wrath, can retard the destruction of the world and the severe chastisement of the children of the Church, who know his will and fail to fulfill it (John 15, 15). But I am much incensed to find so few who condole with me and try to console my Son in his sorrows, as David says (Ps. 68,

21). This hardness of heart will cause great confusion to them on the day of judgment; since they will then see with irreparable sorrow, not only that they were ungrateful, but inhuman and cruel toward my divine Son, toward me and toward themselves.

555. Consider then thy duty, my dearest, and raise thyself above all earthly things and above thyself; for I am calling thee and choose thee to imitate and follow me into the solitude, in which I am left by creatures, whom my Son and I have pursued with so many blessings and favors. Weigh in thy heart, how much it cost my Lord to reconcile mankind to the eternal Father (Colos. 1,22) and regain for them his friendship. Weep and afflict thyself that so many should live in such forgetfulness and that so many should labor with all their might at destroying and losing what was bought by the blood of God itself and all that I from the first moment of my Conception have sought to procure and am procuring for their salvation. Awaken in thy heart the deepest grief, that in his holy Church there should be many followers of the hypocritical and sacrilegious priests who, under cover of a false piety, still condemn Christ; that pride and sumptuousness with other grave vices should be raised to authority and exalted, while humility, truth, justice and all virtues be so oppressed and debased and avarice and vanity should prevail. Few know the poverty of Christ, and fewer embrace it. Holy faith is hindered and is not spread among the nations on account of the boundless ambition of the mighty of this earth; in many Catholics it is inactive and dead; and whatever should be living, is near to death and to eternal perdition. The counsels of the Gospel are forgotten, its precepts trodden under foot, charity almost extinct. My son and true God offers his cheeks in patience and meekness to be buffeted and wounded (Thren. 3, 30). Who pardons an insult for the sake of imitating Him? Just the contrary is set up as law in this

world, not only by the infidels, but by the very children of the faith and of light.

556. In recognizing these sins I desire that thou imitate me in what I did during the Passion and during my whole life, namely practice the virtues opposed to these vices. As a recompense for their blasphemies, I blessed God; for their oaths, I praised Him; for their unbelief, I excited acts of faith, and so for all the rest of the sins committed. This is what I desire thee to do while living in this world. Fly also the dangerous intercourse with creatures, taught by the example of Peter, for thou art not stronger than he, the Apostle of Christ; and if thou fall in thy weakness, weep over thy fault and immediately seek my intercession. Make up for thy ordinary faults and weaknesses by thy patience in adversities, accept them with a joyous mien and without disturbance, no matter what they may be, whether they be sickness or the molestations coming from creatures, or whether they arise from the opposition of the flesh to the spirit, or from the conflicts with visible or invisible enemies. In all these things canst thou suffer and must thou bear up in faith, hope and magnanimous sentiment. I remind thee, that there is no exercise more profitable and useful for the soul than to suffer: for suffering gives light, undeceives, detaches the heart from visible things and raises it up to the Lord. He will come to meet those in suffering, because He is with the afflicted and sends to them his protection and help (Ps. 40, 15).

Chapter XVI

CHRIST IS DRAGGED TO THE HOUSE OF THE PRIEST CAI-
PHAS, WHERE HE IS FALSELY ACCUSED AND ASKED WHETH-
ER HE IS THE SON OF GOD; SAINT PETER DENIES HIM FOR
THE SECOND AND THIRD TIME; WHAT MOST HOLY MARY
DID ON THIS OCCASION, AND OTHER MYSTERIES.

557. After Jesus had been thus insulted and struck in the
house of Annas, He was sent, bound and fettered as He was,
to the priest Caiphas, the son in-law of Annas, who in that
year officiated as the prince and high priest; with him were
gathered the scribes and distinguished men of the Jews in
order to urge the condemnation of the most innocent Lamb
(Matth. 26, 57). The invincible patience and meekness of the
Lord of all virtues (Ps. 23, 10) astounded the demons, and
they were filled with a confusion and fury so great as no
words can describe. Since they could not penetrate into the
interior of the sanctuary of his humanity, and since they
noticed in the meekest Lord no inordinate movement, nor
any sign of complaint, nor any sighing, nor the least attempt
at human relief, by which they are wont to search the hearts
of other men, the dragon was in the utmost torments and
surprised as at something altogether new and unheard of
among weak and imperfect mortals. In his fury he redoubled
his efforts to irritate the scribes and servants of the priests
against Him and excite them to shower their abominable

insults and affronts upon his devoted head. In all that the demon suggested to them they showed themselves most eager and they executed it as far as the divine will allowed.

558. The whole rabble of infernal spirits and merciless foes of Christ left the house of Annas and dragged our Lord Savior through the streets to the house of Caiphas, exercising upon Him all the cruelty of their ignominious fury. The high priests and his attendants broke out in loud derision and laughter, when they saw Jesus brought amid tumultuous noise into their presence and beheld Him now subject to their power and jurisdiction without hope of escape. O mystery of the most exalted wisdom of heaven! O foolishness and ignorance of hell, and blind stupidity of mortals! What a distance immeasurable do I see between the doings of the Most High and yours! At the very time when the King of glory, as the Lord of all virtues and mighty in battles, (Ps. 23, 8), is vanquishing vice, and death, and all sin by the virtues of patience, humility and charity, the world boasts of having overcome and subjected Him to its arrogance and proud presumption! How different were the thoughts of Christ our Lord from those of the ministers of wickedness! The Author of life offered up to the eternal Father the triumph, which his meekness and humility won over sin; He prayed for the priests, the scribes and servants, presenting his patience and sufferings as a compensation for their persecutions and excusing them on account of their ignorance. The same prayer and petition was sent up at the same time by his blessed Mother, for her enemies and the enemies of her divine Son, thus following and imitating the Lord in all his doings; for, as I have many times said, She saw all as if personally present. Between the actions of the Son and the Mother there was a most sweet and wonderful harmony and a correspondence, most pleasing to the eyes of the eternal Father.

559. The high priest Caiphas, filled with a deadly envy and hatred against the Master of life, was seated in his chair of state or throne. With him were Lucifer and all his demons, who had come from the house of Annas. The scribes and pharisees, like bloodthirsty wolves, surrounded the gentle Lamb; all of them were full of the exultation of the envious, who see the object of their envy confounded and brought down. By common consent they sought for witnesses, whom they could bribe to bring false testimonies against Jesus our Savior (Matth. 26, 59). Those that had been procured, advanced to proffer their accusations and testimony; but their accusations neither agreed with each other, nor could any of their slander be made to apply to Him, who of his very nature was innocence and holiness (Mark 25, 56; Heb. 7, 26). In order not to be foiled, they brought two other false witnesses, who deposed, that they had heard Jesus say, He could destroy the temple of God made by the hands of men, and build up another one in three days, not made by them (Mark 16, 58). This testimony did not seem to be of much value, although they founded upon it the accusation, that He arrogated to Himself divine power. Even if this testimony had not been false in itself, the saying, if uttered by the Lord Almighty, would have been infallibly true and could not have been presumptuous or false. But the testimony was false; since the Lord had not uttered these words in reference to the material temple of God, as the witnesses wished to inculcate. At the time when He expelled the buyers and sellers from the temple and when asked by what power He did it, He answered: "Destroy this temple" that is : destroy this sacred humanity, and on the third day I shall restore it, which He certainly did at his Resurrection in testimony of his divine power.

560. Our Savior Jesus answered not a word to all the calumnies and lies brought forward against his innocence.

Caiphas, provoked by the patient silence of the Lord, rose up in his seat and said to Him: "Why dost Thou not answer to what so many witnesses testify against Thee?" But even to this the Lord made no response. For Caiphas and the rest were not only indisposed to believe Him; but they treacherously wished to make use of his answer in order to calumniate Him and satisfy the people in their proceedings against the Galileean, so that they might not be thought to have condemned Him to death without cause. This humble silence, which should have appeased the wicked priest, only infuriated him so much the more because it frustrated his evil purpose. Lucifer, who incited the high priest and all the rest, intently watched the conduct of the Savior. But the intention of the dragon was different from that of the high priest. He merely wanted to irritate the Lord, or to hear some word, by which he could ascertain whether he was true God.

561. With this purpose satan stirred up Caiphas to the highest pitch of rage and to ask in great wrath and haughtiness: "I adjure Thee by the living God, that Thou tell us, if Thou be the Christ, the Son of God." This question of the high priest certainly convicted him at once of the deepest folly and of dreadful blasphemy; for if it was sincere, he had permitted Christ to be brought before his tribunal in doubt whether He was the true God or not, which would make him guilty of the most formidable and audacious crime. The doubt in such a matter should have been solved in quite another way, conformable to the demands of right reason and justice. Christ our Savior, hearing Himself conjured by the living God, inwardly adored and reverenced the Divinity, though appealed to by such sacrilegious lips. Out of reverence for the name of God He therefore answered: "Thou hast said: I am He. Nevertheless I say to you, hereafter you shall see the Son of man (who I am) sitting on the right hand of the power of God, and coming in the clouds of heaven"

(Matth. 26, 64). At this divine answer the demons and the men were affected in different ways. Lucifer and his devils could not bear it; but immediately felt a superior force, which hurled them down into the abyss and oppressed them by the truth it contained. And they would not have dared to come again into the presence of Christ our Savior, if the divine Providence had not allowed them to fall again into doubts, whether this Man Christ had really spoken the truth or had merely sought this means of freeing Himself from the hands of the Jews. This uncertainty gave them new courage and they came forth once more to the battlefield. The ultimate triumph over the demons was reserved to the Cross itself, on which the Savior was to vanquish both them and death, as Zachary had prophesied and as will appear later.

562. But the high priest, furious at the answer of the Lord, instead of looking upon it as a solution of his doubt, rose once more in his seat, and rending his garments as an outward manifestation of his zeal for the honor of God, loudly cried out: "He hath blasphemed; what further need have we of witnesses? Behold, now you have heard the blasphemy: what think you?" (Matth. 26, 65.) The real blasphemy however consisted rather in these words of Caiphas, since he denied the certain fact that Christ was the Son of God by his very nature, and since he attributed to the divine Personality sinfulness, which was directly repugnant to his very nature. Such was the folly of the wicked priest, who by his office should have recognized and proclaimed the universal truth. He made of himself an execrable blasphemer in maintaining that He, who is holiness itself, had blasphemed. Having previously, with satanical instinct, abused his high office in prophesying that the death of one man is better than the ruin of all the people, he now was hindered by his sins from understanding his own prophecy. As the example and the opinions of princes and prelates powerfully stirs up the

flattery and subserviency of inferiors, that whole gathering of wickedness was incensed at the Savior Jesus: all exclaimed in a loud voice: "He is guilty of death (Matth. 26, 66), let Him die, let Him die!" Roused by satanic fury they all fell upon their most meek Master and discharged upon Him their wrath. Some of them struck Him in the face, others kicked Him, others tore out his hair, others spat upon his venerable countenance, others slapped or struck Him in the neck, which was a treatment reserved among the Jews only for the most abject and vile of criminals.

563. Never among men were such outrageous and frightful insults heaped upon anyone as were then heaped upon the Redeemer. Saint Luke and saint Mark say that they covered his face and then struck Him with their hands and fists saying: Prophesy, prophesy to us, Thou Prophet, who was it that struck Thee? The reason for their doing this was mysterious: namely, the joy with which our Savior suffered all these injuries and blasphemies (as I will soon relate) made his face shine forth in extraordinary beauty, and on this account those ministers of wickedness were seized with unbearable consternation and shame. They sought to attribute it to sorcery and magic and, by a resolution befitting also well their unworthiness, they covered the face of the Lord with an unclean cloth, so that they might not be hindered and tormented by its divine light in venting their diabolical wrath. All these affronts, reproaches and insults were seen and felt by the most holy Mary, causing in Her the same pains and wounds in the same parts of her body and at the same time as inflicted upon the Lord. The only difference was, that in our Lord the blows and torments were inflicted by the Jews themselves, while in his most pure Mother they were caused by the Almighty in a miraculous manner and upon request of the Lady. According to natural laws, the vehemence of her interior sorrow and anxiety would have put

an end to her life; but She was strengthened by divine power, so as to be able to continue to suffer with her beloved Son and Lord.

564. The interior acts performed by the Savior under these barbarous and unheard of persecutions, cannot be fathomed by human reason or faculties. Mary alone understood them fully, so as to be able to imitate them with the highest perfection. But as the divine Master now experienced in his own Person, how necessary his sympathy would be for those who were to follow him and practice his doctrine, He exerted Himself so much the more in procuring for them grace and blessings on this occasion, in which He was teaching them by his own example the narrow way of perfection. In the midst of these injuries and torments, and those which followed thereafter, the Lord established for his perfect and chosen souls the beatitudes, which He had promised and proposed to them some time before. He looked upon the poor in spirit, who were to imitate Him in this virtue and said: "Blessed are you in being stripped of the earthly goods; for by my Passion and Death I am to entail upon you the heavenly kingdom as a secure and certain possession of voluntary poverty. Blessed are those who meekly suffer and bear adversities and tribulations; for, besides the joy of having imitated Me, they shall possess the land of the hearts and the good will of men through the peacefulness of their intercourse and the sweetness of their virtues. Blessed are they that weep while they sow in tears; for in them, they shall receive the bread of understanding and life, and they shall afterwards harvest the fruits of everlasting joy and bliss."

565. "Blessed are also those who hunger and thirst for justice and truth; for I shall earn for them satiation far beyond all their desires, as well in the reign of grace as in the reign of glory. Blessed are they, who, imitating Me in my offers of pardon and friendship, mercifully pity those that offend and

persecute them; for I promise them the fullness of mercy from my Father. Blessed be the pure of heart, who imitate Me in crucifying their flesh in order to preserve the purity of their souls. I promise them the vision of peace and of my Divinity, by becoming like unto Me and by partaking of Me. Blessed are the peaceful, who, yielding their rights, do not resist the evil-minded and deal with them with a sincere and tranquil heart without vengeance; they shall be called my children, because they imitate my eternal Father and I shall write them in my memory and in my mind as my adopted sons. Those that suffer persecution for justice's sake, shall be the blessed heirs of my celestial kingdom, since they suffer with Me; and where I am, there also they shall be in eternity. Rejoice, ye poor; be consoled all ye that are and shall be afflicted; glory in your lot, ye little ones and despised ones of this world, you who suffer in humility and longanimity, suffer with an interior rejoicing; since all of you are following Me in the path of truth. Renounce vanity, despise the pomp and haughtiness of the false and deceitful Babylon; pass ye through the fires and the waters of tribulation until you reach Me, who am the light, the truth and your guide to the eternal rest and refreshment."

566. In such divine acts and in other aspirations for the good of sinners, our Savior Jesus occupied Himself, while He was surrounded by his malignant enemies as by ravenous dogs (Ps. 21, 17), who pursued Him and satiated Him with insults, affronts, blasphemies and wounds. The Virgin Mary, who was most attentive to all that passed, accompanied Him in all his acts and petitions; for She made the same petitions for his enemies. She took charge of the blessings lavished by her Son upon the just and the predestined, and constituted Herself as their Mother, their Helper and Protectress. In the name of all of them She composed hymns of praise and thanksgiving, because the Lord had assigned such an exalted

position in the reign of grace to the despised and poor of this
earth. On this account also, and on account of what She
afterwards witnessed in the interior of Christ, She chose anew
labor and contempt, tribulations and pains as her share
during the Passion and during the rest of her most holy life.

567. Saint Peter had followed the Lord Jesus from the
house of Annas to that of Caiphas, although he took care to
walk at some distance behind the crowd of enemies for fear
that the Jews might seize him. He partly repressed this fear
on account of the love of his Master and by the natural
courage of his heart. Among the great multitude which
crowded in and out of the house of Caiphas and in the
darkness, it was not difficult for the Apostle to find entrance
into the house of Caiphas. In the gates of the courtyard a
servant maid, who was a portress as in the house of Annas,
likewise noticed saint Peter; she immediately went up to the
soldiers, who stood at the fire with him and said: "This man
is one of those who were wont to accompany Jesus of Nazareth." One of the bystanders said: "Thou art surely a Galileean and one of them." Saint Peter denied it and added an
oath, that he was not a disciple of Jesus, immediately leaving
the company at the fire. Yet, in his eagerness to see the end,
although he left the courtyard, he did not leave the neighborhood. His natural love and compassion for the Lord still
caused him to linger in the place, where he saw Him suffer so
much. So the Apostle moved about, sometimes nearer,
sometimes farther from the hall of justice for nearly an hour.
Then a relative of that Malchus, whose ear he had severed,
recognized him and said: "Thou art a Galilean and a disciple
of Jesus; I saw thee with Him in the garden." Then Peter
deeming himself discovered, was seized with still greater fear,
and he began to assert with oaths and imprecations, that he
knew not the Man (Matth. 26, 72). Immediately thereupon
the cock crowed the second time, and the prediction of his

divine Master, that he should deny Him thrice before the cock crowed twice, was fulfilled to the letter.

568. The infernal dragon was very anxious to destroy saint Peter. It was Lucifer that incited the two maids, whom he could more easily influence, and afterwards, the soldiers, to molest the Apostle by their attention and inquiries. At the same time as soon as he saw him in his dangerous hesitation and change of mind he tried to disturb saint Peter by vivid imaginations of impending cruelty. Thus tempted, Peter simply denied the Lord at first, added an oath to the second denial, and curses and imprecations against himself at the third. Hence, from one sin he fell into another greater one, yielding to the cruel persecutions of the enemies. But saint Peter, now hearing the crowing of the cock, remembered the warning of his divine Master (Luke 22, 61); for, the great Queen in her gentle love having interceded for him, the Lord now cast upon him a look of boundless mercy. From her oratory in the Cenacle She had witnessed the denials together with all the circumstances and the causes which had brought the Apostle to fall so deeply. She had seen him beset with natural fear and much more by the merciless assaults of Lucifer. She threw Herself upon the ground and tearfully interceded for him, alleging his frailty and appealing to the merits of her divine Son. The Lord himself moved the heart of Peter, and by means of the light sent to him, gently reproached him, exhorting him to acknowledge his fault and deplore his sin. Immediately the Apostle left the house of the high priest, bursting with inmost sorrow into bitter tears over his fall. In order to weep in the bitterness of his heart he betook himself to a cave, even now called that of the Crowing Cock; there he poured forth his sorrow and confusion in a flood of tears. At the end of three hours he had obtained pardon for his crimes; and the holy impulses and inspirations had continued during that whole time until he was again

restored to grace. The most pure Mother and Queen sent to him one of her angels, who secretly consoled him and excited in him the hope of forgiveness, so that he might not delay his full pardon by want of trust in the goodness of God. The angel was ordered not to manifest himself, because the Apostle had so recently committed his sin. Hence the angel fulfilled his commission without being seen by the Apostle. Saint Peter was consoled and strengthened in his great sorrow by these inspirations and thus obtained full pardon through the intercession of most holy Mary.

Words of the Queen

THE VIRGIN MARY SPEAKS TO SISTER MARY OF AGREDA

569. My daughter, the mysterious sacrament of the patience of my Son, by which He bore all the affronts and insults, is a sealed book, which can be opened and understood only by the divine light. Thou hast come to the knowledge of it, as it has been partly laid open for thee, although on account of thy limited powers, thou writest much less than thou hast seen. But as this mystery is being made clear and intelligible to thee in the secret of thy heart, I wish that it be also written there and that thou study by this living example that divine science, which neither flesh nor blood can teach thee. For the world does not know, nor does it merit to know, this science. This philosophy consists in recognizing and loving the happy lot of the poor, the humble, the afflicted, the despised, and those unknown among the children of vanity. This school my most holy and loving Son established in his Church, when He proclaimed and set up the eight beatitudes (Matth. 5, 210). Afterwards, when He himself assumed all the sufferings of his Passion, He became for us a Teacher, who practices what He teaches, as thou hast seen. Nevertheless, although this is set before the eyes of the Catholics, and can be plainly

read by them in this book of life during their whole earthly pilgrimage, there are but few and scattered souls who enter into this school and study this book, while countless are the wayward and foolish, who ignore this science in their unwillingness to be taught.

570. All abhor poverty and thirst after riches, none of them being willing to recognize their emptiness. Infinite is the number of those who are carried away by their anger and vengeance, despising meekness. Few deplore their real miseries and struggle merely for terrestrial consolations; scarcely any love justice, or loyally pursue it in their dealings with the neighbors. Mercy is almost extinct, purity of heart is sullied and infringed upon, peace is constrained. None grant pardon, none wish to suffer for justice's sake, yea not even the least of the many torments and pains, which they have so justly merited. Thus, my dearest, there are few who attain the blessings promised by my divine Son and by me. Many times the just indignation and anger of the Almighty is roused against the professors of the true faith; since in the very sight of the living example of their Master, they live almost like infidels; many of them being even more abominable in their lives; for they are properly those who despise the fruits of the Redemption, which they have come to know and confess. In the land of saints they impiously perform the works of wickedness (Is. 26, 10), and make themselves unworthy of the remedies, which are put at their disposal in more merciful abundance.

571. Of thee I desire, my daughter, that thou labor valiantly for this blessedness, by seeking to imitate me perfectly according to thy grace of so deeply understanding this doctrine, which is hidden from the prudent and wise of this world (Mark 11, 25). Day for day I manifest to thee new secrets of my wisdom, in order that it may be established in thy heart and thou mayest extend thy hands to valiant deeds

(Prov. 31, 19). And now I will tell thee of an exercise which I practiced and which thou canst imitate to a certain degree. Thou knowest already, that from the very first instant of my Conception I was full of grace, without the least stain or participation of the least effect of original sin. On account of this singular privilege I was blessed in all the virtues, without feeling any repugnance or opposition in the exercise of them, and without being conscious of owing satisfaction for any sins of my own. Nevertheless the divine enlightenment taught me, that I was a Daughter of Adam by nature, which in him had sinned, and therefore I felt bound to humiliate myself to the very dust, even though I shared none of the guilt of that sin. And since I also possessed senses of the same kind as those, through which sin and its effects were contracted and which then and afterwards are operative in present human conditions, I thought myself obliged to mortify them, humiliate them and deprive them of the enjoyment proper to their nature, simply on account of this my parentage from Adam. I acted like a most faithful daughter of a family, who assumes the debt of her father and of her brothers as her own, though she had no share in contracting it, and who strives to pay and satisfy for it the more earnestly, the more she loves her family and the more they are unable to satisfy and free themselves from it, not giving herself any rest until she succeeds. This have I done with all the human race, whose miseries and transgressions I bewailed. Because I was a Daughter of Adam I mortified in me the senses and faculties with which he sinned, and I humiliated myself as one that had fallen and one guilty of his sin and disobedience, though I was entirely free from them. All this I did not only for Adam, but for all who by nature are my brethren. Thou canst not imitate me under like conditions, since thou art a partaker in his sin and guilt. But I herewith impose upon thee to labor without ceasing for thyself and for thy neighbor, and to humiliate thyself to the very dust; since a contrite and humble heart draws down mercy from the divine goodness.

Chapter XVII

THE SUFFERINGS OF OUR SAVIOR JESUS CHRIST AFTER THE
DENIAL OF SAINT PETER UNTIL MORNING; AND THE GREAT
SORROW OF HIS MOST HOLY MOTHER.

572. The holy Evangelists pass over in silence what and
where the Savior suffered after the ill-treatment in the house
of Caiphas and the denial of saint Peter. But they all take up
again the thread of events, when they speak of the council
held by them in the morning in order to deliver Him over to
Pilate, as will be related in the next chapter. I had some
doubts as to the propriety of speaking of this intervening
time and of manifesting that which was made known to me
concerning it: for it was intimated to me, that all cannot be
known in this life, nor is it proper that all should be made
known to all men. On the day of judgment these and many
other sacraments of the life and the Passion of our Lord shall
be published to the whole world. I cannot find words for
describing that which I might otherwise manifest: I do not
find adequate expressions for my concepts, and much less for
the reality itself; all is ineffable and above my capacity. But in
order to obey the orders given me, I will say what I am able,
so as not to incur the blame of concealing the truth, which
directly reproaches and confuses our vanity and forgetfulness.
In the presence of heaven I confess my own hardness of
heart, in not dying of sorrow and shame for having commit-

ted such great sins at such a cost to my God, the Originator of my life and being. We cannot ignore the wickedness and gravity of sin, which caused such ravages in the Author of grace and glory. I would be the most ungrateful of all the womanborn, if I would not now abhor sin more than death and as much as even the demon, and I cannot but intimate and assert, that this is the duty likewise of all the children of the holy Catholic church.

573. By the ill-treatment, which the Lord received in the presence of Caiphas, the wrath of this high priest and of all his supporters and ministers was much gratified, though not at all satiated. But as it was already past midnight, the whole council of these wicked men resolved to take good care, that the Savior be securely watched and confined until the morning, lest He should escape while they were asleep. For this purpose they ordered Him to be locked, bound as He was, in one of the subterranean dungeons, a prison cell set apart for the most audacious robbers and criminals of the state. Scarcely any light penetrated into this prison to dispel its darkness. It was filled with such uncleanness and stench, that it would have infected the whole house, if it had not been so remote and so well enclosed; for it had not been cleaned for many years, both because it was so deep down and because of the degradation of the criminals that were confined in it; for none thought it worth while making it more habitable than for mere wild beasts, unworthy of all human kindness.

574. The order of the council of wickedness was executed; the servants dragged the Creator of heaven and earth to that polluted and subterranean dungeon there to imprison Him. As the Lord was still bound with the fetters laid upon Him in the garden, these malicious men freely exercised all the wrathful cruelty with which they were inspired by the prince of darkness; for they dragged Him forward by the ropes, inhumanly causing Him to stumble, and loading Him with

kicks and cuffs amid blasphemous imprecations. From the floor in one corner of the subterranean cavern protruded part of a rock or block, which on account of its hardness had not been cut out. To this block, which had the appearance of a piece of column, they now bound and fettered the Lord Jesus with the ends of the ropes, but in a most merciless manner. For they forced Him to approach it and tied Him to it in a stooping position, so that He could neither seat Himself nor stand upright for relief, forcing Him to remain in a most painful and torturing posture. Thus they left Him bound to the rock, closing the prison door with a key and giving it in charge of one of the most malicious of their number.

575. But the infernal dragon rested not in his ancient pride. In the desire of finding out who this Christ was and of overcoming his imperturbable patience, he invented another scheme, to the execution of which he incited the jailer and some others of the servants. He inspired the one who held the key of the divine Treasure Trove, the greatest in heaven and earth, with the idea of inviting some of his equally evil-minded companions to descend to the dungeon and enter-tain themselves for awhile with the Master of life by forcing Him to speak of prophecy, or do some other strange or unheard of thing; for they believed Him to be a diviner or magician. Moved by this diabolical suggestion, he invited some of the soldiers and servants, who readily consented. While they were discussing this matter, a multitude of angels, who assisted the Redeemer in his Passion, when they saw Him so painfully bound in such an improper and polluted place, prostrated themselves before Him, adoring Him as their true God and Master, and showing Him so much the more reverence and worship the more they admired the love which moved Him to subject Himself to such abuse for the sake of mankind. They sang to Him some of the hymns and canticles which his own Mother had composed in his praise,

as I have mentioned above. The whole multitude of angelic spirits begged Him, in the name of the same Lady, that, since He would not permit his own almighty power to alleviate the sufferings of his humanity, He give them permission to unfetter and relieve Him of this torturing position and to defend Him from that horde of servants now instigated by the demons to heap upon Him new insults.

576. The Lord would not permit the angels to render this service and He said to them: "Ministering spirits of my eternal Father, I do not wish to accept any alleviation in my sufferings at present and I desire to undergo these torments and affronts in order to satiate my burning love for men and leave to my chosen friends this example for their imitation and consolation in their sufferings; and in order that all may properly estimate the treasures of grace, which I am gaining for them in great abundance through my pains. At the same time I wish to justify my cause, so that, on the day of my wrath, all may know how justly the reprobate shall be condemned for despising the most bitter sufferings by which I sought to save them. Tell my Mother to console Herself in this tribulation, since the day of rest and gladness shall come. Let Her accompany Me now in my works and sufferings for men; for her affectionate compassion and all her doings, afford Me much pleasure and enjoyment." Thereupon the holy angels betook themselves to their great Queen and Lady and consoled Her with this message, although She already knew in another way the will of her divine Son and all that happened in the house of Caiphas. When She perceived the new cruelty with which they had left Christ the Lord bound in a posture so painful and hard, She felt in her purest body the same pains; just as She had felt that of the blows and cuffs and other insults inflicted upon the Author of life. All the sufferings of the Lord miraculously reacted upon the virginal body of this sincerest Dove; the same pains beset the

Son and Mother, and the same sword pierced both their hearts; with only this difference, that Christ suffered as Godman and sole Redeemer of mankind, while Mary suffered as a creature and as a faithful helper of her most holy Son.

577. When the blessed Queen perceived that this band of vile miscreants, incited by the devil, would be permitted to enter the dungeon, She wept bitterly at what was to happen. Foreseeing the malicious intentions of Lucifer, She held Herself ready to make use of her sovereign power to prevent the executions of any designs upon the person of Christ that would imply indecency, such as the dragon sought to induce those unhappy men to carry out. For although all they did was most unbecoming and irreverent in his regard, yet there were insults, which would have been still more indecent, and by which the demon, not having succeeded hitherto, desired now to try the meek forbearance of the Lord. So exquisite and rare, wonderful and heroic, were the doings of the Lady at this time and during the whole Passion, that they could not worthily be mentioned or becomingly extolled, even if many books were written for this sole object; and as they are indescribable in this life, we must leave their full revelation to the beatific vision.

578. The ministers of wickedness therefore broke into the dungeon, blasphemously gloating over the expected feast of insult and ridicule, which they were now to hold with the Lord of all creation. Going up to Him they began to defile Him with their loathsome spittle and rain blows and cuffs upon Him with unmentionable and insulting mockery. The Lord opened not his mouth or made any answer; He raised not his divine eyes and lost not the humble serenity of his countenance. The sacrilegious buffoons wished to drive Him to some ridiculous or extraordinary saying or action, so that they might make a laughingstock of Him as a sorcerer; and

when they were compelled to witness his unchanging meekness, they allowed themselves to be incited still more by the demons. They untied the divine Master from the stone block and placed Him in the middle of the dungeon, at the same time blindfolding Him with a cloth; there they began to come up one after the other and strike Him with their fists, or slap or kick Him, each one trying to outdo the other in vehemence of their blasphemous cruelty and asking Him to prophesy who had struck Him. This kind of sacrilegious treatment these servants repeated even more often and continued longer than before the tribunal of Annas, to which saint Matthew (26, 67), saint Mark (14, 65), and saint Luke (22, 64) refer, tacitly including all that followed.

579. The most meek Lamb silently bore this flood of insults and blasphemies. Lucifer, tormented by his anxious desire of seeing some sign of impatience in Him, was lashed into fury at the equanimity with which the Savior bore it all. Therefore he inspired those slaves and friends of his with the project of despoiling the Lord of all his clothes and pursuing their ill-treatment according to suggestions which could only originate in the execrable demon. They readily yielded to this new inspiration and set about its execution. But the most prudent Lady was moved to most tearful prayers and aspirations at this abominable attempt and interfered with her power as the Queen. She asked the eternal Father to withdraw his cooperation with the secondary or created causes toward such a beginning and She commanded the faculties of these servants not to perform their natural functions. Thus it happened that none of the ruffians could execute the indecencies, which the demon or their own malice suggested to them. Some of these suggestions they forgot immediately and others they could not follow up, because their limbs became as it were frozen or paralyzed until they again changed their intent. As soon as they desisted the use of their limbs would

again be restored, for this was not intended as a punishment, but merely in order to prevent their practicing any indecencies. They were left entirely free to practice those cruelties or indulge in other irreverence, which were not so indecent, or were permitted by the Lord.

580. The powerful Queen also commanded the demons to be silent and forbade them to follow out the indecent intentions of Lucifer, their leader. By this command of the powerful Lady the dragon completely lost his power in those matters which Mary wished to include in her prohibition. Neither could he further irritate the foolish anger of those depraved men, nor could they go any further in their indecency than She permitted. But while experiencing within themselves the wonderful and extraordinary effects of her commands, they did not merit to be undeceived or recognize the divine power, although they thus saw themselves alternately paralyzed and suddenly restored to the full use of their powers. They attributed it merely to the sorcery and magic of the Master of truth. In their diabolical infatuation they continued to practice their insulting mockery and tortures upon the person of Christ, until they noticed that the night had already far advanced; then they again tied Him to the column and leaving Him thus bound, they departed with all the demons. It was ordained by the divine Wisdom, that the power of the blessed Mother safeguard propriety and decency due to the person of her most pure Son against the improper intentions of Lucifer and his ministers.

581. Again the Savior was alone in the dungeon, surrounded by the angelic spirits, who were full of admiration at the doings and the secret judgments of the Lord in what He wished to suffer. They adored Him with deepest reverence and magnified his holy name in exalted praise. The Redeemer of the world addressed a long prayer to his eternal Father for the children of the evangelical Church, for the spreading

of the holy faith, and for the Apostles, especially for saint Peter, who during that time was beweeping his sin. He prayed also for those who had injured and tormented Him; above all He included in his prayer his most holy Mother and all those who in imitation of Him were to be afflicted and despised in this world. At the same time He offered up his Passion and his coming Death for these ends. His grief-stricken Mother followed Him in these prayers, offering up the same petitions for the children of the Church and for its enemies without any movements of anger, indignation or dislike toward them. Only against the demon was She incensed, because he was entirely incapable of grace on account of his irreparable obstinacy. In sorrowful complaints She addressed the Lord, saying:

582. "Divine Love of my soul, my Son and Lord, Thou art worthy to be reverenced, honored and praised by all creatures, since Thou art the image of the eternal Father and the figure of his substance (Heb. 1, 3), infinite in thy being and in thy perfections. Thou art the beginning of all holiness (Apoc. 1, 8). But if the creatures are to serve Thee in entire subjection, why do they now, my Lord and God, despise, vilify, insult and torture thy Person, which is worthy of the highest worship and adoration? 'Why has the malice of men risen to such a pitch? Why has pride dared to raise itself even above heaven? How can envy become so powerful? Thou art the only and unclouded Sun of justice, which enlightens and dispels the darkness of sin (John 1, 9). Thou art the fountain of grace, withholding its waters from no one. Thou art the One, who in his liberal love givest being and life to all that live upon this earth, and all things depend upon Thee, while Thou hast need of none (Acts 17, 28). What then have they seen in thy doings, what have they found in thy Passion, that they should treat Thee in so vile a manner? O most atrocious wickedness of sin, which has so disfigured the heavenly

beauty and obscured the light of thy countenance! O cruel sin, which so inhumanly pursues the Repairer of all thy evil consequences! But I understand, my Son and Master, I understand that Thou art the Builder of true love, the Author of human salvation, the Master and Lord of virtues (Ps, 23, 10): Thou wishest to put in practice Thyself what Thou teachest the humble disciples of thy school: Thou wishest to humble pride, confound haughtiness and become the example of eternal salvation to all. And if Thou desirest that all imitate thy ineffable patience and charity, then that is my duty before all others, since I have administered to Thee the material and clothed Thee in this body now subjected to suffering, and wounded, spit upon and buffeted. O would that I alone should suffer these pains, and that Thou, my most innocent Son, be spared! And since this is not possible, let Me suffer with Thee unto death. You, O heavenly spirits, who full of wonder at the longsuffering of my Son recognize his immutable Deity and the innocence and excellence of his humanity, seek ye to compensate for these injuries and blasphemies heaped upon Him by men. Give Him glory and magnificence, wisdom, honor, virtue and power (Apoc. 5, 12). Invite the heavens, the planets and the stars and the elements to acknowledge and confess Him; and see whether there is another sorrow equal to mine!" (Thren. 1, 12). Such and many more were the sorrowful aspirations of the most pure Lady, in giving vent to the bitterness of her grief and pain.

583. Peerless was the patience of the heavenly Princess in the Death and Passion of her beloved Son and Lord; so that what She suffered never seemed to Her much, nor her afflictions equal to those demanded by her affection, which was measured only by the love and the dignity of her Son and the greatness of his sufferings. Nor did She in any of the injuries and affronts against the Lord take any account of their being

committed against Herself. She reflected not on the share which She herself had in them, although She was made to suffer so much by all of them: She deplored them only in so far as they outraged the divine Personality and caused damage to the aggressors. She prayed for them all, that the Most High might pardon them and grant them salvation from the evils of sin and enlightenment for gaining the fruits of Redemption.

Words of the Queen

THE VIRGIN MARY SPEAKS TO SISTER MARY OF AGREDA

584. My daughter, it is written in the holy Gospels (John 5, 57) that the eternal Father has given to his only Son and mine the power to judge and condemn the reprobate on the last day, the day of universal judgment. This was eminently proper, not only in order that all the sinners may see their Judge, who will sentence them according to the most just will of God; but also in order that they may behold and recognize his humanity, by which they were redeemed, and be confronted in it with the torments and injuries it suffered in order to rescue them from eternal damnation. The same Judge and Lord, who shall judge them, shall also advance the charge. As they cannot answer or satisfy for the crimes with which He charges them, their confusion will be only the beginning of the eternal torments, which they merit by their obstinate ingratitude; for then shall become evident to all the world the greatness of his most merciful and kind Redemption and the justice of their damnation. Great was the sorrow, most bitter the grief, of my most holy Son, that not all should make use of the fruits of his Redemption. This same thought also pierced my heart and immensely added to the sorrow of seeing Him spit upon, buffeted, and blasphemed more cruelly than can ever be understood by living man. But

I understood all these sufferings clearly and as they should be understood; therefore my sorrow was great in proportion to this knowledge, just as it was also the measure of my reverence and love of the person of Christ, my Son and Lord. But next to this sorrow, my greatest one was to know, that after all these death dealing sufferings of the Lord, so many men should still damn themselves even within sight of all the infinite treasures of grace.

585. I wish that thou imitate and follow me in this sorrow and that thou lament this fearful misfortune; for among all the losses sustained by men, there is none which deserves to be so deplored, nor which can ever be compared to it. My Son and I look with especial love upon those who imitate this sorrow and afflict themselves on account of the perdition of so many souls. Seek thou, my dearest, to distinguish thyself in this exercise and continue to pray: for thou canst scarcely imagine how acceptable are such prayers to the Almighty. But remember his promise, that those who pray shall receive (Luke 11, 9), and that to those who knock the gates of his infinite treasures shall be opened. In order that thou mayest have something to offer in return, write into thy heart, what my most holy Son and thy Spouse suffered at the hands of those vile and depraved men, and the invincible patience, meekness and silence with which He submitted to their wicked whims. With this example, labor from now on, that no anger, nor any other passion of a daughter of Adam have any sway over thee. Let an interior and ever active horror of pride, and a dread of injuring thy neighbor, be engendered in thy bosom. Solicitously ask the Lord for patience, meekness, and peacefulness and for a love of sufferings and Christ's Cross. Embrace this Cross with a pious affection and follow Christ thy Spouse, in order that thou mayest at last possess Him (Matth, 16, 14).

Chapter XVIII

THE COUNCIL CONVENES ON THE FRIDAY MORNING TO SUBSTANTIATE THE CHARGES AGAINST THE SAVIOR JESUS; THEY SEND HIM TO PILATE; MOST HOLY MARY, WITH SAINT JOHN AND THE THREE MARYS, GOES FORTH TO MEET JESUS.

586. At the dawn of Friday morning, say the Evangelists (Matth. 27, 1; Mark 15, 1; Luke 22, 66; John 11, 47), the ancients, the chief priests and scribes, who according to the law were looked upon with greatest respect by the people, gathered together in order to come to a common decision concerning the death of Christ. This they all desired; however they were anxious to preserve the semblance of justice before the people. This council was held in the house of Caiphas, where the Lord was imprisoned. Once more they commanded Him to be brought from the dungeon to the hall of the council in order to be examined. The satellites of justice rushed below to drag Him forth bound and fettered as He was; and while they untied Him from the column of rock, they mocked Him with great contempt saying: "Well now, Jesus of Nazareth, how little have thy miracles helped to defend Thee. The power which Thou didst vaunt, of being able to rebuild the temple in three days, has failed altogether in securing thy escape. But Thou shalt now pay for thy presumption and thy proud aspirations shall be brought

low. Come now to the chief priests and to the scribes. They are awaiting Thee to put an end to thy imposition and deliver Thee over to Pilate, who will quickly finish Thee." Having freed the Lord from the rock they dragged Him up to the council. The Lord did not open his lips; but the tortures, the blows and the spittle, with which they had covered Him and which He could not wipe off on account of his bonds, had so disfigured Him, that He now filled the members of the council with a sort of dreadful surprise, but not with compassion. Too great was their envious wrath conceived against the Lord.

587. They again asked Him to tell them, whether He was the Christ (Luke 22, 1), that is, the Anointed. Just as all their previous questions, so this was put with the malicious determination not to listen or to admit the truth, but to calumniate and fabricate a charge against Him. But the Lord, being perfectly willing to die for the truth, denied it not; at the same time He did not wish to confess it in such a manner that they could despise it, or borrow out of it some color for their calumny; for this was not becoming his innocence and wisdom. Therefore He veiled his answer in such a way, that if the pharisees chose to yield to even the least kindly feeling, they would be able to trace up the mystery hidden in his words; but if they had no such feeling, then should it become clear through their answer, that the evil which they imputed to Him was the result of their wicked intentions and lay not in his answer. He therefore said to them: "If I tell you that I am He of whom you ask, you will not believe what I say; and if I shall ask you, you will not answer, nor release Me. But I tell you, that the Son of man, after this, shall seat Himself at the right hand of the power of God" (Luke 22, 67). The priests answered: "Then thou art the Son of God?" and the Lord replied: "You say that I am." This was as if He had said: You have made a very correct inference, that I am the Son of

God; for my works, my doctrines, and your own Scripture, as well as what you are now doing with Me, testify to the fact, that I am the Christ, the One promised in the law.

588. But this council of the wicked was not disposed to assent to divine truth, although they themselves inferred it very correctly from the antecedents and could easily have believed it. They would neither give assent nor belief, but preferred to call it a blasphemy deserving death. Since the Lord had now reaffirmed what He had said before, they all cried out: "What need have we of further witnesses, since He himself asserts it by his own lips?" And they immediately came to the unanimous conclusion that He should, as one worthy of death, be brought before Pontius Pilate, who governed Judea in the name of the Roman emperor and was the temporal Lord of Palestine. According to the laws of the Roman empire capital punishment was reserved to the senate or the emperor and his representatives in the remote provinces. Cases of such importance as involved the taking away of life were looked upon as worthy of greater attention and as not to be decided without giving the accused a hearing and an opportunity of defense and justification. In these affairs of justice the Roman people yielded to the requirements of natural reason more faithfully than other nations. In regard to this trial of Christ the priests and scribes were pleased with the prospect of having sentence of death passed upon Christ our Lord by the heathen Pilate, because they could then tell the people, that He was condemned by the Roman governor and that this certainly would not have happened if He were not guilty of death. To this extent had they been blinded by their sins and their hypocrisy, that they failed to see how much more guilty and sacrilegious they would even then be than the gentile judge. But the Lord arranged it thus, in order that by their own behavior before Pilate they might

reveal all their wickedness more plainly, as we shall see immediately.

589. The executioners therefore brought our Savior Jesus Christ to the house of Pilate, in order to present Him, still bound with the same chains and ropes in which they had taken Him from the garden, before his tribunal. The city of Jerusalem was full of strangers, who had come from all Palestine to celebrate the great Pasch of the Lamb and of the unleavened bread. As the rumor of this arrest was already spread among the people, and as the Master of life was known to all of them, a countless multitude gathered in the streets to see Him brought in chains through the streets. They were divided in their opinion concerning the Messiah; some of them shouted out: Let Him die, let Him die, this wicked impostor, who deceives the whole world. Others answered: His doctrines do not appear to be so bad, nor his works; for He has done good to many. Still others, who had believed in Him, were much afflicted and wept; while the whole city was in confusion and uproar concerning the Nazarene. Lucifer and all his demons were very attentive to what was passing; for, seeing himself secretly overcome by the invincible patience and meekness of Christ the Lord, he was stirred to uncontrollable fury by his own pride and haughtiness at the haunting suspicion, that such virtues could not be those of a mere human being. On the other hand, he could not understand how his allowing Himself to be despised and ill-treated and his succumbing to so much bodily weakness and, as it were, total annihilation, could ever harmonize with his being true God; for, if He were God, said the dragon to himself, his Divinity would never consent to such annihilation, and the power inherent in his divine nature and communicated to the humanity, would certainly prevent such weakness. Lucifer argued like one who knew nothing of the suspension of the overflow of the divine upon

the human nature; which the Lord had secretly ordained for the purpose of securing the highest degree of suffering possible, as I have mentioned above (No. 498). By these misgivings, the pride of satan was lashed to still more furious efforts in the persecution of the Lord so as to ascertain who this One was that knew how to suffer torments in such a manner.

590. The sun had already arisen while these things happened and the most holy Mother, who saw it all from afar, now resolved to leave her retreat and follow her divine Son to the house of Pilate and to his death on the Cross. When the great Queen and Lady was about to set forth from the Cenacle, saint John arrived, in order to give an account of all that was happening; for the beloved disciple at that time did not know of the visions, by which all the doings and sufferings of her most holy Son were manifest to the blessed Mother. After the denial of saint Peter, saint John had retired and had observed, more from afar what was going on. Recognizing also the wickedness of his flight in the garden, he confessed it to the Mother of God and asked her pardon as soon as he came into her presence; and then he gave an account of all that passed in his heart and of what he had done and what he had seen in following his Master. Saint John thought it well to prepare the afflicted Mother for her meeting with her most holy Son, in order that She might not be overcome by the fearful spectacle of his present condition. Therefore He sought to impress Her beforehand with some image of his sufferings by saying: "0 my Lady, in what a state of suffering is our divine Master! The sight of Him cannot but break one's heart; for by the buffets and the blows and by the spittle, his most beautiful countenance is so disfigured and defiled, that Thou wilt scarcely recognize Him with thy own eyes." The most prudent Lady listened to his description, as if She knew nothing of the events; but She broke out in bitterest tears of heartrending sorrow. The holy women, who

had came forth with the Lady, also listened to saint John, and all of them were filled with grief and terror at his words. The Queen of heaven asked the Apostle to accompany Her and the devout women, and, exhorting them all, She said: "Let us hasten our steps, in order that my eyes may see the Son of the eternal Father, who took human form in my womb; and you shall see, my dearest friends, to what the love of mankind has driven Him, my Lord and God, and what it costs Him to redeem men from sin and death, and to open for them the gates of heaven."

591. The Queen of heaven set forth through the streets of Jerusalem accompanied by saint John and by some holy women. Of these not all, but only the three Marys and other very pious women, followed Her to the end. With Her were also the angels of her guard, whom She asked to open a way for Her to her divine Son. The holy angels obeyed and acted as her guard. On the streets She heard the people expressing their various opinions and sentiments concerning the sorrowful events now transpiring in reference to Jesus of Nazareth. The more kindly hearted lamented over his fate, and they were fewest in number. Others spoke about the intention of his enemies to crucify Him; others related where He now was and how He was conducted through the streets, bound as a criminal; others spoke of the ill-treatment He was undergoing; others asked, what evil He had done, that He should be so misused; others again in their astonishment and in their doubts, exclaimed: To this then have his miracles brought Him! Without a doubt they were all impostures, since He cannot defend or free Himself! All the streets and squares were full of people and excited talk. But in the midst of this excitement the invincible Queen, though filled with the bitterest sorrow, preserved her constancy and composure, praying for the unbelievers and the evildoers, as if She had no other care than to implore grace and pardon for their sins.

She loved them as sincerely as if She were receiving favors and blessings at their hands. She permitted no indignation or anger to arise in her heart against the sacrilegious ministers of the Passion and Death of her beloved Son, nor any sign of such feelings in her exterior conduct. All of them She looked upon with charity and the desire of doing them good.

592. Some of them that met Her on the streets, recognized Her as the Mother of Jesus of Nazareth and moved by their natural compassion, said: "0 sorrowful Mother! What a misfortune has overtaken Thee! How must thy heart be wounded and lacerated with grief!" Others again impiously said: "Why didst Thou permit Him to introduce such novelties among the people? It would have been better to restrain and dissuade Him; but it will be a warning for other mothers, and they will learn from thy misfortunes, how to instruct their children." These and other more horrible sentiments were expressed in the hearing of this sincerest Dove; but all of them She met with burning charity, accepting the pity of the kindhearted, and suffering the malice of the unbelievers. She was not surprised at the ingratitude of the unresponsive and the ignorant; but implored the eternal Father to impart suitable blessings to all.

593. Through the swarming and confused crowds the angels conducted the Empress of heaven to a sharp turn of the street, where She met her most holy Son. With the profoundest reverence She prostrated Herself before his sovereign Person and adored it more fervently and with a reverence more deep and more ardent than ever was given or ever shall be given to it by all the creatures. She arose and then the Mother and Son looked upon each other with ineffable tenderness, interiorly conversing with each other in transports of an unspeakable sorrow. The most prudent Lady stepped aside and then followed Christ our Lord, continuing at a distance her interior communication with Him and with

the eternal Father. The words of her soul are not for the mortal and corruptible tongue: but among other prayers the afflicted Mother said: "Most high God and my Son, I am aware of thy burning love for men, which leads Thee to hide the infinite power of thy Divinity beneath a form of passible flesh (Phil. 2, 7) formed in my womb. I confess thy incomprehensible wisdom in accepting such affronts and torments, and in sacrificing Thyself, who art the Lord of all creation, for the rescue of man, who is but a servant, dust and ashes (Gen. 3,19). Thy goodness is to be praised, blessed, confessed and magnified by all creatures; but how shall I, thy Mother, ever cease to desire that all these injuries be heaped upon me and not upon thy divine Person, who art the beauty of the angels and the glory of the eternal Father? How shall I cease to desire the end of these pains? With what sorrow is my heart filled to behold Thee so afflicted, thy most beautiful countenance so defiled, and when I see, that to the Creator and Redeemer alone is denied pity and compassion in such bitter suffering? But if it is not possible, that I relieve Thee as Mother, do Thou accept my sorrowful sacrifice in not being able to bring Thee the relief which is due to the true and holy Son of God."

594. The image of her divine Son, thus wounded, defiled and bound, remained so firmly fixed and imprinted in the soul of our Queen, that during her life it was never effaced, and remained in her mind as distinctly, as if She were continually beholding Him with her own eyes. Christ our God arrived at the house of Pilate, followed by many of the council and a countless multitude of the people. The Jews, wishing to preserve themselves as clean before the law as possible for the celebration of the Pasch and the unleavened bread, excused themselves before Pilate for their refusing to enter the pretorium or court of Pilate in presenting Jesus. As most absurd hypocrites they paid no attention to the sacrilegious

uncleanness, with which their souls were affected in becoming the murderers of the innocent Godman. Pilate, although a heathen, yielded to their ceremonious scruples, and seeing that they hesitated to enter his pretorium, he went out to meet them. According to the formality customary among the Romans, he asked them (John 18, 28) : "What accusation have you against this Man ?" They answered: "If He were not a criminal, we would not have brought Him to thee thus bound and fettered." This was as much as to say: We have convinced ourselves of his misdeeds and we are so attached to justice and to our obligations, that we would not have begun any proceedings against Him, if He were not a great malefactor. But Pilate pressed his inquiry and said: "What then are the misdeeds, of which He has made Himself guilty?" They answered: "He is convicted of disturbing the commonwealth, He wishes to make Himself our king and forbids paying tribute to Caesar (Luke 23, 2); He claims to be the son of God, and has preached a new doctrine, commencing in Galilee, through all Judea and Jerusalem." "Take Him then yourselves," said Pilate, "and judge Him according to your laws; I do not find a just cause for proceeding against Him." But the Jews replied: "It is not permitted us to sentence anyone to death, nor to execute such a sentence."

595. The most holy Mary, with saint John and the women who followed Her, was present at this interview; for the holy angels made room for them where they could hear and see all that was passing. Shielded by her mantle She wept tears of blood, pressed forth by the sorrow which pierced her virginal heart. In her interior acts of virtue She faithfully reproduced those practiced by her most holy Son, while in her pains and endurance She copied those of his body. She asked the eternal Father to grant Her the favor of not losing sight of her divine Son, as far as was naturally possible, until his Death; and this was conceded to Her, excepting during

the time in which He was in prison. Considering it but just, that amid all the false accusations of the Jews the innocence of the Savior and the injustice of the sentence should become known, the most prudent Lady fervently prayed, that the judge be not deceived and that he obtain clearest insight into Christ's being delivered over to him by the envy of the priests and scribes. In virtue of this prayer, Pilate clearly saw the truth, was convinced of the innocence of Christ and of his being a victim of their envy (Matth. 28, 18). On her account also the Lord declared Himself more openly to Pilate, although the latter did not cooperate with the truth made known to him. It profited not him, but us; and it served to convict the priests and pharisees of their treachery.

596. In their wrath the Jews were anxious to dispose Pilate favorably toward their project and they wished him to pronounce the sentence of death against Jesus without the least delay. When they perceived his hesitation, they ferociously raised their voices, accusing Jesus over and over again of revolting against the government of Judea, deceiving and stirring up the people (Luke 23, 5), calling Himself Christ, that is an anointed King. This malicious accusation they pressed particularly, hoping to stir Pilate to fear for the temporal welfare of his government, with which he was charged by the Romans. Among the Jews the kings were anointed; therefore they insisted, that Jesus in having called Himself Christ, intended to constitute Himself as King, and, as Pilate was a heathen and knew nothing of the anointing of kings, they wished to persuade him, that calling oneself Christ among the Jews was identical with calling oneself king of the Jews. Pilate asked the Lord: "What dost Thou answer to the accusations which they bring against Thee?" But the Savior answered not one word in the presence of his accusers, causing much wonder in Pilate at such silence and patience. But, desiring to inquire more closely, whether Jesus was truly

a King, he withdrew from the clamoring Jews and brought Jesus into the pretorium. There he asked Him face to face: "Tell me, can it be that Thou art a King of the Jews?" Pilate could not bring himself to think that He was a King in fact; since he knew that Christ was not reigning. Therefore he wished to find out, whether Jesus claimed or really possessed any right to the title of King. Our Savior answered him: "Sayst thou this thing of thyself, or have others told it thee of Me?" (John 18,34). Pilate replied: "Am I a Jew? Thy own nation and the chief priests have delivered Thee up to me. What hast Thou done?" Jesus answered: "My kingdom is not of this world. If my kingdom were of this world, my servants would certainly strive that I be not delivered to the Jews: but now my kingdom is not from hence." The judge partly believed this assertion of Jesus and therefore answered: "Art Thou a king then?" Jesus answered: "Thou sayest that I am a king. For this I was born and for this I came into the world. Every one that is of the Truth, heareth my voice." Pilate wondered at this answer and asked: "What is truth?" But without waiting for an answer, he left Him in the pretorium, and said to the Jews: "I find no cause in Him. But you have a custom, that I should release one unto you at the Pasch: will you, therefore, that I release unto you the King of the Jews, or Barabbas?" This Barabbas was a thief and murderer, who had killed some one in a quarrel. All the people raised their voice and said: "We desire that you release Barabbas, and crucify Jesus." In this demand they persisted until it was granted.

597. Pilate was much disturbed by the answers of Jesus and the obstinacy of the Jews. For on the one hand, seeing that they were so determined on the death of Jesus, he well knew, that it would be difficult to satisfy them without consenting to their demands; and on the other hand, he clearly saw that they persecuted Him out of mortal envy and

that their accusations about his disturbing the people, were false and ridiculous (Matth. Ii, 18). In regard to the imputation, that He had made Himself King, he was likewise satisfied of the contrary by the answers of Christ and by his humility, poverty and patient forbearance toward their calumnies. By the light and grace which Pilate received, he became fully convinced that Jesus was truly innocent, although he never pierced the mystery of his Divinity and the greatness of this innocence. The living words of Christ created an exalted idea of Him in his mind and made him think that some great mystery was connected with Him; therefore he desired to free Him and finally determined to send Him to Herod. But all these shifts failed, because Pilate made himself unworthy by his sin and paid attention only to his worldly prospects, allowing himself to be governed by them and not by the dictates of justice, but more by the suggestions of Lucifer, as I have related above (No. 423), than by the truth, which he so clearly knew. Fully understanding the true circumstances, he acted the part of a wicked judge in continuing to treat the cause of an innocent Man with those who were his declared enemies and false accusers. Thus he committed the still greater crime of condemning Jesus to such an inhuman scourging and then to death, without having any other cause than to satisfy the Jews.

598. But though Pilate for these and other reasons was a most wicked and unjust judge in thus condemning Christ, whom he held to be a mere man, though good and innocent; yet his crime was much smaller than that of the priests and pharisees. And this not only because they were moved by envy, cruelty and other vices, but also because they sinned in not acknowledging Christ as their true Messias and Redeemer, God and Man, such as He had been promised in the Law, which they believed and professed. For their own condemnation the Lord permitted, that in their very accusations they

called Him Christ and anointed King, thus confessing with their lips what they denied and discredited in their proceedings. They were bound to believe this truth, which they confessed in their words, and thus come to the understanding of the true anointment of the Savior, which was an unction prefigured in the kings and priests of the olden times and consisted in the anointment mentioned by David (Ps. 44, 8) and different from theirs; namely, the unction of the Divinity resulting from its union with the humanity and by which Christ's soul was anointed with the gifts of grace and glory corresponding to the hypostatic union. All these mysteries of truth were providentially hidden beneath the accusations of the Jews, although they in their perfidy would not believe them, and in their envy interpreted them falsely. For they imputed to the Savior the desire of making Himself king, without his being one, while just the contrary was really the truth: He was in every respect the supreme Lord, but did not wish to show or make use of the power of a temporal king. He had not come into this world to command men, but to obey (Matth. 20, 28). Still greater was the blindness of the Jews in hoping for a temporal king as their Messias and at the same time calumniously asserting that Jesus made of Himself a king. It seems that they sought for their Messias a King so powerful, that they would not be able to resist Him; although they then would have to receive a king by compulsion and not with the free will benevolently desired by the Lord.

599: Our great Lady profoundly understood these hidden sacraments and the wisdom of her chaste heart made use of them to excite heroic acts of all the virtues. Other children of Adam, conceived in original sin and defiled by their own, are wont to be disturbed and oppressed in proportion to the increase of sorrow and tribulation, and excited to impatience and other inordinate passions; but most holy Mary, who was actuated not by sin or its effects, or by mere nature, was impelled by exalted grace to just the contrary course of action. For the great persecutions and the vast waters of affliction and sorrow extinguished not in her bosom the fire of divine love (Cant. 8, 7); but they were new incentives to the fires of divine love in her soul, breaking forth in petitions for the sinners so much the more ardently, as the malice of men reached greater excesses. O Queen of virtues, Mistress of creatures and sweetest Mother of mercy! How hard of heart am I, how slow and insensible, that my soul is not annihilated by sorrow at what I understand of thy sufferings and those of thy divine Son! That I still live, knowing all I do know, should cause in me a sorrow unto death. It is a crime against love and piety to beg favors from the innocent, whom we see suffering torments. With what truth can we then say as creatures, that we love God, our Redeemer, and Thee, my Queen, who art his Mother, if Thou and He alone drink out the chalice of such torments and pains, while we are draining the chalice of the pleasures of Babylon? O that I might understand this truth! O that it might penetrate into my deepest heart and that it might pierce my very soul at the sight of such inhuman torments of my Savior and his afflicted Mother! How can I conceive, that anyone can do me an injustice in persecuting me, that they offend me by despising me, that they insult me by abhorring me? How can I complain of suffering, even if I am blamed, neglected and contemned by the world? O great Chieftainess of the martyrs, Queen of the courageous, Mistress of all the imitators of thy Son, if I am thy daughter and disciple, as Thou condescendest to call me, and as my Lord wishes me to merit, do not reject my longing desire to follow thy footsteps on the way of the cross. If in my weakness I have fallen, do Thou, my Lady and Mother, obtain for me the courage of a contrite heart, justly humiliated on account of its vile ingratitude. Gain for me through thy prayers the love of the eternal Father, which is so precious, that only thy powerful intercession can obtain it and only my Lord and Redeemer can merit it for me.

Words of the Queen

THE VIRGIN MARY SPEAKS TO SISTER MARY OF AGREDA

600. My daughter, great is the neglect and the inattention of men in failing to consider the works of my most holy Son and to penetrate with humble reverence the mysteries which He has concealed within them for the salvation of all. But many do not know, and others are astonished, that the Lord should have consented to be presented as a criminal before iniquitous judges and be examined by them as a wicked malefactor; that they should have been allowed to treat Him as an ignorant fool; and that He should not have made use of his divine wisdom to defend his innocence, convict the Jews and all his enemies of their malice, since He could so easily have done it. But these sentiments of wonder should be especially united to a deep veneration for the judgments of the Lord, who disposed all things connected with the Redemption according to his equity, goodness and rectitude and in a manner befitting all his attributes, denying none of his enemies sufficient help to follow the good, if only they wished to use their freedom for that purpose. He wished all of them to be saved (I Tim. 2, 4), and if not all of them attained this salvation, no one can justly complain of his superabundant kindness.

601. But besides this, I wish, my dearest, that thou understand the instructive lessons contained in these works; for in each one of them my Son acted as Redeemer and Teacher of men. In the silence and the meekness, which He maintained during his Passion, permitting Himself to be reputed as a wicked and foolish man, He left to mankind a lesson just as

important as it is unnoticed and unpracticed by the children
of Adam. Because they do not heed the contagion of Lucifer
through sin, which is perpetuated in the world, they do not
seek in the Physician the medicine of suffering, which the
Lord in his immense charity has left to the world in word
and deed. Let men then consider themselves conceived in sin
(Ps. 50, 7), and let them realize how strong has grown in
them the hellish seed of pride, of presumption, vanity, self-
esteem, avarice, hypocrisy, deceitfulness, and all other vices.
Each one ordinarily seeks to advance his honor and vainglory, struggling to be applauded and renowned. The learned
and those who think themselves wise, wish to be applauded
and looked up to, bragging about their knowledge. The
unlearned try to appear wise. The rich glory in their riches
and wish to be respected on their account. The poor strive to
be and appear rich, anxious to gain the approbation of the
wealthy. The powerful seek to be feared, worshipped and
obeyed. All of them are pursuing the same deceit of seeking
to appear what they are not in fact, and fail in reality to come
up to what they appear to be. They palliate their faults, extol
their virtues and abilities, they attribute to themselves the
goods and the blessings as if they had not received them from
God. They receive them as if they were their due and not
owing to his liberal kindness; instead of being thankful for
them they abuse them as weapons against God and against
their own selves. Commonly all are swollen up by the mortal
poison of the serpent and so much the more anxious to drink
it, the more deeply they are already wounded and weakened
by his lamentable assaults. The way of the cross and imitation of Christ in humble Christian sincerity is deserted,
because they are so few that walk upon it.

602. In order to crush the head of Lucifer and overcome
pride and arrogance, my Son observed this patient silence in
his Passion, permitting Himself to be treated as an ignorant

and foolish criminal. As the Teacher of this philosophy and as the Physician of the sickness of sin, He would not deny the charges nor defend or justify Himself, nor refute those who accused Him, showing us by his own living example, how to oppose and counteract the intentions of the serpent. In the Lord was that teaching of the wise man put into practice: More precious is a little foolishness in its time than wisdom and glory (Eccles. 10, 1); for it is better that human frailty be at times considered ignorant and wicked, than that it make a vain show of virtue and wisdom. Infinite is the number of those who are entangled in this dangerous error, who, desiring to appear wise, speak much and multiply words like the foolish (Eccles. 1, 14). They only lose what they strive so much to attain, since they become known as foolish. All these vices arise from the pride rooted in human nature. But do thou, my daughter, preserve the doctrine of my divine Son and that which comes from me. Abhor human ostentation, suffer in silence and let the world consider thee ignorant; for it does not know where true wisdom dwells.

Chapter XIX

PILATE SENDS THE JEWS WITH JESUS AND THEIR ACCUSA-
TIONS TO HEROD, WHERE THEY ADVANCE THEIR CHARGES;
HEROD TREATS JESUS WITH CONTEMPT AND SENDS HIM
BACK TO PILATE; MARY FOLLOWS THE SAVIOR; OTHER
HAPPENINGS IN CONNECTION.

603. One of the accusations of the Jews and the priests before
Pilate was that Jesus our Savior had begun to stir up the
people by his preaching in the province of Galilee (Luke 23,
6). This caused Pilate to inquire, whether He was a Galileean; and as they told him, that Jesus was born and raised in
that country, he thought this circumstance useful for the
solution of his difficulties in regard to Jesus and for escaping
the molestations of the Jews, who so urgently demanded his
death. Herod was at that time in Jerusalem, celebrating the
Pasch of the Jews. He was the son of the first Herod, who
had murdered the Innocents to procure the death of Jesus
soon after his birth (Matth 2, 16). This murderer had become a proselyte of the Jews at the time of his marriage with
a Jewish woman. On this account his son Herod likewise
observed the law of Moses, and he had come to Jerusalem
from Galilee, of which he was governor. Pilate was at enmity
with Herod, for the two governed the two principal provinces of Palestine, namely, Judea and Galilee, and a short time
before it had happened that Pilate, in his zeal for the suprem-

acy of the Roman empire, had murdered some Galileens during a public function in the temple, mixing the blood of the insurgents with that of the holy sacrifices. Herod was highly incensed at this sacrilege, and Pilate, in order to afford him some satisfaction without much trouble to himself, resolved to send to him Christ the Lord to be examined and judged as one of the subjects of Herod's sway. Pilate also expected that Herod would set Jesus free as being innocent and a Victim of the malice and envy of the priests and scribes.

604. Christ our Lord therefore went forth from the house of Pilate to the palace of Herod, being still bound and chained as before and accompanied by the scribes and priests as his accusers. There were also a large number of soldiers and servants, who dragged Him along by the ropes and cleared the streets, which had been filled with multitudes of the people to see the spectacle. The military broke their way through the crowds; and as the servants and priests were thirsting so eagerly for the blood of the Savior and wished to shed it on this very day, they hastened with the Lord through the streets nearly on a run and with great tumult. Mary also set forth from the house of Pilate with her company in order to follow her sweetest Son Jesus and accompany Him on the ways, which He was still to go until his death on the Cross. It would not have been possible for the Lady to follow her Beloved closely enough to be in his sight, if She had not ordered her holy angels to open a way for Her. They made it possible for Her to be constantly near her Son, so that She could enjoy his presence, though that also brought with it only a fuller participation in all torments and sorrows. She obtained the fulfillment of all her wishes; for walking along through the streets near the Savior She saw and heard the insults of the servants, the blows they dealt Him, the re-

proaches of the people, expressed either as their own or repeated from hearsay.

605. When Herod was informed that Pilate would send Jesus of Nazareth to him, he was highly pleased. He knew that Jesus was a great friend of John the Baptist, whom he had ordered to be put to death (Mark 6, 27), and had heard many reports of his preaching. In vain and foolish curiosity he harbored the desire of seeing Jesus do something new and extraordinary for his entertainment and wonder (Luke 23, 8). The Author of life therefore came into the presence of the murderer Herod, against whom the blood of the Baptist was calling more loudly to this same Lord for vengeance, than in its time the blood of Abel (Gen. 4, 10). But the unhappy adulterer, ignorant of the terrible judgment of the Almighty, received Him with loud laughter as an enchanter and conjurer. In this dreadful misconception he commenced to examine and question Him, persuaded that he could thereby induce Him to work some miracle to satisfy his curiosity. But the Master of wisdom and prudence, standing with an humble reserve before his most unworthy judge, answered him not a word. For on account of his evildoing he well merited the punishment of not hearing the words of life, which he would certainly have heard if he had been disposed to listen to them with reverence.

606. The princes and priests of the Jews stood around, continually rehearsing the same accusations and charges which they had advanced in the presence of Pilate. But the Lord maintained silence also in regard to these calumnies, much to the disappointment of Herod. In his presence the Lord would not open his lips, neither in order to answer his questions, nor in order to refute the accusations. Herod was altogether unworthy of hearing the truth, this being his greatest punishment and the punishment most to be dreaded by all the princes and the powerful of this earth. Herod was

much put out by the silence and meekness of our Savior and was much disappointed in his vain curiosity. But the unjust judge tried to hide his confusion by mocking and ridiculing the innocent Master with his whole cohort of soldiers and ordering him to be sent back to Pilate. Having made fun of the reserve of the Lord, the servants of Herod joined in treating Him as a fool and as one deficient in mind and they clothed Him in a white garment, in order to mark Him as insane and to be avoided as dangerous. But by the hidden providence of the Most High this dress signified the purity and innocence of the Savior, and these ministers of wickedness were thus unwittingly giving testimony of the truth, which they were trying to obscure in deriding the miraculous power of the Lord.

607. Herod showed himself thankful to Pilate for the courtesy of sending Jesus of Nazareth to be judged before his tribunal. He informed Pilate, that he found no cause in Him, but held Him to be an ignorant man of no consequence whatever. By the secret judgments of divine Wisdom, Herod and Pilate were reconciled on that day and thenceforward remained friends. Conducted by many soldiers, both of Herod and Pilate, amid a still greater concourse, tumult, and excitement of the people, Jesus returned from Herod to Pilate. For the very ones who had some time before hailed and venerated Him as the Savior and Messias, blessed of the Lord (Matth. 21, 9), now perverted by the priests and magistrates, had changed their minds, and they despised and condemned the same Lord, whom they had so shortly before reverenced and glorified. For of such influence is usually the erroneous example of the chiefs in misleading the people. In the midst of all this confusion and ignominy the Lord passed along, repeating within Himself in unspeakable love, humility and patience, those words, which He had long before spoken by the mouth of David: "I am a worm and no man;

the reproach of men and the outcast of people. All they that saw me have laughed me to scorn: they have spoken with their lips and wagged the head" (Ps. 21, 7). The Lord was a worm and no man, not only because He was not engendered like the rest of men, and because He was not merely and solely a man, being true God and man; but also because He was not treated like a man, but like a wretched and despised worm. Amid all the scorn with which He was overwhelmed and trodden under foot, He made no more outcry than an humble wormlet, which is despised and crushed as a most vile and despicable creature. All the innumerable multitudes that saw our Redeemer spoke of Him with wagging heads, as if retracting their previous conception and opinion of this Prophet of Nazareth.

608. Although his afflicted Mother was made interiorly aware of all that happened, She was not present in body when the priests advanced their insulting accusations before Herod, and when he sputtered forth his questions to the Author of life. She remained outside of the hall of judgment, whither they had taken the Lord. But when He came forth from the hall She met him and They looked upon each other in reciprocal sorrow of their souls, such as corresponded to the love between such a Son and Mother. The sight of the white vestment, by which they proclaimed Him fit to be treated only as an insane fool, pierced her heart with new sorrow; though She alone, of all mankind, recognized the mystery of his purity and innocence indicated by this vestment. She adored Him in it with deepest reverence and followed Him through the streets back to the house of Pilate; for in this house was to be executed the divine decree for our salvation. On this way from Herod to Pilate it happened, that on account of the crush of the people and on account of the haste, they tripped Him up and threw Him on the ground several times. By their cruel pulling at the ropes with

which He was bound, they caused the blood to flow from his sacred veins. His hands being tied, He could not easily help Himself to rise from his falls. Therefore the multitudes of the people, who followed and who were neither able, nor cared to stop in their onward rush, stepped upon the divine Lord, treading Him under foot and kicking Him. The blows and wounds He thus received, instead of stirring the compassion of the soldiers, only excited them to loud laughter; for, instigated by the demons, they had become devoid of all human compassion, no less than so many wild beasts.

609. At the sight of such unmeasured cruelty, the most sorrowful and loving Mother was moved to deepest compassion, and turning to her holy angels She commanded them to gather up the divine blood in order that it might not be trodden upon and dishonored by the feet of sinners. This the heavenly servants willingly fulfilled. She commanded also, that if her divine Son should again fall to the earth, they hasten to his assistance and prevent these evildoers from injuring and stepping on his most sacred body. But She was the most prudent of all mortals, She did not wish them to execute her command, unless it met the approval of the Lord; and therefore She urged them to make this proposal themselves and ask his permission, representing to Him at the same time her anguish as his Mother in seeing Him thus irreverently subjected to the feet of sinners. In order to so much the sooner move the Lord to grant this petition, She begged Him through the holy angels, that He commute this humiliation of being trodden upon and crushed by the rabble into an act of obedience in complying with the petition of his afflicted Mother, who at the same time acknowledged Herself as his slave and formed of the dust. All these petitions of his blessed Mother the angels presented to the Lord Christ in her name; not that He was ignorant of them, since He knew all things and was Himself the instigator of them through his

divine grace, but the Lord desires in all these matters a regard
for the due process of reason. The great Lady was aware of
this desire and in her most exalted wisdom practiced virtues
in diverse ways and by diverse activities, unimpeded by the
foreknowledge of the Lord concerning all things.

610. Our Savior Jesus yielded to the desire and petitions
of his most blessed Mother and gave the angels permission to
execute her requests as her ministers. During the rest of the
passage to the house of Pilate they would not permit the
Lord to be tripped or cast to the ground, or to be stepped
upon by the crowd as had happened before. But in regard to
other injuries, He allowed the stupid wrath and blind malice
of the servants of the law and of the populace to vent themselves freely and fully upon his divine Person. His most holy
Mother heard and saw all with an unconquered but lacerated
heart. In a proportionate manner this was also witnessed by
the other Marys and saint John, who with ceaseless tears
followed the Lord in company with his purest Mother. I do
not stop to describe the sorrows of these and other pious
women, who attended upon the Queen, because I would go
too wide of my subject, especially if I were to describe the
doings of Magdalen, most distinguished in her ardent love of
Christ and most pleasing to the Savior. For to her we must
apply, what Christ himself said when He justified Her: that
those love most to whom the greater sins are forgiven (Luke
7, 43).

611. Pilate was again confronted with Jesus in his palace
and was bestormed anew by the Jews to condemn Him to
death of the cross. Convinced of the innocence of Christ and
of the mortal envy of the Jews, he was much put out at
Herod's again referring the disagreeable decision to his own
tribunal. Feeling himself obliged in his quality of judge to
give this decision, he sought to placate the Jews in different
ways. One of these was a private interview with some of the

servants and friends of the high priest and priests. He urged
them to prevail upon their masters and friends, not any more
to ask for the release of the malefactor Barabbas, but instead
demand the release of our Redeemer; and to be satisfied with
some punishment he was willing to administer before setting
Him free. This measure Pilate had taken before they arrived a
second time to press their demand for a sentence upon Jesus.
The proposal to choose between freeing either Barabbas or
Jesus was made to the Jews, not only once, but two or three
times. The first time before sending Him to Herod and the
second time after his return; this is related by the Evangelists
with some variation, though not essentially contradicting
truth (Matth. 27, 17). Pilate spoke to the Jews and said:
"You have brought this Man before me, accusing Him of
perverting the people by his doctrines; and having examined
Him in your presence, I was not convinced of the truth of
your accusations. And Herod, to whom I have sent Him and
before whom you repeated your accusations, refused to
condemn Him to death. It will be sufficient to correct and
chastise Him for the present, in order that He may amend.
As I am to release some malefactor for the feast of the Pasch,
I will release Christ, if you will have Him freed, and punish
Barabbas," But the multitude of the Jews, thus informed how
much Pilate desired to set Jesus free, shouted with one voice:
"Enough, enough, not Christ, but Barabbas deliver unto us."

612. The custom of giving freedom to an imprisoned
criminal at this great solemnity of the Pasch was introduced
by the Jews in grateful remembrance of the release of their
forefathers from servitude by their passage through the Red
Sea, when the Almighty freed them from the power of Pharaoh by killing the firstborn children of the Egyptians and
afterwards annihilating him and his armies in the waters of
the Red sea (Exodus 12, 29). In gratitude for this favor the
Jews always sought out the greatest malefactor and pardoned

him his crimes; while they refused such clemency to those who were less guilty. In their treaties with the Romans they expressly reserved this privilege; and the governors complied with it. But in the present instance they failed to follow out in their demands what they were so loudly proclaiming in regard to Jesus. According to law they were to demand the release of the greatest criminal and this they proclaimed Jesus to be; yet they persisted in demanding the punishment of Christ and the release of Barabbas, whom they judged less guilty. In such blindness and perversity had the wrath and envy of the demon cast them, that they lost the light of reason even in their own affairs and against their own selves.

613. While Pilate was thus disputing with the Jews in the pretorium, his wife, Procula, happened to hear of his doings and she sent him a message telling him: "What hast thou to do with this Man? Let him go free; for I warn thee that I have had this very day some visions in regard to Him!" This warning of Procula originated through the activity of Lucifer and his demons. For they, observing all that was happening in regard to the person of Christ and the unchangeable patience with which He bore all injuries, were more and more confused and staggered in their rabid fury. Although the swollen pride of Lucifer could not explain how his Divinity could ever subject Itself to such great insults, nor how He could permit his body to suffer such ill-treatment, and although he could not come to any certain conviction, whether this Jesus was a Godman or not; yet the dragon was persuaded, that some great mystery was here transpiring among men which would be the cause of great damage and defeat to him and his malice if he did not succeed in arresting its progress in the world. Having come to this conclusion with his demons, he many times suggested to the pharisees the propriety of ceasing their persecutions of Christ. These suggestions, however, since they originated from malice and

were void of any power for good, failed to move the obstinate and perverted hearts of the Jews. Despairing of success the demons betook themselves to the wife of Pilate and spoke to her in dreams, representing to her that this Man was just and without guilt, that if her husband should sentence Him he would be deprived of his rank and she herself would meet with great adversity. They urged her to advise Pilate to release Jesus and punish Barabbas, if she did not wish to draw misfortune upon their house and their persons.

614. Procula was filled with great fear and terror at these visions, and as soon as she heard what was passing between the Jews and her husband, she sent him the message mentioned by saint Matthew, not to meddle with this Man nor condemn One to death, whom she held to be just. The demon also injected similar misgivings into the mind of Pilate and these warnings of his wife only increased them. Yet, as all his considerations rested upon worldly policy, and as he had not cooperated with the true helps given him by the Savior, all these fears retarded his unjust proceedings only so long as no other more powerful consideration arose, as will be seen in effect. But just now he began for the third time to argue (as saint Luke tells us), insisting upon the innocence of Christ our Lord and that he found no crime in Him nor any guilt worthy of death, and therefore he would punish and then dismiss Him (Luke 23, 22). As we shall see in the next chapter, he did really punish Christ in order to see whether the Jews would be satisfied. But the Jews, on the contrary, demanded that Christ be crucified. Thereupon Pilate asked for water and released Barabbas. Then he washed his hands in the presence of all the people, saying: "I have no share in the death of this just Man, whom you condemn. Look to yourselves in what you are doing, for I wash my hands in order that you may understand they are not sullied in the blood of the Innocent." Pilate thought that by this ceremony

he could excuse himself entirely and that he thereby could put its blame upon the princes of the Jews and upon the people who demanded it. The wrath of the Jews was so blind and foolish that for the satisfaction of seeing Jesus crucified, they entered upon this agreement with Pilate and took upon themselves and upon their children the responsibility for this crime. Loudly proclaiming this terrible sentence and curse, they exclaimed: "His blood come upon us and upon our children" (Matth. 27, 25).

615. O most foolish and cruel blindness! O inconceivable rashness! The unjust condemnation of the Just and the blood of the Innocent, whom the judge himself is forced to proclaim guiltless, you wish to take upon yourselves and upon your children, in order that his blood may call out against you to the end of the world! O perfidious and sacrilegious Jews! So lightly then weighs the blood of the Lamb, who bears the sins of the world, and the life of a Man, who is at the same time God! How is it possible you wish to load with it yourselves and your children? If He had been only your brother, your benefactor and master, your audacity would have been tremendous and your malice execrable. Justly indeed do you merit the punishment which you meet; and that the burden, which you have put upon yourselves and your children, allows you no rest or relief in all the world: it is just that this burden should rest upon you heavier than heaven and earth. But, alas! Though this divine Blood was intended to wash and cleanse all the children of Adam, and though it was in effect poured out upon all the children of the holy Church, yet there are many belonging to it who make themselves guilty of this blood by their works in the same manner as the Jews charged themselves with it, both by word and deed. They did not know or believe that it was the blood of the Savior, while Catholics both know and confess that it is their Redeemer's.

616. The sins and depraved lives of the Christians proclaim louder than tongues their abuse of the blood of Christ and their consent to the guilt in his death which they load upon themselves. Let Christ be affronted, spit upon, buffeted, stretched upon a cross, despised, let Him yield to Barabbas and die; let Him be tormented, scourged and crowned with thorns for our sins: let his blood interest us no more than that it flow copiously and be imputed to us for all eternity: let the incarnate God suffer and die; if only we are left free to enjoy the apparent goods of this world, to seize the pleasing hour, to use creatures for our comfort, to be crowned with roses, live in joy; let our power be unrefrained, let no one seek preference before us; be we permitted to despise humility, abhor poverty, hoard up riches, engage in all deceits, forgive no injuries, entertain the delights of carnal pleasures, let our eyes see nothing that they shall not covet. Such be our rule in life without regard for aught else. And if by all this we crucify Christ, let his blood come upon us and upon our children.

617. Ask the damned in hell, whether these were not the sentiments expressed in their works as described by Solomon, and whether it was not because they spoke thus foolishly in their hearts, that they were called impious, and were so in reality. What else except damnation can they expect, who abuse the blood of Christ and waste it upon themselves, not as such who are seeking a remedy? Where do we find, among the children of the Church, anyone that would willingly permit a thief and malefactor to be preferred to him? So little is this doctrine of humility practiced, that one excites surprise if he allows another just as good and honorable as himself, or even more honorable, to take precedence. Though it is certain that no one can be found as good as Christ or as bad as Barabbas, yet there are innumerable men who, in spite of this example, are offended and judge themselves disgraced, if

they are not preferred and exalted by honors, riches and dignities, and in whatever pertains to the ostentation and applause of the world. These are sought after, contended for and solicited; in such things are consumed the thoughts and all the exertions and powers of men, almost from the time in which they can use their faculties until they lose them. The most lamentable misfortune is, that even those who, by their profession and their state, have renounced and turned their backs upon such things, do not free themselves. While the Savior has commanded them to forget their people and the house of their parents (Ps, 44, 11), they devote to them the best part of their human existence, by giving them their attention and solicitude in the direction of their affairs, their best wishes and care in the augmentation of their worldly goods. It seems but a small matter to them to engage themselves in these vanities. Instead of forgetting the house of their father they forget the house of their God in which they live, and where they are divinely assisted to gain a salvation, an honor and esteem never possible in the world, and where they receive their sustenance without any anxiety or worry. They show themselves ungrateful for all these benefits by drifting away from the humility due to their state. Thus the humility of Christ our Savior, his patience, his injuries, the dishonor of the cross, the imitation of Christ's works, the following of his doctrines; all is left to the poor, to the lonely ones, to the weak and humble of this world; while the ways of Sion are deserted and full of wailing, because there are so few who will come to the solemn feast of the imitation of Christ our Lord (Thren. 1, 4).

618. Pilate was not conscious of the absurdity of his pretense, that to have washed his hands and to have charged the Jews with the blood of Christ, was sufficient to clear him before his conscience and before men; for by this ceremony, so full of hypocrisy and deceit, he tried to satisfy both. It is

true that the Jews were the principal actors and more guilty in the condemnation of the innocent Godman, and that they themselves expressly charged themselves with its guilt. But Pilate was not on that account free from it; since, knowing the innocence of Christ our Lord, he should not have allowed a thief and robber to be preferred before Christ; neither should he have chastised, nor pretended to correct Him, who showed nothing that could be corrected or amended (Luke 23, 25). Much less should he have condemned and delivered Him over to his mortal enemies, whose envy and cruelty was so evident. He is not a just judge who is aware of the truth and justice and places it in the balance with his own human respect and his own personal interest; for such a course drags down the right reason of men who are so cowardly of heart. Since they do not possess the strength and perfection of mind necessary to a judge, they cannot resist their greed, or their human respect. In their blind passions they forsake justice in order not to endanger their temporal advantages, as happened to Pilate.

619. In the house of Pilate, through the ministry of the holy angels, our Queen was placed in such a position that She could hear the disputes of the iniquitous judge with the scribes and priests concerning the innocence of Christ our Savior, and concerning the release of Barabbas in preference to Him. All the clamors of these human tigers She heard in silence and admirable meekness, as the living counterpart of her most holy Son. Although She preserved the unchanging propriety and modesty of her exterior, all the malicious words of the Jews pierced her sorrowful heart like a two-edged sword. But the voices of her unspoken sorrows resounded in the ears of the eternal Father more pleasantly and sweetly than the lamentation of the beautiful Rachel who, as Jeremias says, was beweeping her children because they cannot be restored (Jer. 31, 15). Our most beautiful Rachel

the purest Mary, sought not revenge, but pardon for her enemies, who were depriving Her of the Onlybegotten of the Father and her only Son. She imitated all the actions of the most holy Soul of Christ and accompanied Him in the works of most exalted holiness and perfection; for neither could her torments hinder her charity, nor her affliction diminish her fervor, nor could the tumult distract her attention, nor the outrageous injuries of the multitudes prevent her interior recollection: under all circumstances She practiced the most exalted virtues in the most eminent degree.

Words of the Queen

THE VIRGIN MARY SPEAKS TO SISTER MARY OF AGREDA

620. My daughter, in what thou hast written and understood, I see thee astonished to find, that Pilate and Herod exhibited less unkindness and cruelty in the death of my divine Son than the priests, highpriests and pharisees; and thou dwellest much upon the fact that those were secular and gentile judges, while these were teachers of the law and priests of the people of Israel, professing the true faith. In answer to thy thoughts I will remind thee of a doctrine not new, which thou hast understood on former occasions; but I wish that thou refresh it in thy mind and remember it for the rest of thy life. Know then, my dearest, that a fall from the highest position is extremely dangerous and the damage done is either irreparable, or very difficult of redress. Lucifer held an eminent position in heaven, as regards both natural gifts and gifts of grace; for in beauty he excelled all the creatures, and by his sin he fell to the deepest abyss of loathsomeness and misery and into a more hardened obstinacy than all his followers. The first parents of the human race, Adam and Eve, were exalted to the highest dignity and raised to exquisite favor, as coming forth from the hand of the Almighty:

their fall caused perdition to themselves and to all their posterity, and faith teaches what was the cost of their salvation. To restore them and their posterity was the work of an infinite mercy.

621. Many other souls have reached the heights of perfection and have thence fallen most unfortunately, arriving at a state in which they almost despaired or found themselves incapable of rising. This sad state in the creature originates from many causes. The first is the dismay and boundless confusion of one who feels that he has fallen from an exalted state of virtue; for he knows that he has not only lost great blessings, but he does not expect to obtain greater ones than those of the past and those he has lost; nor does he promise himself more firmness in keeping those he can obtain through renewed efforts, than he has shown in those acquired and now lost through his ingratitude. From this dangerous distrust originates lukewarmness, want of fervor and diligence, absence of zeal and devotion; since diffidence extinguishes all these in the soul, just as the sprightliness of ardent hope overcomes many difficulties, strengthens and vivifies weak human creatures to undertake great works. Another obstacle there is, not less formidable, namely: the souls accustomed to the blessings of God, either through their office, as the priests and religious, or by the exercise of virtues and the abundance of divine favors, as spiritual minded persons, usually aggravate their sins by a certain contempt of these very blessings and a certain abuse of the divine things. For by the abundance of the divine favors they fall into a dangerous dullness of mind. They begin to think little of the divine favors and become irreverent. Thus failing to cooperate with God's grace, they hinder its effect. They lose the grace of holy fear of the Lord, which arouses and stimulates the will to obey the divine commandments and to be alert in the avoidance of sin and pursuit of eternal life in the friend-

ship of God. This is an evident danger for lukewarm priests, who frequent the holy Eucharist and other Sacraments, without fear and reverence; also for the learned and wise, and the powerful of this world, who so reluctantly correct and amend their lives. They have lost the appreciation and veneration of the remedial helps of the Church, namely, the Sacraments, preaching and instruction. Thus these medicines, which for other sinners are so salutary and counteract ignorance, weaken those who are the physicians of the spiritual life.

622. There are other reasons for this kind of danger, which must be referred to the Lord himself. For the sins of those souls who, by their state or by their advanced virtues, are more closely bound to their God, are weighed in the balance of God's justice in quite a different way from the sins of those who have been less favored by his mercy. Although the sins of all are more or less essentially the same, yet the circumstances of sin are very different. For the priests and teachers, the powerful and the dignitaries, and those who, on account of their station or by reputation, are supposed to be advanced in a holy life, cause great scandal by their fall or by any sins they commit. There is much more of bold disrespect in their presumption and temerity against God, whom they know better and to whom they owe much more, but whom they offend with more deliberation and knowledge than the ignorant. Hence, as is evident from the tenor of all the holy Scriptures, the sins of Catholics, and especially of those that are instructed and enlightened, are so displeasing to God. As the term of each man's life is preordained for each one as the time in which he is to gain the eternal reward, so the measure or number of sins to be borne by the patience or forbearance of the Lord is likewise preordained. This measure of divine justice is determined not only by the number and quantity of the sins, but also by their quality and weight. Thus it may

happen, that in the souls favored by greater enlightenment and graces of heaven, the grievousness supplies what is wanting in the number of the sins, and that with fewer sins they are forsaken sooner and chastised more severely than others with many more sins. Nor can all expect for themselves the same issue as David (II Reg. 12, 13) and saint Peter; because not all of them have to their credit as many good actions to be remembered by the Lord. Besides the special privileges of some cannot be set up as a rule for all others; because, according to the secret judgments of the Lord, not all are destined for a special office.

623. By this explanation, my dearest, thou wilt be able to satisfy thy doubts and thou wilt understand what a bitter evil so many souls incur, whom the Almighty has redeemed by his blood, placed in the way of light and drawn toward Himself; and how some persons can fall from a more exalted state into more perverse obstinacy than others below them in station. This truth is well illustrated in the mystery of my Son's Passion, in which the priests, scribes and the whole people were much more indebted to their God than the heathens, who knew not of the true religion. I desire that this truth, as exhibited by their example, convince thee of this terrible danger and excite in thee holy fear. And with this fear join humble thanks and an exalted esteem of the favors of the Lord. In the days of abundance, be not unmindful of the hour of want (Eccli, 13, 25). Ponder as well the one as the other within thyself, and remember that thou carriest thy treasure in a fragile vessel, which thou canst easily lose (II Cor. 4, 7). Know well, that the reception of such blessings argues not merit, and the possession of them is not due to thee in justice, but comes to thee by liberality and kindness. That the Most High has favored thee with so much familiar intercourse is no assurance that thou canst not fall, and no license to live carelessly and without reverence and fear. All

things happen to thee according to the number and greatness of thy blessings; for the wrath of the serpent has increased toward thee in proportion, and is more alert against thee than against other souls. He has become aware that the Most High has not been so liberally loving to men of many generations as toward thee, and if thou meet so many blessings and mercies with ingratitude, thou shalt be most wretched and worthy of a rigorous punishment, against which thou canst make no objection.

Chapter XX

OUR SAVIOR, BY ORDER OF PILATE, IS SCOURGED, CROWNED WITH THORNS AND MOCKED. THE BEHAVIOR OF THE MOST HOLY MARY DURING THIS TIME.

624. Pilate, aware of the obstinate hostility of the Jews against Jesus of Nazareth, and unwilling to condemn Him to death, of which he knew Him to be innocent, thought that a severe scourging of Jesus might placate the fury of the ungrateful people and soothe the envy of the priests and the scribes. If He should have failed in anything pertaining to their ceremonies and rites, they would probably consider Him sufficiently chastised and cease in their persecutions and in their clamors for his Death. Pilate was led to this belief by what they had told him in the course of his trial; for they had vainly and foolishly calumniated Christ of not observing the Sabbath and other ceremonies, as is evident from his sermons reported by the Evangelists (John 9, 6). But Pilate was entirely wrong in his judgment and acted like an ignorant man; for neither could the Master of all holiness be guilty of any defect in the observance of that Law, which He had come not to abolish but to fulfill (Matth. 5, 7) ; nor even if the accusation had been true, would He have deserved such an outrageous punishment. For the laws of the Jews, far from demanding such an inhuman and cruel scourging, contained other regulations for atonement of the more common faults.

In still greater error was this judge in expecting any mercy or natural kindness and compassion from the Jews. Their anger and wrath against the most meek Master was not human, not such as ordinarily is appeased by the overthrow and humiliation of the enemy. For men have hearts of flesh, and the love of their own kind is natural and the source of at least some compassion. But these perfidious Jews were clothed in the guise of demons, or rather transformed into demons, who exert the more furious rage against those who are rendered more helpless and wretched; who, when they see anyone most helpless, say: let us pursue him now, since he has none to defend nor free him from our hands.

625. Such was the implacable fury of the priests and of their confederates, the pharisees, against the Author of life. For Lucifer, despairing of being able to hinder his murder by the Jews, inspired them with his own dreadful malice and outrageous cruelty. Pilate, placed between the known truth and his human and terrestrial considerations, chose to follow the erroneous leading of the latter, and order Jesus to be severely scourged, though he had himself declared Him free from guilt (John 19, 1). Thereupon those ministers of satan, with many others, brought Jesus our Savior to the place of punishment, which was a courtyard or enclosure attached to the house and set apart for the torture of criminals in order to force them to confess their crimes. It was enclosed by a low, open building, surrounded by columns, some of which supported the roof, while others were lower and stood free. To one of these columns, which was of marble, they bound Jesus very securely; for they still thought Him a magician and feared his escape.

626. They first took off the white garment with not less ignominy than when they clothed Him therein in the house of the adulterous homicide Herod. In loosening the ropes and chains, which He had borne since his capture in the

garden, they cruelly widened the wounds which his bonds had made in his arms and wrists. Having freed his hands, they commanded Him with infamous blasphemies to despoil Himself of the seamless tunic which He wore. This was the identical garment with which his most blessed Mother had clothed Him in Egypt when He first began to walk, as I have related in its place. Our Lord at present had no other garment, since they had taken from Him his mantle, or cloak, when they seized Him in the garden. The Son of the eternal Father obeyed the executioners and began to unclothe Himself, ready to bear the shame of the exposure of his most sacred and modest body before such a multitude of people. But his tormentors, impatient at the delay which modesty required, tore away the tunic with violence in order to hasten his undressing and, as is said, flay the sheep with the wool. With the exception of a strip of cloth for a cincture, which He wore beneath the tunic and with which his Mother likewise had clothed Him in Egypt, the Lord stood now naked. These garments had grown with his sacred body, nor had He ever taken them off. The same is to be said of his shoes, which his Mother had placed on his feet. However, as I have said on a former occasion, He had many times walked barefooted during his preaching.

627. I understand that some of the doctors have said or have persuaded themselves, that our Savior Jesus at his scourging and at his crucifixion, for his greater humiliation, permitted the executioners to despoil Him of all his clothing. But having again been commanded under holy obedience to ascertain the truth in this matter, I was told that the divine Master was prepared to suffer all the insults compatible with decency; that the executioners attempted to subject his body to this shame of total nakedness, seeking to despoil Him of the cincture, which covered his loins; but in that they failed; because, on touching it, their arms became paralyzed and

stiff, as had happened also in the house of Caiphas, when they attempted to take off his clothes (Chap. XVII). All the six of his tormentors separately made the attempt with the same result. Yet afterwards, these ministers of evil, in order to scourge Him with greater effect, raised some of the coverings; for so much the Lord permitted, but not that He should be uncovered and despoiled of his garments entirely. The miracle of their being hindered and paralyzed in their brutal attempts did not, however, move or soften the hearts of these human beasts; but in their diabolical insanity they attributed it all to the supposed sorcery and witchcraft of the Author of truth and life.

628. Thus the Lord stood uncovered in the presence of a great multitude and the six torturers bound Him brutally to one of the columns in order to chastise Him so much the more at their ease. Then, two and two at a time, they began to scourge Him with such inhuman cruelty, as was possible only in men possessed by Lucifer, as were these executioners. The first two scourged the innocent Savior with hard and thick cords, full of rough knots, and in their sacrilegious fury strained all the powers of their body to inflict the blows. This first scourging raised in the deified body of the Lord great welts and livid tumors, so that the sacred blood gathered beneath the skin and disfigured his entire body. Already it began to ooze through the wounds. The first two having at length desisted, the second pair continued the scourging in still greater emulation; with hardened leather thongs they leveled their strokes upon the places already sore and caused the discolored tumors to break open and shed forth the sacred blood until it bespattered and drenched the garments of the sacrilegious torturers, running down also in streams to the pavement. Those two gave way to the third pair of scourges, who commenced to beat the Lord with extremely tough rawhides, dried hard like osier twigs. They scourged

Him still more cruelly, because they were wounding, not so much his virginal body, as cutting into the wounds already produced by the previous scourging. Besides they had been secretly incited to greater fury by the demons, who were filled with new rage at the patience of Christ.

629. As the veins of the sacred body had now been opened and his whole Person seemed but one continued wound, the third pair found no more room for new wounds. Their ceaseless blows inhumanly tore the immaculate and virginal flesh of Christ our Redeemer and scattered many pieces of it about the pavement; so much so that a large portion of the shoulder bones were exposed and showed red through the flowing blood; in other places also the bones were laid bare larger than the palm of the hand. In order to wipe out entirely that beauty, which exceeded that of all other men (Ps, 44, 3), they beat Him in the face and in the feet and hands, thus leaving unwounded not a single spot in which they could exert their fury and wrath against the most innocent Lamb. The divine blood flowed to the ground, gathering here and there in great abundance. The scourging in the face, and in the hands and feet, was unspeakably painful, because these parts are so full of sensitive and delicate nerves. His venerable countenance became so swollen and wounded that the blood and the swellings blinded Him. In addition to their blows the executioners spirited upon his Person their disgusting spittle and loaded Him with insulting epithets (Thren. 3, 30). The exact number of blows dealt out to the Savior from head to foot was 5,115. The great Lord and Author of all creation who, by his divine nature was incapable of suffering, was, in his human flesh and for our sake, reduced to a man of sorrows as prophesied, and was made to experience our infirmities, becoming the last of men (Is. 53, 3), a man of sorrows and the outcast of the people.

630. The multitudes who had followed the Lord, filled up the courtyard of Pilate's house and the surrounding streets; for all of them waited for the issue of this event, discussing and arguing about it according to each one's views. Amid all this confusion the Virgin Mother endured unheard of insults, and She was deeply afflicted by the injuries and blasphemies heaped upon her divine Son by the Jews and gentiles. When they brought Jesus to the scourging place She retired in the company of the Marys and saint John to a corner of the courtyard. Assisted by her divine visions, She there witnessed all the scourging and the torments of our Savior. Although She did not see it with the eyes of her body nothing was hidden to Her, no more than if She had been standing quite near. Human thoughts cannot comprehend how great and how diverse were the afflictions and sorrows of the great Queen and Mistress of the angels: together with many other mysteries of the Divinity they shall become manifest in the next life, for the glory of the Son and Mother. I have already mentioned in other places of this history, and especially in that of the Passion, that the blessed Mother felt in her own body all the torments of her Son. This was true also of the scourging, which She felt in all the parts of her virginal body, in the same intensity as they were felt by Christ in his body. Although She shed no blood except what flowed from her eyes with her tears, nor was lacerated in her flesh; yet the bodily pains so changed and disfigured Her, that saint John and the holy women failed to find in Her any resemblance of Herself. Besides the tortures of the body She suffered ineffable sorrows of the soul; there sorrow was augmented in proportion to the immensity of her insight (Eccles. 1, 18). For her sorrows flowed not only from the natural love of a mother and a supreme love of Christ as her God, but it was proportioned to her power of judging more accurately than all creatures of the innocence of Christ, the dignity of his

divine Person, the atrocity of the insults coming from the perfidious Jews and the children of Adam, whom He was freeing from eternal death.

631. Having at length executed the sentence of scourging, the executioners unbound the Lord from the column, and with imperious and blasphemous presumption commanded Him immediately to put on his garment. But while they had scourged the most meek Master, one of his tormentors, instigated by the devil, had hidden his clothes out of sight, in order to prolong the nakedness and exposure of his divine Person for their derision and sport. This evil purpose suggested by the devil, was well known to the Mother of the Lord. She therefore, making use of her power as Queen, commanded Lucifer and all his demons to leave the neighborhood, and immediately, compelled by her sovereign power and virtue, they fled. She gave orders that the tunic be brought by the holy angels within reach of her most holy Son, so that He could again cover his sacred and lacerated body. All this was immediately attended to, although the sacrilegious executioners understood not the miracle, nor how it had been wrought; they attributed it all to the sorcery and magic of the demon. During this protracted nakedness our Savior had, in addition to his wounds, suffered greatly from the cold of that morning as mentioned by the Evangelists (Mark 14, 55; Luke 22, 35; John 18, 18). His sacred blood had frozen and compressed the wounds, which had become inflamed and extremely painful; the cold had diminished his powers of resistance, although the fire of his infinite charity strained them to the utmost in order to suffer more and more. Though compassion is so natural in rational creatures, there was none for Him in his affliction and necessity, except that of his sorrowful Mother, who tearfully bewailed and pitied Him in the name of the whole human race.

632. Among other divine mysteries, hidden to the wise of this world, this also causes great astonishment, that the wrath of the Jews, who were men of flesh and blood like ourselves, should not have been appeased at their seeing Christ torn and wounded by 5,115 lashes; that the sight of a person so lacerated should not have moved their natural compassion, but should arouse their envy to inflict new and unheard of tortures upon the Victim. Their implacable fury at once planned another outrageous cruelty. They went to Pilate and in the presence of his counselors said: "This seducer and deceiver of the people, Jesus of Nazareth, in his boasting and vanity, has sought to be recognized by all as the king of the Jews. In order that his pride may be humbled and his presumption be confounded, we desire your permission to place upon Him the royal insignia merited by his fantastic pretensions." Pilate yielded to the unjust demand of the Jews, permitting them to proceed according to their intentions.

633. Thereupon they took Jesus to the pretorium, where, with the same cruelty and contempt, they again despoiled him of his garments and in order to deride Him before all the people as a counterfeit king, clothed Him in a much torn and soiled mantle of purple color. They placed also upon his sacred head a cap made of woven thorns, to serve Him as a crown (John 19, 2). This cap was woven of thorn branches and in such a manner that many of the hard and sharp thorns would penetrate into the skull, some of them to the ears and others to the eyes. Hence one of the greatest tortures suffered by the Lord was that of the crown of thorns. Instead of a scepter they placed into his hands a contemptible reed. They also threw over His shoulders a violet colored mantle, something of the style of capes worn in churches; for such a garment belonged to the vestiture of a king. In this array of a mock king the perfidious Jews decked out Him, who by his nature and by every right was the King of kings and the Lord

of lords (Apoc. 19, 16). Then all the soldiers, in the presence of the priests and pharisees, gathered around Him and heaped upon Him their blasphemous mockery and derision. Some of them bent their knees and mockingly said to Him: God save Thee, King of the Jews. Others buffeted Him; others snatched the cane from his hands and struck Him on his crowned head; others ejected their disgusting spittle upon Him; all of them, instigated by furious demons, insulted and affronted Him in different manners.

634. O charity incomprehensible and exceeding all measure! O patience never seen or imagined among mortals! Who, O my Lord and God, since Thou art the true and mighty God both in essence and in thy works, who could oblige Thee to suffer the humiliation of such unheard of torments, insults and blasphemies? On the contrary, O my God, who among men has not done many things which offend Thee and which should have caused Thee to refuse suffering and to deny them thy favor? Who could ever believe all this, if we knew not of thy infinite goodness. But now, since we see it and in firm faith look upon such admirable blessings and miracles of love, where is our judgment? what effect upon us has the light of truth? What enchantment is this that we suffer, since at the very sight of thy sorrows, scourges, thorns, insults and affronts, we seek for ourselves, without the least shame or fear, the delights, the riches, the ease, the preferments and vanities of this world? Truly, great is the number of fools (Eccles. 1, 15), since the greatest foolishness and dishonesty is to recognize a debt and be unwilling to pay it; to receive blessings and never give thanks for them; to have before one's eyes the greater good, and despise it; to claim it for ourselves and make no use of it; to turn away and fly from life, and seek eternal death. The most innocent Jesus opened not his mouth in those great and many injuries. Nor was the furious wrath of the Jews appeased, either by the

mockery and derision of the divine Master, or by the torments added to the contempt of his most exalted Person.

635. It seemed to Pilate that the spectacle of a man so ill-treated as Jesus of Nazareth would move and fill with shame the hearts of that ungrateful people. He therefore commanded Jesus to be brought from the pretorium to an open window, where all could see Him crowned with thorns, disfigured by the scourging and the ignominious vestiture of a mock king. Pilate himself spoke to the people, calling out to them: "Ecce Homo," "Behold, what a man!" (John 19, 5). See this Man, whom you hold as your enemy! What more can I do with Him than to have punished Him in this severe manner? You certainly have nothing more to fear from Him. I do not find any cause of death in Him. What this judge said was certainly the full truth; but in his own words he condemned his outrageous injustice, since, knowing and confessing that this Man was just and not guilty of death, he had nevertheless ordered Him to be tormented and punished in such a way that, according to the natural course, he should have been killed many times over. O blindness of self love! O hellish malice of estimating only the influence of those, who can confer or take away mere earthly dignities! How deeply do such motives obscure the reason, how much do they twist the course of justice, how completely do they pervert the greatest truths in judging of the just by the standards of the unjust! Tremble, ye judges of the earth (Ps. 2, 10), look to it that the sentences you render are not full of deceit; for you yourselves shall be judged and condemned by your unjust judgments! As the priests and pharisees, in their eager and insatiable hostility, were irrevocably bent upon taking away the life of Christ our Savior, nothing but his Death would content or satisfy them; therefore they answered Pilate: "Crucify Him, Crucify Him!" (John 19,6.)

636. When the Blessed among women, most holy Mary, saw her divine Son as Pilate showed Him to the people and heard him say: "Ecce homo!" She fell upon her knees and openly adored Him as the true Godman. The same was also done by saint John and the holy women, together with all the holy angels of the Queen and Lady; for they saw that not only Mary, as the Mother of the Savior, but that God himself desired them thus to act. The most prudent Lady spoke to the eternal Father, to the angels and especially to her most beloved Son precious words of sorrow, compassion and profound reverence, possible to be conceived only in her chaste and love inflamed bosom. In her exalted wisdom She pondered also the ways and means by which the evidences of his innocence could be made most opportunely manifest at a time when He was so insulted, mocked and despised by the Jews. With this most proper intention She renewed the petitions above mentioned, namely, that Pilate, in his quality of judge, continue to maintain the innocence of Jesus our Redeemer and that all the world should understand, that Jesus was not guilty of death nor of any of the crimes imputed to Him by the Jews.

637. On account of these prayers of the most blessed Mother Pilate was made to feel great compassion at seeing Jesus so horribly scourged and ill treated and regret at having punished Him so severely. Although he was naturally disposed to such emotions by his soft and compassionate disposition; yet they were principally caused by the light he received through the intercession of the Queen and Mother of grace. This same light moved the unjust judge after the crowning of thorns to prolong his parley with the Jews for the release of Christ, as is recorded in the nineteenth chapter of the Gospel of saint John. When they again asked him to crucify the Lord, he answered: "Take Him yourselves and

crucify Him, for I do not find any cause for doing it." They replied:

"According to our law He is guilty of death, for He claims to be the Son of God." This reply threw Pilate into greater consternation, for he conceived it might be true, that Jesus was the Son of God according to his heathen notions of the Divinity. Therefore he withdrew with Jesus into the pretorium, where, speaking with Him alone, he asked whence He was? The Lord did not answer this question; for Pilate was not in a state of mind either to understand or to merit a reply. Nevertheless he insisted and said to the King of heaven: "Dost Thou then not speak to me? Dost Thou not know, that I have power to crucify Thee and power to dismiss Thee?" Pilate sought to move Him to defend Himself and tell what he wanted to know. It seemed to Pilate that a man so wretched and tormented would gladly accept any offer of favor from a judge.

638. But the Master of truth answered Pilate without defending Himself but with unexpected dignity; for He said: "Thou shouldst not have any power against Me, unless it were given thee from above. Therefore, he that hath delivered Me to thee, hath the greater sin." This answer by itself made the condemnation of Christ inexcusable in Pilate; since he could have understood therefore, that neither he nor Caesar had any power of jurisdiction over this man Jesus; that by a much higher decree He had been so unreasonably and unjustly delivered over to his judgment; that therefore Judas and the priests had committed a greater sin than he in not releasing Him; and that nevertheless He too was guilty of the same crime, though not in such high degree. Pilate failed to arrive at these mysterious truths; but he was struck with still greater consternation at the words of Christ our Lord, and therefore made still more strenuous efforts to liberate Him. The priests, who were now abundantly aware of his inten-

tions, threatened him with the displeasure of the emperor, which he would incur, if he permitted this One, who had aspired to be king, to escape death. They said: "If thou freest this Man, thou art no friend of Caesar ; since he who makes a king of himself rises up against his orders and commands." They urged this because the Roman emperors never permitted anyone in the whole empire to assume the title or insignia of a King without their consent and order; if therefore Pilate should permit it, he would contravene the decrees of Caesar, He was much disturbed at this malicious and threatening intimation of the Jews, and seating himself in his tribunal at the sixth hour in order to pass sentence upon the Lord, he once more turned to plead with the Jews, saying: "See there your King!" And all of them answered: "Away with Him, away with Him, crucify Him!" He replied: "Shall I crucify your King?" Whereupon they shouted unanimously: "We have no other king than Caesar."

639. Pilate permitted himself to be overcome by the obstinacy and malice of the Jews. On the day of Parasceve then, seated in his tribunal, which in Greek was called lithostratos, and in Hebrew gabatha, he pronounced the sentence of death against the Author of life, as I shall relate in the following chapter. The Jews departed from the hall in great exultation and joy, proclaiming the sentence of the most innocent Lamb. That they did not realize whom they thus sought to annihilate was the occasion of our Redemption. All this was well known to the sorrowful Mother, who, though outside of the hall of judgment, saw all the proceedings by exalted vision. When the priests and pharisees rushed forth exulting in the condemnation of Christ to the death of the Cross, the pure heart of this most blessed Mother was filled with new sorrow and was pierced and transfixed with the sword of unalleviated bitterness. Since the sorrow of most holy Mary on this occasion surpassed all that can enter the thoughts of

man, it is useless to speak more of it, and it must be referred to the pious meditation of Christians. Just as impossible is it to enumerate her interior acts of adoration, worship, reverence, love, compassion, sorrow and resignation.

Words of the Queen

THE VIRGIN MARY SPEAKS TO SISTER MARY OF AGREDA

640. My daughter, thou reflectest with wonder upon the hardness and malice of the Jews, the weakness of Pilate, who knew of their evil dispositions and permitted himself to be overcome, though fully convinced of the innocence of my Son and Lord. I wish to relieve thee of this astonishment by furnishing thee with instructions and warnings suitable for making thee careful on the path to eternal life. Know then that the ancient prophecies concerning the mysteries of the Redemption and all the holy Scriptures were to be infallibly fulfilled; for sooner shall heaven and earth fall to pieces, than that their words fail of their effect as determined in the divine Mind (Matth. 24, 35; Acts 3, 18). In order that the most ignominious death foretold for my Lord should be brought about (Sap. 2, 20; Jer. 11, 19) it was necessary that He should be persecuted by men. But that these men should happen to be the Jews, the priests and the unjust Pilate, was their own misfortune, not the choice of the Almighty, who wishes to save all (I Tim. 2, 4). Their own wickedness and malice brought them to their ruin; for they resisted the great grace of having in their midst their Redeemer and Master, of knowing Him, of conversing with Him, of hearing his doctrine and preaching, of witnessing his miracles; and they had received such great favors, as none of the ancient Patriarchs had attained by all their longings (Matth. 13,7). Hence the cause of the Savior was justified. He manifestly had cultivated his vineyard by his own hands and showered his

favors upon it (Matth. 21, 33). But it brought Him only thorns and briars, and its keepers took away his life, refusing to recognize Him, as was their opportunity and their duty before all other men.

641. This same, which happened in the head Christ the Lord and Son of God, must happen to all the members of his mystical body, that is, to the just and predestined to the end of the world. For it would be monstrous to see the members incongruous with the Head, the children show no relation with the Father, or the disciples unlike their Master. Although sinners must always exist (Matth. 18, 7), since in this world the just shall always be mingled with the unjust, the predestined with the reprobate, the persecutors with the persecuted, the murderers with the murdered, the afflicting with the afflicted; yet these lots are decided by the malice and the goodness of men. Unhappy shall be he, through whom scandal comes into the world and who thus makes himself an instrument of the demon. This kind of activity was begun in the new Church by the priests and pharisees, and by Pilate, who all persecuted the Head of this mystic body and, in the further course of the world, by all those who persecute its members, the saints and the predestined, imitating and following the Jews and the devil in their evil work.

642. Think well, then, my dearest, which of these lots thou wishest to choose in the sight of my Son and me. If thou seest thy Redeemer, thy Spouse and thy Chief tormented, afflicted, crowned with thorns and saturated with reproaches and at the same time desirest to have a part in Him and be a member of his mystical body, it is not becoming, or even possible, that thou live steeped in the pleasures of the flesh. Thou must be the persecuted and not a persecutor, the oppressed and not the oppressor; the one that bears the cross, that encounters the scandal, and not that gives it; the one that suffers, and at the same time makes none of the neigh-

bors suffer. On the contrary, thou must exert thyself for their conversion and salvation in as far as is compatible with the perfection of thy state and vocation. This is the portion of the friends of God and the inheritance of his children in mortal life ; in this consists the participation in grace and glory, which by his torments and reproaches and by his death of the Cross my Son and Lord has purchased for them. I too have cooperated in this work and have paid the sorrows and afflictions, which thou hast understood and which I wish thou shalt never allow to be blotted out from my inmost memory. The Almighty would indeed have been powerful enough to exalt his predestined in this world, to give them riches and favors beyond those of others, to make them strong as lions for reducing the rest of mankind to their invincible power. But it was inopportune to exalt them in this manner, in order that men might not be led into the error of thinking that greatness consists in what is visible and happiness in earthly goods; lest, being induced to forsake virtues and obscure the glory of the Lord, they fail to experience the efficacy of divine grace and cease to aspire toward spiritual and eternal things. This is the science which I wish thee to study continually and in which thou must advance day by day, putting into practice all that thou learnest to understand and know .

Chapter XXI

PILATE PRONOUNCES THE SENTENCE OF DEATH AGAINST
THE AUTHOR OF LIFE; THE LORD TAKES UP THE CROSS ON
WHICH HE IS TO DIE; HIS MOST HOLY MOTHER FOLLOWS
HIM; WHAT SHE DID ON THIS OCCASION TO RESTRAIN THE
DEVIL, AND OTHER HAPPENINGS.

643. To the great satisfaction and joy of the priests and
pharisees Pilate then decreed the sentence of death on the
Cross against Life itself, Jesus our Savior. Having announced
it to the One they had thus condemned in spite of his innocence, they brought Him to another part of the house of
Pilate, where they stripped Him of the purple mantle, in
which they had derided Him as mock king. All happened by
the mysterious dispensation of God; though on their part it
was due to the concerted malice of the Jews; for they wished
to see Him undergo the punishment of the Cross in his own
clothes so that in them He might be recognized by all. Only
by his garments could He now be recognized by the people,
since his face had been disfigured beyond recognition by the
scourging, the impure spittle, and the crown of thorns. They
again clothed Him with the seamless tunic, which at the
command of the Queen was brought to Him by the angels;
for the executioners had thrown it into a corner of another
room in the house, where they left it to place upon Him the
mocking and scandalous purple cloak. But the Jews neither

understood nor noticed any of these circumstances, since they were too much taken up with the desire of hastening his Death.

644. Through the diligence of the Jews in spreading the news of the sentence decreed against Jesus of Nazareth, the people hastened in multitudes to the house of Pilate in order to see Him brought forth to execution. Since the ordinary number of inhabitants was increased by the gathering of numerous strangers from different parts to celebrate the Pasch, the city was full of people. All of them were stirred by the news and filled the streets up to the very palace of Pilate. It was a Friday, the day of the Parasceve, which in Greek signifies preparation, or getting ready; for on that day the Jews prepared themselves, or got ready, for the ensuing Sabbath, their greatest feast, on which no servile work was to be performed, not even such as cooking meals; all this had to be done on this Friday. In the sight of all these multitudes they brought forth our Savior in his own garments and with a countenance so disfigured by wounds, blood and spittle, that no one would have again recognized Him as the One they had seen or known before. At the command of his afflicted Mother the holy angels had a few times wiped off some of the impure spittle; but his enemies had so persistently continued in their disgusting insults, that now He appeared altogether covered by their vile expectorations. At the sight of such a sorrowful spectacle a confused shouting and clamor arose from the people, so that nothing could be understood, but all formed one uproar and confusion of voices. But above all the rest were heard the shouts of the priests and pharisees, who in their unrestrained joy and exultation harangued the people to become quiet and clear the streets through which the divine Victim was to pass, in order that they might hear the sentence of death proclaimed against Him. The people were divided and confused in their

opinions, according to the suggestions of their own hearts. At this spectacle were present different kinds of people, who had been benefited and succored by the miracles and the kindness of Jesus, and such as had heard and accepted his teachings and had become his followers and friends. These now showed their sympathy, some in bitter tears, others by asking what this Man had done to deserve such punishment; others were dumbfounded and began to be troubled and confused by this universal confusion and tumult.

645. Of the eleven Apostles saint John alone was present. He with the sorrowful Mother and the three Marys stood within sight of the Lord, though in a retired corner. When the holy Apostle saw his divine Master brought forth, the thought of whose love toward himself now shot through his mind, he was so filled with grief, that his blood congealed in his veins and his face took on the appearance of death. The three Marys fell away into a prolonged swoon. But the Queen of virtues remained unconquered and her magnanimous heart, though overwhelmed by a grief beyond all conception of man, never fainted or swooned; She did not share the imperfections or weaknesses of the others. In all her actions She was most prudent, courageous and admirable; calmly She comforted saint John and the pious women. She besought the Lord to strengthen them, in order that She might have their company to the end of the Passion. In virtue of this prayer the Apostle and the holy women were consoled and encouraged, so that they regained their senses and could speak to the Mistress of heaven. Amid all this bitterness and confusion She did nothing unbecoming or inconsiderate, but shed forth incessant tears with the dignity of a Queen. Her attention was riveted upon Her Son, the true God; She prayed to the eternal Father and offered to Him his sorrows and torments, imitating in her actions all that was done by our Savior. She recognized the malice of

sin, penetrated the mysteries of the Redemption, appealed to the angels and interceded for friends and enemies. While giving way to her maternal love and to the sorrows corresponding to it, She at the same time practiced all the virtues, exciting the highest admiration of all heaven and delighting in the highest degree the eternal Godhead. Since it is not possible for me to describe the sentiments filling the heart of this Mother of wisdom, nor those at times also uttered by her lips, I leave them to be imagined by Christian piety.

646. The servants and priests sought to quiet the multitudes, in order that they might be able to hear the sentence pronounced against Jesus of Nazareth; for after it had been made known to Him in person, they desired to have it read before the people and in his presence. When the people had quieted down, they began to read it in a loud voice, so that all could hear it, while Jesus was standing in full view as a criminal. The sentence was proclaimed also in the different streets and at the foot of the Cross; and it was afterwards published and spread in many copies. According to the understanding given to me, the copies were a faithful reproduction, excepting some words which have been added. I will not discuss them, for the exact words of this sentence have been shown me and I give them here without change.

LITERAL RENDERING OF THE SENTENCE OF DEATH PRONOUNCED AGAINST JESUS OF NAZARETH, OUR SAVIOR.

647. "I Pontius Pilate, presiding over lower Galilee and governing Jerusalem, in fealty to the Roman Empire, and being within the executive mansion, judge, decide, and proclaim, that I condemn to death, Jesus, of the Nazarean people and a Galileean by birth, a man seditious and opposed to our laws, to our senate, and to the great emperor Tiberius Cesar. For the execution of this sentence I decree, that his

death be upon the cross and that He shall be fastened thereto with nails as is customary with criminals; because, in this very place, gathering around Him every day many men, poor and rich, He has continued to raise tumults throughout Judea, proclaiming Himself the Son of God and King of Israel, at the same time threatening the ruin of this renowned city of Jerusalem and its temple, and of the sacred Empire, refusing tribute to Caesar; and because He dared to enter in triumph this city of Jerusalem and the temple of Solomon, accompanied by a great multitude of the people carrying branches of palms. I command the first centurion, called Quintus Cornelius, to lead Him for his greater shame through the said city of Jerusalem, bound as He is, and scourged by my orders. Let Him also wear his own garments, that He may be known to all, and let Him carry the Cross on which He is to be crucified. Let Him walk through all the public streets between two other thieves, who are likewise condemned to death for their robberies and murders, so that this punishment be an example to all the people and to all malefactors."

"I desire also and command in this my sentence, that this malefactor, having been thus led through the public streets, be brought outside the city through the pagora gate, now called the Antonian portal, and under the proclamations of the herald, who shall mention all the crimes pointed out in my sentence, He shall be conducted to the summit of the mountain called Calvary, where justice is wont to be executed upon wicked transgressors. There, fastened and crucified upon the Cross, which He shall carry as decreed above, his body shall remain between the aforesaid thieves. Above the Cross, that is, at its top, He shall have placed for Him his name and title in the three languages; namely in Hebrew, Greek and Latin; and in all and each one of them shall be written: THIS IS JESUS OF NAZARETH, KING OF THE JEWS, so that it may be understood by all and become universally known." "At the same time I command, that no one, no matter of what condition, under pain of the loss of his goods and life, and under punishment for rebellion against the Roman empire, presume audaciously to impede the execution of this just sentence ordered by me to be executed with all rigor according to the decrees and laws of the Romans and Hebrews. Year of the creation of the world 5233, the twenty-fifth day of March." Pontius Pilatus Judex et Gubernator Galilaeae inferioris pro Romano Imperio qui supra propria manu. (Pontius Pilate, Judge and Governor of lower Galilee for the Roman Empire, who signed the above with his own hand.)

648. According to the above reckoning the creation of the world happened in March; and from the day on which Adam was created until the Incarnation of the Word 5199 years; adding the nine months, during which He remained in the virginal womb of his most holy Mother, and the thirty-three years of his life, we complete the 5233 years and three months, which according to the reckoning of the Romans intervened between the anniversary of his birth and the 25th of March, the day of his death. According to the reckoning of the Roman Church there are not more than nine months and seven days to the first year, since it begins its count of years with the first of January of the second year of the world. Of all the opinions of the teachers of the Church I have understood the one which corresponds to the reckoning of the Roman Church in the Roman martyrlogy to be the correct one. This I have also stated in the chapter of the Incarnation of Christ our Lord in the first book of the second part, chapter eleventh.

649. The sentence of Pilate against our Savior having been published in a loud voice before all the people, the executioners loaded the heavy Cross, on which He was to be crucified, upon his tender and wounded shoulders. In order

that He might carry it they loosened the bonds holding his hands, but not the others, since they wished to drag Him along by the loose ends of the ropes that bound his body. In order to torment Him the more they drew two loops around his throat. The Cross was fifteen feet long, of thick and heavy timbers. The herald began to proclaim the sentence and the whole confused and turbulent multitude of the people, the executioners and soldiers, with great noise, uproar and disorder began to move from the house of Pilate to mount Calvary through the streets of Jerusalem. The Master and Redeemer of the world, Jesus, before receiving the Cross, looked upon it with a countenance full of extreme joy and exultation such as would be shown by a bridegroom looking at the rich adornments of his bride, and on receiving it, He addressed it as follows:

650. "0 Cross, beloved of my soul, now prepared and ready to still my longings, come to Me, that I may be received in thy arms, and that, attached to them as on an altar, I may be accepted by the eternal Father as the sacrifice of his everlasting reconciliation with the human race. In order to die upon thee, I have descended from heaven and assumed mortal and passible flesh; for thou art to be the sceptre with which I shall triumph over all my enemies, the key with which I shall open the gates of heaven for all the predestined (Is. 22, 22), the sanctuary in which the guilty sons of Adam shall find mercy, and the treasurehouse for the enrichment of their poverty. Upon thee I desire to exalt and recommend dishonor and reproach among men, in order that my friends may embrace them with joy, seek them with anxious longings, and follow Me on the path which I through thee shall open up before them. My Father and eternal God, I confess Thee as the Lord of heaven and earth (Matth. 11, 25), subjecting Myself to thy power and to thy divine wishes, I take upon my shoulders the wood for the sacrifice of my

innocent and passible humanity and I accept it willingly for the salvation of men. Receive Thou, eternal Father, this sacrifice as acceptable to thy justice, in order that from today on they may not any more be servants, but sons and heirs of thy kingdom together with Me" (Rom. 8, 17).

651. None of these sacred mysteries and happenings were hidden from the great Lady of the world, Mary; for She had a most intimate knowledge and understanding of them, far beyond that of all the angels. The events, which She could not see with the eyes of her body, She perceived by her intelligence and revealed science, which manifested to Her the interior operation of her most holy Son. By this divine light She recognized the infinite value of the wood of the Cross after once it had come in contact with the deified humanity of Jesus our Redeemer. Immediately She venerated and adored it in a manner befitting it. The same was also done by the heavenly spirits attending upon the Queen. She imitated her divine Son in the tokens of affections, with which He received the Cross, addressing it in the words suited to her office as Coadjutrix of the Redeemer. By her prayers to the eternal Father She followed Him in his exalted sentiments as the living original and exemplar, without failing in the least point. When She heard the voice of the herald publishing and rehearsing the sentence through the streets, the heavenly Mother, in protest against the accusations contained in the sentence and in the form of comments on the glory and honor of the Lord, composed a canticle of praise and worship of the innocence and sinlessness of her all holy Son and God. In the composing of this canticle the holy angels helped Her, conjointly with them She arranged and repeated it, while the inhabitants of Jerusalem were blaspheming their own Creator and Savior.

652. As all the faith, knowledge and love of creatures, during this time of the Passion, was enshrined in its highest

essence in the magnanimous soul of the Mother of wisdom, She alone had the most proper conception and correct judgment of the suffering and Death of God for men. Without for a moment failing in the attention necessary to exterior actions, her wisdom penetrated all the mysteries of the Redemption and the manner in which it was to be accomplished through the ignorance of the very men who were to be redeemed. She entered into the deepest consideration of the dignity of the One, who was suffering, of what He was suffering, from and for whom He was suffering. Of the dignity of the person of Christ our Redeemer, uniting within Himself the divine and the human natures, of their perfections and attributes, the most blessed Mary alone possessed the highest and intuitive knowledge outside of the Lord himself. On this account She alone among all mere creatures attached sufficient importance to the Passion and Death of her Son and of the true God. Of what He suffered, She was not only an eyewitness, but She experienced it personally within Herself, occasioning the holy envy not only of men, but of the angels themselves, who were not thus favored. But they well knew that their great Queen and Mistress felt and suffered in soul and body the same torments and sorrows as her most holy Son and that the holy Trinity was inexpressibly pleased with Her; and therefore they sought to make up by their praise and worship for the pains which they could not share. Sometimes, when the sorrowful Mother could not personally witness the sufferings of her Son, She was made to feel in her virginal body and in her spirit the effects of his torments before her intelligence made Her aware of them. Thus surprised She would say: "Ah! what new martyrdom have they devised for my sweetest Lord and Master?" And then She would receive the clearest knowledge of what the Lord was enduring. The most loving Mother was so admirably faithful in her sufferings and in imitating the example of

Christ our God, that She never permitted Herself any easement either of her bodily pains, such as rest, or nourishment,
or sleep; nor any relaxation of the spirit, such as any consoling thoughts or considerations, except when She was visited
from on high by divine influence. Then only would She
humbly and thankfully accept relief, in order that She might
recover strength to attend still more fervently to the object of
her sorrows and to the cause of his sufferings. The same wise
consideration She applied to the malicious behavior of the
Jews and their servants, to the needs of the human race, to
their threatening ruin, and to the ingratitude of men, for
whom He suffered. Thus She perfectly and intimately knew
of all these things and felt it more deeply than all the creatures.

653. Another hidden and astonishing miracle was
wrought by the right hand of God through the instrumental-
ity of the blessed Mary against Lucifer and his infernal spirits.
It took place in the following manner:

The dragon and his associates, though they could not understand the humiliation of the Lord, were most attentive to
all that happened in the Passion of the Lord. Now, when He
took upon Himself the Cross, all these enemies felt a new
and mysterious tremor and weakness, which caused in them
great consternation and confused distress. Conscious of these
unwonted and invincible feelings the prince of darkness
feared, that in the Passion and Death of Christ our Lord
some dire and irreparable destruction of his reign was imminent. In order not to be overtaken by it in the presence of
Christ our God, the dragon resolved to retire and fly with all
his followers to the caverns of hell. But when he sought to
execute this resolve, he was prevented by the great Queen
and Mistress of all creation; for the Most High, enlightening
Her and intimating to Her what She was to do, at the same
time invested Her with his power. The heavenly Mother,

turning toward Lucifer and his squadrons, by her imperial command hindered them from flying; ordering them to await and witness the Passion to the end on mount Calvary. The demons could not resist the command of the mighty Queen; for they recognized and felt the divine power operating in Her. Subject to her sway they followed Christ as so many prisoners dragged along in chains to Calvary, where the eternal wisdom had decreed to triumph over them from the throne of the Cross, as we shall see later on. There is nothing which can exemplify the discouragement and dismay, which from that moment began to oppress Lucifer and his demons. According to our way of speaking, they walked along to Calvary like criminals condemned to a terrible death, and seized by the dismay and consternation of an inevitable punishment. This punishment of the demon was in conformity with his malicious nature and proportioned to the evil committed by him in introducing death and sin into the world, to remedy which, God himself was now undergoing Death.

654. Our Savior proceeded on the way to Calvary bearing upon his shoulders, according to the saying of Isaias, his own government and principality (Is. 9, 6), which was none else than his Cross, from whence He was to subject and govern the world, meriting thereby that his name should be exalted above all other names and rescuing the human race from the tyrannical power of the demon over the sons of Adam (Col. 2, 15). The same Isaias calls it the yoke and sceptre of the oppressor and executor, who was imperiously exacting the tribute of the first guilt. In order to destroy this tyrant and break the sceptre of his reign and the yoke of our servitude, Christ our Savior placed the Cross upon his shoulders; namely, upon that place, where are borne both the yoke of slavery and the sceptre of royal power. He wished to intimate thereby, that He despoiled the demon of this power and

transferred it to his own shoulders, in order that thenceforward the captive children of Adam should recognize Him for their legitimate Lord and true King. All mortals were to follow Him in the way of the Cross (Matth. 14, 24) and learn, that by this Cross they were subjected to his power (John 12, 32) and now become his vassals and servants, bought by his own lifeblood (I Cor. 4, 20).

655. But alas, the pity of our most ungrateful forgetfulness! That the Jews and ministers of the Passion should be ignorant of this mystery hidden to princes of this world, and that they should not dare touch the Cross of the Savior, because they considered it the wood of ignominy and shame, was their own fault and a very great one. Yet not so great as our own, since its mystery being already revealed to us, we spend our indignation only on the blindness of those who were persecuting our Lord and God. For, if we blame them for being ignorant of what they ought to have known, how much should we blame ourselves, who, knowing and confessing Christ the Redeemer, persecute and crucify Him by our offenses (Reb. 6, 6)? O my sweetest Love, Jesus, light of my intellect and glory of my soul! Do not, O my Lord, trust in my sluggish torpidity to follow Thee with my Cross on thy way! Take it upon Thee to do me this favor; draw me after Thee, to run after the fragrance of thy sweetest love (Cant. 1, 3) of thy ineffable patience, of thy deepest humility, that I may desire for contempt and anguish, and seek after participation in thy ignominy, insults and sorrows. Let this be my portion and my inheritance in this mortal and oppressing life, let this be my glory and my repose; and outside of the Cross and its ignominy, I desire not to live or be consoled or to partake of any rest or enjoyment. As the Jews and all of that blind multitude avoided the touch of the Cross of Him, who was so innocently sentenced to die upon it, He opened with it a passage and cleared for Himself a way. His perfidi-

ous persecutors looked upon his glorious dishonor as a contagion and they fled from its approach, though all the rest of the streets were full of shouting and clamoring people, who crowded aside as the herald advanced proclaiming the sentence.

656. The executioners, bare of all human compassion and kindness, dragged our Savior Jesus along with incredible cruelty and insults. Some of them jerked Him forward by the ropes in order to accelerate his passage, while others pulled from behind in order to retard it. On account of this jerking and the weight of the Cross they caused Him to sway to and fro and often to fall to the ground. By the hard knocks He thus received on the rough stones great wounds were opened, especially on the two knees and they were widened at each repeated fall. The heavy Cross also inflicted a wound on the shoulder on which it was carried. The unsteadiness caused the Cross sometimes to knock against his sacred head, and sometimes the head against the Cross; thus the thorns of his crown penetrated deeper and wounded the parts, which they had not yet reached. To these torments of the body the ministers of evil added many insulting words and execrable affronts, ejecting their impure spittle and throwing the dirt of the pavement into his face so mercilessly, that they blinded the eyes that looked upon them with such divine mercy. Thus they of their own account condemned themselves to the loss of the graces, with which his very looks were fraught. By the haste with which they dragged Him along in their eagerness to see Him die, they did not allow Him to catch his breath; for his most innocent body, having been in so few hours overwhelmed with such a storm of torments, was so weakened and bruised, that to all appearances He was ready to yield up life under his pains and sorrows.

657. From the house of Pilate the sorrowful and stricken Mother followed with the multitudes on the way of her

divine Son, accompanied by saint John and the pious wom-
en. As the surging crowds hindered Her from getting very
near to the Lord, She asked the eternal Father to be permitted to stand at the foot of the Cross of her blessed Son and
see Him die with her own eyes. With the divine consent She
ordered her holy angels to manage things in such a way as to
make it possible for Her to execute her wishes. The holy
angels obeyed Her with great reverence; and they speedily led
the Queen through some bystreet, in order that She might
meet her Son. Thus it came that both of Them met face to
face in sweetest recognition of each Other and in mutual
renewal of each other's interior sorrows. Yet They did not
speak to one another, nor would the fierce cruelty of the
executioners have permitted such an intercourse. But the
most prudent Mother adored her divine Son and true God,
laden with the Cross; and interiorly besought Him, that,
since She could not relieve Him of the weight of the Cross
and since She was not permitted to command her holy angels
to lighten it, He would inspire these ministers of cruelty to
procure some one for his assistance. This prayer was heard by
the Lord Christ; and so it happened, that Simon of Cyrene
was afterwards impressed to carry the Cross with the Lord
(Matth. 27, 32). The pharisees and the executioners were
moved to this measure, some of them out of natural compassion, others for fear lest Christ, the Author of life, should lose
his life by exhaustion before it could be taken from Him on
the Cross.

658. Beyond all human thought and estimation was the
sorrow of the most sincere Dove and Virgin Mother while
She thus witnessed with her own eyes her Son carrying the
Cross to Mount Calvary; for She alone could fittingly know
and love Him according to his true worth. It would have
been impossible for Her to live through this ordeal, if the
divine power had not strengthened Her and preserved Her

life. With bitterest sorrow She addressed the Lord and spoke to Him in her heart: "My Son and eternal God, light of my eyes and life of my soul, receive, O Lord, the sacrifice of my not being able to relieve Thee of the burden of the Cross and carry it myself, who am a daughter of Adam; for it is I who should die upon it in love of Thee, as Thou now wishest to die in most ardent love of the human race. O most loving Mediator between guilt and justice! How dost Thou cherish mercy in the midst of so great injuries and such heinous offenses! O charity without measure or bounds, which permits such torments and affronts in order to afford it a wider scope for its ardor and efficacy! O infinite and sweetest love, would that the hearts and the wills of men were all mine, so that they could give no such thankless return for all that Thou endurest! O who will speak to the hearts of the mortals to teach them what they owe to Thee, since Thou hast paid so dearly for their salvation from ruin!" Other most prudent and exalted sentiments besides these were conceived by the great Lady, so that I cannot express them by words of mine.

659. As the Evangelist tells us, there were other women among the crowds, who followed the Savior in bitter tears and lamentations (Luke 23, 27). The sweetest Jesus turning toward them, addressed them and said: "Daughters of Jerusalem, weep not over Me; but weep for yourselves and for your children. For behold, the days shall come, wherein they shall say: Blessed are the barren, and the wombs that have not borne, and the pups that have not given suck. Then shall they begin to say to the mountains: Fall upon us, and to the hills: Cover us. For if in the green wood they do these things, what shall be done in the dry?" By these mysterious words the Lord acknowledged the tears shed on account of his Passion, and to a certain extent, by showing his appreciation of them, He approved of them. In these women He wished to teach us for what purpose our tears should be shed so that

they may attain their end. These compassionate disciples of the Lord were at that time ignorant of the true reason for their tears, since they wept over his sufferings and injuries, and not over the cause of these sufferings; and therefore they merited to be instructed and admonished of the truth. It was as if the Savior had said to them: Weep over your sins and over the sins of your children, and attribute what I suffer to those sins. I suffer not for my sins, for I am guilty of none and it is not even possible that I be guilty of any. If I approve of your compassion for Me as good and just, much more do I desire you to weep over your sins, for which I suffer, and by this manner of weeping you shall acquire for yourselves and your children the price of my blood and of my Redemption, ignored by this blind people. For there shall come days, namely the days of universal judgment and chastisement, in which those shall be held fortunate, who have not begotten children; and the foreknown shall call upon the mountains and the hills to shield them against my wrath. For if their sins, now only assumed by Me, have such effects on me, who am innocent, what horrible punishments will they draw upon those, who are so barren and without any fruits of grace and merits?

660. As a reward for their tears and their compassion these women were enlightened so as to understand this doctrine. In fulfillment of the prayerful wish of the blessed Mother the pharisees and ministers were inspired with the resolve to engage some man to help Jesus our Savior in carrying the Cross to mount Calvary. At this juncture, Simon, of Cyrene, the father of the disciples Alexander and Rufus (Mark 15, 21), happened to come along. He was called by this name because he was a native of Cyrene, a city of Libya, and had come to Jerusalem. This Simon was now forced by the Jews to carry the Cross a part of the way. They themselves would not touch it, yea would not even come

near it, as being the instrument of punishment for One whom they held to be a notorious malefactor. By this pretended caution and avoidance of his Cross they sought to impress the people with a horror for Jesus. The Cyrenean took hold of the Cross and Jesus was made to follow between the two thieves, in order that all might believe Him to be a criminal and malefactor like to them. The Virgin Mother walked very closely behind Jesus, as She had desired and asked from the eternal Father. To his divine will She so conformed Herself in all the labors and torments of her Son that, witnessing with her own eyes and partaking of all the sufferings of her Son in her blessed soul and in her body, She never allowed any sentiment or wish to arise interiorly or exteriorly, which could be interpreted as regret for the sacrifice She had made in offering her Son for the death of the Cross and its sufferings. Her charity and love of men, and her grace and holiness, were so great, that She vanquished all these movements of her human nature.

Words of the Queen

THE VIRGIN MARY SPEAKS TO SISTER MARY OF AGREDA

661. I desire that the fruit of the obedience with which thou writest the history of my life shall be, that thou become a true disciple of my most holy Son and of myself. The main purpose of the exalted and venerable mysteries, which are made known to thee, and of the teachings, which I so often repeat to thee, is that thou deny and strip thyself, estranging thy heart from all affection to creatures, neither wishing to possess them nor accept them for other uses. By this precaution thou wilt overcome the impediments, which the devils seek to place in the way of the dangerous softness of thy nature. I who know thee, thus advise and lead thee by the way of instruction and correction as thy Mother and Instruc-

tress. By the divine teaching thou knowest the mysteries of the Passion and Death of Christ and the one true way of life, which is the Cross; and thou knowest that not all who are called, are chosen. Many there are who wish to follow Christ and very few who truly dispose themselves to imitate Him; for as soon as they feel the sufferings of the Cross they cast it aside. Laborious exertions are very painful and averse to human nature according to the flesh; and the fruits of the spirit are more hidden and few guide themselves by the light. On this account there are so many among mortals, who, forgetful of the eternal truths, seek the flesh and the continual indulgence of its pleasures. They ardently seek honors and fly from injuries: they strive after riches, and contemn poverty; they long after pleasure and dread mortification. All these are enemies of the Cross of Christ (Phil. 3, 18), and with dreadful aversion they fly from it, deeming it sheer ignominy, just like those who crucified Christ, the Lord.

662. Another deceit has spread through the world: many imagine that they are following Christ their Master, though they neither suffer affliction nor engage in any exertion or labor. They are content with avoiding boldness in committing sins, and place all their perfection in a certain prudence or hollow self-love, which prevents them from denying anything to their will and from practicing any virtues at the cost of their flesh. They would easily escape this deception, if they would consider that my Son was not only the Redeemer, but their Teacher; and that He left in this world the treasures of his Redemption not only as a remedy against its eternal ruin, but as a necessary medicine for the sickness of sin in human nature. No one knew so much as my Son and Lord; no one could better understand the quality of love than the divine Lord, who was and is wisdom and charity itself; and no one was more able to fulfill all his wishes (I John 4, 16). Nevertheless, although He well could do it, He chose not a

life of softness and ease for the flesh, but one full of labors and pains; for He judged his instructions to be incomplete and insufficient to redeem man, if He failed to teach them how to overcome the demon, the flesh and their own self. He wished to inculcate, that this magnificent victory is gained by the Cross, by labors, penances, mortifications and the acceptance of contempt: all of which are the trademarks and evidences of true love and the special watchwords of the predestined.

663. Thou, my daughter, knowest the value of the holy Cross and the honor which it confers upon ignominies and tribulations; do thou embrace the Cross and bear it with joy in imitation of my Son and thy Master (Matth. 16, 24). In this mortal life let thy glory be in tribulations, persecutions (Rom. 5, 3), contempt, infirmities, poverty, humiliation and in whatever is painful and averse to mortal flesh. And in order that in all thy exercises thou mayest imitate me and give me pleasure, I wish that thou seek no rest or consolation in any earthly thing. Thou must not dwell in thy thoughts upon what thou bearest, nor seek to relieve thyself by enlisting the compassion of others. Much less must thou make much of, or try to impress others with the recital of the persecutions or molestations of creatures, nor should it ever be heard from thy lips, how much thou endurest, nor shouldst thou compare thy sufferings with those of others. I do not wish to say, that it is a sin to accept of some reasonable and moderate alleviation, or to mention thy afflictions. But in thee, my dearest, much alleviation, if not a sin, would be an infidelity to thy Spouse and Lord; for He has put thee personally under more obligation than many generations of men and thy response in suffering and love will be defective and wanting, if it is not complete and loyal in all respects. So faithful does the Lord wish thy correspondence to be, that thou must allow thy weak nature not even one sigh for mere

natural relief and consolation. If love alone impels thee, thou wilt allow thyself to be carried along by its sweet force and rest in it alone; and the love of the Cross would immediately dispense with such natural relief, in the same way as thou knowest I have done in my total self-sacrifice. Let this be to thee a general rule: that all human consolation is an imperfection and a danger, and that thou shouldst welcome only that, which the Most High sends to thee Himself or through his holy angels. And even these favors of the divine right hand thou must accept only in so far as they strengthen thee to suffer more constantly and to withdraw thee from all that ministers to the senses.

Chapter XXII

HOW OUR SAVIOR JESUS WAS CRUCIFIED ON MOUNT CAL-
VARY; THE SEVEN WORDS SPOKEN BY HIM ON THE CROSS
AND THE ATTENDANCE OF HIS SORROWFUL MOTHER AT
HIS SUFFERINGS.

664. Our Savior then, the new and true Isaac, the Son of the
eternal Father, reached the mountain of sacrifice, which is
the same one to which his prototype and figure, Isaac, was
brought by the patriarch Abraham (Gen. 22, 9). Upon the
most innocent Lamb of God was to be executed the rigor of
the sentence, which had been suspended in favor of the son
of the Patriarch. Mount Calvary was held to be a place of
defilement and ignominy, as being reserved for the chastisement of condemned criminals, whose cadavers spread around
it their stench and attached to it a still more evil fame. Our
most loving Jesus arrived at its summit so worn out, wounded, torn and disfigured, that He seemed altogether transformed into an object of pain and sorrows. The power of the
Divinity, which deified his most holy humanity by its hypostatical union, helped Him, not to lighten his pains, but to
strengthen Him against death; so that, still retaining life until
death should be permitted to take it away on the Cross, He
might satiate his love to the fullest extent. The sorrowful and
afflicted Mother, in the bitterness of her soul, also arrived at
the summit of the mount and remained very close to her

divine Son; but in the sorrows of her soul She was as it were beside Herself, being entirety transformed by her love and by the pains which She saw Jesus suffer. Near her were saint John and the three Marys; for they alone, through her intercession and the favor of the eternal Father, had obtained the privilege of remaining so constantly near to the Savior and to his Cross.

665. When the most prudent Mother perceived that now the mysteries of the Redemption were to be fulfilled and that the executioners were about to strip Jesus of his clothes for crucifixion, She turned in spirit to the eternal Father and prayed as follows: "My Lord and eternal God, Thou art the Father of thy onlybegotten Son. By eternal generation He is engendered, God of the true God, namely Thyself, and as man He was born of my womb and received from me this human nature, in which He now suffers. I have nursed and sustained Him at my own breast; and as the best of sons that ever can be born of any creature, I love Him with maternal love. As his Mother I have a natural right in the Person of his most holy humanity and thy Providence will never infringe upon any rights held by thy creatures. This right of a Mother then, I now yield to Thee and once more place in thy hands thy and my Son as a sacrifice for the Redemption of man. Accept, my Lord, this pleasing offering, since this is more than I can ever offer by submitting my own self as a victim or to suffering. This sacrifice is greater, not only because my Son is the true God and of thy own substance, but because this sacrifice costs me a much greater sorrow and pain. For if the lots were changed and I should be permitted to die in order to preserve his most holy life, I would consider it a great relief and the fulfillment of my dearest wishes." The eternal Father received this prayer of the exalted Queen with ineffable pleasure and complacency. The patriarch Abraham was permitted to go no further than to prefigure and attempt

the sacrifice of a son, because the real execution of such a sacrifice God reserved to Himself and to his Onlybegotten. Nor was Sara, the mother of Isaac, informed of the mystical ceremony, this being prevented not only by the promptness of Abraham's obedience, but also because he mistrusted, lest the maternal love of Sara, though she was a just and holy woman, should impel her to prevent the execution of the divine command. But not so was it with most holy Mary, to whom the eternal Father could fearlessly manifest his unchangeable will in order that She might, as far as her powers were concerned, unite with Him in the sacrifice of his Onlybegotten.

666. The invincible Mother finished her prayer and She perceived that the impious ministers were preparing to give to the Lord the drink of wine, myrrh and gall, of which saint Matthew and saint Mark speak (Matth. 27, 34; Mark 15, 23). Taking occasion from the words of Solomon: Give strong drink to the sorrowful and wine to those that suffer bitterness of heart, the Jews were accustomed to give to those about to be executed a drink of strong and aromatic wine in order to raise their vital spirits and to help them to bear their torments with greater fortitude. This custom they now perverted in order to augment the sufferings of the Savior (Prov. 3, 6). The drink, which was intended to assist and strengthen other criminals, by the perfidy of the Jews was now mixed with gall, so that it should have no other effect than to torment his sense of taste by its bitterness. The blessed Mother was aware of their intentions and in her maternal tenderness and compassion asked the Lord not to drink of it. Jesus in deference to the petition of his Mother, without rejecting entirely this new suffering, tasted of the mixture, but would not drink it entirely (Matth. 27, 34)

667. It was already the sixth hour, which corresponds to our noontime, and the executioners, intending to crucify the

Savior naked, despoiled Him of the seamless tunic and of his garments. As the tunic was large and without opening in front, they pulled it over the head of Jesus without taking off the crown of thorns; but on account of the rudeness with which they proceeded, they inhumanly tore off the crown with the tunic. Thus they opened anew all the wounds of his head, and in some of them remained the thorns, which, in spite of their being so hard and sharp, were wrenched off by the violence with which the executioners despoiled Him of his tunic and, with it, of the crown. With heartless cruelty they again forced it down upon his sacred head, opening up wounds upon wounds. By the rude tearing off of the tunic were renewed also the wounds of his whole body, since the tunic had dried into the open places and its removal was, as David says, adding new pains to his wounds (Ps. 68, 27). Four times during the Passion did they despoil Jesus of his garments and again vest Him. The first time in order to scourge Him at the pillar; the second time in order to clothe Him in the mock purple; the third, when they took this off in order to clothe Him in his tunic; the fourth, when they finally took away his clothes. This last was the most painful, because his wounds were more numerous, his holy humanity was much weakened, and there was less shelter against the sharp wind on mount Calvary; for also this element was permitted to increase the sufferings of his death struggle by sending its cold blasts across the mount.

668. To all these sufferings was added the confusion of being bereft of his garments in the presence of his most blessed Mother, of her pious companions, and in full sight of the multitudes gathered around. By his divine power He, however, reserved for Himself the nether garment which his Mother had wound around his loins in Egypt; for neither at the scourging, nor at the crucifixion could the executioners remove it, and He was laid in the sepulcher still covered with

this cloth. That this really happened, has been revealed to me many times. Certainly, He desired to die in the greatest poverty and to take with Him nothing of all that He created and possessed in this world. He would gladly have died entirely despoiled and bereft of even this covering, if it had not been for the desires and the prayers of his blessed Mother, to which Christ wished to yield. On her account He substituted this most perfect obedience of a Son toward his Mother for extreme poverty at his Death. The holy Cross was lying on the ground and the executioners were busy making the necessary preparations for crucifying Him and the two thieves. In the meanwhile our Redeemer and Master prayed to the Father in the following terms:

669. "Eternal Father and my Lord God, to the incomprehensible Majesty of thy infinite goodness and justice I offer my entire humanity and all that according to thy will it has accomplished in descending from thy bosom to assume passible and mortal flesh for the Redemption of men, my brethren. I offer Thee, Lord, with Myself, also my most loving Mother, her love, her most perfect works, her sorrows, her sufferings, her anxious and prudent solicitude in serving Me, imitating Me and accompanying Me unto death. I offer Thee the little flock of my Apostles, the holy Church and congregation of the faithful, such as it is now and as it shall be to the end of the world; and with it I offer to Thee all the mortal children of Adam. All this I place in thy hands as the true and almighty Lord and God. As far as my wishes are concerned, I suffer and die for all, and I desire that all shall be saved, under the condition that all follow Me and profit of my Redemption. Thus may they pass from the slavery of the devil to be thy children, my brethren and coheirs of the grace merited by Me. Especially, O my Lord, do I offer to Thee the poor, the despised and afflicted, who are my friends and who follow Me on the way to the Cross. I desire that the just

and the predestined be written in thy eternal memory. I beseech Thee, my Father, to withhold thy chastisement and not to raise the scourge of thy justice over men; let them not be punished as they merit for their sins. Be Thou from now on their Father as Thou art mine. I beseech Thee also, that they may be helped to ponder upon my Death in pious affection and be enlightened from above; and I pray for those who are persecuting Me, in order that they may be converted to the truth. Above all do I ask Thee for the exaltation of thy ineffable and most holy name."

670. This prayer and supplication of our Savior Jesus were known to the most blessed Mother, and She imitated Him and made the same petitions to the eternal Father in as far as She was concerned. The most prudent Virgin never forgot or disregarded the first word which She had heard from the mouth of her divine Son as an infant: "Become like unto Me, my Beloved." His promise, that in return for the new human existence which She had given Him in her virginal womb, He would, by his almighty power, give Her a new existence of divine and eminent grace above all other creatures, was continually fulfilled. To this favor was due also her deep science and enlightenment concerning all the operations of the sacred humanity of her Son, none of which ever escaped her knowledge and attention. Whatever She thus perceived She imitated; so that She was always anxious to study and penetrate them with deep understanding, to put them promptly into action, and to practice them courageously and zealously during all her life. In this neither sorrow could disturb Her, nor anguish hinder Her, nor persecution detain Her, nor the bitterness of her suffering weaken Her. If the great Queen had assisted at the Passion with the same sentiments as the rest of the just, it would indeed have been admirable; but not so admirable as the way in which She suffered. She was singular and extraordinary in all her suffer-

ings; for, as I have said above, She felt in her own virginal body all the torments of Christ our Lord, both interior and exterior. On account of this conformity we can say, that also the heavenly Mother was scourged, crowned, spit upon, buffeted, laden with the Cross and nailed upon it; for She felt these pains and all the rest in her purest body. Although She felt them in a different manner, yet She felt them with such conformity that the Mother was altogether a faithful likeness of her Son. Besides the greatness of her dignity, which in most holy Mary must, on this account, have corresponded in the highest possible degree with that of Christ, there was concealed therein another mystery. This was, that the desire of Christ to see his exalted love and benignity as exhibited in his Passion copied in all its magnitude in a mere creature, was fulfilled in Her, and no one possessed a greater right to this favor than his own Mother.

671. In order to find the places for the augerholes on the Cross, the executioners haughtily commanded the Creator of the universe. (0 dreadful temerity!), to stretch Himself out upon it. The Teacher of humility obeyed without hesitation. But they, following their inhuman instinct of cruelty, marked the places for the holes, not according to the size of his body, but larger, having in mind a new torture for their Victim. This inhuman intent was known to the Mother of light, and the knowledge of it was one of the greatest afflictions of her chastest heart during the whole Passion. She saw through the intentions of these ministers of sin and She anticipated the torments to be endured by her beloved Son when his limbs should be wrenched from their sockets in being nailed to the Cross. But She could not do anything to prevent it, as it was the will of the Lord to suffer these pains for men. When He rose from the Cross, and they set about boring the holes, the great Lady approached and took hold of one of his hands, adoring Him and kissing it with greatest reverence. The

executioners allowed this because they thought that the sight
of his Mother would cause so much the greater affliction to
the Lord; for they wished to spare Him no sorrow they could
cause Him. But they were ignorant of the hidden mysteries;
for the Lord during his Passion had no greater source of
consolation and interior joy than to see in the soul of his
most blessed Mother, the beautiful likeness of Himself and
the full fruits of his Passion and Death. This joy, to a certain
extent, comforted Christ our Lord also in that hour.

672. Having bored the three holes into the Cross, the executioners again commanded Christ the Lord to stretch
Himself out upon it in order to be nailed to it. The supreme
and almighty King, as the Author of patience, obeyed, and at
the will of the hangmen, placed Himself with outstretched
arms upon the blessed wood. The Lord was so weakened,
disfigured and exhausted, that if the ferocious cruelty of those
men had left the least room for natural reason and kindness,
they could not have brought themselves to inflict further
torments upon the innocent and meek Lamb, humbly suffering such nameless sorrows and pains. But not so with them;
for the judges and their executioners (O terrible and most
hidden judgments of the Lord!) were transformed in their
malice and deathly hatred into demons, void of the feelings
of sensible and earthly men and urged on only by diabolical
wrath and fury.

673. Presently one of the executioners seized the hand of
Jesus our Savior and placed it upon the auger hole, while
another hammered a large and rough nail through the palm.
The veins and sinews were torn, and the bones of the sacred
hand, which made the heavens and all that exists, were forced
apart. When they stretched out the other hand, they found
that it did not reach up to the auger hole; for the sinews of
the other arm had been shortened and the executioners had
maliciously set the holes too far apart, as I have mentioned

above. In order to overcome the difficulty, they took the chain, with which the Savior had been bound in the garden, and looping one end through a ring around his wrist, they, with unheard of cruelty, pulled the hand over the hole and fastened it with another nail. Thereupon they seized his feet, and placing them one above the other, they tied the same chain around both and stretched them with barbarous ferocity down to the third hole. Then they drove through both feet a large nail into the Cross. Thus the sacred body, in which dwelled the Divinity, was nailed motionless to the holy Cross, and the handiwork of his deified members, formed by the Holy Ghost, was so stretched and torn asunder, that the bones of his body, dislocated and forced from their natural position, could all be counted. The bones of his breast, of his shoulders and arms, and of his whole body yielded to the cruel violence and were torn from their sinews.

674. It is impossible for human tongue or words of mouth to describe the torments of our Savior Jesus and what He suffered on this occasion. On the last day alone more will be known, in order that his cause may be justified before sinners and the praise and exaltation of the saints may be so much the greater. But at present, while our faith in this truth gives us occasion and obliges us to apply our reason (if such we possess), I ask, implore and beseech the children of the holy Church, each one for himself, to study this most venerable sacrament. Let us contemplate it and weigh it with all its circumstances, and we shall find powerful motives to abhor and firmly resolve to avoid sin, as the cause of all this suffering to the Author of life. Let us contemplate and look upon his Virgin Mother, so afflicted in spirit and overwhelmed by the torments of her purest body, in order that through this gate of light we may enter to see the Sun that illumines our heart. O Mistress and Queen of virtues! O true Mother of the immortal King of ages become man! It is true, O my

Lady, that the hardness of our ungrateful hearts makes us very unfit and unworthy of suffering thy pains and those of thy most holy Son our Lord; but through thy clemency make us partakers of this favor, which we do not deserve. Purify and free us from this deadening lukewarmness and gross neglect. If we are the cause of these sufferings, what propriety or what justice can there be in visiting them only on Thee and on thy Beloved? Let the chalice pass from the lips of the Innocent, in order that it may be tasted by the guilty who deserve it. But alas! Where is our good sense? Where wisdom and knowledge? Where is the light of our eyes? Who has so entirely deprived us of our understanding? Who has robbed us of our human and sensible hearts? If I, O Lord, had not received from Thee this being according to thy image and likeness; if Thou hadst not given me life and motion; if all the elements and creatures, formed by thy hand for my service (Eccli. 39, 30), were not giving me continual notice of thy immense love: at least thy being nailed so outrageously to the Cross, and all thy torments and sorrows for my salvation, should have sufficed to draw me to Thee with the bonds of compassion and gratitude, of love and confidence in thy ineffable kindness. But if so many voices cannot awaken me, if such love does not enkindle mine, if thy Passion and Death do not move me, if such great benefits cannot oblige me, what end shall I expect as the result of my foolishness?

675. After the Savior was nailed to the Cross, the executioners judged it necessary to bend the points of the nails which projected through the back of the wood, in order that they might not be loosened and drawn out by the weight of the body. For this purpose they raised up the Cross in order to turn it over, so that the body of the Lord would rest face downward upon the ground with the weight of the Cross upon Him. This new cruelty appalled all the bystanders and a shout of pity arose in the crowd. But the sorrowful and

compassionate Mother intervened by her prayers, and asked the eternal Father not to permit this boundless outrage to happen in the way the executioners had intended. She commanded her holy angels to come to the assistance of their Creator. When, therefore, the executioners raised up the Cross to let it fall, with the crucified Lord face downward upon the ground, the holy angels supported Him and the Cross above the stony and fetid ground, so that his divine countenance did not come in contact with the rocks and pebbles. Thus altogether ignorant of the miracle the executioners bent over the points of the nails; for the sacred body was so near to the ground and the Cross was so firmly held by the angels, that the Jews thought it rested upon the hard rock.

676. Then they dragged the lower end of the Cross with the crucified God near to the hole, wherein it was to be planted. Some of them getting under the upper part of the Cross with their shoulders, others pushing upward with their halberds and lances, they raised the Savior on his Cross and fastened its foot in the hole they had drilled into the ground. Thus our true life and salvation now hung in the air upon the sacred wood in full view of the innumerable multitudes of different nations and countries. I must not omit mentioning another barbarity inflicted upon the Lord as they raised Him: for some of them placed the sharp points of their lances and halberds to his body and fearfully lacerating Him under the armpits in helping to push the Cross into position. At this spectacle new cries of protest arose with still more vehemence and confusion from the multitude of people. The Jews blasphemed, the kindhearted lamented, the strangers were astounded, some of them called the attention of the bystanders to the proceedings, others turned away their heads in horror and pity; others took to themselves a warning from this spectacle of suffering, and still others proclaimed Him a

just Man. All these different sentiments were like arrows piercing the heart of the afflicted Mother. The sacred body now shed much blood from the nail wounds, which, by its weight and the shock of the Cross falling into the hole, had widened. They were the fountains, now opened up, to which Isaias invites us to hasten with joy to quench our thirst and wash off the stains of our sins (Is. 12, 3). No one shall be excused who does not quickly approach to drink of them; since the waters are sold without exchange of silver or gold, and they are given freely to those who will but receive them (Is. 54, 1).

677. Then they crucified also the two thieves and planted their crosses to the right and the left of the Savior; for thereby they wished to indicate that He deserved the most conspicuous place as being the greatest malefactor. The pharisees and priests, forgetting the two thieves, turned all the venom of their fury against the sinless and holy One by nature. Wagging their heads in scorn and mockery (Matth. 27, 39) they threw stones and dirt at the Cross of the Lord and his royal Person, saying: "Ah Thou, who destroyest the temple and in three days rebuildest it, save now Thyself; others He has made whole, Himself He cannot save; if this be the Son of God let Him descend from the Cross, and we will believe in Him" (Matth. 27, 42). The two thieves in the beginning also mocked the Lord and said: "If Thou art the Son of God, save Thyself and us." These blasphemies of the two thieves caused special sorrow to our Lord, since they were so near to death and were losing the fruit of their deathpains, by which they could have satisfied in part for their justly punished crimes. Soon after, however, one of them availed himself of the greatest opportunity that a sinner ever had in this world, and was converted from his sins.

678. When the great Queen of the angels, most holy Mary, perceived that the Jews in their perfidy and obstinate

envy vied in dishonoring Him, in blaspheming Him as the most wicked of men and in desiring to blot out his name from the land of the living, as Jeremias had prophesied (Jer. 11, 19), She was inflamed with a new zeal for the honor of her Son and true God. Prostrate before the person of the Crucified, and adoring Him, She besought the eternal Father to see to the honor of his Onlybegotten and manifest it by such evident signs that the perfidy of the Jews might be confounded and their malice frustrated of its intent. Having presented this petition to the Father, She, with the zeal and authority of the Queen of the universe, addressed all the irrational creatures and said: "Insensible creatures, created by the hand of the Almighty, do you manifest your compassion, which in deadly foolishness is denied to Him by men capable of reason. Ye heavens, thou sun, moon and ye stars and planets, stop in your course and suspend your activity in regard to mortals. Ye elements, change your condition, earth lose thy stability, let your rocks and cliffs be rent. Ye sepulchres and monuments of the dead, open and send forth your contents for the confusion of the living. Thou mystical and figurative veil of the temple, divide into two parts and by thy separation threaten the unbelievers with chastisement, give witness to the truth and to the glory of their Creator and Redeemer, which they are trying to obscure."

679. In virtue of this prayer and of the commands of Mary, the Mother of the Crucified, the Omnipotence of God had provided for all that was to happen at the death of his Onlybegotten. The Lord enlightened and moved the hearts of many of the bystanders at the time of these happenings on earth, and even before that time, in order that they might confess Jesus crucified as holy, just and as the true Son of God. This happened, for instance, with the centurion and many others mentioned in the Gospels, who went away from Calvary striking their breasts in sorrow. Among them were

not only those who previously had heard and believed his doctrine, but also a great number of such as had never seen Him or witnessed his miracles. For the same reason Pilate was also inspired not to change the title of the Cross which they had placed over the head of the Savior in Hebrew, Greek and Latin. For when the Jews protested and asked Him not to write: Jesus of Nazareth, King of the Jews; but: This one says, He is King of the Jews; Pilate answered: What is written, is written, and I do not wish it to be changed. All the inanimate creatures, by divine will, obeyed the command of the most holy Mary. From the noon hour until three o'clock in the afternoon, which was called the ninth hour, when the Lord expired, they exhibited the great disturbances and changes mentioned in the Gospels. The sun hid its light, the planets showed great alterations, the earth quaked, many mountains were rent; the rocks shook one against the other, the graves opened and sent forth some of the dead alive. The changes in the elements and in the whole universe were so notable and extraordinary that they were evident on the whole earth. All the Jews of Jerusalem were dismayed and astonished; although their outrageous perfidy and malice made them unworthy of the truth and hindered them from accepting what all the insensible creatures preached to them.

680. The soldiers who had crucified Jesus our Savior, according to a custom permitting the executioners to take possession of the property of those whom they executed, now proceeded to divide the garments of the innocent Lamb. The cloak or outside mantle, which by divine disposition they had brought to mount Calvary and which was the one Christ had laid aside at the washing of the feet, they divided among themselves, cutting it into four parts (John 19, 23). But the seamless tunic, by a mysterious decree of Providence, they did not divide, but they drew lots and assigned it entirely to the one who drew the lot for it; thus fulfilling the prophecy

in the twenty first Psalm. The mysterious signification of the undivided tunic is variously explained by the saints and doctors; one of these explanations being, that though the Jews lacerated and tore with wounds the sacred humanity of Christ our Lord, yet they could not touch or injure the Divinity which was enclosed in the sacred humanity; and whoever should draw the lot of justification by partaking of his Divinity, should thenceforward possess and enjoy it entirely.

681. As the wood of the Cross was the throne of his majesty and the chair of the doctrine of life, and as He was now raised upon it, confirming his doctrine by his example, Christ now uttered those words of highest charity and perfection: "Father, forgive them, for they know not what they do!" (Luke 23, 34.) This principle of charity and fraternal love the divine Teacher had appropriated to Himself and proclaimed by his own lips (John 15, 12; Matth. 15, 44). He now confirmed and executed it upon the Cross, not only pardoning and loving his enemies, but excusing those under the plea of ignorance whose malice had reached the highest point possible to men in persecuting, blaspheming and crucifying their God and Redeemer. Such was the difference between the behavior of ungrateful men favored with so great enlightenment, instruction and blessing; and the behavior of Jesus in his most burning charity while suffering the crown of thorns, the nails, and the Cross and unheard of blasphemy at the hands of men. O incomprehensible love! O ineffable sweetness! a patience inconceivable to man, admirable to the angels and fearful to the devils! One of the two thieves, called Dismas, became aware of some of the mysteries. Being assisted at the same time by the prayers and intercession of most holy Mary, he was interiorly enlightened concerning his Rescuer and Master by the first word on the Cross. Moved by true sorrow and contrition for his sins, he turned to his

companion and said: "Neither dost thou fear God, seeing that thou art under the same condemnation? And we indeed justly, for we receive the due reward of our deeds; but this Man hath done no evil." And thereupon speaking to Jesus, he said: "Lord, remember me when Thou shalt come into thy kingdom!" (Luke 23, 40.)

682. In this happiest of thieves, in the centurion, and in the others who confessed Jesus Christ on the Cross, began to appear the results of the Redemption. But the one most favored was this Dismas, who merited to hear the second word of the Savior on the Cross: "Amen, I say to thee, this day shalt thou be with Me in Paradise. "O fortunate thief, who, of all others, heard those words so much desired by all the saints and just of the earth! Such a word the ancient Patriarchs and Prophets did not hear; they had judged themselves very happy to be allowed to descend into limbo and wait through the long ages for paradise, which thou, in changing so happily thy condition, didst acquire in one moment. Thou hast now ceased to rob earthly possessions of thy neighbor, and immediately snatchest heaven from the hands of thy Master. Thou seizest it in justice and He yields it to thee in grace, since thou wast the last disciple of his doctrine on earth and the most alert of all in practicing it after having heard it from his mouth. Thou hast lovingly corrected thy brother, confessed thy Creator, reprehended those who blasphemed Him, imitated Him in patient suffering, asked Him humbly as thy Redeemer not to forget thy miseries; and He, as thy Exaulter, has at once fulfilled thy desires without delaying the guerdon merited for thee and all the mortals.

683. Having thus justified the good thief, Jesus turned his loving gaze upon his afflicted Mother, who with saint John was standing at the foot of the Cross. Speaking to both, he first addressed his Mother, saying:

"Woman, behold thy son!" and then to the Apostle: "Behold thy Mother!" (John 19, 26.) The Lord called Her Woman and not Mother, because this name of Mother had in it something of sweetness and consolation, the very pronouncing of which would have been a sensible relief. During his Passion He would admit of no exterior consolation, having renounced for that time all exterior alleviation and easement, as I have mentioned above. By this word "woman" he tacitly and by implication wished to say: Woman blessed among all women, the most prudent among all the daughters of Adam, Woman, strong and constant, unconquered by any fault of thy own, unfailing in my service and most faithful in thy love toward Me, which even the mighty waters of my Passion could not extinguish or resist (Cant. 8, 7), I am going to my Father and cannot accompany Thee further; my beloved disciple will attend upon Thee and serve Thee as his Mother, and he will be thy son. All this the heavenly Queen understood. The holy Apostle on his part received Her as his own from that hour on; for he was enlightened anew in order to understand and appreciate the greatest treasure of the Divinity in the whole creation next to the humanity of Christ our Savior. In this light He reverenced and served Her for the rest of her life, as I will relate farther on. Our Lady also accepted him as her son in humble subjection and obedience. Always practicing the highest possible perfection and holiness without failing on any occasion, and not permitting even the immensity of her present suffering to weigh down her magnanimous and most prudent heart, She promised then and there that She would show him this obedience during her whole life.

684. Already the ninth hour of the day was approaching, although the darkness and confusion of nature made it appear to be rather a chaotic night. Our Savior spoke the fourth word from the Cross in a loud and strong voice, so

that all the bystanders could hear it: "My God, my God, why hast thou forsaken Me?" (Matth. 27,46.) Although the Lord had uttered these words in his own Hebrew language, they were not understood by all. Since they began with: "Eli, Elli," some of them thought He was calling upon Elias, and a number of them mocked Him saying: "Let us see whether Elias shall come to free Him from our hands?" But the mystery concealed beneath these words was just as profound as it was unintelligible to the Jews and gentiles; and they have been interpreted in many ways by the doctors of the Church. I shall give the interpretation which has been manifested to me. The dereliction of which Christ speaks, was not one in which the Divinity separated from the humanity, dissolving the hypostatic union, nor including a cessation of the beatific vision in his soul; for both of these He enjoyed from the first moment of his conception by the Holy Ghost in the virginal womb and could never lose. But certainly the sacred humanity was in so far forsaken by the Divinity as it did not ward off death or the most bitter sorrows of his Passion; though, on the other hand, the eternal Father did not forsake Him entirely, since He showed his concern by causing the changes in the visible creation in order to give witness for his honor at his Death. Christ our Savior intimated quite a different dereliction by these words of complaint, one which originated from his immense love for men; namely, from his love of the foreknown as lost and the reprobate, which during his last hour caused in Him the same anguish as it did during his prayer in the garden. He grieved that his copious and superabundant Redemption, offered for the whole human race, should not be efficacious in the reprobate and that He should find Himself deprived of them in the eternal happiness, for which He had created and redeemed them. As this was to happen in consequence of the decree of his Father's eternal will, He lovingly and sorrowfully complained of it in the words: "My God, my God, why hast Thou forsaken Me?" that is, in so far as God deprived Him of the salvation of the reprobate.

685. In confirmation of this sorrow the Lord added: "I thirst!" The sufferings of the Lord and his anguish could easily cause a natural thirst. But for Him this was not a time to complain of this thirst or to quench it; and therefore Jesus would not have spoken of it so near to its expiration, unless in order to give expression to a most exalted mystery. He was thirsting to see the captive children of Adam make use of the liberty, which He merited for them and offered to them, and which so many were abusing. He was athirst with the anxious desire that all should correspond with Him in the faith and love due to Him, that they profit by his merits and sufferings, accept his friendship and grace now acquired for them, and that they should not lose the eternal happiness which He was to leave as an inheritance to those that wished to merit and accept it. This was the thirst of our Savior and Master; and the most blessed Mary alone understood it perfectly and began, with ardent affection and charity, to invite and interiorly to call upon all the poor, the afflicted, the humble, the despised and downtrodden to approach their Savior and thus quench, at least in part, his thirst which they could not quench entirely. But the perfidious Jews and the executioners, evidencing their unhappy hardheartedness, fastened a sponge soaked in gall and vinegar to a reed and mockingly raised it to his mouth, in order that He might drink of it. Thus was fulfilled the prophecy of David: "In my thirst they gave me vinegar to drink" (John 16, 28; Ps. 68, 22). Our most patient Savior tasted of it, partaking of this drink in mysterious submission to the condemnation of the reprobate. But at the instance of his blessed Mother He immediately desisted; because the Mother of grace was to be the portal

and Mediatrix of those who were to profit of the Passion and the Redemption of mankind.

686. In connection with this same mystery the Savior then pronounced the sixth word: "Consumma tum est," "It is consummated" (John 19, 29). Now is consummated this work of my coming from heaven and I have obeyed the command of my eternal Father, who sent Me to suffer and die for the salvation of mankind. Now are fulfilled the holy Scriptures, the prophecies and figures of the old Testament, and the course of my earthly and mortal life assumed in the womb of my Mother. Now are established on earth my example, my doctrines, my Sacraments and my remedies for the sickness of sin. Now is appeased the justice of my eternal Father in regard to the debt of the children of Adam. Now is my holy Church enriched with the remedies for the sins committed by men; the whole work of my coming into the world is perfected in so far as concerns Me, its Restorer; the secure foundation of the triumphant Church is now laid in the Church militant, so that nothing can overthrow or change it. These are the mysteries contained in the few words: "Consummatum est."

687. Having finished and established the work of Redemption in all its perfection, it was becoming that the incarnate Word, just as He came forth from the Father to enter mortal life (John 16, 8), should enter into immortal life of the Father through death. Therefore Christ our Savior added the last words uttered by Him:

"Father, into thy hands I commend my spirit." The Lord spoke these words in a loud and strong voice, so that the bystanders heard them. In pronouncing them He raised his eyes to heaven, as one speaking with the eternal Father, and with the last accent He gave up his spirit and inclined his head. By the divine force of these words Lucifer with all his demons were hurled into the deepest caverns of hell, there they lay motionless, as I shall relate in the next chapter. The invincible Queen and Mistress of all virtues understood these mysteries beyond the understanding of all creatures, as She was the Mother of the Savior and the Coadjutrix of his Passion. In order that She might participate in it to the end, just as She had felt in her own body the other torments of her Son, She now, though remaining alive, felt and suffered the pangs and agony of his death. She did not die in reality; but this was because God miraculously preserved her life, when according to the natural course death should have followed. This miraculous aid was more wonderful than all the other favors She received during the Passion. For this last pain was more intense and penetrating; and all that the martyrs and the men sentenced to death have suffered from the beginning of the world cannot equal what the blessed Mary suffered during the Passion. The great Lady remained at the foot of the Cross until evening, when the sacred body (as I shall relate) was interred. But in return for this last anguish of death, all that was still of this mortal life in the virginal body of the purest Mother, was more than ever exalted and spiritualized.

688. Of many of the sacraments and mysteries connected with the doings of Christ our Savior on the Cross the Evangelists make no mention; and we as Catholics can only form prudent conjectures founded upon the infallible certainty of our faith. But among those which have been manifested to me in this history, and concerning this part of the Passion, is a prayer, which Christ addressed to his eternal Father before speaking the seven words on the Cross recorded by the Evangelists. I call it a prayer because it was addressed to the Father; but in reality it was a last bequest or testament, which He made as a true and most wise Father in order to consign his possessions to his family, that is, to the whole human race. Even natural reason teaches us, that he who is the head

of a family or the lord over many or few possessions, would not be a prudent dispenser of his goods, and inattentive to his office or dignity, if at the hour of his death he would not make known his will in regard to the disposition of his goods and his estate, in order that each one of his family may know what belongs to him and may possess it justly and peacefully without recourse to lawsuits. For this very reason, and in order that they may set their minds at ease in preparation for the hour of death, men of the world make their last testaments. And even the religious resign the things permitted them for daily use, because in that hour earthly matters are apt to fill the mind with anxieties and prevent them from rising toward their Creator. Although earthly things could not disturb our Savior, since He neither possessed them, nor, if He had possessed any, could He be embarrassed by them in his infinite power; yet it was fitting, that He should in that hour dispose of the spiritual riches and treasures which He had amassed for mankind in the course of his pilgrimage.

689. Of these eternal goods the Savior made his last disposition on the Cross, distributing them and pointing out those who should be legitimate heirs and those who should be disinherited, and mentioning the reasons for the one as well as the other. All this He did in conference with his eternal Father, as the supreme Lord and most just Judge of all creatures; for in this testament are rehearsed the mysteries of the predestination of the saints and of the reprobation of the wicked. It was a testament hidden and sealed for mankind; only the blessed Mary understood it, because, in addition to her being informed of the operations of the divine Soul of Christ, She was also to be the universal Heiress of all creation. As She was the Coadjutrix of salvation, She was also to be the testamentary Executrix. For the Son placed all things in her hands, just as the Father had assigned the whole creation to Him. She was to execute his will and she was to

distribute all the treasures acquired and due to her Son as God on account of his infinite merits. This understanding has been given me as part of this history for the exaltation of our Queen and in order that sinners might approach Her as the Custodian of all the treasures gained by her Son and our Redeemer in the sight of his eternal Father. All help and assistance is in the hands of most holy Mary and She is to distribute it according to her most sweet kindness and liberality.

TESTAMENT MADE BY CHRIST OUR LORD ON THE CROSS IN HIS PRAYER TO THE ETERNAL FATHER.

690. When the holy wood of the Cross had been raised on mount Calvary, bearing aloft with it the incarnate Word crucified before speaking any of the seven words, Christ prayed interiorly to his heavenly Father and said: "My Father and eternal God, I confess and magnify Thee from this tree of the Cross, and I offer Thee a sacrifice of praise in my Passion and Death; for, by the hypostatic union with the divine nature, Thou hast raised my humanity to the highest dignity, that of Christ, the Godman, anointed with thy own Divinity. I confess Thee on account of the plenitude of the highest possible graces and glory, which from the first instant of my Incarnation Thou hast communicated to my humanity, and because from all eternity up to this present hour Thou hast consigned to me full dominion of the universe both in the order of grace and of nature. Thou hast made Me the Lord of the heavens and of the elements (Matth. 28, 18), of the sun, the moon and the stars; of fire and air, of the earth and the sea, of all the animate and inanimate creatures therein; Thou hast made Me the Disposer of the seasons, of the days and nights, with full lordship and possession according to my free will, and Thou hast set Me as the Head, the

King and Lord of all angels and men (Ephes, 1,21), to govern and command them, to punish the wicked and to reward the good (John 5, 22); Thou hast given Me the dominion and power of disposing all things from highest heavens to deepest abysses of hell (Apoc. 20, 1). Thou hast placed in my hands the eternal justification of men, the empires, kingdoms and principalities, the great and the little, the rich and the poor; and of all that are capable of thy grace and glory, Thou hast made Me the Justifier, the Redeemer and Glorifier, the universal Lord of all the human race, of life and death, of the holy Church, its treasures, laws and blessings of grace: all hast Thou, my Father, consigned to my hands, subjected to my will and my decrees, and for this I confess, exalt and magnify thy holy name."

691. "Now, at this moment, my Lord and eternal Father, when I am returning from this world to thy right hand through this death on the Cross, by which I completed the task of the Redemption of men assigned to Me, I desire that this same Cross shall be the tribunal of our justice and mercy. Nailed to it, I desire to judge those for whom I give my life. Having justified my cause, I wish to dispense the treasures of my coming into the world and of my Passion and Death to the just and the reprobate according as each one merits by his works of love or hatred. I have sought to gain all mortals and invited them to partake of my friendship and grace; from the first moment of my Incarnation I have ceaselessly labored for them; I have borne inconveniences, fatigues, insults, ignominies, reproaches, scourges, a crown of thorns, and now suffer the bitter death of the Cross; I have implored thy vast kindness upon all of them; I have watched in prayer, fasted and wandered about teaching them the way of eternal life. As far as in Me lay I have sought to secure eternal happiness for all men, just as I merited it for all, without excluding anyone. I have established and built up the law of grace and have

firmly and forever established the Church in which all human beings can be saved."

692. "But in our knowledge and foresight We are aware, my God and Father, that on account of their malice and rebellious obstinacy not all men desire to accept our eternal salvation, nor avail themselves of our mercy and of the way I have opened to them by my labors, life and death; but that many will prefer to follow their sinful ways unto perdition. Thou art just, my Lord and Father, and most equitable are thy judgments (Ps. 68, 137); and therefore it is right, since Thou hast made Me the Judge of the living and the dead, of the good and the bad (Act 10, 3), that I give to the good the reward of having served and followed Me, and to sinners the chastisement of their perverse obstinacy; that the just should share in my goods, and the wicked be deprived of the inheritance, which they refuse to accept. Now then, my eternal Father, in my and thy name and for thy glorification, I make my last bequest according to my human will, which is conformable to thy eternal and divine will. First shall be mentioned my most pure Mother, who gave Me human existence; Her I constitute my sole and universal Heiress of all the gifts of nature, of grace and of glory that are mine. She shall be Mistress and Possessor of them all. The gifts of grace, of which as a mere creature She is capable, She shall actually receive now, while those of glory I promise to confer upon Her in their time. I desire that She shall be Mistress of angels and men, claim over them full possession and dominion and command the service and obedience of all. The demons shall fear Her and be subject to Her. All the irrational creatures, the heavens, the stars, the planets, the elements with all the living beings, the birds, the fishes and the animals contained in them, shall likewise be subject to Her and acknowledge Her as Mistress, exalting and glorifying Her with Me. I wish also that She be the Treasurer and Dispenser of all the goods

in heaven and on earth. Whatever She ordains and disposes in my Church for my children, the sons of men, shall be confirmed by the three divine Persons; and whatever She shall ask for mortals now, afterwards and forever, We shall concede according to her will and wishes;"

693. "To the holy angels, who have obeyed thy holy and just will, I assign as habitation the highest heavens as their proper and eternal abode, and with it the joys of eternal vision and fruition of our Divinity. I desire that they enjoy its everlasting possession together with our company and friendship. I decree, that they recognize my Mother as their legitimate Queen and Lady, that they serve Her, accompany and attend upon Her, bear Her up in their hands in all places and times, obeying Her in all that She wishes to ordain and command. The demons, rebellious to our perfect and holy will, I cast out and deprive of our vision and company; again do I condemn them to our abhorrence, to eternal loss of our friendship and glory, to privation of the vision of my Mother, of the saints and of my friends, the just. I appoint and assign to them as their eternal dwelling the place most remote from our royal throne, namely the infernal caverns, the centre of the earth, deprived of light and full of the horrors of sensible darkness (Jude 6) . I decree this to be their portion and inheritance, as chosen by them in their pride and obstinacy against the divine Being and decrees. In those eternal dungeons of darkness they shall be tormented by everlasting and inextinguishable fire."

694. "From the multitudes of men, in the fullness of my good will, I call, select and separate all the just and the predestined, who through my grace save themselves by imitating Me, doing my will and obeying my holy law. These, next to my most pure Mother, I appoint as the inheritors of all my mysteries, my blessings, my sacramental treasures, of the mysteries concealed in the holy Scriptures; of my

humility, meekness of heart; of the virtues of faith, hope, and charity; of prudence, justice, fortitude and temperance; of my divine gifts and favors; of my Cross, labors, contempt, poverty and nakedness. This shall be their portion and inheritance in this present and mortal life. Since they must choose these in order to labor profitably, I assign to them the trials I have chosen for Myself in this life, as a pledge of my friendship, in order that they may undergo them with joy. I offer them my protection and defense, my holy inspirations, my favors and powerful assistance, my blessings and my justification, according to each one's disposition and degree of love. I promise to be to them a Father, a Brother and a Friend, and they shall be my chosen and beloved children, and as such I appoint them as the inheritors of all my merits and treasures without limitation. I desire that all who dispose themselves, shall partake of the goods of my holy Church and of the Sacraments; that, if they should lose my friendship, they shall be able to restore themselves and recover my graces and blessings through my cleansing blood. For all of them shall be open the intercession of my Mother and of the saints, and She shall recognize them as her children, shielding them and holding them as her own. My angels shall defend them, guide them, protect them and bear them up in their hands lest they stumble, and if they fall, they shall help them to rise" (Ps. 90, 11, 12).

695. "Likewise it is my will that my just and chosen ones shall stand high above the reprobate and the demons, that they shall be feared and obeyed by my enemies; that all the rational and irrational creatures shall serve them; that all the influences of the heavens, the planets and the stars shall favor them and give them life; that the earth, its elements and animals, shall sustain them; all the creatures, that are mine and serve Me, shall be theirs, and shall serve also them as my children and friends (I Cor. 3, 22; Wis. 16, 24), and their

blessing shall be in the dew of heaven and in the fruits of the earth (Genes. 27, 28). I wish to hold with them my delights (Pros. 8, 31), communicate to them my secrets, converse with them intimately and live with them in the militant Church in the species of bread and wine, as an earnest and an infallible pledge of the eternal happiness and glory promised to them; of it, I make them partakers and heirs, in order that they may enjoy it with Me in heaven by perpetual right and in unfailing beatitude."

696. "I consent that the foreknown and reprobate (though they were created for another and much higher end), shall be permitted to possess as their portion and inheritance the concupiscence of the flesh and the eyes (John 1, 216), pride in all its effects; that they eat and be satisfied with the dust of the earth, namely, with riches; with the fumes and the corruption of the flesh and its delights, and with the vanity and presumption of the world. For such possessions have they labored, and applied all the diligence of their mind and body; in such occupations have they consumed their powers, their gifts and blessings bestowed upon them by Us, and they have of their own free will chosen deceit, despising the truth I have taught them in the holy law (Rom. 2, 8). They have rejected the law which I have written in their hearts and the one inspired by my grace; they have despised my teachings and my blessings, and listened to my and their own enemies; they have accepted their deceits, have loved vanity (Ps. 4, 3), wrought injustice, followed their ambitions, sought their delight in vengeance, persecuted the poor, humiliated the just, mocked the simple and the innocent, strove to exalt themselves and desired to be raised above all the cedars of Lebanon in following the laws of injustice" (Ps. 36, 35).

697. "Since they have done all this in opposition to our divine goodness and remained obstinate in their malice, and since they have renounced the rights of sonship merited for

them by Me, I disinherit them of my friendship and glory. Just as Abraham separated the children of the slave, setting aside some possessions for them and reserving the principal heritage for Isaac, the son of the freedwoman Sarah (Gen. 25, 5), thus I set aside their claims on my inheritance by giving them the transitory goods, which they themselves have chosen. Separating them from our company and from that of my Mother, of the angels and saints, I condemn them to the eternal dungeons and the fire of hell in the company of Lucifer and his demons, whom they have freely served, I deprive them forever of all hope of relief. This is, O my Father, the sentence which I pronounce as the Head and the Judge of men and angels (Eph. 4, 15; Col. 2, 10), and this is the testament made at my Death, this is the effect of my Redemption, whereby each one is rewarded with that which he has justly merited according to his works and according to thy incomprehensible wisdom in the equity of thy strictest justice" (II Tim. 4, 8). Such was the prayer of Christ our Savior on the Cross to his eternal Father. It was sealed and deposited in the heart of the most holy Mary as the mysterious and sacramental testament, in order that through her intercession and solicitous care it might at its time, and even from that moment, be executed in the Church, just as it had before this time been prepared and perfected by the wise providence of God, in whom all the past and the future is always one with the present.

Words of the Queen

THE VIRGIN MARY SPEAKS TO SISTER MARY OF AGREDA

698. My daughter, seek with all the powers of thy mind during thy whole life to remember the mysteries manifested to thee in this chapter. I, as thy Mother and thy Instructress, shall ask the Lord by his divine power to impress in thy heart

the knowledge, which I have vouchsafed thee, in order that it may remain fixed and ever present to thee as long as thou livest. In virtue of this blessing keep in thy memory Christ crucified, who is my divine Son and thy Spouse, and never forget the sufferings of the Cross and the doctrine taught by Him upon it. This is the mirror by which thou must arrange all thy adornments and the source from which thou art to draw thy interior beauty, like a true daughter of the Prince (Ps. 44, 14), in order that thou mayest be prepared, proceed and reign as the spouse of the supreme King. As this honorable title obliges thee to seek with all thy power to imitate Him as far as is becoming thy station and possible to thee by his grace, and as this is to be the true fruit of my doctrine, I wish that from today on thou live crucified with Christ, entirely assimilated to thy exemplar and model and dead to this earthly life (II Cor. 5, 15). I desire that in thee shall vanish the effects of the first sin, that thou live only for the operations and movements of divine virtue, and that thou renounce thy inheritance as a daughter of the first Adam, in order that in thee may bear fruit the inheritance of the second Adam, who is Jesus Christ, thy Redeemer and Teacher.

699. Thy state of life must be for thee a most rigid cross on which thou must remain crucified, and thou must not widen thy path by seeking for dispensation and weakening interpretation of thy rules to make it easy and comfortable, but at the same time, insecure and full of imperfections. This is the deception into which the children of Babylon and of Adam fall, that each one according to his state seeks to find ease in the work commanded by the law of God. They set aside the salvation of their soul in their efforts to buy heaven very cheaply, or risk losing it by dreading the restrictions and entire subjection necessary to observe rigorously the divine law and its precepts. Hence arises the desire to find explana-

tions and opinions, which smooth the paths and highways of eternal life, without heeding the doctrine of my divine Son, that the path of life is very narrow (Matth. 7, 14). They forget that the Lord himself has walked these narrow paths, in order that no one might imagine he can reach eternal life over paths more spacious and comfortable to the flesh and to the inclinations vitiated by sins. This danger is greater for ecclesiastics and religious, who by their very state must follow the Master and must accommodate themselves to his life of poverty and must choose for this purpose the way of the Cross. Some of them however are apt to seek the dignities attached to the religious state for their temporal advantage, for the increase of their own honor and praise. In order to secure it they lighten the Cross they have promised to bear, so that they live a carnal life, little restricted and much eased by deceptive dispensations and vain excuses. In their time they shall recognize the truth and that saying of the Holy Ghost: Each one thinks his path secure, but the Lord weighs in his hands the hearts of men (Prov. 21, 2).

700. So far from this deceit, do I wish thee to be, my daughter, that thou must live strictly up to the most rigorous demands of thy profession; in such a way that thou canst not stretch thyself in any way, being nailed immovably to the Cross with Christ. Thou must set aside all temporal advantages, for the least point pertaining to the utmost perfection of thy state. Thy right hand, my daughter, must be nailed to the Cross by obedience, and reserve not for thyself the least movement, the least activity, or word, or thought not controlled by this virtue. Thou must not maintain any position that is of thy own choice, but only such as is willed by others; thou must not appear wise in thy own conceit in anything, but ignorant and blind, in order to follow entirely the guidance of thy superiors (Prov. 3, 7). He that promises, says the wise man (Prov. 6, 1), binds his hands, and by his

words shall he be bound and chained. Thou hast bound thy hand by the vow of obedience and hast thereby lost thy liberty and thy right of wishing or not wishing. Thy left hand thou hast nailed to the Cross by the vow of poverty, depriving thee of all right to follow any inclination toward the objects usually coveted by the eyes; for both in the use and in the desire for such creatures thou must rigorously imitate Christ impoverished and despoiled upon the Cross. By the third vow, that of chastity, thy feet are nailed to the Cross, in order that all thy steps and movements may be pure, chaste and beautiful. For this thou must not permit in thy presence the least word offensive to purity, nor, by looking upon or touching any human creature, allow any sensual image or impression within thee; thy eyes and all thy senses are to remain consecrated to chastity, without making more use of them than to fix them upon Jesus crucified. The fourth vow, of perpetual enclosure, thou wilt maintain in the bosom of my divine Son, to which I consign thee. In order that this doctrine may appear to thee sweet, and this path less narrow, contemplate and consider in thy heart the image of my Son and Lord full of blood, torments, sorrows, and at last nailed to the Cross, no part of his sacred body being exempt from wounds and excruciating pains. The Lord and I were most solicitous and compassionate toward all the children of men; for them We suffered and endured such bitter sorrows, in order that they might be encouraged not to refuse less severe sufferings for their own eternal good and in return for so obliging a love. Therefore let mortals show themselves thankful, willingly entering upon the rough and thorny path and accepting the Cross, to bear it after Christ. Thus will they walk upon the direct path toward heaven and gain an eternal happiness (Matth. 16,24).

Chapter XXIII

THE TRIUMPH OF CHRIST OUR SAVIOR OVER THE DEMON ON THE CROSS; HIS DEATH AND THE PROPHECY OF HABBACUC; THE COUNCIL OF THE DEMONS IN HELL.

701. The hidden and venerable mysteries of this chapter correspond to many others scattered through the whole extent of this history. One of them is, that Lucifer and his demons in the course of the life and miracles of our Savior, never could ascertain fully whether the Lord was true God and Redeemer of the world, and consequently what was the dignity of the most holy Mary. This was so disposed by divine Providence, in order that the whole mystery of the Incarnation and the Redemption of the human race might be more fittingly accomplished. Lucifer, although knowing that God was to assume human flesh, nevertheless knew nothing of the manner and the circumstances of the Incarnation. As he was permitted to form an opinion of this mystery in accordance with his pride, he was full of hallucinations, sometimes believing Christ to be God on account of his miracles, sometimes rejecting such an opinion on account of seeing Him poor, humiliated, afflicted and fatigued. Harassed by these contradicting evidences, he remained in doubt and continued his inquiries until the predestined hour of Christ's Death on the Cross, where, in virtue of the Passion and Death of the sacred humanity, which he had himself

brought about, he was to be both undeceived and vanquished by the full solution of these mysteries.

702. This triumph of Christ our Savior was accomplished in such an exalted and miraculous manner, that I feel the sluggishness and insufficiency of my powers to describe it. It took place in a manner too spiritual and too far removed from the perception of the senses, according to which I must describe its process. In order to manifest it, I should wish we were able to speak and understand one another by means of the simple intercourse and vision peculiar to the angels; for such would be necessary in order to describe and understand correctly this great miracle of the omnipotence of God. I shall say what I can and leave the understanding of it more to the enlightenment of faith than to the signification of my words.

703. In the preceding chapter I have said that Lucifer and his demons, as soon as they saw the Lord taking the Cross upon his sacred shoulders, wished to fly and cast themselves into hell; for at that moment they began to feel with greater force the operations of his divine power. By divine intervention this new torment made them aware that the Death of this innocent Man, whose destruction they had plotted and who could not be a mere man, threatened great ruin to themselves. They therefore desired to withdraw and they ceased to incite the Jews and the executioners, as they had done hitherto. But the command of the most blessed Mary, enforced by the divine power, detained them and, enchained like fiercest dragons, compelled them to accompany Christ to Calvary. The ends of the mysterious chain that bound them were placed into the hands of Mary, the great Queen, who, by the power of her divine Son, held them all in subjection and bondage. Although they many times sought to break away and raged in helpless fury, they could not overcome the power of the heavenly Lady. She forced them to come to

Calvary and stand around the Cross, where She commanded them to remain motionless and witness the end of the great mysteries there enacted for the salvation of men and the ruin of themselves.

704. Lucifer and his infernal hosts were so overwhelmed with pains and torments by the presence of the Lord and his blessed Mother, and with the fear of their impending ruin, that they would have felt greatly relieved to be allowed to cast themselves into the darkness of hell. As this was not permitted them, they fell upon one another and furiously fought with each other like hornets disturbed in their nest, or like a brood of vermin confusedly seeking some dark shelter. But their rabid fury was not that of animals, but that of demons more cruel than dragons. Then the haughty pride of Lucifer saw itself entirely vanquished and all his proud thoughts of setting his throne above the stars of heaven and drinking dry the waters of the Jordan put to shame (Is. 14, 13; Job 40, 18). How weak and annihilated was now he, who so often had presumed to overturn the whole earth. How downcast and confounded he, who had deceived so many souls by false promises and vain threats! How dismayed this unhappy one at the sight of the gibbet, where he had sought to place Mardocheus! (Esther 7, 9). What horrid shame to see the true Esther, most holy Mary, asking for the rescue of her people and the downfall of the traitor and the chastisement of his pride! There our invincible Judith beheaded him (Judith 13, 10); there She trod upon his haughty neck. From now on, O Lucifer, I know that thy arrogance and pride is much greater than thy strength (Is. 16, 6). Instead of splendor now worms clothe thee about (Is. 14, 11), and rottenness envelops and consumes thy carrion corpse! Thou, who hast afflicted the nations, art now more wounded, bound and oppressed than all the world. Thenceforward I do not fear

thy counterfeit threats; I will no longer listen to thy wiles; for I see thee reduced, weakened and entirely helpless.

705. The time had now come for this ancient dragon to be vanquished by the Master of life. As this was to be the hour of his disillusionment, and as this poisonous asp was not to escape it by stopping his ears to the voice of the Enchanter (Ps, 57, 5), the Lord began to speak the seven words from his Cross, at the same time providing that Lucifer and his demons should understand the mysteries therein contained. For it was by this disclosure that the Lord wished to triumph over them, over sin and death, and despoil them of their tyrannous power over the human race. The Savior then pronounced the first word: "Father, forgive them, for they know not what they do!" (Luke 23, 34). By these words the princes of darkness came to the full conviction, that Christ our Lord was speaking to the eternal Father, that He was his natural Son and the true God with Him and the Holy Ghost, that He had permitted death in his most sacred and perfect humanity, united to the Divinity for the salvation of the whole human race; that now He offered his infinitely precious merits for the pardon of the sins of all those children of Adam, who should avail themselves thereof for their rescue, not excepting even the wretches that crucified Him. At this discovery Lucifer and his demons were thrown into such fury and despair that they instantly wished to hurl themselves impetuously to the depths of hell and strained all their powers to accomplish it in spite of the powerful Queen.

706. In the second word spoken by the Lord to the fortunate thief: "Amen I say to thee, today thou shalt be with Me in paradise," the demons understood that the fruits of the Redemption in the justification of sinners ended in the glorification of the just. They were made aware that from this hour the merits of Christ would commence to act with a new force and strength, that through them should be opened the

gates of Paradise, which had been closed by the first sin, and that from now on men would enter upon eternal happiness and occupy their destined heavenly seats, which until now had been impossible for them. They perceived the power of Christ to call sinners, justify and beautify them, and they felt the triumphs gained over themselves by the exalted virtues, the humility, patience, meekness and all the virtues of his life. The confusion and torment of Lucifer at seeing this cannot be explained by human tongue; but it was so great, that he humiliated himself so far as to beg the most blessed Virgin to permit them to descend into hell and be cast out from her presence; but the great Queen would not consent, as the time had not yet arrived.

707. At the third word spoken by the Lord to his Mother: "Woman, behold thy son!" the demons discovered that this heavenly Lady was the true Mother of the Godman, the same Woman whose likeness and prophetic sign had been shown to them in the heavens at their creation, and who was to crush their head as announced by the Lord in the terrestrial paradise. They were informed of the dignity and excellence of this great Lady over all creatures, and of her power which they were even now experiencing. As they had from the beginning of the world and from the creation of the first woman, used all their astuteness to find out who this great woman that was announced in the heavens could be, and as they now discovered Her in Mary, whom they had until now overlooked, these dragons were seized with inexpressible fury; their having been thus mistaken crushed their arrogance beyond all their other torments, and in their fury they raged against their own selves like bloodthirsty lions, while their helpless wrath against the heavenly Lady was increased a thousand fold. Moreover, they discerned that saint John was appointed by Christ our Lord as the angel guardian of his Mother, endowed with the powers of the priesthood. This

they understood to be in the nature of a threat against their own wrath, which was well known to saint John. Lucifer saw not only the power of the Evangelist, but that given to all the priests in virtue of their participation in the dignity and power of our Redeemer; and that the rest of the just, even though not priests, were placed under the special protection of the Lord and made powerful against hell. All this paralyzed the strength of Lucifer and his demons.

708. The fourth word of Christ was addressed to the eternal Father: "God, my God, why hast Thou forsaken Me?" The evil spirits discovered in these words that the charity of God toward men was boundless and everlasting; that, in order to satisfy it, He had mysteriously suspended the influence of the Divinity over his most sacred humanity, thus permitting his sufferings to reach the highest degree and drawing from them the most abundant fruits; that He was aware and lovingly complained of his being deprived of the salvation of a part of the human race; how ready He was to suffer more, if such would be ordained by the eternal Father. Man's good fortune in being so beloved by God increased the envy of Lucifer and his demons, and they foresaw the divine Omnipotence following out this immense love without limitation. This knowledge crushed the haughty malice of the enemies and they were made well aware of their own weakness and helplessness in opposing this love, if men themselves should not choose to neglect its influence.

709. The fifth word of Christ, "I thirst," confirmed Christ's triumph over the devil and his followers; they were filled with wrath and fury because the Lord clearly let them see their total overthrow. By these words they understood Him to say to them: If what I suffer for men and my love for them seem great to you, be assured that my love for them is still unsatiated, that it continues to long for their eternal salvation, and that the mighty waters of torments and suffer-

ings have not extinguished it (Cant. 8, 7). Much more would I suffer for them, if it were necessary, in order to deliver them from your tyranny and make them powerful and strong against your malice and pride.

710. In the sixth word of the Lord: "It is consummated!" Lucifer and his hordes were informed that the mystery of the Incarnation and Redemption was now accomplished and entirely perfected according to the decree of divine wisdom. For they were made to feel that Christ our Redeemer had obediently fulfilled the will of the eternal Father; that He had accomplished all the promises and prophecies made to the world by the ancient Fathers; that his humility and obedience had compensated for their own pride and disobedience in heaven in not having subjected themselves and acknowledged Him as their Superior in human flesh; and that they were now through the wisdom of God justly humbled and vanquished by the very Lord whom they despised. The great dignity and the infinite merits of Christ demanded that in this very hour He should exercise his office and power of Judge over angels and men, such as had been conceded to Him by the eternal Father. He now applied this power by hurling this sentence at Lucifer and all his followers, that, being condemned to eternal fire, they instantly depart into the deepest dungeons of hell. This very sentence was included in the pronouncing of the seventh word: "Father, into thy hands I commend my spirit!" (Luke 23,46.) The mighty Queen and Mother concurred with the will of her Son Jesus and united with his command that Lucifer and all demons depart to the infernal depths. In virtue of these decrees of the supreme King and of the Queen, the evil spirits were routed from Calvary and precipitated to deepest hell more violently and suddenly than a flash of light through the riven clouds.

711. Christ our Savior, as the triumphant Conqueror having vanquished the great enemy, now yielded up his spirit to

the Father and permitted death to approach by inclining his head (John 19, 30). By this permission He also vanquished death, which had been equally deceived in Him with the demons. For death could not attack men, or had any jurisdiction of them, except through the first sin, of which it was a punishment. On this account the Apostle says that the weapon or the sting of death is sin, which opens up the wounds by which death enters into the world of humanity (Rom. 5, 12); and as our Savior paid the debt of sin which He could not commit, therefore, when death took away his life without the shadow of justice, it lost the power which it had over the other sons of Adam (I Cor. 15,55). Thenceforward neither death nor the devil could attack men, unless they, failing to avail themselves of the victory of Christ, should again subject themselves of their own free will. If our first Father Adam had not sinned and we ourselves in him, we would not suffer the punishment of death, but merely pass over to the happiness of the eternal fatherland. But sin has made us its subjects and slaves of the devil. He avails himself of death to deprive us first of the grace, the blessings and the friendship of God. Thereby he also prevents us from reaching eternal life and we remain in the slavery of sin and the devil, subject to his tyrannous power (I John 3, 8). Our Savior Christ despoiled the demon of all these advantages and, in dying without sin and satisfying for our own, merited that our death should be a death of the body only, and not of the soul; that it should have power to take away our temporal life, but not our eternal; the natural, not the spiritual; and that it should thenceforward be merely the portal to the eternal happiness, if we ourselves did not renounce that blessing. Thus the Lord satisfied for the chastisements due to the first sin, at the same time furnishing us a means of offering a compensation in our own name by accepting our natural and bodily death for the love of God. Christ absorbed death (I Cor. 15, 51) and offered his own as a bait for deceiving death (Osee. 13, 14). By his Death He put an end of its power, overcame it, and was the Death of death itself.

712. In this triumph the Savior fulfilled the prophecy contained in the canticle and prayer of Habbacuc, of which I shall select some passages necessary for my purpose. The prophet was informed of the mystery and the power of Christ over death and the devil. In prophetic foresight he prayed that the Lord vivify the work of his hands, that is, man; that in his greatest wrath He remember his mercy. He prophesied that the glory of this miracle should fill the heavens and the praise of it, the earth; that its splendor shall be as that of light; that in his hands He shall embrace the horns, which are the arms of the Cross and wherein is hidden his strength; that death should fly from Him captive and vanquished; that before his feet the devil should be routed and measure the earth (Habac. 3, 25). All this was fulfilled to the letter; for Lucifer departed having his head crushed under the feet of Christ and his blessed Mother, who subdued Him by their sufferings and by their power. Since the devil was forced to cast himself to lowest hell, which is the middle of the earth and farthest removed from its surface, he is said to measure the earth. The rest of the canticle pertains to the triumph of Christ our Lord in the succeeding ages of the Church; but that need not be rehearsed here. It is, however, proper for men to understand that Lucifer and his demons were restricted, lamed and weakened in their power of tempting the rational creatures, unless their sins and their own free will do not again unbind them and encourage them to return for the destruction of the world. All this will be better understood from the proceedings of the infernal council held in hell and from what I shall say further in the course of this history.

COUNCIL HELD BY LUCIFER AND HIS DEMONS IN HELL
AFTER THE DEATH OF CHRIST OUR LORD.

713. The rout of Lucifer and his angels from Calvary to the
abyss of hell was more violent and disastrous than their first
expulsion from heaven. Though, as holy Job says (Job 10,
21), that place is a land of darkness, covered with the shades
of death, full of gloomy disorder, misery, torments and
confusion; yet on this occasion the chaos and disorder was a
thousand fold increased; because the damned were made to
feel new horror and additional punishments at the sudden
meeting of the ferocious demons in their rabid fury. It is
certain that the devils have not the power of assigning the
damned to a place of greater or lesser torment; for all their
torments are decreed by divine justice according to the
measure of the demerits of each of the condemned. But,
besides this essential punishment, the just Judge allows them
to suffer other accidental punishments from time to time
according to occasion; for their sins have left roots in the
world and cause much damage to others, who are damned on
their account, and the new effects still arising from former
sins cause such accidental punishments in the damned. Thus
the demons devised new torments for Judas, for having sold
and brought about the death of Christ. They also understood
then that this place of dreadful punishments, where they had
thrown him and of which I have spoken above, was destined
for the chastisement of those who damned themselves by
refusing to practice their faith in their lives and for those who
purposely refuse to believe and avail themselves of the fruits
of the Redemption. Against these the devils execute a more
furious wrath, similar to the one they have conceived against
Jesus and Mary.

714. As soon as Lucifer was permitted to proceed in these
matters and arise from the consternation in which he remained for some time, he set about proposing to his fellow

demons new plans of his pride. For this purpose he called them all together and placing himself in an elevated position, he spoke to them: "To you, who have for so many ages followed and still follow my standards for the vengeance of my wrongs, is known the injury which I have now sustained at the hands of this Mangod, and how for thirty-three years He has led me about in deceit, hiding his Divinity and concealing the operations of his soul, and how He has now triumphed over us by the very Death which we have brought upon Him. Before He assumed flesh I hated Him and refused to acknowledge Him as being more worthy than I to be adored by the rest of creation. Although on account of this resistance I was cast out from heaven with you and was degraded to this abominable condition so unworthy of my greatness and former beauty, I am even more tormented to see myself thus vanquished and oppressed by this Man and by his Mother. From the day on which the first man was created I have sleeplessly sought to find Them and destroy Them; or if I should not be able to destroy Them, I at least wished to bring destruction upon all his creatures and induce them not to acknowledge Him as their God, and that none of them should ever draw any benefit from his works. This has been my intent, to this all my solicitude and efforts were directed. But in vain, since He has overcome me by his humility and poverty, crushed me by his patience, and at last has despoiled me of the sovereignty of the world by his Passion and frightful Death. This causes me such an excruciating pain, that, even if I succeeded in hurling Him from the right hand of his Father, where He sits triumphant, and if I should draw all the souls redeemed down into this hell, my wrath would not be satiated or my fury placated."

715. "Is it possible that the human nature, so inferior to my own, shall be exalted above all the creatures! That it should be so loved and favored, as to be united to the Crea-

tor in the person of the eternal Word! That He should first make war upon me before executing this work, and afterwards overwhelm me with such confusion! From the beginning I have held this humanity as my greatest enemy; it has always filled me with intolerable abhorrence. O men, so favored and gifted by your God, whom I abhor, and so ardently loved by Him! How shall I hinder your good fortune? How shall I bring upon you my unhappiness, since I cannot destroy the existence you have received? What shall we now begin, O my followers? How shall we restore our reign? How shall we recover our power over men? How shall we overcome them? For if men from now on shall not be most senseless and ungrateful, if they are not worse disposed than we ourselves toward this Godman, who has redeemed them with so much love, it is clear that all of them will eagerly follow Him; none will take notice of our deceits; they will abhor the honors which we insidiously offer them, and will love contempt; they will seek the mortification of the flesh and will discover the danger of carnal pleasure and ease; they will despise riches and treasures, and love the poverty so much honored by their Master; and all that we can offer to their appetites they will abhor in imitation of their true Redeemer. Thus will our reign be destroyed, since no one will be added to our number in this place of confusion and torments; all will reach the happiness which we have lost, all will humiliate themselves to the dust and suffer with patience; and my wrath and haughtiness will avail me nothing."

716. "Ah, woe is me, what torment does this mistake cause me! When I tempted Him in the desert, the only result was to afford Him a chance to leave the example of this victory, by following which men can overcome me so much the more easily. My persecutions only brought out more clearly his doctrine of humility and patience. In persuading Judas to betray Him, and the Jews to subject Him to the

deadly torture of the Cross, I merely hastened my ruin and the salvation of men, while the doctrine I sought to blot out was only the more firmly implanted. How could One who is God humiliate Himself to such an extent? How could He bear so much from men who are evil? How could I myself have been led to assist so much in making this salvation so copious and wonderful? O how godlike is the power of that Man which could torment and weaken me so? And how can this Woman, his Mother and my Enemy, be so mighty and invincible in her opposition to me? New is such power in a mere creature, and no doubt She derived it from the divine Word, whom She clothed in human flesh. Through this Woman the Almighty has ceaselessly waged war against me, though I have hated Her in my pride from the moment I recognized Her in her image or heavenly sign. But if my proud indignation is not to be assuaged, I benefit nothing by my perpetual war against this Redeemer, against his Mother and against men. Now then, ye demons who follow me, now is the time to give way to our wrath against God. Come all of ye to take counsel what we are to do; for I desire to hear your opinions."

717. Some of the principal demons gave their answers to this dreadful proposal, encouraging Lucifer by suggesting diverse schemes for hindering the fruit of the Redemption among men. They all agreed that it was not possible to injure the person of Christ, to diminish the immense value of his merits, to destroy the efficacy of the Sacraments, to falsify or abolish the doctrine which Christ had preached; yet they resolved that, in accordance with the new order of assistance and favor established by God for the salvation of men, they should now seek new ways of hindering and preventing the work of God by so much the greater deceits and temptations. In reference to these plans some of the astute and malicious demons said: "It is true, that men now have at their disposal

a new and very powerful doctrine and law, new and efficacious Sacraments. a new Model and Instructor of virtues, a powerful Intercessor and Advocate in this Woman; yet the natural inclinations and passions of the flesh remain just the same, and the sensible and delectable creatures have not changed their nature. Let us then, making use of this situation with increased astuteness, foil as far as in us lies the effects of what this Godman has wrought for men. Let us begin strenuous warfare against mankind by suggesting new attractions, exciting them to follow their passions in forgetfulness of all else. Thus men, being taken up with these dangerous things, cannot attend to the contrary."

718. Acting upon this counsel they redistributed the spheres of work among themselves, in order that each squadron of demons might, with a specialized astuteness, tempt men to different vices. They resolved to continue to propagate idolatry in the world, so that men might not come to the knowledge of the true God and the Redemption. Wherever idolatry would fail, they concluded to establish sects and heresies, for which they would select the most perverse and depraved of the human race as leaders and teachers of error. Then and there was concocted among these malignant spirits the sect of Mahomet, the heresies of Arius, Pelagius, Nestorius, and whatever other heresies have been started in the world from the first ages of the Church until now, together with those which they have in readiness, but which it is neither necessary nor proper to mention here. Lucifer showed himself content with these infernal counsels as being opposed to divine truth and destructive of the very foundation of man's rescue, namely divine faith. He lavished flattering praise and high offices upon those demons, who showed themselves willing and who undertook to find the impious originators of these errors.

719. Some of the devils charged themselves with perverting the inclinations of children at their conception and birth; others to induce parents to be negligent in the education and instruction of their children, either through an inordinate love or aversion, and to cause a hatred of parents among the children. Some offered to create hatred between husbands and wives, to place them in the way of adultery, or to think little of the fidelity promised to their conjugal partners. All agreed to sow among men the seeds of discord, hatred and vengeance, proud and sensual thoughts, desire of riches or honors, and by suggesting sophistical reasons against all the virtues Christ has taught; above all they intended to weaken the remembrance of his Passion and Death, of the means of salvation, and of the eternal pains of hell. By these means the demons hoped to burden all the powers and the faculties of men with solicitude for earthly affairs and sensual pleasures, leaving them little time for spiritual thoughts and their own salvation.

720. Lucifer heard these different suggestions of the demons, and answering them, he said: "I am much beholden to you for your opinions: I approve of them and adopt them all; it will be easy to put them into practice with those, who do not profess the law given by this Redeemer to men, though with those who accept and embrace these laws, it will be a difficult enterprise. But against this law and against those that follow it, I intend to direct all my wrath and fury and I shall most bitterly persecute those who hear the doctrine of this Redeemer and become his disciples; against these must our most relentless battle be waged to the end of the world. In this new Church I must strive to sow my cockle (Matth. 14, 25), the ambitions, the avarice, the sensuality, and the deadly hatreds, with all the other vices, of which I am the head. For if once these sins multiply and increase among the faithful, they will, with their concomitant malice and ingrati-

tude, irritate God and justly deprive men of the helps of grace left to them by the merits of the Redeemer. If once they have thus despoiled themselves of these means of salvation, we shall have assured victory over them. We must also exert ourselves to weaken piety and all that is spiritual and divine; so that they do not realize the power of the Sacraments and receive them in mortal sin, or at least without fervor and devotion. For since these Sacraments are spiritual, it is necessary to receive them with well-disposed will, in order to reap their fruits. If once they despise the medicine, they shall languish in their sickness and be less able to withstand our temptations; they will not see through our deceits, they will let the memory of their Redeemer and of the intercession' of his Mother slip from their minds. Thus will their foul ingratitude make them unworthy of grace and so irritate their God and Savior, as to deprive them of his helps. In all this I wish, that all of you assist me strenuously, losing neither time nor occasion for executing my commands."

721. It is not possible to rehearse all the schemes of this dragon and his allies concocted at that time against the holy Church and her children, in order that these waters of Jordan might be swallowed up in his throat (Job 40, 18). It is enough to state that they spent nearly a full year after the Death of Christ in conferring and considering among themselves the state of the world up to that time and the changes wrought by Christ our God and Master through his Death and after having manifested the light of his faith by so many miracles, blessings and examples of holy men. If all these labors have not sufficed to draw all men to the way of salvation, it can be easily understood, that Lucifer should have prevailed and that his wrath should be so great, as to cause us justly to say with saint John:

"Woe to the earth, for satan is come down to you full of wrath and fury!" But alas! that truths so infallible and so much to be dreaded and avoided by men, should in our days be blotted from the minds of mortals to the irreparable danger of the whole world! Our enemy is astute, cruel and watchful: we sleepy, lukewarm and careless! What wonder that Lucifer has entrenched himself so firmly in the world, when so many listen to him, accept and follow his deceits, so few resist him, and entirely forget the eternal death, which he so furiously and maliciously seeks to draw upon them? I beseech those, who read this, not to forget this dreadful danger. If they are not convinced of this danger through the evil condition of the world and through the evils each one experiences himself, let them at least learn of this danger by the vast and powerful remedies and helps, which the Savior thought it necessary to leave behind in his Church. For He would not have provided such antidotes if our ailment and danger of eternal death were not so great and formidable.

Words of the Queen

THE VIRGIN MARY SPEAKS TO SISTER MARY OF AGREDA

722. My daughter, by divine enlightenment thou hast received a deep understanding of the glorious triumph of my Son and Lord on the Cross over the demons and of their rout and vanquishment. But thou must remember that thou art yet ignorant of much more than what thou knowest concerning these ineffable mysteries. For in mortal flesh the creature cannot comprehend them in their reality, and divine Providence reserves the full understanding of them as a reward of the saints in heaven and for the beatific vision, in which these mysteries will be comprehended clearly. This insight will also be given to the reprobate, to each one according to his degree, for their confusion and punishment at the end of their career. But what thou hast learned will suffice to apprise thee of the dangers of this mortal life and to enliven thy hope of

overcoming thy enemies. I wish also to warn thee of the new wrath, which the dragon has conceived especially against thee for what thou hast written in this chapter. He has ceaselessly pursued thee with his wrath and has sought to hinder thee from writing my life, as thou hast experienced continually in this work. But now his haughty pride is incensed against thee especially, because thou hast revealed his humiliation, his crushing ruin at the Death of my most blessed Son, the condition in which it left him and the secret counsels for revenging himself upon the children of Adam and especially upon the members of the holy church. All this has excited and disturbed him anew, seeing that these secrets will be revealed to those yet ignorant of them. Thou wilt feel his wrath in the difficulties he will place in thy way, the temptations and persecutions thou hast already encountered. Therefore I warn thee to be wary and circumspect against the rabid fury and cruelty of thy enemy.

723. Thou art astonished, and justly, to see, on the one hand, the power of my Son's merits and of his Redemption, the ruin and weakness caused by the demons in men; and, on the other hand, to see the power of the devil lording it over the world in haughty presumption. Although the light given to thee in writing this history is equal to this astonishment, I wish to add still another point of information, in order that thou mayest guard thyself so much the more carefully against enemies so full of malice. It is certain, that when hell came to the full knowledge of the sacrament of the Incarnation and Redemption, and of the poverty, humility and lowliness of the birth of Jesus, of his life and miracles, ending in the mysterious Passion and Death, and of all the rest of his labors to draw men to Him, Lucifer and his demons were weakened and disabled and they saw that they could not tempt the faithful in the same way as the rest of men and as they ceaselessly desire to do. In the primitive Church this terror and

fear of the baptized, and of the followers of Christ our Lord, continued many years; for the divine virtues shone forth brightly in their imitation of Christ, in their zeal in confessing the faith, in following the teachings of the Gospel, in practicing heroic virtues and most fervent love, humility, patience and contempt of the vanities and deceits of the world. Many shed their blood and gave their life for Christ the Lord; they performed many admirable and exalted deeds for the glory of his name. This invincible fortitude resulted from their living at a time so near to the Passion and Death of their Redeemer and so close to the prodigious example of his patience and humility; but also because they were less tempted by the devils, who could not so soon rise from the crushing defeat brought upon them by the triumph of the crucified God.

724. This close imitation and living reproduction of Christ, confronting the demons in the first children of the Church, they feared so much, that they dared not approach and they precipitously fled from the Apostles and the just ones imbued with the doctrines of my divine Son. In them were offered up to the Almighty the first fruits of grace, and of Redemption. What is seen in the saints and in perfect Christians in those times, would happen in the present times with all the Catholics if they would accept grace and work with it instead of permitting it to go to waste, and if they would seek the way of the Cross; for Lucifer fears it just as much now as in the times thou hast been writing of. But soon the charity, zeal and devotion in many of the faithful began to grow cold and they forgot the blessings of the Redemption; they yielded to their carnal inclinations and desires, they loved vanity and avarice, and permitted themselves to be fascinated and deceived by the false pretenses of Lucifer, obscuring the glory of their Savior and inveigling them into the meshes of their mortal enemies. This foul

ingratitude has thrown the world into the present state and has encouraged the demons to rise up in their pride against God, audaciously presuming to possess themselves of all the children of Adam on account of this forgetfulness and carelessness of Catholics. They presume to plot the destruction of the whole Church by the perversion of so many who have fallen away from it; and by inducing those who are in it, to think little of it, or by hindering them from producing the fruits of the blood and death of their Redeemer. The greatest misfortune is, that many Catholics fail to recognize this great damage and do not seriously think of a remedy, although they can presume that the times, of which Jesus forewarned the women of Jerusalem, have arrived; namely, those in which the sterile should be happy, and in which many would call upon the mountains and the hills to cover and fall upon them, in order not to see the devastation of wickedness cutting down the sons of perdition, the dried trees, barren of all the fruits of virtue. In these evil times dost thou live, my dearest; and in order that thou mayest not be included in the perdition of so many souls, do thou bewail it in the bitterness of thy heart, never forgetting the mysteries of the Incarnation, Passion and Death of my Divine Son. I desire thee to give thanks in compensation for the great number of those, who forget it, and I assure thee that the mere memory and contemplation of these mysteries are terrible to hell, torment and drive away the demons, and that they avoid and fly those who thankfully remember the life and passion of my divine Son.

Chapter XXIV

THE SIDE OF CHRIST IS OPENED WITH A LANCE, AS HIS BODY HANGS ON THE CROSS; HE IS TAKEN DOWN AND BURIED. THE DOINGS OF THE BLESSED MOTHER ON THIS OCCASION, AND UNTIL SHE RETURNED TO THE CENACLE.

725. The Evangelist saint John tells us that near the Cross stood Mary, the most holy Mother of Jesus, with Mary Cleophas and Mary Magdalen. Although this is said of the time before Jesus expired, it must be understood, that the unconquerable Queen remained also afterwards, always standing beneath the Cross and adoring her dead Jesus and his divinity inseparably united to his sacred body. Amid the impetuous floods of sorrow, that penetrated to the inmost recesses of her chastest heart, the great Lady remained immovably constant in the exercise of ineffable virtues, while contemplating within Her the mysteries of man's Redemption and the order in which divine Wisdom disposed of all these sacraments. The greatest affliction of the Mother of mercy was the traitorous ingratitude, which men, to their own great loss, would show toward this extraordinary blessing, so worthy of eternal thanksgiving. But now She was especially solicitous for the burial of the sacred body of her divine Son and how to procure some one to take it down from the Cross. Full of this sorrowful anxiety, keeping her heavenly eyes riveted upon it, She turned to her holy angels

around Her and spoke to them: "Ministers of the Most High, my friends in tribulation, you know that there is no sorrow like unto my sorrow; tell me then, how shall I take down from the Cross, whom my soul loves; how and where shall I give Him honorable burial, since this duty pertains to me as his Mother? Tell me what to do, and assist me on this occasion by your diligence."

726. The holy angels answered: "Our Queen and Mistress, let thy afflicted heart be dilated for what is still to be borne. The omnipotent Lord has concealed his glory and power from mortals in order to subject Himself to the cruelty of man's impious malice and has always permitted the laws established for the course of human events to be fulfilled. One of them is, that the condemned shall not leave the cross without the consent of the judge. We are ready and able to obey Thee and to defend our true God and Creator, but his will restrains us, because He wishes to justify his cause to the end and to shed the rest of the blood still in Him for the benefit of mankind and in order that He may bind them still more firmly to make a return for his copious and redeeming love (Ps. 79, 7). If they do not avail themselves of this blessing as they ought, their punishment shall be deplorable and its severity shall make amends for the longsuffering of God in delaying his vengeance." This answer of the angels increased the sorrow of the afflicted Mother; for it had not been as yet revealed to Her, that her divine Son should be wounded by the lance, and the fear of what should happen to the sacred body renewed her tribulation and anxiety.

727. She soon saw an armed band approaching Calvary; and in her dread of some new outrage against the deceased Savior, She spoke to saint John and the pious women : "Alas, now shall my affliction reach its utmost and transfix my heart! Is it possible, that the executioners and the Jews are not yet satisfied with having put to death my Son and Lord?

Shall they now heap more injury upon his dead body?" It was the evening of the great Sabbath of the Jews, and in order to celebrate it with unburdened minds, they had asked Pilate for permission to shatter the limbs of the three men sentenced, so that, their death being hastened, they might be taken from the crosses and not left on them for the following day. With this intent the company of soldiers, which Mary now saw, had come to mount Calvary. As they perceived the two thieves still alive, they broke their limbs and so hastened their end (John 19, 31). But when they examined Jesus they found Him already dead, and therefore did not break his bones, thus fulfilling the mysterious prophecy in Exodus (Ex. 12, 46), commanding that no bones be broken in the figurative lamb to be eaten for the Pasch. But a soldier, by the name of Longinus, approaching the Cross of Christ, thrust his lance through the side of the Savior. Immediately water and blood flowed from the wound, as saint John, who saw it and who gives testimony of the truth, assures us (John 19, 34).

728. This wounding of the lance, which could not be felt by the sacred and dead body of the Lord, was felt by the most blessed Mother in his stead and in the same manner as if her chaste bosom had been pierced. But even this pain was exceeded by the affliction of her most holy soul, in witnessing the cruel laceration of the breast of her dead Son. At the same time, moved by compassion and love and in forgetfulness of her own sorrow, She said to Longinus: "The Almighty look upon thee with eyes of mercy for the pain thou hast caused to my soul!" So far and no farther went her indignation (or more properly, her most merciful meekness), for the instruction of all of us who are ever injured. For to the mind of this sincerest Dove, this injury to the dead Christ weighed most heavily; and the retribution sought by Her for the delinquent was one of the greatest blessings, namely that God should look upon him with eyes of mercy and return blessings and

gifts of grace for the offense. Thus it also happened; for the Savior, moved by the prayer of his blessed Mother, ordained that some of the blood and water from his sacred side should drop upon the face of Longinus and restore to him his eye-sight, which he had almost lost. At the same time sight was given to his soul, so that he recognized in the Crucified his Savior, whom he had so inhumanly mutilated. Through this enlightenment Longinus was converted; weeping over his sins and having washed them in the blood and water of the side of Christ, he openly acknowledged and confessed Him as the true God and Savior of the world. He proclaimed Him as such in the presence of the Jews, confounding by his testi-mony their perfidy and hardness of heart.

729. The most prudent Queen then perceived the mys-tery of this lance thrust, namely, that in this last pouring forth of the blood and water issued forth the new Church, cleansed and washed by the Passion and Death of Jesus, and that from his sacred side, as from the roots, should now spread out through the whole world the fruits of life eternal. She conferred within Herself also upon the mystery of that rock struck by the rod of divine justice (Exod. 17, 6), in order that the living waters might issue forth, quenching the thirst of all the human race and recreating and refreshing all who betook themselves to drink there from. She considered the coincidence of the five fountains from the wounds of his hands, feet and sides, which opened up the new paradise of the most holy humanity of our Savior, and which were more copious and powerful to fertilize the earth than those of the terrestrial paradise divided into four streams over the surface of the globe (Gen. 2, 10). These and other mysteries the great Lady rehearsed in a canticle of praise, which She com-posed in honor of her divine Son after his being wounded by the lance. Together with this canticle She poured forth a most fervent prayer, that all these mysteries of the Redemp-

tion be verified in the blessings spread over the whole human race.

730. The evening of that day of the parasceve was already approaching, and the loving Mother had as yet no solution of the difficulty of the burial of her dead Son, which She desired so much; but the Lord ordained, that the tribulations of his tenderest Mother should be relieved by Joseph of Arimathea and Nikodemus, whom he had inspired with the thought of caring for the burial of their Master. They were both just men and disciples of the Lord, although not of the seventy-two; for they had not as yet openly confessed themselves as disciples for fear of the Jews, who suspected and hated as enemies all those that followed Christ and acknowledged Him as Teacher. The dispositions of divine Providence concerning the burial of her Son had not been made known to the most prudent Virgin and thus her painful anxiety increased to such an extent, that She saw no way out of the difficulty. In her affliction She raised her eyes to heaven and said: "Eternal Father and my Lord, by the condescension of thy goodness and infinite wisdom I was raised to the exalted dignity of being the Mother of thy Son; and by that same bounty of an immense God Thou hast permitted me to nurse Him at my breast, nourish Him and accompany Him to his death. Now it behooves me as his Mother to give honorable burial to his sacred body, though I can go no farther than to desire it and deeply grieve, because I am unable to fulfill my wishes. I beseech thy divine Majesty to provide some way for accomplishing my desires."

731. This prayer the loving Mother offered up after the sacred body of the Lord was perforated by the lance. Soon after She saw another group of men coming toward Calvary with ladders and other apparatus seemingly for the purpose of taking from the Cross her priceless Treasure; but as She did not know their intentions, She was tortured by new fears

of the cruelty of the Jews, and turning to saint John, She said: "My Son, what may be the object of these people in coming with all these instruments?" The apostle answered: "Do not fear them that are coming, my Lady; for they are Joseph and Nikodemus with some of their servants, all of them friends and servants of thy divine Son and my Lord." Joseph was just in the eyes of the Most High (John 19, 38), a noble decurion in the employment of the government, a member of the council, who as is given us to understand in the Gospel, had not consented to the resolves and the proceedings of the murderers of Christ and who had recognized Jesus as the true Messias. Although Joseph had been a secret disciple of the Lord, yet at his death, in consequence of the efficacious influence of the Redemption, he openly confessed his adherence. Setting aside all fear of the envy of the Jews and caring nothing for the power of the Romans, he went boldly to Pilate and asked for the body of Jesus (Mark 15, 43), in order to take Him down from the Cross and give Him honorable burial. He openly maintained that he was innocent and the true Son of God, as witnessed by the miracles of his life and death.

732. Pilate dared not refuse the request of Joseph, but gave him full permission to dispose of the dead body of Jesus as he thought fit. With this permission Joseph left the house of the judge and called upon Nikodemus. He too was a just man, learned in divine and human letters and in the holy Scriptures, as is evident in what saint John related of him when he visited Christ at Night in order to hear the doctrine of Jesus Christ (John 3, 2). Joseph provided the winding sheets and burial cloths for the body of Jesus, while Nikodemus bought about one hundred pounds of the spices, which the Jews were accustomed to use in the burial of distinguished men (Matth. 27, 59). Provided with these and with other necessaries they took their way to Calvary. They were

accompanied by their servants and some other pious and devout persons, in whom likewise the blood shed for all by the crucified God had produced its salutary effects.

733. They approached most Holy Mary, who, in the company of saint John and the holy women, stood in inconceivable sorrow at the foot of the Cross. Instead of a salute, their sorrow at the sight of so painful a spectacle as that of the divine Crucified, was roused to such vehemence and bitterness, that Joseph and Nikodemus remained for a time prostrate at the feet of the Queen and all of them at the foot of the Cross without speaking a word. All of them wept and sighed most bitterly until the invincible Queen raised them from the ground and animated and consoled them; whereupon they saluted Her in humble compassion. The most observant Mother thanked them kindly, especially for the service they were about to render to their God and Savior, and promised them the reward in the name of Him whose body they were to lay in the tomb. Joseph of Arimathea answered: "Even now, our Lady, do we feel in the secret of our hearts the sweet delight of the divine Spirit, who has moved us to such love, that we never could merit it or succeed in explaining it." Then they divested themselves of their mantles and with their own hands Joseph and Nikodemus placed the ladders to the holy Cross. On these they ascended in order to detach the sacred body, while the glorious Mother stood closely by leaning on the arms of saint John and Mary Magdalen. It seemed to Joseph, that the sorrow of the heavenly Lady would be renewed, when the sacred body should be lowered and She should touch it, and therefore He advised the Apostle to take Her aside in order to draw away her attention. But saint John, who knew better the invincible heart of the Queen, answered that from the beginning She had stood by to witness the torments of the Lord and that

She would not leave him whom She venerated as her God and loved as the Son of her Womb.

734. Nevertheless they continued to urge the expediency of her retiring for a short time, until they should lower their Master from the Cross. But the great Lady responded: "My dearest masters, since I was present, when my sweetest Son was nailed to the Cross, fear not to allow me to be present at his taking down; for this act of piety, though it shall affect my heart with new sorrow, will, in its very performance, afford a great relief." Thereupon they began to arrange for the taking down of the body. First they detached the crown from the head, laying bare the lacerations and deep wounds it had caused. They handed it down with great reverence and amid abundant tears, placing it in the hands of the sweetest Mother. She received it prostrate on her knees, in deepest adoration bathed it with her tears, permitting the sharp thorns to wound her virginal countenance in pressing it to her face. She asked the eternal Father to inspire due veneration toward the sacred thorns in those Christians, who should obtain possession of them in future times.

735. In imitation of the Mother, saint John with the pious women and the other faithful there present, also adored it; and this they also did with the nails, handing them first to most holy Mary for veneration and afterward showing their own reverence. Then the great Lady placed Herself on her knees and held the unfolded cloth in her outstretched arms ready to receive the dead body of her Son. In order to assist Joseph and Nikodemus, saint John supported the head, and Mary Magdalen the feet, of Christ and thus they tearfully and reverently placed Him into the arms of his sweetest Mother. This was to Her an event of mixed sorrow and consolation; for in seeing Him thus wounded and all his beauty disfigured beyond all children of men (Ps. 44, 3), the sorrows of her most chaste heart were again renewed; and in

holding Him in her arms and at her breast, her incomparable sorrow was rejoiced and her love satiated by the possession of her Treasure. She looked upon Him with supreme worship and reverence, shedding tears of blood. In union with Her, as He rested in her arms, all the multitude of her attendant angels worshipped Him, although unseen by all others except Mary. Then saint John first, and after him all those present in their turn, adored the sacred Body. The most prudent Mother, seated on the ground, in the meanwhile held Him in her arms in order that they might satisfy their devotion.

736. In all these proceedings our great Queen acted with such heavenly wisdom and prudence, that She excited the admiration of the angels and men; for all her words were full of the deepest significance, the most winning affection and compassion for her deceased Son, full of tenderness in her lamenting, and full of mystery in sentiment and meaning. Her sorrow exceeded all that could ever be felt by mortals. She moved the hearts to compassion and tears. She enlightened all in the understanding of the sacrament now transpiring under their hands. Above all, without failing in the least of her duties, She preserved her humble dignity and serenity of countenance in the midst of her heartrending affliction. With uniform adaptation to the circumstances She spoke to her beloved Son, to the eternal Father, to the angels, to the bystanders, and to the whole human race, for whose Redemption the Lord had undergone his Passion and Death. I will not detain myself in particularizing the most prudent and sorrowful words of the Lady on this occasion; for Christian piety will be able to conceive many of them, and I cannot stay to enumerate all these mysteries.

737. Some time passed during which the sorrowful Mother held at her breast the dead Jesus, and as evening was far advancing, saint John and Joseph besought Her to allow the burial of her Son and God to proceed. The most prudent

Mother yielded; and they now embalmed the sacred body, using all the hundred pounds of the spices and the aromatic ointments brought by Nikodemus. Thus anointed the deified body was placed on a bier, in order to be carried to the sepulchre. The heavenly Queen, most attentive in her zealous love, called from heaven many choirs of angels, who, together with those of her guard, should accompany the burial of their Creator. Immediately they descended from on high in shapes visible to their Queen and Lady, though not to the rest. A procession of heavenly spirits was formed and another of men, and the sacred body was borne along by saint John, Joseph, Nikodemus and the centurion, who had confessed the Lord and now assisted at his burial. They were followed by the blessed Mother, by Mary Magdalen and the rest of the women disciples. Besides these a large number of the faithful assisted, for many had been moved by the divine light and had come to Calvary after the lance thrust. All of them, in silence and in tears, joined the procession. They proceeded toward a nearby garden, where Joseph had hewn into the rock a new grave, in which nobody had as yet been buried or deposited (John 19, 41). In this most blessed sepulchre they placed the sacred body of Jesus. Before they closed it up with the heavy stone, the devout and prudent Mother adored Christ anew, causing the admiration of men and angels. They imitated Her, all of them adoring the crucified Savior now resting in his grave; thereupon they closed the sepulchre with the stone, which, according to the Evangelist, was very heavy (Matth. 27, 60).

738. At the same time the graves, which had opened at the Death of Christ, were again closed; for among other mysteries of their opening up, was this, that these graves as it were unsealed themselves in order to receive Him, whom the Jews had repudiated, when He was alive and their Benefactor. At the command of the Queen many angels remained to

guard the sepulchre, where She had left her heart. In the same order and silence, in which they had come, they now returned to Calvary. The heavenly Mistress of all virtues approached the holy Cross and worshipped it in deepest reverence. In this Joseph and all the rest of the mourners followed Her. It was already late and the sun had sunk, when the great Lady betook Herself from Calvary to the house of the Cenacle in the company of the faithful. Having brought Her to the Cenacle, saint John, the Marys and the others took leave of Her with many tears and sighs and asked for her benediction. The most humble and prudent Lady thanked them for their service to her divine Son and the consolation afforded Her; She permitted them to depart with many hidden and interior favors and with the blessing of her most amiable and kindest heart.

739. The Jews, confused and disturbed by the events, went to Pilate on the morning of the Sabbath and asked him for soldiers to guard the sepulchre; for Christ, this seducer, they said, had openly announced, that after three days He would arise; hence his disciples might steal the body and then say that He had arisen. Pilate yielded to this malicious measure and gave them the guard they desired, which they stationed at the sepulchre (Matth. 28, 12). But the perfidious priests merely wished to palliate the event, which they feared would really happen, as was manifest afterwards, when they bribed the soldiers of the guard to testify, that Jesus had not arisen, but had been stolen by the disciples. As no counsel will prevail against God (Prov. 21, 30), the Resurrection of Christ became only so much the more public and was the more fully confirmed.

Words of the Queen

THE VIRGIN MARY SPEAKS TO SISTER MARY OF AGREDA

740. My daughter, the lance thrust which my blessed Son received in his side, was cruel and very painful only to me; but its effects and mysteries are most sweet to those souls who know how to taste its sweetness. It was a great affliction to me; but whoever meets with this mysterious favor will find it a great relief and consolation in his sorrows. In order that thou mayest understand this and participate in it, thou must know, that my Son and Lord, on account of his most ardent love for men, in addition to the wounds of the feet and hands, wished to open the wound of his heart, the seat of love, in order that through this port the souls might enter and there receive refuge and relief. This is the only retreat which I wish thee to seek during the time of thy banishment, and which thou must consider as thy habitation upon earth. There thou wilt find the conditions and laws of love for imitating me and learn how for injuries thou must return blessings to all who commit them against thee and thine, just as thou hast seen me do, when I was grieved by the wounding of the side of my dead Son. I assure thee, my dearest, that thou canst not do anything more adapted to the obtaining of the efficacious graces from the Almighty. The prayer, which thou offerest in a forgiving spirit, is powerful not only for thy own good, but for the good of the one that offends thee; for the kind heart of my Son is easily moved, when He sees that creatures imitate Him in pardoning offenders and in praying for them; for they thereby participate in his most ardent charity manifested on the Cross. Write this doctrine in thy heart and in imitation of me practice this virtue, of which I thought so highly. Through this wound look upon the heart of Christ thy Spouse and upon me, sweetly and ardently loving in it thy enemies and all creatures.

741. Consider also the anxious and ever ready providence of the Most High in coming to the aid of the creatures, that call to Him in true confidence. This thou hast seen in my behalf, when I found myself afflicted and at a loss concerning the proper burial of my divine Son. In order to come to my assistance in this plight, the Lord showed his sweet love by moving the hearts of Joseph and Nikodemus and of the other faithful to assist me in burying Him. By their opportune help I was so much consoled in this tribulation, that on account of their behavior and my prayer the Most High filled them with wonderful influences of the Divinity, by which they were regaled during the time of taking Jesus from the Cross and his burial; and from that time on these faithful were enlightened and filled with the mysteries of the Redemption. This is the admirable disposition of the sweet and powerful providence of God, that in order to bind Himself to do good to some of his creatures, He sends affliction upon others, thus giving an occasion for the practice of benevolence, so that at the same time those in necessity may be benefited. Thus the benefactor, on account of the good work he does and on account of the prayer of the poor, is rewarded by receiving graces of which he otherwise would not be worthy. The Father of mercies, who inspires and assists the good work done, afterwards pays for it as if it were due in justice. For we can correspond to his inspirations merely according to our insignificant abilities, while all that is really good, comes entirely from his hands (James 1, 17).

742. Consider also the equity maintained by this Providence in compensating the injuries received in patient suffering. For after my divine Son had suffered death amid the contempt, dishonor and blasphemies of men, the Most High at once provided for an honorable burial and moved many to confess Him as the true God and Redeemer, to proclaim Him as holy, innocent and just, and, at the very time when

they had finished their frightful crucifixion, to adore Him as the Son of God. Even his enemies were made to feel within themselves the horror and confusion of their sin in persecuting Him. Although these benefits availed not all men, yet all of them were effects of the innocent Death of the Lord. I also concurred in my prayers, in order that the Lord might be acknowledged and honored by those known to me.

Chapter XXV

HOW THE QUEEN OF HEAVEN CONSOLED SAINT PETER AND THE OTHER APOSTLES; HOW PRUDENTLY SHE ACTED AFTER THE BURIAL OF HER SON; HOW SHE SAW HIS DIVINE SOUL DESCEND TO THE LIMBO OF THE HOLY PATRIARCHS.

743. The fullness of wisdom in the soul of our great Queen and Lady amid all her sorrows permitted no defect or remissness in noticing and attending to all the duties of each occasion and at all times. By this heavenly foresight She met her obligations and practiced the highest and most eminent of all the virtues. As I have said, the Queen retired, after the burial of Christ, to the house of the Cenacle. Remaining in the hall of the last Supper in the company of saint John, the Marys, and the other women who had followed Christ from Galilee, She spoke to them and the Apostle, thanking them in profound humility and abundant tears for persevering with Her up to this time throughout the Passion of her beloved Son and promising them in his name the reward of having followed Him with so much constancy and devotion. At the same time She offered Herself as a servant and as a friend to those holy women. All of them with Saint John acknowledged this great favor, kissed her hands and asked for her blessing. They also begged her to take some rest and some bodily refreshment. But the Queen answered: "My rest and my consolation shall be to see my Son and Lord arisen from

the dead. Do you, my dearest friends, satisfy your wants according to your necessities, while I retire alone with my Son."

744. Thereupon She retired with saint John and being with him alone, She fell upon her knees and said: "Do thou not forget the words which my Son spoke to us on the Cross. He condescended to call thee my son, and me thy mother. Thou art my master, art priest of the Most High; and on account of this dignity, it is meet that I obey thee in all that I am to do; and from this hour I wish that thou order and command me in all things, remembering that I shall always be thy servant and that all my joy shall be to serve thee as such until my death." This the Lady said with many tears. And among many other things, the Apostle said: "My Mistress and Mother of the Redeemer and Lord, I am the one who should be subject to thy authority, for the name of a son implies devotion and subjection to his mother. He that has made me priest, has made Thee his Mother and was subject to thy authority, though He was the Creator of the universe (Luke 2, 51). It is reasonable that I should likewise be so, and that I labor with all my powers to make myself worthy of the office He has conferred upon me, to serve Thee as thy son, for which I would desire to be rather an angel than a creature of earth." This answer of the Apostle was most appropriate; but it did not avail to overcome the humility of the Mother of virtues, who answered: "My son John, my consolation shall be to obey thee as my superior, since such thou art. In this life I must always have a superior, to whom I can render my will in obedience: for this purpose thou art the minister of the Most High, and as my son thou owest me this as a consolation in my solitude." "Let then thy will be done, my Mother," said saint John, "for in this lies my own security.' Without further answer the heavenly Mother then asked permission to remain alone in meditating on the mysteries of

her divine Son; and She asked him also to provide some refreshment for the holy women, who had accompanied Her, and that he assist them and console them. She reserved only the Marys, because they wished to persevere in their fast until they should see the Lord arisen; and She asked saint John to allow them to fulfill their pious desire.

745. Saint John then parted from Her in order to console the Marys and to execute the commands of the great Lady. Having attended to their wants, these pious women all retired to spend that night in sorrowful and mournful meditation concerning the mysteries of the Lord's Passion. In such heavenly wisdom the blessed Mary labored amid the floods of her anxieties and afflictions, without ever forgetting the least point of the most perfect obedience, humility, charity and prudent foresight for all that was necessary. She did not forget to attend to the necessities of these pious women, nor did She on their account forget anything that was necessary to the exercise of the highest perfection in Herself. She approved of the fast of the Marys as being strong and fervent in their love; and She took heed of the weakness of the others. She instructed the Apostle in his duties toward Herself and, proceeded in all things as the Instructress of perfection and the Mistress of grace. All this She did when the waters of tribulation had entered to her very soul (Ps. 68, 2). Then, remaining alone in her retreat, She let loose the impetuous floods of her afflicted love and permitted Herself to be possessed interiorly and exteriorly by the bitterness of her soul. She renewed in her mind the recollection of her divine Son's frightful death; the mysteries of his life, his preaching and his miracles, the infinite value of the Redemption; the new Church which He had founded and adorned with the riches of the Sacraments and the treasures of grace; the happiness of the human race, now so copiously and gloriously redeemed; the inestimable fortune of the predestined, who

should really obtain that happiness; the dreadful misfortune of the reprobate, who by their own fault would make themselves unworthy of the eternal glory, merited for them by her Son.

746. In the deep consideration of these high and hidden sacraments the great Lady passed that whole night, weeping and sighing, praising and glorifying the works of her divine Son, his Passion, his hidden judgments, and the rest of the high mysteries of divine wisdom and unsearchable providence of the Lord. All of them, as the Mother of true wisdom, She contemplated and understood, conferring sometimes with the holy angels, at others with the Lord himself concerning what the divine influences caused Her to feel in her own purest heart. On the following sabbath morning, after four o'clock, saint John entered to console the sorrowful Mother. Falling on her knees before him, She asked him for his blessing, as from her superior and a priest. Her new son on his part asked it of Her with tears in his eyes, and thus they gave their blessing one to the other. The heavenly Queen begged saint John to meet saint Peter, who was looking for him on the way to the city. She ordered saint John to receive and console him kindly, and bring him to her presence. The same he was to do with the other Apostles, giving them hope of pardon and offering them her friendship. Saint John issued from the Cenacle and shortly met saint Peter, who, full of shame and in tears, was timidly seeking the presence of the great Queen. He had just come from the cave, where he had bewept his denials; but he was now consoled by saint John and encouraged by the message from the heavenly Mother. Then these two went in search of the other Apostles. Having found some they together betook themselves to the Cenacle, hoping for pardon. Saint Peter entered first and alone to the presence of the Mother of grace, and falling at her feet, he said with great sorrow: "I

have sinned, Lady, I have sinned before my God, and have offended my Master and Thee!" He could not speak another word, further speech being stifled with tearful sobs and sighs which came from the depths of his oppressed heart.

747. The most prudent Virgin, seeing Peter prostrate on the ground and considering him on the one hand as doing penance for sins so recently committed, and on the other hand as the head of the church, chosen by her divine Son as his vicar, did not deem it proper to prostrate Herself before the pastor, who had just denied his Master; but neither would her humility suffer Her to withhold the reverence due to his office. In order to conform her action to both these circumstances, She resolved to show him proper reverence without disclosing her motive. For this purpose, She fell on her knees to do him reverence, at the same time concealing her intention by saying: "Let us ask pardon for thy guilt from my Son and thy Master." She prayed for him, revived his hope by reminding him of the merciful behavior of the Lord in regard to wellknown sinners, and pointing out his own obligation as head of the apostolic college to give the example of constancy in the confession of the faith. By these and other arguments of great force and sweetness She confirmed Peter in the hope of pardon. Then also the other Apostles presented themselves, prostrating themselves before the most blessed Mary and asking pardon for their cowardice in forsaking her divine Son during his sufferings. They wept bitterly over their sin, being moved to greater sorrow by the presence of this Mother so full of sorrowful pity. Her wonderfully sweet countenance caused in them divine movements of contrition for their sins and of love of their Master. The great Lady raised them up and encouraged them, promising them the pardon they sought and her intercession to obtain it. Then all of them in their turn related what had happened to each in his flight. Though the blessed Lady

knew all even to the last particulars concerning these events, She heard them all kindly, taking occasion from what they said to touch their hearts and confirm them in their faith in their Redeemer and Master and of arousing in them divine love. In this the heavenly Lady completely succeeded; for they all went away from this conference burning with new fervor and justified by new increase of graces.

748. These were the occupations of the heavenly Queen during a part of the sabbath. At the approach of evening She again retired, leaving the Apostles now renewed in spirit and full of consolation and joy in the Lord, yet also full of grief for the Passion of their Master. In her retirement during this evening the great Lady contemplated the doings of the most holy soul of her Son after it left the sacred body. For from the first the blessed Mother knew that the soul of Christ, united to the Divinity, descended to limbo in order to release the holy Fathers from the subterranean prison, where they had been detained since the death of the first just man that had died in expectance of the advent of the Redeemer of the whole human race. In order to speak about this mystery, which is one of the articles of faith pertaining to the most sacred humanity of Christ our Lord, it seemed best to mention that which has been given me to understand about this limbo and its situation. I say then, that the diameter of the earth's sphere, passing through the centre from one surface to the other, measures two thousand, five hundred and two leagues; and from the surface to the centre, one thousand, two hundred and fiftyone leagues; and according to the diameter is to be calculated the circumference of this globe. In the centre is the hell of the damned, as in the heart of the earth. This hell is a chaotic cavern, which contains many darksome dwellings for diverse punishments, all of them dreadful and terrible. All of these together form a vast globe like a huge round jar, with an opening or mouth of vast

expansion. In this horrible dungeon filled with confusion and torments were the demons and all the damned, and shall be there for all eternity, as long as God is God; for in hell there is no redemption (Matth, 25,41).

749. To one side of hell is purgatory, where the souls of the just are purged and where they cleanse themselves, if they have not satisfied for their faults in this life, or have not departed from this earthly life entirely free from the defects incapacitating them for the beatific vision. This cavern is also large, but not so large as hell; and though there are severe punishments in purgatory, they have no connection with those of hell. To the other side is limbo with two different divisions: The one for the children, who die unbaptized and tainted only with original sin, without either good or bad works of their own election. The other served as a retreat for the just, who had already satisfied for their sins; for they could not enter heaven, nor enjoy the vision of God until the Redemption of man was accomplished and until Christ our Savior should open the gates of heaven closed by the sin of Adam (Ps. 23, 9). This cavern is likewise smaller than hell, and has no connection with it, nor are there in it the pains of the senses like in purgatory. For it was destined for the souls already cleansed in purgatory and implied only the absence of beatific vision or pain of privation; there also stayed all those who died in the state of grace until the death of the Redeemer. This is the place to which Christ's soul descended with the Divinity and which we refer to in saying that He descended into hell. For the word "hell" may be used to signify any of the infernal regions in the depths of the earth, though commonly we apply it only to the hell of the demons and the damned. This is the most notable meaning of this word, just as "heaven" ordinarily signifies the empyrean, the habitation of the saints, where they are to dwell forever, while the damned remain forever in hell. The other parts of hell have

also the more particular names of purgatory and limbo. After the final judgment heaven and hell only are to be inhabited, since purgatory shall become unnecessary and since even the infants shall be transported to another dwellingplace.

750. To this cavern of limbo then the most holy soul of Christ our Lord betook itself in the company of innumerable angels, who gave glory, fortitude and Divinity to their victorious and triumphant King. In accordance with his greatness and majesty they commanded the portals of this ancient prison to be opened, in order that the King of glory, powerful in battles and Lord of virtues, might find them unlocked and open at his entrance. At their command some of the rocks of the passage were rent and shattered; although this was not really necessary, since the King and his army were immaterial spirits. By the presence of the most holy Soul this obscure cavern was converted into a heaven and was filled with a wonderful splendor; and to the souls therein contained was imparted the clear vision of the Divinity. In one instant they passed from the state of longdeferred hope to the possession of glory, and from darkness to the inaccessible light, which they now began to enjoy. All of them recognized their true God and Redeemer, and gave him thanks and glory, breaking forth in canticles of praise saying: "The Lamb that was slain is worthy to receive power and Divinity, and wisdom, and strength, and honor, and glory and benediction. Thou hast redeemed us, Lord, in thy blood, out of every tribe, and tongue, and people, and nation; and hast made us to our God a kingdom and priests, and we shall reign on the earth (Apoc. 59, 12). Thine is, O Lord, the power, thine the reign, and thine is the glory of thy works." Then the Lord commanded the angels to bring all the souls in purgatory, and this was immediately done. As if in earnest of the human Redemption they were absolved then and there by the Redeemer from the punishments still due to them, and they

were glorified with the other souls of the just by the beatific vision. Thus on that day of the presence of the King were depopulated the prison houses of both limbo and purgatory.

751. But for the damned in hell this was a terrible day; because by the disposition of the Most High all of them were made to see and feel the descent of the Redeemer into limbo, and also the holy Fathers and the just were made witnesses of the terror caused by this mystery to the demons and the damned. The demons were yet terrorized and oppressed by the ruin which they had undergone on Mount Calvary, as related above; and when they heard (according to their manner of hearing and speaking) the voices of the angels advancing before their King to limbo, they were confounded and terrified anew. Like serpents pursued, they hid themselves and clung to the most remote caverns of hell. The damned were seized with confusion upon confusion, becoming still more deeply conscious of their aberration and of the loss of salvation, now secured to the just. As Judas and the impenitent thief had so recently and signally shared this misfortune, so their torments were greater; and the demons were the more highly incensed against them. Then and there the infernal spirits resolved to persecute and torment more grievously the Catholics, and chastise more severely those who should deny or repudiate the Catholic faith. For they concluded that these merited greater punishment than the infidels, to whom it is not preached.

752. Of all these mysteries and of other secrets, which I cannot mention, the great Lady of the world had a clear knowledge and vision from her retreat. Although this knowledge, in the higher parts of her being or in her soul where this knowledge originated, caused Her exquisite joy; yet She did not permit it to overflow in her virginal body, in her senses or inferior faculties, to which it should naturally have been communicated. On the contrary, when She felt

that some of this joy overflowed to the inferior parts of her being, She besought the eternal Father to retard this overflow; for She did not wish to permit such enjoyment to her body, as long as that of her divine Son rested in the grave and was not yet glorified. Such a careful and faithful love was that of the blessed Mother toward her Son and Lord, that She strove to be a living, true and perfect image of the deified humanity in all respects. Attending thus minutely to the smallest particulars, She was rejoiced exceedingly in her soul, while She still felt the sorrows and depression of her body in imitation of the state of Christ our Savior. During this vision She composed songs of praise magnifying the mysteries of this triumph and the most loving and wise providence of the Redeemer, who as an affectionate Father and omnipotent King wished, in his own Person, to take possession of the new reign, given to Him by the Father, and who now rescued his subjects by his own presence in order that they might commence immediately to enjoy the reward merited for them. For these reasons, and others recognized by Her in this sacrament, She rejoiced and glorified the Lord as his Helper and as the Mother of the Conqueror.

Words of the Queen

THE VIRGIN MARY SPEAKS TO SISTER MARY OF AGREDA

753. My daughter, attend to the teaching of this chapter as being the most appropriate and necessary for the state assigned to thee by the Most High and for the correspondence in love which thou owest Him. This requires of thee, that in the midst of thy labors and intercourse with the creatures, whether in commanding or governing as superior, or obeying as a subject, thou do not permit thyself by any of these duties or other exterior occupations to neglect the attention due to the presence of thy Savior in the secret and higher parts of

thy soul; nor withdraw thyself from the light of the holy Spirit and his constant communications. For my divine Son seeks, in the secrets of thy heart, such ways as are hidden to the demon and to which thy passions have no access; for they lead to the sanctuary, whither the Highpriest alone can enter (Heb. 9, 7) and where the soul enjoys the hidden embraces of its King and Spouse, as soon as it prepares for Him his chamber of rest with a single and eager mind. There shalt thou find thy Lord propitious, the Most High, liberal, thy Creator, merciful, thy sweet Spouse and Redeemer, loving; then wilt thou not fear the powers of darkness, nor the effects of sin, which are unknown in that region of light and truth. But the soul disordered by anxiety for the visible things, or careless in the observance of the divine law will close up these ways; it will be embarrassed by the disorderly attachments of the passions; it will be hindered by useless cares, and much more by restlessness of mind and by the want of serenity and interior peace; for the heart must be untrammeled, pure and detached from all that is not truth and light.

754. Thou hast well understood and experienced this doctrine, and moreover I have shown it to thee in practice as in the clearest mirror, namely in my behavior amid the sorrows, sighs and afflictions of the Passion of my divine Son, and amid the solicitous cares, occupations and watchings during his burial and during the assistance rendered to the Apostles and the holy women. During my whole life thou hast seen me act in the same manner, uniting the works of the spirit with exterior occupations without friction or hindrance. In order then to imitate me in all this as I require, it is necessary, that neither by the unavoidable intercourse with creatures, nor by the labors of thy state of life, nor by the hardships of this life of exile, nor by the temptations or malice of the demon, thou permit thy heart to desire anything that will hinder thee, or pay attention to anything

which destroys thy recollection. And I warn thee, my dearest, that if thou art not very vigilant and careful in this matter, thou wilt lose much time, abuse immense and extraordinary blessings, frustrate the high and holy purposes of the Lord, and wilt grieve me and the angels; since all of Us desire that thy conversation be with Us. Thou wilt lose the quiet of thy spirit and the interior consolations, many degrees of grace, the desired increase of divine love, and finally the most copious reward in heaven. So much does it concern thee to listen to me and obey me in all that I teach thee with a Mother's kindness. Consider it, my daughter, ponder it, and bend upon it thy mind, so that through my intercession and by divine grace thou mayest put it into practice. Take heed also to imitate me in the faithful love, by which I abstained from the sweets of inferior delights in imitation of my Master. Do thou praise Him for this and for the blessings He brought to the saints in limbo, when his most holy soul descended to free them and fill them with joy at his sight, all of which were operations of his infinite love.

Chapter XXVI

THE RESURRECTION OF CHRIST OUR SAVIOR AND HIS APPARITION TO HIS MOST BLESSED MOTHER IN COMPANY WITH THE HOLY FATHERS OF LIMBO.

755. The divine soul of Christ our Redeemer remained in limbo from half past three of Friday afternoon, until after three of the Sunday morning following. During this hour He returned to the Sepulchre as the victorious Prince of the angels and of the saints, whom He had delivered from those nether prisons as spoils of his victory and as an earnest of his glorious triumph over the chastised and prostrate rebels of hell. In the sepulchre were many angels as its guard, venerating the sacred body united to the Divinity. Some of them, obeying the command of their Queen and Mistress, had gathered the relics of the sacred blood shed by her divine Son, the particles of flesh scattered about, the hair torn from his divine face and head, and all else that belonged to the perfection and integrity of his most sacred humanity. On these the Mother of prudence lavished her solicitous care. The angels took charge of these relics, each one filled with joy at being privileged to hold the particles, which he was able to secure. Before any change was made, the body of the Redeemer was shown to the holy Fathers, in the same wounded, lacerated and disfigured state in which it was left by the cruelty of the Jews. Beholding Him thus disfigured in

death, the Patriarchs and Prophets and other saints adored Him and again confessed Him as the incarnate Word, who had truly taken upon Himself our infirmities and sorrows (Is. 53, 4) and paid abundantly our debts, satisfying in his innocence and guiltlessness for what we ourselves owed to the justice of the eternal Father. There did our first parents Adam and Eve see the havoc wrought by their disobedience, the priceless remedy it necessitated, the immense goodness and mercy of the Redeemer. As they felt the effects of his copious Redemption in the glory of their souls, they praised anew the Omnipotent and Saint of saints, who had with such marvelous wisdom wrought such a salvation.

756. Then, in the presence of all those saints, through the ministry of those angels, were united to the sacred body all the relics, which they had gathered, restoring it to its natural perfection and integrity. In the same moment the most holy soul reunited with the body, giving it immortal life and glory. Instead of the windingsheets and the ointments, in which it had been buried, it was clothed with the four gifts of glory, namely: with clearness, impassibility, agility and subtility (John 19, 40). These gifts overflowed from the immense glory of the soul of Christ into the sacred body. Although these gifts were due to it as a natural inheritance and participation from the instant of its conception, because from that very moment his soul was glorified and his whole humanity was united to the Divinity; yet they had been suspended in their effects upon the purest body, in order to permit it to remain passible and capable of meriting for us our own glory. In the Resurrection these gifts were justly called into activity in the proper degree corresponding to the glory of his soul and to his union with the Divinity. As the glory of the most holy soul of Christ our Savior is in comprehensible and ineffable to man, it is also impossible entirely to describe in our words or by our examples the glorious gifts

of his deified body; for in comparison to its purity, crystal would be obscure. The light inherent and shining forth from his body so far exceeds that of the others, as the day does the night, or as many suns the light of one star; and all the beauty of creatures, if it were joined, would appear ugliness in comparison with his, nothing else being comparable to it in all creation.

757. The excellence of these gifts in the Resurrection were far beyond the glory of his Transfiguration or that manifested on other occasions of the kind mentioned in this history. For on these occasions He received it transitorily and for special purposes, while now He received it in plenitude and forever. Through impassibility his body became invincible to all created power, since no power can ever move or change Him. By subtility the gross and earthly matter was so purified, that it could now penetrate other matter like a pure spirit. Accordingly He penetrated through the rocks of the sepulchre without removing or displacing them, just as He had issued forth from the womb of his most blessed Mother. Agility so freed Him from the weight and slowness of matter, that it exceeded the agility of the immaterial angels, while He himself could move about more quickly than they, as shown in his apparitions to the Apostles and on other occasions. The sacred wounds, which had disfigured his body, now shone forth from his hands and feet and side so refulgent and brilliant, that they added a most entrancing beauty and charm. In all this glory and heavenly adornment the Savior now arose from the grave; and in the presence of the saints and Patriarchs He promised universal resurrection in their own flesh and body to all men, and that they moreover, as an effect of his own Resurrection, should be similarly glorified. As an earnest and as a pledge of the universal resurrection, the Lord commanded the souls of many saints there present to reunite with their bodies and rise up to immortal life.

Immediately this divine command was executed, and their bodies arose, as is mentioned by saint Matthew, in anticipation of this mystery (Matthew 27, 52). Among them was saint Anne, saint Joseph and saint Joachim, and others of the ancient Fathers and Patriarchs, who had distinguished themselves in the faith and hope of the Incarnation, and had desired and prayed for it with greater earnestness to the Lord. As a reward for their zeal, the resurrection and glory of their bodies was now anticipated.

758. 0 how powerful and wonderful, how victorious and strong, appeared even now this Lion of Juda, the son of David! None ever woke from sleep so quickly as Christ from death (Ps. 3, 4). At his imperious voice the dry and scattered bones of the ancient dead were joined together, and the flesh, which had long ago turned to dust, was united to the bones, renewed their former life, and adorned by the gifts of glory communicated to it by the liferestoring soul. In one instant all these saints gathered around their Savior, more refulgent and brilliant than the sun, pure, transparent, beauteous and agile, fit to follow Him everywhere and by their own good fortune they now confirmed the prophecy of Job, that, in our own flesh and with our own eyes, and not with those of others, we shall see our Redeemer for our consolation (Job 19, 26). Of all these mysteries the great Queen of heaven was aware and She participated in them from her retreat in the Cenacle. In the same instant in which the most holy soul of Christ entered and gave life to his body the joy of her immaculate soul, which I mentioned in the foregoing chapter as being restrained and, as it were, withheld, overflowed into her immaculate body. And this overflow was so exquisite in its effects, that She was transformed from sorrow to joy, from pain to delight. from grief to ineffable jubilation and rest. It happened that just at this time the Evangelist John, as he had done on the previous morning, stepped in to visit Her and

console Her in her bitter solitude, and thus unexpectedly, in the midst of splendor and glory, met Her, whom he had before scarcely recognized on account of her overwhelming sorrow. The Apostle now beheld Her with wonder and deepest reverence and concluded that the Lord had risen, since his blessed Mother was thus transfigured with joy.

759. In this new joy and under the divine influences of her supernatural vision the great Lady began to prepare Herself for the visit of the Lord, which was near at hand. While eliciting acts of praise, and in her canticles and prayers, She immediately felt within Her a new kind of jubilation and celestial delight, reaching far beyond the first joy, and corresponding in a wonderful manner to the sorrows and tribulations She had undergone in the Passion; and this new favor was different and much more exalted than the joys overflowing naturally from her soul into her body. Moreover She perceived within Herself another, third and still more different effect, implying new divine favors. Namely She felt infused into her being the heavenly light heralding the advent of beatific vision, which I will not here explain, since I have descanted on it in the first part (Part I, No. 620). I merely add here, that the Queen, on this occasion, received these divine influences more abundantly and in a more exalted degree; for now the Passion of Christ had gone before and She had acquired the merits of this Passion. Hence the consolations from the hands of her divine Son corresponded to the multitude of her sorrows.

760. The blessed Mary being thus prepared, Christ our Savior, arisen and glorious, in the company of all the Saints and Patriarchs, made his appearance. The ever humble Queen prostrated Herself upon the ground and adored her divine Son; and the Lord raised Her up and drew Her to Himself. In this contact, which was more intimate than the contact with the humanity and the wounds of the Savior

sought by Magdalen, the Virgin Mother participated in an extraordinary favor, which She alone, as exempt from sin, could merit. Although it was not the greatest of the favors She attained on this occasion, yet She could not have received it without failing of her faculties, if She had not been previously strengthened by the angels and by the Lord himself. This favor was, that the glorious body of the Son so closely united itself to that of his purest Mother, that He penetrated into it or She into his, as when, for instance, a crystal globe takes up within itself the light of the sun and is saturated with the splendor and beauty of its light. In the same way the body of the most holy Mary entered into that of her divine Son by this heavenly embrace; it was, as it were, the portal of her intimate knowledge concerning the glory of the most holy soul and body of her Lord. As a consequence of these favors, constituting higher and higher degrees of ineffable gifts, the spirit of the Virgin Mother rose to the knowledge of the most hidden sacraments. In the midst of them She heard a voice saying to Her: "My beloved, ascend higher!" (Luke 18, 10). By the power of these words She was entirely transformed and saw the Divinity clearly and intuitively, wherein She found complete, though only temporary, rest and reward for all her sorrows and labors. Silence alone here is proper, since reason and language are entirely inadequate to comprehend or express what passed in the blessed Mary during this beatific vision, the highest She had until then enjoyed. Let us celebrate this day in wonder and praise, with congratulations and loving and humble thanks for what She then merited for us, and for her exaltation and joy.

761. For some hours the heavenly Princess continued to enjoy the essence of God with her divine Son, participating now in his triumph as She had in his torments. Then by similar degrees She again descended from this vision and found Herself in the end reclining on the right arm of the

most sacred humanity and regaled in other ways by the right hand of his Divinity (Cant. 2, 6). She held sweetest converse with her Son concerning the mysteries of his Passion and of his glory. In these conferences She was again inebriated with the wine of love and charity, which now She drank unmeasured from the original fount. All that a mere creature can receive was conferred upon the blessed Mary on this occasion; for, according to our way of conceiving such things, the divine equity wished to compensate the injury (thus I must call it, because I cannot find a more proper word), which a Creature so pure and immaculate had undergone in suffering the sorrows and torments of the Passion. For, as I have mentioned many times before, She suffered the same pains as her Son, and now in this mystery She was inundated with a proportionate joy and delight.

762. Then, still remaining in her exalted state, the great Lady turned to the holy Patriarchs and all the just, recognizing them and speaking to each in succession, praising the Almighty in his liberal mercy to each one of them. She was filled with an especial delight in speaking to her parents, saint Joachim and Anne, with her spouse, saint Joseph, with saint John the Baptist, and with them She conversed more particularly than with the Patriarchs and Prophets and with the first parents, Adam and Eve. All of them prostrated themselves before the heavenly Lady, acknowledging Her as the Mother of the Redeemer of the world, as the cause of their rescue and the Coadjutrix of their Redemption. The divine wisdom impelled them thus to venerate and honor Her. But the Queen of all virtues and the Mistress of Humility prostrated Herself on the ground and reverenced the saints according to their due. This the Lord permitted because the saints, although they were inferior in grace, were superior in their state of blessedness, endowed with imperishable and eternal glory, while the Mother of grace was yet in mortal life and a pilgrim

and had not as yet assumed the state of fruition. The presence of Christ our Savior continued during all the conference of Mary with the holy Fathers. The most blessed Mary invited all the angels and saints there present to praise the Victor over death, sin and hell. Whereupon all sang new songs, psalms, hymns of glory and magnificence, until the hour arrived, when the risen Savior was to appear in other places, as I shall relate in the following chapter.

Words of the Queen

THE VIRGIN MARY SPEAKS TO SISTER MARY OF AGREDA

763. My daughter, rejoice in thy very anxiety of not being able to explain in words what thy interior faculties perceive concerning the exalted mysteries recorded in thy writing. To acknowledge oneself conquered by such sovereign sacraments as these must be looked upon as a victory for creatures, and as redounding to the glory of God; and in mortal flesh still more so. I felt the pains of my divine Son, and, although I did not lose my life, I endured the agonies of death mysteriously; therefore I experienced in myself also this wonderful and mystical resurrection to a most exalted state of grace and activity. The essence of God is infinite; and although the creature can participate in it so highly, yet there remains much to understand, love and enjoy. In order that now thou mayest by the help of thy understanding trace something of the glory of Christ my Son, of my own and of the saints, I wish to give thee some rules, by which thou canst pass on from the consideration of the gifts of the glorified body to those of the soul. Thou already knowest that the gifts of the soul are vision, comprehension and fruition, while thou hast already mentioned those of the body as being: clearness, impassibility, subtility and agility.

764. Each of these gifts are correspondingly augmented in him who in the state of grace performs the least meritorious work, even if it be no more than removing a straw or giving a cup of water for the love of God (Matth. 10, 42). For each of the most insignificant works the creature gains an increase of these gifts; an increase of clearness exceeding many times the sunlight and added to its state of blessedness; an increase of impassibility, by which man recedes from human and earthly corruption farther than what all created efforts and strength could ever effect in resisting or separating itself from such infirmity or changefulness; an increase of subtility, by which he advances beyond all that could offer it resistance and gains new power of penetration; an increase of agility, surpassing all the activity of birds, of winds, and all other active creatures, such as fire and the elements tending to their centre. From this increase of the gifts of the body merited by good works, thou wilt understand the augmentation of the gifts of the soul; for those of the body are derived from those of the soul and correspond with them. In the beatific vision each merit secures greater clearness and insight into the divine attributes and perfections than that acquired by all the doctors and enlightened members of the Church. Likewise the gift of apprehension, or possession of the divine Object, is augmented; for the security of the possession of the highest and infinite Good makes the tranquillity and rest of its enjoyment more estimable than if the soul possessed all that is precious and rich, desirable and worthy of attainment in all creation, even if possessed all at one time. Fruition, the third gift of the soul, on account of the love with which man performs the smallest acts, so exalts the degrees of fruitional love, that the greatest love of men here on earth can never be compared thereto; nor can the delight resulting therefrom ever be compared with all the delights of this mortal life.

765. Elevate therefore now thy thoughts, my daughter, and from these wonderful rewards, gained by one little deed done for God, consider what shall be the lot of the saints, who for the love of God have performed such heroic and magnificent works, and have suffered such cruel torments and martyrdom as are known in the Church of Christ. And if these things happen in mere men, subject to faults and imperfections that retard merit, imagine, as far as thou canst, the exaltation of my divine Son. Then thou wilt feel how limited is human capacity, especially in mortal life, to comprehend worthily this mystery and to conceive in a becoming manner such greatness. The most holy soul of my Lord was united substantially to the Divinity and on account of this hypostatic union the ocean of his Divinity necessarily communicated Itself to his divine and human personality, beatifying it as participating in the very essence of God in an ineffable manner. Although his glory depended not on merits, since it was given to Him as consequent upon the hypostatical union from the first instant of his conception in my womb; yet the works of the thirtythree years of his life, his being born in poverty, living in labor, loving as a pilgrim, operating in all the virtues, redeeming the human race, founding the Church and the doctrines of the faith: all this demanded, that the glory of his body be measured by that of his soul. And therefore his greatness is ineffable and immense, to be manifested only in eternal life. In connection with the magnificent exaltation of my divine Son, the right hand of the Almighty wrought also in me effects proportionate to a mere creature, and in them I forgot all the tribulations and sorrows of the Passion. Similar was the lot of the Fathers of limbo and the other saints, when they received their rewards. I forgot the bitterness and labors I had suffered; for the great joy drove out pain, though I never lost from view what my Son had suffered for the human race.

CITY OF GOD: VOLUME III "THE TRANSFIXION"   689

Chapter XXVII

SOME APPARITIONS OF CHRIST OUR SAVIOR TO THE MARYS AND TO THE APOSTLES; THE PRUDENCE OF THE QUEEN IN LISTENING TO THEIR REPORTS CONCERNING THESE APPARITIONS OF THE LORD.

766. After Jesus our Savior, arisen and glorified, had visited and filled with glory his most blessed Mother, He resolved, as the loving Father and Pastor, to gather the sheep of his flock, which the scandal of his sufferings had disturbed and scattered. The holy Patriarchs and all whom He had rescued from limbo continually remained in his company, although they did not manifest themselves and remained invisible during his apparitions; only our great Queen was privileged to see them, know them and speak to them all during the time intervening between the Resurrection and the Ascension of her divine Son. Whenever the Lord did not appear to others, He remained with his beloved Mother in the Cenacle; nor did She ever leave this place during all the forty days. There She enjoyed the presence of the Redeemer of the world and of the choir of Prophets and Saints, by whom the King and Queen were attended. For the purpose of making his Resurrection known to his Apostles, He began by showing Himself to the women, not on account of their weakness, but because they were stronger in their belief and in their hope of

the Resurrection; for this is the reason why they merited the privilege of being the first to see Him arisen.

767. The Evangelist Mark (Mark 15, 47) mentions the special notice, which Mary Magdalen and Mary Joseph took of the place where they had seen the body of Jesus deposited. Accordingly they, with other holy women, went forth on the evening of the Sabbath from the Cenacle to the city and bought additional ointments and spices in order to return, early the following morning, to the sepulchre, and show their veneration by visiting and anointing the holy body once more. On the Sunday, entirely ignorant of the grave's having been sealed and placed under guard by order of Pilate (Matth. 27, 65), they arose before dawn in order to execute their pious design. On their way they thought only of the difficulty of removing the large stone, which they now remembered had been rolled before the opening of the sepulchre; but their love made light of this hindrance, though they did not know how to remove it. When they came forth from the house of the Cenacle, it was yet dark, but before they arrived at the sepulchre the sun had already dawned and risen; for on that day the three hours of darkness which had intervened at the Death of the Savior, were compensated by an earlier sunrise. This miracle will harmonize the statements of saint Mark and of saint John, of whom the one says, that the Marys came after sunrise, and the other that it was yet dark (Mark 16, 2; John 20, 1); for both speak truly: That they went forth very early and before dawn, and that the sun, by its more sudden and accelerated flight, had already risen at their arrival at the grave, though they tarried not on the short way. The sepulchre was in an arched vault, as in a cave, the entrance to which was covered by a large stone slab. Within, somewhat to one side and raised from the ground, was the hollow slab wherein the body of the Savior rested.

768. A little before the Marys thought and spoke of the difficulty of removing the stone, a violent and wonderful quaking or trembling of the earth took place; at the same time an angel of the Lord opened the sepulchre and cast aside the stone that covered and obstructed the entrance (Matth. 28, 2). At this noise and the earthquake the guards of the sepulchre fell prostrate to the earth, struck motionless with fear and consternation, although they did not see the Lord. For the body of the Lord was no more in the grave; He had already arisen and issued from the monument before the angel cast aside the stone. The Marys, though in some fear, took heart and were encouraged by God to approach and enter the vault. Near the entrance they saw the angel who had thrown aside the stone, seated upon it, refulgent in countenance and in snowwhite garments (Mark 16, 5). He spoke to them saying: "Be not affrighted; you seek Jesus of Nazareth, who was crucified: He is risen, He is not here; behold the place where they laid Him." The holy women entered, and seeing the sepulchre vacant they were filled with grief; for as yet they were more deeply affected at seeing the Lord absent, than by the words of the angel. Then they saw two other angels seated at each end of the slab, who said to them: "Why seek you the Living with the dead? Remember how He spoke unto you, when he was yet in Galilee (Luke 26, 45), that He was to rise on the third day. But go, tell his disciples and Peter, that He goeth before you into Galilee, there shall you see Him" (Mark 16, 7).

769. Being thus reminded by the angels the Marys remembered what their divine Master had said. Assured of his Resurrection they hastened away from the sepulchre and gave an account to the eleven Apostles and other followers of the Lord. But many of these were so shaken in their faith and so forgetful of the words of their Master and Redeemer, that they thought this story of the holy women a mere hallucina-

tion (Luke 24, 11). While the holy women, full of trembling and joy, related to the Apostles what they had seen, the sentinels at the grave awoke from their stupor and regained the use of their senses. As they saw the sepulchre open and emptied of the sacred body, they fled to give notice of the event to the princes and priests (Matth. 11, 14). These were cast into great consternation and called a meeting in order to determine what they could do in order to palliate the miracle, which was so patent that it could not remain hidden. They concluded to offer to the soldiers much money to induce them to say that during their sleep the disciples of Jesus had come and stolen the body from the grave. The priests, having assured the guards of immunity and protection, spread this lie among the Jews. Many were so foolish as to believe it; and there are some in our own day, who are obstinate and blind enough to give it credit and who prefer to accept the testimony of witnesses, who acknowledged that they were asleep during the time of which they testify.

770. Although the disciples and Apostles considered the tale of the Marys mere preposterous talk, saint Peter and saint John, desirous of convincing themselves with their own eyes, departed in all haste to the sepulchre, closely followed by the holy women (John 20, 3). Saint John arrived first, and without entering saw the windingsheets laid to one side. He waited for the arrival of saint Peter, who, passing the other Apostle, entered first. Both of them saw that the sacred body was not in the tomb. Saint John then was assured of what he had begun to believe, when he had seen the great change in the Queen of heaven, as I have related in the foregoing chapter, and he then professed his belief. The two Apostles returned to give an account of the wonder they had seen in the sepulchre. The Marys remained in a place apart from the sepulchre and wonderingly commented on the events. Mary Magdalen, in great excitement and tears, reentered the

sepulchre to reconnoitre. Although the Apostles had not seen the angels, she saw them and they asked her: "Woman, why dost thou weep?" (John 20, 5). She answered: "Because they have taken away my Lord; and I know not where they have laid Him." With this answer she left the garden where the sepulchre was, and met the Lord. She did not know Him, but thought it was the gardener. And the Lord also asked her: "Woman, why weepest thou? Whom dost thou seek?" (John 15). Magdalen, ignorant of his being the Lord, answered Him as if He were the gardener and, without further reflection, said: "Sir, if thou hast taken Him hence, tell me where thou hast laid Him, and I will take Him away." Then the loving Master said: "Mary," and in pronouncing her name He permitted Himself to be recognized by the tone of his voice.

771. As soon as Magdalen recognized Jesus she was aflame with joyous love and aswered saying: "Rabboni, my Master!" Throwing herself at his feet, she was about to touch and kiss them, as being used to that favor. But the Lord prevented her and said: "Do not touch Me, for I am not yet ascended to my Father whence I came; but return and tell my brethren, the Apostles, that I am going to my Father and theirs." Then Magdalen left, filled with consolation and jubilee. Shortly she met the other Marys. Scarcely had they heard what had happened to her and how she had seen Jesus arisen from the grave, and while they were yet standing together conferring with each other in wonder and tears of joy, He appeared to them and said: "God save you." They all recognized Him and, as saint Matthew tells us, they worshipped his sacred feet. The Lord again commanded them to go to the Apostles and tell them, that they had seen Him and that they should go to Galilee, where they should see Him arisen (Matth. 22, 9). Jesus then disappeared and the holy women hastened to the Cenacle to tell the Apostles all that

had happened to them; but the Apostles continued to hesitate in their belief (Luke 24, 11). Then the women sought the Queen of Heaven in order to tell Her of the events. Although Mary knew all that had happened by intellectual vision, She listened to them with admirable tenderness and prudence. While listening to the Marys, She took occasion to confirm their faith in the mysteries and high sacraments of the Incarnation and in the passages of holy Scriptures pertaining thereto. But the heavenly Queen did not tell them what had happened, although She was the Teacher of these faithful and devout disciples, just as the Lord was the Teacher of the Apostles in holy faith.

772. The Evangelists do not state when the Lord appeared to saint Peter, although saint Luke supposes it; but it was after He had appeared to the women. He appeared to him in private as the head of the Church and before He appeared to all of the Apostles together or to anyone of them. This happened on that same day, after the holy women had informed him of his apparition to them. Soon after also happened the apparition of the Lord to the two disciples going that afternoon to Emmaus, which is related minutely by saint Luke (Luke 24, 13). This town is sixty stadia from Jerusalem; four Palestinian miles and about two Spanish leagues. The one of them was called Cleophas and the other was saint Luke himself. It took place in the following manner: The two disciples left Jerusalem, after they had heard the reports of the women. On the way they continued to converse about the events of the Passion, the holiness of their Master and the cruelty of the Jews. They wondered that the Almighty should permit so holy and innocent a Man to suffer such wrongs and torments. The one said: "When was ever such meekness and gentleness seen?" and the other coincided, saying: "Who ever saw or heard of such patience, without a word of complaint or the least sign of perturbation

in outward appearance or bearing? His doctrine was holy, his life blameless, his words those of etemallife, his doings for the welfare of all. What then could the priests see in him to warrant such hatred ?" The other answered: "Truly He was wonderful in all respects; and no one can deny, that He was a great Prophet; He performed many miracles, gave sight to the blind, health to the sick, life to the dead, and conferred wonderful benefits upon all. But He said He would rise on the third day after his Death, which is today, and this we do not see fulfilled." The other one replied: "He also said that He would be crucified, and it was fulfilled to the word" (Matth. 20, 19).

773. In the midst of this and similar conversation Jesus appeared to them in the habit of a pilgrim and as one who happened to meet them on the way. He saluted them and said: "Of what do you speak, for it seems to Me you are sad?" Cleophas answered: "Art Thou the only stranger in Jerusalem, that Thou dost not know what has happened during these days in the city?" The Lord said: "What has happened, then?" to which the disciple replied: "Dost thou not know what the princes and priests have done to Jesus of Nazareth, a Man holy and powerful in words and deeds; how they condemned and crucified him? We had hopes that He would redeem Israel by rising from the dead; now the third day has already come, and we do not know what has happened. And some of the women of our party have terrified us, since they went early this morning to the sepulchre and did not find the body. They maintain that they saw some angels who told them that He had risen. Then some of our associates went to the grave and found true, what the women had said. We are going to Emmaus in order to await the drift of these events." Then the Lord answered: "0 foolish and slow of heart to believe; since you do not understand, that it must be so, that

Christ suffer all these pains and so frightful a death in order to enter into his glory!"

774. Following up these mysteries the divine Master then explained to them his life and death for the Redemption of the human race; He interpreted to them different types of holy Scripture: of the lamb which Moses commanded to be slain and eaten, after the thresholds should have been marked with its blood (Exod. 12, 7) ; the death of the highpriest Aaron (Numb. 20, 23), the death of Samson through the amours of his spouse Delila (Judges 16, 30), many psalms of David pointing out the wicked council, the crucifixion and the division of his garments (Ps. 21, 17, 19; 15, 10), and that his body shall not see corruption; what is said in Wisdom (Wisdom 2, 20) and more clearly in Isaias (Is. 53, 2) and Jeremias (11, 19) concerning his Passion; namely, that He should appear as a leper and a man of sorrows, that He should be borne to slaughter like a lamb without opening his mouth; and in Zacharias, who saw Him pierced with many wounds; and many other passages of the holy Prophets, which clearly manifest the mysteries of his life and death. By the fervor of these arguments the disciples were gradually enkindled with love and enlightened in the faith, which they had permitted to be obscured. And when they were already near to the castle of Emmaus, the divine Master gave them to understand, that He was to pass on in his journey; but they eagerly begged Him to stay with them, as it was getting late in the evening. The Lord yielded and, invited by the disciples, sat down to supper with them according to the manner of the Jews. The Lord took the bread, blessing it and breaking it as usual, He imparted to them, with it, the certainty that He was their Redeemer and Master.

775. They knew Him, because He opened the eyes of their souls. In the same instant He disappeared from their bodily eyes and they saw Him no more. But they were left in

a state of wonder and full of joy, conferring with each other about the ardors of charity they had felt on the way, when He had conversed with them and explained to them the Scriptures. Without delay they returned to Jerusalem (Luke 24, 33), although night had already set in. They went to the house, where the rest of the Apostles had secreted themselves for fear of the Jews and they found them discussing the news of the risen Savior and how He had already appeared to Peter. To this the two disciples added all that had happened to them on the way to Emmaus, and how they had recognized the Savior at the breaking of the bread in the castle of Emmaus. At this meeting was present also saint Thomas, who, although hearing the arguments of the Apostles and the testimony of saint Peter asserting that he had seen the Master risen, refused credit to the three disciples and the women, persevering in doubt and unbelief. In a somewhat hasty manner, caused by his incredulity, he left their company. Shortly after, when Thomas had left and the doors had been locked, the Lord entered and appeared to the others. In their midst He saluted them, saying: "Peace be with you. It is I; do not fear."

776. At this sudden apparition, the Apostles feared lest what they saw was a ghost or phantasm, and the Lord added: "Why are you troubled, and why do thoughts arise in your hearts? See my hands and feet, that it is I myself; handle and see: for a spirit hath no flesh and bones, as you see Me have." The Apostles were so excited and confused, that though they saw Him and touched the wounded hands of the Savior, they could not realize, that it was He to whom they spoke and whom they touched. The loving Master in order to assure them still more, said to them: "Give Me to eat, if you have aught." Joyfully they offered Him some fried fish and a comb of honey. He ate part of these, and divided the rest among them, saying: "Do you not know, that all that has happened

with Me is the same that has been written by Moses and the Prophets, in the Psalms and holy Scriptures, and that all must necessarily be fulfilled in Me as it was prophesied?" And at these words He opened their minds, and they knew Him, and understood the sayings of the Scriptures concerning his Passion, Death and Resurrection on the third day. Having thus instructed them, He said again: "Peace be with you. As the Father has sent me, so I send you, in order that you may teach the world the knowledge of the truth, of God and of eternal life, preaching repentance for sins and forgiveness of them in my name." Breathing upon them, He added and said: "Receive ye the Holy Ghost, in order that the sins which you forgive may be forgiven, and those which you do not forgive, may not be forgiven. Preach ye to all nations, beginning in Jerusalem." Then the Savior, having thus consoled and confirmed them in faith, and having given them and all priests the power to forgive sins, disappeared from their midst.

777. All this took place in the absence of Thomas; but soon after, the Lord so disposing, he returned to the assembly, and the Apostles told him what had happened during his absence. Yet, though he found them so changed in joyful exultation, he remained incredulous and obstinate, maintaining, that he would not believe what all of them affirmed, unless he himself should see with his own eyes and touch with his own hands and fingers the wounds of the Savior's side and those of the nails (John 20, 25). In this obstinacy the incredulous Thomas persevered for eight days, when the Savior again returned through locked doors and appeared in the midst of the Apostles including Thomas. He saluted them as usual, saying: "Peace be with you," and then calling Thomas, He sweetly reprimanded him. "Come, Thomas, and with your hands touch the openings of my hands and of my side, and be not so incredulous, but convinced and

believing." Thomas touched the divine wounds and was interiorly enlightened to believe and to acknowledge his ignorance. Prostrating himself to the ground he said: "My Lord and my God!" to which the Lord replied: "Because thou hast seen Me, thou hast believed; but blessed are those who do not see Me and believe Me." The Lord then disappeared, leaving the Apostles and Thomas filled with light and joy. They immediately sought most holy Mary in order to relate to Her what had happened, just as they had done after the first apparition of the Lord.

778. The Apostles were at that time not yet able to comprehend the great wisdom of the Queen of heaven and earth, and much less to understand the knowledge She had of all that happened to them and of all the works of her divine Son; She therefore listened to them with highest prudence and with the loving sweetness of a Mother and Queen. After the first apparition some of the Apostles told Her of the obstinacy of Thomas, and that he would not believe their unanimous testimony concerning the Resurrection of the Master. During the eight days in which his incredulity continued, the indignation of some of the Apostles against him grew more intense. They went to the heavenly Lady and accused him before Her of being an obstinate and stubborn transgressor, a man too dull to be enlightened. The loving Princess listened to them sweetly, and seeing that the anger of the Apostles, who were as yet all imperfect, was still increasing, She spoke to those most indignant and quieted them by arguing that the judgments of the Lord were deeply hidden and that the incredulity of Thomas would occasion great benefit to others and glory to God; that they should wait and hope and not be disturbed so easily. The heavenly Mother offered up most fervent prayers and petitions for Thomas and on that account the Lord hastened the cure of the incredulous Apostle. When He yielded and all of them

brought the news to Mary, their Mistress and Lady, She confirmed them in their faith, at the same time admonishing and correcting them. She told them to give thanks to the Most High for this blessing, and to be constant in temptation, since all were subject to the danger of falling. Many other sweet words of correction, instruction and warning did She add, preparing them for what was yet to be done in the establishment of the new Church.

779. There were other apparitions and doings of the Lord, as the Evangelist saint John gives us to understand; but only those are mentioned, which suffice to establish the fact of the Resurrection. The same Evangelist describes the apparition of the Lord at the sea of Tiberias to saint Peter, Thomas, Nathanael, the sons of Zebedee, and two other disciples, which, as it is so mysterious, I thought I ought not pass over unmentioned in this chapter. The apparition happened in the following manner: the Apostles, after the above events in Jerusalem, betook themselves to Galilee; for the Lord had so commanded them and had promised, that they should there see Him. Saint Peter, happening to be with the seven Apostles and disciples on the shores of that sea, proposed that they pass the time in fishing, as that was his trade. All of them accompanied him and they spent the night in casting out their nets; but they caught not a single fish. In the morning our Savior Jesus appeared on the bank without making Himself known. He was near the boat on which they were fishing and He asked them: "Have you something to eat?" They answered: "We have nothing." The Lord replied: "Throw out your net on the right side, and you shall make a catch." They complied and their net became so filled, that they could not lift it into the boat. This miracle caused saint John to recognize the Lord Christ, and going nearer to saint Peter, he said: "It is the Lord who speaks to us from the bank." Then saint Peter likewise recognized Jesus; and im-

mediately seized with his accustomed fervor, he hastily girded himself with the tunic, which he had laid off, and cast himself into the sea, walking on the waters to the Master of life, while the others followed in their boat.

780. They sprang ashore and found that the Lord had already prepared for them a meal; for they saw a fire and upon its glimmering ashes bread and a fish. The Lord however told them to bring some of those they had caught. Saint Peter then drew out the catch and found, that they had secured one hundred and fifty-three fishes; and that even with that great number the net had not been torn. The Lord commanded them to eat. Although He was so familiar and affable in his behavior to them, no one ventured to ask who He was; for the miracles and the majesty of the Lord filled them with great reverence. He divided among them the fish and the bread. As soon as they had finished eating, He turned to saint Peter and said to him: "Simon, son of John, dost thou love Me more than these do?" Saint Peter answered: "Yea, Lord, Thou knowest that I love Thee." The Lord replied: "Feed my lambs." Immediately He asked again: "Simon, son of John, dost thou love me?" Saint Peter gave the same answer: "Lord, Thou knowest that I love Thee." And the Lord put the same question the third time: "Simon, son of John, lovest thou me?" At this third repetition Peter grieved and answered: "Lord, Thou knowest all things, and also that I love Thee." Christ our Savior then answered the third time: "Feed my sheep." By these words he made Peter the sole head of his only and universal Church, giving him the supreme vicarious authority over all men. On this account He had questioned him so often concerning his love, as if that alone could make him capable of the supreme dignity, and of itself sufficed for its worthy exercise.

781. Then the Lord intimated to him the duties of the office He had given him and said: "Truly I assure thee, that

when thou art old, thou shalt not gird thyself as now, nor shalt thou go where thou listest; for another shall gird thee and lead thee where thou wouldst not." Saint Peter understood, that the Lord held in store for him the death of the cross in which he was to imitate and follow his Lord. But as saint John was so beloved, Peter was desirous of knowing what would become of him, and he asked the Savior:" And what shalt Thou do with this one so beloved by Thee?" The Lord answered: "What is it to thee to know this? If I desire that he remain thus until I come again to the world, it will be in my hands. Follow thou Me, and do not concern thyself with what I desire to do with him." On account of these words a report was spread among the Apostles, that John was not to die. But the Evangelist himself remarks, that Christ had not said positively, he should not die, as is plain from the words, but He seems to have expressly desired to conceal his will concerning the death of the Evangelist, reserving this secret to Himself at that time. The most holy Mary, by her clear intuition so often mentioned, had a full intelligence of all these mysteries and apparitions of the Lord. Being the archive of the works of the Lord and the treasure house of the mysteries of his Church, She preserved and conferred them within her own most prudent and chaste heart. The Apostles, and especially her new son John, informed Her of all that happened to them. The great Lady persevered in her retirement for the forty days after the Resurrection and there enjoyed the sight of her divine Son and of the angels and saints. They in tum sang hymns to the Lord, which She composed; and the angels as it were gathered them from her mouth, celebrating the glories and the virtues of the Lord.

Words of the Queen

THE VIRGIN MARY SPEAKS TO SISTER MARY OF AGREDA

782. My daughter, the instruction which I shall give thee in this chapter shall be also an answer to thy desire of knowing why my divine Son appeared at one time as a gardener, at another as a stranger, and why He did not always make Himself known at first sight. Know then, my dearest, that the Marys and the Apostles, although they were followers of Christ and at that time privileged and perfect in comparison with the rest of men; yet they had withal arrived only at a low degree of perfection and holiness and not far enough advanced in the school of their Master. They were weak in faith and in other virtues; they were less constant and fervent than was due to their vocation and to the graces they had received. The little faults in souls favored and chosen for the friendship and familiar intercourse with God weigh more in the scales of his most righteous equity, than some great ones in other souls not selected for these privileges. Hence, although the Apostles and the Marys were friends of the Savior, yet, on account of their faults and their weaknesses, their lukewarm and faltering love, they were not prepared for the immediate effects of the full knowledge and presence of their Master. In this paternal love He therefore created in them the proper dispositions by enlightening them and enkindling them with words of eternal life before He manifested Himself to them. When their hearts had been thus prepared by faith and love, He made known and communicated to them the abundance of his Divinity together with other admirable gifts and graces by which they were renewed and raised above themselves. When they had enjoyed his favors, He again disappeared, in order that they might desire so much the more earnestly the sweetness of his communications and intercourse. This was the secret of his appearing in disguise to Magdalen, to the

Apostles, and to the disciples at Emmaus. The same course He pursues respectively with many other souls, whom He chooses for intimate converse and communication.

783. By the consideration of these admirable tactics of divine Providence thou wilt be instructed and reprehended for the doubts and incredulity with which thou hast so often met the divine blessings and favors of my Son. Thou wilt learn that it is time thou moderate thy constant fears, lest thou pass from doubt to obstinacy and to slowness of heart in giving thanks. Thou wilt also draw a very useful lesson if thou worthily contemplate, how quickly the immense charity of the Most High responds to those who are contrite and humble of heart (Ps. 33, 19), and how ready He is, immediately to assist those who seek Him in love, who meditate and speak of his Passion and Death (Wis. 6, 13). All this thou seest well exemplified in saint Peter, Mary Magdalen and in the disciples. Imitate then, my dearest, the fervor of Magdalen in search for her Master, who did not permit herself to be diverted even by the angels, or leave the sepulchre with the others, or rest until she found Him so full of sweetness and kindness. This she also earned by having accompanied Me through all the Passion with an ardent and unfaltering heart. Similar was also the conduct of the other Marys, who thus merited before so many others the joys of the Resurrection. Next to them the humility and contrition of saint Peter in bewailing his denial, secured the same reward; immediately the Lord bent down to console him and commissioned the women to tell especially him of his Resurrection and shortly after, He visited him, confirmed him in faith and filled him with joy and the gifts of grace. Then before appearing to others, He showed Himself to the two disciples, because, although in doubt, they were conversing regretfully of his Death. I assure thee, my daughter, that none of the works of men done with a good intention and righteous heart, shall

remain without an immediate reward. For neither fire will in its greatest intensity so quickly consume the driest tow, nor will a stone, freed from hindrance, so quickly fall to its centre, nor the waves of the sea rush on with so great an impulse and force, as the goodness of the Most High and his grace to those souls, who are well disposed and have cleared away the hindrances of sin. This is a truth which causes the greatest wonder in the saints, who are made aware of it in heaven. Praise Him for this goodness and also for his drawing vast good out of evil, as He did out of the incredulity of the Apostles. For through it He manifested his mercy to them and has made his Resurrection plain to all men, and evident his kindness in pardoning the Apostles. He showed his willingness to forget their faults, his readiness to seek them and appear to them, dealing humanely with them as a father, enlightening them and instructing them according to their needs and the weakness of their faith.

Chapter XXVIII

SOME HIDDEN AND DIVINE MYSTERIES IN THE LIFE OF
MARY DURING THE DAYS AFTER THE RESURRECTION OF
THE LORD; SHE RECEIVES THE TITLE OF MOTHER AND
QUEEN OF THE CHURCH; THE APPARITION OF CHRIST
BEFORE AND IN PREPARATION FOR THE ASCENSION.

784. During the whole course of this history the abundance
and vastness of its mysteries have made me feel destitute of
proper words. Vast is that which is offered to the understanding in the divine light, and insignificant what can be expressed in language. On account of this inequality and defect
arising from the fecundity of the intellect and the sterility of
words, my faculties have suffered a great strain; for the want
of correspondence between the results of the spoken word
and the conception of the mind continually causes a mistrust
and dissatisfaction with the words, as falling short of the
meaning and as making me hopelessly incapable of correcting
the deficiency or of filling up the discrepancy between the
things said and those perceived. I find myself in this state just
now, when I am to describe what has been made known to
me concerning the hidden mysteries and exalted sacraments
of the life of Mary during the forty days after the Resurrection of her Son and our Redeemer until the time He ascended into heaven. The state in which the divine power placed
Her after the Passion and Resurrection was new and more

exalted: her operations were more mysterious, the favors conferred upon Her were proportionate to her eminent holiness and to the will of Him who wrought them; for according to this rule He proceeded. If I were obliged to describe all that has been manifested to me, it would be necessary to extend this history into many large volumes. From what I shall say something can be gathered concerning these most divine mysteries for the glory of that great Queen and Lady.

785. It has already been said at the beginning of the last chapter, that during the forty days after the Resurrection the Lord remained in the Cenacle and in the company of his most holy Mother whenever He was not absent in appearing to some of his chosen friends. All the rest of the time He spent in her presence. Anyone can prudently conjecture, that all this time, in which these two Sovereigns of the world were together, They spent in works altogether divine and above all the conceptions of the human mind. What has been made known to me of these works is ineffable; for often They would engage in sweetest colloquy of inscrutable wisdom and this conversation was for the loving Mother a joy, which though inferior to the beatific vision, was consoling and delightful beyond all that is imaginable. At other times the great Queen, the Patriarchs and Saints, who there assisted in their glorified state, occupied themselves in the praise and exaltation of the Most High. Mary had a deep knowledge of all the works and merits of the saints; of the blessings, favors and gifts each one had received from the Omnipotent; of the mysteries, figures and prophecies which had gone before in the ancient Patriarchs. All this She was Mistress of, and it was present to her mind in contemplation more completely, than the Hail Mary is known to us for recitation. The exalted Lady considered all the great motives of these saints for praising and blessing the Author of all good. Though they,

enjoying the beatific vision, fulfilled and are fulfilling this duty without cessation, yet in their conversations and intercourse with the heavenly Princess, they were constantly urged by Her to magnify and praise the divine Majesty for all these blessings and operations so evident to the eyes of her soul.

786. All this sacred choir of the saints joined with their Queen and began to engage in these divine exercises according to a stated order; so that all of them formed a choir, in which each one of the blessed recited a verse, while the Mother of wisdom answered with another. In their frequent exercise of these sweet alternating songs, the great Lady by Herself produced as many hymns and canticles of praise, as all the saints and angels together; for also the angels entered into this competition of new songs, admirable to them and to all the blessed. For the wise worship of God practiced by the heavenly Princess in this life exceeded that of all other creatures, including those who already enjoyed the beatific vision. All that the blessed Mary did during these days is beyond the capacity and estimation of men. But her exalted thoughts and motives were prudently measured by her most faithful love; for, knowing that her divine Son tarried in this world principally in order to assist and console Her, She resolved to compensate Him as far as it was possible. Therefore She did all in her power to provide for the Lord the same praises and honors as the saints furnish Him in heaven. By concurring in these praises Herself She at once raised them to the highest worth and changed the house of the Cenacle into a heaven.

787. In such exercises She consumed the greater part of the forty days and during that time were composed more canticles and hymns than all the saints and Prophets have left for our use. Sometimes this heavenly gathering made use of the psalms of David or the prophecies of the Scripture, commenting, as it were, or expatiating on these so divine and profound mysteries; and the holy fathers, who had been the

authors of the prophecies, when they recognized the gifts and favors of the right hand of God and the revelations of such numerous and great sacraments, referred them especially to our Queen. Admirable was also the delight She drew from her conversation with her holy mother, her father Joachim, saint Joseph, saint John the Baptist, and the great Patriarchs. In mortal flesh no state can be imagined, which approaches so close to the beatific fruition as the one enjoyed at that time by the great Lady and Queen. Another wonder happened during those days, which was: that all the souls of the just who died in grace within those forty days, gathered in the Cenacle, and those who had no debt to pay, were there beatified. But those who were subject to purgatory were obliged to wait in the same place without seeing the Lord, some three, some five days, others again for a shorter or longer period. For the Mother of mercy satisfied for their defects by genuflections, prostrations or some work of satisfaction, but much more by the ardent charity with which She wrought for them and applied to them the infinite merits of her divine Son. Thus She helped to abbreviate their punishment and the pain of not seeing the Lord (for they suffered no sensible pains) and soon they were beatified and admitted to the choir of the saints. For each one that thus joined their ranks, the great Lady composed new hymns of praise to the Lord.

788. Amidst all these delights and jubilations the kindest Mother, with ineffable generosity, did not forget the misery and poverty of the children of Eve deprived of this glory; but like a true Mother of mercy, turning her eyes upon the condition of mortals, She offered for all of them her most fervent prayers. She besought the eternal Father for the spreading of the new Law through all the world; the multiplication of the children of the Church; for its defense and protection and for the extension of the fruits of the Redemp-

tion to all men. The fulfillment of this petition was regulated by the eternal decrees of the divine wisdom; but as far as the desires and affections of the most loving Queen were concerned She wished the Redemption and eternal life to be extended to the whole human race. Besides these general petitions, She made special ones for the Apostles, and particularly for saint John and saint Peter: for the one, as her son; for the other, as the head of the Church. She prayed also for Magdalen and the Marys, and all the other faithful then belonging to the Church. Finally She prayed for the exaltation of the faith and of the name of her divine Son Jesus.

789. A few days before the Ascension of the Lord, while the blessed Mary was engaged in the one of the abovementioned exercises, the eternal Father and the Holy Ghost appeared in the Cenacle upon a throne of ineffable splendor surrounded by the choirs of angels and saints there present and other heavenly spirits, which had now come with the divine Persons. Then the incarnate Word ascended the throne and seated Himself with the other Two. The ever humble Mother of the Most High, prostrate in a corner of a room, in deepest reverence adored the most blessed Trinity, and in it her own incarnate Son. The eternal Father commanded two of the highest angels to call Mary, which they did by approaching Her, and in sweetest voices intimating to Her the divine will. She arose from the dust with the most profound humility, modesty and reverence. Accompanied by the angels She approached the foot of the Throne, humbling herself anew. The eternal Father said to Her: "Beloved, ascend higher!" (Luke 14, 10). As these words at the same time effected what they signified, She was raised up and placed on the throne of royal Majesty with the three divine Persons. New admiration was caused in the saints to see a mere Creature exalted to such dignity. Being made to understand the sanctity and equity of the works of the Most High,

they gave new glory and praise proclaiming Him immense, Just, Holy and Admirable in all his counsels.

790. The Father then spoke to the blessed Mary saying: "My Daughter, to Thee do I entrust the Church founded by my Onlybegotten, the new law of grace He established in the world, and the people, which He redeemed: to Thee do I consign them all." Thereupon also the Holy Ghost spoke to Her: "My Spouse, chosen from all creatures, I communicate to Thee my wisdom and grace together with which shall be deposited in thy heart the mysteries, the works and teachings and all that the incarnate Word has accomplished in the world." And the Son also said: "My most beloved Mother, I go to my Father and in my stead I shall leave Thee and I charge Thee with the care of my Church; to Thee do I recommend its children and my brethren, as the Father has consigned them to Me." Then the three Divine Persons, addressing the choir of holy angels and the other saints, said: "This is the Queen of all created things in heaven and earth; She is the Protectress of the Church, the Mistress of creatures, the Mother of piety, the Intercessor of the faithful, the Advocate of sinners, the Mother of beautiful love and holy hope (Eccli. 24, 24); She is mighty in drawing our will to mercy and clemency. In Her shall be deposited the treasures of our grace and her most faithful heart shall be the tablet whereon shall be written and engraved our holy law. In Her are contained the mysteries of our Omnipotence for the salvation of mankind. She is the perfect work of our hands, through whom the plenitude of our desires shall be communicated and satisfied without hindrance in the currents of our divine perfections. Whoever shall call upon Her from his heart shall not perish; whoever shall obtain her intercession shall secure for himself eternal life. What She asks of Us, shall be granted, and We shall always hear her requests and prayers and fulfill her will; for She has consecrated Herself perfectly

to what pleases Us." The most blessed Mary, hearing Herself thus exalted, humiliated Herself so much the deeper the more highly She was raised by the right hand of the Most High above all the human and angelic creatures. As if She were the least of all, She adored the Lord and offered Herself, in the most prudent terms and in the most ardent love, to work as a faithful servant in the Church and to obey promptly all the biddings of the divine will. From that day on She took upon Herself anew the care of the evangelical Church, as a loving Mother of all its children; She renewed all the petitions She had until then made, so that during the whole further course of her life they were most fervent and incessant, as we shall see in the third part, where will appear more clearly what the Church owes to this great Queen and Lady, and what blessings She gained and merited for it. By the favor now vouchsafed to Mary and by those conferred upon Her later, She was raised to a participation in the being of her Son beyond all possibility of words to explain; for He communicated his attributes and perfections to Her in correspondence to her ministry as Instructress and Mother of the Church and as supplying his own ministry. He elevated Her into a new state of knowledge and power, by means of which nothing was to be hidden from Her either of the divine mysteries or of the inmost secrets of the human heart. She was made to understand and know when and how She was to use this communicated power of the Divinity in her dealings with men, with the demons and with all creatures. In short, all that can possibly be conferred upon a mere creature was received and given over in all its fullness and excellence to our great Queen and Lady. Of these sacramental operations saint John was to a certain extent made aware, in order that he might form an estimate, how much he was to esteem and appreciate the inestimable Treasure consigned to his care.

From that day on he venerated and served the great Lady with new solicitude and reverence.

791. Other wonderful favors the Most High wrought for Mary in those forty days, and there was none of them, in which He did not show forth his beneficent power and holiness toward his Mother and his solicitude to enrich Her more and more before his Ascension into heaven. When the preordained time for the return of the eternal Wisdom to his Father had arrived, after having proved his Resurrection by many apparitions and by many arguments (as saint Luke says, Acts 1, 3), He resolved to appear and manifest Himself once more to that whole gathering of Apostles and disciples, numbering one hundred and twenty persons. This apparition took place in the Cenacle on the very day of the Ascension and in addition to the one mentioned by saint Mark in the last chapter (Mark 16, 14); for all this happened on one and the same day. After the sojourn of the Apostles in Galilee, whither the Lord had commanded them to go and where He appeared to them close to the sea of Tiberias, after they had seen and adored Him on the mountain, as mentioned by Mark, and after He had been seen by the five hundred according to saint Paul, the disciples returned to Jerusalem in order to be present according to the wishes of the Lord, at his wonderful Ascension. While the eleven Apostles were reclining at their meal, as is related by saint Mark and saint Luke in the Acts, the Lord entered and ate with them, moderating, with admirable affability and condescension, the splendors of his beauty and glory in order that He might be looked upon by all. Having finished their meal He spoke to them in earnest yet sweetly tempered majesty.

792. "Know ye, my disciples, that my eternal Father has given Me all power in heaven and on earth, and I wish to communicate it to you in order that you may establish my new Church throughout the whole world. You have been

slow and tardy in believing my Resurrection; but it is now time that as true and faithful disciples, you be the teachers of the faith to all men. Preaching my Gospel as you have heard it from my lips, you shall baptize all that believe, giving them Baptism in the name of the Father, and of the Son (who am I) and of the Holy Ghost. Those that shall believe and be baptized, shall be saved, and those that shall not believe, shall be damned. Teach the believers to observe all that concerns my holy Law. In confirmation thereof the faithful shall perform signs and wonders; they shall cast out the demons from their habitations; they shall speak new tongues; they shall cure the bites of serpents; if they drink aught poisonous, it shall not hurt them; and they shall cure the sick by the laying on of hands." Such miracles Christ our Savior promised for the foundation of the Church in the preaching of the Gospel; and all of them were verified in the first ages of the Church. For the propagation of the faith in the rest of the world and for the preservation of the Church where it exists, He continues the same signs, when and how his Providence deems it necessary; for He never will forsake the holy Church, his most beloved spouse.

793. On that same day, by divine dispensation, while the Lord was at table with the eleven Apostles, other disciples and pious women gathered at the Cenacle to the number of one hundred and twenty; for the divine Master wished them to be present at his Ascension. Moreover, just as He had instructed the Apostles, so He now wanted to instruct these faithful respectively in what each was to know before his leaving them and ascending into heaven. All of them being thus gathered and united in peace and charity within those walls in the hall of the last Supper, the Author of life manifested Himself to them as a kind and loving Father and said to them:

794. "My sweetest children, I am about to ascend to my Father, from whose bosom I descended in order to rescue and save men. I leave with you in my stead my own Mother as your Protectress, Consoler and Advocate, and as your Mother, whom you are to hear and obey in all things. Just as I have told you, that he who sees Me sees my Father, and he who knows Me, knows also Him; so I now tell you, that He who knows my Mother, knows Me; he who hears Her, hears Me; and who honors Her, honors Me. All of you shall have Her as your Mother, as your Superior and Head, and so shall also your successors. She shall answer your doubts, solve your difficulties; in Her, those who seek Me shall always find Me; for I shall remain in Her until the end of the world, and I am in Her now, although you do not understand how." This the Lord said, because He was sacramentally present in the bosom of his Mother; for the sacred species, which She had received at the last Supper, were preserved in Her until consecration of the first Mass, as I shall relate further on. The Lord thus fulfilled that which He promised in saint Matthew: "I am with you to the consummation of the world" (Matth. 28, 20). The Lord added and said: "You will have Peter as the supreme head of the Church, for I leave him as my Vicar; and you shall obey him as the chief highpriest. Saint John you shall hold as the son of my Mother; for I have chosen and appointed him for this office on the Cross." The Lord then looked upon his most beloved Mother, who was there present, and intimated his desire of expressly commanding that whole congregation to worship and reverence Her in a manner suited to the dignity of Mother of God, and of leaving this command under form of a precept for the whole Church. But the most humble Lady besought her Onlybegotten to be pleased not to secure Her more honor than was absolutely necessary for executing all that He had charged Her with; and that the new children of the Church

should not be induced to show Her greater honor than they had shown until then. On the contrary, She desired to divert all the sacred worship of the Church immediately upon the Lord himself and to make the propagation of the Gospel redound entirely to the exaltation of his holy name. Christ our Savior yielded to this most prudent petition of his Mother, reserving to Himself the duty of spreading the knowledge of Her at a more convenient and opportune time; yet in secret He conferred upon Her new extraordinary favors, as shall appear in the rest of this history.

795. In considering the loving exhortations, of their divine Master, the mysteries which He had revealed to them, and the prospect of his leaving them, that whole congregation was moved to their inmost hearts; for He had enkindled in them the divine love by the vivid faith of his Divinity and humanity. Reviving within them the memory of his words and his teachings of eternal life, the delights of his most loving intercourse and company, and sorrowfully realizing, that they were now all at once to be deprived of these blessings, they wept most tenderly and sighed from their inmost souls. They longed to detain Him, although they could not, because they saw it was not befitting; words of parting rose to their lips, but they could not bring themselves to utter them; each one felt sentiments of sorrow arising amid feelings both of joy and yet also of pious regret. How shall we live without such a Master? they thought. Who can ever speak to us such words of life and consolation as He? Who will receive us so lovingly and kindly? Who shall be our Father and protector? We shall be helpless children and orphans in this world. Some of them broke their silence and exclaimed: "0 most loving Lord and Father! O joy and life of our souls! Now that we know Thee as our Redeemer, Thou departest and leavest us! I Take us along with Thee, 0 Lord; banish us not from thy sight. Our blessed Hope, what shall we do without thy

presence? Whither shall we turn, if Thou goest away? Whither shall we direct our steps, if we cannot follow Thee, our Father, our Chief, and our Teacher?" To these and other pleadings the Lord answered by bidding them not to leave Jerusalem and to persevere in prayer until He should send the Holy Spirit, the Consoler, as promised by the Father and as already foretold to the Apostles at the last Supper. Thereupon happened, what I shall relate in the next chapter.

Words of the Queen

THE VIRGIN MARY SPEAKS TO SISTER MARY OF AGREDA

796. My daughter, it is just, that in thy admiration of the hidden favors vouchsafed to me by the right hand of the Almighty, thy love be awakened in eternal benedictions and praise of his wonderful operations. Although I withhold from thy knowledge many of them, which thou shalt know after leaving mortal flesh; yet I wish, that from now on thou consider it thy especial duty to praise and magnify the Lord, because, in spite of my being formed of the same material as Adam (Luke 1, 51), He has raised me from the dust and has manifested to me the power of his arm, operating in me such great things as can never be merited. In order to exercise thyself in these praises of the Most High, repeat many times over the canticle of the Magnificat, in which I have briefly comprehended them. When thou art alone, say it prostrate and upon thy knees; and above all, let it be done with the sincerest love and veneration. This exercise shall be especially agreeable and pleasing in my eyes; and I shall present it to the Lord, if thou perform it in the manner I tell thee.

797. As thou art now again astonished, that the Evangelists should not have made any mention of these wonderful favors of the Lord toward me, I will repeat what I have already told thee; for I wish that all mortals should remember

the reason for the reticence of the Gospels. I myself have commanded the Evangelists not to write anything about my privileges except what is contained in the articles of faith and in the commandments of the divine law and what was necessary for the establishment of the Church. For, as the Teacher of the Church, I knew by the infused science of the Most High, what would then be proper for its beginning. The manifestation of my prerogatives, being included in the dignity of Mother of God and in my being full of grace, was reserved by the divine Providence for a more opportune and convenient time; namely, when the faith should be better known and established. In the course of the centuries some mysteries pertaining to me have been made plain; but the plenitude of light has been given to thee, who art a poor and insignificant creature; and this has been done on account of the necessities and unhappy state of the world. God in his kindness wishes to offer this opportune remedy to men, in order that all of them may seek help and eternal salvation through my intercession. This thou hast always understood, and thou shalt understand it still better. But above all I desire, that thou occupy thyself entirely in the imitation of my life and in the continual contemplation of my virtues and works, in order that thou mayest gain the desired victory over my and thy enemies.

Chapter XXIX

CHRIST OUR REDEEMER ASCENDS INTO HEAVEN FOL-
LOWED BY ALL THE SAINTS IN HIS COMPANY; HE ASSUMES
WITH HIM HIS MOST HOLY MOTHER AND PUTS HER IN
POSSESSION OF GLORY.

798. The most auspicious hour, in which the Onlybegotten
of the eternal Father, after descending from heaven in order
to assume human flesh, was to ascend by his own power and
in a most wonderful manner to the right hand of God, the
Inheritor of his eternities, one and equal with Him in nature
and infinite glory. He was to ascend, also, because He had
previously descended to the lowest regions of the earth, as the
Apostle says (Ephes. 4, 9), having fulfilled all that had been
written and prophesied concerning his coming into the
world, his Life, Death and the Redemption of man, and
having penetrated, as the Lord of all, to the very centre of the
earth. By this Ascension he sealed all the mysteries and
hastened the fulfillment of his promise, according to which
He was, with the Father, to send the Paraclete upon his
Church after He himself should have ascended into heaven
(John 16, 7). In order to celebrate this festive and mysterious
day, Christ our Lord selected as witnesses the hundred and
twenty persons, to whom, as related in the foregoing chapter,
He had spoken in the Cenacle. They were the most holy
Mary, the eleven Apostles, the seventy-two disciples, Mary

Magdalen, Lazarus their brother, the other Marys and the faithful men and women making up the abovementioned number of one hundred and twenty.

799. With this little flock our divine Shepherd Jesus left the Cenacle, and, with his most blessed Mother at his side, He conducted them all through the streets of Jerusalem. The Apostles and all the rest in their order, proceeded in the direction of Bethany, which was less than half a league over the brow of mount Olivet. The company of angels and saints from limbo and purgatory followed the Victor with new songs of praise, although Mary alone was privileged to see them. The Resurrection of Jesus of Nazareth was already divulged throughout Jerusalem and Palestine. Although the perfidious and malicious princes and priests had spread about the false testimony of his being stolen by the disciples, yet many would not accept their testimony, nor give it any credit. It was divinely provided, that none of the inhabitants of the city, and none of the unbelievers or doubters, should pay any attention to this holy procession, or hinder it on its way from the Cenacle. All, except the one hundred and twenty just, who were chosen by the Lord to witness his Ascension into heaven, were justly punished by being prevented from noticing this wonderful mystery, and the Chieftain and Head of this procession remained invisible to them.

800. The Lord having thus secured them this privacy, they all ascended mount Olivet to its highest point. There they formed three choirs, one of the angels, another of the saints, and a third of the Apostles and faithful, which again divided into two bands, while Christ the Savior presided. Then the most prudent Mother prostrated Herself : at the feet of her Son and, worshipping Him with admirable humility, She adored Him as the true God and as the Redeemer of the world, asking his last blessing. All the faithful there present imitated Her and did the same. Weeping and sigh-

ing, they asked the Lord, whether He was now to restore the kingdom of Israel (Acts 1, 6). The Lord answered, that this was a secret of the eternal Father and not to be made known to them; but, for the present, it was necessary and befitting, that they receive the Holy Ghost and preach, in Jerusalem, in Samaria and in all the world, the mysteries of the Redemption of the world.

801. Jesus, having taken leave of this holy and fortunate gathering of the faithful, his countenance beaming forth peace and majesty, joined his hands and, by his own power, began to raise Himself from the earth, leaving thereon the impression of his sacred feet. In gentlest motion He was wafted toward the aerial regions, drawing after Him the eyes and the hearts of those firstborn children, who amid sighs and tears vented their affection. And as, at the moving of the first Cause of all motion, it is proper that also the nether spheres should be set in motion, so the Savior Jesus drew after Him also the celestial choirs of the angels, the holy Patriarchs and the rest of the glorified saints, some of them with body and soul, others only as to their soul. All of them in heavenly order were raised up together from the earth, accompanying and following their King, their Chief and Head. The new and mysterious sacrament, which the right hand of the Most High wrought on this occasion for his most holy Mother, was that He raised Her up with Him in order to put Her in possession of the glory, which He had assigned to Her as his true Mother and which She had by her merits prepared and earned for Herself. Of this favor the great Queen was capable even before it happened; for her divine Son had offered it to Her during the forty days which He spent in her company after his Resurrection. In order that this sacrament might be kept secret from all other living creatures at that time, and in order that the heavenly Mistress might be present in the gathering of the Apostles and the

faithful in their prayerful waiting upon the coming of the Holy Ghost (Acts 1, 14), the divine power enabled the blessed Mother miraculously to be in two places at once; remaining with the children of the Church for their comfort during their stay in the Cenacle and at the same time ascending with the Redeemer of the world to his heavenly throne, where She remained for three days. There She enjoyed the perfect use of all her powers and faculties, whereas She was more restricted in the use of them during that time in the Cenacle.

802. The most blessed Lady was raised up with her divine Son and placed at the right hand in fulfillment of what David said: "The Queen was at his right hand in vestments gilded by the splendors of his glory and surrounded by the variety of his gifts and graces in the sight of the ascending angels and saints" (Ps. 44, 10). In order that this astounding mystery may excite the devotion and enliven the faith of the faithful, and that it may draw them to magnify the Author of this extraordinary and inconceivable miracle, I again inform those who read of it, that, from the time in which the Most High commissioned me, and afterward repeatedly, through many years, expressly commanded me to write this history, He has revealed to me many diverse mysteries and great sacraments, both already written and yet to be written; for the exalted nature of this history demanded such a preparation and predisposition. I have not received all these revelations at once; for the limitation of a creature is not capable of such abundance. But in order that I might be enabled to write, new enlightenment was given me for each mystery in particular. The enlightenments concerning each were usually given to me on the feasts of the Christ our Lord and of the heavenly Lady. Especially the great sacrament of Mary's being raised to heaven with her divine Son at his Ascension and of her remaining at the same time in the Cenacle in a

wonderful manner, was shown to me in several consecutive years on that feast day.

803. When the divine truth is known and contemplated in God himself, in whom there is all light without mixture of darkness and where as well the object as its cause is evident, it creates a certainty without a touch of doubt (I John 1, 5). But those who hear these mysteries told by others, must excite their piety in order to ask for belief in what is obscure. On this account I would feel a hesitation in writing of the hidden sacrament of this celestial visit of our Queen, if the omission of such a great and important wonder and prerogative were not so serious a defect in this history. This hesitation occurred to me, when I was made aware of this mystery for the first time; but now, after I have already related in the first part, that the child Mary at its birth was elevated to the empyrean heavens, and, in this second part, that She was twice thus elevated during the nine days of preparation for the incarnation of the divine Word, I have no such hesitation in writing of this miracle. If the divine power conferred such admirable favors on the blessed Virgin before She became the Mother of God in preparation for this dignity; it is much more credible, that He should repeat it after She had been consecrated by bearing Him in her virginal womb, after giving Him human form from her own purest blood, after nursing Him at her breast and raising Him as a true Son, after serving Him for thirty-three years, following Him and imitating Him in his life, in his Passion and Death with a fidelity inexpressible to human tongue.

804. In the investigation of these mysteries and special favors of the blessed Mother the reason why the Most High operated them, is quite a different thing from the cause of their being kept secret for so many centuries in the Church. In inquiring into the first, we must be guided by our knowledge of the divine power and of the love of God for his

Mother, as well as by our knowledge of his desire of raising
Her to a dignity above all other creatures. As men in their
mortal flesh can never perfectly know the dignity of that
Mother, nor her love, nor the love of her Son, or of the
blessed Trinity, nor the merits and holiness conferred upon
Her by the Almighty, their ignorance tends to set limits to
the divine power in its operations. God did for Her all He
could, and that was as much as He wished. But he communicated Himself to Her in such a special manner, as to become
her Son of her substance, hence it necessarily follows, that in
the order of grace He dealt with Her in an extraordinary
manner, and as befitted no one else, not even the whole
human race. Hence to Her were due not only extraordinary
favors, benefits and blessings of the Almighty; but the rule of
judging about them must be, that, after his own most holy
humanity, nothing, that could in any manner redound to her
glory and holiness, was denied Her.

805. But in regard to the revelation of these wonders in
his Church, the high providence of God, which governs it
and procures new splendors for it according to the circumstances of the times, is guided by other reasons. For the
happy day of grace, which dawned upon the world in the
Incarnation of the Word and in the Redemption of man, has
its morning and its noontide as also its eventide, and all this
the divine Wisdom disposes when and how it becomes
opportune. Although all the mysteries of Christ and his
Mother are revealed in the holy Scriptures; yet not all of
them are manifested at the same time, but little by little the
Lord withdraws the veil of figures, metaphors and enigmas,
under which many of the sacraments have been hidden. Like
the rays of the sun under a passing cloud, they were covered
and concealed until some of the many rays of divine light
should fall upon men; since even the angels, though they
were made aware of the Incarnation in a general way as being

the end of all their ministry to man, were not informed of all the conditions, effects and circumstances of this mystery: they gradually came to know many of them during the five thousand two hundred years from the creation to the Incarnation. This acquisition of new knowledge gave occasion for continued admiration and renewed praise and glory to the Author of these mysteries, as I have shown in the whole course of this history. I mention this example in answer to any wonder, which might be caused in those that hear of this mysterious exaltation of the most blessed Mary, which, with many others already described and to be described, was hidden until the Most High was willing to make them manifest.

806. Before I was capable of these reasonings and when I first came to know of this mystery of Christ's having taken his blessed Mother to heaven with Him, I was not a little astounded, not only on my own account, but on account of those who should hear it. Among other things which I then heard the Lord tell me, was that I should remember what saint Paul has left recorded of himself in the Church, when he refers to his rapture into the third heaven, which is that of the blessed, and how he was in doubt whether he was taken up in the body or out of the body, daring to affirm neither the one or the other, but supposing that it could have happened in either manner. This at once cleared up my difficulties; for if such a thing as being taken bodily to heaven could happen to the Apostle in the beginning of his conversion and when he had no merits, but only sins to his credit; and if the concession of such a privilege entailed no danger or inconvenience to God's Church; how can anyone doubt that the Lord showed the same favor to his Mother, especially after her attaining to such ineffable merit and holiness? The Lord also added, that if some of the saints, who rose in their body with the resurrected Christ, were privileged to ascend in their

body with the Savior, surely there was a better reason for showing this favor to his purest Mother. Even if none of the mortals ever should have enjoyed this distinction, it was due to the most blessed Mary, because She had suffered with the Lord. It was reasonable that She should share with Him his triumph and glory in taking possession of it at the right hand of the Most High; since She, as his Mother, had, from her own substance, given Him his human nature, in which He now triumphantly ascended into heaven. And just as it was befitting, that She should not be separated from her Son in glory, so it was also due to Her that none of the human race should come body and soul to the enjoyment of eternal glory before most blessed Mary, not even excepted her mother or father, or her spouse Joseph, or any of the rest. All of them, and the Savior himself, her Son Jesus, would have been deprived of this accidental increase of their joy, if the most blessed Mary, as the Mother of the Redeemer and as the Queen of all creation, who merited such a favor and blessing more than all the rest, had not ascended with them into heaven on that day.

807. These arguments seem to me sufficient to establish the knowledge and excite the pious joy and consolation of this mystery and of others to be mentioned in the third part in the further history of the life of Mary. Returning now to my history, I say that the Lord took with Him his blessed Mother in his Ascension into heaven and, amid incredible rejoicing and admiration, filled Her with splendor and glory in the sight of the angels and saints. It was also very appropriate, that the Apostles and the other faithful, for the time being, should be ignorant of this mystery; for if they had seen their Mother and Mistress ascend with Christ, their affliction would have been beyond all bounds and without recourse or relief. Nothing could ever console them for the departure of Christ more fully than to feel that they had still with them

their most blessed Lady and kindest Mother. Even then their sighs and sobbing, and their tears welled up from their inmost hearts, when they saw their beloved Master and Redeemer disappearing through the aerial regions. And when they had almost lost sight of Him, a most resplendent cloud interposed itself between Him and those He had left upon earth (Acts 1, 9), intercepting Him altogether from their view. In it the Person of the eternal Father descended from heaven to the regions of the air in order to meet the Son and the Mother. who had furnished the new mode of existence in which He now returned. Coming to Them the eternal Father received Them in his embrace of infinite love, to the joy of the angels, who had accompanied the Father in innumerable choirs from his heavenly seat. In a short space of time, penetrating the elements and the celestial orbs, that whole divine procession arrived at the supreme regions of the empyrean. At their entrance the angels, who had ascended from the earth with their Sovereigns Jesus and Mary, and those who had joined them in the aerial regions, spoke to those who had remained in the heavenly heights and repeated those words of David and many others referring to this mystery, saying:

808. "Open, ye princes, open your gates eternal; let them be raised and opened up, and receive into his dwelling the great King of glory, the Lord of virtues, the Powerful in battle, the Strong and Invincible, who comes triumphant and victorious over all his enemies. Open the gates of the heavenly paradise, and let them remain open and free forever, since the new Adam is coming, the Repairer of the whole human race, rich in mercy, overflowing with the merits of his copious Redemption wrought by his Death in the world. He has restored our loss and has raised human nature to the supreme dignity of his own immensity. He comes with the reign of the elect and the redeemed, given to Him by his eternal Father. Now his liberal mercy has given to mortals the power

of regaining in justice the right lost by their sin, to merit, by the observance of his law, as his brothers and coinheritors of the goods of his Father eternal life; and, for his greater glory and to our greater rejoicing, He brings with Him and at his side the Mother of piety, who gave Him the form of man for overcoming the demon; She comes as our charming and beautiful Queen delighting all that behold Her. Come forth, come forth, ye heavenly courtiers, and you shall see our most beautiful King with the crown given to Him by his Mother, and his Mother crowned with the glory conferred upon Her by her Son."

809. Amidst this jubilee and other rejoicings exceeding all our conceptions that new divinely arranged procession approached the empyrean heavens. Between the two choirs of angels and saints, Christ and his most blessed Mother made their entry. All in their order gave supreme honor to Each respectively and to Both together, breaking forth in hymns of praise in honor of the Authors of grace and of life. Then the eternal Father placed upon the throne of his Divinity at his right hand, the incarnate Word, and in such glory and majesty, that He filled with new admiration and reverential fear all the inhabitants of heaven. In clear and intuitive vision they recognized the infinite glory and perfection of the Divinity inseparably and substantially united in one personality to the most holy humanity, beautified and exalted by the preeminence and glory due to this union, such as eyes have not seen, nor ears heard, nor ever has entered into the thoughts of creatures (Is. 54, 4).

810. On this occasion the humility and wisdom of our most prudent Queen reached their highest point; for, overwhelmed by such divine and admirable favors, She hovered at the footstool of the royal throne, annihilated in the consciousness of being a mere earthly creature. Prostrate She adored the Father and broke out in new canticles of praise for

the glory communicated to his Son and for elevating in Him the deified humanity to such greatness and splendor. Again the angels and saints were filled with admiration and joy to see the most prudent humility of their Queen, whose living example of virtue, as exhibited on that occasion, they emulated among themselves in copying. Then the voice of the eternal Father was heard saying: "My Daughter, ascend higher!" Her divine Son also called Her, saying: "My Mother, rise up and take possession of the place, which I owe Thee for having followed and imitated Me." The Holy Ghost said: "My Spouse and Beloved, come to my eternal embraces!" Immediately was proclaimed to all the blessed the decree of the most holy Trinity, by which the most blessed Mother, for having furnished her own lifeblood toward the Incarnation and for having nourished, served, imitated and followed Him with all the perfection possible to a creature, was exalted and placed at the right hand of her Son for all eternity. None other of the human creatures should ever hold that place or position, nor rival Her in the unfailing glory connected with it; but it was to be reserved to the Queen and to be her possession by right after her earthly life, as of one who preeminently excelled all the rest of the saints.

811. In fulfillment of this decree, the most blessed Mary was raised to the throne of the holy Trinity at the right hand of her Son. At the same time She, with all the saints, was informed, that She was given possession of this throne not only for all the ages of eternity, but that it was left to her choice to remain there even now and without returning to the earth. For it was the conditional will of the divine Persons, that as far as they were concerned, She should now remain in that state. In order that She might make her own choice, She was shown anew the state of the Church upon earth, the orphaned and necessitous condition of the faithful, whom She was left free to assist. This admirable proceeding

of the divine Providence was to afford the Mother of mercy an occasion of going beyond, so to say, even her own Self in doing good and in obliging the human race with an act of tenderest love similar to that of her Son in assuming a passable state and in suspending the glory due to his body during and for our Redemption. The most blessed Mother imitated Him also in this respect, so that She might be in all things like the incarnate Word. The great Lady therefore, having clearly before her eyes all the sacrifices included in this proposition, left the throne and, prostrating Herself at the feet of the Three Persons, said: "Eternal and almighty God, my Lord, to accept at once this reward, which thy condescending kindness offers me, would be to secure my rest; but to return to the world and continue to labor in mortal life for the good of the children of Adam and the faithful of thy holy Church, would be to the glory and according to the pleasure of thy Majesty and would benefit my sojourning and banished children on earth. I accept this labor and renounce for the present the peace and joy of thy presence. Well do I know, what I possess and receive, but I will sacrifice it to further the love Thou hast for men. Accept, Lord and Master of all my being, this sacrifice and let thy divine strength govern me in the undertaking confided to me. Let faith in Thee be spread, let thy holy name be exalted, let thy holy Church be enlarged, for Thou hast acquired it by the blood of thy Onlybegotten and mine; I offer myself anew to labor for thy glory and for the conquest of the souls, as far as I am able."

812. Such was the sacrifice made by the most loving Mother and Queen, one greater than ever was conceived by creature, and it was so pleasing to the Lord, that He immediately rewarded it by operating in Her those purifications and enlightenments, which I have at other times mentioned as necessary to the intuitive vision of the Divinity; for so far She had on this occasion seen It only by abstractive vision. Thus

elevated She partook of the beatific vision and was filled with splendor and celestial gifts, altogether beyond the power of man to describe or conceive in mortal life.

813. The Most High renewed in Her all the gifts, which until then He had communicated to Her and confirmed and sealed them anew in the degree then befitting, in order to send Her back as Mother and Instructress of holy Church, confirming all the titles He had conferred upon Her as the Queen of all creation, as the Advocate and Mistress of all the faithful; and just as wax receives the form of the seal, so the blessed Mary, by the divine Omnipotence, became the image of the humanity of Christ, in order that She might thus return to the militant Church and be the true garden, locked and sealed to preserve the waters of grace (Cant. 4, 12). o secrets of the highest Majesty, worthy of all reverence ! 0 mysteries, as venerable as they are exalted! O charity and kindness of the most holy Mary, never comprehended by the ignorant children of Eve! The choice made by God of this only and sweetest Mother for a refuge of his faithful children was not without its great mystery; it was a contrivance for manifesting to us this maternal love, which perhaps in her other great deeds we would not succeed in finding out. It was in accordance with the divine decree, by which neither She should be deprived of an occasion to attain such excellence, nor we be deprived of the blessed obligation of imitating her example. To whom should it now seem much in comparison with this excess of love, when he sees the saints and the martyrs rejecting momentary contentment in order to arrive at their eternal rest, since our most loving Mother has deprived Herself of this complete beatitude in order to succour her little children? How can we avoid direst confusion, when, neither in gratitude for this favor, nor for the imitation of her example, nor in order to please this Lady, nor in order to secure us Her company or that of her Son, we on our part

will not deny ourselves of a slight and deceitful pleasure, that brings us only their enmity and death itself? Blessed be that Woman, let all the heavens praise Her, and let all generations call her fortunate and happy (Luke 1, 48).

814. I finished up the first part of this history with the thirtyfirst chapter of the parables of Solomon, setting forth in its explanation the exalted virtues of this great Lady, the only strong Woman of the Church, and by referring to the same chapter I close this second part. For the Holy Ghost includes all concerning Her in the mysterious fecundity of the words of that passage. The great sacrament, of which I have here spoken that fecundity is verified more particularly in the supreme exaltation of the most blessed Mary consequent upon this blessing. But I will not tarry to repeat what I have there said; for much of what I could say can be understood by the perusal of that portion. There I said, that this Queen is the strong Woman, whose price and value is as of things from afar (Prov. 31, to), from the farthest confines of the empyrean heavens, measured by the esteem shown Her by the most blessed Trinity; and the heart of her Man was not deceived, since She failed in nothing that He had expected of Her. She was the ship of the merchant, who brought from heaven the sustenance of his Church; She was the One who planted it by the fruit of her hands; She, who girded Herself with strength; it was She who put forth her arms to great things; She who extended her hands to the poor, and opened her palms to the destitute; She, who tasted and saw how good was this negotiation, seeing with her own eyes the reward of eternal beatitude; She, who clothed her servants in double garments; it was She, whose light was not extinguished in the night of tribulation, and needed not to fear the rigor of temptation. Before descending from the heavens, She, in order to fulfill these offices, besought the eternal Father for his power, the Son for his wisdom, and the Holy

Ghost for the fire of his love, and all the three divine Persons, for their assistance and their blessing. This They gave Her, as She prostrated Herself before the throne, and They filled Her with new influences and communications of the Divinity. Then They lovingly permitted Her to depart with ineffable treasures of grace. The holy angels and saints magnified Her in wonderful exaltation and praise and She returned to the earth, as I will relate in the third part. There I shall also relate all that She did in the holy Church during the time of her stay; and her doings were the admiration of heaven and of exceeding benefit to men; for all her labors and sufferings were undergone to secure eternal felicitude for her children. As She had come to know the excellence of charity in its origin and source, namely in the eternal God, who is charity (I John 4, 16), She continued to be inflamed by its ardors, and her bread day and night, was charity. Like a busy bee She descended from the triumphant to the militant Church, charged with the flowerdust of charity, to construct the honeycomb of the love of God for the nourishment of the little children of the primitive Church. She raised them up to manhood, so robust and consummate in perfection that they formed a foundation abundantly strong enough for the high edifice of the holy Church (Ephes. 2, 20).

815. In order to finish this chapter, and with it this second part, I return to the congregation of the faithful, whom we left so sorrowful on mount Olivet. The most holy Mary did not forget them in the midst of her glory; as they stood weeping and lost in grief and, as it were, absorbed in looking into the aerial regions, into which their Redeemer and Master had disappeared, She turned her eyes upon them from the cloud on which She had ascended, in order to send them her assistance. Moved by their sorrow, She besought Jesus lovingly to console these little children, whom He had left as orphans upon the earth. Moved by the prayers of his Mother,

the Redeemer of the human race sent down two angels in white and resplendent garments, who appeared to all the disciples and the faithful and spoke to them: "Ye men of Galilee, do not look up to heaven in so great astonishment, for this Lord Jesus, who departed from you and has ascended into heaven, shall again return with the same glory and majesty in which you have just seen Him" (Acts 1,11). By such words and others which they added they consoled the Apostles and disciples and all the rest, so that they might not grow faint, but in their retirement hope for the coming and the consolation of the Holy Ghost promised by their divine Master.

816. But I must remark, that these words of the angels, though they consoled these men and women, at the same time contained a reproach of their want of faith. For if their faith had been wellfounded and permeated by the pure love and charity, it would not have been necessary to remain there with their gaze so intently fixed on the heavens, since they could not see their Master, nor detain Him by the outward and sensible demonstration of their love, which they showed in looking up in the air where they had seen Him disappear; but they should have enlivened their faith and looked for Him and sought Him there, where He really was and where they would certainly have found Him. Theirs was a useless and imperfect manner of seeking Him; for in order to obtain the presence and assistance of his grace, it was not necessary that they should see and converse with Him corporally. That they did not understand this truth was a blamable defect in men so enlightened and perfected. For a long time had the Apostles and disciples attended the school of Christ our God and they had drawn the doctrine of perfection from its very fount, from a source so pure and exquisite, that they should have been far advanced in spirituality and highest perfection. But this is the misfortune of our nature, that in its depend-

ence upon the senses and its satisfaction in exercising its lower faculties, it wishes to love and enjoy even the most divine spiritual blessings in a sensible manner. Accustomed to this grossness, it is very dilatory in purifying and cleansing itself from those lower elements; and sometimes it is thus deceived, even when it firmly and eagerly pursues the highest aims. This truth was well exemplified for our instruction in the Apostles, who had been taught by the Lord that He was the light and the truth, and at the same time the way (John 14, 6), and that they were to come to the knowledge of the eternal Father through Him, the true way; since light shines not merely for its own self, and a road is not made for the purpose of resting upon it.

817. This teaching, so often repeated in the Gospels, heard from the lips of its Author, and confirmed by the example of his life, should have raised the hearts and the understanding of the Apostles to its comprehension and practice. But the very pleasure which they found for their spirit and for their senses in the intercourse and conversation with their Master, the security of their love, and the assurance of the just love of their Master, kept the forces of their will bound to their senses, so that they did not know how to free themselves from the encroachments of their lower faculties, nor ever became aware how much of self-seeking there really was in their piety and how much they were carried away by the spiritual delight coming only from the senses. If their divine Master had not left them by ascending into heaven, they could not have separated from Him without great bitterness and sorrow, and therefore would not have been as fit to preach the Gospel; for this was to be preached throughout the world at the cost of much labors and difficulties, and at the risk of life itself. This could not be the work of small-minded men, but of men courageous and strong in love, men not hampered or softened by the sensible delights

clinging to the spirit, but ready to go through abundance or want, infamy or renown, honors or dishonors, sorrows or joys, preserving throughout it all their love and zeal for the Lord, and a magnanimous heart, superior to all prosperity and adversity (II Cor. 6, 8). After they had therefore been admonished by the angels they left mount Olivet and returned to the Cenacle with most holy Mary, persevering in prayer and in their expectation of the coming of the Holy Ghost, as we shall see in the last part.

Words of the Queen

THE VIRGIN MARY SPEAKS TO SISTER MARY OF AGREDA

818. My daughter, thou wilt appropriately close this second part of my life by remembering the lesson concerning the most efficacious sweetness of the divine love and the immense liberality of God with those souls, that do not hinder its flowing. It is in conformity with the inclinations of his holy and perfect will to regale rather than afflict creatures, to console them rather than cause them sorrow, to reward them rather than to chastise them, to rejoice rather than grieve them. But mortals ignore this divine science, because they desire from the hands of the Most High such consolations, delights and rewards, as are earthly and dangerous, and they prefer them to the true and more secure blessings. The divine Love then corrects this fault by the lessons conveyed in tribulations and punishments. Human nature is slow, coarse and uneducated; and if it is not cultivated and softened, it gives no fruit in season, and on account of its evil inclinations, will never of itself become fit for the most loving and sweet intercourse with the highest Good. Therefore it must be shaped and reduced by the hammer of adversities, refined in the crucible of tribulation, in order that it may become fit and capable of the divine gifts and favors and may learn to

despise terrestrial and fallacious goods, wherein death is concealed.

819. I counted for little all that I endured, when I saw the reward which the divine Goodness had prepared for me; and therefore He ordained, in his admirable Providence, that I should return to the militant Church of my own free will and choice. This I knew would redound to my greater glory and to the exaltation of his holy name, while it would provide assistance to his Church and to his children in an admirable and holy manner (I Tim. 1, 17). It seemed to me a sacred duty, that I deprive myself of the eternal felicity of which I was in possession and, returning from heaven to earth, gain new fruits of labor and love for the Almighty; all this lowed to the divine Goodness, which had raised me up from the dust. Learn therefore, my beloved, from my example, and excite thyself to imitate me most eagerly during these times, in which the holy Church is so disconsolate and over-whelmed by tribulations and in which there are none of her children to console her. In this cause I desire that thou labor strenuously, ready to suffer in prayer and supplication, and crying from the bottom of thy heart to the Omnipotent. And if it were necessary thou shouldst be willing to give thy life. I assure thee, my daughter, thy solicitude shall be very pleasing in the eyes of my divine Son and in mine.

820. Let it all be for the glory and honor of the Most High, the King of the ages, the Immortal and Invisible (I Tim. 1, 17), and for that of his Mother, the most blessed Mary, through all the eternities!

CATHOLIC WAY PUBLISHING

QUALITY PAPERBACKS AND E-BOOKS

THE MYSTICAL CITY OF GOD
BY VENERABLE MARY OF AGREDA

The Conception
Volume I, Part I, Books I & II in one Book:
Paperback 5" x 8" Edition: ISBN-13: 978-1-78379-280-1
Kindle E-Book Edition:....................................ISBN-13: 978-1-78379-281-8
EPUB E-Book Edition: ISBN-13: 978-1-78379-282-5

The Incarnation
Volume II, Part II, Books III & IV in one Book:
Paperback 5" x 8" Edition: ISBN-13: 978-1-78379-283-2
Kindle E-Book Edition:....................................ISBN-13: 978-1-78379-284-9
EPUB E-Book Edition: ISBN-13: 978-1-78379-285-6

The Transfixion
Volume III, Part II, Books V & VI in one Book:
Paperback 5" x 8" Edition: ISBN-13: 978-1-78379-286-3
Kindle E-Book Edition:....................................ISBN-13: 978-1-78379-287-0
EPUB E-Book Edition: ISBN-13: 978-1-78379-288-7

The Coronation
Volume IV, Part III, Books VII & VIII in 1 Book:
Paperback 5" x 8" Edition: ISBN-13: 978-1-78379-289-4
Kindle E-Book Edition:....................................ISBN-13: 978-1-78379-290-0
EPUB E-Book Edition: ISBN-13: 978-1-78379-291-7

Popular Abridgement
Paperback 5" x 8" Edition: ISBN-13: 978-1-78379-063-0
Kindle E-Book Edition:....................................ISBN-13: 978-1-78379-064-7
EPUB E-Book Edition: ISBN-13: 978-1-78379-065-4

True Devotion to Mary: With Preparation for Total Consecration
by Saint Louis de Montfort
6" x 9" Hardback:...ISBN–13: 978-1-78379-004-3
6" x 9" Paperback: ISBN–13: 978-1-78379-011-1
5" x 8" Paperback: ISBN–13: 978-1-78379-000-5
MOBI E-Book:...ISBN–13: 978-1-78379-001-2
EPUB E-Book: ISBN–13: 978-1-78379-002-9

www.catholicwaypublishing.com
London, England, UK
2013